THE POEMS
OF
JOHN DONNE

EDITED FROM THE OLD EDITIONS

AND NUMEROUS MANUSCRIPTS

WITH INTRODUCTIONS & COMMENTARY

BY

HERBERT J. C. GRIERSON M.A.

CHALMERS PROFESSOR OF ENGLISH LITERATURE

IN THE UNIVERSITY OF ABERDEEN

VOL. I
THE TEXT OF THE POEMS
WITH APPENDIXES

OXFORD UNIVERSITY PRESS

Oxford University Press, Ely House, London W.I

GLASGOW NEW YORK TORONTO MELBOURNE WELLINGTON
CAPE TOWN SALISBURY IBADAN NAIROBI LUSAKA ADDIS ABABA
BOMBAY CALCUTTA MADRAS KARACHI LAHORE DACCA
KUALA LUMPUR HONG KONG TOKYO

FIRST EDITION 1912
REPRINTED LITHOGRAPHICALLY IN GREAT BRITAIN
BY LOWE AND BRYDONE (PRINTERS) LTD., LONDON
FROM SHEETS OF THE FIRST EDITION
1929, 1938, 1951, 1953, 1958, 1963, 1966, 1968

PREFACE

THE present edition of Donne's poems grew out of my
work as a teacher. In the spring of 1907, just after I had
published a small volume on the literature of the early
seventeenth century, I was lecturing to a class of Honours
students on the 'Metaphysical poets'. They found Donne
difficult alike to understand and to appreciate, and accord-
ingly I undertook to read with them a selection from his
poems with a view to elucidating difficult passages and
illustrating the character of his 'metaphysics', the
Scholastic and scientific doctrines which underlie his
conceits. The only editions which we had at our disposal
were the modern editions of Donne's poems by Grosart
and Chambers, but I did not anticipate that this would
present any obstacle to the task I had undertaken. About
the same time the Master of Peterhouse asked me to
undertake the chapter on Donne, as poet and prose-artist,
for the *Cambridge History of English Literature*. The result
was that though I had long been interested in Donne,
and had given, while at work on the poetry of the seven-
teenth century, much thought to his poetry as a centre of
interest and influence, I began to make a more minute
study of the text of his poems than I had yet attempted.

The first result of this study was the discovery that
there were several passages in the poems, as printed
in Mr. Chambers' edition, of which I could give no
satisfactory explanation to my class. At the close of the
session I went to Oxford and began in the Bodleian
a rapid collation of the text of that edition with the
older copies, especially of 1633. The conclusion to which

I came was that, excellent in many ways as that edition is, the editor had too often abandoned the reading of 1633 for the sometimes more obvious but generally weaker and often erroneous emendations of the later editions. As he records the variants this had become clear in some cases already, but an examination of the older editions brought out another fact,—that by modernizing the punctuation, while preserving no record of the changes made, the editor had corrupted some passages in such a manner as to make it impossible for a student, unprovided with all the old editions, to recover the original and sometimes quite correct reading, or to trace the error to its fountain-head.

My first proposal to the Delegates of the Clarendon Press was that I should attempt an edition of Donne's poems resting on a collation of the printed texts ; that for all poems which it contains the edition of 1633 should be accepted as the authority, to be departed from only when the error seemed to be obvious and certain, and that all such changes, however minute, should be recorded in the notes. In the case of poems not contained in the edition of 1633, the first edition (whether 1635, 1649, 1650, or 1669) was to be the authority and to be treated in the same fashion. Such an edition, it was hoped, might be ready in a year. I had finished my first collation of the editions when a copy of the Grolier Club edition came into my hands, and I included it in the number of those which I compared throughout with the originals.

While the results of this collation confirmed me in the opinion I had formed as to the superiority of the edition of 1633 to all its successors, it showed also that that edition was certainly not faultless, and that the text of those poems which were issued only in the later editions was in general very carelessly edited and corrupt, especially of those poems which were added for the first time in 1669. This raised the question, what use was to be made of the manuscript copies of the poems in correcting the errors of the edition? Grosart had based his whole text on one or two manuscripts in preference to the editions. Mr. Chambers, while wisely refusing to do this, and adopting the editions as the basis of his text, had made frequent reference to the manuscripts and adopted corrections from them. Professor Norton made no use of the manuscripts in preparing the text of his edition, but he added in an Appendix an account of one of these which had come into his hands, and later he described some more and showed clearly that he believed corrections were to be obtained from this source. Accordingly I resolved to examine tentatively those which were accessible in the British Museum, especially the transcript of three of the *Satyres* in Harleian MS. 5110.

A short examination of the manuscripts convinced me that it would be very unsafe to base a text on any single extant manuscript, or even to make an eclectic use of a few of them, taking, now from one, now from another, what seemed a probable emendation. On the other hand it became clear that if as wide a collation as possible of extant manuscripts were made one would be able to establish in many cases what was, whether right or wrong, the traditional reading before any printed edition appeared.

A few experiments further showed that one, and a very important, result of this collation would be to confirm the trustworthiness of 1633, to show that in places where modern editors had preferred the reading of some of the later editions, generally 1635 or 1669, the text of 1633 was not only intrinsically superior but had the support of tradition, i. e. of the majority of the manuscripts. If this were the case, then it was also possible that the traditional, manuscript text might afford corrections when 1633 had fallen into error. At the same time a very cursory examination of the manuscripts was sufficient to show that many of them afforded an infinitely more correct and intelligible text of those poems which were not published in 1633 than that contained in the printed editions.

Another possible result of a wide collation of the manuscripts soon suggested itself, and that was the settlement of the canon of Donne's poems. One or two of the poems contained in the old editions had already been rejected by modern editors, and some of these on the strength of manuscript ascriptions. But on the one hand, no systematic attempt had been made to sift the poems, and on the other, experience has shown that nothing is more unsafe than to trust to the ascriptions of individual, unauthenticated manuscripts. Here again it seemed to the present editor that if any definite conclusion was to be obtained it must be by as wide a survey as possible, by the accumulation of evidence. No such conclusion might be attainable, but it was only thus that it could be sought.

The outcome of the investigation thus instituted has been fully discussed in the article on the *Text and Canon of Donne's Poems* in the second volume, and I shall not attempt to summarize it here. But it may be convenient for the student to have a quite brief statement of what it is that the notes in this volume profess to set forth.

Their first aim is to give a complete account of the variant readings of the original editions of 1633, 1635, 1639, 1649–50–54 (the text in these three is identical), and 1669. This was the aim of the edition as originally planned, and though my opinion of the value of many of the variants of the later editions has undergone considerable abatement since I was able to study them in the light afforded by the manuscripts, I have endeavoured to complete my original scheme; and I trust it may be found that nothing more important has been overlooked than an occasional misprint in the later editions. But I know from the experience of examining the work of my precursors, and of revising my own work, that absolute correctness is almost unattainable. It has been an advantage to me in this part of the work to come after Mr. Chambers and the Grolier Club editors, but neither of these editions records changes of punctuation.

The second purpose of the notes is to set forth the evidence of the manuscripts. I have not attempted to give anything like a full account of the variant readings of these, but have recorded so much as is sufficient for four different purposes.

(1) To vindicate the text of 1633. I have not thought it necessary to detail the evidence in cases where no one has disputed the 1633 reading. If the note simply records the readings of the editions it may be assumed that the manuscript evidence, so far as it is explicit (the manuscripts frequently abound in absurd errors), is on the side of 1633. In other cases, when there is something to be said for the text of the later editions, and especially when modern editors have preferred the later reading (though I have not always called attention to this) I have set forth the evidence in some detail. At times I have mentioned each manuscript, at others simply *all the MSS.*, occasionally just *MSS.* This last means generally that all the positive evidence before me was in favour of the reading, but that my collations were silent as to some of the manuscripts. My collators, whether myself or those who worked for me, used Mr. Chambers' edition because of its numbered lines. Now if Mr. Chambers had already adopted a 1635 or later reading the tendency of the collator—especially at first, before the importance of certain readings had become obvious—was to pass over

the agreement of the manuscript with this later reading in silence.   In all important cases I have verified the reading by repeated reference to the manuscripts, but in some of smaller importance I have been content to record the general trend of the evidence.   I have tried to cite no manuscript unless I had positive evidence as to its reading.

(2) The second use which I have made of the manuscript evidence is to justify my occasional departures from the text of the editions, whether 1633 (and these are the departures which call for most justification) or whatever later edition was the first to contain the poem.   In every such case the reader should see at a glance what was the reading of the first edition, and on what authority it has been altered.   My aim has been a true text (so far as that was attainable), not a reprint ; but I have endeavoured to put the reader in exactly the same position as I was myself at each stage in the construction of that text.   If I have erred, he can (in a favourite phrase of Donne's) 'control' me.   This applies to spelling and punctuation as well as to the words themselves.   But two warnings are necessary. When I note a reading as found in a number of editions, e. g. 1635 to 1654 (1635–54), or in *all* the editions (1633–69), it must be understood that the spelling is not always the same throughout.   I have generally noted any variation in the use of capitals, but not always.   The spelling and punctuation of each poem is that of the *first* edition in which it was published, or of the manuscript from which I have printed, all changes being recorded. Again, if, in a case where the words and not the punctuation is the matter in question, I cite the reading of an edition or some editions followed by a list of agreeing manuscripts, it will be understood that any punctuation given is that of the editions.   If a list of manuscripts only

is given, the punctuation, if recorded, is that of one or two of the best of these.

In cases where punctuation is the matter in question the issue lies between the various editions and my own sense of what it ought to be. Wherever it is not otherwise indicated the punctuation of a poem is that of the first edition in which it appeared or of the manuscript from which I have printed it. I have not recorded every variant of the punctuation of later editions, but all that affect the sense while at the same time not manifestly absurd. The punctuation of the manuscripts is in general negligible, but of a few manuscripts it is good, and I have occasionally cited these in support of my own view as to what the punctuation should be.

(3) A third purpose served by my citation of the manuscripts is to show clearly that there are more versions than one of some poems. A study of the notes to the *Satyres, The Flea, The Curse, Elegy XI: The Bracelet*, will make this clear.

(4) A fourth, subordinate and occasional, purpose of my citation of the manuscripts is to show how Donne's poems were understood or misunderstood by the copyists. Occasionally a reading which is probably erroneous throws light upon a difficult passage. The version of *P* at p. 34, ll. 18–19, elucidates a difficult stanza. The reading of Q in *The Storme*, l. 38,

Yea, and the Sunne

for the usual

I, and the Sunne

suggests, what is probably correct but had not been suspected by any editor, that 'I' here, as often, is not the pronoun, but 'Aye'.

The order of the poems is that of the editions of 1635 onwards with some modifications explained in the

Introduction. In Appendix B I have placed all those poems which were printed as Donne's in the old editions (1633 to 1669), except Basse's *Epitaph on Shakespeare*, and a few found in manuscripts connected with the editions, or assigned to Donne by competent critics, all of which I believe to be by other authors. The text of these has been as carefully revised as that of the undoubted poems. In Appendix C I have placed a miscellaneous collection of poems loosely connected with Donne's name, and illustrating the work of some of his fellow-wits, or the trend of his influence in the occasional poetry of the seventeenth century.

The work of settling the text, correcting the canon, and preparing the Commentary has been done by myself. It was difficult to consult others who had not before them all the complex mass of evidence which I had accumulated. On some five or six places in the text, however, where the final question to be decided was the intrinsic merits of the readings offered by the editions and by the manuscripts, or the advisability of a bolder emendation, I have had the advantage of comparing my opinion with that of Sir James Murray, Sir Walter Raleigh, Dr. Henry Bradley, Mr. W. A. Craigie, Mr. J. C. Smith, or Mr. R. W. Chapman.

For such accuracy as I have secured in reproducing the old editions, in the text and in the notes, I owe much to the help of three friends, Mr. Charles Forbes, of the Post Office, Aberdeen, who transcribed the greater portion of my manuscript; Professor John Purves, of University College, Pretoria, who during a visit to this country read a large section of my proofs, comparing them with the editions in the British Museum; and especially to my assistant, Mr. Frederick Rose, M.A., now Douglas Jerrold Scholar, Christ Church, Oxford, who has revised my proofs throughout with minute care.

I am indebted to many sources for the loan of necessary

material.   In the first place I must acknowledge my debt
to the Carnegie Trust for the Universities of Scotland for
allowing me a grant of £40 in 1908–9, and of £30 in
1909–10, for the collation of manuscripts.   Without this
it would have been impossible for me to collate, or have
collated for me, the widely scattered manuscripts in London,
Petworth, Oxford, Cambridge, Manchester, and Boston.
Some of my expenses in this connexion have been met by
the Delegates of the Clarendon Press, who have also been
very generous in the purchase of necessary books, such as
editions of the Poems and the Sermons.   At the outset
of my work the Governing Body of Christ Church,
Oxford, lent me the copy of the edition of 1633 (origin-
ally the possession of Sir John Vaughan (1603–1674)
Chief Justice of the Common Pleas) on which the present
edition is based, and also their copies of the editions of
1639, 1650, and 1654.   At the same time Sir Walter
Raleigh lent me his copy of the edition of 1669.   At an
early stage of my work Captain C. Shirley Harris, of
90 Woodstock Road, Oxford, communicated with me
about Donne's use of the word 'Mucheron', and he
was kind enough to lend me both his manuscript, *P*, and
the transcript which he had caused to be made.   By
the kindness of Lord Ellesmere I was permitted to
collate his unique copy of the 1611 edition of the
Anatomy of the World and *Funerall Elegie*.   While
I was doing so, Mr. Strachan Holme, the Librarian,
drew my attention to a manuscript collection of Donne's
poems (*B*), and with his kind assistance I was enabled to
collate this at Walkden, Manchester, and again at Bridge-
water House.   Mr. Holme has also furnished a photo-
graph of the title-page of the edition of 1611.   To the
authorities of Trinity College, Dublin, and of Trinity
College, Cambridge, I am indebted not only for permission

to collate their manuscripts on the spot, but for kindly lending them to be examined and compared in the Library at King's College, Aberdeen ; and I am indebted for a similar favour to the authorities of Queen's College, Oxford. In Dublin I met Professor Edward Dowden, and no one has been a kinder friend to my enterprise. He put at my disposal his interesting and valuable manuscript (*D*) and all his collection of Donne's works. He drew my attention to a manuscript (*O'F*) in Ellis and Elvey's catalogue for 1903. Mr. Warwick Bond was good enough to lend me the notes he had made upon this manuscript, which ultimately I traced to Harvard College Library. With Professor Dowden, Mr. Edmund Gosse has given me the most generous and whole-hearted assistance. He lent me, as soon as ever I applied to him, his valuable and unique Westmoreland MS., containing many poems which were not included in any of the old editions. Some of these Mr. Gosse had already printed in his own delightful *Life and Letters of John Donne* (1899), but he has allowed me to reprint these and to print the rest of the unpublished poems for the first time. From his manuscript (*G*) of the *Progresse of the Soule*, or *Metempsychosis*, I have also obtained important emendations of the text. This is the most valuable manuscript copy of this poem. It will be seen that Mr. Gosse is a very material contributor to the completeness and interest of the present edition.

To the Marquess of Crewe I am indebted for permission to examine the manuscript *M*, to which a note of Sir John Simon's had called my attention ; and to Lord Leconfield for a like permission to collate a manuscript in his possession, of which a short description is given in the *Hist. MSS. Commission, Sixth Report*, p. 312, No. 118. With Mr. Whitcomb's aid I was enabled to do this carefully, and he has subsequently verified references. Another interesting manuscript (*JC*) was lent me by Mr. Elkin Mathews, who has also put at my disposal his various editions of the *Lives* of Walton and other books connected with Donne. Almost at the eleventh hour, Mr. Geoffrey Keynes, of St. Bartholomew's Hospital, discovered for me a copy of the 1612 edition of the *Anniversaries*, for which I had asked in vain in *Notes and Queries*. I owe to him, and to the kind permission of Mr. Edward Huth and the Messrs. Sotheby, a careful collation and a photograph of the title-page.

For the Commentary Dr. Norman Moore supplied me with a note on the Galenists and Paracelsians ; and Dr. Gaster with the materials for a note on Donne's use of Jewish Apocrypha. Professor Picavet, of the Sorbonne, Paris, was kind enough to read in proof my notes on Donne's allusions to Scholastic doctrines, and to make suggestions. But I have added to these notes as they passed through the Press, and he must not be made responsible for my errors. Mr. W. Barclay Squire and Professor C. Sanford Terry have revised my transcripts and proofs of the music.

I desire lastly to express my gratitude to the officials of the Clarendon Press for the care with which they have checked my proofs, the patience with which they have accepted my changes and additions, and the trouble they have taken to secure photographs, music, and other details. Whatever faults may be found—and I doubt not they will be many—in my part of the work, I think the part for which the Press is responsible is wellnigh faultless.

H. J. C. GRIERSON.

Langcroft,
Dinnet, Aberdeenshire.
  July 15, 1912.

NOTE

The typography of the edition of 1633 has been closely followed, in its use for example of 'u' and 'v'; and of long 'ſ', which is avoided in certain combinations, e. g. 'sk' (but P. 12, l. 27. 'aſkes' 1633) and frequently 'sb'; nor is it generally used when the letter following 's' is elided; but there are one or two exceptions to this.

In the following places I have printed a full 'and' where 1633 contracts to '&' owing to the length of the line :

Page 12, l. 4. & whõ; P. 15, l. 40. & drove; P. 65, l. 8. & nought; P. 153, l. 105. & almes; P. 158, l. 101. & name; do , l. 107. & rockes, &; P. 159, l. 30. & black; P. 171, l. 83. & lawes; P. 183, l. 18. & Courts; P. 184, l. 29. & God; P. 205, l. 2. & pleasure; P. 240, l. 288. & ſinke; P. 254, l. 107. & thinke; do., l. 113. & think; P. 280, l. 24. & Mines; P. 297, l. 56. & lands; do., l. 62. & brow ; P. 306, l. 290. & lents; P. 327 (xii), l. 8. & feed; P. 337, l. 35. & thou; P. 360, l. 188. & turn'd; P. 384, l. 78. & face.

In the following places 'm' or 'n', indicated by a contraction, has been printed in full : Page 12, l. 4. Her whõ; do. & whõ ; P. 37, l. 17. whẽ (bis); P. 82, l. 46. thẽ; P. 90, l. 2. frõ; P. 128, l. 28. Valẽtine; P. 141, l. 8. whẽ; P. 150, l. 16. thẽ; P. 159, l. 30. ſträge; P. 169, l. 31. whõ; P. 257, l. 210. ſucceſſiõ; P. 266, l. 513. anciẽt; P. 305, l. 255. thẽ; P. 336, l. 10. whẽ; P. 343, l. 126. Frõ; P. 345, l. 169. thẽ; P. 387, l. 71. Pẽbrooke.

There are a few examples of the same changes in the poems printed from the later editions, but I have not reproduced any of these editions so completely as 1633, every poem in which, with the exception of Basse's *An Epitaph upon Shakespeare* (1633. p. 149 i. e. 165) has been here reprinted.

CONTENTS OF VOL. I

EPITHALAMIONS, OR MARRIAGE SONGS

SATYRES

LETTERS TO SEVERALL PERSONAGES

AN ANATOMIE OF THE WORLD

OF THE PROGRESSE OF THE SOULE

EPICEDES AND OBSEQUIES UPON THE DEATHS OF SUNDRY PERSONAGES

APPENDIX A

LATIN POEMS AND TRANSLATIONS

APPENDIX B

POEMS ATTRIBUTED TO JOHN DONNE IN THE OLD EDITIONS (1633–1669) AND THE PRINCIPAL MS. COLLECTIONS, ARRANGED ACCORDING TO THEIR PROBABLE AUTHORS.

I

POEMS. Probably by Sir John Roe, Knt.

Contents. xxi

PLATES

LIST OF EDITIONS REGULARLY CITED IN NOTES.

1633, 1635, 1639, 1650, 1654, 1669.

Contractions :—
    1633–54 i. e. All editions between and including these dates.
    1633–69 i. e. All the editions.
                Etc.

EDITIONS OCCASIONALLY CITED.

1649, in lists of editions and MSS. appended to poems first published in that edition. Textually it is identical with *1650–54*.

1719, Tonson's edition.

1855, The Boston edition of that year—cited once.

Grosart, A. B. Grosart's edition of 1872–3.

Grolier, The Grolier Club edition of Professor Norton and Mrs. Burnett, 1895.

Chambers, Mr. E. K. Chambers' edition of 1896.

LIST OF MS. SIGLA.

A10   Additional MS. 10,309, British Museum.
A11   ,,   ,,   11,811,   ,,
A18   ,,   ,,   18,646,   ,,
A23   ,,   ,,   23,229,   ,,
A25   ,,   :,   25,707,   ,,
A34   ,,   ,,   34,744,   ,,
Ash 38   Ashmole MS. 38, Bodleian Library.
B   Bridgewater MS., Bridgewater House.
Bur   Burley MS., formerly at Burley-on-the-Hill House, Rutland
C   Cambridge University Library MS.
Cy   Carnaby MS., Harvard College.
D   Dowden MS., belonging to Professor Edward Dowden.
E20   Egerton MS. 2013, British Museum.
E22   ,,   ,,   2230,   ,,
G   Gosse MS. of *Metempsychosis*, belonging to Mr. Edmund Gosse.
H39   Harleian MS. 3910, British Museum.
H40   ,,   ,,   4064,   ,,
H49   ,,   ,,   4944,   ,,
H51   ,,   ,,   5110,   ,,
HN   Hawthornden MS., Library of Society of Antiquaries, Edinburgh.
JC   John Cave MS., belonging to Mr. Elkin Mathews.
L74   Lansdowne MS. 740, British Museum.
L77   ,,   ,,   777,   ,,
Lec   Leconfield MS., at Petworth House.
M   Monckton-Milnes MS., belonging to the Marquis of Crewe.
N   Norton MS., Harvard College.
O'F   O'Flaherty MS., Harvard College.
P   Phillipps MS., belonging to Captain C. Shirley Harris.
Q   Queen's College MS., Queen's College, Oxford.
RP31   Rawlinson Poetical MS. 31, Bodleian Library, Oxford.
RP61   ,,   ,,   ,,   61,   ,,   ,,   ,,
S   Stephens MS., Harvard College.
S96   Stowe MS. 961, British Museum.
TCC   Trinity College, Cambridge, MS.
TCD   Trinity College, Dublin, MS. G. 2. 21.
TCD (II)   A second collection of poems in the same MS.
W   Westmoreland MS., belonging to Mr. Edmund Gosse.

The following groups are important:—
   D, H49, Lec,

and

   A18, N, TC, where *TC* represents *TCC* and *TCD*.

THE
PRINTER
TO THE
UNDERSTANDERS.

Or this time I muſt ſpeake only to you : at another, *Readers* may perchance ſerve my turne ; and I thinke this a way very free from exception, in hope that very few will have a minde to confeſſe themſelves ignorant.

If you looke for an Epiſtle, as you have before ordinary publications, I am ſory that I muſt deceive you ; but you will not lay it to my charge, when you ſhall conſider that this is not ordinary, for if I ſhould ſay it were the beſt in this kinde, that ever this Kingdome hath yet·ſeene ; he that would doubt of it muſt goe out of the Kingdome to enforme himſelfe, for the beſt judgments, within it, take it for granted.

You may imagine (if it pleaſe you) that I could endeare it unto you, by ſaying, that importunity drew it on ; that had it not beene preſented here, it would have come to us from beyond the Seas ; (which perhaps is true enough,) That my charge and paines in procuring of it hath beene ſuch, and ſuch. I could adde hereto, a promiſe of more correctneſſe, or enlargement in the next Edition, if you ſhall in the meane time content you with this. But theſe

---

The Printer &c. *1633–49:* om. *1650–69, which ſubſtitute Dedication* To the &c. *(p. 4)* 2 you : *1635–49:* you, *1633*

things

things are ſo common, as that I ſhould profane this Peece
by applying them to it ; A Peece which who ſo takes not
as he findes it, in what manner ſoever, he is unworthy of
it, ſith a ſcattered limbe of this Author, hath more amiable-
neſſe in it, in the eye of a diſcerner, then a whole body of
ſome other ; Or, (to expreſſe him beſt by himſelfe)

In the   —*A hand, or eye,*
Storme.   *By* Hilyard *drawne, is worth a hiſtory*
            By a worſe Painter made;—

If any man (thinking I ſpeake this to enflame him for the
vent of the Impreſſion) be of another opinion, I ſhall as
willingly ſpare his money as his judgement.   I cannot loſe
ſo much by him as hee will by himſelfe.   For I ſhall
ſatisfie my ſelfe with the conſcience of well doing, in
making ſo much good common.

    Howſoever it may appeare to you, it ſhall ſuffice mee to
enforme you, that it hath the beſt warrant that can bee,
publique authority, and private friends.

    There is one thing more wherein I will make you of
my counſell, and that is, That whereas it hath pleaſed
ſome, who had ſtudyed and did admire him, to offer to the
memory of the Author, not long after his deceaſe, I have
thought I ſhould do you ſervice in preſenting them unto
you now ; onely whereas, had I placed them in the
beginning, they might have ſerv'd for ſo many Encomiums
of the Author (as is uſuall in other workes, where perhaps
there is need of it, to prepare men to digeſt ſuch ſtuffe as
follows after,) you ſhall here finde them in the end, for
whoſoever reades the reſt ſo farre, ſhall perceive that there
is no occaſion to uſe them to that purpoſe ; yet there they
are, as an atteſtation for their ſakes that knew not ſo much
before, to let them ſee how much honour was attributed
to this worthy man, by thoſe that are capable to give it.
Farewell.

    The Printer to the Vnderſtanders. *1635–69:* The Printer to the
Reader. *1633.   See note*   28 here *1635–69 : om. 1633*

                                  Hexaſtichon

Hexaſtichon Bibliopolae.

I See in his laſt preach'd, and printed Booke,
  His Picture in a ſheet ; in *Pauls* I looke,
And ſee his Statue in a ſheete of ſtone,
And ſure his body in the grave hath one :
Thoſe ſheetes preſent him dead, theſe if you buy,
You have him living to Eternity.

Jo. MAR.

Hexaſtichon ad Bibliopolam.
Incerti.

I*N thy Impreſsion of* Donnes *Poems rare,*
 For his Eternitie thou haſt ta'ne care:
'Twas well, and pious ; And for ever may
He live : Yet ſhew I thee a better way;
Print but his Sermons, and if thoſe we buy,
He, We, *and Thou ſhall live i' Eternity.*

Hexaſtichon Bibliopolae. *1633–69*
Hexaſtichon ad Bibliopolam. *1635–69*

Dedication

To the Right Honourable
William Lord *Craven* Baron of
Hamſted-Marſham.

My Lord,

MAny of theſe Poems have, for ſeverall impreſſions, wandred up and down truſting (as well they might) upon the Authors reputation ; neither do they now complain of any injury but what may proceed either from the kindneſſe of the Printer, or the curteſie of the Reader ; the one by adding ſomething too much, left any ſpark of this ſacred fire might periſh undiſcerned, the other by putting ſuch an eſtimation upon the wit & fancy they find here, that they are content to uſe it as their own: as if a man ſhould dig out the ſtones of a royall Amphitheatre to build a ſtage for a countrey ſhow. Amongſt all the monſters this unlucky age has teemed with, I finde none ſo prodigious, as the Poets of theſe later times, wherein men as if they would level underſtandings too as well as eſtates, acknowledging no inequality of parts and Judgements, pretend as indifferently to the chaire of wit as to the Pulpit, & conceive themſelves no leſſe inſpired with the ſpirit of Poetry then with that of Religion : ſo it is not onely the noiſe of Drums and Trumpets which have drowned the Muſes harmony, or the feare that the Churches ruine wil deſtroy their Prieſts likewiſe, that now frights them from this Countrey, where they have been ſo ingenuouſly received, but theſe rude pretenders to excellencies they unjuſtly own who profanely ruſhing into *Minervaes* Temple, with noyſome Ayres blaſt the lawrell

w^{ch}

wch thunder cannot hurt. In this ſad condition theſe learned ſiſters are fled over to beg your *L*^ps. protection, who have been ſo certain a patron both to arts and armes, and who in this generall confuſion have ſo intirely preſerved your Honour, that in your Lordſhip we may ſtill read a moſt perfect character of what *England* was in all her pompe and greatneſſe, ſo that although theſe poems were formerly written upon ſeverall occaſions, and to ſeverall perſons, they now unite themſelves, and are become one pyramid to ſet your Lordſhips ſtatue upon, where you may ſtand like Armed *Apollo* the defendor of the Muſes, encouraging the Poets now alive to celebrate your great Acts by affording your countenance to his poems that wanted onely ſo noble a ſubject.

My Lord,

Your moſt humble ſervant

JOHN DONNE.

TO JOHN DONNE.

DOnne, *the delight of Phoebus, and each Muſe,*
    Who, to thy one, all other braines refuſe;
Whoſe every work, of thy moſt early wit,
    Came forth example, and remaines ſo, yet:
Longer a knowing, than moſt wits doe live;
    And which no'n affection praiſe enough can give!
To it, thy language, letters, arts, beſt life,
    Which might with halfe mankind maintain a ſtrife;
All which I mean to praiſe, and, yet, I would;
    But leave, becauſe I cannot as I ſhould!

B. JONS.

To John Donne. *1650-69, following the* Hexaſtichon ad Bibliopolam.

To

To Lucy, Countesse of Bedford, with M. Donnes Satyres.

L *Vcy*, you brightneſſe of our Spheare, who are
    Life of the *Muſes* day, their morning Starre!
If works (not th'Authors) their own grace ſhould look
Whoſe poems would not wiſh to be your book?
But theſe, deſir'd by you, the makers ends
Crown with their own. Rare Poems ask rare friends.
Yet, *Satyres*, ſince the moſt of mankind bee
Their unavoided ſubject, feweſt ſee:
For none ere took that pleaſure in ſins ſenſe,
But, when they heard it tax'd, took more offence.
They, then, that living where the matter is bred,
Dare for theſe Poems, yet, both ask, and read,
And like them too; muſt needfully, though few,
Be of the beſt: and 'mongſt thoſe beſt are you;
Lucy, you brightneſſe of our Spheare, who are
The *Muſes* evening, as their morning-Starre.

B. Jon.

To John Donne.

W Ho ſhall doubt, *Donne*, where I a *Poet* bee,
    When I dare ſend my *Epigrammes* to thee?
That ſo alone canſt judge, ſo'alone do'ſt make:
And, in thy cenſures, evenly, doſt take
As free ſimplicity, to diſ-avow,
As thou haſt beſt authority, t'allow.
Read all I ſend: and, if I finde but one
Mark'd by thy hand, and with the better ſtone,
My title's ſeal'd. Thoſe that for claps doe write,
Let punees, porters, players praiſe delight,
And, till they burſt, their backs, like aſſes load:
A man ſhould ſeek great glory, and not broad.

B. Jon.

To Lucy &c.   To John Donne &c. *1650–69, in sheets added 1650.*
See Text and Canon &c.

SONGS

This was for youth, Strength, Mirth, and wit that Time
Most count their golden Age; but t'was not thine.
Thine was thy later yeares, so much refind
From youths Drosse, Mirth, & wit; as thy pure mind
Thought (like the Angels) nothing but the Praise
Of thy Creator, in those last, best Dayes.
    Witnes this Booke, (thy Embleme) which begins
    With Love; but endes, with Sighes, & Teares for sins.

Will: Marshall sculpsit.   IZ: WA:

JOHN DONNE

From the engraving prefixed to the Poems in the
Editions of 1635, 1639, 1649, 1650, 1654

SONGS
AND
SONETS.

The good-morrow.

I Wonder by my troth, what thou, and I
Did, till we lov'd? were we not wean'd till then?
But fuck'd on countrey pleafures, childifhly?
Or fnorted we in the feaven fleepers den?
T'was fo ; But this, all pleafures fancies bee.   5
If ever any beauty I did fee,
Which I defir'd, and got, t'was but a dreame of thee.

And now good morrow to our waking foules,
Which watch not one another out of feare;
For love, all love of other fights controules,   10
And makes one little roome, an every where.
Let fea-discoverers to new worlds have gone,
Let Maps to other, worlds on worlds have fhowne,
Let us poffeffe one world, each hath one, and is one.

My face in thine eye, thine in mine appeares,   15
And true plaine hearts doe in the faces reft,
Where can we finde two better hemifpheares
Without fharpe North, without declining West?

SONGS AND SONETS. *1635–69: no division into sections, 1633*
The good-morrow. *1633–69, A18, L74, N, TCC, TCD: no title, A25, B, C,
D, H40, H49, JC, Lec, O'F, P, S:* Elegie. *S96*   2 lov'd? *1639–69:* lov'd,
1633–35   3 countrey pleafures, childifhly? *1633–54, D, H40, H49, Lec:*
childifh pleafures feelily? *1669, A18, A25, B, JC, L74, N, O'F, P, S, S96, TC*
4 fnorted *1633–54, D, H40, H49, Lec, O'F, S96:* flumbred *1669, A18,
A25, JC, L74, N, P, TC*   feaven fleepers *1633:* feven-fleepers *1635–69*
5 this,] as *1669*   10 For *1633–69, D, H40, H49, Lec:* But *rest of MSS.*
13 to other, worlds on *1633–54:* to other worlds our *1669:* to others,
worlds on *D, H49, Lec, and other MSS.*   14 one world *1633–69, D,
H49, Lec:* our world *rest of MSS.*   17 better *1633, D, H40, H49, Lec:*
fitter *1635–69, and rest of MSS.*

What

What ever dyes, was not mixt equally;
If our two loves be one, or, thou and I   20
Love fo alike, that none doe flacken, none can die.

Song.

GOe, and catche a falling ftarre,
    Get with child a mandrake roote,
Tell me, where all paft yeares are,
    Or who cleft the Divels foot,
Teach me to heare Mermaides finging,   5
    Or to keep off envies ftinging,
        And finde
        What winde
Serves to advance an honeft minde.

If thou beeft borne to ftrange fights,   10
    Things invifible to fee,
Ride ten thoufand daies and nights,
    Till age fnow white haires on thee,
Thou, when thou retorn'ft, wilt tell mee
All ftrange wonders that befell thee,   15
        And fweare
        No where
Lives a woman true, and faire.

---

19 was not] is not *1669*   20–1 or, thou and I . . . can die. *1633,*
D,H40,H49,Lec: or, thou and I . . can flacken, . can die.*Chambers :*
                both thou and I
    Love juft alike in all, none of thefe loves can die. *1635–69, JC, O'F, P:*
            or thou and I
    Love juft alike in all, none of thefe loves can die.
A18, A25, B, L74, S96, TC   As thou and I *&c. H40:* And thou
and I *&c. S*
    Song. *1633–69:* Song, A Songe, *or no title, A18, A25, B, C, Cy, D,*
H40,H49, JC, L74,Lec, N, O'F, P, S, S96,TCC,TCD   3 paft yeares]
times paft *1669:* paft times *P*   11 to fee] go fee *1669, S, S96:* fee
most other MSS.

                                              If

If thou findſt one, let mee know,
   Such a Pilgrimage were ſweet;   20
Yet doe not, I would not goe,
   Though at next doore wee might meet,
Though ſhee were true, when you met her,
And laſt, till you write your letter,
          Yet ſhee   25
          Will bee
Falſe, ere I come, to two, or three.

Womans conſtancy.

NOw thou haſt lov'd me one whole day,
  To morrow when thou leav'ſt, what wilt thou ſay?
Wilt thou then Antedate ſome new made vow?
      Or ſay that now
We are not juſt thoſe perſons, which we were?   5
Or, that oathes made in reverentiall feare
Of Love, and his wrath, any may forſweare?
Or, as true deaths, true maryages untie,
So lovers contracts, images of thoſe,
Binde but till ſleep, deaths image, them unlooſe?   10
      Or, your owne end to Juſtifie,
For having purpoſ'd change, and falſehood; you
Can have no way but falſehood to be true?
Vaine lunatique, againſt theſe ſcapes I could
         Diſpute, and conquer, if I would,   15
        Which I abſtaine to doe,
For by to morrow, I may thinke ſo too.

   20 ſweet; *1669:* ſweet, *1633–54*   24 laſt, till] laſt ſo till *O'F, S, S96*
27 Falſe, . . . three] Falſe, ere ſhe come to two or three. *1669*
    Womans conſtancy. *1633–69, A18, L74, N, O'F, TCC, TCD: no title,*
B, D, H40, H49, Lec, P, S   8 Or, *1633, 1669:* For, *1635–54*
(ll. 8–10 in brackets)

VOL. I. C   *The*

The undertaking.

I Have done one braver thing
    Then all the *Worthies* did,
And yet a braver thence doth fpring,
    Which is, to keepe that hid.

It were but madnes now t'impart   5
    The skill of fpecular ftone,
When he which can have learn'd the art
    To cut it, can finde none.

So, if I now fhould utter this,
    Others (becaufe no more   10
Such ftuffe to worke upon, there is,)
    Would love but as before.

But he who lovelineffe within
    Hath found, all outward loathes,
For he who colour loves, and skinne,   15
    Loves but their oldeft clothes.

If, as I have, you alfo doe
    Vertue'attir'd in woman fee,
And dare love that, and fay fo too,
    And forget the Hee and Shee;   20

And if this love, though placed fo,
    From prophane men you hide,
Which will no faith on this beftow,
    Or, if they doe, deride:

Then you have dóne a braver thing   25
    Then all the *Worthies* did;
And a braver thence will fpring,
    Which is, to keepe that hid.

The undertaking. *1635–69: no title, 1633, B, D, H40, H49, JC, Lec,*
O'F, P, S: Platonique Love. *A18, N, TCC, TCD*   2 *Worthies*] worthies
1633   3 And yet] Yet *B, D, H49, Lec*   7–8 art . . . it, *1669:*
art, . . . it *1633–54*   16 their] her *B*   18 Vertue'attir'd in *1633, A18,*
B, D, H40, H49, JC, Lec, N, S, TC: Vertue in *1635–69, O'F, Chambers*
26 did; *Ed:* did. *1633–39:* did, *1650–69*   27 fpring.] fpring *1633–39*
The

The Sunne Rising.

B Ufie old foole, unruly Sunne,
    Why doft thou thus,
Through windowes, and through curtaines call on us?
Muft to thy motions lovers feafons run?
    Sawcy pedantique wretch, goe chide   5
    Late fchoole boyes, and fowre prentices,
Goe tell Court-huntfmen, that the King will ride,
Call countrey ants to harveft offices;
Love, all alike, no feafon knowes, nor clyme,
Nor houres, dayes, moneths, which are the rags of time.

    Thy beames, fo reverend, and ftrong   11
    Why fhouldft thou thinke?
I could eclipfe and cloud them with a winke,
But that I would not lofe her fight fo long:
    If her eyes have not blinded thine,   15
    Looke, and to morrow late, tell mee,
Whether both the'India's of fpice and Myne
Be where thou leftft them, or lie here with mee.
Aske for thofe Kings whom thou faw'ft yefterday,
And thou fhalt heare, All here in one bed lay.   20

    She'is all States, and all Princes, I,
    Nothing elfe is.
Princes doe but play us; compar'd to this,
All honor's mimique; All wealth alchimie.

The Sunne Rifing. *1633–69:* Sunne Rising. *A18,L74,N,TCC,TCD:*
Ad Solem. *A25,D,H49,JC,O'F,S,S96:* To the Sunne. *Cy,Lec,O'F*
(*as a second title*)*: no title, B*   3 call] look *1669*   6 and] or *1669*
fowre] flowe *B,Cy,P*   8 offices;] offices, *1633*   11–14 Thy
beames, ... fo long: *1633 and all MSS.:*
        Thy beames fo reverend, and ftrong
        Doft thou not thinke
      I could eclipfe and cloude them with a winke,
     But that I would not lofe her fight fo long? *1635–69*
17 fpice] fpace *1650–54*   **18** leftft *1633:* left *1635–69*   **23** us;]
us, *1633*   **24** wealth] wealth's *A25,C,P* alchimie. *Ed:* alchimie;
1633–69

                           Thou

Thou funne art halfe as happy'as wee,   25
 In that the world's contracted thus;
 Thine age askes eafe, and fince thy duties bee
 To warme the world, that's done in warming us.
Shine here to us, and thou art every where;
This bed thy center is, thefe walls, thy fpheare.   30

The Indifferent.

I Can love both faire and browne,
 Her whom abundance melts,and her whom want betraies,
Her who loves loneneffe beft,and her who maskes and plaies,
Her whom the country form'd, and whom the town,
Her who beleeves, and her who tries,   5
Her who ftill weepes with fpungie eyes,
And her who is dry corke, and never cries;
I can love her, and her, and you and you,
I can love any, fo fhe be not true.

Will no other vice content you?   10
Wil it not ferve your turn to do, as did your mothers?
Or have you all old vices fpent, and now would finde out
      others?
Or doth a feare, that men are true, torment you?
Oh we are not, be not you fo,
Let mee, and doe you, twenty know.   15
Rob mee, but binde me not, and let me goe.
Muft I, who came to travaile thorow you,
Grow your fixt fubject, becaufe you are true?

26 thus; *Ed:* thus. *1633–69*
  The Indifferent. *1633–69,A18,N,TCC,TCD:* A Songe, Songe, *or no
title,* B,D,H40,H49,JC,Lec,O'F,S,S96: Sonnet. *P*   3 loneneffe]
lovers *1669*   maskes] fports *1669,S*   and *1669:* & *1633–39:* om.
1650–54   12 fpent] worn *1669*   15 mee, *1633:* me; *1635–69*
17 travaile] *spelt* travell, travel *1635–69*

Venus

Venus heard me figh this fong,
And by Loves fweeteft Part, Variety, fhe fwore,   20
She heard not this till now; and that it fhould be fo no more.
She went, examin'd, and return'd ere long,
And faid, alas, Some two or three
Poore Heretiques in love there bee,
Which thinke to ftablifh dangerous conftancie.   25
But I have told them, fince you will be true,
You fhall be true to them, who'are falfe to you.

Loves Vfury.

FOr every houre that thou wilt fpare mee now,
    I will allow,
Ufurious God of Love, twenty to thee,
When with my browne, my gray haires equall bee;
Till then, Love, let my body raigne, and let   5
Mee travell, fojourne, fnatch, plot, have, forget,
Refume my laft yeares relict: thinke that yet
    We'had never met.

Let mee thinke any rivalls letter mine,
    And at next nine   10
Keepe midnights promife; miftake by the way
The maid, and tell the Lady of that delay;
Onely let mee love none, no, not the fport;
From country graffe, to comfitures of Court,
Or cities quelque chofes, let report   15
    My minde tranfport.

19 figh] fing *1669*   20 fweeteft Part,] fweeteft fweet, *1669, P, S*
21 and that it *1633, B, D, H49, Lec, S :* it *1635–69, H40, P :* and it *A18,
JC, N, O'F, S96, TC*
    Loves Vfury. *1633–69, L74 : no title, B, Cy, D, H40, H49, Lec, O'F,
P, S :* Elegie. *S96*   5 raigne, *1633, B, Cy, D, H40, H49, L74, Lec,
P, S :* range, *1635–69, O'F, S96.   See note*   6 fnatch, *1633, 1669 :*
match, *1635–54*   7 relict] relique *1669*   12 that] her *1669*   13
fport; *1669 :* fport *1633–54 :* fport, *most MSS.*   15 let report *1633,
1669, B, Cy, D, H40, H49, L74, Lec, P, S :* let not report *1635–54, O'F,
S96, Chambers.   See note*

                                                This

This bargaine's good; if when I'am old, I bee
    Inflam'd by thee,
If thine owne honour, or my fhame, or paine,
Thou covet moft, at that age thou fhalt gaine.   20
Doe thy will then, then fubject and degree,
And fruit of love, Love I fubmit to thee,
Spare mee till then, I'll beare it, though fhe bee
    One that loves mee.

The Canonization.

FOr Godfake hold your tongue, and let me love,
    Or chide my palfie, or my gout,
My five gray haires, or ruin'd fortune flout,
    With wealth your ftate, your minde with Arts improve,
        Take you a courfe, get you a place,   5
        Obferve his honour, or his grace,
Or the Kings reall, or his ftamped face
    Contemplate, what you will, approve,
    So you will let me love.

Alas, alas, who's injur'd by my love?   10
    What merchants fhips have my fighs drown'd?
Who faies my teares have overflow'd his ground?
    When did my colds a forward fpring remove?
        When did the heats which my veines fill
        Adde one more to the plaguie Bill?   15
Soldiers finde warres, and Lawyers finde out ftill
    Litigious men, which quarrels move
    Though fhe and I do love.

19 or. paine *1633,1669, and most MSS.:* and paine *1635–54, O'F*   22
fruit] fruites *B,D,H49,Lec,O'F,S96*   24 loves *1633,1669 and all the
MSS.:* love *1635–54*
    The Canonization. *1633–39,A18,Cy,D,H49,Lec,N,O'F,P,TCC,TCD:*
Canonization. *1650–69,S:* Canonizatio. *S96: no title, B,H40,JC*   3
five *1633,1669:* true *1635–54*   fortune] fortunes *1669*   4 improve,
1650–69: improve *1633–39*   7 reall] Roiall *Lec*   14 veines] reynes
1669   15 more, *1633–54,Lec:* man *1669,A18,B,Cy,D,H40,H49,JC,
N,O'F,P,S,S96,TC*   17 which] whom *1669*   18 Though]
While *1669*

Call

Call us what you will, wee are made fuch by love;
　Call her one, mee another flye,　　　　　　　20
We'are Tapers too, and at our owne coft die,
　And wee in us finde the'Eagle and the Dove.
　　The Phœnix ridle hath more wit
　　By us, we two being one, are it.
So to one neutrall thing both fexes fit,　　　　25
　Wee dye and rife the fame, and prove
　Myfterious by this love.

Wee can dye by it, if not live by love,
　And if unfit for tombes and hearfe
Our legend bee, it will be fit for verfe;　　　30
　And if no peece of Chronicle wee prove,
　　We'll build in fonnets pretty roomes;
　　As well a well wrought urne becomes
The greateft afhes, as halfe-acre tombes,
　And by thefe hymnes, all fhall approve　　35
　Us *Canoniz'd* for Love:

And thus invoke us; You whom reverend love
　Made one anothers hermitage;
You, to whom love was peace, that now is rage;
　Who did the whole worlds foule contract, and drove 40
　　Into the glaffes of your eyes
　　(So made fuch mirrors, and fuch fpies,
That they did all to you epitomize,)
　Countries, Townes, Courts: Beg from above
　A patterne of your love!　　　　　　　45

22 Dove. *Ed: dove, 1633–69*　24 are it. *1633–69:* are it; *Chambers and Grolier*　25 So *1650–69:* So, *1633–39. See note*　fit, *D, H49, Lec:* fit. *1633–69. See note*　29 tombes and *1633–54:* tomb or *1669*　30 legend] legends *1633*　35 thefe *1633:* thofe *1635–69*　36 Love:] Love. *1633*　39 rage; *Ed:* rage, *1633–69*　40 contract] extract *A18, B, Cy, D, H40, H49, Lec, N, O'F, S, S96, TCC*　41 eyes *1633–69:* eyes; *Chambers*　42–3 brackets, *Ed*　44 Courts: Beg] Courts Beg *1669:* courts beg *Chambers. See note*　from] frow *1633*　45 your *1669, A18, B, H40, JC, N, O'F, P, S96, TC:* our *1633–54, D, H49, Lec*　love ! *Ed:* love. *1633–69*

　　　　　　　　　　　　　　　　The

The triple Foole.

I Am two fooles, I know,
For loving, and for faying fo
    In whining Poëtry;
But where's that wifeman, that would not be I,
    If fhe would not deny?   5
Then as th'earths inward narrow crooked lanes
Do purge fea waters fretfull falt away,
    I thought, if I could draw my paines,
Through Rimes vexation, I fhould them allay,
Griefe brought to numbers cannot be fo fierce,   10
For, he tames it, that fetters it in verfe.

    But when I have done fo,
Some man, his art and voice to fhow,
    Doth Set and fing my paine,
And, by delighting many, frees againe   15
    Griefe, which verfe did reftraine.
To Love, and Griefe tribute of Verfe belongs,
But not of fuch as pleafes when'tis read,
    Both are increafed by fuch fongs:
For both their triumphs fo are publifhed,   20
And I, which was two fooles, do fo grow three;
Who are a little wife, the beft fooles bee.

    The triple Foole. *1633–69, A18, L74, N, TCC, TCD:* Song *or no title*,
B, Cy, D, H40, H49, HN, JC, Lec, O'F, P, S, S96   4 the wifer
man, *1669*   5 If he fhould not deny? *P*   6 narrow *om, P:*
crooked *om. B*   lanes] vaines *Cy, P*   9 allay, *1633–39:* allay. *1650–69,*
Chambers   10 numbers] number *1669*   11 For, he tames it] He
tames it much *B*   13 and] or *1669*

Lovers infiniteneſſe.

IF yet I have not all thy love,
  Deare, I ſhall never have it all,
I cannot breath one other ſigh, to move,
Nor can intreat one other teare to fall,
And all my treaſure, which ſhould purchaſe thee,   5
Sighs, teares, and oathes, and letters I have ſpent.
Yet no more can be due to mee,
Then at the bargaine made was ment,
If then thy gift of love were partiall,
That ſome to mee, ſome ſhould to others fall,   10
  Deare, I ſhall never have Thee All.

Or if then thou gaveſt mee all,
All was but All, which thou hadſt then;
But if in thy heart, ſince, there be or ſhall,
New love created bee, by other men,   15
Which have their ſtocks intire, and can in teares,
In ſighs, in oathes, and letters outbid mee,
This new love may beget new feares,
For, this love was not vowed by thee.
And yet it was, thy gift being generall,   20
The ground, thy heart is mine, what ever ſhall
  Grow there, deare, I ſhould have it all.

Yet I would not have all yet,
Hee that hath all can have no more,
And ſince my love doth every day admit   25
New growth, thou ſhouldſt have new rewards in ſtore;

Lovers infiniteneſſe. *1633–69:* Mon Tout. *A25, C: no title, B, D, H40,*
H49, JC, Lec, O'F, P, S: Elegie. *S96*   *Query* Loves infinitenesse.
3 move, *Ed:* move; *1633–69*   4 fall, *Ed:* fall. *1633:* fall; *1635–69*
6 teares,] teares *1633*   ſpent. *Ed:* ſpent, *1633–69 and Grolier:* spent;
Chambers   8 Then *1633–35, 1669:* That *1639–54*   9 were] was
1669   partiall] generall *A25, C*   11 Thee *1633:* It *1635–69*
(it *1669*)   12 gaveſt] giveſt *1669*   13 then; *1635–54:* then, *1633*
17 and letters *1633:* in letters *1635–69*   19 thee. *1639–69:* thee,
1633–35   20 it] is *1633*   21 is *1633, 1669:* was *1635–54*   25–6
And ſince my heart doth every day beget New love, *&c. A25.*
                                                    Thou

Thou canſt not every day give me thy heart,
If thou canſt give it, then thou never gaveſt it:
Loves riddles are, that though thy heart depart,
It ſtayes at home, and thou with loſing ſaveſt it: 30
But wee will have a way more liberall,
Then changing hearts, to joyne them, ſo wee ſhall
   Be one, and one anothers All.

Song.

SWeeteſt love, I do not goe,
   For wearineſſe of thee,
Nor in hope the world can ſhow
   A fitter Love for mee;
    But ſince that I   5
Muſt dye at laſt, 'tis beſt,
To uſe my ſelfe in jeſt
    Thus by fain'd deaths to dye ;

29-30   Except mine come when thine doth part
    And in ſuch giving it, thou ſaveſt it : *A25, C*
    Perchance mine comes, when thine doth parte,
    And by ſuch loſing it, *&c. JC*
31 have] love *1669 :* find *A25, C*   32 them] us *1669*
   Song. *1633–69 :* Song. *or no title,* A18, A25, B, C, D, H40, H49, JC,
Lec, N, O'F, P, S, S96, TCC, TCD : *in* A18, N, TCC, TCD, *this with* Send
home my long ſtray'd eyes *and* The Bait *are given as* Songs which
were made to certain ayres which were made before.   1-4 *In most*
MSS. these lines are written as two long lines, and so with ll. 9–12, 17–20,
25–28, 33–36   4 mee ; *1650–69 :* mee, *1633–39*   5–8 But ſince
. . . dye ; *1633,* A18, A25, B, D, H40, H49, JC, Lec, N, P, S, S96, TC :
             At the laſt muſt part 'tis beſt,
             Thus to uſe my ſelfe in jeſt
               By fained deaths to dye ; *1635–54, O'F :*
             Muſt dye at laſt, 'tis beſt,
             Thus to uſe my ſelf in jeſt
               By fained death to dye ; *1669*
                              Yeſternight

Yesternight the Sunne went hence,
    And yet is here to day,   10
He hath no desire nor sense,
    Nor halfe so short a way :
        Then feare not mee,
But beleeve that I shall make
Speedier journeyes, since I take   15
    More wings and spurres then hee.

O how feeble is mans power,
    That if good fortune fall,
Cannot adde another houre,
    Nor a lost houre recall !   20
        But come bad chance,
And wee joyne to'it our strength,
And wee teach it art and length,
    It selfe o'r us to'advance.

When thou sigh'st, thou sigh'st not winde,   25
    But sigh'st my soule away,
When thou weep'st, unkindly kinde,
    My lifes blood doth decay.
        It cannot bee
That thou lov'st mee, as thou say'st,   30
If in thine my life thou waste,
    Thou art the best of mee.

Let not thy divining heart
    Forethinke me any ill,
Destiny may take thy part,   35
    And may thy feares fulfill ;
        But thinke that wee
Are but turn'd aside to sleepe ;
They who one another keepe
    Alive, ne'r parted bee.   40

15 Speedier] Hastier *1669*   20 recall ! *Ed:* recall ? *1633–69*   25 not
wind *1633:* no wind *1635–69*   32 Thou *1633 and MSS. generally :*
That *1635–54:* Which *1669*   best *1633–54:* life *1669*   36 may
1633–35,1669: make *1639–54*   fulfill ; *Ed:* fulfill, *1633–69*
38 turn'd] lai'd *1669*

                                     The

The Legacie.

WHen I dyed laſt, and, Deare, I dye
　　As often as from thee I goe,
　Though it be but an houre agoe,
And Lovers houres be full eternity,
I can remember yet, that I　　　　　　　　　　　　5
　Something did ſay, and ſomething did beſtow;
Though I be dead, which ſent mee, I ſhould be
Mine owne executor and Legacie.

I heard mee ſay, Tell her anon,
　That my ſelfe, (that is you, not I,)　　　　　　　10
　Did kill me, and when I felt mee dye,
I bid mee ſend my heart, when I was gone,
But I alas could there finde none,
　When I had ripp'd me,'and ſearch'd where hearts did lye;
It kill'd mee againe, that I who ſtill was true,　　15
In life, in my laſt Will ſhould cozen you.

Yet I found ſomething like a heart,
　But colours it, and corners had,
　It was not good, it was not bad,
It was intire to none, and few had part.　　　　　20
As good as could be made by art
　It ſeem'd ; and therefore for our loſſes ſad,
I meant to ſend this heart in ſtead of mine,
But oh, no man could hold it, for twas thine.

The Legacie. *1633–69*: Legacie. *L74*: Song. *or no title*, *A25, B, Cy,*
D, H40, H49, Lec, O'F, P, S, S96: Elegie. *A18, N, TCC, TCD*　　1
When I dyed laſt,] When laſt I dyed, *1669*　　　1–4 (and deare . . .
eternity) *Grolier.*　　7 ſent *1633, 1669:* meant *1635–54*　　ſhould be]
might be *1669*　　10 that is *1635–69:* that's *1633: brackets from A18,*
N, TC　　13 none, *1633–69:* none. *Chambers and Grolier*　　14 When
. . . did *1633, A25* (doe), *D, H40, H49, Lec, S, S96:* When I had ripp'd, and
ſearch'd where hearts ſhould *1635–69, A18, L74, N, TC*　　lye; *Ed:* lye,
1633–69, Chambers and Grolier. See note　　18 But] For *1650–69*　　20
part. *1633–39:* part: *1650–69*　　22 ſeem'd; *Ed:* ſeem'd, *1633–69,*
Grolier, and Chambers　　our loſſes ſad, *1633–54, A18, A25, L74, N, O'F,*
P, S96, TC: our lofs be ſad. *1669:* our lofs be ye ſad. *B, Cy, D, H40,*
H49, Lec, S: our losses sad; *Grolier:* our loss be sad. *Chambers*　　23
meant] thought *A18, L74, N, O'F, TC*　　this *1633:* that *1635–69*

A

A Feaver.

OH doe not die, for I ſhall hate
 All women ſo, when thou art gone,
That thee I ſhall not celebrate,
 When I remember, thou waſt one.

But yet thou canſt not die, I know;   5
 To leave this world behinde, is death,
But when thou from this world wilt goe,
 The whole world vapors with thy breath.

Or if, when thou, the worlds foule, goeſt,
 It ſtay, tis but thy carkaſſe then,   10
The faireſt woman, but thy ghoſt,
 But corrupt wormes, the worthyeſt men.

O wrangling ſchooles, that ſearch what fire
 Shall burne this world, had none the wit
Unto this knowledge to aſpire,   15
 That this her feaver might be it ?

And yet ſhe cannot waſt by this,
 Nor long beare this torturing wrong,
For much corruption needfull is
 To fuell ſuch a feaver long.   20

Theſe burning fits but meteors bee,
 Whoſe matter in thee is ſoone ſpent.
Thy beauty,'and all parts, which are thee,
 Are unchangeable firmament.

Yet t'was of my minde, ſeiſing thee,   25
 Though it in thee cannot perſever.
For I had rather owner bee
 Of thee one houre, then all elſe ever.

A Feaver. *1633-69, D, H40, H49, Lec, S96:* Of a fever. *L74:* The
Fever. *B, Cy, O'F, P:* Fever. *A18, N, TCC, TCD:* no title, *JC*   5
know ; *Ed:* know, *1633-69*   8 with] in *1669*   16 might] muſt *TCC*
18 beare] endure *1669*   torturing] tormenting *JC, O'F (corr. from*
torturing)   19 For much *1633, A18, B, D, H40, H49, JC, L74, Lec,*
N, S, S96, TC : For more *1635-69, O'F:* Far more *Cy, P*   22 is
ſoon] ſoon is *1669*   24 Are] Are an *1669, P, S96*   25 Yet
'twas of *1633-54:* And here as *1669*   27 For] Yet *1669*

             Aire

Aire and Angels.

TWice or thrice had I loved thee,
   Before I knew thy face or name;
So in a voice, fo in a fhapeleffe flame,
Angells affect us oft, and worfhip'd bee;
   Still when, to where thou wert, I came,   5
Some lovely glorious nothing I did fee.
   But fince my foule, whofe child love is,
Takes limmes of flefh, and elfe could nothing doe,
   More fubtile then the parent is,
Love muft not be, but take a body too,   10
   And therefore what thou wert, and who,
      I bid Love aske, and now
That it affume thy body, I allow,
And fixe it felfe in thy lip, eye, and brow.

Whilft thus to ballaft love, I thought,   15
And fo more fteddily to have gone,
With wares which would finke admiration,
I faw, I had loves pinnace overfraught,
   Ev'ry thy haire for love to worke upon
Is much too much, fome fitter muft be fought;   20
   For, nor in nothing, nor in things
Extreme, and fcatt'ring bright, can love inhere;
   Then as an Angell, face, and wings
Of aire, not pure as it, yet pure doth weare,
   So thy love may be my loves fpheare;   25
      Juft fuch difparitie
As is twixt Aire and Angells puritie,
'Twixt womens love, and mens will ever bee.

Aire and Angels. *1633–69, A18, D, H49, JC, Lec, N, O'F, P, S, S96,*
TCC, TCD: no title, B, H40   4 bee; *Ed:* bce, *1633–69*   5 came,]
came *1633*   6 I did] did I *1669*   fee. *Ed:* fee, *1633–69*   7 fince
Ed: fince, *1633–69*   11 who, *Ed:* who *1633–69*   14 lip, eye,]
lips, eyes, *1669, Chambers*   19 Ev'ry thy *1633–39, A18, B*(Even), *D,*
H40, H49, JC, Lec, N, O'F, S(Ever), *S96, TC:* Thy every *1650–69*   22
fcatt'ring *Ed:* fcattring *1633–35:* fcattering *1639–69*   27 Aire *1633–54*
and all MSS.: Airs *1669, Chambers*

Breake

Breake of day.

'TIs true, 'tis day; what though it be?
⎿ O wilt thou therefore rife from me?
Why fhould we rife, becaufe 'tis light?
Did we lie downe, becaufe 'twas night?
Love which in fpight of darkneffe brought us hether,   5
Should in defpight of light keepe us together.

Light hath no tongue, but is all eye;
If it could fpeake as well as fpie,
This were the worft, that it could fay,
That being well, I faine would ftay,   10
And that I lov'd my heart and honor fo,
That I would not from him, that had them, goe.

Muft bufineffe thee from hence remove?
Oh, that's the worft difeafe of love,
The poore, the foule, the falfe, love can   15
Admit, but not the bufied man.
He which hath bufineffe, and makes love, doth doe
Such wrong, as when a maryed man doth wooe.

Breake of day. *1633–69, A18, L74, N, TCC, TCD: no title or* Sonnet,
B, D, H40, H49, JC, Lec, O'F, P, S, S96 : A Songe. *A25*   1 day;] day,
1633   5 in fpight *1633–39, 1669, A25, JC, S96:* in difpight *1650–54,*
A18, D, H40, H49, L74, Lec, N, S, TC   6 in defpight *1633, 1650–69:* in
fpight *1635–39*   keepe] holde *A18, L74, N, S96, TC*   9 were]
is *A18, L74, N, O'F, S, TC*   11 I lov'd] I love *JC, N, O'F, TC*   12
him, that had them, *1633–54, D, H49, Lec, S:* him that hath them (*or* it)
A25, B, C, L74, N, O'F, TC: her, that had them, *1669:* her that hath
them *B, JC* (it), *S96*   15 foule.] foole, *H40*   18 as when . . . doth
1633, 1669, A25, C, D, H40, H49, Lec, S, S96: as if . . . fhould *A18,*
B, JC, L74, N, O'F, TC: as when . . . fhould *1635–54*

The Anniverfarie.

ALL Kings, and all their favorites,
   All glory of honors, beauties, wits,
The Sun it felfe, which makes times, as they paffe,
Is elder by a yeare, now, then it was
When thou and I firft one another faw: 5
All other things, to their deftruction draw,
   Only our love hath no decay;
This, no to morrow hath, nor yefterday,
Running it never runs from us away,
But truly keepes his firft, laft, everlafting day.   10

Two graves muft hide thine and my coarfe,
   If one might, death were no divorce.
Alas, as well as other Princes, wee,
(Who Prince enough in one another bee,)
Muft leave at laft in death, thefe eyes, and eares,   15
Oft fed with true oathes, and with fweet falt teares;
   But foules where nothing dwells but love
(All other thoughts being inmates) then fhall prove
This, or a love increafed there above,
When bodies to their graves, foules from their graves
   remove.   20

The Anniverfarie. *1633–69, A18, N, TCC, TCD:* no title, *B, Cy, D,
H40, H49, JC, Lec, O'F, P, S:* Ad Liviam. *S96*   3 times, as they
paffe, *1633,1669 (which brackets* which . . . pafs), *MSS.:* times, as thefe
pafs, *1635–54:* time, as they pass, *Chambers, who attributes to 1633, 1669*
12 divorce. *Ed:* divorce, *1633–69*   17 love *Ed:* love; *1633–69*   20
to their graves] to their grave *1635–39*

And then wee ſhall be throughly bleſt,
  But wee no more, then all the reſt;
Here upon earth, we'are Kings, and none but wee
Can be ſuch Kings, nor of ſuch ſubjeĉts bee.
Who is ſo ſafe as wee? where none can doe   25
Treaſon to us, except one of us two.
  True and falſe feares let us refraine,
Let us love nobly, and live, and adde againe
Yeares and yeares unto yeares, till we attaine
To write threeſcore: this is the ſecond of our raigne.   30

A Valediĉtion : of my name, in the window.

I.

MY name engrav'd herein,
Doth contribute my firmneſſe to this glaſſe,
  Which, ever ſince that charme, hath beene
  As hard, as that which grav'd it, was;
Thine eye will give it price enough, to mock   5
  The diamonds of either rock.

---

22 wee *A18, B, Cy, D, H40, H49, JC, Lec, N, O'F, P, S, S96, TC:* now *1633–69. See note*   reſt; *Ed:* reſt. *1633–69*   23 none *om. 1669, D, H40, H49, JC, Lec, S, S96*   24 None are ſuch Kings, *1669, D, H40, H49, JC, Lec, S, S96*   nor] and *D, H40, H49, JC, Lec, S, S96*   bee. *Ed:* bee; *1633–69*   27 refraine,] refraine. *1669*   30 threeſcore : *Grolier:* threeſcore, *1633–69*
  A Valediĉtion : Of *&c. D, H49:* A Valediĉtion of *&c. 1633–69, H40, Lec:* Valediĉtion of *&c. A18, N, TCC, TCD:* A Valediĉtion of my name in the Glaſſe Window *Cy:* A Valediĉtion to *&c. B:* Valediĉtion 4 : of Glaſſe *O'F:* Valediĉtion in Glaſſe *P:* The Diamond and Glaſſe *S:* Vpon the ingravinge of his name with a Diamonde in his miſtris windowe when he was to travel. *S96 (This is added to the title in O'F.):* ſimilarly, *JC* 4 was; *Ed:* was, *1633–69*   5 eye] eyes *A18, B, Cy, JC, N, O'F, P, S, S96, TC*

II.

II.

'Tis much that Glaffe fhould bee
As all confeffing, and through-fhine as I,
  'Tis more, that it fhewes thee to thee,
  And cleare reflects thee to thine eye.   10
But all fuch rules, loves magique can undoe,
    Here you fee mee, and I am you.

III.

As no one point, nor dafh,
Which are but acceffaries to this name,
  The fhowers and tempefts can outwafh,   15
  So fhall all times finde mee the fame;
You this intireneffe better may fulfill,
    Who have the patterne with you ftill.

IIII.

Or, if too hard and deepe
This learning be, for a fcratch'd name to teach,
  It, as a given deaths head keepe,   20
  Lovers mortalitie to preach,
Or thinke this ragged bony name to bee
    My ruinous Anatomie.

V.

Then, as all my foules bee,   25
Emparadif'd in you, (in whom alone
  I underftand, and grow and fee,)
  The rafters of my body, bone
Being ftill with you, the Mufcle, Sinew, and Veine,
    Which tile this houfe, will come againe.   30

8 I, *1633–54:* I *1669*   12 am you.] fee you. *1669*   14
acceffaries *1633–69,* O'*F,* S: acceffary A*18,* B, C*y,* D, H*40,* H*49,* JC, L*ec,* N,
P, S*96,* TC   15 tempefts *1633, 1669:* tempeft *1635–54*   19 Or, *Ed:*
Or *1633–69*

VI.

VI.

Till my returne, repaire
And recompact my fcattered body fo.
　As all the vertuous powers which are
　Fix'd in the ftarres, are faid to flow
Into fuch characters, as graved bee　　　　　　35
　　When thefe ftarres have fupremacie:

VII.

So, fince this name was cut
When love and griefe their exaltation had,
　No doore 'gainft this names influence fhut;
　As much more loving, as more fad,　　　　　40
'Twill make thee; and thou fhouldft, till I returne,
　　Since I die daily, daily mourne.

VIII.

When thy inconfiderate hand
Flings ope this cafement, with my trembling name,
　To looke on one, whofe wit or land,　　　　　45
　New battry to thy heart may frame,
Then thinke this name alive, and that thou thus
　　In it offendft my Genius.

IX.

And when thy melted maid,
Corrupted by thy Lover's gold, and page,　　　　50
　His letter at thy pillow'hath laid,
　Difputed it, and tam'd thy rage,
And thou begin'ft to thaw towards him, for this,
　　May my name ftep in, and hide his.

32 fo. *1633–35:* fo, *1639–69, Chambers. See note*　　34 flow *Ed:*
flow, *1633–69*　　36 thefe *1633 :* thofe *1635–69*　　have] had *1669*
fupremacie: *1633–39:* fupremacie. *1650–69. See note*　　37 So, *Ed:* So
1633–69　　39 fhut; *Ed:* fhut, *1633–69*　　44 ope *1633–69, O'F,*
S96: out *A18, B, D, H40, H49, JC, Lec, N, P, S, TC*　　48 offendft]
offends *1669*　　50 and] or *1669, JC, O'F, S96*
52–3　　Difputed thou it, and tame thy rage.
　　　If thou to him begin'ft to thaw for this, *1669*

X.

X.

And if this treafon goe 55
To an overt act, and that thou write againe;
  In fuperfcribing, this name flow
Into thy fancy, from the pane.
So, in forgetting thou remembreft right,
    And unaware to mee fhalt write. 60

XI.

But glaffe, and lines muft bee,
No meanes our firme fubftantiall love to keepe;
  Neere death inflicts this lethargie,
And this I murmure in my fleepe;
Impute this idle talke, to that I goe, 65
    For dying men talke often fo.

Twicknam garden.

BLafted with fighs, and furrounded with teares,
  Hither I come to feeke the fpring,
    And at mine eyes, and at mine eares,
Receive fuch balmes, as elfe cure every thing;
  But O, felfe traytor, I do bring 5
The fpider love, which tranfubftantiates all,
    And can convert Manna to gall,
And that this place may thoroughly be thought
  True Paradife, I have the ferpent brought.

---

55 goe] growe *JC,O'F,S* 56 againe; *1633:* againe: *1635–69* 57
this] my *1669* 58 pane. *1633:* Pen, *1635–69,O'F,S* 60 unaware|
unawares *B,N,O'F,P,S,S96,TC* 64 this] thus *1635–69,O'F,P,S,S96*
Twicknam garden. *1633–69: do.* or Twitnam Garden. *A18,L74 (in
margin),N,O'F,P,S,S96,TCC,TCD:* In a Garden. *B: no title, A25,
Cy,D,H40,H49,JC,Lec,P* 3 eares] years *1669* 4 balms . . .
cure *1633,A25,D,H49:* balm . . . cures *1635–69,A18,B,Cy,L74,N,
O'F,P,S,S96,TC* thing; *Ed:* thing, *1633:* thing : *1635–69* 6
fpider] fpiders *1669* 8 thoroughly *1633–39:* throughly *1650–69*
                                         'Twere

'Twere wholſomer for mee, that winter did   10
   Benight the glory of this place,
   And that a grave froſt did forbid
Theſe trees to laugh, and mocke mee to my face;
   But that I may not this diſgrace
Indure, nor yet leave loving, Love let mee   15
   Some ſenſleſſe peece of this place bee;
Make me a mandrake, ſo I may groane here,
   Or a ſtone fountaine weeping out my yeare.

Hither with chriſtall vyals, lovers come,
   And take my teares, which are loves wine,   20
   And try your miſtreſſe Teares at home,
For all are falſe, that taſt not juſt like mine;
   Alas, hearts do not in eyes ſhine,
Nor can you more judge womans thoughts by teares,
   Then by her ſhadow, what ſhe weares.   25
O perverſe ſexe, where none is true but ſhee,
   Who's therefore true, becauſe her truth kills mee.

A Valediction : of the booke.

I'Ll tell thee now (deare Love) what thou ſhalt doe
  To anger deſtiny, as ſhe doth us,
   How I ſhall ſtay, though ſhe Eſloygne me thus
And how poſterity ſhall know it too;

12 did] would *A18, A25, N, TC*   13 laugh,] laugh *1633*   14 that
I may not] ſince I cannot *1669*   15 nor yet leave loving, *1633:* om.*D,*
H40, H49, Lec: nor leave this garden, *1635–69, A18, A25, Cy, JC, L74, N,*
O'F, P, S, S96, TC   17 groane *A18, D, H40, H49, N, TC:* grow
1633–69, B, L74, Lec, O'F, P, S, S96   18 my yeare, *1633, 1669, D, H40,*
H49, Lec: the yeare. *1635–54, A18, A25, L74, N, O'F, P, TC*   20 loves]
lovers *1639*   24 womans *A18, D, H40, H49, L74, N, TC:* womens
1633–69, Lec, P, S96
   A Valediction: of &c. *Ed:* A Valediction of the Booke *A18, N, TCC,*
TCD: Valediction of the booke. *D, H49, Lec:* Valediction 3: Of the
Booke *O'F:* The Booke *Cy, P:* Valediction to his booke. *1633–69, S:*
A Valediction of a booke left in a windowe. *JC*
                                                 How

How thine may out-endure   5
Sybills glory, and obfcure
Her who from Pindar could allure,
And her, through whofe helpe *Lucan* is not lame,
And her, whofe booke (they fay) *Homer* did finde, and name.

Study our manufcripts, thofe Myriades   10
Of letters, which have paft twixt thee and mee,
Thence write our Annals, and in them will bee
To all whom loves fubliming fire invades,
Rule and example found ;
There, the faith of any ground   15
No fchifmatique will dare to wound,
That fees, how Love this grace to us affords,
To make, to keep, to ufe, to be thefe his Records.

This Booke, as long-liv'd as the elements,
Or as the worlds forme, this all-graved tome   20
In cypher writ, or new made Idiome,
Wee for loves clergie only'are inftruments :
When this booke is made thus,
Should againe the ravenous
Vandals and Goths inundate us,   25
Learning were fafe ; in this our Univerfe
Schooles might learne Sciences, Spheares Mufick, Angels
Verfe.

Here Loves Divines, (fince all Divinity
Is love or wonder) may finde all they feeke,
Whether abftract fpirituall love they like,   30
Their Soules exhal'd with what they do not fee,

---

18 Records, *1633–69:* records, *Grolier*   20 tome *1633–35:* to me
1639–54: Tomb. *1669, A18, Cy, Lec, N, S*   21 Idiome, *Ed:* Idiome;
1633–69   22 inftruments: *Ed:* inftruments, *1633–69. See note*   25
and Goths inundate us, *A18, B, Cy, D, H40, H49, Lec, N, TC:* and the
Goths invade us, *1633–54, S:* and Goths invade us, *1669, H40, JC* (or), *O'F,*
P   26 were fafe; *1633: rest omit semicolon.*   Univerfe *1633–39:*
Univerfe, *1650–69*   30 abftract] abftracted *1669*

Or,

Or, loth fo to amuze
Faiths infirmitie, they chufe
Something which they may fee and ufe;
For, though minde be the heaven, where love doth fit, 35
Beauty a convenient type may be to figure it.

Here more then in their bookes may Lawyers finde,
  Both by what titles Miftreffes are ours,
  And how prerogative thefe ftates devours,
Transferr'd from Love himfelfe, to womankinde,   40
    Who though from heart, and eyes,
    They exact great fubfidies,
    Forfake him who on them relies,
  And for the caufe, honour, or confcience give,
Chimeraes, vaine as they, or their prerogative.   45

Here Statefmen, (or of them, they which can reade,)
  May of their occupation finde the grounds :
  Love and their art alike it deadly wounds,
If to confider what 'tis, one proceed,
    In both they doe excell   50
    Who the prefent governe well,
    Whofe weakneffe none doth, or dares tell;
  In this thy booke, fuch will their nothing fee,
As in the Bible fome can finde out Alchimy.

Thus vent thy thoughts; abroad I'll ftudie thee,   55
  As he removes farre off, that great heights takes ;
  How great love is, prefence beft tryall makes,
But abfence tryes how long this love will bee ;

32 Or, . . . amuze *Ed:* Or . . . amuze, *1633–69*　　33 infirmitie,]
infirmities, *1669, D, H49, Lec*　　38 titles] titles, *1633*　　39 thefe ftates]
thofe rites *A18, N, TC*　　40 womankinde, *Ed:* womankinde. *1633–54:*
womankinde: *1669*　　43 relies, *Ed:* relies *1633:* relies; *1635–69*　　44
give,] give; *1635–69*　　46 Statefmen] Tradefmen *Cy, P*　　47 grounds:
Ed: grounds, *1633–69*　　49 'tis, one] 'tis on, *1669*　　53 their nothing
1635–54, A18, B, Cy, D, H40, H49, JC (nothings), *Lec, N, O'F, S, TC* (*but
the MSS. waver between* their *and* there)*:* there fomething *1633, 1669, P*
55 vent *1633, 1669:* went *1635–54*　　thoughts; abroad] thoughts abroad:
1669　　56 great heights] fhadows *O'F*

To

　　To take a latitude
　　Sun, or ſtarres, are fitlieſt view'd   60
　　　At their brighteſt, but to conclude
Of longitudes, what other way have wee,
But to marke when, and where the darke eclipſes bee?

Communitie.

GOod wee muſt love, and muſt hate ill,
　For ill is ill, and good good ſtill,
　　But there are things indifferent,
Which wee may neither hate, nor love,
But one, and then another prove,
　　As wee ſhall finde our fancy bent.   5

If then at firſt wiſe Nature had
Made women either good or bad,
　　Then ſome wee might hate, and ſome chuſe,
But ſince ſhee did them ſo create,
That we may neither love, nor hate,   10
　　Onely this reſts, All, all may uſe.

If they were good it would be ſeene,
Good is as viſible as greene,
　　And to all eyes it ſelfe betrayes:
If they were bad, they could not laſt,   15
Bad doth it ſelfe, and others waſt,
　　So, they deſerve nor blame, nor praiſe.

　　63 *1669 omits* darke
　　Communitie. *1635–69: no title, 1633, A18, B, Cy, D, H40, H49, JC,*
L74, Lec, N, O'F, P, S, S96, TCC, TCD　　3 there *1635–69, A18, B, N,*
O'F, S, TC, &c.: theſe *1633, D, Cy, H49, Lec*　　7 had *Ed:* had, *1633–39*
12 All, all *1633–54:* All men *1669*　　15 betrayes: *1650–69:* betrayes,
1633–39

　　　　　　　　　　　　　　　　　　　　　　But

But they are ours, as fruits are ours,
He that but tafts, he that devours,   20
    And he that leaves all, doth as well:
Chang'd loves are but chang'd forts of meat,
And when hee hath the kernell eate,
    Who doth not fling away the fhell?

Loves growth.

I Scarce beleeve my love to be fo pure
    As I had thought it was,
      Becaufe it doth endure
Viciffitude, and feafon, as the graffe;
Me thinkes I lyed all winter, when I fwore,   5
My love was infinite, if fpring make'it more.

But if this medicine, love, which cures all forrow
With more, not onely bee no quinteffence,
But mixt of all ftuffes, paining foule, or fenfe,
And of the Sunne his working vigour borrow,   10
Love's not fo pure, and abftract, as they ufe
To fay, which have no Miftreffe but their Mufe,
But as all elfe, being elemented too,
Love fometimes would contemplate, fometimes do.

And yet no greater, but more eminent,   15
      Love by the fpring is growne;
      As, in the firmament,

---

21 well: *Ed:* well, *1633–69*
    Loves growth. *1633–69, A18, N, TCC, TCD:* The Spring. *or* Spring. *B,*
Cy, D, H49, Lec, O'F, P, S, S96: no title, JC   9 paining *1633, A18, B,*
D, H49, JC, Lec, N, S96, TC: vexing *1635–69, Cy, O'F, P, S*   10 working
1633 and MSS. as above: active *1635–69 and MSS. as above*   11 pure,
and] pure an *1669, O'F*   14 do.] do *1633*

Starres

Starres by the Sunne are not inlarg'd, but fhowne.
Gentle love deeds, as bloffomes on a bough,
From loves awakened root do bud out now.   20
If, as in water ftir'd more circles bee
Produc'd by one, love fuch additions take,
Thofe like fo many fpheares, but one heaven make,
For, they are all concentrique unto thee.
And though each fpring doe adde to love new heate,   25
As princes doe in times of action get
New taxes, and remit them not in peace,
No winter fhall abate the fprings encreafe.

Loves exchange.

Love, any devill elfe but you,
    Would for a given Soule give fomething too.
At Court your fellowes every day,
Give th'art of Riming, Huntfmanfhip, or Play,
For them which were their owne before;   5
Onely I have nothing which gave more,
But am, alas, by being lowly, lower.

I afke no difpenfation now
To falfifie a teare, or figh, or vow,
I do not fue from thee to draw   10
A *non obftante* on natures law,
Thefe are prerogatives, they inhere
In thee and thine; none fhould forfweare
Except that hee *Loves* minion were.

18–19 Starres . . . fhowne. Gentle love *Ed:* Starres . . . fhowne,
Gentle love *1633–69*:
                Stars are not by the funne enlarg'd; but fhowne
                Greater; Loves deeds *P. See note*
24 thee. *Ed:* thee, *1633–69*   28 the *1633, A18, B, D, H49, JC, Lec,
N, S96, TC:* this *1635–69, Cy, O'F, P, S*
    Loves exchange. *1633–69, A18, N, TCC, TCD: no title, B, D, H40, H49,
JC, Lec, O'F, P*   4 or] and *most MSS.*   Play *D:* play *1633–69*   9
or figh, or vow, *1633–54:* a figh, a vow, *1669*

                                                        Give

Give mee thy weakneſſe, make mee blinde,   15
Both wayes, as thou and thine, in eies and minde;
Love, let me never know that this
Is love, or, that love childiſh is;
Let me not know that others know
That ſhe knowes my paines, leaſt that ſo   20
A tender ſhame make me mine owne new woe.

If thou give nothing, yet thou'art juſt,
Becauſe I would not thy firſt motions truſt;
Small townes which ſtand ſtiffe, till great ſhot
Enforce them, by warres law *condition* not.   25
Such in loves warfare is my caſe,
I may not article for grace,
Having put Love at laſt to ſhew this face.

This face, by which he could command
And change the Idolatrie of any land,   30
This face, which whereſoe'r it comes,
Can call vow'd men from cloiſters, dead from tombes,
And melt both Poles at once, and ſtore
Deſerts with cities, and make more
Mynes in the earth, then Quarries were before.   35

For this, Love is enrag'd with mee,
Yet kills not. If I muſt example bee
To future Rebells; If th'unborne
Muſt learne, by my being cut up, and torne:
Kill, and diſſect me, Love; for this   40
Torture againſt thine owne end is,
Rack't carcaſſes make ill Anatomies.

18 is; *Ed:* is. *1633–69*   20 paines] paine *A18, B, D, H40, H49,
JC, Lec, O'F, P, TC*   21 *1669 omits* new   28 Love *D:* love *1633–69*
this] his *1669*   36 For this, *Ed:* For, this *1633–69*   Love *D:* love
1633–69   37 not. If *Ed:* not; if *1633–39:* not: if *1650–69*

Confined Love.

SOme man unworthy to be poſſeſſor
Of old or new love, himſelfe being falſe or weake,
  Thought his paine and ſhame would be leſſer,
If on womankind he might his anger wreake,
        And thence a law did grow,   5
        One might but one man know;
        But are other creatures ſo?

  Are Sunne, Moone, or Starres by law forbidden,
To ſmile where they liſt, or lend away their light?
  Are birds divorc'd, or are they chidden   10
If they leave their mate, or lie abroad a night?
        Beaſts doe no joyntures loſe
        Though they new lovers chooſe,
        But we are made worſe then thoſe.

  Who e'r rigg'd faire ſhip to lie in harbors,   15
And not to ſeeke new lands, or not to deale withall?
  Or built faire houſes, ſet trees, and arbors,
Only to lock up, or elſe to let them fall?
        Good is not good, unleſſe
        A thouſand it poſſeſſe,   20
        But doth waſt with greedineſſe.

Confined Love. *1635–69 : no title, 1633, A18, B, D, H49, JC, L74, Lec,*
N, O'F, TCC, TCD: To the worthieſt of all my lovers. *Cy:* To the
of all my loves my virtuous miſtriſs. *P*   3 his] this *1669*   leſſer]
the leſſer *A18, Cy, JC, P*   6 might *1633–69:* ſhould *B, Cy, D, H49,*
JC, L74, Lec, O'F, S, TC   9 lend] bend *1669*   11 mate, *1633–39:*
meate, *1650:* meat, *1669*   a night (*i.e.* a-night) *1633–54:* all night *1669*
12 Beaſts] Beaſt *1635*   15 ſhip] ſhips *1669, Chambers*   16 ſeeke
new lands *1633–35 and MSS.:* ſeeke lands *1639–69, Chambers, whose note*
is incorrect   withall *1633:* with all *1635–69*   17 built *1633–35 :*
build *1639–69*

The

The Dreame.

DEare love, for nothing leſſe then thee
Would I have broke this happy dreame,
    It was a theame
For reaſon, much too ſtrong for phantaſie,
Therefore thou wakd'ſt me wiſely; yet   5
My Dreame thou brok'ſt not, but continued'ſt it,
Thou art ſo truth, that thoughts of thee ſuffice,
To make dreames truths; and fables hiſtories;
Enter theſe armes, for ſince thou thoughtſt it beſt,
Not to dreame all my dreame, let's act the reſt.   10

As lightning, or a Tapers light,
Thine eyes, and not thy noiſe wak'd mee;
    Yet I thought thee
(For thou loveſt truth) an Angell, at firſt ſight,
But when I ſaw thou ſaweſt my heart,   15
And knew'ſt my thoughts, beyond an Angels art,
When thou knew'ſt what I dreamt, when thou knew'ſt when
Exceſſe of joy would wake me, and cam'ſt then,
I muſt confeſſe, it could not chuſe but bee
Prophane, to thinke thee any thing but thee.   20

Comming and ſtaying ſhow'd thee, thee,
But riſing makes me doubt, that now,
    Thou art not thou.
That love is weake, where feare's as ſtrong as hee;

The Dreame. *1633–69*: *do. or similarly*, *A18,A25,B,C,Cy,D,H49,L74,*
Lec,N,O'F,P,RP31,S,S96,TCC,TCD   6 brok'ſt . . . continued'ſt]
breakeſt . . . continueſt *1669,A25,C,P,S*   7 ſo truth, *1633,A18,D,*
H49,L74,Lec,N,TC: ſo true, *1635–69,A25,B,C,Cy,O'F,P,S. See note*
10 act] doe *A25,B,Cy,D,H49,L74,Lec,O'F,P,S,S96*   14 an
Angell,] but an Angell, *A18,D,H49,L74,Lec,N,TC*   16 thoughts,]
om. comma Grolier and Chambers. See note   17 then thou knew'ſt when
1669   19 muſt] doe *A18,A25,B,Cy,D,H49,Lec,N,O'F,P,TC*   20
Prophane,] Profaneſs *A18,D,H49,L74,Lec,N,S96,TC*   24 feare's
as ſtrong *1633–54,A18,D,H49,L74,Lec,TCC*: feares are ſtrong *1669,*
B,Cy,O'F,P,S,S96: feare is ſtrong *N,TCD*

                                      'Tis

'Tis not all fpirit, pure, and brave,   25
If mixture it of *Feare, Shame, Honor,* have.
Perchance as torches which muft ready bee,
Men light and put out, fo thou deal'ft with mee,
Thou cam'ft to kindle, goeft to come; Then I
Will dreame that hope againe, but elfe would die.   30

A Valediction : of weeping.

LEt me powre forth
My teares before thy face, whil'ft I ftay here,
For thy face coines them, and thy ftampe they beare,
And by this Mintage they are fomething worth,
    For thus they bee   5
    Pregnant of thee;
Fruits of much griefe they are, emblemes of more,
When a teare falls, that thou falft which it bore,
So thou and I are nothing then, when on a divers fhore.

    On a round ball   10
A workeman that hath copies by, can lay
An Europe, Afrique, and an Afia,
And quickly make that, which was nothing, *All,*
    So doth each teare,
    Which thee doth weare,   15
A globe, yea world by that impreffion grow,
Till thy teares mixt with mine doe overflow
This world, by waters fent from thee, my heaven diffolved fo.

---

26 have. *1669:* have; *1633–54*   29 cam'ft] com'ft *1669*   Then
I] Thus I *A18, D, H49, L74, Lec, N, TC (RP31 agrees with this group
throughout)*

A Valediction: of *&c. Ed:* A Valediction of weeping. *1633–69:* Vale-
diction of Weeping. *A18, N, TCC, TCD:* A Valediction. *B, D, H40, H49,
L74, Lec:* A Valediction of Teares. *Cy, S, S96:* Valediction 2. Of Tears.
O'F: no title, JC   3 beare, *1633:* beare; *1635–69*   6 thee; *Ed:* thee,
1633–69   8 falft *1633–69:* falls *A18, D, H49, JC, L74, Lec, N, S, TC*
9 fhore.] fhore, *1633*   13 *All, 1633:* All *1635:* All. *1639:* All :
1650–69   16 world] would *1669*

O more

O more then Moone,
Draw not up feas to drowne me in thy fpheare,   20
Weepe me not dead, in thine armes, but forbeare
To teach the fea, what it may doe too foone;
   Let not the winde
   Example finde,
To doe me more harme, then it purpofeth;   25
Since thou and I figh one anothers breath,
Who e'r fighes moft, is cruelleft, and hafts the others death.

Loves Alchymie.

SOme that have deeper digg'd loves Myne then I,
Say, where his centrique happineffe doth lie:
  I have lov'd, and got, and told,
But fhould I love, get, tell, till I were old,
I fhould not finde that hidden myfterie;   5
  Oh, 'tis impofture all:
And as no chymique yet th'Elixar got,
   But glorifies his pregnant pot,
   If by the way to him befall
Some odoriferous thing, or medicinall,   10
 So, lovers dreame a rich and long delight,
 But get a winter-feeming fummers night.

Our eafe, our thrift, our honor, and our day,
Shall we, for this vaine Bubles fhadow pay?
   Ends love in this, that my man,   15
Can be as happy'as I can; If he can

 20 up feas] thy feas *1669* 22 foone; *Ed:* foone, *1633–69* 25
purpofeth; *Ed:* purpofeth, *1633–69*
 Loves Alchymie. *1633–69:* Mummye. *A18,B,Cy,D,H40,H49,JC,
L74*(or Alchymy. *added in a later hand), Lec,N,O'F,S,S96,TCC,TCD:*
Elegie. *P: no title, A25* 14 Bubles] Bublefs *1669* 15 my *1633–69*
and *MSS.:* any *S96, 1855,* and Grolier *(perhaps from some copy of 1633)*
              Endure

Endure the fhort fcorne of a Bridegroomes play ?
    That loving wretch that fweares,
'Tis not the bodies marry, but the mindes,
    Which he in her Angelique findes,   20
    Would fweare as juftly, that he heares,
In that dayes rude hoarfe minftralfey, the fpheares.
    Hope not for minde in women ; at their beft
    Sweetneffe and wit, they'are but *Mummy*, poffeft.

The Flea.

MArke but this flea, and marke in this,
  How little that which thou deny'ft me is ;
It fuck'd me firft, and now fucks thee,
And in this flea, our two bloods mingled bee ;
Thou know'ft that this cannot be faid   5
A finne, nor fhame, nor loffe of maidenhead,
    Yet this enjoyes before it wooe,
    And pamper'd fwells with one blood made of two,
    And this, alas, is more then wee would doe.

Oh ftay, three lives in one flea fpare,   10
Where wee almoft, yea more then maryed are.
This flea is you and I, and this
Our mariage bed, and mariage temple is ;

23–4 *punctuation from MSS :*   at their beft,
       Sweetneffe, and wit they'are, but, *Mummy*, poffeft. *1633–54:*
1669 omits all punctuation in these lines
    The Flea *is placed here in the 1633 edition : 1635–69 place it at beginning
of* Songs and Sonets: The Flea. *or no title,* A18, A25, B, C, Cy, D, H40,
H49, L74, Lec, N, O'F, P, S, S96, TCC, TCD   3 It fuckt mee firft,
1633–54, D, H49 Lec, S96: Mee it fuck'd firft, *1669,* A18, A25, B, C, Cy,
L74, N, P, S, TC   and now fucks] and now it fucks *1669*   5 Thou
know'ft that *1633–54, D, H49, Lec:* Confefs it.   This cannot be faid *1669,*
A18, A25, B, Cy, H40, L74, N, O'F, P, S, S96, TC   6 nor fhame, nor
loffe *1633–54* (fhame *1633*), D, H49, Lec: *or* fhame, or lofs *1669,* A18,
A25, B, Cy, H40, L74, N, O'F, P, TC   9 would] could *1669*   11 yea,
1633–54, D, H49, Lec: nay, *1669,* A18, A25, B, C, H40, L74, N, O'F, S, TC
                                              Though

Though parents grudge, and you, w'are met,
And cloyſterd in theſe living walls of Jet.   15
   Though uſe make you apt to kill mee,
   Let not to that, ſelfe murder added bee,
   And ſacrilege, three ſinnes in killing three.

Cruell and ſodaine, haſt thou ſince
Purpled thy naile, in blood of innocence?   20
Wherein could this flea guilty bee,
Except in that drop which it ſuckt from thee?
Yet thou triumph'ſt, and ſaiſt that thou
Find'ſt not thy ſelfe, nor mee the weaker now;
   'Tis true, then learne how falſe, feares bee;   25
   Juſt ſo much honor, when thou yeeld'ſt to mee,
   Will waſt, as this flea's death tooke life from thee.

The Curſe.

WHo ever gueſſes, thinks, or dreames he knowes
    Who is my miſtris, wither by this curſe;
   His only, and only his purſe
    May ſome dull heart to love diſpoſe,
And ſhee yeeld then to all that are his foes;   5
   May he be ſcorn'd by one, whom all elſe ſcorne,
   Forſweare to others, what to her he'hath ſworne,
   With feare of miſſing, ſhame of getting, torne:

16 you] thee *A18, Cy, N, O'F, S, S96, TC*   21 Wherein] In what
A18, A25, B, Cy, L74, N, O'F, S, S96, TC   22 drop] blood *1669*
   The Curſe. *1633–69:* A Curſe. *or* The Curſe. *A18, A25, B, C, D,
H40, H49, JC, L74, Lec, N, O'F, S, TCC, TCD:* Dirae. *P, Q*   2 curſe]
courſe *1669*   3 His only, and only his purſe *1633–54, A18, A25, B,
C, D, H40, H49, JC, L74, Lec, N, O'F, S, TC:* Him, only for his purſe
1669, Chambers: His one and his onely purſe *P*   4 heart *1633–54
and MSS.:* whore *1669 and Chambers*   5 And ſhe yeeld then to
1633–54 and MSS.: And then yield unto *1669, Chambers*   8 getting,
Ed: getting *1633–69*   torne: *Ed:* torne; *1633–54:* torne. *1669. Compare
16 and 24*

                                 Madneſſe

Madneſſe his ſorrow, gout his cramp, may hee
Make, by but thinking, who hath made him ſuch: 10
    And may he feele no touch
    Of conſcience, but of fame, and bee
Anguiſh'd, not that'twas ſinne, but that'twas ſhee:
  In early and long ſcarceneſſe may he rot,
  For land which had been his, if he had not   15
  Himſelfe inceſtuouſly an heire begot:

May he dreame Treaſon, and beleeve, that hee
Meant to performe it, and confeſſe, and die,
    And no record tell why:
    His ſonnes, which none of his may bee,   20
Inherite nothing but his infamie:
  Or may he ſo long Paraſites have fed,
  That he would faine be theirs, whom he hath bred,
  And at the laſt be circumciſ'd for bread:

The venom of all ſtepdames, gamſters gall,   25
What Tyrans, and their ſubjects interwiſh,
    What Plants, Mynes, Beaſts, Foule, Fiſh,
    Can contribute, all ill which all
Prophets, or Poets ſpake; And all which ſhall
  Be annex'd in ſchedules unto this by mee,   30
  Fall on that man; For if it be a ſhee
  Nature before hand hath out-curſed mee.

---

  9 cramp,] cramps, *1669, Chambers, and most MSS.*   10 him *1633–54*
and MSS.: them *1669, Chambers*   12 fame,] ſhame; *A18,A25,N,P,TC*
14–16 In early and lóng ſcarceneſs . . . an heire begot: *1633,B,D,H40,*
H49,Lec,O'F (which gives alternate version in margin), S:
          Or may he for her vertue reverence
          One that hates him onely for impotence,
          And equall Traitors be ſhe and his ſenſe.
                     1635–69,A18,A25,C,JC,N,P,Q,S,TC
18 Meant] Went *A18,N,TC*   26 Tyrans, *1633–35:* Tyrants, *1639:*
tyrants, *1650–69*   27 Mynes, *A18,A25,B,H40,JC,L74,N,O'F,*
P,Q,S,TC: Myne, *1633–69,D,H49,Lec*   28 ill *1669:* ill, *1633–54*

The Meſſage.

SEnd home my long ſtrayd eyes to mee,
Which (Oh) too long have dwelt on thee;
Yet ſince there they have learn'd ſuch ill,
    Such forc'd faſhions,
    And falſe paſſions,   5
        That they be
        Made by thee
Fit for no good ſight, keep them ſtill.

Send home my harmleſſe heart againe,
Which no unworthy thought could ſtaine;   10
But if it be taught by thine
    To make jeſtings
    Of proteſtings,
        And croſſe both
        Word and oath,   15
Keepe it, for then 'tis none of mine.

Yet ſend me back my heart and eyes,
That I may know, and ſee thy lyes,
And may laugh and joy, when thou
    Art in anguiſh
    And doſt languiſh   20
        For ſome one
        That will none,
Or prove as falſe as thou art now.

The Meſſage. *1635–69: no title, 1633:* Song. *or no title,* A25, B, Cy, D, H49, JC, Lec, O'F, S, S96: Sonnet. *P:* Songes wᶜʰ were made to &c. (*vid. sup. p.* 18) A18, N, TCC, TCD   2 thee; *Ed:* thee, *1633–69*   3 But if they there *1669*, S   10 ſtaine;] ſtaine, *1633–69*   11 But *1635–69:* Which *1633*, A18, A25, D, H49, Lec, N, TC   14 croſſe A18, A25, B, Cy, D, H49, JC, Lec, N, O'F, P, S, S96, TC: breake *1633–69*   16 Keep it ſtill 'tis *1669*   19 And may laugh, when that Thou D, H49, Lec 24 art'now.] doſt now. *1669*

A noc-

A noƈturnall upon S. Lucies day,
Being the ſhorteſt day.

TIs the yeares midnight, and it is the dayes,
　Lucies, who ſcarce ſeaven houres herſelf unmaskes,
　The Sunne is ſpent, and now his flasks
　Send forth light ſquibs, no conſtant rayes;
　　　The worlds whole ſap is ſunke:　　　　　　　　5
The generall balme th'hydroptique earth hath drunk,
Whither, as to the beds-feet, life is ſhrunke,
Dead and enterr'd; yet all theſe ſeeme to laugh,
Compar'd with mee, who am their Epitaph.

Study me then, you who ſhall lovers bee　　　　　10
At the next world, that is, at the next Spring:
　　For I am every dead thing,
　　In whom love wrought new Alchimie.
　　　For his art did expreſſe
A quinteſſence even from nothingneſſe,　　　　　15
From dull privations, and leane emptineſſe:
He ruin'd mee, and I am re-begot
Of abſence, darkneſſe, death; things which are not.

All others, from all things, draw all that's good,
Life, ſoule, forme, ſpirit, whence they beeing have;　20
　　I, by loves limbecke, am the grave
　　Of all, that's nothing. Oft a flood
　　　Have wee two wept, and ſo
Drownd the whole world, us two; oft did we grow
To be two Chaoſſes, when we did ſhow　　　　　25
Care to ought elſe; and often abſences
Withdrew our ſoules, and made us carcaſſes.

　A noƈturnal *&c. 1633–69, A18, N, O'F, TCC, TCD*　　　7 beds-
feet,] beds-feet *1633–69*　　12 every *1633, A18, N, O'F (altered to* a very),
TC: a very *1635–69*　　16 emptineſſe: *1719:* emptineſſe; *Chambers
and Grolier:* emptineſſe *1633–54:* emptineſſe, *1669. See note*　　20
have; *Ed:* have, *1633–69.*

　　　　　　　　　　　　　　　　　　　　　　　But

But I am by her death, (which word wrongs her)
Of the firſt nothing, the Elixer grown;
   Were I a man, that I were one,   30
   I needs muſt know; I ſhould preferre,
      If I were any beaſt,
Some ends, ſome means; Yea plants, yea ſtones deteſt,
And love; All, all ſome properties inveſt;
If I an ordinary nothing were,   35
As ſhadow, a light, and body muſt be here.

But I am None; nor will my Sunne renew.
You lovers, for whoſe ſake, the leſſer Sunne
   At this time to the Goat is runne
   To fetch new luſt, and give it you,   40
      Enjoy your ſummer all;
Since ſhee enjoyes her long nights feſtivall,
Let mee prepare towards her, and let mee call
This houre her Vigill, and her Eve, ſince this
Both the yeares, and the dayes deep midnight is.   45

Witchcraft by a picture.

I Fixe mine eye on thine, and there
  Pitty my picture burning in thine eye,
My picture drown'd in a tranſparent teare,
   When I looke lower I eſpie;
     Hadſt thou the wicked skill   5
By pictures made and mard, to kill,
How many wayes mightſt thou performe thy will?

31 know;] know, *1633*   32 beaſt,] beast; *Grolier*   34 love;
All, all *Ed:* love, all, all *1633–69*   inveſt; *Ed:* inveſt, *1633:* inveſt
1635–69   37 renew. *1633:* renew, *1635–69*   41 all; *Ed:* all,
1633–69 and Chambers, who places a full stop after festivall   44 Eve,
1650–69: eve, *1633–39*
    Witchcraft *&c. 1633–69, A18, N, TCC, TCD:* The Picture. *or* Picture.
Cy, JC, O'F, P, S96: A Songe. *B*   4 eſpie; *Ed:* eſpie, *1633–69*
6 to kjll, *Ed:* to kill? *1633–39 :* to kill; *1650–69*

                                            But

But now I have drunke thy fweet falt teares,
  And though thou poure more I'll depart;
My picture vanifh'd, vanifh feares,   10
  That I can be endamag'd by that art;
    Though thou retaine of mee
One picture more, yet that will bee,
Being in thine owne heart, from all malice free.

The Baite.

COme live with mee, and bee my love,
  And wee will fome new pleafures prove
Of golden fands, and chriftall brookes,
With filken lines, and filver hookes.

There will the river whifpering runne   5
Warm'd by thy eyes, more then the Sunne.
And there the'inamor'd fifh will ftay,
Begging themfelves they may betray.

When thou wilt fwimme in that live bath,
Each fifh, which every channell hath,
Will amoroufly to thee fwimme,   10
Gladder to catch thee, then thou him.

    9 · And though] Although *1669*   And though thou therefore poure more
will depart; *B, H40*   10 vanifh'd, vanifh feares, *1633, A18, B, Cy, H40,
JC, N, P, S96, TC:* vanifhed, vanifh all feares *1635–54, O'F:* vanifh, vanifh
fears, *1669*   11 that] thy *JC, O'F, S96*   14 all] thy *B, H40, S96*
    The Baite. *1635–69: no title, 1633:* Song. or no title, *D, H49, JC, Lec,
O'F, P, S96, Walton's* Complete Angler: *Fourth Day: Chap. XII.:*
Songs that were made *&c.* (*vid. sup. p.* 18) *A18, N, TCC, TCD*   2 fome
new] all the *P*   3 brookes, *Ed:* brookes: *1633–69*   5 whifpering
1633: whifpring *1635–69*   6 thy] thine *1669, A18, N, TC*   7
inamor'd] enamelled *Walton*   ftay] play *1669*   11 to] unto *JC, O'F,
P:* to see *N:* Moft amoroufly to thee will fwim *Walton*

If

If thou, to be fo feene, beeft loath,
By Sunne, or Moone, thou darkneft both,
And if my felfe have leave to fee,   15
I need not their light, having thee.

Let others freeze with angling reeds,
And cut their legges, with fhells and weeds,
Or treacheroufly poore fifh befet,
With ftrangling fnare, or windowie net: 20

Let coarfe bold hands, from flimy neft
The bedded fifh in banks out-wreft,
Or curious traitors, fleavefilke flies
Bewitch poore fifhes wandring eyes.

For thee, thou needft no fuch deceit,   25
For thou thy felfe art thine owne bait;
That fifh, that is not catch'd thereby,
Alas, is wifer farre then I.

The Apparition.

WHen by thy fcorne, O murdreffe, I am dead,
    And that thou thinkft thee free
From all folicitation from mee,
Then fhall my ghoft come to thy bed,
And thee, fain'd veftall, in worfe armes fhall fee;   5

15 my felfe] mine eyes *Walton*: my heart *A18, N, TC*   18 with]
which *1633*   20 fnare,] fnares, *Walton*   windowie] winding *1669. See
note*   23 Or *1633–69 :* Let *Walton*   fleavefilke *1635 :* fleave filke
1639–69 and Walton : fleaveficke *1633*   24 To witch poor wandring
fifhes eyes. *Walton*   25 thou needft] there needs *D, H49, Lec, S96*
26 bait; *Ed :* bait, *1633–69*   27 catch'd *1633–69 :* catch't *Walton :*
caught *P*   28 Is wifer far, alas *Walton*
    The Apparition. *1633–69 :* do. or An Apparition. *A18, A25, B, Cy,
D, H40, H49, Lec, N, O'F, P, S, S96, TCC, TCD*   2 that thou thinkft]
thou fhalt think *1669*   3 folicitation] folicitations *JC, O'F*   5 thee,
. . . veftall, *Ed :* thee . . . veftall *1633–39 :* thee . . . Veftall *1650–69*
                                             Then

Then thy ſicke taper will begin to winke,
And he, whoſe thou art then, being tyr'd before,
Will, if thou ſtirre, or pinch to wake him, thinke
    Thou call'ſt for more,
And in falſe ſleepe will from thee ſhrinke,   10
And then poore Aſpen wretch, neglected thou
Bath'd in a cold quickſilver ſweat wilt lye
    A veryer ghoſt then I;
What I will ſay, I will not tell thee now,
Leſt that preſerve thee'; and ſince my love is ſpent,   15
I'had rather thou ſhouldſt painfully repent,
Then by my threatnings reſt ſtill innocent.

The broken heart.

HE is ſtarke mad, who ever ſayes,
    That he hath beene in love an houre,
Yet not that love ſo ſoone decayes,
    But that it can tenne in leſſe ſpace devour;
Who will beleeve mee, if I ſweare   5
That I have had the plague a yeare?
    Who would not laugh at mee, if I ſhould ſay,
    I ſaw a flaske of *powder burne a day?*

Ah, what a trifle is a heart,
    If once into loves hands it come!   10
All other griefes allow a part
    To other griefes, and aske themſelves but ſome;

7 then] *1669 omits*   10 in falſe ſleepe will from *1633, Cy, D, H49,*
Lec, S: in falſe ſleepe from *1635–54:* in a falſe ſleepe even from *1669:*
in a falſe ſleepe from *A25, P:* in a falſe ſleepe will from *A18, N, TC*
13 I;] I, *1633, some copies*   17 reſt ſtill] keep thee *A25, Cy, JC, O'F, P*
    The broken heart. *1633–69:* Broken Heart. *L74:* Song. *or no title, A18,*
A25, B, Cy, D, H49, JC, Lec, N, O'F, S, TCC, TCD: Elegie. *P, S96*   8
flaske *1633, A25, B, C, Cy, D, H40, Lec, O'F*(*corrected from* flaſh), *P, S:*
flaſh *1635–69, A18, H49, N, TC*   10 come! *Ed:* come? *1633–69*
12 ſome; *Ed:* ſome, *1633–69*

                                        They

They come to us, but us Love draws,
Hee fwallows us, and never chawes:
 By him, as by chain'd fhot, whole rankes doe dye,   15
 He is the tyran Pike, our hearts the Frye.

If 'twere not fo, what did become
 Of my heart, when I firft faw thee?
I brought a heart into the roome,
 But from the roome, I carried none with mee: 20
If it had gone to thee, I know
Mine would have taught thine heart to fhow
 More pitty unto mee: but Love, alas,
 At one firft blow did fhiver it as glaffe.

Yet nothing can to nothing fall,   25
 Nor any place be empty quite,
Therefore I thinke my breaft hath all
 Thofe peeces ftill, though they be not unite;
And now as broken glaffes fhow
A hundred leffer faces, fo   30
 My ragges of heart can like, wifh, and adore,
 But after one fuch love, can love no more.

A *Valediction : forbidding mourning.*

AS virtuous men paffe mildly away,
 And whifper to their foules, to goe,
Whilft fome of their fad friends doe fay,
 The breath goes now, and fome fay, no :

15 chain'd fhot] chain-fhott *A18, A25, N, TC*   16 tyran] Tyrant
1669   our hearts] and we *1669*   17 did] could *A18, A25, B, C, L74,*
O'F, N, TC: would *B, Cy, M, S*   20 mee: *1650–69:* mee; *1633–39*
23 alas,] alas *1633*   24 firft] fierce *A18, B, N, TC*   30 hundred]
thoufand *A18, A25, B, Cy, L74, M, N, P, S, TC*
 A Valediction: forbidding *&c. Ed:* A Valediction forbidding *&c.*
1633–69: Valediction forbidding *&c. A18, N, TCC, TCD:* Valediction
agaynft *&c. A25, C:* A Valediction. *B, Cy, D, H40, H49, Lec:* Vpon
the partinge from his Miftris. *O'F, S96:* To his love upon his departure
from her. *JC:* Elegie. *L74, P: also in Walton's* Life of Donne (1675)
4 The breath goes now, *1633–54, and all the MSS.:* Now his breath
goes, *1669, Chambers*   no: *Ed:* no. *1633–54:* No; *1669*

              So

So let us melt, and make no noife,   5
   No teare-floods, nor figh-tempefts move,
T'were prophanation of our joyes
   To tell the layetie our love.

Moving of th'earth brings harmes and feares,
   Men reckon what it did and meant,   10
But trepidation of the fpheares,
   Though greater farre, is innocent.

Dull fublunary lovers love
   (Whofe foule is fenfe) cannot admit
Abfence, becaufe it doth remove   15
   Thofe things which elemented it.

But we by a love, fo much refin'd,
   That our felves know not what it is,
Inter-affured of the mind,
   Care leffe, eyes, lips, and hands to miffe.   20

Our two foules therefore, which are one,
   Though I muft goe, endure not yet
A breach, but an expanfion,
   Like gold to ayery thinneffe beate.

If they be two, they are two fo   25
   As ftiffe twin compaffes are two,
Thy foule the fixt foot, makes no fhow
   To move, but doth, if the'other doe.

   6 No wind-fighs or tear-floods us move, *Walton*   8 layetie our love.
1633–69 (love· *1633*), *A25*, *D, C, H49, Lec, S :* layetie of our love. *A18, B,*
Cy, JC, L74, N, O'F, P, S96, TC   9 Moving . . . brings] Movings . . .
caufe *Walton, O'F*   10 it] they *Walton*   15 Abfence, becaufe
1633–54 and MSS. : Of abfence, caufe *1669*   16 Thofe things
1633–54 and all MSS. : The thing *1669, Chambers. See note*   17
much] far *1669*   18 our felves] our fouls *Walton*   20 Care leffe,
1633–35, 1669 : Careleffe, *1639–54*   lips, and hands *1669 and all*
MSS.: lips, hands *1633*

                                                   And

And though it in the center fit,
　　Yet when the other far doth rome,　　　　　　　30
It leanes, and hearkens after it,
　　And growes erect, as that comes home.

Such wilt thou be to mee, who muft
　　Like th'other foot, obliquely runne;
Thy firmnes makes my circle juft,　　　　　　　　35
　　And makes me end, where I begunne.

The Extafie.

WHere, like a pillow on a bed,
　　　A Pregnant banke fwel'd up, to reft
The violets reclining head,
　　Sat we two, one anothers beft.
Our hands were firmely cimented　　　　　　　　5
　　With a faft balme, which thence did fpring,
Our eye-beames twifted, and did thred
　　Our eyes, upon one double ftring;
So to'entergraft our hands, as yet
　　Was all the meanes to make us one,　　　　　10
And pictures in our eyes to get
　　Was all our propagation.
As 'twixt two equall Armies, Fate
　　Sufpends uncertaine victorie,
Our foules, (which to advance their ftate,　　　15
　　Were gone out,) hung 'twixt her, and mee.

30 the other] my other *Walton*　　31 It] Thine *Walton*　　32 that]
mine *Walton*　　34 runne; *Ed:* runne. *1633–69*　　35 circle] circles
1639–54　　36 makes me] me to *Walton*
　　The Extafie. *1633–69:* do. or Extafie. *A18, A25, B, D, H40, H49,*
JC, Lec, N, O'F, P, S, S96, TCC, TCD　　3 reclining *1633–54:* de-
clining *1669*　　4 beft. *Ed:* beft; *1633–54*　　　Sate we on one
anothers breafts. *1669*　　6 With *1633, A18, A25, B, D, H49, JC, Lec,*
P, S, TC: By *1635–69, Chambers*　　8 ftring; *Ed:* ftring, *1633–69*
9 to'entergraft *1633, A18, D, H40, H49, Lec, N, P, S, TC:* to engraft *1635–*
69, A25, JC, O'F, Chambers　　11 in *1633–69, P:* on *A18, A25, B, D,*
H40, H49, JC, Lec, N, O'F, S, TC　　15 their *1633 and most MSS.:*
our *1635–69, O'F, P*

And

And whil'ſt our ſoules negotiate there,
  Wee like ſepulchrall ſtatues lay;
All day, the ſame our poſtures were,
  And wee ſaid nothing, all the day.   20
If any, ſo by love refin'd,
  That he ſoules language underſtood,
And by good love were growen all minde,
  Within convenient diſtance ſtood,
He (though he knew not which ſoule ſpake,   25
  Becauſe both meant, both ſpake the ſame)
Might thence a new concoction take,
  And part farre purer then he came.
This Extaſie doth unperplex
  (We ſaid) and tell us what we love,   30
Wee ſee by this, it was not ſexe,
  Wee ſee, we ſaw not what did move:
But as all ſeverall ſoules containe
  Mixture of things, they know not what,
Love, theſe mixt ſoules, doth mixe againe,   35
  And makes both one, each this and that.
A ſingle violet tranſplant,
  The ſtrength, the colour, and the ſize,
(All which before was poore, and ſcant,)
  Redoubles ſtill, and multiplies.   40
When love, with one another ſo
  Interinanimates two ſoules,
That abler ſoule, which thence doth flow,
  Defects of lonelineſſe controules.
Wee then, who are this new ſoule, know,   45
  Of what we are compos'd, and made,
For, th'Atomies of which we grow,
  Are ſoules, whom no change can invade.

18 lay; *Ed:* lay, *1633–69*   25 knew *1635–69,A18,A25,B,H40,*
H49,JC,N,P,TC: knowes *1633,D,Lec*   29 doth] do *1669*   31 ſexe,
1669: ſexe *1633–54*   42 Interinanimates *A18,A25,B,H40,H49,*
JC,N,O'F,P,TC: Interanimates *1633–69,D,Lec*   44 lonelineſs]
lovelineſs *1669*   46 made, *1633–39:* made: *1650–69*   47 Atomies
1633–54: Atomes *1669*   48 are ſoules, *1633,1669:* are ſoule, *1635–54*
                                                              But

But O alas, fo long, fo farre
  Our bodies why doe wee forbeare ?   50
They are ours, though they are not wee, Wee are
  The intelligences, they the fpheare.
We owe them thankes, becaufe they thus,
  Did us, to us, at firft convay,
Yeelded their forces, fenfe, to us,   55
  Nor are droffe to us, but allay.
On man heavens influence workes not fo,
  But that it firft imprints the ayre,
Soe foule into the foule may flow,
  Though it to body firft repaire.   60
As our blood labours to beget
  Spirits, as like foules as it can,
Becaufe fuch fingers need to knit
  That fubtile knot, which makes us man:
So muft pure lovers foules defcend   65
  T'affections, and to faculties,
Which fenfe may reach and apprehend,
  Elfe a great Prince in prifon lies.
To'our bodies turne wee then, that fo
  Weake men on love reveal'd may looke;   70
Loves myfteries in foules doe grow,
  But yet the body is his booke.
And if fome lover, fuch as wee,
  Have heard this dialogue of one,
Let him ftill marke us, he fhall fee   75
  Small change, when we'are to bodies gone.

51 though they are not *A18, A25, B, D, H40, H49, JC, Lec, N, O'F, S,*
S96, TC: though not *1633–69*   52 fpheare. *A18, A25, B, D, H40,*
H49, JC, Lec, N, O'F, P, S, S96, TC: fpheares. *1633–69*   55 forces, fenfe,
A18, A25, D, H40, H49, JC, Lec, N, O'F, S, S96, TC: fenfes force *1633–69*
59 Soe *A18, A25, B, H40, JC, N, P, S, S96, TC:* For *1633–69, D, H49,*
Lec   64 makes] make *1635–39*   72 his] the *1669*   76 gone. *1633,*
A18, A25, B, D, H49, JC, Lec, O'F, S, TC: growne. *1635–69, P, S96*

Loves

Loves Deitie.

I Long to talke with fome old lovers ghoft,
  Who dyed before the god of Love was borne:
I cannot thinke that hee, who then lov'd moft,
  Sunke fo low, as to love one which did fcorne.
But fince this god produc'd a deftinie,   5
And that vice-nature, cuftome, lets it be;
  I muft love her, that loves not mee.

Sure, they which made him god, meant not fo much,
  Nor he, in his young godhead practis'd it;
But when an even flame two hearts did touch,   10
  His office was indulgently to fit
Actives to paffives. Correfpondencie
Only his fubject was; It cannot bee
  Love, till I love her, that loves mee.

But every moderne god will now extend   15
  His vaft prerogative, as far as Jove.
To rage, to luft, to write to, to commend,
  All is the purlewe of the God of Love.
Oh were wee wak'ned by this Tyrannie
To ungod this child againe, it could not bee   20
  I fhould love her, who loves not mee.

Rebell and Atheift too, why murmure I,
  As though I felt the worft that love could doe?
Love might make me leave loving, or might trie
  A deeper plague, to make her love mee too,   25
Which, fince fhe loves before, I'am loth to fee;
Falfhood is worfe then hate; and that muft bee,
  If fhee whom I love, fhould love mee.

Loves Deitie. *1633–69, A18, A25, B, Cy, D, H40, H49, JC, L74, Lec,
N, O'F, S, S96, TCC, TCD*: Elegye. *P*   8 much, *1639–69*: much:
1633: much? *1635*   9 it; *Ed:* it. *1633–69*   13 fubject] *Subject
1669*   14 Love, ... mee. *1633, 1669, A25, B, C, Cy, D, H40*(who),
H49, JC, L74, N, P, S(lov'd),*TCD*: Love, if I love, who loves not me.
1635–54, O'F   19 Oh ... wak'ned] Were we not weak'ned *1669*
21 That I fhould love, who loves not me. *A18, A25, C, Cy, D, H49,
JC, L74, Lec, N, P, S, S96, TC*: O'F *reads as these but alters to as in
printed edd.*   24 might make *A18, A25, B, Cy, D, H40, H49, JC, L74,
N, P, S, S96, TC*: may make *1633–69, Lec*   26 Which,] Which *1633*
                                                                    Loves

Loves diet.

TO what a comberſome unwieldineſſe
  And burdenous corpulence my love had growne,
  But that I did, to make it leſſe,
  And keepe it in proportion,
Give it a diet, made it feed upon   5
That which love worſt endures, *diſcretion*.

Above one ſigh a day I'allow'd him not,
Of which my fortune, and my faults had part;
  And if ſometimes by ſtealth he got
  A ſhe ſigh from my miſtreſſe heart,   10
And thought to feaſt on that, I let him ſee
'Twas neither very ſound, nor meant to mee.

If he wroung from mee'a teare, I brin'd it ſo
With ſcorne or ſhame, that him it nouriſh'd not;
  If he ſuck'd hers, I let him know   15
  'Twas not a teare, which hee had got,
His drinke was counterfeit, as was his meat;
For, eyes which rowle towards all, weepe not, but ſweat.

What ever he would dictate, I writ that,
But burnt my letters; When ſhe writ to me,   20
  And that that favour made him fat,
  I ſaid, if any title bee
Convey'd by this, Ah, what doth it availe,
To be the fortieth name in an entaile?

  Loves diet. *1633–69, A18, A25, B, C, Cy, D, H40, H49, L74, Lec, N,*
O'F, P, S, TCC (torn out of TCD): Amoris Dieta. *S96*   12 mee.
Ed: mee ; *1633–35 :* mee : *1639–69*   18 For,] Her *1669*   19
Whatever . . . that, *1633–39, 1669 :* Whate'er might him diſtaſt I ſtill
writ that, *1650–54 :* Whatſoever hee would diſtaſt I writt that, *A18, N, TC*
20 But burnt my letters ; When ſhe writ to me, *1633 :* But burnt her
letters when ſhe writ to me, *1635 :* But burnt her letters when ſhe writ to
me ; *1639–54, Chambers :* But burnt my letters which ſhe writ to me ; *1669*
21 that that *1633 :* if that *1635–69. See note*   24 name] man *1669*
                                                      Thus

Thus I reclaim'd my buzard love, to flye   25
At what, and when, and how, and where I chufe;
   Now negligent of fport I lye,
   And now as other Fawkners ufe,
I fpring a miftreffe, fweare, write, figh and weepe:
And the game kill'd, or loft, goe talke, and fleepe.   30

The Will.

BEfore I figh my laft gafpe, let me breath,
  Great love, fome Legacies; Here I bequeath
  Mine eyes to *Argus*, if mine eyes can fee,
  If they be blinde, then Love, I give them thee;
  My tongue to Fame; to'Embaffadours mine eares;   5
    To women or the fea, my teares.
  Thou, Love, haft taught mee heretofore
By making mee ferve her who'had twenty more,
That I fhould give to none, but fuch, as had too much
    before.

  My conftancie I to the planets give;   10
  My truth to them, who at the Court doe live;
  Mine ingenuity and openneffe,
  To Jefuites; to Buffones my penfiveneffe;
  My filence to'any, who abroad hath beene;
    My mony to a Capuchin.   15
  Thou Love taught'ft me, by appointing mee
To love there, where no love receiv'd can be,
Onely to give to fuch as have an incapacitie.

   25 reclaim'd *1635–69*, *A18*, *A25*, *B*, *D*, *H40*, *H49*, *L74*, *N*, *O'F*, *S*, *TCC*:
redeem'd *1633*, *Lec*   26 chufe] chofe *1669*   27 fport *1635–69*, *A18*,
B, *D*, *H40*, *H49*, *L74*, *Lec*, *S*, *S96*, *TCC*: fports *1633*   30 and *1633*
and most MSS.: or *1635–69*, *Cy*, *O'F*, *S*
   The Will. *1633–69*: do. *or* A Will. *A25*, *B*, *C*, *Cy*, *D*, *H40*, *H49*.
Lec, *M*, *O'F*, *P*: Loves Will. *L74*: Loves Legacies. *A18*, *N*, *TCC*
(*torn out of TCD*), *S*: Teftamentum. *S96*: His Laft Will and Teftament.
JC   2 Here I *1633–54*: I here *1669*, *Chambers*   6 teares. *Ed*:
teares; *1633–69*   8 ferve her] love her *1669*   10 give; *Ed*:
give, *1633–69*   10–27 *These stanzas printed without a break*, *1669*
 14 hath] have *1669*   18 an incapacitie.] no good Capacity. *1669*
                                              My

My faith I give to Roman Catholiques;
All my good works unto the Schifmaticks   20
Of Amfterdam; my beft civility
And Courtfhip, to an Univerfitie;
My modefty I give to fouldiers bare;
   My patience let gamefters fhare.
Thou Love taughtft mee, by making mee   25
Love her that holds my love difparity,
Onely to give to thofe that count my gifts indignity.

I give my reputation to thofe
Which were my friends; Mine induftrie to foes;
To Schoolemen I bequeath my doubtfulneffe;   30
My fickneffe to Phyfitians, or exceffe;
To Nature, all that I in Ryme have writ;
   And to my company my wit.
Thou Love, by making mee adore
Her, who begot this love in mee before,   35
Taughtft me to make, as though I gave, when I did but
   reftore.

To him for whom the paffing bell next tolls,
I give my phyfick bookes; my writen rowles
Of Morall counfels, I to Bedlam give;
My brazen medals, unto them which live   40
In want of bread; To them which paffe among
   All forrainers, mine Englifh tongue.
Thou, Love, by making mee love one
Who thinkes her friendfhip a fit portion
For yonger lovers, doft my gifts thus difproportion.   45

Therefore I'll give no more; But I'll undoe
The world by dying; becaufe love dies too.
Then all your beauties will bee no more worth
Then gold in Mines, where none doth draw it forth;

19-27 *omitted,* A18,A25,B,Cy,D,H40,H49,JC,L74 (*added later*),
Lec,M(*added later*),N,P,TCC: *given in* O'F,S, *and all editions*   33
wit. *Ed:* wit; *1633-69*   34 Love, *1650-69:* love, *1633-39*   36 did
1633 and MSS.: do *1635-69,O'F*   45 gifts *1633-35,1669:* gift *1639-54*
46 more; But *1633:* more, but *1635-69*   49-51 forth; . . . grave.
1669: forth. . . . grave, *1633-39 by interchange:* forth . . . grave. *1650-54*

And all your graces no more ufe fhall have   50
    Then a Sun dyall in a grave.
  Thou Love taughtft mee, by making mee
Love her, who doth neglect both mee and thee,
To'invent, and practife this one way, to'annihilate all three.

The Funerall.

WHo ever comes to fhroud me, do not harme
            Nor queftion much
That subtile wreath of haire, which crowns my arme;
The myftery, the figne you muft not touch,
            For'tis my outward Soule,   5
Viceroy to that, which then to heaven being gone,
            Will leave this to controule,
And keepe thefe limbes, her Provinces, from diffolution.

For if the finewie thread my braine lets fall
            Through every part,   10
Can tye thofe parts, and make mee one of all;
Thefe haires which upward grew, and ftrength and art
            Have from a better braine,
Can better do'it; Except fhe meant that I
            By this fhould know my pain,   15
As prifoners then are manacled, when they'are condemn'd
            to die.

54 all three. *1633–39*, three *being below the line in 1633 and above in*
1635–39 : al. three *1650–54, the full stop having fallen from* three *to* all *below*
it : annihilate thee. *1669*
    The Funerall. *1633–69, A18, B, Cy, D, H49, L74, Lec, N, O'F, P, S, S96,*
TCC, TCD   3 which . . . arme ;] about mine arm ; *1669*   6
then to *A18, B, Cy, D, H49, L74, Lec, N, O'F, P, S, S96, TC*: unto *1633–69*
1 2 Thefe *A18, B, Cy, D, H49, L74, N, S* (The), *S96, TC*: Thofe *1633–69,*
Lec, O'F   grew, *1633–39*: grow, *1650–69*   16 condemn'd] con-
dem'nd *1633*

                                                What

What ere fhee meant by'it, bury it with me,
  For fince I am
Loves martyr, it might breed idolatrie,
If into others hands thefe Reliques came;   20
  As'twas humility
To afford to it all that a Soule can doe,
  So,'tis fome bravery,
That fince you would fave none of mee, I bury fome of
  you.

The Bloſſome.

Little think'ft thou, poore flower,
 Whom I have watch'd fixe or feaven dayes,
And feene thy birth, and feene what every houre
Gave to thy growth, thee to this height to raife,
And now doft laugh and triumph on this bough, 5
  Little think'ft thou
That it will freeze anon, and that I fhall
To morrow finde thee falne, or not at all.

 Little think'ft thou poore heart
  That labour'ft yet to neftle thee,   10
And think'ft by hovering here to get a part
In a forbidden or forbidding tree,
And hop'ft her ftiffeneffe by long fiege to bow:
  Little think'ft thou,
That thou to morrow, ere that Sunne doth wake, 15
Muft with this Sunne, and mee a journey take.

17 with me, *1635–69 and MSS.:* by me, *1633* 24 fave *A18, B,
Cy, D, H49, L74, N, P, TC:* have *1633–69, Lec, O'F, S96:* om. *S*
 The Bloffome. *1633–69, A18, B, D, H49, JC, Lec, N, O'F, S, S96, TCC,
TCD: no title, A25* 9–13 poore heart . . . bow:] *in brackets 1650–69*
10 labour'ft *A18, N, TC:* laboureft *1635–69:* labours *1633* 15 that
Sunne *1633:* the Sunne *1635–69*
                But

But thou which lov'ft to bee
  Subtile to plague thy felfe, wilt fay,
Alas, if you muft goe, what's that to mee ?
Here lyes my bufineffe, and here I will ftay: 20
You goe to friends, whofe love and meanes prefent
              Various content
To your eyes, eares, and tongue, and every part.
If then your body goe, what need you a heart ?

Well then, ftay here ; but know,   25
  When thou haft ftayd and done thy moft ;
A naked thinking heart, that makes no fhow,
Is to a woman, but a kinde of Ghoft ;
How fhall fhee know my heart ; or having none,
              Know thee for one?   30
Practife may make her know fome other part,
But take my word, fhee doth not know a Heart.

Meet mee at London, then,
  Twenty dayes hence, and thou fhalt fee
Mee frefher, and more fat, by being with men,   ·35
Then if I had ftaid ftill with her and thee.
For Gods fake, if you can, be you fo too:
              I would give you
There, to another friend, whom wee fhall finde
As glad to have my body, as my minde.   40

18 wilt] will *1669*   23 tongue *A18, A25, B, D, H49, JC, Lec,*
N, O'F, S96, TC : om. *S :* taft *1633-69*   24 need you a heart ? *A25,*
B, D, H49, Lec, N, O'F, S, S96, TC : need you have a heart ? *JC :* need
your heart ? *1633-69*   38 I would *A18, A25, B, D, H49, JC, N, O'F,*
S, S96, TC : I will *1633-69, Lec*

The Primroſe, being at Montgomery Caſtle, upon the hill, on which it is ſituate.

VPon this Primroſe hill,
    Where, if Heav'n would diſtill
A ſhoure of raine, each ſeverall drop might goe
To his owne primroſe, and grow Manna ſo;
And where their forme, and their infinitie   5
    Make a terreſtriall Galaxie,
      As the ſmall ſtarres doe in the skie:
I walke to finde a true Love; and I ſee
That'tis not a mere woman, that is ſhee,
But muſt, or more, or leſſe then woman bee.   10

    Yet know I not, which flower
      I wiſh; a ſixe, or foure;
For ſhould my true-Love leſſe then woman bee,
She were ſcarce any thing; and then, ſhould ſhe
Be more then woman, ſhee would get above   15
    All thought of ſexe, and thinke to move
      My heart to ſtudy her, and not to love;
Both theſe were monſters; Since there muſt reſide
Falſhood in woman, I could more abide,
She were by art, then Nature falſify'd.   20

    Live Primroſe then, and thrive
      With thy true number five;
And women, whom this flower doth repreſent,
With this myſterious number be content;
Ten is the fartheſt number; if halfe ten   25

The Primroſe. *1633, A18, B, D, H49, Lec, N, O'F, S, S96, TCC, TCD:* The Primroſe, being at *&c. 1635–69* 16 ſexe, *1633:* ſexe; *1635–69* 17 and not] and om. *1635–39, A18, N, S, TC* 23 women] woman *Chambers* 25 number; *Ed:* number, *1633–69*
                              Belonge

Belonge unto each woman, then
        Each woman may take halfe us men ;
Or if this will not ferve their turne, Since all
Numbers are odde, or even, and they fall
Firft into this, five, women may take us all.   30

The Relique.

WHen my grave is broke up againe
        Some fecond gheft to entertaine,
        (For graves have learn'd that woman-head
        To be to more then one a Bed)
                And he that digs it, fpies   5
A bracelet of bright haire about the bone,
        Will he not let'us alone,
And thinke that there a loving couple lies,
Who thought that this device might be fome way
To make their foules, at the laft bufie day,   10
Meet at this grave, and make a little ftay ?

        If this fall in a time, or land,
        Where mif-devotion doth command,
        Then, he that digges us up, will bring
        Us, to the Bifhop, and the King,   15
                To make us Reliques ; then
Thou fhalt be a Mary Magdalen, and I
        A fomething elfe thereby ;

26 Belonge *all the MSS.*: Belongs *1633–69. See note*   27 men ;
Ed: men, *1633–39*: men: *1650–69*   28 their *1633–39*: the
1650–69   29 and *1633*: fince *1635–69*   30 this, *Ed*: this *1633,
A18, B, D, H49, Lec, N, S, S96, TC*: om. *1635–69, O'F, Chambers*
    The Relique. *1633–69, A18, B, D, H49, JC, Lec, N, O'F, S, S96, TCC,
TCD: no title, A25*   13 mif-devotion *1633–54, A18, A25, B, D, H49,
JC, Lec, N, O'F, S, S96, TC*: maff-devotion *1669, Chambers*   15 and
1633–54 and MSS.: or *1669, Chambers*   17 Thou fhalt be] You fhal
be *A25, D, H49, JC, Lec, S. See note*

All

All women fhall adore us, and fome men;
And fince at fuch time, miracles are fought,   20
I would have that age by this paper taught
What miracles wee harmeleffe lovers wrought.

    Firft, we lov'd well and faithfully,
    Yet knew not what wee lov'd, nor why,
    Difference of fex no more wee knew,   25
    Then our Guardian Angells doe;
        Comming and going, wee
Perchance might kiffe, but not between thofe meales;
        Our hands ne'r toucht the feales,
Which nature, injur'd by late law, fets free: 30
Thefe miracles wee did; but now alas,
All meafure, and all language, I fhould paffe,
Should I tell what a miracle fhee was.

The Dampe.

WHen I am dead, and Doctors know not why,
    And my friends curiofitie
Will have me cut up to furvay each part,
When they fhall finde your Picture in my heart,
    You thinke a fodaine dampe of love   5
    Will through all their fenfes move,
And worke on them as mee, and fo preferre
Your murder, to the name of Maffacre.

---

20 time] times *JC,O'F*   21 have that age] that age were *A18,*
N,TC   25–26 Difference . . . doe, *1633,A18,N,TC* :
        Difference of Sex we never knew,
        No more then Guardian Angells do, *1635–69* :
        Difference of Sex we never knew,
        More then our Guardian Angells do. *A25,B, D,H49,JC,*
           Lec,S,S96 (No more then our *&c. B,S96*)
26 doe; *Ed:* doe, *1633–69*   27 wee *Ed:* wee, *1633–69*   28 not]
yet *1669*   meales; *Ed:* meales. *1633*: meales *1635–69, following some*
copies of 1633   30 fets] fet *1669*   free: *1650–69*: free, *1633–39*
    The Dampe.   *1633–69,A18,B,D,H49,JC,Lec,N,O'F,P,S,S96,*
TCC,TCD   4 When] And *1669*   my *1633–39*: mine *1650–69*
                                                  Poore

Poore victories ! But if you dare be brave,
   And pleasure in your conquest have,   10
First kill th'enormous Gyant, your *Disdaine*,
And let th'enchantresse *Honor*, next be slaine,
  And like a Goth and Vandall rize,
  Deface Records, and Histories
Of your owne arts and triumphs over men,   15
And without such advantage kill me then.

For I could muster up as well as you
   My Gyants, and my Witches too,
Which are vast *Constancy*, and *Secretnesse*,
But these I neyther looke for, nor professe;   20
  Kill mee as Woman, let mee die
  As a meere man; doe you but try
Your passive valor, and you shall finde than,
In that you'have odds enough of any man.

The Dissolution.

SHee'is dead; And all which die
 To their first Elements resolve;
And wee were mutuall Elements to us,
  And made of one another.
 My body then doth hers involve,   5
And those things whereof I consist, hereby
In me abundant grow, and burdenous,
  And nourish not, but smother.

9 victories! *1650–69*: victories; *1633–39*   10 your] the *1669*   conqueſt] conqueſts *JC*   13 and Vandall *1633-54, A18, B, D, H49, JC, Lec, N, O'F, P, S, S96, TC*: or Vandall *1669, Chambers*   15 arts] acts *1669, JC*   20 professe; *Ed*: professe, *1633–69*   24 In that *1633, A18, N, TC*: Naked *1635–69, B, D, H49, Lec, JC, O'F, P, S*
 The Dissolution. *1633–69, A18, N, TCC, TCD*

                My

My fire of Paſſion, ſighes of ayre,
Water of teares, and earthly ſad deſpaire,   10
     Which my materialls bee,
But neere worne out by loves ſecuritie,
Shee, to my loſſe, doth by her death repaire,
   And I might live long wretched ſo
But that my fire doth with my fuell grow.   15
     Now as thoſe Active Kings
   Whoſe foraine conqueſt treaſure brings,
Receive more, and ſpend more, and ſooneſt breake :
This (which I am amaz'd that I can ſpeake)
     This death, hath with my ſtore   20
     My uſe encreas'd.
And ſo my ſoule more earneſtly releas'd,
Will outſtrip hers ; As bullets flowen before
A latter bullet may o'rtake, the pouder being more.

A Ieat Ring ſent.

THou art not ſo black, as my heart,
  Nor halfe ſo brittle, as her heart, thou art ;
What would'ſt thou ſay ? ſhall both our properties by thee
    bee ſpoke,
Nothing more endleſſe, nothing ſooner broke ?

     Marriage rings are not of this ſtuffe ;   5
  Oh, why ſhould ought leſſe precious, or leſſe tough
Figure our loves ? Except in thy name thou have bid it ſay,
  I'am cheap, and nought but faſhion, fling me'away.

  10 earthly *1633, A18, N, TC :* earthy *1635–69*   12 neere *1635–
69* (But . . . ſecuritie *bracketed 1669*) : ne'r *1633*   24 latter] later *1669*
  A Ieat Ring ſent. *1633–69, A18, N, O'F, TCC, TCD :* To a Jeat Ring
ſent to me. *W* (*among the* Epigrams)   7 loves] love *O'F*   ſay, *Ed :*
ſay *1633–69*
                                           Yet

Yet ftay with mee fince thou art come,
Circle this fingers top, which did'ft her thombe.   10
Be juftly proud, and gladly fafe, that thou doft dwell with
          me,
She that, Oh, broke her faith, would foon breake thee.

Negative love.

I Never ftoop'd fo low, as they
  Which on an eye, cheeke, lip, can prey,
   Seldome to them, which foare no higher
   Then vertue or the minde to'admire,
For fenfe, and underftanding may   5
   Know, what gives fuell to their fire:
My love, though filly, is more brave,
For may I miffe, when ere I crave,
If I know yet, what I would have.

If that be fimply perfecteft   10
Which can by no way be expreft
   But *Negatives*, my love is fo.
   To All, which all love, I fay no.
If any who deciphers beft,
   What we know not, our felves, can know,   15
Let him teach mee that nothing; This
As yet my eafe, and comfort is,
Though I fpeed not, I cannot miffe.

   Negative love. *1633–69*, *A18*, *N*, *TCC*, *TCD*: Negative Love: or the
Nothing. *O'F*: The Nothing. *A25*, *C*   4 to'admire, *1633–39*: to'admire;
1650–69   5 For] Both *A25*, *C*   11 way] means *1669*, *O'F*
16 nothing; *1633*: nothing. *1635–69*

The

The Prohibition.

Take heed of loving mee,
At leaſt remember, I forbade it thee;
Not that I ſhall repaire my'unthrifty waſt
Of Breath and Blood, upon thy ſighes, and teares,
By being to thee then what to me thou waſt;   5
But, ſo great Joy, our life at once outweares,
Then, leaſt thy love, by my death, fruſtrate bee,
If thou love mee, take heed of loving mee.

Take heed of hating mee,
Or too much triumph in the Victorie.   10
Not that I ſhall be mine owne officer,
And hate with hate againe retaliate;
But thou wilt loſe the ſtile of conquerour,
If I, thy conqueſt, periſh by thy hate.
Then, leaſt my being nothing leſſen thee,   15
If thou hate mee, take heed of hating mee.

Yet, love and hate mee too,
So, theſe extreames ſhall neithers office doe;
Love mee, that I may die the gentler way;
Hate mee, becauſe thy love is too great for mee;   20
Or let theſe two, themſelves, not me decay;
So ſhall I, live, thy Stage, not triumph bee;

The Prohibition. *1633–69, A18, N, TCC, TCD : no title, B, Cy, D, H40, H49, JC, O'F, S96: in B first two verses headed J. D., last verse* T. R.: *in A18, N, S96, TCC, TCD the* last stanza is omitted   3 repaire my'unthrifty waſt] repay in unthrifty a waſt, *1669*   5 By . . . waſt; *Ed :* By . . . waſt, *1635–69, B, Cy, H40, O'F, P, RP31, S96* (mee *for thee B, P): By being to mee then that which thou waſt ; 1633: om. A18, D, H40, H49, N, TC*   18 neithers *Ed:* neythers *D, H40, H49, JC:* neyther *O'F, RP31:* neyther their *Cy:* ne'r their *1633–69, B*   20 thy *1635–69:* my *1633* (thy *in some copies*)   22 I, live, *Ed:* I live *1633–69* Stage, *1635–69, B, Cy, H40, O'F:* ſtay, *1633, JC:* ſtaye, *D, H49*   not] and *H40*

Left

Left thou thy love and hate and mee undoe,
To let mee live, O love and hate mee too.

The Expiration.

SO, fo, breake off this laft lamenting kiffe,
  Which fucks two foules, and vapors Both away,
Turne thou ghoft that way, and let mee turne this,
  And let our felves benight our happieft day,
We ask'd none leave to love; nor will we owe   5
  Any, fo cheape a death, as faying, Goe;

Goe; and if that word have not quite kil'd thee,
  Eafe mee with death, by bidding mee goe too.
Oh, if it have, let my word worke on mee,
  And a juft office on a murderer doe.   10
Except it be too late, to kill me fo,
  Being double dead, going, and bidding, goe.

23–4 Left thou thy love and hate and mee undoe
      To let mee live, Oh (of *in some copies*) *love and hate mee too. 1633, B*
      Then left thou thy love hate, and mee thou undoe
      O let me live, yet love and hate me too. 1635–54, Cy, D, H40, H49,
          JC, O'F (*MSS. omitting first* thou *and some with* Oh *for* yet)
      Left thou thy love, and hate, and me thou undo,
      O let me live, yet love and hate me too. 1669.
    The Expiration. *1633–69:* An Expiration. *A18, N, TCC, TCD:*
Valediction. *B:* Valedictio. *O'F:* Valedictio Amoris. *S:* Valedico. *P: no*
title, A25, C, JC   1 So, fo,] So, go *1669*   5 ask'd *A18, A25, B, C,*
JC, N, O'F, S96, TC: aske *1633–69, P, S*   9 Oh, *1633, A18, A25, JC,*
N, TC: Or, *1635–69, B, O'F, S, S96*

The Computation.

FOr the firſt twenty yeares, ſince yeſterday,
   I ſcarce beleev'd, thou could'ſt be gone away,
For forty more, I fed on favours paſt,
   And forty'on hopes, that thou would'ſt, they might laſt.
Teares drown'd one hundred, and ſighes blew out two,   5
   A thouſand, I did neither thinke, nor doe,
   Or not divide, all being one thought of you;
   Or in a thouſand more, forgot that too.
Yet call not this long life; But thinke that I
Am, by being dead, Immortall; Can ghoſts die?   10

The Paradox.

NO Lover ſaith, I love, nor any other
   Can judge a perfeét Lover;
Hee thinkes that elſe none can, nor will agree
   That any loves but hee:
I cannot ſay I lov'd, for who can ſay   5
   Hee was kill'd yeſterday?
Love with exceſſe of heat, more yong then old,
   Death kills with too much cold;
Wee dye but once, and who lov'd laſt did die,
   Hee that ſaith twice, doth lye: 10
For though hee ſeeme to move, and ſtirre a while,
   It doth the ſenſe beguile.

  The Computation. *1633–69, A18, N, TCC, TCD:* no title, *B, O'F, S*
1 For *1633–54:* From *1669*   the *1633, A18, N, TC:* my *1635–69, B,*
O'F, S, Chambers   3 For] And *1669*   6 One thouſand
I did think nothing nor doe, *S, O'F* (nothing think) doe, *1635–69:* doe. *1633*
7 divide, *1633, 1669:* deem'd, *1635–54, O'F*   8 a] one *O'F, S: line*
dropped A18, N, TC   forgot] forget *1669, A18, N, O'F, S, TC*
  The Paradox. *1635–69:* no title, *1633, A18, H40, L74, N, O'F, S, S96*
TCC, TCD   3 can, nor will agree *A18, H40, N, O'F, S, TC:* can or
will agree, *1633–69*   6 yeſterday?] yeſterday. *1633–39*

                                       Such

Such life is like the light which bideth yet
  When the lights life is fet,
Or like the heat, which fire in folid matter   15
  Leaves behinde, two houres after.
Once I lov'd and dy'd; and am now become
  Mine Epitaph and Tombe.
Here dead men fpeake their laft, and fo do I;
  Love-flaine, loe, here I lye.   20

Farewell to love.

W<small>Hilft</small> yet to prove,
I thought there was fome Deitie in love
  So did I reverence, and gave
Worfhip; as Atheifts at their dying houre
Call, what they cannot name, an unknowne power, 5
  As ignorantly did I crave:
    Thus when
Things not yet knowne are coveted by men,
  Our defires give them fafhion, and fo
As they waxe leffer, fall, as they fife, grow.   10

  But, from late faire
His highneffe fitting in a golden Chaire,
  Is not leffe cared for after three dayes
By children, then the thing which lovers fo
Blindly admire, and with fuch worfhip wooe;   15
  Being had, enjoying it decayes:
    And thence,
What before pleas'd them all, takes but one fenfe,
  And that fo lamely, as it leaves behinde
A kinde of forrowing dulneffe to the minde.   20

14 lights life *H40, L74, RP31, S:* lifes light *1633–69, A18, N, O'F, S96,*
TC 15 which *Ed:* which, *1633–69* 17 lov'd *A18, H40, L74,*
N, O'F, S, TC: love *1633–69* dy'd] dyed *1633–69* 20 lye.
H40, RP31, S, S96: dye. *1633–69, A18, L74, N, O'F, TC*
 Farewell to love. *1635–69 (following* Soules joy : *p. 429), O'F, S96* 4
Worfhip; *Ed:* Worfhip, *1635–69* 10 fife, *1635–69, O'F:* rife *S96*
                    Ah

Ah cannot wee,
As well as Cocks and Lyons jocund be,
   After fuch pleafures? Unleffe wife
Nature decreed (fince each fuch Act, they fay,
Diminifheth the length of life a day)   25
    This, as fhee would man fhould defpife
        The fport;
Becaufe that other curfe of being fhort,
   And onely for a minute made to be,
⟨Eagers defire⟩ to raife pofterity.   30

    Since fo, my minde
Shall not defire what no man elfe can finde,
   I'll no more dote and runne
To purfue things which had indammag'd me.
And when I come where moving beauties be,   35
    As men doe when the fummers Sunne
        Growes great,
Though I admire their greatneffe, fhun their heat;
   Each place can afford fhadowes. If all faile,
'Tis but applying worme-feed to the Taile.   40

A Lecture upon the Shadow.

STand ftill, and I will read to thee
 A Lecture, Love, in loves philofophy.
    Thefe three houres that we have fpent,
    Walking here, Two fhadowes went

   23 pleafures? *Ed:* pleafures, *1635–69*   **26** This, *Ed:* This;
1635–69   **27** fport; *Ed:* fport, *1635–69*   **29** to be, *Ed:*
to be *1635–69*   **30** ⟨Eagers defire⟩ *Ed:* Eager, defires *1635–69*. *See*
note   **36** fummers *1635–39 :* fummer *1650–69*
   A Lecture *&c. 1650–69 :* Lecture *&c,* A18, N, TCC, TCD: Song.
1635–39 (*following* Dear Love continue: *p.* 412): The Shadowe. O'F,
P: Shadowe. S96: Loves Lecture. S: Loves Lecture upon the Shaddow.
L74: Loves Philofophy. JC: *no title,* A25, B, C, D, H40, H49, Lec
 4 Walking *1635–69,* A18, A25, N, TC: In walking B, D, H40, H49, JC,
Lec, S96   here, *1719:* here; *1635–39:* here: *1650–69*

                                          Along

Along with us, which we our felves produc'd;   5
But, now the Sunne is juft above our head,
  We doe thofe fhadowes tread;
  And to brave clearneffe all things are reduc'd.
So whilft our infant loves did grow,
Difguifes did, and fhadowes, flow,   10
From us, and our cares; but, now 'tis not fo.

That love hath not attain'd the high'ft degree,
Which is ftill diligent left others fee.

Except our loves at this noone ftay,
We fhall new fhadowes make the other way.   15
  As the firft were made to blinde
  Others; thefe which come behinde
Will worke upon our felves, and blind our eyes.
If our loves faint, and weftwardly decline;
  To me thou, falfly, thine,   20
  And I to thee mine actions fhall difguife.
 The morning fhadowes weare away,
 But thefe grow longer all the day,
 But oh, loves day is fhort, if love decay.

Love is a growing, or full conftant light;   25
And his firft minute, after noone, is night.

Sonnet.   *The Token.*

SEnd me fome token, that my hope may live,
 Or that my eafeleffe thoughts may fleep and reft;
Send me fome honey to make fweet my hive,
 That in my paffion I may hope the beft.

9 loves *1635–54, A18, L74, N, TC*: love *1669, B, D, H40, H49, JC,
Lec, O'F, S* 12 high'ft] leaft *B, D, H40, H49, JC, Lec, O'F, S, S96*
14 loves *1635–69, A18, A25, L74, N, TC*: love *B, D, H40, H49, JC, Lec,
O'F, S, S96* 19 If our loves faint *1635–69, A25, O'F* (love), *P, S96* (love),
TC: If once love faint *B, D, H40, H49, JC, S* 26 firft *A18, A25,
B, D, H40, H49, JC, L74, Lec, N, O'F, P, S96, TC*: fhort *1635–69*
 Sonnet. The Token. *1649–69* (*following* Vpon Mr. Thomas Coryats
Crudities. *at close of* Epicedes): Ad Lefbiam. *S96: no title, B, Cy*:
Sonnet. *O'F*: Elegie. *P* 1 token *B, O'F, S96*: Tokens *1650–69, P*
4 paffion *S96*: paffions *1650–69, B, P*

I beg

I beg noe ribbond wrought with thine owne hands,   5
   To knit our loves in the fantaftick ftraine
Of new-toucht youth; nor Ring to fhew the ftands
   Of our affection, that as that's round and plaine,
So fhould our loves meet in fimplicity;
   No, nor the Coralls which thy wrift infold,   10
Lac'd up together in congruity,
   To fhew our thoughts fhould reft in the fame hold;
No, nor thy picture, though moft gracious,
   And moft defir'd, becaufe beft like the beft;
Nor witty Lines, which are moft copious,   15
   Within the Writings which thou haft addreft.

  Send me nor this, nor that, t'increafe my ftore,
  But fwear thou thinkft I love thee, and no more.

⟨*Selfe Love.*⟩

HE that cannot chufe but love,
   And ftrives againft it ftill,
Never fhall my fancy move;
   For he loves 'gaynft his will;
Nor he which is all his own,   5
   And can att pleafure chufe,
When I am caught he can be gone,
   And when he lift refufe.
Nor he that loves none but faire,
   For fuch by all are fought;   10
Nor he that can for foul ones care,
   For his Judgement then is nought:

5 noe *B,O'F,P,S96:* nor *1650–69*   9 fimplicity; *Ed:* fimplicity.
1650–69   11 in *1650–69:* with *B,O'F,S96*   12 hold; *Ed:* hold.
1650–69   14 defir'd becaufe . . . beft; *B, O'F, S96:* defired 'caufe 'tis
like thee beft; *1650–54:* defired 'caufe 'tis like the beft; *1669, Chambers*
17 ftore, *B,O'F,P,S96:* fcore, *1650–69*

⟨Selfe Love.⟩ *title given by Chambers:* no title, *1650–69* (*in appendix*),
JC,O'F   4 'gaynft *JC,O'F:* againft *1650–69*   6 And
can . . . chufe, *JC:* And cannot pleafure chufe, *1650–69:* And can all
pleafures chufe, *O'F*   11 foul ones] foulnefs *O'F*

                 Nor

Nor he that hath wit, for he
Will make me his jeſt or ſlave ;
Nor a fool, for when others . . .,   15
He can neither . . . . . .
Nor he that ſtill his Miſtreſſe payes,
For ſhe is thrall'd therefore :
Nor he that payes not, for he ſayes
Within, ſhee's worth no more.   20
Is there then no kinde of men
Whom I may freely prove ?
I will vent that humour then
In mine own ſelfe love.

14 ſlave; *1719:* ſlave *1650–69*   15 fool, *1719:* fool *1650–69*
17 payes, *JC, O'F:* prays, *1650–69*   19 payes not,] payes, not, *1650–69*
20 Within, *Ed:* Within *1650–69*

The end of the Songs and Sonets.

EPIGRAMS.

EPIGRAMS.

Hero and *Leander*.

BOth rob'd of aire, we both lye in one ground,
Both whom one fire had burnt, one water drownd.

Pyramus and *Thisbe*.

TWo, by themfelves, each other, love and feare
Slaine, cruell friends, by parting have joyn'd here.

Niobe.

BY childrens births, and death, I am become
So dry, that I am now mine owne fad tombe.

A burnt fhip.

OUt of a fired fhip, which, by no way
But drowning, could be refcued from the flame,
Some men leap'd forth, and ever as they came
Neere the foes fhips, did by their fhot decay;
So all were loft, which in the fhip were found,
    They in the fea being burnt, they in the burnt fhip
        drown'd.

Hero and Leander. *1633–69, A18, HN, N, O'F, TCC, TCD, W*
Pyramus   and   Thisbe.   *1633–69, A18, Cy, HN, N, O'F, TCC, TCD, W*
1 feare] feare, *Chambers, and Grolier (which drops all the other commas*)
    Niobe. *1633–69, A18, HN, N, O'F, TCC, TCD, W*   2 mine owne
fad tombe. *1633–69:* mine owne tombe. *A18, N, TC:* made mine owne
tombe. *HN, W*
    A burnt fhip. *1633–69, A18, N, TCC, TCD :* Nave arfa. *W:* De
Nave arfa. *O'F. See note*

Fall

Fall of a wall.

VNder an undermin'd, and ſhot-bruis'd wall
A too-bold Captaine periſh'd by the fall,
Whoſe brave misfortune, happieſt men envi'd,
That had a towne for tombe, his bones to hide.

A lame begger.

I Am unable, yonder begger cries,
To ſtand, or move ; if he ſay true, hee *lies*.

Cales and Guyana.

IF you from ſpoyle of th'old worlds fartheſt end
To the new world your kindled valors bend,
What brave examples then do prove it trew
That one things end doth ſtill beginne a new.

Sir Iohn Wingefield.

BEyond th'old Pillers many have travailed
Towards the Suns cradle, and his throne, and bed :
A fitter Piller our Earle did beſtow
In that late Iſland ; for he well did know
Farther then Wingefield no man dares to goe.

A ſelfe accuſer.

YOur miſtris, that you follow whores, ſtill taxeth you :
'Tis ſtrange that ſhe ſhould thus confeſſe it, though'it
be true.

Fall of a wall. *1633–69, A18, N, TCC, TCD :* Caſo d'un muro. *O'F,
W*   4 towne *1633 and MSS.:* towre *1635–69*   bones *1633–69,
A18, N, TC :* corpſe *B, HN, O'F, W*
   A lame begger. *1633–69, A18, N, TC :* A beggar. *HN : no title, P :*
Zoppo. *O'F, W*
   Cales and Guyana. *O'F :* Calez *&c. W : first printed in Gosse's* Life
and Letters of John Donne (1899)
   Sir Iohn Wingefield. *Ed :* Il Cavalliere Gio: Wingef: *W :* On Cavallero
Wingfield. *O'F : first printed in Gosse's* Life and Letters of John Donne
(1899)   2 throne *W :* grave *O'F*   4 late *W :* Lady *O'F*
   A ſelfe accuſer. *1633–69 :* A Miſtriſſe. *HN : no title, B, O'F, W*
2 that] *om. HN, O'F, W*   thus] *om. HN, O'F, W*   it] *om. HN, O'F*
                                                      A licentious

A licentious perſon.

THy ſinnes and haires may no man equall call,
For, as thy ſinnes increaſe, thy haires doe fall.

Antiquary.

IF in his Studie he hath ſo much care
To'hang all old ſtrange things, let his wife beware.

Diſinherited.

THy father all from thee, by his laſt Will,
Gave to the poore; Thou haſt good title ſtill.

Phryne.

THy flattering picture, *Phryne,* is like thee,
Onely in this, that you both painted be.

An obſcure writer.

PHilo, with twelve yeares ſtudy, hath beene griev'd
To be underſtood; when will hee be beleev'd?

Klockius.

KLockius ſo deeply hath ſworne, ne'r more to come
In bawdie houſe, that hee dares not goe home.

A licentious perſon. *1633–69, A18, N, TCC, TCD:* Whore. *HN: no title, O'F, RP31, W* 1 Thy] His *and so throughout, RP31*
Antiquary. *1633–69, A18, N, P, TCC, TCD, W:* Hammon. *HN: no title, Bur, Cy, O'F:* Epigram. *S96* 1 he hath ſo much *1633–69:* he have such *A18, N, TC:* Hamon hath such *B, Cy, HN* (have), *O'F, S96, W* 2 ſtrange *om. B, HN, O'F* all *om. Bur*
Diſinherited. *1633–69:* One diſinherited. *HN: no title, Cy, O'F, P, W* 1 Will, *Ed:* Will *1633–69*
Phryne. *1633–69, A18, N, TCC, TCD: no title, O'F* 1 like thee,] like to thee, *1650–69*
An obſcure writer. *1633–69, A18, N, TCC, TCD: no title, O'F* 1 griev'd *Ed:* griev'd, *1633–69* 2 To be *Ed:* To'be *1633–69* under-ſtood; *Ed:* underſtood, *1633–69* beleev'd?] beleev'd. *1633*
Klockius. *HN: no title, 1633–69, Bur, O'F* 1 *Klockius*] Rawlings *Bur* 2 In bawdie] In a bawdie *HN*

Raderus.

Raderus.

WHy this man gelded *Martiall* I mufe,
    Except himfelfe alone his tricks would ufe,
As *Katherine*, for the Courts fake, put downe Stewes.

Mercurius Gallo-Belgicus.

LIke *Efops* fellow-flaves, O *Mercury*,
    Which could do all things, thy faith is; and I
Like *Efops* felfe, which nothing; I confeffe
I fhould have had more faith, if thou hadft leffe;
Thy credit loft thy credit: 'Tis finne to doe,
In this cafe, as thou wouldft be done unto,
To beleeve all: Change thy name: thou art like
Mercury in ftealing, but lyeft like a *Greeke*.

Ralphius.

COmpaffion in the world againe is bred:
    Ralphius is fick, the broker keeps his bed.

The Lier.

THou in the fields walkft out thy fupping howers,
    And yet thou fwear'ft thou haft fupp'd like a king:
Like Nebuchadnezar perchance with grafs and flowers,
    A fallet worfe then Spanifh dieting.

Raderus. *1633–69, A18, N, TCD*: Randerus. *TCC*: Martial: caftrat*us.*
W   1 *Martiall* I mufe, *1633–54*: *Martiall*, I amufe, *1669*
    Mercurius Gallo-Belgicus. *1633–69, A18, B, N, O'F, S, TCC, TCD, W*
8 but lyeft *1633–69*: and lyeft *B, W*
    Ralphius. *HN*: *no title, 1633–69, O'F*
    The Lier. *HN*: *no title, B, Bur, Cy, O'F, P, W*   2 fwear'ft *HN, W*:
fay'ft *B, Cy, O'F*   3 grafs] hearbes *Bur*   fupp'd like] fupp'd and like *HN*

ELEGIES.

ELEGIES.

ELEGIE I.

Iealofie.

FOnd woman, which would'ft have thy hufband die,
  And yet complain'ft of his great jealoufie;
If fwolne with poyfon, hee lay in'his laft bed,
His body with a fere-barke covered,
Drawing his breath, as thick and fhort, as can   5
The nimbleft crocheting Mufitian,
Ready with loathfome vomiting to fpue
His Soule out of one hell, into a new,
Made deafe with his poore kindreds howling cries,
Begging with few feign'd teares, great legacies,   10
Thou would'ft not weepe, but jolly,'and frolicke bee,
As a flave, which to morrow fhould be free;
Yet weep'ft thou, when thou feeft him hungerly
Swallow his owne death, hearts-bane jealoufie.
O give him many thanks, he'is courteous,   15
That in fufpecting kindly warneth us.
Wee muft not, as wee us'd, flout openly,
In fcoffing ridles, his deformitie;
Nor at his boord together being fatt,
With words, nor touch, fcarce lookes adulterate.   20
Nor when he fwolne, and pamper'd with great fare,
Sits downe, and fnorts, cag'd in his basket chaire,
Muft wee ufurpe his owne bed any more,
Nor kiffe and play in his houfe, as before.

Elegie I. Iealofie. *1635–54:* Elegie I. *1633 and 1669 : no title or*
Elegie *(numbered variously, according to scheme adopted)* A18, A25, B, Cy,
D, H49, JC, Lec, N, O'F, P, S, S96, TCC, TCD, W   1 woman,] woman
1633   4 fere-barke *1633–54,* B, Cy, H49, Lec, O'F, S, W: fere-cloth
1669, D, P: fore barke A18, A25, JC, N, TC   10 few] fome few A18,
N, TC   12 free; *Ed:* free, *1633–69:* free. D   16 us.
1633–35: us, *1639–69*   21 great *1633–54,* A18, A25, D, H49, JC, Lec,
N, S, TC, W: high *1669,* B, O'F, P, S96: his Cy   fare, *Ed:* fare *1633–69*

Now I fee many dangers ; for that is   25
His realme, his caftle, and his dioceffe.
But if, as envious men, which would revile
Their Prince, or coyne his gold, themfelves exile
Into another countrie,'and doe it there,
Wee play'in another houfe, what fhould we feare?   30
There we will scorne his houfhold policies,
His feely plots, and penfionary fpies,
As the inhabitants of Thames right fide
Do Londons Major; or Germans, the Popes pride.

ELEGIE II.

The Anagram.

MArry, and love thy *Flavia*, for, fhee
Hath all things, whereby others beautious bee,
For, though her eyes be fmall, her mouth is great,
Though they be Ivory, yet her teeth be jeat,
Though they be dimme, yet fhe is light enough,   5
And though her harfh haire fall, her skinne is rough ;
What though her cheeks be yellow, her haire's red,
Give her thine, and fhe hath a maydenhead.
Thefe things are beauties elements, where thefe
Meet in one, that one muft, as perfe&, pleafe.   10

25 Now . . . dangers ;] Now do I fee my danger ; *1669*   that *all*
MSS.: it *1633–69*   26 dioceffe] Diocys *D:* Diocis *W*   27–29
(as envious . . . do it there,) *1669*   30 another] anothers *1669*
We into fome third place retired were *B, O'F, P, S96*   34 Major ;
1650–54: Major, *1633–39:* Mayor ; *1669*
    Eleg. II. The Anagram. *1635–54 :* Elegie II. *1633,1669 :* Elegie.
(*numbered varioufly*) *A18, A25, B, Cy, D, H49, JC, L74, Lec, M, N, O'F, P,
S, S96, TCC, TCD, W*   4 they] theirs *1669, S96*   teeth be *1633–69, D,
H49, JC, Lec:* teeth are *A18, A25, B, Cy, L74, M, N, O'F, S, TC, W*   6
hair fall] hair's foul *1669*   is rough *1633,1669, A18, A25, B, D, H49,
JC, L74, Lec, M, N, P, S, TC, W:* is tough *1635–54, O'F, Chambers*

If

If red and white and each good quality
Be in thy wench, ne'r aske where it doth lye.
In buying things perfum'd, we aske; if there
Be muske and amber in it, but not where.
Though all her parts be not in th'ufuall place, 15
She'hath yet an Anagram of a good face.
If we might put the letters but one way,
In the leane dearth of words, what could wee fay?
When by the Gamut fome Mufitions make
A perfect fong, others will undertake, 20
By the fame Gamut chang'd, to equall it.
Things fimply good, can never be unfit.
She's faire as any, if all be like her,
And if none bee, then fhe is fingular.
All love is wonder; if wee juftly doe 25
Account her wonderfull, why not lovely too?
Love built on beauty, foone as beauty, dies,
Chufe this face, chang'd by no deformities.
Women are all like Angels; the faire be
Like thofe which fell to worfe; but fuch as fhee, 30
Like to good Angels, nothing can impaire:
'Tis leffe griefe to be foule, then to'have beene faire.
For one nights revels, filke and gold we chufe,
But, in long journeyes, cloth, and leather ufe.
Beauty is barren oft; beft hufbands fay, 35
There is beft land, where there is fouleft way.
Oh what a foveraigne Plaifter will fhee bee,
If thy paft finnes have taught thee jealoufie!
Here needs no fpies, nor eunuches; her commit
Safe to thy foes; yea, to a Marmofit. 40
When Belgiaes citties, the round countries drowne,
That durty fouleneffe guards, and armes the towne:

16 an Anagram] the Anagrams *1669* 18 the *1633:* that *1635–69*
words *1633–69, A25, B, L74, M, N, O'F, P, S, TC:* letters *D, Cy, H49, W*
22 unfit. *D:* unfit; *1633–69* 28 deformities.] deformities; *1633*
29 faire] fairer *S, S96* 35 fay,] fay *1633* 37 bee,] bee *1633*
41–2 When Belgiaes … towne: *1633–54:* Like Belgia's cities when the

So

So doth her face guard her; and fo, for thee,
Which, forc'd by bufineffe, abfent oft muft bee,
Shee, whofe face, like clouds, turnes the day to night,   45
Who, mightier then the fea, makes Moores feem white,
Who, though feaven yeares, fhe in the Stews had laid,
A Nunnery durft receive, and thinke a maid,
And though in childbeds labour fhe did lie,
Midwifes would fweare,'twere but a tympanie,   50
Whom, if fhee accufe her felfe, I credit leffe
Then witches, which impoffibles confeffe,
Whom Dildoes, Bedftaves, and her Velvet Glaffe
Would be as loath to touch as Jofeph was:
One like none, and lik'd of none, fitteft were,   55
For, things in fafhion every man will weare.

ELEGIE III.

Change.

ALthough thy hand and faith, and good workes too,
Have feal'd thy love which nothing fhould undoe,
Yea though thou fall backe, that apoftafie
Confirme thy love; yet much, much I feare thee.
Women are like the Arts, forc'd unto none,   5
Open to'all fearchers, unpriz'd, if unknowne.

Country is drown'd, That .. towns; *1669:* Like Belgia's cities the round
country drowns, That .. towns, *Chambers: MSS. agree with 1633–54, but
before* countries *read variously* round (*A18, A25, Cy, D, H49, JC, L74, Lec,
M, N, P, TC, W*), lowe (*B*), foul (*O'F, S, S96, which read* country drowns ...
towns)   49 childbeds *1633–54, Lec, W:* childbirths *1669, A18, A25, B,
Cy, D, H49, JC, L74, O'F, P, S, S96, TC*   52 confeffe, *Ed:* confeffe.
1633–69   53–4 Whom ... Joseph was: *1669 and all MSS* [or a
Velvet *1669*]: *om. 1633–54*
   Eleg. III. Change. *1635–54:* Elegie III. *1633, 1669: no title or* Elegye
(*numbered variously*) *A18, A25, B, Cy, D, H49, JC, L74, Lec, N, O'F, P, S,
S96, TCC, TCD, W*   1 workes] word *1669*   4 Confirme]
Confirms *1669, A25, L74, P*   5 Women] Women, *1633*   forc'd unto
none] forbid to none *B*

If

If I have caught a bird, and let him flie,
Another fouler ufing thefe meanes, as I,
May catch the fame bird; and, as thefe things bee,
Women are made for men, not him, nor mee.   10
Foxes and goats; all beafts change when they pleafe,
Shall women, more hot, wily, wild then thefe,
Be bound to one man, and did Nature then
Idly make them apter to'endure then men?
They'are our clogges, not their owne; if a man bee   15
Chain'd to a galley, yet the galley'is free;
Who hath a plow-land, cafts all his feed corne there,
And yet allowes his ground more corne fhould beare;
Though Danuby into the fea muft flow,
The fea receives the Rhene, Volga, and Po.   20
By nature, which gave it, this liberty
Thou lov'ft, but Oh! canft thou love it and mee?
Likeneffe glues love: and if that thou fo doe,
To make us like and love, muft I change too?
More then thy hate, I hate'it, rather let mee   25
Allow her change, then change as oft as shee,
And foe not teach, but force my'opinion
To love not any one, nor every one.
To live in one land, is captivitie,
To runne all countries, a wild roguery;   30
Waters ftincke foone, if in one place they bide,
And in the vaft fea are more putrifi'd:
But when they kiffe one banke, and leaving this
Never looke backe, but the next banke doe kiffe,
Then are they pureft; Change'is the nurfery   35
Of muficke, joy, life, and eternity.

8 thefe *1633–54, D, H49, Lec*: thofe *1669, A18, A25, B, Cy, JC, L74,
N, P, TC, W*   11 Foxes and goats; all beafts *1633–54*: Foxes, goats
and all beafts *1669*   13 did] bid *1669*   17 a plow-land] plow-
lands *P*   18 corne] feed *P*   20 Rhene,] Rhine, *1669*   Po. *1633*:
Po, *1635–69*   21 liberty *1633*: libertie. *1635–69*   23 and ... doe,]
then if fo thou do, *A18, A25, B, Cy, D, H49. JC, L74, Lec, N, O'F, P, S96,
TC, W*   24 like *i.e.* alike *as in A18, N, TC*   31 bide] abide *1669*
32 more putrifi'd *1633–39*: more purifi'd *1650–54*: worfe purifi'd *1669*:
worfe putrifi'd *A18, A25, Cy, D, L74, Lec, N, O'F, P, S, S96, TC, W*: worft
putrifi'd *B, H49, JC*

ELEGIE

ELEGIE IV.

The Perfume.

ONce, and but once found in thy company,
　All thy ſuppos'd eſcapes are laid on mee;
And as a thiefe at barre, is queſtion'd there
By all the men, that have beene rob'd that yeare,
So am I, (by this traiterous meanes ſurpriz'd)　　　　　5
By thy Hydroptique father catechiz'd.
Though he had wont to ſearch with glazed eyes,
As though he came to kill a Cockatrice,
Though hee hath oft ſworne, that hee would remove
Thy beauties beautie, and food of our love,　　　　　10
Hope of his goods, if I with thee were ſeene,
Yet cloſe and ſecret, as our ſoules, we'have beene.
Though thy immortall mother which doth lye
Still buried in her bed, yet will not dye,
Takes this advantage to ſleepe out day-light,　　　　　15
And watch thy entries, and returnes all night,
And, when ſhe takes thy hand, and would ſeeme kind,
Doth ſearch what rings, and armelets ſhe can finde,
And kiſſing notes the colour of thy face,
And fearing leaſt thou'art ſwolne, doth thee embrace;　　　20
To trie if thou long, doth name ſtrange meates,
And notes thy paleneſſe, bluſhing, ſighs, and ſweats;
And politiquely will to thee confeſſe
The ſinnes of her owne youths ranke luſtineſſe;
Yet love theſe Sorceries did remove, and move　　　　　25

Eleg. IV.　The Perfume. *1635–54 :* Elegie IV. *1633, 1669 :* Elegie.
(*numbered variouſly*) *A18, A25, C, D, H49, JC, L74, Lec, N, O'F, P, S, S96,
TCC, TCD, W :* Diſcovered by a Perfume. *B : no title, Cy, HN*　　2 ſuppos'd eſcapes] ſuppoſed ſcapes *1669, P*　　4 By] For *P*　　7–8 *1635–69 and MSS. generally :* om. *1633, D, H49, Lec*　　9 hath] have *A18, A25, L74, N, P, TC, W*　　15 Takes] Take *A18, A25, N, P, TC, W*　　21 To trie &c. *1633, D, H49, S* (doſt long) : And to trie &c. *1635–69, A18, A25, L74, N, O'F, S96* (longeſt), *TC*　　meates, *1635–69 :* meates. *1633*　　22 bluſhing *1633–54, A18, A25, JC, N, TC :* bluſhes *1669 :* bluſhings *B, D, H49, HN, L74, Lec. O'F, P, W*

Thee

Thee to gull thine owne mother for my love.
Thy little brethren, which like Faiery Sprights
Oft skipt into our chamber, thofe fweet nights,
And kift, and ingled on thy fathers knee,
Were brib'd next day, to tell what they did fee: 30
The grim eight-foot-high iron-bound ferving-man,
That oft names God in oathes, and onely than,
He that to barre the firft gate, doth as wide
As the great Rhodian Coloffus ftride,
Which, if in hell no other paines there were,   35
Makes mee feare hell, becaufe he muft be there:
Though by thy father he were hir'd to this,
Could never witneffe any touch or kiffe.
But Oh, too common ill, I brought with mee
That, which betray'd mee to my enemie: 40
A loud perfume, which at my entrance cryed
Even at thy fathers nofe, fo were wee fpied.
When, like a tyran King, that in his bed
Smelt gunpowder, the pale wretch fhivered.
Had it beene fome bad fmell, he would have thought   45
That his owne feet, or breath, that fmell had wrought.
But as wee in our Ile emprifoned,
Where cattell onely,'and diverfe dogs are bred,
The pretious Vnicornes, ftrange monfters call,
So thought he good, ftrange, that had none at all.   50
I taught my filkes, their whiftling to forbeare,
Even my oppreft fhoes, dumbe and fpeechleffe were,
Onely, thou bitter fweet, whom I had laid
Next mee, mee traiteroufly haft betraid,
And unfufpeéted haft invifibly   55
At once fled unto him, and ftaid with mee.
Bafe excrement of earth, which doft confound

29 ingled] dandled *1669*   30 fee: *1635–69* : fee. *1633*   31 grim
eight-foot-high iron-bound *Ed:* grim-eight-foot-high-iron-bound *1633–69*
37 to *1633–69* : for *MSS.*   38 kiffe.] kiffe ; *1633*   40 my *1633* :
mine *1635–69*   44 Smelt] Smells *1669*   fhivered. *A18, D. H49.I.74,*
N,TC,W: fhivered; *1633–69* : shivered, *Chambers and Grolier. See note*
46 that fmell] the fmell *1669*   49 monfters *Ed:* monfters, *1633–69*
50 good,] fweet *1669*   53 bitter fweet, *1633–39* : bitter-fweet, *1650–69*
                                                                    Senfe,

Senſe, from diſtinguiſhing the ſicke from ſound;
By thee the ſeely Amorous ſucks his death
By drawing in a leprous harlots breath;   60
By thee, the greateſt ſtaine to mans eſtate
Falls on us, to be call'd effeminate;
Though you be much lov'd in the Princes hall,
There, things that ſeeme, exceed ſubſtantiall;
Gods, when yee fum'd on altars, were pleas'd well, 65
Becauſe you'were burnt, not that they lik'd your ſmell;
You'are loathſome all, being taken ſimply alone,
Shall wee love ill things joyn'd, and hate each one?
If you were good, your good doth ſoone decay;
And you are rare, that takes the good away.   70
All my perfumes, I give moſt willingly
To'embalme thy fathers corſe; What? will hee die?

ELEGIE V.

His Picture.

HEre take my Picture; though I bid farewell,
Thine, in my heart, where my ſoule dwels, ſhall dwell.
'Tis like me now, but I dead, 'twill be more
When wee are ſhadowes both, then'twas before.
When weather-beaten I come backe; my hand,   5
Perhaps with rude oares torne, or Sun beams tann'd,
My face and breſt of hairecloth, and my head
With cares raſh ſodaine ſtormes, being o'rſpread,

60 breath; *1650–69:* breath, *1633–39*   64 ſubſtantiall; *Ed:* ſub-
ſtantiall. *1633–69*   66 you'were] you'er *1669*   ſmell; *1635–39:*
ſmell, *1633, 1669:* ſmel *1650–54*   71 All] And *Chambers*
    Eleg. V. His Picture. *1635–54:* Elegie V. *1633, 1669:* Elegye.
(*numbered variously*) *A18, A25, Cy, D, H49, JC, Lec, N, O'F, S, S96, TCC,
TCD, W:* The Picture. *P:* Travelling he leaves his Picture with his
myſtris. *B*   1 Picture; . . . farewell, *Ed:* Picture, . . . farewell;
1633: rest semicolon or colon after each   8 With cares raſh ſodaine
ſtormes, being o'rſpread, *1633. A18, N, TC:* With cares raſh, cruel, ſudden
ſtorms o'erſpread *P:* With cares raſh-ſudden cruel-ſtorms o'erpreſt *B:*
                                                     My

My body'a facke of bones, broken within,
And powders blew ftaines fcatter'd on my skinne;   10
If rivall fooles taxe thee to'have lov'd a man,
So foule, and courfe, as, Oh, I may feeme than,
This fhall fay what I was: and thou fhalt fay,
Doe his hurts reach mee? doth my worth decay?
Or doe they reach his judging minde, that hee   15
Should now love leffe, what hee did love to fee?
That which in him was faire and delicate,
Was but the milke, which in loves childifh ftate
Did nurfe it: who now is growne ftrong enough
To feed on that, which to difufed tafts feemes tough.   20

ELEGIE VI.

OH, let mee not ferve fo, as thofe men ferve
Whom honours fmoakes at once fatten and fterve;
Poorely enrich't with great mens words or lookes;
Nor fo write my name in thy loving bookes
As thofe Idolatrous flatterers, which ftill   5
Their Princes ftiles, with many Realmes fulfill

With cares rafh fudden ftorms o'erpreffed *S*, *S96*: With cares rafh fudden
ftorms o'erfpread *Cy*, *D*, *H49*, *Lec*: With cares rafh fodaine horinefs o'er-
fpread *A25*, *JC*, *W*: With cares harfh fodaine horineffe o'rfpread, *1635–
69*, *O'F*   16 now love leffe, *1633–69*, *A18*, *N*, *TC*: like and love
lefs *A25*, *B*, *Cy*, *D*, *H49*, *JC*, *Lec*, *O'F*, *P*, *S*, *S96*, *W*   19 nurfe] nourifh
A18, *N*, *P*, *S*, *TC*   ftrong] tough *P*   20 difufed *Ed*: difus'd
1633–39, *A18*, *A25*, *B*, *Cy*, *D*, *H49*, *JC*, *Lec*, *N*, *O'F*, *P*, *S*, *S96*, *TC*, *W*: weake
1650–69   tough.] rough. *P*
   Eleg. VI. *1635–69*: Elegie VII. *1633* (Elegie VI. *being* Sorrow who
to this houfe *&c.* *See* Epicedes *&c.*, *p.* 287): Elegie. (*numbered vari-
oufly*) *A18*, *A25*, *B*, *Cy*, *D*, *H49*, *JC*, *L74*, *Lec*, *N*, *O'F*, *P*, *S*, *S96*, *TCC*,
TCD, *W*   2 fatten] flatter *1669*, *A18*, *B*, *Cy*, *L74*, *N*, *TC*   3 or] and
A18, *Cy*, *L74*, *N*, *P*, *TC*   6 ftiles, *1633–69*, *A18*, *B*, *Cy*, *D*, *H49*, *JC*,
L74, *Lec*, *N*, *P*, *S96*, *TC*, *W*: ftyle *A25*, *O'F*, *S*, *Chambers and Grosart*   with
all MSS., *Chambers and Grosart*: which (*probably by confufion of* w[ch] *and*
w[th]) *1633–69*   Realmes] names *1669*

Whence

Whence they no tribute have, and where no fway.
Such fervices I offer as fhall pay
Themfelves, I hate dead names: Oh then let mee
Favorite in Ordinary, or no favorite bee.   10
When my Soule was in her owne body fheath'd,
Nor yet by oathes betroth'd, nor kiffes breath'd
Into my Purgatory, faithleffe thee,
Thy heart feem'd waxe, and fteele thy conftancie:
So, careleffe flowers ftrow'd on the waters face,   15
The curled whirlepooles fuck, fmack, and embrace,
Yet drowne them; fo, the tapers beamie eye
Amoroufly twinkling, beckens the giddie flie,
Yet burnes his wings; and fuch the devill is,
Scarce vifiting them, who are intirely his.   20
When I behold a ftreame, which, from the fpring,
Doth with doubtfull melodious murmuring,
Or in a fpeechleffe flumber, calmely ride
Her wedded channels bofome, and then chide
And bend her browes, and fwell if any bough   25
Do but ftoop downe, or kiffe her upmoft brow;
Yet, if her often gnawing kiffes winne
The traiterous banke to gape, and let her in,
She rufheth violently, and doth divorce
Her from her native, and her long-kept courfe,   30
And rores, and braves it, and in gallant fcorne,
In flattering eddies promifing retorne,
She flouts the channell, who thenceforth is drie;
Then fay I; that is fhee, and this am I.
Yet let not thy deepe bitterneffe beget   35
Careleffe defpaire in mee, for that will whet
My minde to fcorne; and Oh, love dull'd with paine

7 where] bear *1669*   14 conftancie: *1635–69:* conftancie. *1633*
24 then *1633, B, D, H49, Lec, S, S96, W:* there *1635–69, A18, A25, Cy, JC,*
N, O'F, P, TC, Chambers   26 upmoft *1633 and most MSS:* utmoft
1635–69, O'F, Chambers   brow; *Ed:* brow: *1633–39:* brow. *1650–69*
28 banke *A18, D, H49, JC, N, S, TC, W:* banks *1633–69, Lec, O'F*   33
the *1633, D, H49, Lec:* her *1635–69, A18, N, TC*   who *1633, A18, A25,*
B, Cy, D, JC, H49, L74, Lec, N, P, S, S96, TC: which *1635–69, O'F*   37
Oh,] Ah, *1669*

Was

Was ne'r so wise, nor well arm'd as disdaine.
Then with new eyes I shall survay thee,'and spie
Death in thy cheekes, and darknesse in thine eye.   40
Though hope bred faith and love; thus taught, I shall
As nations do from Rome, from thy love fall.
My hate shall outgrow thine, and utterly
I will renounce thy dalliance: and when I
Am the Recusant, in that resolute state,   45
What hurts it mee to be'excommunicate?

ELEGIE VII.

NAtures lay Ideot, I taught thee to love,
   And in that sophistrie, Oh, thou dost prove
Too subtile: Foole, thou didst not understand
The mystique language of the eye nor hand:
Nor couldst thou judge the difference of the aire   5
Of sighes, and say, this lies, this sounds despaire:
Nor by the'eyes water call a maladie
Desperately hot, or changing feaverously.
I had not taught thee then, the Alphabet
Of flowers, how they devisefully being set   10
And bound up, might with speechlesse secrecie
Deliver arrands mutely, and mutually.

39 thee,'] *om. 1669*   40 eye. *Ed:* eye; *1633–54:* eye: *1669:*
eye, *Chambers*   41 Though . . . love ; *1633:* Though . breed . .
love : *1635–39:* Though . breed . . love *1650–69* (Through . *1669*)   42
fall. *1633–35:* fall *1639–69*   43 outgrow] o'ergrow *Cy, P*
    Elegie VII. *1635–69:* Elegie VIII. *1633:* Elegye. (*numbered variously*)
A18, A25, B, Cy, D, H49, JC, Lec, M, N, O'F, P, S, TCC, TCD, W   2
Oh, . . prove] Oh, how . . prove *1669*   6 despaire: *1635–69:* despaire.
1633   7 call *1633, A18, A25, B, Cy, D, H49, JC, Lec, M, N, O'F* (*cor-
rected from* know), *P, TC, W:* know *1635–69:* cast *S, Chambers and Grosart*
10 they devisefully being set] their devise in being set *Cy, P*   12 arrands
1633: errands *1635–69:* meet errands *B*

Remember fince all thy words us'd to bee
To every fuitor; *I, if my friends agree*;
Since, houfehold charmes, thy hufbands name to teach, 15
Were all the love trickes, that thy wit could reach;
And fince, an houres difcourfe could fcarce have made
One anfwer in thee, and that ill arraid
In broken proverbs, and torne fentences.
Thou art not by fo many duties his,   20
That from the worlds Common having fever'd thee,
Inlaid thee, neither to be feene, nor fee,
As mine: who have with amorous delicacies
Refin'd thee'into a blif-full Paradife.
Thy graces and good words my creatures bee;   25
I planted knowledge and lifes tree in thee,
Which Oh, fhall ftrangers tafte? Muft I alas
Frame and enamell Plate, and drinke in Glaffe?
Chafe waxe for others feales? breake a colts force
And leave him then, beeing made a ready horfe?   30

ELEGIE VIII.

The Comparifon.

A S the fweet fweat of Rofes in a Still,
As that which from chaf'd muskats pores doth trill,
As the Almighty Balme of th'early Eaft,
Such are the fweat drops of my Miftris breaft,
And on her ⟨brow⟩ her skin fuch luftre fets,   5
They feeme no fweat drops, but pearle coronets.

14 *agree*; *Ed: agree. 1633–69*   21–2 That ... nor fee,] *in brackets*
1669   24 Paradife] paradife *1633*   25 words *1633–54, A25, B, Cy,*
JC, N, O'F, P, W: works *1669, A18, D, H49, Lec, TC*   bee; *Ed:* bee,
1633–69   26 thee, *1633:* thee: *1635–69*   28 Glaffe? *Ed:* glaffe.
1633–69
    Eleg. VIII. The Comparifon. *1635–54:* Elegie VIII. *1669:* Elegie.
1633: Elegie. (*numbered varioufly*) *A18, A25, B, C, Cy, JC, L74, N, O'F, P,*
S, S96, TCC, TCD, W   2 muskats] muskets *1669*   4 breaft, *1635–69:*
breaft. *1633*   5 ⟨brow⟩ *Ed:* necke *1633–69 and MSS. See note* · 6
coronets. *1633–69, A18, B, Cy, L74, M, N, O'F, S96, TC:* carcanets. *A25,*
C, JC, S, W: carolettes. *P*

                                                    Ranke

Ranke fweaty froth thy Miftreffe's brow defiles,
Like fpermatique iffue of ripe menftruous boiles,
Or like the skumme, which, by needs lawleffe law
Enforc'd, Sanferra's ftarved men did draw   10
From parboild fhooes, and bootes, and all the reft
Which were with any foveraigne fatnes bleft,
And like vile lying ftones in faffrond tinne,
Or warts, or wheales, they hang upon her skinne.
Round as the world's her head, on every fide,   15
Like to the fatall Ball which fell on Ide,
Or that whereof God had fuch jealoufie,
As, for the ravifhing thereof we die.
Thy *head* is like a rough-hewne ftatue of jeat,
Where marks for eyes, nofe, mouth, are yet fcarce fet;   20
Like the firft Chaos, or flat feeming face
Of Cynthia, when th'earths fhadowes her embrace.
Like Proferpines white beauty-keeping cheft,
Or Joues beft fortunes urne, is her faire breft.
Thine's like worme eaten trunkes, cloth'd in feals skin,   25
Or grave, that's duft without, and ftinke within.
And like that flender ftalke, at whofe end ftands
The wood-bine quivering, are her armes and hands.
Like rough bark'd elmboughes, or the ruffet skin
Of men late fcurg'd for madnes, or for finne,   30
Like Sun-parch'd quarters on the citie gate,
Such is thy tann'd skins lamentable ftate.
And like a bunch of ragged carrets ftand
The fhort fwolne fingers of thy gouty hand.
Then like the Chymicks mafculine equall fire,   35
Which in the Lymbecks warme wombe doth infpire
Into th'earths worthleffe durt a foule of gold,

8 boiles, *Ed:* boiles. *1633–69: in MSS. generally spelt as pronounced,*
biles *or* byles   13 vile lying ftones *1635–54 and MSS.:* vile ftones lying
1633,1669   14 they hang *A18, B, JC, L74, M, N, O'F (altered to* it), *S,
TC, W:* it hangs *1633–69*   19 a] *om. 1635–39*   26 grave] grav'd *1669*
duft *1633–69, W:* durt *A18, A25, JC, M, N, O'F, P, S, TC*   28 hands. *W:*
hands, *1633–69*   34 thy gouty hand. *1635–69, A18, A25, B, L74, N, O'F,
P, S96, TC, W* (hand; *1635–69):* her gouty hand; *1633, JC, S:* thy
miftrefs hand; *1669*   37 durt *1635–69:* part *1633, from next line*
                                                               Such

Such cherifhing heat her beft lov'd part doth hold.
Thine's like the dread mouth of a fired gunne,
Or like hot liquid metalls newly runne   40
Into clay moulds, or like to that Ætna
Where round about the graffe is burnt away.
Are not your kiffes then as filthy, and more,
As a worme fucking an invenom'd fore?
Doth not thy fearefull hand in feeling quake,   45
As one which gath'ring flowers, ftill feares a fnake?
Is not your laft act harfh, and violent,
As when a Plough a ftony ground doth rent?
So kiffe good Turtles, fo devoutly nice
Are Priefts in handling reverent facrifice,   50
And fuch in fearching wounds the Surgeon is
As wee, when wee embrace, or touch, or kiffe.
Leave her, and I will leave comparing thus,
She, and comparifons are odious.

ELEGIE IX.

The Autumnall.

N O *Spring*, nor *Summer* Beauty hath fuch grace,
    As I have feen in one *Autumnall* face.
Yong *Beauties* force our love, and that's a *Rape*,
    This doth but *counfaile*, yet you cannot fcape.

46 feares] fear'd *A18, L74, N, O'F, TC, W*   48 when *1635–69 and MSS.:* where *1633*   50 Are Priefts . . . facrifice,] A Prieft is in his handling Sacrifice, *1669*   51 fuch *A18, A25, B, JC, L74, N, O'F, P, S, S96, TC, W:* nice *1633–69*
   Eleg. IX. The Autumnall. *1635–54:* Elegie. The Autumnall. *1633:* Elegie IX. *1669:* Elegie. *A18, N, TCC, TCD:* Elegie Autumnall. *D, H40, H49, JC, Lec:* An autumnall face: On the Ladie Sr Edward Herbart mothers Ladie Danvers. *B:* On the Lady Herbert afterwards Danvers. *O'F:* Widdow. *M, P:* A Paradox of an ould Woman. *S:* Elegie Autumnall on the Lady Shandoys. *S96: no title, L74*   1 *Summer 1633:* Summers *1635–69*   2 face. *Ed:* face, *1633–69*   3 our love, *1633, D, H49, Lec, S:* our Loves, *1669:* your love, *1635–54, A18, A25, B, H40, L74, M, N, O'F, P, S96, TC*

If t'were a *shame* to love, here t'were no *shame,*   5
  Affection here takes *Reverences* name.
Were her firſt yeares the *Golden Age*; That's true,
  But now ſhee's *gold* oft tried, and ever new.
That was her torrid and inflaming time,
  This is her tolerable *Tropique clyme.*   10
Faire eyes, who askes more heate then comes from hence,
  He in a fever wiſhes peſtilence.
Call not theſe wrinkles, *graves*; If *graves* they were,
  They were *Loves graves*; for elſe he is no where.
Yet lies not Love *dead* here, but here doth ſit   15
  Vow'd to this trench, like an *Anachorit.*
And here, till hers, which muſt be his *death,* come,
  He doth not digge a *Grave,* but build a *Tombe.*
Here dwells he, though he ſojourne ev'ry where,
  In *Progreſſe,* yet his ſtanding houſe is here.   20
Here, where ſtill *Evening* is; not *noone,* nor *night*;
  Where no *voluptuouſneſſe,* yet all *delight.*
In all her words, unto all hearers fit,
  You may at *Revels,* you at *Counſaile,* ſit.
This is loves timber, youth his under-wood;   25
  There he, as wine in *Iune,* enrages blood,
Which then comes ſeaſonablieſt, when our taſt
  And appetite to other things, is paſt.
Xerxes ſtrange *Lydian* love, the *Platane* tree,
  Was lov'd for age, none being ſo large as ſhee,   30
Or elſe becauſe, being yong, nature did bleſſe
  Her youth with ages glory, *Barrenneſſe.*
If we love things long ſought, *Age* is a thing
  Which we are fifty yeares in compaſſing.

6 *Affection* . takes *A18,A25,B,D,H40,H49,L74,Lec,M,N,P,S,*
S96,TC: Affections . take *1633–69,JC,O'F*   8 ſhee's *1635–69,A18,A25,*
B,D,H40,H49,JC,L74,Lec,M,N,O'F,P,S,S96,TC :   they'are *1633*
10 tolerable *1633,D,H40,H49,Lec,S:*   habitable *1635–69,A18,A25,*
L74,M,N,O'F,P,TC   14 for *1633:* or *1635–69*   15 Love]
love *1633*   22 Where] Where's *O'F,S*   23 unto all] to all her *P*
24 *Counſaile,* Ed: *counſaile, 1633–54: counſails 1669*   26 enrages]
bringes *D,H49:* breeds *Lec*   27 ſeaſonablieſt, *1633:* ſeaſonableſt,
1635–69   28 paſt.] paſt; *1633*   30 large *1633:* old *1635–69*

                                                 If

If tranſitory things, which ſoone decay,   35
   Age muſt be lovelyeſt at the lateſt day.
But name not *Winter-faces*, whoſe skin's ſlacke;
   Lanke, as an unthrifts purſe ; but a ſoules ſacke;
Whoſe *Eyes* ſeeke light within, for all here's ſhade;
   Whoſe *mouthes* are holes, rather worne out, then made; 40
Whoſe every tooth to a ſeverall place is gone,
   To vexe their ſoules at *Reſurrection*;
Name not theſe living *Deaths-heads* unto mee,
   For theſe, not *Ancient*, but *Antique* be.
I hate extreames; yet I had rather ſtay   45
   With *Tombs*, then *Cradles*, to weare out a day.
Since ſuch loves naturall lation is, may ſtill
   My love deſcend, and journey downe the hill,
Not panting after growing beauties, ſo,
   I ſhall ebbe out with them, who home-ward goe.   50

---

37 not] noe *several MSS.*   38 ſoules ſacke ; *1633, 1669, and MSS.:*
fooles ſack ; *1635-54*   40 made ; *Ed:* made *1633-54:* made, *1669*
42 their ſoules] the ſoul *1669*   43 *Deaths-heads 1633:* Death-heads
1635-69, Chambers: death-shades *H40*   44 *Ancient, ... Antique 1633,*
1669, D, H49, Lec: Ancients, . Antiques *1635-54, B, O'F, S:* ancient .
antiques *A18, A25, H40, L74, M, N, TC*   be. *Ed:* be; *1633*   46 a]
the *1669, M, P*   47 naturall lation *A18, A25, B, D, H40, H49, L74, M,*
N, P, S, TC (sometimes thus, natural-lation): motion naturall *1633:* naturall
ſtation *1635-69, Lec, O'F*   50 ebbe out *1633:* ebbe on *1635-69, A18,*
A25, B, D, H40, H49, JC, L74, Lec, M, N, O'F, P, S, TC

ELEGIE

ELEGIE X.

The Dreame.

IMage of her whom 1 love, more then fhe,
  Whofe faire impreffion in my faithfull heart,
Makes mee her *Medall*, and makes her love mee,
  As Kings do coynes, to which their ftamps impart
The value: goe, and take my heart from hence,   5
  Which now is growne too great and good for me:
Honours oppreffe weake fpirits, and our fenfe
  Strong objects dull; the more, the leffe wee fee.
When you are gone, and *Reafon* gone with you,
  Then *Fantafie* is Queene and Soule, and all;   10
She can prefent joyes meaner then you do;
  Convenient, and more proportionall.
So, if 1 dreame I have you, I have you,
  For, all our joyes are but fantafticall.
And fo I fcape the paine, for paine is true;   15
  And fleepe which locks up fenfe, doth lock out all.
After a fuch fruition I fhall wake,
  And, but the waking, nothing fhall repent;
And fhall to love more thankfull Sonnets make,
  Then if more *honour, teares*, and *paines* were fpent.   20
But deareft heart, and dearer image ftay;
  Alas, true joyes at beft are *dreame* enough;
Though you ftay here you paffe too faft away:
  For even at firft lifes *Taper* is a fnuffe.
Fill'd with her love, may 1 be rather grown   25
Mad with much *heart*, then *ideott* with none.

  Eleg. X. The Dreame. *1635–54:* Elegie X. *1669:* Elegie. *1633:*
Picture. *S96:* Elegie. *or no title, A18, B, D, H40, H49, L74, Lec, N, O'F,
P, S, S96, TCC, TCD*   7 fenfe] fenfe, *1633*   8 dull; *1635–69:*
dull, *1633*   16 out] up *B, P, S*   17 a fuch *1633–54:* fuch a *1669*
22 *dreame*] dreams *1669*

ELEGIE

ELEGIE XI.

The Bracelet.

*Vpon the loſſe of his Miſtreſſes Chaine, for which
he made ſatisfaction.*

NOt that in colour it was like thy haire,
  For Armelets of that thou maiſt let me weare:
Nor that thy hand it oft embrac'd and kiſt,
For ſo it had that good, which oft I miſt:
Nor for that ſilly old moralitie,   5
That as theſe linkes were knit, our love ſhould bee:
Mourne I that I thy ſeavenfold chaine have loſt;
Nor for the luck ſake; but the bitter coſt.
O, ſhall twelve righteous Angels, which as yet
No leaven of vile ſoder did admit;   10
Nor yet by any way have ſtraid or gone
From the firſt ſtate of their Creation;
Angels, which heaven commanded to provide
All things to me, and be my faithfull guide;
To gaine new friends, t'appeaſe great enemies;   15
To comfort my ſoule, when I lie or riſe;
Shall theſe twelve innocents, by thy ſevere
Sentence (dread judge) my ſins great burden beare?
Shall they be damn'd, and in the furnace throwne,
And puniſht for offences not their owne?   20
They ſave not me, they doe not eaſe my paines,
When in that hell they'are burnt and tyed in chains.

Elégie XI. *&c. Ed.:* Eleg. XII. The Bracelet. *&c. 1635* (Eleg. XI.
being Death, *for which see p.* 284): Eleg. XII. Vpon *&c. 1639–54* (Eleg.
IV. *1650–54, a misprint*) : Elegie XII. *1669* : Elegie (*numbered variously*).
The Bracelett. *or* The Chaine. *A25,B,C,Cy,D,H49,JC,L74,Lec,M,N,
O'F,P,S,S96,TCD,W*   2 For ... weare :] Armelets of that thou maiſt
ſtill let me weare: *1669*   6 were knit, *1635–69:* are knit *Cy:* are tyde
A25,D,H49,Lec,N,O'F,P,R212,S,S96,TCD,W: were tyde *L74*   love]
loves *1669*   11 way *1635–69:* taynt *S96,O'F,W:* taynts *B:* fault *A25,
Cy,D,H49,L74,Lec,M,N,P,S,TCD*   15 great] old *1669*   16
riſe; *Ed:* riſe. *1635–69*   22 chains. *Ed.:* chains: *1635–69*

Were

Were they but Crownes of France, I cared not,
For, moſt of theſe, their naturall Countreys rot
I think poſſeſſeth, they come here to us,   25
So pale, ſo lame, ſo leane, ſo ruinous;
And howſoe'r French Kings moſt Chriſtian be,
Their Crownes are circumcis'd moſt Iewiſhly.
Or were they Spaniſh Stamps, ſtill travelling,
That are become as Catholique as their King,   30
Thoſe unlickt beare-whelps, unfil'd piſtolets
That (more than Canon ſhot) availes or lets;
Which negligently left unrounded, looke
Like many angled figures, in the booke
Of ſome great Conjurer that would enforce   35
Nature, as theſe doe juſtice, from her courſe;
Which, as the ſoule quickens head, feet and heart,
As ſtreames, like veines, run through th'earth's every part,
Viſit all Countries, and have ſlily made
Gorgeous *France*, ruin'd, ragged and decay'd;   40
Scotland, which knew no State, proud in one day:
And mangled ſeventeen-headed *Belgia*.
Or were it ſuch gold as that wherewithall
Almighty *Chymiques* from each minerall,
Having by ſubtle fire a ſoule out-pull'd;   45
Are dirtely and deſperately gull'd:
I would not ſpit to quench the fire they'are in,
For, they are guilty of much hainous Sin.
But, ſhall my harmleſſe angels periſh? Shall
I loſe my guard, my eaſe, my food, my all?   50

    24 theſe *1635–54:* them *1669*   their naturall Countreys *Cy, O'F:*
their Countreys naturall *1635–54, P:* their naturall Countrey *1669, and rest
of MSS.*   26 ruinous; *Ed:* ruinous. *1635–69*   28 Iewiſhly. *Ed:*
Iewiſhly; *1635–69*   35 great] dread *1669*   36 courſe; *Ed:* courſe.
1635–69   38 ſtreames, *Ed:* ſtreames *1635–69*   40 ruin'd, ragged
and decay'd; *1669, and MSS., but end stop varies:* ruin'd: ragged and
decay'd *1635:* ruin'd: ragged and decay'd, *1639–54*   42 *Belgia. Ed:*
Belgia: 1635–69   45 ſoule] Mercury *B*   47 they'are in, *1635–69:*
therein, *Cy, P:* they were in, *rest of MSS.*

                                                                    Much

Much hope which they fhould nourifh will be dead,
Much of my able youth, and luftyhead
Will vanifh; if thou love let them alone,
For thou wilt love me leffe when they are gone;
And be content that fome lowd fqueaking Cryer   55
Well-pleas'd with one leane thred-bare groat, for hire,
May like a devill roare through every ftreet;
And gall the finders confcience, if they meet.
Or let mee creepe to fome dread Conjurer,
That with phantaftique fcheames fils full much paper;   60
Which hath divided heaven in tenements,
And with whores, theeves, and murderers ftuft his rents,
So full, that though hee paffe them all in finne,
He leaves himfelfe no roome to enter in.
But if, when all his art and time is fpent,   65
Hee fay 'twill ne'r be found; yet be content;
Receive from him that doome ungrudgingly,
Becaufe he is the mouth of deftiny.

    Thou fay'ft (alas) the gold doth ftill remaine,
Though it be chang'd, and put into a chaine;   70
So in the firft falne angels, refteth ftill
Wifdome and knowledge; but,'tis turn'd to ill:
As thefe fhould doe good works; and fhould provide
Neceffities; but now muft nurfe thy pride.
And they are ftill bad angels; Mine are none;   75
For, forme gives being, and their forme is gone :
Pitty thefe Angels; yet their dignities
Paffe Vertues, Powers, and Principalities.

    51 dead, *Ed: dead. 1635-69*   52 luftyhead *Ed: lufty head 1635-69*
53 vanifh; *Ed: vanifh, 1635-69*   if thou love let them alone, *1635-39:*
if thou Love let them alone, *1650-69:* if thou, Love, let them alone;
Grolier (conjecturing atone)   54-5 gone ; And *Ed: gone, And
1635-69, Cy, P:* gone. Oh, *rest of MSS.*   58 confcience, if they
meet. *1669 and MSS.:* confcience, if hee meet. *1635-54, JC, L74, P*
60 fcheames *D, H49, JC, Lec, O'F, S96, W:* fcenes *1635-69, Cy, L74, P,
TCD*   63 paffe] place *1669*   65 *new par. 1635-69* But *1635-69,
Cy, P:* And *rest of MSS.*   66 yet *1635-69, Cy, P:* Oh *rest of MSS.*
67 that *1635-54, Cy, P:* the *1669 and rest of MSS.*   70 chaine; *Ed:*
chaine, *1635-69*   74 pride. *Ed:* pride, *1635-69*   76 being, *Ed:*
being: *1635-69*   77 Angels; yet *Cy, D, H49, N, P, S, TCD:* Angels
yet; *1635-69, W*

But,

But, thou art refolute; Thy will be done!
Yet with fuch anguifh, as her onely fonne   80
The Mother in the hungry grave doth lay,
Vnto the fire thefe Martyrs I betray.
Good foules, (for you give life to every thing)
Good Angels, (for good meffages you bring)
Deftin'd you might have beene to fuch an one,   85
As would have lov'd and worfhip'd you alone :
One that would fuffer hunger, nakedneffe,
Yea death, ere he would make your number leffe.
But, I am guilty of your fad decay ;
May your few fellowes longer with me ftay.   90
   But ô thou wretched finder whom I hate
So, that I almoft pitty thy eftate :
Gold being the heavieft metal amongft all,
May my moft heavy curfe upon thee fall :
Here fetter'd, manacled, and hang'd in chains,   95
Firft mayft thou bee; then chaind to hellifh paines ;
Or be with forraine gold brib'd to betray
Thy Countrey, and faile both of that and thy pay.
May the next thing thou ftoop'ft to reach, containe
Poyfon, whofe nimble fume rot thy moift braine ;   100
Or libels, or fome interdicted thing,
Which negligently kept, thy ruine bring.
Luft-bred difeafes rot thee ; and dwell with thee
Itching defire, and no abilitie.
May all the evils that gold ever wrought ;   105
All mifchiefes that all devils ever thought ;
Want after plenty ; poore and gouty age ;
The plagues of travellers ; love ; marriage
Afflict thee, and at thy lives laft moment,

79 done! *Ed:* done ; *1635–39 :* done : *1650–54 :* done? *1669*   90
few fellowes] few-fellowes *1635–69*   92 So, that *1635–69, Cy, P:* So
much that *A25, D, H49, JC* (as), *L74, Lec, N, S, S96* (as), *TCD, W* (as):
So much *B*   eftate] ftate *D, H49, &c.*   93 metal amongft all,]
amongft metals all, *1669, Cy*   95 Here] Her *1639*   98 that
MSS.: it *1635–69*   thy] om. *1669*   104 Itching] Itchy *MSS.*
105 evils that gold ever *1635–69, P:* hurt that ever gold hath *rest of MSS.*
106 mifchiefes *all MSS.:* mifchiefe *1635–69*   108 love ; marriage
1635–54, Cy, P: love and marriage *1669, and rest of MSS.*   109 at]
that *1669*

May thy fwolne finnes themfelves to thee prefent. 110
　But, I forgive; repent thee honeft man:
Gold is Reftorative, reftore it then:
But if from it thou beeft loath to depart,
Becaufe 'tis cordiall, would twere at thy heart.

ELEGIE XII.

His parting from her.

Since fhe muft go, and I muft mourn, come Night,
Environ me with darknefs, whilft I write:
Shadow that hell unto me, which alone
I am to fuffer when my Love is gone.
Alas the darkeft Magick cannot do it, 5
Thou and greate Hell to boot are fhadows to it.
Should *Cinthia* quit thee, *Venus*, and each ftarre,
It would not forme one thought dark as mine are.
I could lend thee obfcurenefs now, and fay,
Out of my felf, There fhould be no more Day, 10
Such is already my felt want of fight,
Did not the fires within me force a light.
Oh Love, that fire and darknefs fhould be mixt,
Or to thy Triumphs foe ftrange torments fixt?
Is't becaufe thou thy felf art blind, that wee 15
Thy Martyrs muft no more each other fee?

110 thee] thou *1669*　113 But if from it . . . depart, *1635–54, Cy, P:* But if that from it . . . part, *1669:* Or if with it . . . depart *rest of MSS.*
　Elegie. XII. *&c. Ed:* Eleg. XIIII *&c. 1635–54* (Eleg. XIII. *being* Come, Fates, *&c., p.* 407): Elegie XIIII. *1669:* At her Departure. *A25:* At his Miftris departure. *B:* Elegie. *H40,O'F,P,S96, TCD (II)*　1 Night, *Ed:* night *1635–69*　4 Love] foule *1635–54*　5–44 *omit, 1635–54, A25, B*　6 Thou and greate Hell *H40,O'F,P, S96:* And that great Hell *1669*　to boot are *1669, H40,O'F:* are nought but *P,S96*　7 thee, *Ed:* thee *1669*　9 thee *H40:* them *1669, P,S96,TCD*　10 Day, *Ed:* Day. *1669*　11 felt want *H40,O'F, P,S96,TCD:* felf-want *1669*　fight, *Ed:* fight *1669*　12 fires *H40, S96,TCD:* fire *1669, P*　14 Or] Are *S96:* And *TCD*　foe *H40, O'F,P,S96,TCD:* fuch *1669*

Or

Or tak'ft thou pride to break us on the wheel,
And view old Chaos in the Pains we feel?
Or have we left undone fome mutual Right,
Through holy fear, that merits thy defpight? 20
No, no. The falt was mine, impute it to me,
Or rather to confpiring deftinie,
Which (fince I lov'd for forme before) decreed,
That I fhould fuffer when I lov'd indeed:
And therefore now, fooner then I can fay, 25
I faw the golden fruit, 'tis rapt away.
Or as I had watcht one drop in a vaft ftream,
And I left wealthy only in a dream.
Yet Love, thou'rt blinder then thy felf in this,
To vex my Dove-like friend for my amifs: 30
And, where my own fad truth may expiate
Thy wrath, to make her fortune run my fate:
So blinded Juftice doth, when Favorites fall,
Strike them, their houfe, their friends, their followers all.
Was't not enough that thou didft dart thy fires 35
Into our blouds, inflaming our defires,
And made'ft us figh and glow, and pant, and burn,
And then thy felf into our flame did'ft turn?
Was't not enough, that thou didft hazard us
To paths in love fo dark, fo dangerous: 40
And thófe fo ambufh'd round with houfhold fpies,
And over all, thy hufbands towring eyes

17 the *H40,O'F,P,S96,TCD:* thy *1669*   20 Through holy fear,
that merits (caufes *S96*) thy defpight (meriteth thy fpight *P*)*H40,O'F,P,
S96,TCD:* That thus with parting thou feek'ft us to fpight? *1669*   21
was *H40,S96:* is *1669,P,TCD*   23 Which ... decreed, *H40,O'F,
S96:* Which (fince I lov'd) for me before decreed, *1669,P,TCD:*
Which, fince I lov'd in jeft before, decreed *H-K, which Chambers follows*
25 now, fooner *all the MSS.:* fooner now *1669*   rapt] wrapt *1669*
27 a vaft *H40,O'F,P,S96,TCD:* the vaft *1669*   29 thy felf] myself
Chambers   31 my own *H40,O'F,P,S96:* one *1669*   fad *1669*: glad
H40,O'F,P,S96,TCD   32 fate: *Ed:* fate. *1669*   33 blinded]
blindeft *H40*   34 followers *H40,P,TCD:* favourites *1669,S96*
37 glow *H40,S96,P,TCD:* blow *1669*   38 flame *H40,S96,P,TCD:*
flames *1669*   40 fo dangerous *H40,P,S96,TCD:* and dangerous
1669   42 all, *Ed:* all *1669*   towring *1669,TCD:* towred *O'F,P,
S96:* lowering *Grolier*   the towred husbands eyes *H40:* the Loured,
husbandes eyes *RP31*

That

That flam'd with oylie sweat of jealousie:
Yet went we not still on with Constancie?
Have we not kept our guards, like spie on spie?   45
Had correspondence whilst the foe stood by?
Stoln (more to sweeten them) our many blisses
Of meetings, conference, embracements, kisses?
Shadow'd with negligence our most respects?
Varied our language through all dialects,   50
Of becks, winks, looks, and often under-boards
Spoak dialogues with our feet far from our words?
Have we prov'd all these secrets of our Art,
Yea, thy pale inwards, and thy panting heart?
And, after all this passed Purgatory,   55
Must sad divorce make us the vulgar story?
First let our eyes be rivited quite through
Our turning brains, and both our lips grow to:
Let our armes clasp like Ivy, and our fear
Freese us together, that we may stick here,   60
Till Fortune, that would rive us, with the deed
Strain her eyes open, and it make them bleed:
For Love it cannot be, whom hitherto
I have accus'd, should such a mischief doe.
Oh Fortune, thou'rt not worth my least exclame,   65
And plague enough thou hast in thy own shame.
Do thy great worst, my friend and I have armes,

43 That flam'd with oylie *H40, O'F, P, S96, TCD:* Inflam'd with
th'ouglie *1669*   jealousie: *Ed:* jealousie, *1669*   44 with *H40,O'F,P,
S96,TCD:* in *1669*   45 Have we not kept our guards, *H40,O'F,
P,S96,TCD:* Have we for this kept guards, *1669*   on *1669:* o'r
1635-54   49 most *1635-69,H40,O'F,P,S96,TCD:* best *1669*
50 our] thy *RP31*   52 from our words? *1669:* from words? *1635-54*
53 these secrets *MSS.:* the secrets *1635-69*   our] thy *RP31*   54
Yea . . . panting heart? *1635-69,A25:* Yea thy pale colours inward as
thy heart? *H40,O'F,P,S96,TCD*   56 sad] rude *P,TCD*   57-66
om. *1635-54,A25,B*   58 brains] beams *P:* brain *Chambers*   61
Fortune, *Ed:* fortune, *1669*   would rive us, with *H40,O'F,S96,TCD:*
would ruine us with *1669*   62 her *H40:* his *1669*   it] yet *1669*
bleed: *Ed:* bleed. *1669*   65 Oh Fortune,] Oh fortune, *1669, S96:*
And Fortune *H40,P*   66 shame. *H40,O'F,P,S96:* name. *1669*   67
Do thy great worst &c. *1669:* Fortune, doe thy worst &c. *1635-54 (after*
56 the vulgar story?)   armes, *1635-69,H40,O'F,P,S,TCD:* charmes
H-K (Grosart and Chambers)

                                          Though

Though not againſt thy ſtrokes, againſt thy harmes.
Rend us in ſunder, thou canſt not divide
Our bodies ſo, but that our ſouls are ty'd,   70
And we can love by letters ſtill and gifts,
And thoughts and dreams; Love never wanteth ſhifts.
I will not look upon the quickning Sun,
But ſtraight her beauty to my ſenſe ſhall run;
The ayre ſhall note her ſoft, the fire moſt pure;   75
Water ſuggeſt her clear, and the earth ſure.
Time ſhall not loſe our paſſages; the Spring
How freſh our love was in the beginning;
The Summer how it ripened in the eare;
And Autumn, what our golden harveſts were.   80
The Winter I'll not think on to ſpite thee,
But count it a loſt ſeaſon, ſo ſhall ſhee.
And deareſt Friend, ſince we muſt part, drown night
With hope of Day, burthens well born are light.
Though cold and darkneſs longer hang ſomewhere,   85
Yet *Phoebus* equally lights all the Sphere.
And what he cannot in like Portions pay,
The world enjoyes in Maſs, and ſo we may.
Be then ever your ſelf, and let no woe
Win on your health, your youth, your beauty: ſo   90
Declare your ſelf baſe fortunes Enemy,
No leſs by your contempt then conſtancy:
That I may grow enamoured on your mind,
When my own thoughts I there reflected find.

69 Rend us in ſunder, *1669 and MSS.*: Bend us, in ſunder *1635–54*
72 ſhifts. *1635*: ſhifts, *1639–69*   76 Water *H40,P,TCD*: Waters
1635–69,A25,S96   ſure. *Ed*: ſure; *1635–69*   77 Time] Times
H40,TCD   Spring *Ed*: ſpring *1635–69*   79 ripened in the eare;
B,H40,O'F,P,S96,TCD: ripened in the yeare; *1635*: inripened the
yeare; *1639–69*   83–94 *omit 1635–54, A25, B*   85 Though *H40,*
P,TCD: The *1669, S96*   87 he . . . Portions *Ed*: he . . . portions
H40: he . . . portion *O'F,P,TCD*: we . . . Portion *1669*: he can't in
like proportion *H-K (Grosart)*   88 enjoyes] yet joys *H40*   89 ever
your] your fayreſt *H40,TCD*   92 by your contempt then con-
ſtancy: *H40,S96*: be your contempt then conſtancy: *O'F,H-K (Grosart),*
P,TCD: be your contempt then her inconſtancy: *1669*   94 there
reflected *H40,O'F,P,S,TCD*: here neglected *1669*: there neglected
H-K (Grosart, probably wrongly)

                                                                    For

For this to th'comfort of my Dear I vow,   95
My Deeds ſhall ſtill be what my words are now;
The Poles ſhall move to teach me ere I ſtart;
And when I change my Love, I'll change my heart;
Nay, if I wax but cold in my deſire,
Think, heaven hath motion loſt, and the world, fire: 100
Much more I could, but many words have made
That, oft, ſuſpected which men would perſwade;
Take therefore all in this: I love ſo true,
As I will never look for leſs in you.

ELEGIE XIII.

Iulia.

HArke newes, ô envy, thou ſhalt heare deſcry'd
My *Iulia*; who as yet was ne'r envy'd.
To vomit gall in ſlander, ſwell her vaines
With calumny, that hell it ſelfe diſdaines,
Is her continuall practice; does her beſt,   5
To teare opinion even out of the breſt
Of deareſt friends, and (which is worſe than vilde)
Sticks jealouſie in wedlock; her owne childe
Scapes not the ſhowres of envie, To repeate
The monſtrous faſhions, how, were, alive, to eate   10
Deare reputation. Would to God ſhe were
But halfe ſo loath to act vice, as to heare

95-104 *om. TCD*   95 For *H40, S96:* And *1635-69*   96 my
words are now; *H40, P:*   my deeds are now; *1635-69, O'F, S96:*   my
thoughts are now; *A25*   102 oft, *1633-54:* oft *1669*   would
1635-54, A25, B, H40, O'F, S96: moſt *1669*
  Elegie XIII. *&c. Ed:*   Eleg. XV. *&c. 1635-54:* Elegie XV. *1669:*
Iulia. *B:* Elegy. Iulia. *O'F*   5 practice; *Ed:* practice, *1635-69*
7 vilde) *Ed:* vile) *1635-69:* vilde *is the regular ſpelling of this word in the
Donne MSS.*   8 in wedlock;] in the ſheets of wedlock; *B*
10 how, *1635:* how; *1639-69*

                                                         My

My milde reproofe. Liv'd *Mantuan* now againe,
That fœmall Maſtix, to limme with his penne
This ſhe *Chymera*, that hath eyes of fire,   15
Burning with anger, anger feeds deſire,
Tongued like the night-crow, whoſe ill boding cries
Give out for nothing but new injuries,
Her breath like to the juice in *Tenarus*
That blaſts the ſprings, though ne'r ſo proſperous,   20
Her hands, I know not how, us'd more to ſpill
The food of others, then her ſelfe to fill.
But oh her minde, that *Orcus,* which includes
Legions of miſchiefs, countleſſe multitudes
Of formleſſe curſes, projeĉts unmade up,   25
Abuſes yet unfaſhion'd, thoughts corrupt,
Miſhapen Cavils, palpable untroths,
Inevitable errours, ſelf-accuſing oaths:
Theſe, like thoſe Atoms ſwarming in the Sunne,
Throng in her boſome for creation.   30
I bluſh to give her halfe her due; yet ſay,
No poyſon's halfe ſo bad as *Iulia*.

ELEGIE XIV.

A Tale of a Citizen and his Wife.

I Sing no harme good ſooth to any wight,
To Lord or foole, Cuckold, begger or knight,
To peace-teaching Lawyer, Proĉtor, or brave
Reformed or reduced Captaine, Knave,

  14 That fœmall Maſtix, *1635: 1639–69 and Chambers drop comma. But
see note*   18 injuries, *1635–39* : injuries. *1650–69*   20 proſperous, *Ed:*
proſperous. *1635–69*   24 miſchiefs *O'F:* miſchiefe, *1635–69*   28
oaths : *B, H-K (Grosart)*: loathes: *1635–69, O'F*   31 give but half *B :*
give half her *O'F*   yet ſay,] only this ſay, *B :* but this ſay *O'F*
  Elegie XIV. *&c. Ed:*   Eleg. XVI. A Tale *&c. 1635–54:*   Elegie
XVI. *1669:*   Elegie XV. *O'F: no title, B*   2 or foole,] to fool, *1669*

Officer, Iugler, or Iuftice of peace,   5
Iuror or Iudge; I touch no fat fowes greafe,
I am no Libeller, nor will be any,
But (like a true man) fay there are too many.
I feare not *ore tenus*; for my tale,
Nor Count nor Counfellour will redd or pale.   10
A Citizen and his wife the other day
Both riding on one horfe, upon the way
I overtooke, the wench a pretty peate,
And (by her eye) well fitting for the feate.
I faw the lecherous Citizen turne backe   15
His head, and on his wifes lip fteale a fmacke,
Whence apprehending that the man was kinde,
Riding before, to kiffe his wife behinde,
To get acquaintance with him I began
To fort difcourfe fit for fo fine a man: 20
I ask'd the number of the Plaguy Bill,
Ask'd if the Cuftome Farmers held out ftill,
Of the Virginian plot, and whether Ward
The traffique of the I⟨n⟩land feas had marr'd,
Whether the Brittaine *Burfe* did fill apace,   25
And likely were to give th'Exchange difgrace;
Of new-built *Algate*, and the *More-field* croffes,
Of ftore of Bankerouts, and poore Merchants loffes
I urged him to fpeake; But he (as mute
As an old Courtier worne to his laft fuite)   30
Replies with onely yeas and nayes; At laft
(To fit his element) my theame I caft
On Tradefmens gaines; that fet his tongue agoing:
Alas, good fir (quoth he) *There is no doing*
In Court nor City now ; fhe fmil'd and I,   35
And (in my confcience) both gave him the lie

5 Iugler, *1635–39:* Iudge, *1650–69*   9 *tenus*; *Ed:* tenus, *1635–69*
10 will redd or pale. *1669, B, O'F*(fhall): will looke redd or pale. *1635–54*
14 feate. *Ed:* feate, *1635–69*   16 fteale] feale *O'F*   21 Plaguy *1669,*
B, O'F: Plaguing *1635–54*   22 Cuftome] cuftome *1635*   24
I⟨n⟩land *Ed:* Iland *1635–54:* Midland *1669, O'F:* the land, the feas *B,*
but later hand has inserted mid *above the line:* Island *Chambers and Grolier*
27 *More-field*] Moorefields *B*   32 To fit] To hit *O'F*   33 agoing:
Ed: agoing, *1635–69*   35 *In . . . now; Ed:* roman *1635–69*

                                                              In

In one met thought: but he went on apace,
And at the prefent time with fuch a face
He rail'd, as fray'd me; for he gave no praife,
To any but my Lord of *Effex* dayes;   40
Call'd thofe the age of action; true (quoth Hee)
There's now as great an itch of bravery,
And heat of taking up, but cold lay downe,
For, put to pufh of pay, away they runne;
Our onely City trades of hope now are   45
Bawd, Tavern-keeper, Whore and Scrivener;
The much of Privileg'd kingfmen, and the ftore
Of frefh protections make the reft all poore;
In the firft ftate of their Creation,
Though many ftoutly ftand, yet proves not one   50
A righteous pay-mafter. Thus ranne he on
In a continued rage: fo void of reafon
Seem'd his harfh talke, I fweat for feare of treafon.
And (troth) how could I leffe? when in the prayer
For the protection of the wife Lord Major,   55
And his wife brethrens worfhips, when one prayeth,
He fwore that none could fay Amen with faith.
To get him off from what I glowed to heare,
(In happy time) an Angel did appeare,
The bright Signe of a lov'd and wel-try'd Inne,   60
Where many Citizens with their wives have bin
Well us'd and often; here I pray'd him ftay,
To take fome due refrefhment by the way.
Looke how hee look'd that hid the gold (his hope)
And at's returne found nothing but a Rope,   65

38 time *1669*: times *O'F*   41 thofe... (quoth Hee) *1669,B,O'F:*
that...(quoth I) *1635–54*   46 Bawd, ... Scrivener; *B,O'F:* Bawds,
Tavernkeepers, Whores and Scriveners, *1635–54:* Bawds, Tavernkeepers,
Whore and Scrivener *1669*   47 kingfmen, and the ftore *1669,B,*
O'F(kingfman): kinfmen, and ftore *1635–54*   58 him off *O'F:* off
him *1669:* him *1635–54*   61 have bin *B,O'F:* had beene, *1635–69*
64 the gold (his hope)] his gold, his hope *1669*   65 at's *1669:* at
1635–54 •

                                                         So

So he on me, refus'd and made away,
Though willing ſhe pleaded a weary day:
I found my miſſe, ſtruck hands, and praid him tell
(To hold acquaintance ſtill) where he did dwell;
He barely nam'd the ſtreet, promis'd the Wine,   70
But his kinde wife gave me the very Signe.

ELEGIE XV.

The Expoſtulation.

TO make the doubt cleare, that no woman's true,
  Was it my fate to prove it ſtrong in you?
Thought I, but one had breathed pureſt aire,
  And muſt ſhe needs be falſe becauſe ſhe's faire?
Is it your beauties marke, or of your youth,   5
  Or your perfection, not to ſtudy truth?
Or thinke you heaven is deafe, or hath no eyes?
  Or thoſe it hath, ſmile at your perjuries?
Are vowes ſo cheape with women, or the matter
  Whereof they are made, that they are writ in water,   10
And blowne away with winde? Or doth their breath
  (Both hot and cold at once) make life and death?
Who could have thought ſo many accents ſweet
  Form'd into words, ſo many ſighs ſhould meete
As from our hearts, ſo many oathes, and teares   15
  Sprinkled among, (all ſweeter by our feares

---

66 on *1669, B:* at *1635–54*   me,] me: *1635–54*   67 day: *1669, B, O'F:* ſtay. *1635–39:* ſtay: *1650–54*   69 dwell; *1635:* dwell *1639–54:* dwell, *1669*
  Elegie XV. *Ed:* Eleg. XVII. The Expostulation. *1635–54:* Elegie XVII. *1669:* Elegie. *1633, B, Cy, H40, HN, M, N, O'F, P, RP31, S, S96, TCD, Jonson's* Underwoods   2 ſtrong] full *Und*   3 pureſt] the purer *Und*   6 Or your *1633–69:* Or of your *H40*   8 it hath,] ſhe hath *B, H40, M, N, P, S96*   12 (Both hot and cold at once) *RP31:* Both . . . at once, *Und:* (Both . . . cold) at once *1633–69, S96:* Both heate and coole at once *M*   make] threat *Und*   14 Form'd into] Tun'd to our *Und*   15 As] Blowne *Und*   16–18 (all ſweeter . . . the rest) *1633, B, Cy, M, N, O'F, P, RP31:* (all ſweetend &c. *1635, which does not complete the bracket:* (all ſweetend by our fears) &c. *1639–69, L74* (ſweeter), *P* (ſweeter), *S96* (ſweetned)

And

And the divine impreſſion of ſtolne kiſſes,
    That ſeal'd the reſt) ſhould now prove empty bliſſes?
Did you draw bonds to forfet? ſigne to breake?
    Or muſt we reade you quite from what you ſpeake,   20
And finde the truth out the wrong way? or muſt
    Hee firſt deſire you falſe, would wiſh you juſt?
O I prophane, though moſt of women be
    This kinde of beaſt, my thought ſhall except thee;
My deareſt love, though froward jealouſie,   25
    With circumſtance might urge thy'inconſtancie,
Sooner I'll thinke the Sunne will ceaſe to cheare
    The teeming earth, and *that* forget to beare,
Sooner that rivers will runne back, or Thames
    With ribs of Ice in June would bind his ſtreames,   30
Or Nature, by whoſe ſtrength the world endures,
    Would change her courſe, before you alter yours.
But O that treacherous breaſt to whom weake you
    Did truſt our Counſells, and wee both may rue,
Having his falſhood found too late, 'twas hee   35
    That made me *caſt* you guilty, and you me,
Whilſt he, black wretch, betray'd each ſimple word
    Wee ſpake, unto the cunning of a third.
Curſt may hee be, that ſo our love hath ſlaine,
    And wander on the earth, wretched as *Cain*,   40
Wretched as hee, and not deſerve leaſt pitty;
    In plaguing him, let miſery be witty;
Let all eyes ſhunne him, and hee ſhunne each eye,
    Till hee be noyſome as his infamie;
May he without remorſe deny God thrice,   45
    And not be truſted more on his Soules price;

22 wiſh] have *P*   24 This kinde of beaſt,] The common Monſter,
Und   my thought *1633:* my thoughts *1635–69, HN, S96*   25
though froward] how ever *RP31, Und*   26 thy'inconſtancie,] the
contrarie. *Und*   28 beare, *1633:* beare: *1635–69*   30 would *1633,*
Und: will *1635–69*   ſtreames, *Ed:* ſtreames; *1633–69*   32 yours.]
yours; *1633*   34 truſt *1633–69:* drift *Chambers*   37 wretch]
wrech *1633*   38 third. *Ed:* third; *1633–69*   39 love] loves *RP31*
40 wretched as *Cain, 1633–69, B, Cy, N, O'F:* as wretched Cain, *P:* as
curſed Cain, *S:* wretched on the Earth, as Cain: *Und*

                                        And

And after all felfe torment, when hee dyes,
   May Wolves teare out his heart, Vultures his eyes,
Swine eate his bowels, and his falfer tongue
   That utter'd all, be to fome Raven flung,   50
And let his carrion coarfe be a longer feaft
   To the Kings dogges, then any other beaft.
Now have I curft, let us our love revive;
   In mee the flame was never more alive;
I could beginne againe to court and praife,   55
   And in that pleafure lengthen the fhort dayes
Of my lifes leafe; like Painters that do take
   Delight, not in made worke, but whiles they make;
I could renew thofe times, when firft I faw
   Love in your eyes, that gave my tongue the law   60
To like what you lik'd; and at maskes and playes
   Commend the felfe fame Actors, the fame wayes;
Aske how you did, and often with intent
   Of being officious, be impertinent;
All which were fuch foft paftimes, as in thefe   65
   Love was as fubtilly catch'd, as a difeafe;
But being got it is a treafure fweet,
   Which to defend is harder then to get:
And ought not be prophan'd on either part,
   For though'tis got by *chance*,'tis kept by *art*.   70

52 dogges, . . . beaft.] dogges ; . . . beaft; *1633*   53 have I] I have *1669* revive] receive *Und*   58 worke, *1633-39, most MSS.:* works, *1650-69, S96, Und*   61 and playes] or playes *Und*   64 be] grow *Und*   65 foft] loft *Und*

ELEGIE

ELEGIE XVI.

On his Miſtris.

B Y our firſt ſtrange and fatall interview,
By all deſires which thereof did enſue,
By our long ſtarving hopes, by that remorſe
Which my words maſculine perſwaſive force
Begot in thee, and by the memory   5
Of hurts, which ſpies and rivals threatned me,
I calmly beg: But by thy fathers wrath,
By all paines, which want and divorcement hath,
I conjure thee, and all the oathes which I
And thou have ſworne to ſeale joynt conſtancy,   10
Here I unſweare, and overſwear them thus,
Thou ſhalt not love by wayes ſo dangerous.
Temper, ô faire Love, loves impetuous rage,
Be my true Miſtris ſtill, not my faign'd Page;
I'll goe, and, by thy kinde leave, leave behinde   15
Thee, onely worthy to nurſe in my minde,
Thirſt to come backe; ô if thou die before,
My ſoule from other lands to thee ſhall ſoare.
Thy (elſe Almighty) beautie cannot move
Rage from the Seas, nor thy love teach them love,   20
Nor tame wilde Boreas harſhneſſe; Thou haſt reade
How roughly hee in peeces ſhivered
Faire Orithea, whom he ſwore he lov'd.

Elegie XVI. *&c. Ed:* Elegie on his Miſtris. *1635–54 where, and in
1669, it appears among* Funerall Elegies *:* Elegie. *1669: among* Elegies
with or without heading or number, A18,A25,B,D,H49, JC, Lec, M,N,O'F,
P,S,TCC,TCD,W: B heads His wife would have gone as his page.
1 interview, *Ed:* interview *1635–69*   3 ſtarving] ſtriving *1669,B,P:*
ſtarvling *A18,N,TC*   7 beg: *D:* beg. *1635–69*   fathers *1635–69,O'F:*
Parents *A18,A25,B,D,H49, JC, Lec, M,N,P,S,TC,W*   11 Here I]
I here *1669*   12 wayes *1635–54,O'F:* means *1669, and reſt of MSS.*
14 ſtill . . . faign'd] *1669 om.* ſtill *and reads* faigned   18 My ſoule
. . . to thee] From other lands my ſoule towards thee *A18,A25,B,D,
H49, JC, Lec,M*(to),*N,P,S,TC,W*   ſoare. *Ed:* ſoare, *1635–69*   21
harſhneſs] raſhneſs *P. Compare* Elegy V, 8   23 Faire Orithea] The
fair Orithea *1669*

Fall

Fall ill or good, 'tis madneſſe to have prov'd
Dangers unurg'd; Feed on this flattery,　　　　　　25
That abſent Lovers one in th'other be.
Diſſemble nothing, not a boy, nor change
Thy bodies habite, nor mindes; bee not ſtrange
To thy ſelfe onely; All will ſpie in thy face
A bluſhing womanly diſcovering grace;　　　　　　30
Richly cloath'd Apes, are call'd Apes, and as ſoone
Ecclips'd as bright we call the Moone the Moone.
Men of France, changeable Camelions,
Spittles of diſeaſes, ſhops of faſhions,
Loves fuellers, and the righteſt company　　　　　　35
Of Players, which upon the worlds ſtage be,
Will quickly know thee, and no leſſe, alas!
Th'indifferent Italian, as we paſſe
His warme land, well content to thinke thee Page,
Will hunt thee with ſuch luſt, and hideous rage,　　　40
As *Lots* faire gueſts were vext. But none of theſe
Nor ſpungy hydroptique Dutch ſhall thee diſpleaſe,
If thou ſtay here. O ſtay here, for, for thee
England is onely a worthy Gallerie,
To walke in expectation, till from thence　　　　　　45
Our greateſt King call thee to his preſence.
When I am gone, dreame me ſome happineſſe,
Nor let thy lookes our long hid love confeſſe,
Nor praiſe, nor diſpraiſe me, nor bleſſe nor curſe
Openly loves force, nor in bed fright thy Nurſe　　　50
With midnights ſtartings, crying out, oh, oh
Nurſe, ô my love is ſlaine, I ſaw him goe

26 Lovers] friends *P*　　　　28 mindes; *A18, A25, B, JC, N, TC, W:*
minde, *1635–69, D, H49, Lec, O'F, P*　　　　29 onely; *A18, D, N, TC:*
onely. *1635–69*　　　35 Loves fuellers,] Lyves fuellers, *1669, B, D, H49,*
JC, Lec, S96, P　　　37 Will quickly know thee, and no leſſe, alas! *1635–54,*
O'F: Will too too quickly know thee; and alas, *1669:* Will quickly
know thee, and know thee, and alas *A18, N, S (omitting second* and),
TCD, W: Will quickly know thee, and thee, and alas *A25:* Will quickly
know thee, and alas *D, H49, JC, Lec, P, S96, TCC*　　　39 Page, *Ed:* Page
1635–39　　40 hunt *1635–69, O'F:* haunt *most MSS.*　　42 hydroptique]
Aydroptique *1669*　　46 greateſt *1635–69, B, O'F, P:* greate *A18, A25,*
D, H49, JC, Lec, N, S, TC　　call] doe call *A18, N, TC*　　to] in to *A25,*
JC, S　　49 me, nor bleſſe] me; Bleſſe *A18, D, H49, JC, Lec, N, TC, W*
　　　　　　　　　　　　　　　　　　　　　　　　　O'

O'r the white Alpes alone; I faw him I,
Affail'd, fight, taken, ftabb'd, bleed, fall, and die.
Augure me better chance, except dread *Iove*   55
Thinke it enough for me to'have had thy love.

ELEGIE XVII.

Variety.

THe heavens rejoyce in motion, why fhould I
  Abjure my fo much lov'd variety,
And not with many youth and love divide?
Pleafure is none, if not diverfifi'd:
The fun that fitting in the chaire of light   5
Sheds flame into what elfe fo ever doth feem bright,
Is not contented at one Signe to Inne,
But ends his year and with a new beginnes.
All things doe willingly in change delight,
The fruitfull mother of our appetite: 10
Rivers the clearer and more pleafing are,
Where their fair fpreading ftreames run wide and farr;
And a dead lake that no ftrange bark doth greet,
Corrupts it felf and what doth live in it.
Let no man tell me fuch a one is faire,   15
And worthy all alone my love to fhare.
Nature in her hath done the liberall part
Of a kinde Miftreffe, and imploy'd her art
To make her loveable, and I aver
Him not humane that would turn back from her: 20

Elegie XVII. Variety. *Ed: printed for first time without title in appendix
to 1650 and so in 1669 and 1719:* An Elegie. *A10:* Elegie 17ᵗʰᵉ. *JC*
1 motion, why *Ed:* motion why, *1650–69*   3 love divide? *MSS.:* lov'd
divide? *1650–69*   4 diverfifi'd: *Ed:* diverfifi'd *1650–69*   6 what
elfe fo ever doth feem *1650–69:* what elfe is not fo *A10*   12 fair-
fpreading *1650–69, JC:* broad filver *A10*   and farr; *A10, JC:* and cleare;
1650–69   14 it felf and *1650–69:* it felf, kills *A10*   16 And
only worthy to be paft compare; *A10*   19 aver] ever *1650–69*   20
would turn back from *1650–69:* could not fancy *A10*

I love

I love her well, and would, if need were, dye
To doe her fervice. But followes it that I
Muſt ferve her onely, when I may have choice
Of other beauties, and in change rejoice?
The law is hard, and ſhall not have my voice.   25
The laſt I ſaw in all extreames is faire,
And holds me in the Sun-beames of her haire;
Her nymph-like features ſuch agreements have
That I could venture with her to the grave:
Another's brown, I like her not the worſe,   30
Her tongue is ſoft and takes me with diſcourſe.
Others, for that they well deſcended are,
Do in my love obtain as large a ſhare;
And though they be not fair, 'tis much with mee
To win their love onely for their degree.   35
And though I faile of my required ends,
The attempt is glorious and it ſelf commends.
How happy were our Syres in ancient times,
Who held plurality of loves no crime!
With them it was accounted charity   40
To ſtirre up race of all indifferently;
Kindreds were not exempted from the bands:
Which with the Perſian ſtill in uſage ſtands.
Women were then no ſooner asked then won,
And what they did was honeſt and well done.   45
But ſince this title honour hath been us'd,
Our weake credulity hath been abus'd;
The golden laws of nature are repeald,
Which our firſt Fathers in ſuch reverence held;
Our liberty's revers'd, our Charter's gone,   50
And we're made ſervants to opinion,

24 Of other beauties, and in change rejoice? *A10: om. 1650–69*   25–36 *omitted in A10*   30 brown, *Ed:* brown *1650–69*   32 are *JC:* were *1650–69*   39 crime! *Ed:* crime? *1650–69*   43 Perſian *1650–54, JC:* Perſians *1669, A10*   46 title *A10, JC:* little *1650–69*   50 liberty's *Ed:* liberty *1650–69, JC*   revers'd, our *A10:* revers'd and *1650–69, JC*   51 we're *A10:* we *1650–69, JC*

A

A monfter in no certain fhape attir'd,
And whofe originall is much defir'd,
Formleffe at firft, but goeing on it fafhions,
And doth prefcribe manners and laws to nations. 55
Here love receiv'd immedicable harmes,
And was difpoiled of his daring armes.
A greater want then is his daring eyes,
He loft thofe awfull wings with which he flies;
His finewy bow, and thofe immortall darts 60
Wherewith he'is wont to bruife refifting hearts.
Onely fome few ftrong in themfelves and free
Retain the feeds of antient liberty,
Following that part of Love although depreft,
And make a throne for him within their breft, 65
In fpight of modern cenfures him avowing
Their Soveraigne, all fervice him allowing.
Amongft which troop although I am the leaft,
Yet equall in perfection with the beft,
I glory in fubjection of his hand, 70
Nor ever did decline his leaft command:
For in whatever forme the meffage came
My heart did open and receive the fame.
But time will in his courfe a point difcry
When I this loved fervice muft deny, 75
For our allegiance temporary is,
With firmer age returnes our liberties.
What time in years and judgement we repos'd,
Shall not fo eafily be to change difpos'd,

53 whofe originall *1650–69, JC:* one whofe origin *A10*   54 goeing
on it fafhions *A10:* growing on it fafhions *JC:* growing on its fafhions,
1650–69   55 manners and laws to *1650–69, JC:* Lawes, Manners
unto *A10*   57 armes. *A10:* armes, *1650–69*   58 is *1650–69:* of
A10   61 bruife *1650–69:* wound *A10*   hearts. *Ed:* hearts;
1650–69   63 feeds of antient *1650–69, JC:* feed of priftine *A10*
64 Love] love *1650–69*   70 of his *1650–69:* under's *A10*   71
Nor . . . decline *1650–69:* Never declining from *A10*   72–7 *omitted
in A10*   73 fame. *Ed:* fame: *1650–69:* flame *JC*   75 deny,
Ed: deny. *1650–69*   79 difpos'd, *Ed:* difpos'd *1650–69*

Nor

Nor to the art of feverall eyes obeying;   80
But beauty with true worth fecurely weighing,
Which being found affembled in fome one,
Wee'l love her ever, and love her alone.

ELEGIE XVIII.

Loves Progress.

WHo ever loves, if he do not propofe
　　The right true end of love, he's one that goes
To fea for nothing but to make him fick:
Love is a bear-whelp born, if we o're lick
Our love, and force it new ftrange fhapes to take,   5
We erre, and of a lump a monfter make.
Were not a Calf a monfter that were grown
Face'd like a man, though better then his own?
Perfection is in unitie: preferr
One woman firft, and then one thing in her.   10
I, when I value gold, may think upon
The ductilnefs, the application,
The wholfomnefs, the ingenuitie,
From ruft, from foil, from fire ever free:
But if I love it, 'tis becaufe 'tis made   15
By our new nature (Ufe) the foul of trade.
　All thefe in women we might think upon
(If women had them) and yet love but one.

80 obeying; *Ed:* obeying, *1650–69*   81 fecurely *1650–69:* un-
partially *A10*   82 being *1650–69:* having *A10*   one, *Ed:* one
1650–69   83 Wee'l love her ever, *Ed:* Wee'l leave her ever, *1650–69,*
JC: Would love for ever, *A10*
　Elegie XVIII. &c. Ed: Elegie XVIII. *1669, where it is first included
among the Elegies. It had already been printed in* Wit and Drollery. By
Sir J. M., J. S., Sir W. D., J. D., *and the most refined Wits of the Age. 1661.
It appears in* A18, A25, B, Cy, D, H49, Lec, N, O'F, S, S96, TC, *with title*
Loves Progref., *or* Elegie. on Loves Progreffe., *or with no title*   4
Love is a *1669:* And Love's a *MSS.*   5 ftrange *1661 and MSS.:*
ftrong *1669*   11 I,] I *1669*   14 ever *1669:* for ever *O'F, S, S96*
16. (our new nature) use, *1661*   17 thefe *1669 and MSS.:* this *1661,*
Cy, P, Chambers

Can

Can men more injure women then to fay
They love them for that, by which they're not they? 20
Makes virtue woman? muft I cool my bloud
Till I both be, and find one wife and good?
May barren Angels love fo. But if we
Make love to woman; virtue is not fhe:
As beauty'is not nor wealth: He that ftrayes thus 25
From her to hers, is more adulterous,
Then if he took her maid. Search every fpheare
And firmament, our *Cupid* is not there:
He's an infernal god and under ground,
With *Pluto* dwells, where gold and fire abound: 30
Men to fuch Gods, their facrificing Coles
Did not in Altars lay, but pits and holes.
Although we fee Celeftial bodies move
Above the earth, the earth we Till and love:
So we her ayres contemplate, words and heart, 35
And virtues; but we love the Centrique part.
    Nor is the foul more worthy, or more fit
For love, then this, as infinite as it.
But in attaining this defired place
How much they erre; that fet out at the face? 40
The hair a Foreft is of Ambufhes,
Of fpringes, fnares, fetters and manacles:
The brow becalms us when 'tis fmooth and plain,
And when 'tis wrinckled, fhipwracks us again.
Smooth, 'tis a Paradice, where we would have 45
Immortal ftay, and wrinkled 'tis our grave.
The Nofe (like to the firft Meridian) runs
Not 'twixt an Eaft and Weft, but 'twixt two funs;
It leaves a Cheek, a rofie Hemifphere

   20 them] *om. 1661*   25 beauty'is not *1661 and MSS.:* beauties
no *1669*   thus] thus: *1669*   27 Then if he took] Then he that
took *1661,* B (takes), *Cy,O'F,P,S*   fpheare] fphear *1669*   30
abound: *Ed:* abound, *1669*   32 in *A18,B,D,H49,Lec,N,TC:*
on *1669,A25*   holes.] holes: *1669*   38 infinite] infinit *1669*
40 erre *1661-69,S,S96:* ftray *A18,A25,B,Cy,D,H49,JC,N,O'F,P,TC*
42 fpringes, *H49 and some MSS.:* fprings, *1669*   46 and *1661, A18,*
A25,B,C,D,H49,Lec,N,P,S96,TC: but *1669*   our *1661, MSS.:* a
1669   47 firft Meridian *1661 and MSS.:* fweet Meridian *1669.*
                                                        On

On either fide, and then directs us where   50
Upon the Iflands fortunate we fall,
(Not faynte *Canaries*, but *Ambrofiall*)
Her fwelling lips; To which when wee are come,
We anchor there, and think our felves at home,
For they feem all: there Syrens fongs, and there   55
Wife Delphick Oracles do fill the ear;
There in a Creek where chofen pearls do fwell,
The Remora, her cleaving tongue doth dwell.
Thefe, and the glorious Promontory, her Chin
Ore paft; and the ftreight *Hellefpont* betweene   60
The *Seftos* and *Abydos* of her breafts,
(Not of two Lovers, but two Loves the neafts)
Succeeds a boundlefs fea, but yet thine eye
Some Ifland moles may fcattered there defcry;
And Sailing towards her *India*, in that way   65
Shall at her fair Atlantick Navell ftay;
Though thence the Current be thy Pilot made,
Yet ere thou be where thou wouldft be embay'd,
Thou fhalt upon another Foreft fet,
Where many Shipwrack, and no further get.   70
When thou art there, confider what this chace
Mifpent by thy beginning at the face.
      Rather fet out below; practice my Art,
Some Symetry the foot hath with that part
Which thou doft feek, and is thy Map for that   75

52–3 (Not ... Ambrofiall) ... lips *&c. 1661* and *MSS.* (*not always with brackets and sometimes with* No *for* Not *and* Canary): Not ... Ambrofiall. Unto her fwelling lips when we are come, *1669*   55 For they feem all: there *1669, A18, B, D, H49, JC, Lec, N, S, TC:* For they fing all their *1661, Cy, P*   57 There *1661* and *MSS.:* Then *1669*   fwell, *Ed:* fwell *1669*   58 Rhemora *1669*   59 the glorious Promontory,] *brackets and no comma, 1669*   60 Ore paft; ... betweene *1661* and *MSS.:* Being paft the Straits of *Hellefpont* between *1669*   62 Loves] loves *1669*   63 yet] that *D, H49, Lec, and other MSS.*   65 Sailing] Sailng *1669*   66 Navell] Naval *1669*   67 thence *A18, A25, B, Cy, D, H49, Lec, O'F, S, S96, TC:* there *1661-9, N*(?): hence *P*   thy *all MSS.:* the *1661-9*   68 wouldft *A18, A25, B, Cy, H49, JC, Lec, N, O'F, P, S, S96, TC:* fhouldft *1669*   70 many *1669:* fome doe *A18, A25, B, Cy, D, H49, JC, Lec, N, P*   73 my *1669, A25, B, Cy, D, H49, N, O'F, P, S, S96, TCD:* thy *Chambers:* thine *A18, TCC*

Lovely

Lovely enough to ſtop, but not ſtay at:
Leaſt ſubject to diſguiſe and change it is;
Men ſay the Devil never can change his.
It is the Emblem that hath figured
Firmneſs; 'tis the firſt part that comes to bed.   80
Civilitie we ſee refin'd: the kiſs
Which at the face began, tranſplanted is,
Since to the hand, ſince to the Imperial knee,
Now at the Papal foot delights to be:
If Kings think that the nearer way, and do   85
Riſe from the foot, Lovers may do ſo too;
For as free Spheres move faſter far then can
Birds, whom the air reſiſts, ſo may that man
Which goes this empty and Ætherial way,
Then if at beauties elements he ſtay.   90
Rich Nature hath in women wiſely made
Two purſes, and their mouths averſely laid:
They then, which to the lower tribute owe,
That way which that Exchequer looks, muſt go:
He which doth not, his error is as great,   95
As who by Clyſter gave the Stomack meat.

ELEGIE XIX.

Going to Bed.

COme, Madam, come, all reſt my powers defie,
Until I labour, I in labour lie.
The foe oft-times having the foe in ſight,
Is tir'd with ſtanding though he never fight.

80 the] *bis 1669*   81–2 Civilitie, we ſee, refin'd the kiſſe Which at the face begonne, tranſplanted is *D, H49, Lec*   83 Imperial] imperial *1669*
86 too;] too. *1669.*   90 elements *1661 and MSS.:* enemies *1669*   91 hath] *Chambers omits*   93 owe,] owe *1669*   96 Clyſter gave *A18, D, H49, Lec, N, TC:* gliſter gives *1669*
Elegie XIX. &c. *Ed: in 1669, A18, A25, B, Cy, D, H49, JC, L74, N, O'F, P, S, S96, TCC, TCD, W   Appeared in 1669 edition after the Elegies, unnumbered but with the heading* To his Miſtris going to Bed. *The MSS. include it among the Elegies either with no heading, or simply* Elegye, *or numbered according to the scheme adopted: B gives title which I have adopted as consistent with other titles*   4 he *1669:* they *A18, D, H49, JC, L74, Lec, N, TC*

Off with that girdle, like heavens Zone glittering,　　5
But a far fairer world incompaſſing.
Unpin that ſpangled breaſtplate which you wear,
That th'eyes of buſie fooles may be ſtopt there.
Unlace your ſelf, for that harmonious chyme,
Tells me from you, that now it is bed time.　　10
Off with that happy busk, which I envie,
That ſtill can be, and ſtill can ſtand ſo nigh.
Your gown going off, ſuch beautious ſtate reveals,
As when from flowry meads th'hills ſhadow ſteales.
Off with that wyerie Coronet and ſhew　　15
The haiery Diademe which on you doth grow:
Now off with thoſe ſhooes, and then ſafely tread
In this loves hallow'd temple, this ſoft bed.
In ſuch white robes, heaven's Angels us'd to be
Receavd by men; Thou Angel bringſt with thee　　20
A heaven like Mahomets Paradiſe; and though
Ill ſpirits walk in white, we eaſly know,
By this theſe Angels from an evil ſprite,
Thoſe ſet our hairs, but theſe our fleſh upright.

　　Licence my roaving hands, and let them go,　　25
Before, behind, between, above, below.
O my America! my new-found-land,
My kingdome, ſaflieſt when with one man man'd,
My Myne of precious ſtones, My Emperie,

　　5 glittering] gliſtering *MSS.*　　　　8 That I may ſee my ſhrine that
ſhines ſo fair. *Cy, P*　　　10 it is *1669:* 'tis your *MSS.*　　　11 which]
whom *A18, D, H49, L 74, Lec, S, TC, W*　　　14 from *MSS.:* through
1669　　　ſhadow] ſhadows *1669*　　　16 Diademe . . . grow:
A25, B, Cy, D, H49, JC, L74, Lec, N, O'F, P, TC: Diadem which on your
head doth grow: *1669:* Diadems which on you do grow. *S, Chambers*
17 Now . . . ſhooes, *1669, JC, W:* Off . . ſhoes *A18, D, H49, Lec, N, TC:*
Off with thoſe hoſe and ſhoes *S*　　　ſafely *A18, A25, B, L74, N, O'F, S,*
S96, TC, W: ſoftly *1669, Cy, D, H49, JC, Lec, P*　　　20 Receavd by
men; Thou *all MSS.:* Reveal'd to men; thou *1669*　　　21 Paradiſe; *Ed:*
Paradice, *1669*　　　22 Ill *1669, A18, D, H49, L74, Lec, N, S, S96,*
TC, W: All *B, O'F, P, and Chambers' conjecture*　　　ſpirits *1669, A18, B, D,*
H49, N, S: angels *O'F, S96*　　　white, *Ed:* white; *1669*　　　26 below. *Ed:*
below, *1669*　　　28 kingdome, *MSS.:* Kingdom's *1669*　　　ſafelieſt *A18,*
D, H49, Lec, N, TC: ſafeſt, *1669*　　　man'd, *Ed:* man'd. *1669*　　　29
ſtones, *Ed:* ſtones: *1669*

　　　　　　　　　　　　　　　　　　　　　　　　How

How bleft am I in this difcovering thee! 30
To enter in thefe bonds, is to be free;
Then where my hand is fet, my feal fhall be.
   Full nakednefs! All joyes are due to thee,
As fouls unbodied, bodies uncloth'd muft be,
To tafte whole joyes. Gems which you women ufe 35
Are like Atlanta's balls, caft in mens views,
That when a fools eye lighteth on a Gem,
His earthly foul may covet theirs, not them.
Like pictures, or like books gay coverings made
For lay-men, are all women thus array'd; 40
Themfelves are myftick books, which only wee
(Whom their imputed grace will dignifie)
Muft fee reveal'd. Then fince that I may know;
As liberally, as to a Midwife, fhew
Thy felf: caft all, yea, this white lynnen hence, 45
There is no pennance due to innocence.
   To teach thee, I am naked firft; why than
What needft thou have more covering then a man.

30 How bleft am I *all MSS.*: How am I bleft *1669*   this *A18*,
B,Cy,D,H49,JC,Lec,N,O'F,P,TC,W: thus *1669,A25,L74,S*   dif-
covering] difcovery *B,O'F*   thee! *Ed:* thee? *1669*   be.] be, *1669*
35 Gems] Jems *1669: and so* 37   36 like *1669:* as *MSS.*   balls,
MSS.: ball: *1669*   38 covet *A18,A25,B,D,H49,JC,L74,Lec,N,TC,*
W: court *1669,Cy,P,S,S96*   theirs, *A18,A25,Cy,D,H49,JC,L74,*
Lec,N,P,S96,TC,W: thofe *S:* that, *1669,B,O'F*   them.]them: *1669*
39 pictures, *Ed:* pictures *1669*   made *Ed:* made,*1669*   40 lay-men,
Ed: lay-men *1669*   array'd; *Ed:* arrayed.*1669*   41 Themfelves … only
wee *A18,Cy,D,H49,JC,L74,Lec,N,O'F,P,S,S96,TC,W:* Themfelves
are only myftick books, which we, *1669,B*   43 fee] be *A18,A25,D,*
H49,Lec,N,TC   reveal'd] revealed *1669*   44 a *all MSS.*:
thy *1669*   Midwife, *Ed:* Midwife *1669*   45 hence, *Ed:* hence
1669   46 pennance due to innocence. *1669,B,Cy,JC,O'F,P,S:*
pennance, much lefs innocence; *A18,A25,D,H49,L74,Lec,N,S96,W*
47 thee, *Ed:* thee *1669*   firft; *Ed:* firft, *1669*

           ELEGIE

ELEGIE XX.

Loves Warre.

Till I have peace with thee, warr other men,
   And when I have peace, can I leave thee then?
All other Warrs are fcrupulous; Only thou
O fayr free Citty, maift thyfelfe allowe
To any one: In Flanders, who can tell   5
Whether the Mafter preffe; or men rebell?
Only we know, that which all Ideots fay,
They beare moft blows which come to part the fray.
France in her lunatique giddines did hate
Ever our men, yea and our God of late;   10
Yet fhe relyes upon our Angels well,
Which nere returne; no more then they which fell.
Sick Ireland is with a ftrange warr poffeft
Like to an Ague; now raging, now at rest;
Which time will cure: yet it muft doe her good   15
If fhe were purg'd, and her head vayne let blood.
And Midas joyes our Spanifh journeys give,
We touch all gold, but find no food to live.
And I fhould be in the hott parching clyme,
To duft and afhes turn'd before my time.   20
To mew me in a Ship, is to inthrall
Mee in a prifon, that weare like to fall;
Or in a Cloyfter ; fave that there men dwell
In a calme heaven, here in a fwaggering hell.

Elegy XX &c. *Ed: First published in F. G. Waldron's* A Collection of
Miscellaneous Poetry, *1802, from a MS. dated 1625 ; then by Sir J. Simeon
in his* Philobiblon Society *volume of 1856. It is included among Donne's
Elegies in A18, A25, B, Cy, D, H49, JC, L74, Lec, N, O'F, P, S, S96, TCC,
TCD, W. In B it has the title* Making of Men. *The present text is based on
W*   7 all *A18, B, Cy, D, H49, L74, Lec, O'F, S, S96, TC, W:* moft
JC, Chambers   8 They beare moft blows which (*or that*) *A18, B, D,
H49, JC, L74, Lec, S, S96, TC, W:* They must bear blows, which *Chambers*
9 giddinefs] guidings *Sim:* giddinge *Wald*   11 well,] well *W*   13
a ftrange] straying *Sim*   16 head] dead *Sim*   19 the *A18, B, Cy, D, H49,
N, S, S96, TC, W:* that *Chambers, A25, JC, L74, O'F*   24 fwaggering]
swaying *Chambers*

Long

Long voyages are long confumptions,   25
And fhips are carts for executions.
Yea they are Deaths; Is't not all one to flye
Into an other World, as t'is to dye?
Here let mee warr; in thefe armes lett mee lye;
Here lett mee parlee, batter, bleede, and dye.   30
Thyne armes imprifon me, and myne armes thee;
Thy hart thy ranfome is; take myne for mee.
Other men war that they their reft may gayne;
But wee will reft that wee may fight agayne.
Thofe warrs the ignorant, thefe th'experienc'd love,   35
There wee are alwayes under, here above.
There Engins farr off breed a juft true feare,
Neere thrufts, pikes, ftabs, yea bullets hurt not here.
There lyes are wrongs; here fafe uprightly lye;
There men kill men, we'will make one by and by.   40
Thou nothing; I not halfe fo much fhall do
In thefe Warrs, as they may which from us two
Shall fpring. Thoufands wee fee which travaile not
To warrs; But ftay swords, armes, and shott
To make at home; And fhall not I do then   45
More glorious fervice, ftaying to make men?

25 confumptions,] confumptions *W : line omitted, Wald*   29 lye] *fpelt* ly
W : and fo 30 dy   33 gayne;] gayne *W*   37 There] Thefe *Sim*
and, that, with, which] *contracted throughout, W*

HEROICALL

HEROICALL EPISTLE.

Sapho to *Philænis*.

WHere is that holy fire, which *Verſe* is ſaid
   To have? is that inchanting force decai'd?
Verſe that drawes *Natures* workes, from *Natures* law,
   Thee, her beſt worke, to her worke cannot draw.
Have my teares quench'd my old *Poetique* fire;   5
   Why quench'd they not as well, that of *deſire?*
Thoughts, my mindes creatures, often are with thee,
   But I, their maker, want their libertie.
Onely thine image, in my heart, doth ſit,
   But that is waxe, and fires environ it.   10
My fires have driven, thine have drawne it hence;
   And I am rob'd of *Picture*, *Heart*, and *Senſe.*
Dwells with me ſtill mine irkſome *Memory*,
   Which, both to keepe, and loſe, grieves equally.
That tells me'how faire thou art: Thou art ſo faire,   15
   As, *gods*, when *gods* to thee I doe compare,
Are grac'd thereby; And to make blinde men ſee,
   What things *gods* are, I ſay they'are like to thee.
For, if we juſtly call each ſilly *man*
   A *litle world*, What ſhall we call thee than?   20
Thou art not ſoft, and cleare, and ſtrait, and faire,
   As *Down*, as *Stars*, *Cedars*, and *Lillies* are,

Heroicall Epiſtle.] *In 1633* Sapho to Philaenis *follows Basse's* Epitaph
upon Shakeſpeare. *and precedes* The Annuntiation and Paſſion. *In 1635
it was placed with some other miscellaneous and dubious poems among the*
Letters to ſeverall Perſonages, *where it has appeared in all subsequent
editions. I have transferred it to the neighbourhood of the* Elegies *and given
it the title which seems to describe exactly the genre to which it belongs. In*
JC *it is entitled* Elegie 18th. *The other MSS. are* A18, A25, O'F, N, P,
TCC, TCD. *In* A25, JC, *and* P, ll. 31–54 *are omitted*   **2** have?
1650–69: have, *1633–39*   **3** workes, *1633–39:* worke, *1650–69, O'F*
8 maker, *1635–69:* maker; *1633*   **17** thereby; And *1635–69:* thereby.
And *1633, some copies*   **22** As *Down, 1633–69,* A18, N, TC : As dowves
P : As downs O'F. *See note*   Cedars,] as Cedars, A18, N, O'F, TC
                                             But

But thy right hand, and cheek, and eye, only
  Are like thy other hand, and cheek, and eye.
Such was my *Phao* awhile, but fhall be never,   25
  As thou, waft, art, and, oh, maift be ever.
Here lovers fweare in their *Idolatrie*,
  That I am fuch; but *Griefe* difcolors me.
And yet I grieve the leffe, leaft *Griefe* remove
  My beauty, and make me'unworthy of thy love.   30
Plaies fome foft boy with thee, oh there wants yet
  A mutuall feeling which fhould fweeten it.
His chinne, a thorny hairy unevenneffe
  Doth threaten, and fome daily change poffeffe.
Thy body is a naturall *Paradife*,   35
  In whofe felfe, unmanur'd, all pleafure lies,
Nor needs *perfection*; why fhouldft thou than
  Admit the tillage of a harfh rough man?
Men leave behinde them that which their fin fhowes,
  And are as theeves trac'd, which rob when it fnows.   40
But of our dallyance no more fignes there are,
  Then *fifhes* leave in ftreames, or *Birds* in aire.
And betweene us all fweetneffe may be had;
  All, all that *Nature* yields, or *Art* can adde.
My two lips, eyes, thighs, differ from thy two,   45
  But fo, as thine from one another doe;
And, oh, no more; the likeneffe being fuch,
  Why fhould they not alike in all parts touch?
Hand to ftrange hand, lippe to lippe none denies;
  Why fhould they breft to breft, or thighs to thighs?   50
Likeneffe begets fuch ftrange felfe flatterie,
  That touching my felfe, all feemes done to thee.
My felfe I embrace, and mine owne hands I kiffe,
  And amoroufly thanke my felfe for this.
Me, in my glaffe, I call thee; But alas,   55

---

26 maift be ever. *1633, A18, A25, N, TC:* maift thou be ever. *1635-69,*
O'F: fhalt be for ever. *P:* mayft thou be for ever. *JC*   33 thorny
hairy *1633-69:* thorney-hairy *TCD:* thorny, hairy *modern edd.*   40 are
Ed: are, *1633-69*

When

When I would kiffe, teares dimme mine *eyes,* and *glaffe.*
O cure this loving madneffe, and reftore
  Me to mee; thee, my *halfe,* my *all,* my *more.*
So may thy cheekes red outweare fcarlet dye,
  And their white, whiteneffe of the *Galaxy,*   60
So may thy mighty, amazing beauty move
  Envy'in all *women,* and in all *men, love,*
And fo be *change,* and *fickneffe,* farre from thee,
  As thou by comming neere, keep'ft them from me.

58 me to mee; thee, *1635–69, A18, A25, JC, N, P, TC (generally* mee,
in MSS.): me to mee; fhee, *1633:* me to thee, thee *Chambers*   *halfe,*]
harte *A25, JC, P*
59–60   So may thy cheekes outweare all fcarlet dye
             May bliffe and thee be one eternallye *P: om. JC*
61 mighty, amazing *Ed:* mighty amazing *1633–69:* almighty amazing *P*

EPITHA-

EPITHALAMIONS,

MARRIAGE SONGS.

An Epithalamion, Or mariage Song on the Lady Elizabeth,
and Count Palatine *being married on St.* Valentines *day.*

I.

H Aile Biſhop Valentine, whoſe day this is,
  All the Aire is thy Diocis,
  And all the chirping Choriſters
And other birds are thy Pariſhioners,
  Thou marryeſt every yeare   5
The Lirique Larke, and the grave whiſpering Dove,
The Sparrow that neglects his life for love,
The houſehold Bird, with the red ſtomacher,
  Thou mak'ſt the black bird ſpeed as ſoone,
As doth the Goldfinch, or the Halcyon;   10
The huſband cocke lookes out, and ſtraight is ſped,
And meets his wife, which brings her feather-bed.
This day more cheerfully then ever ſhine,
This day, which might enflame thy ſelf, Old Valentine.

II.

Till now, Thou warmd'ſt with multiplying loves   15
  Two larkes, two ſparrowes, or two Doves,
   All that is nothing unto this,
For thou this day coupleſt two Phœnixes;
   Thou mak'ſt a Taper ſee
What the ſunne never ſaw, and what the Arke   20

Epithalamions, &c. *1635–69: no general title, 1633.*   An Epithalamion,
*&c. 1633–69, A25, B, C, D, H49, Lec, N, O'F, P, S96, TCD (most of the
MSS. have the full title but with slight verbal variations)*   13 ſhine, *Ed :*
ſhine. *1633–69*   14 enflame] enfläe *1633*   18 Phœnixes; *Ed:*
Phœnixes, *1633:* Phœnixes. *1635–69*

               (Which

(Which was of foules, and beaſts, the cage, and park,)
Did not containe, one bed containes, through Thee,
     Two Phœnixes, whoſe joyned breaſts
Are unto one another mutuall neſts,
Where motion kindles ſuch fires, as ſhall give   25
Yong Phœnixes, and yet the old ſhall live.
Whoſe love and courage never ſhall decline,
But make the whole year through, thy day, O Valentine.

III.

Up then faire Phœnix Bride, fruſtrate the Sunne,
     Thy ſelfe from thine affection   30
       Takeſt warmth enough, and from thine eye
All leſſer birds will take their Jollitie.
       Up, up, faire Bride, and call,
Thy ſtarres, from out their ſeverall boxes, take
Thy Rubies, Pearles, and Diamonds forth, and make   35
Thy ſelfe a conſtellation, of them All,
       And by their blazing, ſignifie,
That a Great Princeſs falls, but doth not die;
Bee thou a new ſtarre, that to us portends
Ends of much wonder; And be Thou thoſe ends.   40
Since thou doſt this day in new glory ſhine,
May all men date Records, from this thy Valentine.

IIII.

Come forth, come forth, and as one glorious flame
     Meeting Another, growes the ſame,
      So meet thy Fredericke, and ſo   45
To an unſeparable union growe.
     Since ſeparation

21 foules, *1633*: fowle, *1635–69*   22 Thee, *1633, 1650–69*: Thee:
1635–39   37 their blazing *1633–69*, D, *Lec*: this blazing *A25*, B, H*49*,
JC, N, *O'F* (*altered to* their), P, *TCD*   40 ends. *1635–69*: ends, *1633*
42 this thy *1633–54*, B, D, H*49*, *Lec*, N, *O'F*, P, *S96*, *TCD*: this day *1669*,
A25, *JC*, *Chambers*   46 growe. *A25*, B, D, H*49*, *JC*, N, *O'F*, P, *S96*,
TCD: goe, *1633–69*, *Lec*

Falls not on such things as are infinite,
Nor things which are but one, can disunite,
You'are twice inseparable, great, and one;   50
      Goe then to where the Bishop staies,
To make you one, his way, which divers waies
Must be effected; and when all is past,
And that you'are one, by hearts and hands made fast,
You two have one way left, your selves to'entwine,   55
Besides this Bishops knot, or Bishop Valentine.

V.

But oh, what ailes the Sunne, that here he staies,
      Longer to day, then other daies?
      Staies he new light from these to get?
And finding here such store, is loth to set?   60
      And why doe you two walke,
So slowly pac'd in this procession?
Is all your care but to be look'd upon,
And be to others spectacle, and talke?
      The feast, with gluttonous delaies,   65
Is eaten, and too long their meat they praise,
The masquers come too late, and'I thinke, will stay,
Like Fairies, till the Cock crow them away.
Alas, did not Antiquity assigne
A night, as well as day, to thee, O Valentine?   70

VI.

They did, and night is come; and yet wee see
      Formalities retarding thee.
      What meane these Ladies, which (as though
They were to take a clock in peeces,) goe
      So nicely about the Bride;   75

49 disunite, *Grolier*: disunite. *1633–69 and Chambers*   56 Bishops knot, or Bishop Valentine. *A25, B, D, H49, JC, Lec, N, O'F, P*(our), *S96, TC* Bishops knot, O Bishop Valentine. *1633–54*: Bishops knot of Bishop Valentine. *1669*: Bishops knot, of Bishop Valentine. *Chambers*   60 store. *1633, A25, B, D, H49, JC, Lec, N, P, S96, TCD*: starres, *1635–69, O'F, Chambers*   67 come too late, *1633*: come late, *1635–69* 70 O Valentine? *1633–54, A25, B, D, H49, JC, Lec, N, O'F, P, S96, TCD*: old Valentine? *1669*

                                        A Bride,

A Bride, before a good night could be faid,
Should vanifh from her cloathes, into her bed,
As Soules from bodies fteale, and are not fpy'd.
   But now fhe is laid; What though fhee bee?
Yet there are more delayes, For, where is he?   80
He comes, and paffes through Spheare after Spheare,
Firft her fheetes, then her Armes, then any where.
Let not this day, then, but this night be thine,
Thy day was but the eve to this, O Valentine.

VII.

Here lyes a fhee Sunne, and a hee Moone here,   85
  She gives the beft light to his Spheare,
  Or each is both, and all, and fo
They unto one another nothing owe,
  And yet they doe, but are
So juft and rich in that coyne which they pay,   90
That neither would, nor needs forbeare, nor ftay;
Neither defires to be fpar'd, nor to fpare,
  They quickly pay their debt, and then
Take no acquittances, but pay again;
They pay, they give, they lend, and fo let fall   95
No fuch occafion to be liberall.
More truth, more courage in thefe two do fhine,
Then all thy turtles have, and fparrows, Valentine.

VIII.

And by this act of thefe two Phenixes
  Nature againe reftored is,   100
  For fince thefe two are two no more,
Ther's but one Phenix ftill, as was before.
  Reft now at laft, and wee

81 paffes *1633–39*: paffeth *1650–69* Spheare, *Ed*: Spheare. *1633*:
Spheare: *1635–69* 82 where. *1650–69*: where, *1633–39* 85 here,
1633–39, A25, B, D, H49, JC, Lec, N, TCD: there, *1650–69, O'F, P, S96*
91 ftay;] ftay, *1633* 92 fpare, *1633–54*: fpare. *1669* 94 acquittances,
1635–69: acquittance, *1633* 96 fuch] *om. 1669*

As

As Satyres watch the Sunnes uprife, will ftay
Waiting, when your eyes opened, let out day,   105
Onely defir'd, becaufe your face wee fee;
    Others neare you fhall whifpering fpeake,
And wagers lay, at which fide day will breake,
And win by'obferving, then, whofe hand it is
That opens firft a curtaine, hers or his;   110
This will be tryed to morrow after nine,
Till which houre, wee thy day enlarge, O Valentine.

ECCLOGVE.

1613. *December* 26.

Allophanes *finding* Idios *in the country in Chriftmas
time, reprehends his abfence from court, at the mariage
Of the Earle of Sommerfet,* Idios *gives an account of
his purpofe therein, and of his abfence thence.*

Allophanes.

VNfeafonable man, ftatue of ice,
    What could to countries folitude entice
Thee, in this yeares cold and decrepit time?
    Natures inftinct drawes to the warmer clime
Even fmall birds, who by that courage dare,   5
    In numerous fleets, faile through their Sea, the aire.
What delicacie can in fields appeare,
    Whil'ft Flora'herfelfe doth a freeze jerkin weare?
Whil'ft windes do all the trees and hedges ftrip
    Of leafes, to furnifh roddes enough to whip   10

104 As . . . uprife,] *brackets 1650–69*   105 day,] day. *1633*
    ECCLOGVE. *&c. 1633–69: similarly,* A18, A23, B, D, H49, Lec, N,
O'F, S96, TCC, TCD   his abfence thence. *1633, Lec:* his Actions there.
1635–69, A18, H49, N, O'F, TC: his abfence then. D, S96   2 countries]
country A18, N, TC   4 clime *1633–39:* clime : *1650–69:* clime. D
5 fmall *1633,* A18, B, D, H49, Lec, N, O'F, TC: fmaller *1635–69.* Chambers
                                       Thy

Thy madneſſe from thee; and all ſprings by froſt
    Have taken cold, and their ſweet murmure loſt;
If thou thy faults or fortunes would'ſt lament
    With juſt ſolemnity, do it in Lent;
At Court the ſpring already advanced is,   15
    The Sunne ſtayes longer up; and yet not his
The glory is, farre other, other fires.
    Firſt, zeale to Prince and State; then loves deſires
Burne in one breſt, and like heavens two great lights,
    The firſt doth governe dayes, the other nights.   20
And then that early light, which did appeare
    Before the Sunne and Moone created were,
The Princes favour is defus'd o'r all,
    From which all Fortunes, Names, and Natures fall;
Then from thoſe wombes of ſtarres, the Brides bright
      eyes,   25
    At every glance, a conſtellation flyes,
And ſowes the Court with ſtarres, and doth prevent
    In light and power, the all-ey'd firmament;
Firſt her eyes kindle other Ladies eyes,
    Then from their beames their jewels luſters riſe,   30
And from their jewels torches do take fire,
    And all is warmth, and light, and good deſire;
Moſt other Courts, alas, are like to hell,
    Where in darke plotts, fire without light doth dwell:
Or but like Stoves, for luſt and envy get   35
    Continuall, but artificiall heat;
Here zeale and love growne one, all clouds diſgeſt,
    And make our Court an everlaſting Eaſt.
And can'ſt thou be from thence?

Idios.   No, I am there.
As heaven, to men diſpos'd, is every where,   40

12 Have *1633:* Having *1635–69*   murmure *A18,A23,B,D,H49,*
N,O'F,TC: murmures *1633–69*   22 were, *Ed:* were; *1633–69*
29 kindle] kindles *1633*   34 plotts, *1635–69,A18,B,D,H49,N,O'F,*
S96,TC: places, *1633,1669,Lec*   37 diſgeſt, *1633–39:* digeſt, *1650–69*
39 there. *D:* there *1633–69*   40 where, *1633:* where: *1635–69,*
owing to the dropping of stop in previous line

So

So are thofe Courts, whofe Princes animate,
 Not onely all their houfe, but all their State.
Let no man thinke, becaufe he is full, he hath all,
 Kings (as their patterne, God) are liberall
Not onely in fulneffe, but capacitie,   45
 Enlarging narrow men, to feele and fee,
And comprehend the bleffings they beftow.
 So, reclus'd hermits often times do know
More of heavens glory, then a worldling can.
 As man is of the world, the heart of man,   50
Is an epitome of Gods great booke
 Of creatures, and man need no farther looke;
So is the Country of Courts, where fweet peace doth,
 As their one common foule, give life to both,
I am not then from Court.

Allophanes.
        Dreamer, thou art.   55
 Think'ft thou fantaftique that thou haft a part
In the East-Indian fleet, becaufe thou haft
 A little fpice, or Amber in thy tafte?
Becaufe thou art not frozen, art thou warme?
 Seeft thou all good becaufe thou feeft no harme?   60
The earth doth in her inward bowels hold
 Stuffe well difpos'd, and which would faine be gold,
But never fhall, except it chance to lye,
 So upward, that heaven gild it with his eye;
As, for divine things, faith comes from above,   65
 So, for beft civill ufe, all tinctures move
From higher powers; From God religion fprings,
 Wifdome, and honour from the ufe of Kings.
Then unbeguile thy felfe, and know with mee,
 That Angels, though on earth employd they bee,   70

42 State.] State, *1633*   54 one *1633, A18, D, H49, N, O'F, TC:* own
1635-69, Lec   55 I am . . . Court. *1633, A18, B, D, H49, N, S96, TC:*
And am I then from Court? *1635-69*   art. *1650-69:* art, *1633-39*   57
East-Indian *A18, A23, B, D, H49, Lec, N, O'F, S96, TC:* Indian *1633-69*
61 inward *A18, A23, B, D, H49, Lec, N, O'F, S96, TC:* inner *1633-69*
                  Are

Are ftill in heav'n, fo is hee ftill at home
  That doth, abroad, to honeft actions come.
Chide thy felfe then, O foole, which yefterday
  Might'ft have read more then all thy books bewray;
Haft thou a hiftory, which doth prefent   75
  A Court, where all affections do affent
Unto the Kings, and that, that Kings are juft?
  And where it is no levity to truft?
Where there is no ambition, but to'obey,
  Where men need whifper nothing, and yet may;   80
Where the Kings favours are fo plac'd, that all
  Finde that the King therein is liberall
To them, in him, becaufe his favours bend
  To vertue, to the which they all pretend?
Thou haft no fuch; yet here was this, and more,   85
  An earneft lover, wife then, and before.
Our little Cupid hath fued Livery,
  And is no more in his minority,
Hee is admitted now into that breft
  Where the Kings Counfells and his fecrets reft.   90
What haft thou loft, O ignorant man?

Idios.

                              I knew
All this, and onely therefore I withdrew.
To know and feele all this, and not to have
  Words to expreffe it, makes a man a grave
Of his owne thoughts; I would not therefore ftay   95
  At a great feaft, having no Grace to fay.
And yet I fcap'd not here; for being come
  Full of the common joy, I utter'd fome;
Reade then this nuptiall fong, which was not made
  Either the Court or mens hearts to invade,   100

75 prefent] reprefent *A18, N, TC*   78 truft? *Ed:* truft. *1633–39:*
truft, *1650–69*   84 pretend? *Ed:* pretend. *1633–69*   85 more, *1633:*
more. *1635–69*   86 before. *1633–69:* before, *Chambers. See note*
92 withdrew.] withdrew *1633*   96 fay. *1635–69:* fay, *1633*   98
joy, . . . fome; *Ed:* joy; . . . fome, *1633:* joy; . . . fome. *1635–69*

                                                                But

But fince I'am dead, and buried, I could frame
  No Epitaph, which might advance my fame
So much as this poore fong, which teftifies
  I did unto that day fome facrifice.

EPITHALAMION.

I.

The time of the Mariage.

THou art repriv'd old yeare, thou fhalt not die,   105
  Though thou upon thy death bed lye,
    And fhould'ft within five dayes expire,
Yet thou art refcu'd by a mightier fire,
    Then thy old Soule, the Sunne,
When he doth in his largeft circle runne.   110
The paffage of the Weft or Eaft would thaw,
And open wide their eafie liquid jawe
To all our fhips, could a Promethean art
Either unto the Northerne Pole impart
The fire of thefe inflaming eyes, or of this loving heart. 115

II.

Equality of perfons.

But undifcerning Mufe, which heart, which eyes,
  In this new couple, doft thou prize,
    When his eye as inflaming is
As hers, and her heart loves as well as his?
    Be tryed by beauty, and than   120
The bridegroome is a maid, and not a man.
If by that manly courage they be tryed,
Which fcornes unjuft opinion; then the bride

EPITHALAMION. *D, H49, Lec, O'F, S96: om. 1633–69. See note*
107 expire,] expire *1633–39*   108 by *1633:* from *1635–69*   121
man. *1669, D:* man, *1633–39:* man; *1650–54*

                                                      Becomes

Becomes a man. Should chance or envies Art
Divide thefe two, whom nature fcarce did part?   125
Since both have both th'enflaming eyes, and both the
    loving heart.

III.

Rayfing of the Bridegroome.

Though it be fome divorce to thinke of you
    Singly, fo much one are you two,
    Yet let me here contemplate thee,
Firft, cheerfull Bridegroome, and firft let mee fee,   130
    How thou prevent'ft the Sunne,
And his red foming horfes doft outrunne,
How, having laid downe in thy Soveraignes breft
All bufineffes, from thence to reinveft
Them, when thefe triumphs ceafe, thou forward art   135
To fhew to her, who doth the like impart,
The fire of thy inflaming eyes, and of thy loving heart.

IIII.

Raifing of the Bride.

But now, to Thee, faire Bride, it is fome wrong,
    To thinke thou wert in Bed fo long,
    Since Soone thou lyeft downe firft, tis fit   140
Thou in firft rifing fhould'ft allow for it.
    Pouder thy Radiant haire,
Which if without fuch afhes thou would'ft weare,

124 or] our *1669*   126 both th'enflaming eyes, *A18, B, D, H49,*
N, O'F, S96, TC : th'enflaming eye, *1633 :* the enflaming eye, *1635–69*
128 Singly, *A18, A23, B, D, H49, N, O'F, S96, TC :* Single, *1633–69, Lec*
129 Yet let *A23, O'F :* Let *1633–69*   141 fhould'ft] fhould *1669*
it. *1635–69 :* it, *1633*

                                              Thou

Thou, which to all which come to looke upon,
Art meant for Phœbus, would'ft be Phaëton. 145
For our eafe, give thine eyes th'unufual part
Of joy, a Teare; fo quencht, thou maift impart,
To us that come, thy inflaming eyes, to him, thy loving
heart.

V.

Her Apparrelling.

Thus thou defcend'ft to our infirmitie,
Who can the Sun in water fee. 150
Soe doft thou, when in filke and gold,
Thou cloudft thy felfe; fince wee which doe behold,
Are duft, and wormes, 'tis juft
Our objects be the fruits of wormes and duft;
Let every Jewell be a glorious ftarre, 155
Yet ftarres are not fo pure, as their fpheares are.
And though thou ftoope, to'appeare to us in part,
Still in that Picture thou intirely art,
Which thy inflaming eyes have made within his loving
heart.

VI.

Going to the Chappell.

Now from your Eafts you iffue forth, and wee, 160
As men which through a Cipres fee
The rifing fun, doe thinke it two,
Soe, as you goe to Church, doe thinke of you,

---

144 Thou, which *D:* Thou, which, *1633:* Thou which, *1635–69*   145
Art *A18, B, S96, TCC:* Are *1633, D, H49, Lec, N, TCD:* Wert *1635–69,*
O'F   for] for, *1633*   Phaëton. *1635–69:* Phaëton, *1633*   146 eafe,
. . . eyes *1635–69:* eafe, . . . eyes, *1633*   150 fee. *1633–69:* see;
Grolier. But see note   157 ftoope, . . . us *1635–69:* ftoope, . . .
us, *1633*

But that vaile being gone,
By the Church rites you are from thenceforth one.   165
The Church Triumphant made this match before,
And now the Militant doth ſtrive no more;
Then, reverend Prieſt, who Gods Recorder art,
Doe, from his Dictates, to theſe two impart
All bleſſings, which are ſeene, or thought, by Angels eye
        or heart.   170

VII.

The Benediction.

Bleſt payre of Swans, Oh may you interbring
        Daily new joyes, and never ſing,
        Live, till all grounds of wiſhes faile,
Till honor, yea till wiſedome grow ſo ſtale,
        That, new great heights to trie,   175
It muſt ſerve your ambition, to die;
Raiſe heires, and may here, to the worlds end, live
Heires from this King, to take thankes, you, to give,
Nature and grace doe all, and nothing Art.
May never age, or error overthwart   180
With any Weſt, theſe radiant eyes, with any North, this
        heart.

VIII.

Feaſts and Revells.

But you are over-bleſt. Plenty this day
        Injures; it cauſeth time to ſtay;
        The tables groane, as though this feaſt
Would, as the flood, deſtroy all fowle and beaſt.   185

---

167 more; *Ed:* more, *1633:* more. *1635–69*   170 or thought]
Or thought *1633*   172 ſing, *1633:* ſing : *1635–69*   178 you,]
yours, *A23, B, D, O'F, S96*   give, *1633:* give. *1635–69*   179
Art. *Ed:* Art, *1633–69*

And

And were the doctrine new
That the earth mov'd, this day would make it true;
For every part to dance and revell goes.
They tread the ayre, and fal not where they rose.
Though fix houres fince, the Sunne to bed did part,   190
The masks and banquets will not yet impart
A funfet to thefe weary eyes, A Center to this heart.

IX.

The Brides going to bed.

What mean'ft thou Bride, this companie to keep?
    To fit up, till thou faine wouldft fleep?
    Thou maift not, when thou art laid, doe fo.   195
Thy felfe muft to him a new banquet grow,
    And you muft entertaine
And doe all this daies dances o'r againe.
Know that if Sun and Moone together doe
Rife in one point, they doe not fet fo too;   200
Therefore thou maift, faire Bride, to bed depart,
Thou art not gone, being gone; where e'r thou art,
Thou leav'ft in him thy watchfull eyes, in him thy loving
    heart.

X.

The Bridegroomes comming.

As he that fees a ftarre fall, runs apace,
    And findes a gellie in the place,
    So doth the Bridegroome haft as much,   205
Being told this ftarre is falne, and findes her fuch.

194 wouldft] would *1669*   200 too; *Ed:* too. *1635–69:* to. *1633*
202 being gone; *Ed:* being gone, *1633–39:* being gone *1650–69*   207
fuch. *1635–69:* fuch, *1633*

And

And as friends may looke ftrange,
By a new fafhion, or apparrells change,
Their foules, though long acquainted they had beene, 210
Thefe clothes, their bodies, never yet had feene;
Therefore at firft fhee modeftly might ftart,
But muft forthwith furrender every part,
As freely, as each to each before, gave either eye or heart.

XI.

The good-night.

Now, as in Tullias tombe, one lampe burnt cleare, 215
    Unchang'd for fifteene hundred yeare,
      May thefe love-lamps we here enfhrine,
In warmth, light, lafting, equall the divine.
      Fire ever doth afpire,
And makes all like it felfe, turnes all to fire, 220
But ends in afhes, which thefe cannot doe,
For none of thefe is fuell, but fire too.
This is joyes bonfire, then, where loves ftrong Arts
Make of fo noble individuall parts
One fire of foure inflaming eyes, and of two loving hearts. 225

    Idios.

As I have brought this fong, that I may doe
    A perfect facrifice, I'll burne it too.

    Allophanes.

No S^r. This paper I have juftly got,
    For, in burnt incenfe, the perfume is not
His only that prefents it, but of all; 230
    What ever celebrates this Feftivall

211 feene; *Ed:* feene. *1633–69*   214 eye] hand *1650–69*   215
burnt] burn *1669*   218 divine. *1635–69:* divine; *1633*   230 all;
1635–69: all, *1633*

                                Is

Is common, fince the joy thereof is fo.
  Nor may your felfe be Prieft: But let me goe,
Backe to the Court, and I will lay'it upon
  Such Altars, as prize your devotion.   235

Epithalamion made at Lincolnes Inne.

THe Sun-beames in the Eaft are fpred,
  Leave, leave, faire Bride, your folitary bed,
    No more fhall you returne to it alone,
It nourfeth fadneffe, and your bodies print,
Like to a grave, the yielding downe doth dint;   5
      You and your other you meet there anon;
        Put forth, put forth that warme balme-breathing thigh,
Which when next time you in thefe fheets wil fmother,
        There it muft meet another,
            Which never was, but muft be, oft, more nigh; 10
Come glad from thence, goe gladder then you came,
To day put on perfeêtion, and a womans name.

Daughters of London, you which bee
Our Golden Mines, and furnifh'd Treafurie,
    You which are Angels, yet ftill bring with you   15
Thoufands of Angels on your mariage daies,
Help with your prefence and devife to praife
    Thefe rites, which alfo unto you grow due;
      Conceitedly dreffe her, and be affign'd,
By you, fit place for every flower and jewell,   20
      Make her for love fit fewell
        As gay as Flora, and as rich as Inde;
So may fhee faire, rich, glad, and in nothing lame,
To day put on perfeêtion, and a womans name.

Epithalamion &c. *1633–69, A18, N, TCC, TCD*   Epithalamion on a
Citizen. *A34, B, O'F, S, S96: do.* of the La: Eliz: *P:* Epithalamion. *W*
4 bodies *1635–69 and MSS.:* body *1633*   8 fmother, *1650–69:*
fmother *1633–39*   17 prefence *Ed:* prefence, *1633–69. See note*
22 faire, rich, glad, and in *A18, N, TC, W:* faire and rich, in *1633–69, B,*
O'F, P, S96

                                                            And

And you frolique Patricians,   25
Sonns of thefe Senators wealths deep oceans,
   Ye painted courtiers, barrels of others wits,
Yee country men, who but your beafts love none,
Yee of thofe fellowfhips whereof hee's one,
   Of ftudy and play made ftrange Hermaphrodits,   30
   Here fhine; This Bridegroom to the Temple bring.
Loe, in yon path which ftore of ftraw'd flowers graceth,
   The fober virgin paceth;
       Except my fight faile, 'tis no other thing;
Weep not nor blufh, here is no griefe nor fhame,   35
To day put on perfection, and a womans name.

Thy two-leav'd gates faire Temple unfold,
And thefe two in thy facred bofome hold,
   Till, myftically joyn'd, but one they bee;
Then may thy leane and hunger-ftarved wombe   40
Long time expect their bodies and their tombe,
   Long after their owne parents fatten thee.
   All elder claimes, and all cold barrenneffe,
All yeelding to new loves bee far for ever,
     Which might thefe two diffever,   45
       All wayes all th'other may each one poffeffe;
For, the beft Bride, beft worthy of praife and fame,
To day puts on perfection, and a womans name.

Oh winter dayes bring much delight,
Not for themfelves, but for they foon bring night;   50
   Other fweets wait thee then thefe diverfe meats,
Other difports then dancing jollities,
Other love tricks then glancing with the eyes,
   But that the Sun ftill in our halfe Spheare fweates;

25 Patricians,] Patricians *1633*   26 Sonns of . . . deep oceans, *Ed:*
Some of thefe Senators wealths deep oceans, *1633, A18, N, TC:* Sonnes of
thefe Senatours, wealths deep oceans *W:* Sonnes of thofe Senatours,
wealths deepe oceans, *1635–69, B, O'F, S96* (*but* Senators *O'F, S96*). *See
note*   29 thofe fellowfhips] that Fellowfhip *S96*   31 bring. *W:* bring
1633–39: bring, *1650–69*   32 ftraw'd] ftrow'd *1669*   42 thee.
1635–69: thee; *1633*   46 All wayes *W:* Alwaies, *1633:* Alwayes,
1635–69   49 Oh winter dayes *A34, B, O'F, P, S96, W:* Winter dayes
1633–69, A18, N, TC   53 eyes, *1635–69:* eyes; *1633*

Hee

   Hee flies in winter, but he now ftands ftill.   55
Yet fhadowes turne; Noone point he hath attain'd,
  His fteeds nill bee reftrain'd,
    But gallop lively downe the Wefterne hill;
Thou fhalt, when he hath runne the worlds half frame,
To night put on perfection, and a womans name.   60

The amorous evening ftarre is rofe,
Why then fhould not our amorous ftarre inclofe
  Her felfe in her wifh'd bed? Releafe your ftrings
Muficians, and dancers take fome truce
With thefe your pleafing labours, for great ufe   65
  As much wearineffe as perfection brings;
    You, and not only you, but all toyl'd beafts
Reft duly; at night all their toyles are difpenfed;
But in their beds commenced
    Are other labours, and more dainty feafts;   70
She goes a maid, who, leaft fhe turne the fame,
To night puts on perfection, and a womans name.

Thy virgins girdle now untie,
And in thy nuptiall bed (loves altar) lye
  A pleafing facrifice; now difpoffeffe   75
Thee of thefe chaines and robes which were put on
T'adorne the day, not thee; for thou, alone,
  Like vertue'and truth, art beft in nakedneffe;
    This bed is onely to virginitie
A grave, but, to a better ftate, a cradle;   80
Till now thou waft but able
    To be what now thou art; then that by thee
No more be faid, *I may bee*, but, *I am*,
To night put on perfection, and a womans name.

  55 ftill. *W:* ftill, *1633–69*   57 nill *W:* will *1633–69 and rest of MSS.: B inserts* not. *See note*   59 runne the worlds halfe frame, *A34,B,S96,W:* runne the Heavens halfe frame, *1635–69, O'F:* come the worlds half frame, *1633, A18, N, TC*   60 put] *but 1633*   72 puts] put *1669*   73 Thy virgins girdle *1633–69, W:* The Virgin Girdle *B,O'F,S96:* Thy Virgin girdle *P*   74 [loves alter] *1633–69*   76 were] wee *some copies of 1633, Grolier*   78 art] are *1669*
                                              Even

Even like a faithfull man content,   85
That this life for a better ſhould be ſpent,
  So, ſhee a mothers rich ſtile doth preferre,
And at the Bridegroomes wiſh'd approach doth lye,
Like an appointed lambe, when tenderly
    The prieſt comes on his knees t'embowell her;   90
        Now ſleep or watch with more joy; and O light
Of heaven, to morrow riſe thou hot, and early;
This Sun will love ſo dearely
        Her reſt, that long, long we ſhall want her ſight;
Wonders are wrought, for ſhee which had no maime,   95
To night puts on perfeŒion, and a womans name.

    86 ſpent, *Ed:* ſpent ; *1633:* ſpent : *1635–69*   95 maime, *1633, W :*
name, *1635–69, A18, A34, B, N, P, S96, TC*

SATYRES.

Satyre I.

AWay thou fondling motley humorift,
Leave mee, and in this ftanding woodden cheft,
Conforted with thefe few bookes, let me lye
In prifon, and here be coffin'd, when I dye;
Here are Gods conduits, grave Divines; and here   5
Natures Secretary, the Philofopher;
And jolly Statefmen, which teach how to tie
The finewes of a cities miftique bodie;
Here gathering Chroniclers, and by them ftand
Giddie fantaftique Poëts of each land.   10
Shall I leave all this conftant company,
And follow headlong, wild uncertaine thee?
Firft fweare by thy beft love in earneft
(If thou which lov'ft all, canft love any beft)
Thou wilt not leave mee in the middle ftreet,   15
Though fome more fpruce companion thou doft meet,
Not though a Captaine do come in thy way
Bright parcell gilt, with forty dead mens pay,
Not though a briske perfum'd piert Courtier
Deigne with a nod, thy courtefie to anfwer.   20

Satyre I. *1633–69, D, H49, JC, Lec, P, Q, S, W:* Satyre the Second. *or*
Satyre 2. *A25, B, O'F:* Satyre. *or* A Satyre of Mr. John Donnes. *Cy, L74,*
S96: no title (but placed first), H51, N, TCD   1 fondling *1633, L74, Lec,*
N, S, TCD: changeling *1635–69, A25, B, Cy, D, H49, H51, JC, O'F, P, Q,*
S96, W   5 conduits, ... Divines; *1650–69, Q:* conduits ; ... Divines,
1633–39   6 Is Natures Secretary, *1669, S96*   Philofopher; *Ed:*
Philofopher. *1633–39:* Philofopher : *1659–69*   7 jolly *1633, A25,*
B, Cy, D, H49, H51, JC, L74, N, Q, S, S96, TCD, W: wily *1635–69, O'F:*
with *P*   12 headlong, wild uncertaine thee? *1633:* om. comma *1635–69*
and Grolier   13 love in earneft *1633, A25, B, Cy, D, H49, H51, JC, L74,*
Lec, N, P, Q, S, S96, TCD, W: love, here, in earneft *1635–69, O'F*   16
doft meet,] doe meet. *H51, Q, W*   19 Not *1633–69, A25, Lec, P, Q:* Nor
Cy, D, H49, L74, N, O'F, S, S96, TCD, W   piert] neat *Q*

Nor

Nor come a velvet Juftice with a long
Great traine of blew coats, twelve, or fourteen ftrong,
Wilt thou grin or fawne on him, or prepare
A fpeech to Court his beautious fonne and heire!
For better or worfe take mee, or leave mee: 25
To take, and leave mee is adultery.
Oh monftrous, fuperftitious puritan,
Of refin'd manners, yet ceremoniall man,
That when thou meet'ft one, with enquiring eyes
Doft fearch, and like a needy broker prize   30
The filke, and gold he weares, and to that rate
So high or low, doft raife thy formall hat:
That wilt confort none, untill thou have knowne
What lands hee hath in hope, or of his owne,
As though all thy companions fhould make thee   35
Jointures, and marry thy deare company.
Why fhould'ft thou (that doft not onely approve,
But in ranke itchie luft, defire, and love
The nakedneffe and bareneffe to enjoy,
Of thy plumpe muddy whore, or proftitute boy)   40
Hate vertue, though fhee be naked, and bare?
At birth, and death, our bodies naked are;
And till our Soules be unapparrelled
Of bodies, they from bliffe are banifhed.
Mans firft bleft ftate was naked, when by finne   45
Hee loft that, yet hee was cloath'd but in beafts skin,

23 Wilt *1633-69, L74, Lec, N, TCD*: Shalt *A25, B, D, H49, H51, JC,*
O'F, P, Q, S, S96, W   24 heire! *Ed*: heire? *1633-69*   25 or worfe
1633-69, Cy, D, L74, Lec, N, O'F, Q, TCD: and worfe *A25, B, H49, H51,*
S96, W: or for worfe *P*: and for worfe *JC*   27 Oh monftrous,]
A (*i.e.* Ah) *or* O Monfter, *B, D, H49, H51, JC, W*   29 eyes *1635-69*:
eyes; *1633*   32 raife *1633-69, D, H49, H51, L74, Lec, N, TCD*:
vaile *A25, B, Cy, JC, O'F, P, Q, S, W*   hat:] hate: *1633*   33 confort
none,] confort with none, *Cy, O'F, P, S, S96*   untill] till *1669*   37-40
brackets 1650-69, Q: that . . . boy *1633*: that . . . boy; *1635-39*
39 bareneffe *A25, B, D, H49, H51, JC, O'F, Q, W*: barrenneffe *1633-69,*
L74, Lec, N, P, S, TCD   40 Of] of *1633*: or *1633, 1669*: om. *1635-54*
41 bare? *1635-69*: bare, *1633*   45 firft bleft *1633-69, Cy, D, H49, L74,*
Lec, N, TCD, W: firft beft *A25, B, H51, JC, O'F, P, Q, S*   46 yet *1633,*
A25, B, D, H49, H51, JC, L74, Lec, N, Q, S, TCD: om. *1635-69, Cy, O'F, P*

And

And in this courfe attire, which I now weare,
With God, and with the Mufes I conferre.
But fince thou like a contrite penitent,
Charitably warn'd of thy finnes, doft repent   50
Thefe vanities, and giddineffes, loe
I fhut my chamber doore, and come, lets goe.
But fooner may a cheape whore, who hath beene
Worne by as many feverall men in finne,
As are black feathers, or musk-colour hofe,   55
Name her childs right true father, 'mongft all thofe:
Sooner may one gueffe, who fhall beare away
The Infanta of London, Heire to an India;
And fooner may a gulling weather Spie
By drawing forth heavens Scheme tell certainly   60
What fafhioned hats, or ruffes, or fuits next yeare
Our fubtile-witted antique youths will weare;
Then thou, when thou depart'ft from mee, canft fhow
Whither, why, when, or with whom thou wouldft go.
But how fhall I be pardon'd my offence   65
That thus have finn'd againft my confcience?
Now we are in the ftreet; He firft of all
Improvidently proud, creepes to the wall,
And fo imprifoned, and hem'd in by mee
Sells for a little ftate his libertie;   70
Yet though he cannot skip forth now to greet

    47 weare, *1650-69:* weare *1633-39*   50 warn'd] warm'd *1633*
52 goe. *1635-69:* goe, *1633*   54 Worne by] Worne out by *1650-69*
55 musk-colour *1633-35, D, H49, L74, Lec, N, TCD, W:* musk-coloured
1639-69, A25, P, Q   58 The Infanta . . . India; *Ed:* The Infanta
. . . India, *A25, O'F, Q:* The infant . . . India, *1633-54 and MSS.*
generally: The Infantry of London, hence to India: *1669*   60
Scheme *1635-69, A25, B, D, H49, H51, JC, Q:* fchemes *L74, S:* fceames
N: Sceanes *1633, Cy, Lec, TCD:* fcene *P*   62 fubtile-witted *D, H49:*
fubtile wittied *1633-54, L74, N, TCD:* fupple-witted *A25, JC (altered to*
fubtle), *H51, O'F, P, Q, S, W:* giddy-headed *1669*   youths] youth *1669*
63 depart'ft from mee] depart'ft from hence *Cy, D, H49, H51, O'F, S, W:*
departeft hence *A25, Q, S96*   canft *JC, Q:* can *1633-69 and many MSS.*
66 conscience?] conscience. *1633*   70 ftate] room *H51* his *1635-69*
and all MSS.: high *1633, Chambers*   libertie;] libertie, *1633*

Every

Every fine filken painted foole we meet,
He them to him with amorous fmiles allures,
And grins, fmacks, fhrugs, and fuch an itch endures,
As prentifes, or fchoole-boyes which doe know   75
Of fome gay fport abroad, yet dare not goe.
And as fidlers ftop loweft, at higheft found,
So to the moft brave, ftoops hee nigh'ft the ground.
But to a grave man, he doth move no more
Then the wife politique horfe would heretofore,   80
Or thou O Elephant or Ape wilt doe,
When any names the King of Spaine to you.
Now leaps he upright, Joggs me, & cryes, Do you fee
Yonder well favoured youth? Which? Oh, 'tis hee
That dances fo divinely; Oh, faid I,   85
Stand ftill, muft you dance here for company?
Hee droopt, wee went, till one (which did excell
Th'Indians, in drinking his Tobacco well)
Met us; they talk'd; I whifpered, let'us goe,
'T may be you fmell him not, truely I doe;   90
He heares not mee, but, on the other fide
A many-coloured Peacock having fpide,
Leaves him and mèe; I for my loft fheep ftay;
He followes, overtakes, goes on the way,
Saying, him whom I laft left, all repute   95
For his device, in hanfoming a fute,
To judge of lace, pinke, panes, print, cut, and plight,
Of all the Court, to have the beft conceit;
Our dull Comedians want him, let him goe;

73 them] then *1633*   78 ftoops *1635–69, A25, Cy, D, H49, H51,*
O'F, Q: ftoopeth *B, P:* ftoopt *1633, L74, Lec, N, TCD*   nigh'ft the
ground.] nigheft ground. *D, H49, P, Q, W*   81–2 *om. 1633*   84
youth? *1635–69:* youth; *1633*   Oh,] Yea, *A25, B, H51, JC, Q, W*   86
here] fo *H51*   89 us ; *Ed:* us: *1635–69:* us, *1633*   whifpered, let'us goe,
Ed: whifpered, let us goe, *1633–54:* whifperd, let us goe, *1669:* whifpered
(letts goe) *Q. See note*   90 'T may be] May be *Cy, D, H49, JC, Lec,*
O'F, P, Q, S, S96, W   94 goes on the way,] goes, on the way *D, H49,*
Q(in), *W*(in)   95 all repute *1635–69 and MSS. generally:* s'all repute
1633, Lec   97 print, cut, and plight (pleite, *1635–39:* pleit, *1650–69*),
1633–69, L74, Lec, N, TCD: cut, print, or pleate (pleight *&c.*), *A25, B,*
Cy, D, H49, H51, JC, O'F, P, Q. S96, W

But

But Oh, God ſtrengthen thee, why ſtoop'ſt thou ſo?   100
Why? he hath travayld; Long? No; but to me
(Which underſtand none,) he doth ſeeme to be
Perfeᐸt French, and Italian; I replyed,
So is the Poxe; He anſwered not, but ſpy'd
More men of ſort, of parts, and qualities;   105
At laſt his Love he in a windowe ſpies,
And like light dew exhal'd, he flings from mee
Violently raviſh'd to his lechery.
Many were there, he could command no more;
Hee quarrell'd, fought, bled; and turn'd out of dore   110
    Direᐸtly came to mee hanging the head,
    And conſtantly a while muſt keepe his bed.

Satyre II.

Sir; though (I thanke God for it) I do hate
Perfeᐸtly all this towne, yet there's one ſtate
In all ill things ſo excellently beſt,
That hate, toward them, breeds pitty towards the reſt.

100 ſtoop'ſt   *1633, 1669, A25, B, D, H49, H51, JC, L74, Lec, N, P, Q,
TCD:* ſtop'ſt *1635-54, O'F*   101 Why? he hath travayld; Long?
No; but to me *S96:* Why: he hath travayld.   Long? No: but to mee
W: Why, hee hath travayl'd.   Long? no.   But to mee *H49:* Why he hath
travayld; Longe? Noe: but to mee *JC:* Why, he hath travailed (traveled
1635-39) long? no, but to me *1633-39:* Why hath he travelled long?
no, but to me *1650-54, P:* Why.   He hath travelled long; no, but to me
1669. See note   102 underſtand] underſtood *1669: brackets from Q.
See note*   105 and qualities;] of qualities; *Lec, P, Q, S96*   106
a] *om. 1669*   108 lechery. *1635-69 and MSS:* liberty; *1633*   109
were there, *1633-39:* there were, *1650-69*
    Satyre II. *1633-69, D, H49, H51, HN* (after C. B. copy *in margin*),
JC, Lec, Q, S, W: Satyre 3rd. *A25:* Law Satyre. *P:* Satire. *or no title,
B, Cy, L74, N, O'F, S96, TCD*
                                            there is one
2-3   All this towne perfeᐸtly yet in every ſtate
                In all ill things ſo excellently beſt
           There are ſome found ſo villainouſly beſt, *H51*
           All this towne perfeᐸtly yet everie ſtate
           Hath in't one found ſo villainouſly beſt *S96*
4 toward] towards *1669 and MSS.*   them,] that *A25*   towards] toward
1653-54   reſt.] reſt; *1633*
                                                            Though

Though Poëtry indeed be such a sinne   5
As I thinke that brings dearths, and Spaniards in,
Though like the Pestilence and old fashion'd love,
Ridlingly it catch men; and doth remove
Never, till it be sterv'd out; yet their state
Is poore, disarm'd, like Papists, not worth hate.   10
One, (like a wretch, which at Barre judg'd as dead,
Yet prompts him which stands next, and cannot reade,
And saves his life) gives ideot actors meanes
(Starving himselfe) to live by his labor'd sceanes;
As in some Organ, Puppits dance above   15
And bellows pant below, which them do move.
One would move Love by rithmes; but witchcrafts charms
Bring not now their old feares, nor their old harmes:
Rammes, and slings now are seely battery,
Pistolets are the best Artillerie.   20
And they who write to Lords, rewards to get,
Are they not like singers at doores for meat?
And they who write, because all write, have still
That excuse for writing, and for writing ill;
But hee is worst, who (beggarly) doth chaw   25
Others wits fruits, and in his ravenous maw
Rankly digested, doth those things out-spue,
As his owne things; and they are his owne, 'tis true,
For if one eate my meate, though it be knowne
The meate was mine, th'excrement is his owne: 30

6 As I thinke that *1633*: As I thinke That *1635–54*: As, I think,
that *1669*: As I'ame afraid brings *H51*   dearths, *A25, H51, HN, L74,*
Lec, N, TCD, W: dearth, *1633–69, D, H49*   7 and] or *A25, D, H49,*
H51, O'F, P, S96, W   8 Ridlingly it *1633–69, L74, Lec, N, TCD*: It
riddlinglie *rest of MSS.*   10 hate. *Ed*: hate: *1633–69*   12 cannot
1633–69, L74, Lec, N, TCD: could not *rest of MSS.*   14 sceanes;
Ed: sceanes. *1633–69 and Chambers*   15 Organ *1633–54, L74, Lec,*
N, TCD: Organs *1669 and rest of MSS.*   16 move. *1633–69*: move,
Chambers. See note   17 rithmes; *1633–69, Lec, Q, TCD*: rimes;
A25, B, Cy(rime), *D, H49, H51, HN, JC, L74, N, O'F, P, W*   18
harmes: *Ed*: harmes. *1633–69*   19 Rammes, and slings] Rimes and
songs *P*   22 singers at doores *1633–69, L74, Lec, N, TCD*: Boyes
singing at dore (*or* dores) *B, Cy, D, H49, H51, HN, JC, O'F*(*corrected from*
singers), *P, Q*(at a dore), *S, W*: singers at mens dores *A25*   24
excuse] scuse *MSS.*

But

But thefe do mee no harme, nor they which ufe
To out-doe Dildoes, and out-ufure Jewes;
To out-drinke the fea, to out-fweare the Letanie;
Who with finnes all kindes as familiar bee
As Confeffors; and for whofe finfull fake,   35
Schoolemen new tenements in hell muft make:
Whofe ftrange finnes, Canonifts could hardly tell
In which Commandements large receit they dwell.
But thefe punifh themfelves; the infolence
Of Cofcus onely breeds my juft offence,   40
Whom time (which rots all, and makes botches poxe,
And plodding on, muft make a calfe an oxe)
Hath made a Lawyer, which was (alas) of late
But a fcarce Poët; jollier of this ftate,
Then are new benefic'd minifters, he throwes   45
Like nets, or lime-twigs, wherefoever he goes,
His title of Barrifter, on every wench,
And wooes in language of the Pleas, and Bench:
A motion, Lady; Speake Cofcus; I have beene
In love, ever fince *tricefimo* of the Queene,   50
Continuall claimes I have made, injunctions got
To ftay my rivals fuit, that hee fhould not
Proceed; fpare mee; In Hillary terme I went,
You faid, If I return'd next fize in Lent,

32 To out-doe Dildoes, *1635-69, B, H51, L74, Lec, N, P, Q, TCD:* To
out-doe ———; *1633:* To out-fwive dildoes *Cy, D, H49, HN, O'F, S,
S96, W* 33 Letanie; *Ed:* Letanie, *1669 and all MSS.:* ———
1633: simply omit, 1635-39: gallant, he *1650-54. See note* 34 finnes
all kindes *1635-69, A25, B, D, H49, H51, HN, JC, L74, N, O'F, Q, S, TCD,
W:* finnes of all kindes *1633, Cy*(kind), *Lec, P* 35-6 fake, Schoolemen
1669: fake Schoolemen, *1633-54* 40 juft *1633-69, L74, Lec, N, TCD:*
great *A25, B, Cy, D, H49, H51, HN, O'F, P, Q, S, S96, W:* harts *JC* 43
Lawyer, *Ed:* Lawyer; *1633-69* which was (alas) of late *Ed:* which
was alas of late *1633:* which, (alas) of late *1635-69* 44 a fcarce
A25, H49, H51, HN, JC (altered in margin), L74, Q, S96, TCD, W: fcarce
a *1633-69, D, Lec, P* Poet; *1635-69:* Poët, *1633* this *1633-69:* that
A25, Cy, H51, Q: his *HN, JC, O'F, S* 49 Lady; *Ed:* Lady,
1633: Lady. *1635-39:* Lady: *1650-69* Cofcus; *1633:* Cofcus. *1635-69*
53 Proceed; *1669:* Proceed, *1633-54* 54 return'd] Returne *1633*
next fize *1633-69, L74, Lec, N, O'F, TCD:* this fize *rest of MSS.*

I fhould

I fhould be in remitter of your grace;   55
In th'interim my letters fhould take place
Of affidavits: words, words, which would teare
The tender labyrinth of a foft maids eare,
More, more, then ten Sclavonians fcolding, more
Then when winds in our ruin'd Abbeyes rore.   60
When ficke with Poëtrie, and poffeft with mufe
Thou waft, and mad, I hop'd; but men which chufe
Law practife for meere gaine, bold foule, repute
Worfe then imbrothel'd ftrumpets proftitute.
Now like an owlelike watchman, hee muft walke   65
His hand ftill at a bill, now he muft talke
Idly, like prifoners, which whole months will fweare
That onely furetifhip hath brought them there,
And to every fuitor lye in every thing,
Like a Kings favourite, yea like a King;   70
Like a wedge in a blocke, wring to the barre,
Bearing-like Affes; and more fhameleffe farre
Then carted whores, lye, to the grave Judge; for
Bastardy abounds not in Kings titles, nor
Symonie and Sodomy in Churchmens lives,   75
As thefe things do in him; by thefe he thrives.
Shortly (as the fea) hee will compaffe all our land;
From Scots, to Wight; from Mount, to Dover ftrand.
And fpying heires melting with luxurie,
Satan will not joy at their finnes, as hee.   80

58 foft maids eare, *Ed:* foft maids eare. *1633–54 and MSS.:* Maids
foft ear *1669*   59 fcolding] fcolding's *1669*   60 rore.] rore; *1633*
63 gaine, bold foule, repute *Ed:* gaine; bold foule repute *1633–69, B, Cy,*
D, H49, H51, HN, L74, P, W: gayne (bold foule) repute: *Q:* gain, bold
fouls repute *1719 and Chambers:* gayne, hold foule repute *A25, N, S, TCD,*
and Lowell's conjecture in Grolier.   See note   68 That] The *Chambers*
69–70 *These lines represented by dashes,* 1633   70 yea *A25, B, Cy, D,*
H49, H51, HN, JC, L74, Lec, N, O'F, P, Q, S, S96, TCD, W: or *1635–69*
72 Bearing-like Affes; *Ed:* Bearing like Affes, *1633–69 and MSS.*
73 whores, *1633–69:* whores; *Chambers and Grolier.   See note*   74–5
These lines represented by dashes, 1633   77 our land;] our land, *A25, B,*
Cy, D, H49, H51, HN, JC, L74, Lec, N, O'F, P, S, S96, TCD, W: the land;
1633–69, Q   79 luxurie, *1633–69, A25, JC, L74, Lec, N, O'F(corr.*
fr. Gluttony), *P, Q, TCD:* Gluttony *B, Cy, D, H49, H51, HN, S, S96, W*
80 will] would *A25, Q*

For as a thrifty wench fcrapes kitching-ftuffe,
And barrelling the droppings, and the fnuffe,
Of wafting candles, which in thirty yeare
(Relique-like kept) perchance buyes wedding geare;
Peecemeale he gets lands, and fpends as much time   85
Wringing each Acre, as men pulling prime.
In parchments then, large as his fields, hee drawes
Affurances, bigge, as glofs'd civill lawes,
So huge, that men (in our times forwardneffe)
Are Fathers of the Church for writing leffe.   90
Thefe hee writes not; nor for thefe written payes,
Therefore fpares no length; as in thofe firft dayes
When Luther was profeft, He did defire
Short *Pater nofters,* faying as a Fryer
Each day his beads, but having left thofe lawes,   95
Addes to Chrifts prayer, the Power and glory claufe.
But when he fells or changes land, he'impaires
His writings, and (unwatch'd) leaves out, *fes heires,*
As flily as any Commenter goes by
Hard words, or fenfe; or in Divinity   100
As controverters, in vouch'd Texts, leave out
Shrewd words, which might againft them cleare the doubt.
Where are thofe fpred woods which cloth'd hertofore
Thofe bought lands? not built, nor burnt within dore.
Where's th'old landlords troops, and almes? In great hals
Carthufian fafts, and fulfome Bachanalls   106

84 Relique-like *A25, B, D, H49, H51, L74, N, O'F, Q, S, S96, TCD, W*:
Reliquely *1633–69, Cy, JC, Lec, P*   geare;] chear; *1669 (which brackets
from* 81 *as to end of* 84), *Cy*   86 men] Maids *1669*   87 parchments
A25, B, Cy, D, H49, H51, JC, Q, W: parchment *1633–69, L74, Lec, N, O'F,
P, S, S96, TCD*   his] the *1669*   98 *fes 1633–69, B, L74, Lec, Q, and
other MSS.*: his *Cy, D, H49, H51, P*   heires,] heires *1633*   99 As]
And *1669*   by] by, *1633*   102 doubt.] doubt: *1633*   105 Where's
&c. Ed: Where's th'old landlords troops, and almes, great hals? *1633, Lec,
N, TCD (but* hals *MSS.*): Where the old landlords troops, and almes?
In hals *1635–69, L74, O'F:* Where the old landlords troopes and almes?
In great halls *A25, B, Cy, D, H49, H51, HN, P, Q, S, W (but the punctuation
is very irregular, and some have* 's *after* Where). *See note*

Equally

Equally I hate; meanes bleſſe; in rich mens homes
I bid kill ſome beaſts, but no Hecatombs,
None ſtarve, none ſurfet ſo; But (Oh) we allow,
Good workes as good, but out of faſhion now,   110
Like old rich wardrops; but my words none drawes
Within the vaſt reach of th'huge ſtatute lawes.

Satyre III.

K Inde pitty chokes my ſpleene; brave ſcorn forbids
Thoſe teares to iſſue which ſwell my eye-lids;
I muſt not laugh, nor weepe ſinnes, and be wiſe,
Can railing then cure theſe worne maladies?
Is not our Miſtreſſe faire Religion,   5
As worthy of all our Soules devotion,
As vertue was to the firſt blinded age?
Are not heavens joyes as valiant to aſſwage
Luſts, as earths honour was to them? Alas,
As wee do them in meanes, ſhall they ſurpaſſe   10
Us in the end, and ſhall thy fathers ſpirit
Meete blinde Philoſophers in heaven, whoſe merit
Of ſtrict life may be imputed faith, and heare
Thee, whom hee taught ſo eaſie wayes and neare

107 Equally I hate;] Equallie hate, *Q*   hate; *Ed:* hate, *1633:* hate.
1635–69   meanes blefs; *1633, A25, B, D, H49, H51, JC, L74, N, O'F, P,*
Q, TCD, W: Meane's bleſt. *1635–69, Cy, S, S96*(*altered to* is bleſt). *See note*
111 wardrops; *1633:* wardrobes. *1635–69*   112 ſtatute lawes. *1633–54*
and all MSS.: ſtatutes jawes. *1669, Chambers*
   Satyre III. *1633–69, B, D, H49, H51* (*with title* Of Religion.), *JC, Lec,*
O'F, Q, S, W: Satire the 4th. *A25, Cy:* ˌSatyre the Second. *P:* A Satire.
L74: no title, N, TCD   1 chokes] checks *1635–54:* cheeks *1669*
eye-lids; *Ed:* eye-lids, *1633–39:* eyelids. *1650–69*   3 and] but *1669*
7 to *1635–69, A25, B, Cy, D, H49, H51, JC, L74, O'F, P, Q, S, W:* in *1633,*
Lec, N, TCD   9 honour was] honours were *Cy, D, H49, S*   14 ſo
eaſie wayes and neare *1633–69, L74, Lec, N, P, TCD:* wayes eaſie and neere
A25, B, Cy, D, H49, H51, JC, Q, S, W: wayes ſo eaſy and neere *O'F*

To follow, damn'd? O if thou dar'ft, feare this;   15
This feare great courage, and high valour is.
Dar'ft thou ayd mutinous Dutch, and dar'ft thou lay
Thee in fhips woodden Sepulchers, a prey
To leaders rage, to ftormes, to fhot, to dearth?
Dar'ft thou dive feas, and dungeons of the earth?   20
Haft thou couragious fire to thaw the ice
Of frozen North difcoueries? and thrife
Colder then Salamanders, like divine
Children in th'oven, fires of Spaine, and the line,
Whofe countries limbecks to our bodies bee,   25
Canft thou for gaine beare? and muft every hee
Which cryes not, Goddeffe, to thy Miftreffe, draw,
Or eate thy poyfonous words? courage of ftraw!
O defperate coward, wilt thou feeme bold, and
To thy foes and his (who made thee to ftand   30
Sentinell in his worlds garrifon) thus yeeld,
And for forbidden warres, leave th'appointed field?
Know thy foes: The foule Devill (whom thou
Striveft to pleafe,) for hate, not love, would allow
Thee faine, his whole Realme to be quit; and as   35
The worlds all parts wither away and paffe,

15 this;]'this.*1633* 16 is.]is; *1633* 17 Dutch,and dar'ft *1633–69,L74,*
Lec,N,P,TCD: Dutch? dar'ft *A25,B,Cy,D,H49,H51,JC,O'F,Q,S,W*
22–3 difcoueries? . . Salamanders, *Ed:* difcoueries, . . Salamanders?
1633–69 28 words?] words, *1633* 31 Sentinell *1633–69,L74,*
Lec,N,P,TCD: Souldier *A25,B,Cy,D,H49,H51,JC,Q,S,W* his
1633–54: this *1669,A25,H51,P,Q* 32 forbidden *1633 and most*
MSS. forbid *1635–69,H51*
33–4   Know thy foes; the foule Devell whom thou
      Striveft to pleafe &c.
H51,Q and generally (but with varying punctuation and sometimes foe), A25,
B,Cy,D,H49,JC,O'F,P,W:
    Know thy foe, the foule devill h'is, whom thou
    Striveft to pleafe: for hate, not love, would allow
            1633, L74(is),*Lec,N*(his),*S*(is),*TCD*(his):
    Know thy foes: The foule devill, he, whom thou
    Striv'ft to pleafe, for hate, not love, would allow
            1635–69 (he, . . . pleafe, *bracketed, 1669*)
35 quit *1633–69,L74,Lec,N,P,S,TCD:* ridd *A25,B,Cy,D,H51,*
JC,O'F,Q,W

So the worlds felfe, thy other lov'd foe, is
In her decrepit wayne, and thou loving this,
Doft love a withered and worne ftrumpet; laft,
Flefh (it felfes death) and joyes which flefh can tafte,   40
Thou loveft; and thy faire goodly foule, which doth
Give this flefh power to tafte joy, thou doft loath.
Seeke true religion. O where? Mirreus
Thinking her unhous'd here, and fled from us,
Seekes her at Rome; there, becaufe hee doth know   45
That fhee was there a thoufand yeares agoe,
He loves her ragges fo, as wee here obey
The ftatecloth where the Prince fate yefterday.
Crantz to fuch brave Loves will not be inthrall'd,
But loves her onely, who at Geneva is call'd   50
Religion, plaine, fimple, fullen, yong,
Contemptuous, yet unhanfome; As among
Lecherous humors, there is one that judges
No wenches wholfome, but courfe country drudges.
Graius ftayes ftill at home here, and becaufe   55
Some Preachers, vile ambitious bauds, and lawes
Still new like fafhions, bid him thinke that fhee
Which dwels with us, is onely perfect, hee
Imbraceth her, whom his Godfathers will
Tender to him, being tender, as Wards ftill   60
Take fuch wives as their Guardians offer, or
Pay valewes. Carelefle Phrygius doth abhorre
All, becaufe all cannot be good, as one
Knowing fome women whores, dares marry none.
Graccus loves all as one, and thinkes that fo   65
As women do in divers countries goe

40 (it felfes death) *1635–69, A25, B, H51, L74, Lec, N, O'F, P, Q, TCD,
W:* (it felfe death) *1633, Cy, D, S*   42 loath.] loath ; *1633*   44 here,]
her, *1633*   45 Rome ; *Ed:* Rome, *1633–69*   47 He *1633,1669:*
And *1635–54*   her *D, H49, H51, Lec, O'F, P, S, W:* the *1633–69, L74,
N, P, TCD*   49 Crantz *W:* Crants *1633–54, A25, H51, JC, Lec, N, TCD:*
Grants *or* Grauntes *1669, L74, O'F, P:* Grant *Cy, D, H49:* Crates *Q*
52 unhanfome; *Ed:* unhanfome. *1633–69*   54 drudges.] drudges : *1633*
57 bid *or* bidd *MSS.:* bids *1633–69*   62 Prigas *H51:* Phrygas *W:*
Phrigias *A25*

In

In divers habits, yet are ſtill one kinde,
So doth, ſo is Religion; and this blind-
neſſe too much light breeds; but unmoved thou
Of force muſt one, and forc'd but one allow;   70
And the right; aske thy father which is ſhee,
Let him aske his; though truth and falſhood bee
Neare twins, yet truth a little elder is ;
Be buſie to ſeeke her, beleeve mee this,
Hee's not of none, nor worſt, that ſeekes the beſt.   75
To adore, or ſcorne an image, or proteſt,
May all be bad; doubt wiſely; in ſtrange way
To ſtand inquiring right, is not to ſtray;
To ſleepe, or runne wrong, is. On a huge hill,
Cragged, and ſteep, Truth ſtands, and hee that will   80
Reach her, about muſt, and about muſt goe;
And what the hills ſuddennes reſiſts, winne ſo ;
Yet ſtrive ſo, that before age, deaths twilight,
Thy Soule reſt, for none can worke in that night.
To will, implyes delay, therefore now doe: 85
Hard deeds, the bodies paines; hard knowledge too
The mindes indeavours reach, and myſteries
Are like the Sunne, dazling, yet plaine to all eyes.
Keepe the truth which thou haſt found; men do not ſtand
In ſo ill caſe here, that God hath with his hand   90
Sign'd Kings blanck-charters to kill whom they hate,
Nor are they Vicars, but hangmen to Fate.

67 kinde, *Ed:* kinde; *1633–69*   70 muſt . . . but *in reverse order* Q
73 is; *1633:* is. *1635–69*   74 her, *1633:* her; *1635–69*   77 wiſely;
Ed: wiſely, *1633–69, Cy, D, L74, Lec, N, O'F, S,*
TCD, W: ſtaye; *A25, B, H49, H51, JC, P, Q*   79 is. On] is: on *1633*
huge] high *B, Cy, D, H51, O'F, Q, W*   80 Cragged, *1669, L74, N, P,*
TCD: Cragg'd, *1633–54, Lec:* Ragged *A25, B, Cy, D, H49, JC, O'F, S, W:*
Ruggued *H51, Q*   81 about muſt goe ; *1633–54, O'F:* about it goe ;
1669: about goe *A25, Cy, D, H49, H51, L74, N, P, Q, W*   84 Soule
1633–69, L74, N, P, TCD: minde *rest of MSS.*   that night. *Ed:* that
night, *1633, 1669:* the night. *1635–54*   85 doe: *Ed:* doe *1633,*
Chambers and Grolier: doe. *1635–69, D, W. See note*   86 too *H51,*
S, W: ſpelt to *1633–69, many MSS.:* to (*prep.*) *Chambers*   88 eyes.]
eyes ; *1633*   90 In ſo ill (evil *H51*) caſe here, *A25, B, Cy, D, H49,*
H51, JC, L74, O'F, P, Q. S, W: here *om. 1633–69, N, TCD*

Foole

Foole and wretch, wilt thou let thy Soule be tyed
To mans lawes, by which fhe fhall not be tryed
At the laft day? Oh, will it then boot thee   95
To fay a Philip, or a Gregory,
A Harry, or a Martin taught thee this?
Is not this excufe for mere contraries,
Equally ftrong? cannot both fides fay fo?
That thou mayeft rightly obey power, her bounds know; 100
Thofe paft, her nature, and name is chang'd; to be
Then humble to her is idolatrie.
As ftreames are, Power is; thofe bleft flowers that dwell
At the rough ftreames calme head, thrive and do well,
But having left their roots, and themfelves given   105
To the ftreames tyrannous rage, alas, are driven
Through mills, and rockes, and woods, and at laft, almoft
Confum'd in going, in the fea are loft:
So perifh Soules, which more chufe mens unjuft
Power from God claym'd, then God himfelfe to truft.   110

Satyre IIII.

WEll; I may now receive, and die; My finne
Indeed is great, but I have beene in
A Purgatorie, fuch as fear'd hell is
A recreation to, and fcarfe map of this.

94 mans *1633–69, A25, L74, Lec, N, O'F, P, Q, TCD:* mens *B, Cy, D,*
H49, H51, JC, S, W not *om. 1635–54* 95 Oh, will it then boot thee *Ed:*
Will . . boot thee *1633, L74, N, P, TCD:* Or . . . boot thee *1635–69:* Oh
will it then ferve thee *A25, B, Cy, D, H49, H51, O'F(Or), Q, S, W*   97
thee] me *1669*   99 ftrong? *Ed:* ftrong *1633:* ftrong; *1635–69*
101 is] are *1669*   chang'd;] chang'd *1633*   to be *Ed:* to be, *1633–69*
102 idolatrie.] idolatrie; *1633*   103 is;] is, *1633*   104 do well
1633–69, Lec, N, P, TCD: prove well *A25, B, Cy, D, H49, H51, JC, L74,*
O'F, Q, S, W   106 alas,] alas *1633*   107 mills, and rockes, *1633,*
L74, N, P, TCD: Mils, rocks, *1635–69, and rest of MSS.*
Satyre IIII. *1633–69, B, D, H49, HN* (anno 1594 *in margin*), *JC, Lec,*
O'F, P, Q, S, W: Mr. Dunns firft Satire. *A25:* Another Satire by the fame.
J: D: *Cy* (*where it is the third*): Satyre. *S96:* no title, *L74, N, TCD* (*in*
L74 it is second, in N, TCD third in order)   2 but I *1633, A25, D, H49,*
HN, JC, L74, Lec, N, P, Q, S, W: but yet I *1635–69, Cy, O'F, S96*   4 A
recreacion to, and fcarfe *Q:* A recreation, and fcant *1633–69, and other MSS.*
                                                                                    My

My minde, neither with prides itch, nor yet hath been   5
Poyfon'd with love to fee, or to bee feene,
I had no fuit there, nor new fuite to fhew,
Yet went to Court; But as Glaze which did goe
To'a Maffe in jeft, catch'd, was faine to difburfe
The hundred markes, which is the Statutes curfe;   10
Before he fcapt, So'it pleas'd my deftinie
(Guilty of my fin of going,) to thinke me
As prone to all ill, and of good as forget-
full, as proud, as luftfull, and as much in debt,
As vaine, as witleffe, and as falfe as they   15
Which dwell at Court, for once going that way.
Therefore I fuffered this; Towards me did runne
A thing more ftrange, then on Niles flime, the Sunne
E'r bred; or all which into Noahs Arke came;
A thing, which would have pos'd Adam to name;   20
Stranger then feaven Antiquaries ftudies,
Then Africks Monfters, Guianaes rarities.
Stranger then ftrangers; One, who for a Dane,
In the Danes Maffacre had fure beene flaine,
If he had liv'd then; And without helpe dies,   25
When next the Prentifes'gainft Strangers rife.
One, whom the watch at noone lets fcarce goe by,
One, to whom, the examining Juftice fure would cry,
Sir, by your priefthood tell me what you are.
His cloths were ftrange, though coarfe; and black, though
    bare;   30

5 neither *1633–69:* nor *some MSS. and Chambers, who wrongly attributes
to 1635–39*   8 Glaze *1633*, D, H49, HN, Lec: Glare *1635–69, and rest
of MSS.*   9 To'a mafs A25, B, D, H49, HN, JC, L74, N, S, S96,
TCD, W: To Maffe *1633–69,* Cy, Q, Lec   10–11 curfe; . . . fcapt,
1633–39: curfe, . . . fcapt, *1650–69*   12 of going, *1633, 1669,* B, Cy,
D, H49, JC, L74, Lec, N, S, TCD, W: in going, *1635–54,* A25, O'F   14
as luftfull,] as om. *1635–69 and many MSS.*   16 at Court, A25, B, Cy,
D, HN, JC, L74, N, O'F, P, Q, S, S96, TCD, W: in Court, *1633–69,*
Lec   18 Niles] Nilus D, H49, L74, Lec, N, TCD   19 bred; W:
bred, *1633–69* came; W: came: *1633–69*   20 name; W: name, *1633:*
name: *1635–69*   22 rarities. W: rarities, *1633–69*   23 then
ftrangers; *1633–69,* A25, B, Cy, HN, L74, Lec, N, P, Q, TCD, W: then
ftrangeft. D, H49, JC (*corr. from* ftrangers), S

                                   Sleeveleffe

Sleeveleffe his jerkin was, and it had beene
Velvet, but'twas now (fo much ground was feene)
Become Tufftaffatie; and our children fhall
See it plaine Rafhe awhile, then nought at all.
This thing hath travail'd, and faith, fpeakes all tongues   35
And only knoweth what to all States belongs.
Made of th'Accents, and beft phrafe of all thefe,
He fpeakes no language; If ftrange meats difpleafe,
Art can deceive, or hunger force my taft,
But Pedants motley tongue, fouldiers bumbaft,   40
Mountebankes drugtongue, nor the termes of law
Are ftrong enough preparatives, to draw
Me to beare this: yet I muft be content
With his tongue, in his tongue, call'd complement:
In which he can win widdowes, and pay fcores,   45
Make men fpeake treafon, cofen fubtleft whores,
Out-flatter favorites, or outlie either
Jovius, or Surius, or both together.
He names mee, and comes to mee; I whifper, God!
How have I finn'd, that thy wraths furious rod,   50
This fellow chufeth me? He faith, Sir,
I love your judgement; Whom doe you prefer,
For the beft linguift? And I feelily
Said, that I thought Calepines Dictionarie;
Nay, but of men, moft fweet Sir; Beza then,   55
Some other Jefuites, and two reverend men
Of our two Academies, I named; There
He ftopt mee, and faid; Nay, your Apoftles were

32 ground] the ground *HN*   35 This *1633:* The *1635-69* faith,
1633-54, A25, B, Cy, D, H49, HN (fayeth), *JC, L74, Lec, O'F, P, Q, S* (faith
he), *TCD, W:* faith, *1669, Chambers and Grolier, without note*   36 be-
longs.] belongs, *1633*   37 th'Accents,] the antient, *HN:* the ancients,
(*prob. for* ancientest, *but corrected to* accents,) *L74*   38 no language;
A25, Q: one language; *1633-69, and MSS. generally*   43 beare]
hear *1669* this: *Q:* this, *1633-69*   44 With his tongue, *1669, Q:*
With his tongue: *1633-54*   47 or] and *Cy, D, H49 HN, JC, O'F, Q, W*
48 Surius,] Sleydon *O'F* (*corrected to* Surius), *Q:* Snodons, *A25. See note*
51 chufeth] chafeth *P, Q*   55 Sir; *Ed:* Sir. *1633-69*   56 Some
other *HN:* Some *1633-69 and most MSS.:* two other *S*   57 There
1633 (T *faintly printed*): here *1635-69*

Good

Good pretty linguiſts, and ſo Panurge was;
Yet a poore gentleman, all theſe may paſſe   60
By travaile. Then, as if he would have ſold
His tongue, he prais'd it, and ſuch wonders told
That I was faine to ſay, If you'had liv'd, Sir,
Time enough to have beene Interpreter
To Babells bricklayers, ſure the Tower had ſtood.   65
He adds, If of court life you knew the good,
You would leave loneneſſe. I ſaid, not alone
My loneneſſe is, but Spartanes faſhion,
To teach by painting drunkards, doth not laſt
Now; Aretines pictures have made few chaſt;   70
No more can Princes courts, though there be few
Better pictures of vice, teach me vertue;
He, like to a high ſtretcht lute ſtring ſqueakt, O Sir,
'Tis ſweet to talke of Kings. At Weſtminſter,
Said I, The man that keepes the Abbey tombes,   75
And for his price doth with who ever comes,
Of all our Harries, and our Edwards talke,
From King to King and all their kin can walke:
Your eares ſhall heare nought, but Kings; your eyes meet
Kings only; The way to it, is Kingſtreet.   80
He ſmack'd, and cry'd, He's baſe, Mechanique, coarſe,
So are all your Engliſhmen in their diſcourſe.
Are not your Frenchmen neate? Mine? as you ſee,
I have but one Frenchman, looke, hee followes mee.

59 Good pretty *1633-69:* Pretty good *Cy, O'F, Q, S, S96*   Panurge
1635-54: Panirge *1633:* Panurgus *1669 (omitting* and), *JC, O'F, Q*   60
gentleman, all *Ed:* gentleman ; All *1633-69*   60-1 paſſe By travaile.
1633-54: paſs. But travaile *1669*   62 prais'd *Ed:* praiſed *1633-69*
wonders *1635-69 and most MSS.:* words *1633, Lec, N, TCD*   67 lone-
neſſe. *1635-69, A25, B, Cy, D, H49, HN, JC, O'F, P, Q, W:*   lonelineſſe ;
1633, L74, Lec, N, TCD   68 loneneſſe *1635-69, A25, &c.:* lonelineſſe
1633, L74, &c.   faſhion, *1633:* faſhion. *1635-69*   69 laſt *1633, 1669*,
D, H49, HN, JC, L74, Lec, N, P, TCD, W: taſte *1635-54, O'F, Q* (taſt), *S,*
S96   80 Kingſtreet. *1633:* Kingsſtreet. *1635-39:* Kings ſtreet. *1650-69*
83 Mine? *1635-54 and MSS.:* Fine, *1633:* Mine, *1669*   84 French-
man, *Ed:* frenchman, *1633 and most MSS.:* Sir, *1635-69, Q:* here, *Cy*
                                                               Certes

Certes they are neatly cloth'd; I, of this minde am,   85
Your only wearing is your Grogaram.
Not fo Sir, I have more. Under this pitch
He would not flie; I chaff'd him; But as Itch
Scratch'd into fmart, and as blunt iron ground
Into an edge, hurts worfe: So, I (foole) found,   90
Croffing hurt mee; To fit my fullenneffe,
He to another key, his ftile doth addreffe,
And askes, what newes? I tell him of new playes.
He takes my hand, and as a Still, which ftaies
A Sembriefe, 'twixt each drop, he nigardly,   95
As loth to enrich mee, fo tells many a lye.
More then ten Hollensheads, or Halls, or Stowes,
Of triviall houfhold trafh he knowes; He knowes
When the Queene frown'd, or fmil'd, and he knowes what
A fubtle States-man may gather of that;   100
He knowes who loves; whom; and who by poyfon
Hafts to an Offices reverfion;
He knowes who'hath fold his land, and now doth beg
A licence, old iron, bootes, fhooes, and egge-
fhels to tranfport; Shortly boyes fhall not play   105
At fpan-counter, or blow-point, but they pay
Toll to fome Courtier; And wifer then all us,
He knowes what Ladie is not painted; Thus

     85–6 cloth'd; I, . . . Grogaram. *Ed:* cloth'd. I, . . . Grogaram; *1633:*
cloth'd. I, . . . Grogaram. *1635–69*   86 your Grogaram *1633–69, L74,
Lec, N, TCD:* this Grogaram *A25, B, Cy, D, H49, HN, JC, O'F, Q, S, W:*
the Grogaram *P*   89 ground *Ed:* grown'd *1633:* grownd *1635–69*
90 (foole)] *no bracket 1633*   92 addreffe, *N, TCD:* addreffe. *1633:*
dreffe. *1635–39, D, W:* dreffe; *1650–69*   96 lye. *D, H49, W:*
lie, *1633–69*   98 trafh he knowes; He knowes *D, H49, W:* trafh;
He knowes; He knowes *1633:* trafh. He knowes; He knowes *1635–39:*
trafh, He knowes; He knowes *1650–69*   101 loves; whom; *1633:*
loves; whom, *1635–54:* loves, whom; *1669:* loves whom; *Chambers and
Grolier*   104 and *1633–69, L74, Lec, N, S96, TCD:* or *A25, B, Cy, D,
H49, HN, JC, O'F, Q, W*   106 At blow-point or fpan-counter *A25, B, D,
H49, HN, JC, O'F, Q, S, S96, W*   they pay *Cy, D, H49, HN, Lec, N, O'F,
P, Q, S, S96, TCD, W:* fhall pay *1633–69, JC*   108 what *1633–69, Cy,
L74, Lec, N, TCD:* which *A25, B, D, H49, HN, JC, O'F, P, Q, S, W*

                                                                  He

He with home-meats tries me; I belch, fpue, fpit,
Looke pale, and fickly, like a Patient; Yet   110
He thrufts on more; And as if he'd undertooke
To fay Gallo-Belgicus without booke
Speakes of all States, and deeds, that have been fince
The Spaniards came, to the loffe of Amyens.
Like a bigge wife, at fight of loathed meat,   115
Readie to travaile: So I figh, and fweat
To heare this Makeron talke: In vaine; for yet,
Either my humour, or his owne to fit,
He like a priviledg'd fpie, whom nothing can
Difcredit, Libells now'gainft each great man.   120
He names a price for every office paid;
He faith, our warres thrive ill, becaufe delai'd;
That offices are entail'd, and that there are
Perpetuities of them, lafting as farre
As the laft day; And that great officers,   125
Doe with the Pirates fhare, and Dunkirkers.
Who wafts in meat, in clothes, in horfe, he notes;
Who loves whores, who boyes, and who goats.
I more amas'd then Circes prifoners, when
They felt themfelves turne beafts, felt my felfe then   130
Becomming Traytor, and mee thought I faw
One of our Giant Statutes ope his jaw
To fucke me in; for hearing him, I found
That as burnt venome Leachers do grow found
By giving others their foares, I might growe   135
Guilty, and he free: Therefore I did fhew

109 tries *1633, A25, D, H49, HN, L74, N, Q, TCD, W:* cloyes *1635–69,*
O'F, S: tyres *Cy, JC, P*   111 thrufts on more; *1633–69, O'F:* thrufts
more; *A25, B, D, H49, HN, JC, P, Q, W:* thrufts me more; *L74, Lec,*
N, S, TCD: thrufts me *P*   as if he'd undertooke *most MSS.:* as if
he'undertooke *1633, N, TCD:* as he'had undertooke *1635–69*   113
have] hath *1633, Lec*   117 this] his *B, L74, O'F, TCD, W*   talke:
In vaine; for *D, W, and other MSS.:* talke in vaine: For *1633, Q:* talke,
in vaine: For *1635–69*   123 entail'd, and that there *1633:* entailed, and
there *1635–54:* intailed and that there *1669*   128 whores, *Ed:* Whores,
1633–69   132 Statutes] Statues *1639*   133 in; for hearing him,
1669, N, P, TCD: in, for hearing him, *1650–54:* in, for hearing him.
1633–39, A25, D, H49, L74, O'F, S, W   134–6 (That . . . free :) *represented*
by dashes in 1633   134 venome *1635–54:* venomous *1669:* venomd *many*
MSS.

All

All fignes of loathing; But fince I am in,
I muft pay mine, and my forefathers finne
To the laft farthing; Therefore to my power
Toughly and ftubbornly I beare this crofle; But the'houre   140
Of mercy now was come; He tries to bring
Me to pay a fine to fcape his torturing,
And faies, Sir, can you fpare me; I faid, willingly;
Nay, Sir, can you fpare me a crowne? Thankfully I
Gave it, as Ranfome; But as fidlers, ftill,   145
Though they be paid to be gone, yet needs will
Thruft one more jigge upon you: fo did hee
With his long complementall thankes vexe me.
But he is gone, thankes to his needy want,
And the prerogative of my Crowne: Scant   150
His thankes were ended, when I, (which did fee
All the court fill'd with more ftrange things then hee)
Ran from thence with fuch or more haft, then one
Who feares more actions, doth make from prifon.
At home in wholefome folitarineffe   155
My precious foule began, the wretchedneffe
Of fuiters at court to mourne, and a trance
Like his, who dreamt he faw hell, did advance
It felfe on mee, Such men as he faw there,
I faw at court, and worfe, and more; Low feare   160
Becomes the guiltie, not the accufer; Then,
Shall I, nones flave, of high borne, or raif'd men
Feare frownes? And, my Miftreffe Truth, betray thee
To th'huffing braggart, puft Nobility?
No, no, Thou which fince yefterday haft beene   165
Almoft about the whole world, haft thou feene,

141 mercy now *1633–69*: my redemption *Cy, P*: redemption now *Q, S*
145 Gave] Give *Cy, D, H49*   146 Though] Thou *1635*   152
more . . then] fuch . . as *1669*   154 make *B, Cy, D, H49, HN, JC,*
L74, O'F, P, Q, S96, W: hafte *1633–69, Lec, N, S, TCD (from previous line)*:
om. *A25*   prifon.] prifon; *1633*   156 precious *1633, L74, Lec, N, TCD*:
piteous *1635–69 and reft of MSS.*   159 on *1633, Cy, L74, Lec, N, O'F,*
P, S, TCD: o'r *1635–69, A25, B, D, H49, Q, S96, W*   162 nones] none
1669   164 th'huffing braggart, *1669, A25, B, Cy, D, H49, HN, JC,*
L74, O'F, P, Q, S, S96, W (but no commas in MSS.): huffing, braggart,
1633–54, Lec, N, TCD   th'huffing, braggart, *1719*   Nobility?]
Nobility. *1633*

O Sunne,

O Sunne, in all thy journey, Vanitie,
Such as fwells the bladder of our court? I
Thinke he which made your waxen garden, and
Tranfported it from Italy to ftand   170
With us, at London, flouts our Prefence, for
Juft fuch gay painted things, which no fappe, nor
Taft have in them, ours are ; And naturall
Some of the ftocks are, their fruits, baftard all.
'Tis ten a clock and paft ; All whom the Mues,   175
Baloune, Tennis, Dyet, or the ftewes,
Had all the morning held, now the fecond
Time made ready, that day, in flocks, are found
In the Prefence, and I, (God pardon mee.)
As frefh, and fweet their Apparrells be, as bee   180
The fields they fold to buy them; For a King
Thofe hofe are, cry the flatterers; And bring
Them next weeke to the Theatre to fell;
Wants reach all ftates; Me feemes they doe as well
At ftage, as court; All are players; who e'r lookes   185
(For themfelves dare not goe) o'r Cheapfide books,
Shall finde their wardrops Inventory. Now,
The Ladies come; As Pirats, which doe know
That there came weak fhips fraught with Cutchannel,
The men board them; and praife, as they thinke, well, 190

169 your *1633–69, L74, Lec, N, TCD :* yon *A25, B, JC, O'F, Q, W :* the
Cy, D, H49, P, S, S96   170 Tranfported *1633–69, L74, Lec, N, P, Q,
TCD :* Tranfplanted *B, Cy, D, H49, JC, O'F, S, S96, W*   to ftand] to
Strand *L74* (ftand *being struck through*), *S*   171 our Prefence, *1633,
L74, Lec, N, P, TCD :* our Court here, *A25, B, Cy, D, H49, HN, JC, Q, S,
W :* our Courtiers, *1635–69, O'F*   173 are;] are, *1633*   178 are found
1633, 1669 : were found *1635–54*   179 I, (God pardon mee.) *1633 :*
I. (God pardon mee.) *1635 :* I. (God pardon me) *1639–69 :* aye—God
pardon me— *Chambers*   180 their Apparrells] th'apparells *B, Cy, D,
H49, L74, W*   182 cry the flatterers; *1633 :* cry his flatterers ; *1635–54,
P :* cryes his flatterers ; *Cy, D, H49, JC, Q, S, W :* cryes the flatterer ; *1669,
L74* (flatterers *is changed to* flatterer), *Lec* (flatterers)   185 players;]
players, *1633*   187 wardrops *1633 :* wardrobes *1635–69*   Inventory.]
Inventory ; *1633*   188 doe know *1633–69, Lec, N, Q, TCD :* did know
Cy, D, H49, HN, JC, P, S, S96, W   190 (as they think) *1669*

Their

Their beauties; they the mens wits; Both are bought.
Why good wits ne'r weare fcarlet gownes, I thought
This caufe, Thefe men, mens wits for fpeeches buy,
And women buy all reds which fcarlets die.
He call'd her beauty limetwigs, her haire net;   195
She feares her drugs ill laid, her haire loofe fet.
Would not Heraclitus laugh to fee Macrine,
From hat to fhooe, himfelfe at doore refine,
As if the Prefence were a Mofchite, and lift
His skirts and hofe, and call his clothes to fhrift,   200
Making them confeffe not only mortall
Great ftaines and holes in them; but veniall
Feathers and duft, wherewith they fornicate:
And then by *Durers* rules furvay the ftate
Of his each limbe, and with ftrings the odds trye   205
Of his neck to his legge, and waft to thighe.
So in immaculate clothes, and Symetrie
Perfect as circles, with fuch nicetie
As a young Preacher at his firft time goes
To preach, he enters, and a Lady which owes   210
Him not fo much as good will, he arrefts,
And unto her protefts protefts protefts,
So much as at Rome would ferve to have throwne
Ten Cardinalls into the Inquifition;
And whifperd by Jefu, fo often, that A   215
Purfevant would have ravifh'd him away

194 fcarlets] fcarlett *D,H49,Lec,O'F,P,Q,W*   195 call'd] calls
A25,HN,O'F,P,Q   195–6 net; . . . fet.] net. . . . fet; *1633*   198
hat] hat, *1633–54*   199 As if the Prefence . . . Mofchite, *1633–69,*
Lec(colon *1635–69*): As the Prefence . . . Mofchite, (or Mefchite,) *A25, B,*
Cy, HN, JC, L74, O'F, P, Q, W: As the Queenes Prefence . . . Mefchite,
D, H49: As if the Queenes Prefence . . . mefchite, *S*   203 fornicate:]
fornicate. *1633*   204 furvay *1633–69,N,O'F,P,Q,TCD*: furvayes *B,*
Cy, D, H49, JC, S, W   205 trye *Ed:* tryes *1633–69 and MSS.*   206
to thighe. *Ed:* to thighes. *1633–69 and MSS.:* to his thighes. *Q*   211
he arrefts, *1633–69,L74,Lec,N,TCD:* ftraight arrefts, *A25, Cy, D, H49,*
HN, O'F, P, Q, S, S96, W   215 whifperd *1633, D, H49, L74, N, TCD, W:*
whifpers *1635–69*   216 Topcliffe would have ravifh'd him quite away
JC, O'F, Q (*JC* and *O'F* alter *to* Purfevant)

For

For ſaying of our Ladies pſalter; But'tis fit
That they each other plague, they merit it.
But here comes Glorius that will plague them both,
Who, in the other extreme, only doth   220
Call a rough careleſſeneſſe, good faſhion;
Whoſe cloak his ſpurres teare; whom he ſpits on
He cares not, His ill words doe no harme
To him; he ruſheth in, as if arme, arme,
He meant to crie; And though his face be as ill   225
As theirs which in old hangings whip Chriſt, ſtill
He ſtrives to looke worſe, he keepes all in awe;
Jeaſts like a licenc'd foole, commands like law.
Tyr'd, now I leave this place, and but pleas'd ſo
As men which from gaoles to'execution goe,   230
Goe through the great chamber (why is it hung
With the ſeaven deadly ſinnes?). Being among
Thoſe Askaparts, men big enough to throw
Charing Croſſe for a barre, men that doe know
No token of worth, but Queenes man, and fine   235
Living, barrells of beefe, flaggons of wine;
I ſhooke like a ſpyed Spie. Preachers which are
Seas of Wit and Arts, you can, then dare,
Drowne the ſinnes of this place, for, for mee
Which am but a ſcarce brooke, it enough ſhall bee   240

217 of *om.* Cy,D,H49,HN,JC,P,Q,S,W   222 whom *1633,A25,B,D,*
H49,L74,N, P, Q, S, S96,TCD,W: or whom *1635–69, O'F*   223 He
cares not, His *1633 and MSS.:* He cares not hee. His *1635–69*   224
ruſheth] ruſhes *1639–69*   226 ſtill *1635–69, Q, and other MSS.:* yet
ſtill *1633,L74,N,TCD*   229 I leave] Ile leave *B,Cy, D,H49,W*
230 men which from *A25,B,Cy, D,H49,HN, JC,L74,Lec,N,O'F,P,*
Q,S, S96,TCD,W: men from *1633–69*   232 ſinnes?). Being *Ed:*
ſinnes) being *1633–39:* ſinnes?) being *1650–69: all the editions and some*
MSS. close the sentence at 236 wine.   236 Living barrells of beefe,
flaggons of wine. *1633–54:* Living, barrels of beef, and flaggons of wine.
1669   237 Spie.] Spie; *1633*   238 Seas of Wit and Arts, *B,Cy,*
L74,N,P,Q,TCD: Seas of Wits and Arts, *1633,D,H49,JC,Lec,S:* Seas
of witt and art, *A25,HN:* Great ſeas of witt and art, *O'F,S96:* Seas of
all Wits and Arts, *conj. Lowell*   239 Drowne] To drowne *O'F,S96*
240 Which] Who *MSS.*   am but a ſcarce brooke, *1633,L74,Lec,N,TCD:*
am but a ſcant brooke, *1635–69:* am a ſcant brooke, *B,HN,JC,O'F,P,Q,*
W: am a ſhallow brooke, *Cy,D,H49,S,S96*

To

To wafh the ftaines away; Although I yet
With *Macchabees* modeftie, the knowne merit
Of my worke leflen: yet fome wife man fhall,
I hope, efteeme my writs Canonicall.

Satyre V.

THou fhalt not laugh in this leafe, Mufe, nor they
 Whom any pitty warmes; He which did lay
Rules to make Courtiers, (hee being underftood
May make good Courtiers, but who Courtiers good?)
Frees from the fting of jefts all who in extreme   5
Are wreched or wicked: of thefe two a theame
Charity and liberty give me. What is hee
Who Officers rage, and Suiters mifery
Can write, and jeft? If all things be in all,
As I thinke, fince all, which were, are, and fhall   10
Bee, be made of the fame elements:
Each thing, each thing implyes or reprefents.
Then man is a world; in which, Officers
Are the vaft ravifhing feas; and Suiters,
Springs; now full, now fhallow, now drye; which, to   15
That which drownes them, run: Thefe felfe reafons do
Prove the world a man, in which, officers
Are the devouring ftomacke, and Suiters
The excrements, which they voyd. All men are duft;
How much worfe are Suiters, who to mens luft   20

 241 the *1633–69*: their *A25,B,Cy,D,HN,JC,O'F,Q,S,W*: thefe *L74,*
N,TCD   Although] though *1633 and MSS*.   242 the knowne merit
1633–69, JC, Lec, N, O'F, Q, TCD: known *om. B, Cy, D, H49, HN, L74,*
P, S, W   243 wife man] wife men *1650–69, B, HN, L74, P, TCD, W*
 Satyre V. *1633–69, A25, B, D, JC, Lec, O'F, Q, S, W*: Satyre the third.
P: no title, L74, N, TCD (in L74 it is third, in N, TCD fourth in order)
1 fhalt] fhal *1669*   9 and] in *1669*   12 implyes *1635–69: spelt* employes
1633 and some MSS. reprefents. *1635–69*: reprefents, *1633*   13 Officers]
Officers, *1633–69*   14 ravifhing *1633–69*: ravenous *Q*: ravening *P, S*
19 voyd. All *1669*: voyd; all *1633–54*   duft; *W*: duft, *1633–69*

                     Are

Are made preyes? O worfe then duft, or wormes meat,
For they do eate you now, whofe felves wormes fhall eate.
They are the mills which grinde you, yet you are
The winde which drives them; and a waftfull warre
Is fought againft you, and you fight it; they   25
Adulterate lawe, and you prepare their way
Like wittals; th'iffue your owne ruine is.
Greateft and faireft Empreffe, know you this?
Alas, no more then Thames calme head doth know
Whofe meades her armes drowne, or whofe corne o'rflow: 30
You Sir, whofe righteoufnes fhe loves, whom I
By having leave to ferve, am moft richly
For fervice paid, authoriz'd, now beginne
To know and weed out this enormous finne.
O Age of rufty iron! Some better wit   35
Call it fome worfe name, if ought equall it;
The iron Age *that* was, when juftice was fold; now
Injuftice is fold dearer farre. Allow
All demands, fees, and duties, gamfters, anon
The mony which you fweat, and fweare for, is-gon   40
Into other hands: So controverted lands
Scape, like Angelica, the ftrivers hands.
If Law be in the Judges heart, and hee
Have no heart to refift letter, or fee,
Where wilt thou appeale? powre of the Courts below   45
Flow from the firft maine head, and thefe can throw

21 preyes? *1669*: preyes. *1633–54*   26 their *1633, D, L74, Lec, N,*
S, TCD, W: the *1635–69, O'F, P, Q*   27 wittals; *W*: wittals, *1633–69*
is.] is; *1633*   33 authoriz'd, *1635–54*: authorized, *1633*: authoriz'd. *1669*
35–6 Some ... equall it;] *in brackets 1635–54*
37–9 The iron Age *that* was, when juftice was fold, now
     Injuftice is fold deerer farre; allow
     All demands, fees, and duties; gamfters, anon   *1633, D, JC* (All
        claym'd fees), *Lec, N, Q* (All claym'd fees), *TCD, W* (All
        claym'd fees):
     The iron Age *that* was, when juftice was fold (now
     Injuftice is fold dearer) did allow
     All claim'd fees and duties. Gamefters, anon *1635–54, B, O'F, P* (*the
        last two omit* that was), *Chambers* (*no italics*):
     The iron Age was, when juftice was fold, now
     Injuftice is fold dearer far, allow
     All claim'd fees and duties, Gamefters, anon *1669*
46 Flow] Flows *O'F, Chambers. See note*   Thee,

Thee, if they fucke thee in, to mifery,
To fetters, halters; But if the injury
Steele thee to dare complaine, Alas, thou go'ft
Againft the ftream, when upwards: when thou art moft 50
Heavy and moft faint; and in thefe labours they,
'Gainft whom thou fhould'ft complaine, will in the way
Become great feas, o'r which, when thou fhalt bee
Forc'd to make golden bridges, thou fhalt fee
That all thy gold was drown'd in them before;   55
All things follow their like, only who have may have more.
Judges are Gods; he who made and faid them fo,
Meant not that men fhould be forc'd to them to goe,
By meanes of Angels; When fupplications
We fend to God, to Dominations,   60
Powers, Cherubins, and all heavens Courts, if wee
Should pay fees as here, Daily bread would be
Scarce to Kings; fo 'tis. Would it not anger
A Stoicke, a coward, yea a Martyr,
To fee a Purfivant come in, and call   65
All his cloathes, Copes; Bookes, Primers; and all
His Plate, Challices; and miftake them away,
And aske a fee for comming? Oh, ne'r may
Faire lawes white reverend name be ftrumpeted,
To warrant thefts: fhe is eftablifhed   70
Recorder to Deftiny, on earth, and fhee
Speakes Fates words, and but tells us who muft bee
Rich, who poore, who in chaires, who in jayles:
Shee is all faire, but yet hath foule long nailes,

    49 complaine,] complaine; *1633*   go'ft] goeft *1633–39*   50 when
upwards: *1633–54,A25,B,D,JC,L74,Lec,N,O'F,P,Q,S,TCD,W:* up-
wards, *1669, Chambers*   52 the *1633:* thy *1635–69*   56 only who have]
only, who have, *1633*   more.] more *1633*   57 he . . . fo, *1633–54:*
and he who made them fo, *1669:* he . . and cal'd (*changed to* ftil'd) them fo,
O'F   58 that] *om. 1669*   59 fupplications] fupplication *1635–54*
61 Courts, *1635–69, B, JC, L74, O'F, P, Q, W:* Court, *1633, D, Lec, N,*
S, TCD   63 'tis. Would *1669:* 'tis, would *1633:* 'tis; Would *1635–54*
68 aske *1669, A25, B, D, JC, L74, N, O'F, P, Q, S, W:* lack *1633–54, Lec*
comming?] comming; *1633*   72 Speakes Fates words, and but tells us
&c. *Q, W, Chambers:* Speakes Fates words, and tells who muft bee *1633–69*
                                                      With

With which fhe fcracheth Suiters; In bodies   75
Of men, fo in law, nailes are th'extremities,
So Officers ftretch to more then Law can doe,
As our nailes reach what no elfe part comes to.
Why bareft thou to yon Officer? Foole, Hath hee
Got thofe goods, for which erft men bar'd to thee?   80
Foole, twice, thrice, thou haft bought wrong, and now hungerly
Beg'ft right; But that dole comes not till thefe dye.
Thou had'ft much, and lawes Urim and Thummim trie
Thou wouldft for more; and for all haft paper
Enough to cloath all the great Carricks Pepper.   85
Sell that, and by that thou much more fhalt leefe,
Then Haman, when he fold his Antiquities.
O wretch that thy fortunes fhould moralize
Efops fables, and make tales, prophefies.
Thou'art the fwimming dog whom fhadows cofened,   90
And div'ft, neare drowning, for what's vanifhed.

76 men,] men; *1633*   th'extremities, *A25, B, D, JC, L74, Lec, N, O'F,*
P, Q, S, TCD, W: extremities, *1633:* extremities. *1635-69*   78 comes to.]
can come to. *Q*   80 which erft men bar'd *1635-69, B, O'F, Q, S, W:*
which men bared *1633, D, Lec, N, TCD:* which men erft bar'd *A25, L74, P*
85 great] *om. Q*   Carricks *1633-35:* Charricks *1639-69*   87 Haman,
1633: Hammon, *1635-69, P: MSS. generally vary between* Haman *and*
Hammond   when *1633, 1669, D, L74, Lec, N, P, TCD:* if *1635-54, A25,*
B, JC, O'F, Q, S   90 Thou'art *Ed:* Thou art *1633-69*   cofened,]
cozeneth, *1669*   91 And *1633:* Which *1635-69:* Whoe *Q*   div'ft,
1633-54, N, P, S, TCD: div'ft *1669:* div'dft *D, L74, Lec (altered from*
div'ft), *W:* div'd *A25, B, JC, O'F, S (Grosart), Q*   what's vanifhed. *N:*
what vanifhed. *1633-54 and rest of MSS.:* what vanifheth. *1669*

Vpon Mr. Thomas Coryats Crudities.

OH to what height will love of greatneſſe drive
Thy leavened ſpirit, *Seſqui-ſuperlative?*
Venice vaſt lake thou hadſt ſeen, and would ſeek than
Some vaſter thing, and found'ſt a Curtizan.
That inland Sea having diſcovered well,					5
A Cellar gulfe, where one might ſaile to hell
From Heydelberg, thou longdſt to ſee: And thou
This Booke, greater then all, produceſt now.
Infinite worke, which doth ſo far extend,
That none can ſtudy it to any end.					10
'Tis no one thing, it is not fruit nor roote;
Nor poorely limited with head or foot.
If man be therefore man, becauſe he can
Reaſon, and laugh, thy booke doth halfe make man.
One halfe being made, thy modeſtie was ſuch,					15
That thou on th'other half wouldſt never touch.
When wilt thou be at full, great Lunatique?
Not till thou exceed the world? Canſt thou be like
A proſperous noſe-borne wenne, which ſometimes growes
To be farre greater then the Mother-noſe?					20
Goe then; and as to thee, when thou didſt go,
Munſter did Townes, and *Geſner* Authors ſhow,
Mount now to *Gallo-belgicus*; appear
As deepe a States-man, as a Gazettier.
Homely and familiarly, when thou com'ſt back,					25
Talke of *Will. Conquerour*, and *Preſter Iack.*
Go baſhfull man, leſt here thou bluſh to looke
Vpon the progreſſe of thy glorious booke,
To which both Indies ſacrifices ſend;
The Weſt ſent gold, which thou didſt freely ſpend,					30

Vpon Mr. *&c. 1649, where it was placed with* The Token (*p. 72*),
at the end of the Funerall Elegies*: appeared originally in* Coryats Crudities
(*1611: see note*) *with heading* Incipit Joannes Donne.   2 leavened
1611: learned *1649-69 and mod. edd.*   7 longdſt *1611:* long'ſt
1649-69   19 ſometimes] ſometime *1611*   24 Gazettier. *1611:*
Garretteir *1649-69*   28 booke,] booke. *1611*

(Meaning

(Meaning to fee't no more) upon the preffe.
The Eaft fends hither her delicioufneffe;
And thy leaves muft imbrace what comes from thence,
The Myrrhe, the Pepper, and the Frankincenfe.
This magnifies thy leaves; but if they ftoope   35
To neighbour wares, when Merchants do unhoope
Voluminous barrels; if thy leaves do then
Convey thefe wares in parcels unto men;
If for vaft Tons of Currans, and of Figs,
Of Medicinall and Aromatique twigs,   40
Thy leaves a better method do provide,
Divide to pounds, and ounces fub-divide;
If they ftoope lower yet, and vent our wares,
Home-*manufactures*, to thick popular Faires,
If *omni-praegnant* there, upon warme ftalls,   45
They hatch all wares for which the buyer calls;
Then thus thy leaves we juftly may commend,
That they all kinde of matter comprehend.
Thus thou, by means which th'Ancients never took,
A Pandect makeft, and Vniversall Booke.   50
The braveft Heroes, for publike good,
Scattered in divers Lands their limbs and blood.
Worft malefactors, to whom men are prize,
Do publike good, cut in Anatomies;
So will thy booke in peeces; for a Lord   55
Which cafts at Portefcues, and all the board,
Provide whole books; each leafe enough will be
For friends to paffe time, and keep company.
Can all caroufe up thee? no, thou muft fit
Meafures; and fill out for the half-pint wit: 60
Some fhall wrap pils, and fave a friends life fo,
Some fhall ftop mufkets, and fo kill a foe.
Thou fhalt not eafe the Criticks of next age
So much, at once their hunger to affwage:
Nor fhall wit-pirats hope to finde thee lye   65
All in one bottome, in one Librarie.

37 barrels; *1649-69:* barrels, *1611*   56 board, *1611:* board *1649-69*

Some Leaves may paste strings there in other books,
And so one may, which on another looks,
Pilfer, alas, a little wit from you;
But hardly* much; and yet I think this true;
As *Sibyls* was, your booke is mysticall,
For every peece is as much worth as all.
Therefore mine impotency I confesse,
The healths which my braine bears must be far lesse:
Thy Gyant-wit'orethrowes me, I am gone;
And rather then read all, I would reade none.

> * I meane 70
> from one
> page which
> shall paste
> strings in a
> booke.[1]

> 75

I. D.

In eundem Macaronicon.

Quot, dos haec, Linguists *perfetti, Disticha* fairont,
Tot cuerdos States=men, *hic* livre fara *tuus.*
Es *sat* a my l'honneur estre hic inteso; Car J leave
L'honra, de personne nestre creduto, *tibi.*

Explicit Joannes Donne.

---

[1] I meane *&c. side-note in 1611*
In eundem *&c. 1611, concluding the above*

Viri seraphici Joannis Donne Qua =
dragenarij Effigies vera, Qui post
eam ætatem Sacris initiatus Ec=
clesiæ Sti Pauli Decanus obijt.
Anō { Dōm 1631°
       Ætatis suæ 59°

Lombart Sculp Londre

JOHN DONNE, 1613

From the engraving prefixed to his son's edition of the
Letters to Several Persons of Honour 1651, 1654

LETTERS

TO SEVERALL PERSONAGES.

THE STORME.

To Mr. *Chriſtopher Brooke.*

THou which art I, ('tis nothing to be foe)
  Thou which art ſtill thy ſelfe, by theſe ſhalt know
Part of our paſſage; And, a hand, or eye
By *Hilliard* drawne, is worth an hiſtory,
By a worſe painter made; and (without pride)   5
When by thy judgment they are dignifi'd,
My lines are ſuch: 'Tis the preheminence
Of friendſhip onely to'impute excellence.
England to whom we'owe, what we be, and have,
Sad that her ſonnes did ſeeke a forraine grave   10
(For, Fates, or Fortunes drifts none can ſoothſay,
Honour and miſery have one face and way.)
From out her pregnant intrailes ſigh'd a winde
Which at th'ayres middle marble roome did finde
Such ſtrong reſiſtance, that it ſelfe it threw   15
Downeward againe; and ſo when it did view
How in the port, our fleet deare time did leeſe,
Withering like priſoners, which lye but for fees,
Mildly it kiſt our ſailes, and, freſh and ſweet,
As to a ſtomack ſterv'd, whoſe inſides meete,   20
Meate comes, it came; and ſwole our ſailes, when wee
So joyd, as *Sara*'her ſwelling joy'd to ſee.

  The Storme. To Mr. Chriſtopher Brooke. *1633* (*1635–69 add* from
the Iland voyage with the Earle of Essex)*:* The Storme, A Storme *or*
Storme; *A25,B,Cy,D,H49,HN,JC,L74,Lec,N,O'F,P,Q,S,TCD,W:*
some add To Mr. C: B: *or a longer note to the same effect as 1635–69:* to
Sr Baſil Brooke *JC,S*   2 theſe *1633 and most MSS.:* this *1635–69,*
O'F,S   4 an *1633:* a *1635–69*   7 ſuch: *Ed:* ſuch. *1633–69*   11
ſoothſay, *1650–54: spelt* Southſay *1633–39:* gainſay *1669*   12 and
way. *1633,1669:* one way. *1635–54*   18 lye] laie *Q*   19
freſh *W:* freſh, *1633–69*   20 As *W:* As, *1633–69*

                                          But

But 'twas but fo kinde, as our countrimen,
Which bring friends one dayes way, and leave them then.
Then like two mighty Kings, which dwelling farre   25
Afunder, meet againft a third to warre,
The South and Weft winds joyn'd, and, as they blew,
Waves like a rowling trench before them threw.
Sooner then you read this line, did the gale,
Like fhot, not fear'd till felt, our failes affaile;   30
And what at firft was call'd a guft, the fame
Hath now a ftormes, anon a tempefts name.
Ionas, I pitty thee, and curfe thofe men,
Who when the ftorm rag'd moft, did wake thee then;
Sleepe is paines eafieft falue, and doth fullfill   35
All offices of death, except to kill.
But when I wakt, I faw, that I faw not;
I, and the Sunne, which fhould teach mee'had forgot
Eaft, Weft, Day, Night, and I could onely fay,
If 'the world had lafted, now it had beene day.   40
Thoufands our noyfes were, yet wee'mongft all
Could none by his right name, but thunder call:
Lightning was all our light, and it rain'd more
Then if the Sunne had drunke the fea before.
Some coffin'd in their cabbins lye,'equally   45
Griev'd that they are not dead, and yet muft dye;
And as fin-burd'ned foules from graves will creepe,
At the laft day, fome forth their cabbins peepe:
And tremblingly'aske what newes, and doe heare fo,
Like jealous hufbands, what they would not know.   50

23 'twas *1650–69*: 'twas, *1633–39*   30 fear'd] fear'd, *1633*   37
not; *Ed*: not. *1633–69*   38 I, and the Sunne, *1633–69 and most MSS.*:
yea, and the Sunne, *Q*   39 Day, Night, *D, W*: day, night, *1633–69*
could onely fay *1633–69*: could but fay *Cy, HN, JC, L74, Q, N, S, TCD, W*:
could then but fay *O'F*: could fay *H49, Lec*: should say *D*   40 lafted,
now *1633, 1669*: lafted, yet *1635–54*: Lafted yet, *O'F*   42 his] this *1669*
44 before.] before; *1633*   46 dye; *Ed*: dye. *1633–69*   47 graves *1669*,
A25, B, D, H49, JC, L74, Lec, N, O'F, P, S, TCD, W: grave *1633–54, Cy*
49 tremblingly *1633, A25, D, H49, HN, L74, Lec, N, TCD, W*: trembling
1635–69, Cy, JC, O'F, P, S   50 Like *1633, D, H49, HN, JC, L74, Lec,*
N, TCD, W: As *1635–69*

Some

Some fitting on the hatches, would feeme there,
With hideous gazing to feare away feare.
Then note they the fhips ficknesses, the Maft
Shak'd with this ague, and the Hold and Waft
With a falt dropfie clog'd, and all our tacklings   55
Snapping, like too-high-ftretched treble ftrings.
And from our totterd failes, ragges drop downe fo,
As from one hang'd in chaines, a yeare agoe.
Even our Ordinance plac'd for our defence,
Strive to breake loofe, and fcape away from thence.   60
Pumping hath tir'd our men, and what's the gaine?
Seas into feas throwne, we fuck in againe;
Hearing hath deaf'd our faylers; and if they
Knew how to heare, there's none knowes what to fay.
Compar'd to thefe ftormes, death is but a qualme,   65
Hell fomewhat lightfome, and the'Bermuda calme.
Darkneffe, lights elder brother, his birth-right
Claims o'r this world, and to heaven hath chas'd light.
All things are one, and that one none can be,
Since all formes, uniforme deformity   70
Doth cover, fo that wee, except God fay
Another *Fiat*, fhall have no more day.
So violent, yet long thefe furies bee,
That though thine abfence fterve me,'I wifh not thee.

53 Then] There *1669*   54 this] an *1635–69*   56 too-high-ftretched
1633, A25, Cy, D, H49, JC, L74, Lec, N, P, S, TCD, W (*MS. spelling generally
to and* ftretcht): too-too-high-ftretch'd *1635–54:* to too-high-ftretch'd *1669,
B, O'F*   59 Even our Ordinance *1633 and MSS.:* Yea even our Ordinance
1635–69   60 Strive *1633, D, H49, HN, JC, L74, Lec, S, TCD, W:* Strives
1635–69, Chambers: Striv'd *A25, B, Cy*   66 Hell] Hell's *S*   lightfome]
light *B, Cy*   and the'Bermuda *1633, D, H49, L74, Lec, N, TCD, W:* and the
Bermudas *B, Cy, HN, P, S, Q:* the Bermudas *1635–54 O'F:* the *Bermuda's
1669*   67 elder *A25, Cy, D, H49, HN, JC, L74, N, O'F, P, Q, S, TCD, W:*
eldeft *1633–69, B, Lec*   68 Claims *1635–69 and MSS.:* Claim'd *1633*
this *1633, D, H49, HN, L74, Lec, N, TCD:* the *1635–69, A25, B, Cy, O'F,
P, Q, S*

THE

THE CALME.

OUr ftorme is paft, and that ftorms tyrannous rage,
A ftupid calme, but nothing it, doth fwage.
The fable is inverted, and farre more
A blocke afflicts, now, then a ftorke before.
Stormes chafe, and foone weare out themfelves, or us;   5
In calmes, Heaven laughs to fee us languifh thus.
As fteady'as I can wifh, that my thoughts were,
Smooth as thy miftreffe glaffe, or what fhines there,
The fea is now. And, as the Iles which wee
Seeke, when wee can move, our fhips rooted bee.   10
As water did in ftormes, now pitch runs out:
As lead, when a fir'd Church becomes one fpout.
And all our beauty, and our trimme, decayes,
Like courts removing, or like ended playes.
The fighting place now feamens ragges fupply;   15
And all the tackling is a frippery.
No ufe of lanthornes; and in one place lay
Feathers and duft, to day and yefterday.
Earths hollowneffes, which the worlds lungs are,
Have no more winde then the upper valt of aire.   20
We can nor loft friends, nor fought foes recover,
But meteorlike, fave that wee move not, hover.
Onely the Calenture together drawes
Deare friends, which meet dead in great fifhes jawes:
And on the hatches as on Altars lyes   25
Each one, his owne Prieft, and owne Sacrifice.
Who live, that miracle do multiply

The Calme. *1633–69: similarly,* A25, B, Cy, D, H49, HN, JC, L74, Lec,
N, O'F, P, Q, S, TCD   4 ftorke] ftroke *1639*   7 can wifh, that my
1633, A25, Cy, D, H49, JC, L74, Lec, N, P, S, TCD: could wifh that my
Q: could wifh my *1635–69, Chambers, who makes no note of 1633 reading*
9 the Iles *1633–69:* thefe ifles D, H49, Lec, Chambers (*no note*): thofe
Iles B, Cy, HN, JC, L74, N, P, Q, TCD   11 out: *1635–69:* out *1633*
14 ended] ending *1669*   15 ragges] rage *1669*   17 No] Now *1669*
21 loft] lefte Cy, D, H49, L74, Lec, N, P, TCD   24 jawes: *1633,* A25,
B, D, H49, HN, JC, L74, Lec, N, Q, S, TCD: mawes, *1635–69,* O'F, P,
Chambers

Where

Where walkers in hot Ovens, doe not dye.
If in defpite of thefe, wee fwimme, that hath
No more refrefhing, then our brimftone Bath,   30
But from the fea, into the fhip we turne,
Like parboyl'd wretches, on the coales to burne.
Like *Bajazet* encag'd, the fhepheards fcoffe,
Or like flacke finew'd *Sampfon*, his haire off,
Languifh our fhips. Now, as a Miriade   35
Of Ants, durft th'Emperours lov'd fnake invade,
The crawling Gallies, Sea-goales, finny chips,
Might brave our Pinnaces, now bed-ridde fhips.
Whether a rotten ftate, and hope of gaine,
Or to difufe mee from the queafie paine   40
Of being belov'd, and loving, or the thirft
Of honour, or faire death, out pufht mee firft,
I lofe my end: for here as well as I
A defperate may live, and a coward die.
Stagge, dogge, and all which from, or towards flies,   45
Is paid with life, or pray, or doing dyes.
Fate grudges us all, and doth fubtly lay
A fcourge,'gainft which wee all forget to pray,
He that at fea prayes for more winde, as well
Under the poles may begge cold, heat in hell.   50
What are wee then? How little more alas
Is man now, then before he was? he was

29 thefe,] this, *L74, Q, TCD*   30 our *1633, B, D, H49, HN, JC, L74,*
Lec, N, S, TCD: a *1635–69, A25, P*   33 fhepheards *1650–69:* fheepheards
1633–39   37 Sea-goales, (*or* gayles *&c.*) *1633, 1669, Cy, D, H49, HN,*
L74, Lec, N, P, S, TCD: Sea-gulls, *1635–54, O'F, Chambers:* Sea-fnayles,
B, JC   38 our Pinnaces, now *1635–54, B, O'F:* our venices, now *1633,*
A25, Cy, D, H49, JC, L74, Lec, N, P, Q, S, TCD: with *Vinice's,* our *1669*
40 Or] Or, *1633–69*   44 and a coward *1633, MSS.:* and coward
1635–69: a coward *P, S*   45 and all] and each *B, Q, S*   48 forget
1633–54, D, H49, Lec, P, S: forgot *1669, A25, HN, JC, L74, N, Q, TCD*
50 poles] pole *JC, Q*   52–3 he was? he was Nothing; for us, wee are
for nothing fit; *1633, N, P, S, TCD* (*but MSS. have no stop after* Nothing):
he was, he was? Nothing; for us, wee are for nothing fit; *1635–54:* he
was, he was? Nothing for us, we are for nothing fit; *1669, A25, B, Cy, D,*
H49, HN, JC, L74, Lec, O'F, Q: but *the MSS. have not all got a mark of*
interrogation or other stop after second he was. *See note*

Nothing;

Nothing; for us, wee are for nothing fit;
Chance, or our felves ftill difproportion it.
Wee have no power, no will, no fenfe; I lye,   55
I fhould not then thus feele this miferie.

To Sr *Henry Wotton.*

SIr, more then kiffes, letters mingle Soules;
For, thus friends abfent fpeake. This eafe controules
The tedioufneffe of my life: But for thefe
I could ideate nothing, which could pleafe,
But I fhould wither in one day, and paffe   5
To'a bottle'of Hay, that am a locke of Graffe.
Life is a voyage, and in our lifes wayes
Countries, Courts, Towns are Rockes, or Remoraes;
They breake or ftop all fhips, yet our ftate's fuch,
That though then pitch they ftaine worfe, wee muft touch. 10
If in the furnace of the even line,
Or under th'adverfe icy poles thou pine,
Thou know'ft two temperate Regions girded in,
Dwell there: But Oh, what refuge canft thou winne
Parch'd in the Court, and in the country frozen?   15
Shall cities, built of both extremes, be chofen?
Can dung and garlike be'a perfume? or can
A Scorpion and Torpedo cure a man?

To Sr Henry Wotton. *1633–69* (Sir *1669*): *same or no title,* A18, A25,
Cy, D, H49, JC, Lec, N, O'F, P, S, S96, TCC, TCD: To Mr H. W. B, W
(B *adds* J. D.). *See note*   4 I could invent nothing at all to pleafe,
1669   6 bottle] botle *1633* To a lock of hay, that am a Bottle of
grafs. *1669*   7 lifes *1633:* lives *1635–69*   10 though . . . worfe, *in
brackets 1650–69*   11 even *1669,* A18, A25, B, Cy, D, H49, HN, JC, Lec,
N, O'F, S96, TC, W: raging *1633–54:* other P: over S   12 poles A25,
B, Cy, D, H49, JC, Lec, P, O'F, S, W: pole *1633–69,* A18, HN, N, TC   16
cities, . . . extremes, *Ed:* cities . . . extremes *1633–69*   17 dung and
garlike *1633,* A18, B, D, H49, JC, Lec, N, TC, W (dung, *1633*): dung, or gar-
like *1635–69,* A25, Cy, O'F, P, S   a perfume] a *om. 1635–54, Chambers*   18
Scorpion *Ed:* Scorpion, *1633–69*   and Torpedo A18, D, H49, N, TC, W:
or Torpedo *1633–69,* A25, B, Cy, JC, Lec, O'F, P, S. *See note*

Cities

Cities are worſt of all three; of all three
(O knottie riddle) each is worſt equally.   20
Cities are Sepulchers; they who dwell there
Are carcaſes, as if no ſuch there were.
And Courts are Theaters, where ſome men play
Princes, ſome ſlaves, all to one end, and of one clay.
The Country is a deſert, where no good,   25
Gain'd (as habits, not borne,) is underſtood.
There men become beaſts, and prone to more evils;
In cities blockes, and in a lewd court, devills.
As in the firſt Chaos confuſedly
Each elements qualities were in the'other three;   30
So pride, luſt, covetize, being ſeverall
To theſe three places, yet all are in all,
And mingled thus, their iſſue inceſtuous.
Falſhood is denizon'd. Virtue is barbarous.
Let no man ſay there, Virtues flintie wall   35
Shall locke vice in mee, I'll do none, but know all.
Men are ſpunges, which to poure out, receive,
Who know falſe play, rather then loſe, deceive.
For in beſt underſtandings, ſinne beganne,
Angels ſinn'd firſt, then Devills, and then man.   40

19 of all three *1633:* of all three? *1635–69*   22 no ſuch *1633, A18,*
A25, B, D, H49, JC, N, S, TC, W: none ſuch *1635–69, O'F, P*   there were.
1635–69, A25, B, D, H49, JC, O'F, P, S, W: they were. *1633, Lec:* then
were *A18, N, TC*   24 and of one clay. *1633 and MSS. generally:* of one
clay. *1635–39:* of one day. *1650–54:* and at one daye. *A25:* Princes, some
slaves, and all end in one day. *1669*
25–6 The Country is a deſert, where no good,
      Gain'd, as habits, not borne, is underſtood. *1633, 1669, A18, B, Cy,*
D, H49, HN, JC, Lec, N, S96, TC, W
      The Country is a deſert, where the good,
      Gain'd inhabits not, borne, is not underſtood. *1635–54, O'F, P, S*
      The Country is a deſert, where noe good
      Gain'd doth inhabit, nor born's underſtood. *A25*
27 more *1633, A25, W:* meere *Cy, D, H49, JC, Lec, S96:* men *(a slip for*
mere) A18, N, TC: all *1635–69. See note*   33 iſſue inceſtuous. *1633,*
A18, D, H49, JC, Lec, N, TC, W: iſſue is inceſtuous. *1635–69, P, S:* iſſues
monſterous. *A25*   35 there] then *Lec*

                                                            Onely

Onely perchance beafts finne not; wretched wee
Are beafts in all, but white integritie.
I thinke if men, which in thefe places live
Durft looke for themfelves, and themfelves retrive,
They would like ftrangers greet themfelves, feeing than 45
Utopian youth, growne old Italian.
  Be thou thine owne home, and in thy felfe dwell;
Inne any where, continuance maketh hell.
And feeing the fnaile, which every where doth rome,
Carrying his owne houfe ftill, ftill is at home,   50
Follow (for he is eafie pac'd) this fnaile,
Bee thine owne Palace, or the world's thy gaile.
And in the worlds fea, do not like corke fleepe
Upon the waters face; nor in the deepe
Sinke like a lead without a line: but as   55
Fifhes glide, leaving no print where they paffe,
Nor making found; fo clofely thy courfe goe,
Let men difpute, whether thou breathe, or no.
Onely'in this one thing, be no Galenift: To make
Courts hot ambitions wholefome, do not take   60
A dramme of Countries dulneffe; do not adde
Correctives, but as chymiques, purge the bad.
But, Sir, I advife not you, I rather doe
Say o'er thofe leffons, which I learn'd of you:
Whom, free from German fchifmes, and lightneffe   65
Of France, and faire Italies faithlefneffe,
Having from thefe fuck'd all they had of worth,
And brought home that faith, which you carried forth,
I throughly love. But if my felfe, I'have wonne
To know my rules, I have, and you have   70

                                                DONNE:

  44 for themfelves, *A18, A25, B, D, H49, HN, JC, Lec, N, S, S96, TC,
W:* in themfelves, *1633–69:* into themfelves, themfelves retrive, *Cy, O'F, P*
45 than] then *1633*   45–6 than . . . Italian.] that . . . Italianate. *Cy, P*
47 Be thou *1633, Lec:* Be then *1635–69 and MSS.*   50 home, *Ed:* home.
1633: home: *1635–69*   52 gaile. *1635–69:* goale; *1633*   57 fo
D, W: fo, *1633–69*   58–9 breathe,] breath, *1633*   or no. Onely'in this
one thing, be no Galenift: *Ed:* or no: Onely . . . Galenift. *1633, A18, B, D,
H49, JC, Lec, N, TC, W:* or no: Onely in this be no Galenift. *1635–69.
Cy, O'F, S*   64 you:] ycu. *1633*   65 German *1633 and all MSS.:*
Germanies *1635–69, Grosart and Chambers (without note)*

                                                   To

To Sr *Henry Goodyere.*

WHo makes the Paſt, a patterne for next yeare,
    Turnes no new leafe, but ſtill the ſame things reads,
Seene things, he ſees againe, heard things doth heare,
    And makes his life, but like a paire of beads.

A Palace, when'tis that, which it ſhould be,   5
    Leaves growing, and ſtands ſuch, or elſe decayes:
But hee which dwels there, is not ſo; for hee
    Strives to urge upward, and his fortune raiſe;

So had your body'her morning, hath her noone,
    And ſhall not better; her next change is night: 10
But her faire larger gueſt, to'whom Sun and Moone
    Are ſparkes, and ſhort liv'd, claimes another right.

The noble Soule by age growes luſtier,
    Her appetite, and her digeſtion mend,
Wee muſt not ſterve, nor hope to pamper her   15
    With womens milke, and pappe unto the end.

Provide you manlyer dyet; you have ſeene
    All libraries, which are Schools, Camps, and Courts;
But aske your Garners if you have not beene
    In harveſts, too indulgent to your ſports.   20

Would you redeeme it? then your ſelfe tranſplant
    A while from hence. Perchance outlandiſh ground
Beares no more wit, then ours, but yet more ſcant
    Are thoſe diverſions there, which here abound.

To Sir Henry Goodyere. *1633-69: so with* Goodyere *variously spelt* *A25, B, C, Cy, D, H49, Lec:* To Sr Henry Goodyere (H: G: *A18, N, TC*) moveing him to travell. *A18, N, O'F, TC*   1 Paſt, *1633-54, A18, A25, B, Cy, D, H49, Lec, N, O'F, TC:* Laſt *1669, Chambers*   2 reads,] read, *1650-54*   6 decayes:] decayes, *1633*   16 womens] womans *1669* 17 dyet; *Ed:* dyet, *1633 (with a larger interval than is usually given to a comma), 1669:* dyet. *1635-54*   20 harveſts, *1633-54, A18, B, D, H49, Lec, TC:* harveſt, *1669, A25, C, Cy, N, O'F, Chambers*

To

To be a ſtranger hath that benefit,   25
    Wee can beginnings, but not habits choke.
Goe; whither? Hence; you get, if you forget;
    New faults, till they preſcribe in us, are ſmoake.

Our ſoule, whoſe country'is heaven, and God her father,
    Into this world, corruptions ſinke, is ſent,   30
Yet, ſo much in her travaile ſhe doth gather,
    That ſhe returnes home, wiſer then ſhe went;

It payes you well, if it teach you to ſpare,
    And make you,'aſham'd, to make your hawks praiſe,
        yours,
Which when herſelfe ſhe leſſens in the aire,   35
    You then firſt ſay, that high enough ſhe toures.

However, keepe the lively taſt you hold
    Of God, love him as now, but feare him more,
And in your afternoones thinke what you told
    And promiſ'd him, at morning prayer before.   40

Let falſhood like a diſcord anger you,
    Elſe be not froward. But why doe I touch
Things, of which none is in your practiſe new,
    And Tables, or fruit-trenchers teach as much;

But thus I make you keepe your promiſe Sir,   45
    Riding I had you, though you ſtill ſtaid there,
And in theſe thoughts, although you never ſtirre,
    You came with mee to Micham, and are here.

---

27 Goe; *A18,B,TC:* Goe, *1633–69*   Hence; *A18,TC:* hence;
1633: hence *1635–54:* Hence. *1669*   28 in us, *1633, A18, A25, C,*
Cy, D, H49, Lec, N, TC: to us, *1635–69, B, O'F*   34 you,'aſham'd, *Ed:*
you'aſham'd, *1633–69:* you asham'd *Chambers and Grolier. See note*
37 However, *1633–39:* However *1650–69:* Howſoever *A18, B, D, N, O'F,*
TC   38 as] *om. 1639–69*   42 froward.] froward; *1633*   44
Tables *1633–54, Lec:* Fables *1669, A18, A25, B, Cy, D, H49, N, O'F, TC*
45 make] made *A18, N, TC*   48 with mee to] to mee at *A18, N, TC*

To

To M[r] *Rowland Woodward.*

Like one who'in her third widdowhood doth profeſſe
  Her ſelfe a Nunne, tyed to retirednesse,
So'affects my muſe now, a chaſt fallowneſſe;

Since ſhee to few, yet to too many'hath ſhowne
How love-ſong weeds, and Satyrique thornes are growne 5
Where ſeeds of better Arts, were early ſown.

Though to uſe, and love Poëtrie, to mee,
Betroth'd to no'one Art, be no'adulterie;
Omiſſions of good, ill, as ill deeds bee.

For though to us it ſeeme,' and be light and thinne,   10
Yet in thoſe faithfull ſcales, where God throwes in
Mens workes, vanity weighs as much as ſinne.

If our Soules have ſtain'd their firſt white, yet wee
May cloth them with faith, and deare honeſtie,
Which God imputes, as native puritie.   15

There is no Vertue, but Religion:
Wiſe, valiant, ſober, juſt, are names, which none
Want, which want not Vice-covering diſcretion.

    To M[r] Rowland Woodward. *1633–69: similarly or without heading,* A18,
Cy, D, H40, H49, JC, L74, Lec, N, O'F, P, S, S96, TCC, TCD: A Letter
of Doctor Dunne to one that deſired ſome of his papers. B: To M[r] R. W. W
1 profeſſe] profeſſe, *1633*   2 retirednesse, *1633–69,* B, Cy, D; H40,
H49, JC, O'F, P, S: a retirednesse, A18, L74, N, TC, W   3 fallowneſſe;
Ed: fallowneſſe. *1633–54:* fallownes, *1669:* holineſſe Cy, P, S96   4
too] ſo W ſhowne *1633, 1669:* ſlowne, *1635–54*   5 How love-ſong
weeds, *1633:* How long loves weeds, *1635–54,* O'F: How Love-ſong weeds,
1669   6 ſown. *1633, 1669:* sown? *1635–54:* ſown; *Chambers, who
retains the full-stop after* fallownesse   10 to us it] to uſe it, Cy, P,
S96 ſeeme,'and be light *1633,* A18, B, D, H40, H49, L74, N, S, S96, TC,
W: ſeem but light *1635–69,* Cy, OF, P, *and Chambers, who attributes to
1633 the reading* seem and be but light   13 white] whites Cy, O'F, P
14 honeſtie] integritie Cy, P, S, S96   15 puritie.] puritie, *1633*   16
Religion: *1669:* Religion, *1633:* Religion. *1635–54*

Seeke wee then our felves in our felves; for as
Men force the Sunne with much more force to paffe,   20
By gathering his beames with a chriftall glaffe;

So wee, If wee into our felves will turne,
Blowing our fparkes of vertue, may outburne
The ftraw, which doth about our hearts fojourne.

You know, Phyfitians, when they would infufe   25
Into any'oyle, the Soules of Simples, ufe
Places, where they may lie ftill warme, to chufe.

So workes retirednefle in us; To rome
Giddily, and be every where, but at home,
Such freedome doth a banifhment become.   30

Wee are but farmers of our felves, yet may,
If we can ftocke our felves, and thrive, uplay
Much, much deare treafure for the great rent day.

Manure thy felfe then, to thy felfe be'approv'd,
And with vaine outward things be no more mov'd,   35
But to know, that I love thee'and would be lov'd.

23 our] the *A18, L74, N, TC*   fparkes *1633-54, B, Cy, D, H49,*
JC, L74, Lec, N, O'F, P, S96, TC, W: fpark *1669, A18, H40, S, Chambers*
25 infufe] infufe *1633*   26 Soules *1633-69, Cy, P*: foule *B, D, H40*
JC, Lec, N, O'F, S, S96, TC, W   28 To *1635-69*: to *1633*   29
Giddily, *1669*: Giddily *1633-54*   31 farmers *1635-69, and all MSS.,*
where it is generally fpelt feimers: teimers *1633*   33 deare *1633, and*
most MSS.: good *1635-69, Cy, O'F, P, S96*   34 approv'd *1633-54,*
A18, Cy, D, H40, H49, JC, L74, Lec, N, O'F, P, S, S96, TC, W: improv'd
1669, B, Chambers   36 lov'd. *1633-69*: belov'd. *A18, L74, N, P, S,*
S96, TC

To

To Sr *Henry Wootton.*

HEre's no more newes, then vertue,'I may as well
Tell you *Cales,* or St *Michaels* tale for newes, as tell
That vice doth here habitually dwell.

Yet, as to'get ftomachs, we walke up and downe,
And toyle to fweeten reft, fo, may God frowne,   5
If, but to loth both, I haunt Court, or Towne.

For here no one is from the'extremitie
Of vice, by any other reafon free,
But that the next to'him, ftill, is worfe then hee.

In this worlds warfare, they whom rugged Fate,   10
(Gods Commiffary,) doth fo throughly hate,
As in'the Courts Squadron to marfhall their ftate:

If they ftand arm'd with feely honefty,
With wifhing prayers, and neat integritie,
Like Indians'gainft Spanifh hofts they bee.   15

Sufpitious boldneffe to this place belongs,
And to'have as many eares as all have tongues;
Tender to know, tough to acknowledge wrongs.

To Sr Henry Wootton. *1633–69: do. or* A Letter to *&c. B, Cy, D,
H49, L74, Lec, S, S96 (of these Cy and S add* From Court *and* From y^e
Court): From Court. *P:* To Mr H. W. 20 Jul. 1598 at Court. *HN:*
To Mr H. W. 20 July 15098 *(sic)* At Court. *W:* Jo: D: to M^r H: W:
A18, N, TC: Another Letter. *JC* 1 newes] new *1669* 2 Tell you
Cales, (*Calis, 1633*) or *St Michaels* tale for newes, as tell *1633, A18, B* (tales),
Cy (and St Michaels tales), *D, H49, JC, L74, N, O'F* (tales), *P, S, S96* (tales),
TC. W (*MSS. waver in spelling—but* Cales *Cy, HN, P*): Tell you *Calis,* or
Saint Michaels tales, as tell *1635–54, Chambers* (Calais): Tell *Calis,* or Saint
Michaels Mount, as tell *1669:* Tell you Calais, or Saint Michaels Mount as
tell *1719: All modern editions read* Calais   6 or] and *1669*   9
to'him, ftill, *1633:* to him, ftill, *1635–69:* to him is ftill *A18, L74, N,
O'F, TC*   12 ftate: *1635–69:* ftate *1633*   14 wifhing prayers,
1633. A18, D, H49, JC, L74, Lec, N, S, S96, TC, W: wifhing, prayers, *1669,
HN:* wifhes, prayers, *1635–54, B, Cy, O'F, P, Chambers*

Beleeve

Beleeve mee Sir, in my youths giddieſt dayes,
When to be like the Court, was a playes praiſe,   20
Playes were not ſo like Courts, as Courts'are like playes.

Then let us at theſe mimicke antiques jeaſt,
Whoſe deepeſt projeᴄts, and egregious geſts
Are but dull Moralls of a game at Cheſts.

But now'tis incongruity to ſmile,   25
Therefore I end ; and bid farewell a while,
At Court; though *From Court*, were the better ſtile.

H: W: in Hiber: belligeranti.

WEnt you to conquer? and have ſo much loſt
Yourſelf, that what in you was beſt and moſt,
Reſpeᴄtive friendſhip, ſhould ſo quickly dye?
In publique gaine my ſhare'is not ſuch that I
Would loſe your love for Ireland : better cheap   5
I pardon death (who though he do not reap
Yet gleanes hee many of our frends away)
Then that your waking mind ſhould bee a prey
To lethargies. Lett ſhott, and boggs, and skeines
With bodies deale, as fate bids and reſtreynes ;   10
Ere ſickneſſes attack, yong death is beſt,
Who payes before his death doth ſcape arreſt.

---

20 playes] players *1639-69*   21 are like *1633, A18,* D, *H49, L74,*
Lec, N, S, S96 (are now like), *TC, W :* are om. (*metri causa*) *1635-69. B. Cy.*
JC, O'F
23-4   are egregeous gueſts,
          And but dull Morals at a game of Cheſts. *1669*
25 now'tis] 'tis an *1669*   27 *At Court*; though, *From Court, &c. W :*
At Court, though from Court, *&c. 1633-69*
     H: W: *&c. Burley MS.* (JD *in margin*) *i. e.* Henrico Wottoni in Hibernia
belligeranti   2 that] yᵗ *Bur, and similarly* yᵉ (the), yʳ (your), wᶜʰ
(which), wᵗʰ (with) *throughout*   2-3 moſt, Reſpeᴄtive friendſhip,] *no
commas, Bur*   4 ſhare'is] ſhare is *Bur*   9 lethargies.] letargies. *Bur*
10 reſtreynes ;] reſtreynes *Bur*   11 attack,] attack *Bur*   beſt,] beſt *Bur*
                                                                    Lett

Lett not your foule (at firſt with graces fill'd,
And ſince, and thorough crooked lymbecks, ſtill'd
In many ſchools and courts, which quicken it,)   15
It ſelf unto the Iriſh negligence ſubmit.
I aske not labored letters which ſhould weare
Long papers out: nor letters which ſhould feare
Diſhoneſt carriage: or a ſeers art:
Nor ſuch as from the brayne come, but the hart.   20

To the Counteſſe of Bedford.

MADAME,

R Eaſon is our Soules left hand, Faith her right,
  By theſe wee reach divinity, that's you;
Their loves, who have the bleſſings of your light,
Grew from their reaſon, mine from faire faith grew.

But as, although a ſquint lefthandedneſſe   5
Be'ungracious, yet we cannot want that hand,
So would I, not to encreaſe, but to expreſſe
My faith, as I beleeve, ſo underſtand.

Therefore I ſtudy you firſt in your Saints,
Thoſe friends, whom your election glorifies,   10
Then in your deeds, acceſſes, and reſtraints,
And what you reade, and what your ſelfe devize.

But ſoone, the reaſons why you'are lov'd by all,
Grow infinite, and ſo paſſe reaſons reach,
Then backe againe to'implicite faith I fall,   15
And reſt on what the Catholique voice doth teach;

13 (at firſt] *Bur closes bracket after* firſt *and again after* 15 quicken it,
14 ſince,] ſince *Bur*   19 art:] art *Bur*
   To the Counteſſe of Bedford. *1633-69:* do. *or* To the Counteſſe of B.
B,Cy,D,H49,L74,Lec,M,N,O'F,RP31,S,S96,TCD   3 bleſſings
1633,D,H49,Lec: bleſſing *1635-69,B,Cy,L74,N,O'F,S,S96,TCD*
light, *1633-69:* ſight, *B,Cy,D,H49,L74,Lec,N,O'F,RP31,S,TCD*
4 faire *1633-69,L74,N,TCD:* farr *B,Cy,D,H49,Lec,M,O'F,RP31,S,*
S96   16 what] that *Chambers*   voice *1635-69,B,Cy,D,H49,L74,*
Lec,M,N,O'F,S96,TCD: faith *1633,RP31,S*

That

That you are good: and not one Heretique
Denies it: if he did, yet you are fo.
For, rockes, which high top'd and deep rooted fticke,
Waves wafh, not undermine, nor overthrow.   20

In every thing there naturally growes
A *Balfamum* to keepe it frefh, and new,
If'twere not injur'd by extrinfique blowes;
Your birth and beauty are this Balme in you.

But you of learning and religion,   25
And vertue,'and fuch ingredients, have made
A methridate, whofe operation
Keepes off, or cures what can be done or faid.

Yet, this is not your phyficke, but your food,
A dyet fit for you; for you are here   30
The firft good Angell, fince the worlds frame ftood,
That ever did in womans fhape appeare.

Since you are then Gods mafterpeece, and fo
His Factor for our loves; do as you doe,
Make your returne home gracious; and beftow   35
This life on that; fo make one life of two.
    For fo God helpe mee,'I would not miffe you there
    For all the good which you can do me here.

19 high top'd and deep rooted *1633, N, TCD:* high to fenfe deepe-rooted
1635–54, O'F, Chambers (who has overlooked 1633 reading): high to fenfe and
deepe-rooted *S96:* high to fun and deepe-rooted *L74, RP31, S:* high do
feem, deep-rooted *1669, Cy (but MS. with and):* high to fome, and deepe-
rooted *D, H49, Lec:* high to feeme, and deepe-rooted *B. See note* 25
But *Ed:* But, *1633–69*   36 This *1635–69, B, Cy, D, H49, L74, Lec,
N, O'F, RP31, S, TCD, Grosart and Chambers:* Thy *1633, Grolier. See note*

To the Counteſſe of Bedford.

MADAME,

YOu have refin'd mee, and to worthyeſt things
   (Vertue, Art, Beauty, Fortune,) now I ſee
Rareneſſe, or uſe, not nature value brings ;
And ſuch, as they are circumſtanc'd, they bee.
    Two ills can ne're perplexe us, ſinne to'excuſe ;   5
    But of two good things, we may leave and chuſe.

Therefore at Court, which is not vertues clime,
(Where a tranſcendent height, (as, lowneſſe mee)
Makes her not be, or not ſhow) all my rime
Your vertues challenge, which there rareſt bee ;   10
    For, as darke texts need notes : there ſome muſt bee
    To uſher vertue, and ſay, *This is ſhee.*

So in the country'is beauty ; to this place
You are the ſeaſon (Madame) you the day,
'Tis but a grave of ſpices, till your face   15
Exhale them, and a thick cloſe bud diſplay.
    Widow'd and reclus'd elſe, her ſweets ſhe'enſhrines ;
    As China, when the Sunne at Braſill dines.

Out from your chariot, morning breaks at night,
And falſifies both computations ſo ;   20
Since a new world doth riſe here from your light,
We your new creatures, by new recknings goe.
    This ſhowes that you from nature lothly ſtray,
    That ſuffer not an artificiall day.

To the Counteſſe of Bedford. *1633–69: similarly or with no title,* B, Cy,
D, H40, H49, Lec, N, O'F, TCD   2 (Vertue, . . Fortune,)] *brackets Ed :*
Fortune, *1633:* Fortune; *1635–69, Grolier :* Fortune. *Chambers. See note*
5 ne're] nere *1633*   6 and] or *1669*   8–9 *1633 begins to bracket*
(Where . . . not ſhow) *but does not finish, putting a colon after* ſhow : *the
others drop the larger brackets, retaining the smaller* (as . . . mee)   9 be]
ſee *1669*   ſhow] ſhow : *1633–54:* ſhow. *1669*   11 notes : there
ſome *1633–54:* notes ſome : there *1669*   17 enſhrines ; *1719:* enſhrines
1633–69   20 computations ſo ; *1633–69:* computations ; so, *Chambers*

In

In this you'have made the Court the Antipodes, 25
And will'd your Delegate, the vulgar Sunne,
To doe profane autumnall offices,
Whilft here to you, wee facrificers runne;
 And whether Priefts, or Organs, you wee'obey,
 We found your influence, and your Dictates fay. 30

Yet to that Deity which dwels in you,
Your vertuous Soule, I now not facrifice;
Thefe are *Petitions,* and not *Hymnes*; they fue
But that I may furvay the edifice.
 In all Religions as much care hath bin 35
 Of Temples frames, and beauty,'as Rites within.

As all which goe to Rome, doe not thereby
Efteeme religions, and hold faft the beft,
But ferve difcourfe, and curiofity,
With that which doth religion but inveft, 40
 And fhunne th'entangling laborinths of Schooles,
 And make it wit, to thinke the wifer fooles:

So in this pilgrimage I would behold
You as you'are vertues temple, not as fhee,
What walls of tender chriftall her enfold, 45
What eyes, hands, bofome, her pure Altars bee;
 And after this furvay, oppofe to all
 Bablers of Chappels, you th'Efcuriall.

Yet not as confecrate, but merely'as faire,
On thefe I caft a lay and country eye. 50
Of paft and future ftories, which are rare,
I finde you all record, and prophecie.
 Purge but the booke of Fate, that it admit
 No fad nor guilty legends, you are it.

42 fooles:] fooles. *1633*   48 Bablers *1633:* Bablers *1635-54:*
Builders *1669* 49 faire, *Ed:* faire; *1633-69* 50 eye.] eye, *1633*
52 and prophecie] all prophecye *B, D, H49, Lec, N, O'F, TCD* pro-
phecie.] prophecie, *1633 some copies*

                        If

If good and lovely were not one, of both   55
You were the tranſcript, and originall,
The Elements, the Parent, and the Growth,
And every peece of you, is both their All:
  So'intire are all your deeds, and you, that you
  Muſt do the ſame thinge ſtill; you cannot two.   60

But theſe (as nice thinne Schoole divinity
Serves hereſie to furder or repreſſe)
Taſt of Poëtique rage, or flattery,
And need not, where all hearts one truth profeſſe;
  Oft from new proofes, and new phraſe, new doubts grow,
  As ſtrange attire aliens the men wee know.   66

Leaving then buſie praiſe, and all appeale
To higher Courts, ſenſes decree is true,
The Mine, the Magazine, the Commonweale,
The ſtory of beauty, in Twicknam is, and you.   70
  Who hath ſeene one, would both; As, who had bin
  In Paradiſe, would ſeeke the Cherubin.

To Sʳ *Edward Herbert.* at *Iulyers.*

MAn is a lumpe, where all beaſts kneaded bee,
  Wiſdome makes him an Arke where all agree;
The foole, in whom theſe beaſts do live at jarre,
  Is ſport to others, and a Theater;

57 Parent] Parents *1669*   Growth, *1669*: Growth *1633-54*   58 both
1633 and *MSS.*: worth *1635-69*, *O'F*   All: *Ed*: All, *1633-69*   60
thinge *B, Cy, D, H40, H49, N, O'F*: things *1633-69, Lec*   61 nice thinne
1633-54: niceſt *1669*   66 aliens *1633, 1669* and *MSS.*: alters *1635-54*,
O'F   67 and] end *1669, not* lend *as in Chambers' note*   appeale
Ed: appeale, *1633-69*   68 true, *1633*: true. *1635-69*   71 had bin
1633-35: hath bin *1639-69*. *See note*
  To Sʳ Edward *&c. 1633, D, H49, Lec, O'F*: A Letter to Sʳ Edward
Herbert (*or* Harbert). *B, Cy* (*which adds* Incerti Authoris), *S96*: To Sir
E. H. *A18, N, TC*: *no title, P*: Elegia Vicesima Tertia. *S*: To Sʳ Edward
Herbert, now (ſince *1669*) Lord Herbert of Cherbury, being at the ſiege of
Iulyers. *1635-69*   4 Theater; *Ed*: Theater, *1633-69*: Theater. *D*
Nor

Nor ſcapes hee ſo, but is himſelfe their prey,   5
  All which was man in him, is eate away,
And now his beaſts on one another feed,
  Yet couple'in anger, and new monſters breed.
How happy'is hee, which hath due place aſſign'd
  To'his beaſts, and diſaforeſted his minde!   10
Empail'd himſelfe to keepe them out, not in;
  Can ſow, and dares truſt corne, where they have bin;
Can uſe his horſe, goate, wolfe, and every beaſt,
  And is not Aſſe himſelfe to all the reſt.
Elſe, man not onely is the heard of ſwine,   15
  But he's thoſe devills too, which did incline
Them to a headlong rage, and made them worſe:
  For man can adde weight to heavens heavieſt curſe.
As Soules (they ſay) by our firſt touch, take in
  The poyſonous tincture of Originall ſinne,   20
So, to the puniſhments which God doth fling,
  Our apprehenſion contributes the ſting.
To us, as to his chickins, he doth caſt
  Hemlocke, and wee as men, his hemlocke taſte;
We do infuſe to what he meant for meat,   25
  Corroſiveneſſe, or intenſe cold or heat.
For, God no ſuch ſpecifique poyſon hath
  As kills we know not how; his fierceſt wrath
Hath no antipathy, but may be good
  At leſt for phyſicke, if not for our food.   30
Thus man, that might be'his pleaſure, is his rod,
  And is his devill, that might be his God.
Since then our buſineſſe is, to rectifie
  Nature, to what ſhe was, wee'are led awry
By them, who man to us in little ſhow;   35
  Greater then due, no forme we can beſtow

5 prey, *Ed:* prey; *1633–69*   8 breed.] breed; *1633*   10 minde!
Ed: minde? *1633–69*   17 a headlong] a *om. 1669:* an headlong *1635–54*
24 taſte; *Ed:* taſte. *1633–69*   28 we know *1633 and MSS.:* men know
1635–69, O'F   35 ſhow; *1669:* ſhow, *1633–54, Chambers*   36
due, *1633–69:* due; *Chambers. See note*

On

On him ; for Man into himfelfe can draw
    All ; All his faith can fwallow,'or reafon chaw.
All that is fill'd, and all that which doth fill,
    All the round world, to man is but a pill,   40
In all it workes not, but it is in all
    Poyfonous, or purgative, or cordiall,
For, knowledge kindles Calentures in fome,
    And is to others icy *Opium.*
As brave as true, is that profeffion than   45
    Which you doe ufe to make ; that you know man.
This makes it credible ; you have dwelt upon
    All worthy bookes, and now are fuch an one.
Actions are authors, and of thofe in you
    Your friends finde every day a mart of new.   50

To the Counteſſe of Bedford.

T'Have written then, when you writ, feem'd to mee
    Worft of fpirituall vices, Simony,
And not t'have written then, feemes little leffe
    Then worft of civill vices, thankleffeneffe.
In this, my debt I feem'd loath to confeffe,   5
    In that, I feem'd to fhunne beholdingneffe.
But 'tis not foe ; *nothings,* as I am, may
    Pay all they have, and yet have all to pay.
Such borrow in their payments, and owe more
    By having leave to write fo, then before.   10
Yet fince rich mines in barren grounds are fhowne,
    May not I yeeld (not gold) but coale or ftone ?

---

38 All; All *1669:* All : All *1635–54:* All, All *1633*   chaw. *1633:*
chaw, *1635–69, Grolier*   39 fill, *1633–54:* fill *1669:* fill ; *Grolier*
44 icy] jcy *1633*   47–8 credible ; . . . bookes, *Ed:* credible, . . .
bookes ; *1633–69:* credible . . . bookes *Grolier*
    To the *&c. 1633–69:* To the Counteffe of B. *N, O'F, TCD*   5 debt
1669, N, O'F, TCD: doubt *1633–54*   7 foe ; *Ed:* foe, *1633–54:* foe.
1669 *nothings, 1635–54:* nothing, *1633, N, TCD:* Nothing *1669*   may]
may, *1633*

Temples

Temples were not demolifh'd, though prophane:
　Here *Peter Ioves*, there *Paul* hath *Dian's* Fane.
So whether my hymnes you admit or chufe,　　　　　15
　In me you'have hallowed a Pagan Mufe,
And denizend a ftranger, who miftaught
　By blamers of the times they mard, hath fought
Vertues in corners, which now bravely doe
　Shine in the worlds beft part, or all It ; You.　　20
I have beene told, that vertue in Courtiers hearts
　Suffers an Oftracifme, and departs.
Profit, eafe, fitneffe, plenty, bid it goe,
　But whither, only knowing you, I know ;
Your (or you) vertue two vaft ufes ferves,　　　　25.
　It ranfomes one fex, and one Court preferves.
There's nothing but your worth, which being true,
　Is knowne to any other, not to you :
And you can never know it ; To admit
　No knowledge of your worth, is fome of it.　　　30
But fince to you, your praifes difcords bee,
　Stoop, others ills to meditate with mee.
Oh! to confeffe wee know not what we fhould,
　Is halfe excufe ; wee know not what we would :
Lightneffe depreffeth us, emptineffe fills,　　　　35
　We fweat and faint, yet ftill goe downe the hills.
As new Philofophy arrefts the Sunne,
　And bids the paffive earth about it runne,
So wee have dull'd our minde, it hath no ends ;
　Onely the bodie's bufie, and pretends ;　　　　　40
As dead low earth ecclipfes and controules

　　14 hath] have *1633*: om. *N, TCD* (have *inserted*)　　*Dian's 1635–54*:
Dian's 1633: *Dina's 1669*　　　　20 or all It; You. *1635–54*: or
all it, you. *1669, N, O'F, TCD*: or all, in you. *1633* (you, *some copies*)
25 Your (or you) vertue *O'F*: Your, or you vertue, *1633–54*: You, or
you vertue, *1669*　　　26 preferves. *Ed*: preferves; *1633–69*　　　28
you :] you. *1633–39*　　　30 is fome] it fome *1633*　　　32 Stoop, others
ills] Stoop (Stop *1633*) others ills, *1633–54*: Stoop others ills *1669*
34 excufe; *Ed*: excufe, *1633–69, Grosart* (*who transposes* should *and*
would), *Chambers*: excuse *Grolier. See note*　　　would: *Ed*: would]
1633–69　　　36 the hills. *Ed*: the hills; *1633–69*　　　37 Philofophy.
Phylofophy *1633 some copies,1669*
　　　　　　　　　　　　　　　　　　　　　　　　The

The quick high Moone: fo doth the body, Soules.
In none but us, are fuch mixt engines found,
　　As hands of double office: For, the ground
We till with them; and them to heav'n wee raife;　　45
　　Who prayer-leffe labours, or, without this, prayes,
Doth but one halfe, that's none; He which faid, *Plough*
　　And looke not back, to looke up doth allow.
Good feed degenerates, and oft obeyes
　　The foyles difeafe, and into cockle ftrayes;　　50
Let the minds thoughts be but tranfplanted fo,
　　Into the body,'and baftardly they grow.
What hate could hurt our bodies like our love?
　　Wee (but no forraine tyrants could) remove
Thefe not ingrav'd, but inborne dignities,　　55
　　Caskets of foules; Temples, and Palaces:
For, bodies fhall from death redeemed bee,
　　Soules but preferv'd, not naturally free.
As men to'our prifons, new foules to us are fent,
　　Which learne vice there, and come in innocent.　　60
Firft feeds of every creature are in us,
　　What ere the world hath bad, or pretious,
Mans body can produce, hence hath it beene
　　That ftones, wormes, frogges, and fnakes in man are
　　　　feene:
But who ere faw, though nature can worke foe,　　65
　　That pearle, or gold, or corne in man did grow?
We'have added to the world Virginia,'and fent
　　Two new ftarres lately to the firmament;

45 raife;] raife *1633*　　46 this,] these *1669*　　50 ftrayes; *Ed:*
ftrayes. *1633–69*　　51 Let] Let but *1669*　　54 Wee (but no forraine
tyrants could) remove *Ed:* Wee but no forraine tyrants could, remove *O'F:*
Wee but no forraigne tyrants could remove, *1633–54* (tyrans *1633*):
We, but no forrain tyrants, could remove *1669, Chambers and Grolier. See
note*　　55 dignities, *Ed:* dignities *1633–69*　　56 Palaces: *1633–35:*
Palaces. *1639–69*　　58 not naturally free. *Ed:* not naturally free; *1633,
N, TCD:* borne naturally free; *1635–69, O'F*　　59 prifons, new foules
1633: prifons now, foules *1635–69, O'F:* prifons, now foules *N. TCD*
60 vice *1635–69, O'F:* it *1633, N, TCD*　　66 That] That, *1633*　　grow?
1639–69: grow. *1633–35*

Why

Why grudge wee us (not heaven) the dignity
   T'increafe with ours, thofe faire foules company.   70
But I muft end this letter, though it doe
   Stand on two truths, neither is true to you.
Vertue hath fome perverfeneffe; For fhe will
   Neither beleeve her good, nor others ill.
Even in you, vertues beft paradife,   75
   Vertue hath fome, but wife degrees of vice.
Too many vertues, or too much of one
   Begets in you unjuft fufpition;
And ignorance of vice, makes vertue leffe,
   Quenching compaffion of our wrechedneffe.   80
But thefe are riddles; Some afperfion
   Of vice becomes well fome complexion.
Statefmen purge vice with vice, and may corrode
   The bad with bad, a fpider with a toad:
For fo, ill thralls not them, but they tame ill   85
   And make her do much good againft her will,
But in your Commonwealth, or world in you,
   Vice hath no office, or good worke to doe.
Take then no vitious purge, but be content
   With cordiall vertue, your knowne nourifhment.   90

To the Counteſſe of Bedford.

On New-yeares day.

THis twilight of two yeares, not paft nor next,
   Some embleme is of mee, or I of this,
Who Meteor-like, of ftuffe and forme perplext,
   Whofe *what,* and *where,* in difputation is,
   If I fhould call mee *any thing,* fhould miffe.   5

74 ill.] ill, *1633-35*   75 you, *1669:* you *1635-54:* your *1633*
78 fufpition; *Ed:* fufpition. *1633-69*   79 makes] make *1635-39*   87
Commonwealth, . . . you,] *no commas 1633*
. To the *&c. 1633-69:* To the Counteffe of B. at New-yeares tide. *N,*
O'F,TCD   3-4 (Meteor-like, . . . difputation is,) *1635-69*
I fumme

I fumme the yeares, and mee, and finde mee not
  Debtor to th'old, nor Creditor to th'new,
That cannot fay, My thankes I have forgot,
    Nor truft I this with hopes, and yet fcarce true
    This bravery is, fince thefe times fhew'd mee you.   10

In recompence I would fhow future times
  What you were, and teach them to'urge towards fuch.
Verfe embalmes vertue;'and Tombs, or Thrones of rimes,
    Preferve fraile tranfitory fame, as much
    As fpice doth bodies from corrupt aires touch.   15

Mine are fhort-liv'd; the tincture of your name
  Creates in them, but diffipates as faft,
New fpirits: for, ftrong agents with the fame
    Force that doth warme and cherifh, us doe waft;
    Kept hot with ftrong extracts, no bodies laft: 20

So, my verfe built of your juft praife, might want
  Reafon and likelihood, the firmeft Bafe,
And made of miracle, now faith is fcant,
    Will vanifh foone, and fo poffeffe no place,
    And you, and it, too much grace might difgrace.   25

When all (as truth commands affent) confeffe
  All truth of you, yet they will doubt how I,
One corne of one low anthills duft, and leffe,
    Should name, know, or expreffe a thing fo high,
    And not an inch, meafure infinity.   30

I cannot tell them, nor my felfe, nor you,
  But leave, left truth b'endanger'd by my praife,
And turne to God, who knowes I thinke this true,

  9 true *Ed:* true, *1633:* true. *1635–69*   10 is, *Ed:* is *1633–69 (in
1633 the interval shows that a comma was intended)*   times] time *1633*
12 fuch. *Ed:* fuch, *1633–69*   16 fhort-liv'd] fhort liv'd *1633*   17
faft,] faft *1633*   18 fpirits: *Ed:* fpirit: *1633:* fpirits; *1635–69*   19
cherifh, us doe *1633:* cherifh us, doe *1635–69*   27 I, *Ed:* I *1633–69*
28 (One corne . . . and leffe,) *1635–69*   29 name, know,] *no commas*
1633–69   30 And not an inch, *1633:* And (not an inch) *1635–69*
infinity.] infinite. *1669*
                         And

And useth oft, when such a heart mis-sayes,
    To make it good, for, such a praiser prayes.   35

Hee will best teach you, how you should lay out
    His stock of *beauty, learning, favour, blood*;
He will perplex security with doubt,
    And cleare those doubts; hide from you,'and shew you
        good,
    And so increase your appetite and food;   40

Hee will teach you, that good and bad have not
    One latitude in cloysters, and in Court;
Indifferent there the greatest space hath got;
    Some pitty'is not good there, some vaine disport,
    On this side sinne, with that place may comport.   45

Yet he, as hee bounds seas, will fixe your houres,
    Which pleasure, and delight may not ingresse,
And though what none else lost, be truliest yours,
    Hee will make you, what you did not, possesse,
    By using others, not vice, but weakenesse.   50

He will make you speake truths, and credibly,
    And make you doubt, that others doe not so:
Hee will provide you keyes, and locks, to spie,
    And scape spies, to good ends, and hee will show
    What you may not acknowledge, what not know.   55

For your owne conscience, he gives innocence,
    But for your fame, a discreet warinesse,
And though to scape, then to revenge offence
    Be better, he showes both, and to represse
    Ioy, when your state swells, *sadnesse* when'tis lesse.   60

---

35 praiser prayes. *1635–69, O'F:* prayer prayes. *1633:* prayer praise. *N,
TCD*   37 *blood;*] blood, *1633*   39 doubts;] doubts, *1633*   42
Court; *Ed:* Court, *1633–69*   43 got; *Ed:* got, *1633–69*   44 pitty'
1633–69: piety *James Russell Lowell, in Grolier note. See note*   45 On
this side sinne, *Ed (from Chambers):* On this side, sinne; *1633:* On this
side, sin, *1635–69. See note*   46 he, *Ed:* he *1633–69*   47 Which]
With *1633*   55 may] will *1669*   58–9 (though to scape . . . Be
better,) *1635–69*

From

From need of teares he will defend your foule,
  Or make a rebaptizing of one teare;
Hee cannot, (that's, he will not) dif-inroule
  Your name; and when with active joy we heare
  This private Ghofpell, then'tis our New Yeare.   65

To the Counteſſe of Huntingdon.

Madame,

MAn to Gods image ; *Eve,* to mans was made,
  Nor finde wee that God breath'd a foule in her,
Canons will not Church functions you invade,
  Nor lawes to civill office you preferre.

Who vagrant tranfitory Comets fees,   5
  Wonders, becaufe they'are rare ; But a new ftarre
Whofe motion with the firmament agrees,
  Is miracle ; for, there no new things are ;

In woman fo perchance milde innocence
  A feldome comet is, but active good   10
A miracle, which reafon fcapes, and fenfe ;
  For, Art and Nature this in them withftood.

As fuch a ftarre, the *Magi* led to view
  The manger-cradled infant, God below :
By vertues beames by fame deriv'd from you,   15
  May apt foules, and the worft may, vertue know.

If the worlds age, and death be argued well
  By the Sunnes fall, which now towards earth doth bend,
Then we might feare that vertue, fince fhe fell
  So low as woman, fhould be neare her end.   20

65 New Yeare.] new yeare, *1633*
  To the &c. *1633–69,O'F:* To the C. of H. *N,TCD*   1 image ;]
image, *1633*   mans] man *1650–69*   9 woman] women *1669*   13
the] which *1633*   *Magi*] Magis *N,O'F,TCD: compare p.* 243, *l.* 390
14 below : *Ed:* below. *1633–69*   15 beames by . . . you, *1633 :* beames
(by . . . you) *1635–69*   16 may, *Ed:* may *1633–69*

But fhe's not ftoop'd, but rais'd; exil'd by men
    She fled to heaven, that's heavenly things, that's you;
She was in all men, thinly fcatter'd then,
    But now amafs'd, contracted in a few.

She guilded us: But you are gold, and Shee;   25
    Us fhe inform'd, but tranfubftantiates you;
Soft difpofitions which ductile bee,
    Elixarlike, fhe makes not cleane, but new.

Though you a wifes and mothers name retaine,
    'Tis not as woman, for all are not foe,   30
But vertue having made you vertue,'is faine
    T'adhere in thefe names, her and you to fhow,

Elfe, being alike pure, wee fhould neither fee;
    As, water being into ayre rarify'd,
Neither appeare, till in one cloud they bee,   35
    So, for our fakes you do low names abide;

Taught by great conftellations, which being fram'd,
    Of the moft ftarres, take low names, *Crab*, and *Bull*,
When fingle planets by the *Gods* are nam'd,
    You covet not great names, of great things full.   40

So you, as woman, one doth comprehend,
    And in the vaile of kindred others fee;
To fome ye are reveal'd, as in a friend,
    And as a vertuous Prince farre off, to mee.

To whom, becaufe from you all vertues flow,   45
    And 'tis not none, to dare contemplate you,
I, which doe so, as your true fubject owe
    Some tribute for that, fo thefe lines are due.

    22 you; *Ed:* you, *1633–69*   24 amafs'd, *1633, O'F:* a maffe *1635–69,*
N, TCD   25–6 But you are gold, and Shee; . . . tranfubftantiates
you; *Ed:* But you are gold, and Shee, . . . tranfubftantiates you, *1633:*
        but you are gold; and fhe,
      Informed us, but tranfubftantiates you, *1635–69, Chambers* (*but no comma
after* and fhe *and colon or full stop after* you *1650–69, Chambers*)   33 fee;
Ed: fee, *1633–69*   37–9 (which being . . . are nam'd) *1635–69*   42
vaile] vale *1669*   43 ye *1633:* you *1635–69*   47 doe so, *1635–69,*
O'F: doe *N, TCD:* to you *1633*   48 due.] due, *1633*

If you can thinke thefe flatteries, they are,
    For then your judgement is below my praife,   50
If they were fo, oft, flatteries worke as farre,
    As Counfels, and as farre th'endeavour raife.

So my ill reaching you might there grow good,
    But I remaine a poyfon'd fountaine ftill;
But not your beauty, vertue, knowledge, blood   55
    Are more above all flattery, then my will.

And if I flatter any,'tis not you
    But my owne judgement, who did long agoe
Pronounce, that all thefe praifes fhould be true,
    And vertue fhould your beauty,'and birth outgrow.   60

Now that my prophefies are all fulfill'd,
    Rather then God fhould not be honour'd too,
And all thefe gifts confefs'd, which hee inftill'd,
    Your felfe were bound to fay that which I doe.

So I, but your Recorder am in this,   65
    Or mouth, or Speaker of the univerfe,
A minifteriall Notary, for'tis
    Not I, but you and fame, that make this verfe;

I was your Prophet in your yonger dayes,
And now your Chaplaine, God in you to praife.   70

To Mʳ *T. W.*

ALl haile fweet Poët, more full of more ftrong fire,
  Then hath or fhall enkindle any fpirit,
    I lov'd what nature gave thee, but this merit
Of wit and Art I love not but admire;

    55 But *1633,N,O'F,TCD:* And *1635-69, Chambers*   64 that]
thar *1633*   66 or Speaker *1633 :* and Speaker *1635-69*   67 Notary,]
notary, *1633*
    To Mʳ T. W. *P,S,W:* To M. I. W. *1633-69,A18,N,TCC,TCD:* A
Letter. To Mʳ T. W. *O'F:* Ad amicum. *S96: no title, B,Cy*   1 more full]
and full *1669*   2 any fpirit, *1633,A18,Cy,N,P,TC,W:* my dull fpirit,
1635-69,B,O'F,S   3 this merit *1633,A18,Cy,N,P,S,TC,W:* thy
merit *1635-69, B,O'F, Chambers*

                                       Who

Who have before or fhall write after thee, 5
Their workes, though toughly laboured, will bee
Like infancie or age to mans firme ftay,
Or earely and late twilights to mid-day.

Men fay, and truly, that they better be
    Which be envyed then pittied: therefore I, 10
    Becaufe I wifh thee beft, doe thee envie:
O wouldft thou, by like reafon, pitty mee!
But care not for mee: I, that ever was
In Natures, and in Fortunes gifts, alas,
    (Before thy grace got in the Mufes Schoole 15
    A monfter and a begger,) am now a foole.

Oh how I grieve, that late borne modefty
    Hath got fuch root in eafie waxen hearts,
    That men may not themfelves, their owne good parts
Extoll, without fufpect of furquedrie, 20
For, but thy felfe, no fubject can be found
Worthy thy quill, nor any quill refound
    Thy worth but thine : how good it were to fee
    A Poëm in thy praife, and writ by thee.

Now if this fong be too'harfh for rime, yet, as 25
    The Painters bad god made a good devill,

11 thee . . thee] the . . the *1669*   12 mee! *Ed:* mee. *W:* mee,
1633–69   13 mee: *Ed:* mee, *1633–69*   ever was] never was *B, P, S96*
14–16 In Natures, and in Fortunes gifts, alas,
        (Before . . . and a begger,) *Ed:*
        In Natures, and in fortunes gifts, (alas,
        Before thy grace got in the Mufes Schoole)
        A monfter and a begger, *1633 (some copies: others read* 15 Before
by thy grace *&c., which is also the Grolier conjecture), A18, Cy, N, P, S,
TC, W (but W and some of the other MSS. have no brackets):*
        In Natures, and in fortunes gifts, alas,
        (But for thy grace got in the Mufes Schoole)
        A Monfter and a beggar, *1635–69, O'F, Chambers*
        In fortunes, nor (or *S96*) in natures gifts alas,
        But by thy grace, *&c. B, S96. See note*
16 am now a foole. *Cy, O'F, P, S, S96, W:* am a foole. *1633–69, A18, B,
N, TC*   23 worth *1669, B, Cy, O'F, P, S, S96, W:* worke *1633–54,
A18, N, TC*

'Twill

'Twill be good profe, although the verfe be evill,
If thou forget the rime as thou doft paffe.
Then write, that I may follow, and fo bee
Thy debter, thy'eccho, thy foyle, thy zanee.   30
    I fhall be thought, if mine like thine I fhape,
    All the worlds Lyon, though I be thy Ape.

To M *T. W.*

HAft thee harfh verfe, as faft as thy lame meafure
    Will give thee leave, to him, my pain and pleafure.
I have given thee, and yet thou art too weake,
    Feete, and a reafoning foule and tongue to fpeake.
Plead for me, and fo by thine and my labour   5
    I am thy Creator, thou my Saviour.
Tell him, all queftions, which men have defended
    Both of the place and paines of hell, are ended ;
And 'tis decreed our hell is but privation
    Of him, at leaft in this earths habitation: 10
And 'tis where I am, where in every ftreet
    Infections follow, overtake, and meete:
Live I or die, by you my love is fent,
    And you'are my pawnes, or elfe my Teftament.

    27 evill, *W:* evill. *1633–69, Chambers*   28 paffe. *W:* paffe,
1633–69, Chambers   29 that I *1669, B, Cy, N, O'F, P, S, W:* then I
1633–54, A18, N, TC   30 Thy debter, thy'eccho *1633–54:* Thy
eccho, thy debtor *1669*   thy zanee.] and thy Zanee. *A18, N, TC*
31 if . . . shape] *brackets 1635–69*
    To Mr T. W. *O'F, W:*   To M. T. W. *1633–69, A18, N, TCC, TCD*
1 verfe, *1669:* verfe *1633–54*   2 to him, my pain and pleafure. *W,*
and *Chambers (without comma):* to him ; My pain, and pleafure *1633–69:*
to him. My pain and pleasure, *Grolier*   4 Feete, . . . foule *W: no*
comma *1633:* Feete . . . foule, *1635–69*   5–6 *These lines only in W*
9 our] that *W*   14 And you'are *1633, A18, N, TC, W:* You are
1635–69, O'F   pawnes] *om. with space, W*

To Mr *T. W.*

PRegnant again with th'old twins Hope, and Feare,
  Oft have I askt for thee, both how and where
Thou wert, and what my hopes of letters were;

As in our ſtreets ſly beggers narrowly
Watch motions of the givers hand and eye,   5
And evermore conceive ſome hope thereby.

And now thy Almes is given, thy letter'is read,
The body riſen againe, the which was dead,
And thy poore ſtarveling bountifully fed.

After this banquet my Soule doth ſay grace,   10
And praiſe thee for'it, and zealouſly imbrace
Thy love; though I thinke thy love in this caſe
    To be as gluttons, which ſay 'midſt their meat,
    They love that beſt of which they moſt do eat.

To Mr *T. W.*

AT once, from hence, my lines and I depart,
  I to my ſoft ſtill walks, they to my Heart;
I to the Nurſe, they to the child of Art;

Yet as a firme houſe, though the Carpenter
Periſh, doth ſtand: As an Embaſſadour   5
Lyes ſafe, how e'r his king be in danger:

So, though I languiſh, preſt with Melancholy,
My verſe, the ſtrict Map of my miſery,
Shall live to ſee that, for whoſe want I dye.

To Mr T. W. *O'F,W:* To M. T. W. *1633–69,A18,N,TCC,TCD*
5 Watch] Marke *W*   and eye, *A18,A23,N,O'F,TC,W:* or eye,
1633–69   12 love; *Ed:* love, *1633–69*
    To Mr T. W. *W:* An Old Letter. *D,H49:* A Letter. *S96:* Letter.
*O'F: no heading, and following the preceding without any interval, 1633,A18,
N,TC:* Incerto. *1635–69*   5 As *W:* as *1633–69*   7 Melancholy]
Malancholy *1633*

Therefore

Therefore I envie them, and doe repent,   10
That from unhappy mee, things happy'are fent;
Yet as a Picture, or bare Sacrament,
    Accept thefe lines, and if in them there be
    Merit of love, beftow that love on mee.

To Mr *R. W.*

ZEaloufly my Mufe doth falute all thee,
  Enquiring of that miftique trinitee
Whereof thou,'and all to whom heavens do infufe
Like fyer, are made; thy body, mind, and Mufe.
Doft thou recover ficknes, or prevent?   5
Or is thy Mind travail'd with difcontent?
Or art thou parted from the world and mee,
In a good skorn of the worlds vanitee?
Or is thy devout Mufe retyr'd to fing
Vpon her tender Elegiaque ftring?   10
Our Minds part not, joyne then thy Mufe with myne,
For myne is barren thus devorc'd from thyne.

To Mr *R. W.*

MVfe not that by thy mind thy body is led:
  For by thy mind, my mind's diftempered.
So thy Care lives long, for I bearing part
It eates not only thyne, but my fwolne hart.
And when it gives us intermiffion   5
We take new harts for it to feede upon.
But as a Lay Mans Genius doth controule
Body and mind; the Mufe beeing the Soules Soule

14 of love,] of love *1633*
   To Mr R. W. *A23,W: first printed in Gosse's* Life and Letters of
John Donne, *&c.,* 1899   1 thee,] thee *W*
   To Mr R. W. *A23,W: printed here for the first time*

                                                     Of

Of Poets, that methinks fhould eafe our anguifh,
Although our bodyes wither and minds languifh.   10
Wright then, that my griefes which thine got may bee
Cured by thy charming soveraigne melodee.

To Mr *C. B.*

THy friend, whom thy deferts to thee enchaine,
  Urg'd by this unexcufable occafion,
   Thee and the Saint of his affection
Leaving behinde, doth of both wants complaine;
And let the love I beare to both fuftaine   5
  No blott nor maime by this divifion,
   Strong is this love which ties our hearts in one,
And ftrong that love purfu'd with amorous paine;
But though befides thy felfe I leave behind
  Heavens liberall, and earths thrice-fairer Sunne,   10
  Going to where fterne winter aye doth wonne,
Yet, loves hot fires, which martyr my fad minde,
   Doe fend forth fcalding fighes, which have the Art
   To melt all Ice, but that which walls her heart.

To Mr *E. G.*

EVen as lame things thirft their perfection, fo
  The flimy rimes bred in our vale below,
Bearing with them much of my love and hart,
Fly unto that Parnaffus, where thou art.

To Mr C. B. *A23,W:* To M. C. B. *1633–69,A18,N,O'F,TCC,
TCD* 9 thy felf] my felf *1669* 10 liberall,] liberall *1633* earths
1633,1669,A18,A23,N,O'F,TC,W: the *1635–54, Chambers* thrice fairer
A23,W: thrice-faire *1633–69,A18,N,TC* 11 fterne *1633,A18,A23,
N,TC,W:* fterv'd *1635–69,O'F* 13 forth] out *A18,N,TC*
To Mr E. G. *W: first printed in Gosse's* Life and Letters of John
Donne, *&c.* 1899

There

There thou orefeeft London : Here I have beene,   5
By ftaying in London, too much overfeene.
Now pleafures dearth our City doth poffes,
Our Theaters are fill'd with emptines;
As lancke and thin is every ftreet and way
As a woman deliver'd yefterday.   10
Nothing whereat to laugh my fpleen efpyes
But bearbaitings or Law exercife.
Therefore I'le leave it, and in the Country ftrive
Pleafure, now fled from London, to retrive.
Do thou fo too: and fill not like a Bee   15
Thy thighs with hony, but as plenteoufly
As Ruffian Marchants, thy felfes whole veffell load,
And then at Winter retaile it here abroad.
Bleffe us with Suffolks fweets; and as it is
Thy garden, make thy hive and warehoufe this.   20

To Mr *R. W.*

IF, as mine is, thy life a flumber be,
    Seeme, when thou read'ft thefe lines, to dreame of me,
Never did Morpheus nor his brother weare
    Shapes foe like thofe Shapes, whom they would appeare,
As this my letter is like me, for it   5
    Hath my name, words, hand, feet, heart, minde and wit;
It is my deed of gift of mee to thee,
    It is my Will, my felfe the Legacie.
So thy retyrings I love, yea envie,
    Bred in thee by a wife melancholy,   10
That I rejoyce, that unto where thou art,
    Though I ftay here, I can thus fend my heart,

   5–6 beene, . . . London,] *no commas, W*   6 ftaying] ftaing *W*
7 dearth] dirth *W*   7–8 poffes, . . . emptines;] poffes . . . emptines. *W*
   To Mr R. W. *A18, A23, N, O'F, TCC, TCD, W:* To M. R. W.
1633–69: no breaks, W: two stanzas of fourteen lines and a quatrain, 1633:
twenty-eight lines continuous and a quatrain, 1635–69   3 brother *1633–69,*
A18, N, O'F, TC : brethren *W*   6 hand,] hands *O'F, TC*

                          As

As kindly'as any enamored Patient
   His Picture to his abfent Love hath fent.

All newes I thinke fooner reach thee then mee;   15
   Havens are Heavens, and Ships wing'd Angels be,
The which both Gofpell, and fterne threatnings bring;
   Guyanaes harveft is nip'd in the fpring,
I feare ; And with us (me thinkes) Fate deales fo
   As with the Jewes guide God did; he did fhow   20
Him the rich land, but bar'd his entry in:
   Oh, flownes is our punifhment and finne.
Perchance, thefe Spanifh bufineffe being done,
   Which as the Earth betweene the Moone and Sun
Eclipfe the light which Guyana would give,   25
   Our difcontinued hopes we fhall retrive:
But if (as all th'All muft) hopes fmoake away,
   Is not Almightie Vertue'an India ?

If men be worlds, there is in every one
   Some thing to anfwere in fome proportion   30
All the worlds riches: And in good men, this,
   Vertue, our formes forme and our foules foule, is.

To Mr R. W.

Kindly I envy thy fongs perfection
   Built of all th'elements as our bodyes are:
That Litle of earth that is in it, is a faire
Delicious garden where all fweetes are fowne.

21 in: *1650–69,W:* in, *1633–39*   22 Oh, *A23,N,O'F,TC:* Ah, *W:*
Our *1633–69*   finne. *W:* finne; *1633–69*   23 bufineffe *1633,A18,*
N,TC: bufneffes *W:* bufineffes *1635–69*   done] donne *W*   27 all
th'All *W:* All th'All *1633–69*   31 men, this, *Ed:* men, this *1633–69*
32 foules foule, is. *Chambers:* foules foule is. *1633–69*
   To Mr R. W. *W: publifhed here for the firft time*

In

In it is cherifhing fyer which dryes in mee 5
   Griefe which did drowne me: and halfe quench'd by it
   Are fatirique fyres which urg'd me to have writt
In fkorne of all: for now I admyre thee.
   And as Ayre doth fullfill the hollownes
   Of rotten walls; fo it myne emptines, 10
Where toft and mov'd it did beget this found
Which as a lame Eccho of thyne doth rebound.
   Oh, I was dead ; but fince thy fong new Life did give,
   I recreated, even by thy creature, live.

To Mʳ S. B.

O Thou which to fearch out the fecret parts
  Of the India, or rather Paradife
Of knowledge, haft with courage and advife
Lately launch'd into the vaft Sea of Arts,
Difdaine not in thy conftant travailing 5
   To doe as other Voyagers, and make
   Some turnes into leffe Creekes, and wifely take
Frefh water at the Heliconian fpring ;
I fing not, Siren like, to tempt; for I
   Am harfh ; nor as thofe Scifmatiques with you, 10
   Which draw all wits of good hope to their crew ;
But feeing in you bright fparkes of Poetry,
   I, though I brought no fuell, had defire
   With thefe Articulate blafts to blow the fire.

6 which] wᶜʰ *W, and so always*   10 emptines,] emptines. *W*
13–14 Oh, . . . give, . . . recreated, . . . creature,] *no commas, W*
  To Mʳ S. B. *O'F:* To M. S. B. *1633–69, A18, N, TCC, TCD, W*
10 harfh ; *1650–69:* harfh, *1633–39*   12 feeing] feing *1633 :* feene
TCD, W: feeme *TCC*   13 I, though] I thought *1650–54*   had]
but *1650–54*

To Mr *I. L.*

OF that fhort Roll of friends writ in my heart
   Which with thy name begins, fince their depart,
Whether in the Englifh Provinces they be,
   Or drinke of Po, Sequan, or Danubie,
There's none that fometimes greets us not, and yet   5
   Your Trent is Lethe; that paft, us you forget.
You doe not duties of Societies,
   If from the'embrace of a lov'd wife you rife,
View your fat Beafts, ftretch'd Barnes, and labour'd fields,
   Eate, play, ryde, take all joyes which all day yeelds,   10
And then againe to your embracements goe :
   Some houres on us your frends, and fome beftow
Upon your Mufe, elfe both wee fhall repent,
   I that my love, fhe that her guifts on you are fpent.

To Mr *B. B.*

IS not thy facred hunger of fcience
   Yet fatisfy'd ? Is not thy braines rich hive
   Fulfil'd with hony which thou doft derive
From the Arts fpirits and their Quinteffence ?
Then weane thy felfe at laft, and thee withdraw   5
   From Cambridge thy old nurfe, and, as the reft,
   Here toughly chew, and fturdily digeft
Th'immenfe vaft volumes of our common law;
And begin foone, left my griefe grieve thee too,
   Which is, that that which I fhould have begun   10

To Mr I. L. *W:* To M. I. L. *1633–69:* To M. I. L. *A18,N,TCC,
TCD:* To Mr T. L. *O'F*   5 fometimes] fometime *1635–39, Chambers*
6 Lethe; *W:* Lethe', *1633–69*   forget. *1639–69,W:* forget, *1633–35*
13 your] thy *W*   14 you] thee *W*   fpent.] fpent *1633*
   To Mr B. B. *O'F,W:* To M. B. B. *1633–69,A18,N,TCC,TCD*

In

In my youthes morning, now late muſt be done;
And I as Giddy Travellers muſt doe,
    Which ſtray or ſleepe all day, and having loſt
    Light and ſtrength, darke and tir'd muſt then ride poſt.

If thou unto thy Muſe be marryed,   15
    Embrace her ever, ever multiply,
    Be far from me that ſtrange Adulterie
To tempt thee and procure her widowhed.
My Muſe, (for I had one,) becauſe I'am cold,
    Divorc'd her ſelfe: the cauſe being in me,   20
    That I can take no new in Bigamye,
Not my will only but power doth withhold.
Hence comes it, that theſe Rymes which never had
    Mother, want matter, and they only have
    A little forme, the which their Father gave;   25
They are prophane, imperfeᴄt, oh, too bad
    To be counted Children of Poetry
    Except confirm'd and Biſhoped by thee.

To Mʳ *I. L.*

BLeſt are your North parts, for all this long time
    My Sun is with you, cold and darke'is our Clime;
Heavens Sun, which ſtaid ſo long from us this yeare,
    Staid in your North (I thinke) for ſhe was there,
And hether by kinde nature drawne from thence,   5
    Here rages, chafes, and threatens peſtilence;

12 I . . . Travellers *1650–69*: I, . . . Travellers, *1633–39*   13
ſtray] ſtay *W: compare* Sat. III. 78   16 ever, ever multiply, *1633–69,*
A18, N, O'F, TC: ſtill: encreaſe and multiply; *W*   18 widowhed.
W: widdowhood, *1633–39: widdowhood; 1650–69*   19 Muſe,
A18, N, O'F, TC, W: nurſe, *1633–69*   20 ſelfe: *W:* ſelfe, *1633–69*
in me, *1633–69:* in me; *Grolier:* in me. *Chambers. See note*
    To Mʳ I. L. *Ed:* To M. I. L. *A18, N, TCC, TCD, W:* To Mʳ T. L.
O'F: To M. I. P. *1633–69*   6 rages, chafes, *Ed:* rages chafes
1633–39: rages, chafes *1650–69:* rages, burnes, *W*

                                           Yet

Yet I, as long as fhee from hence doth ftaie,
   Thinke this no South, no Sommer, nor no day.
With thee my kinde and unkinde heart is run,
   There facrifice it to that beauteous Sun: 10
And fince thou art in Paradife and need'ft crave
   No joyes addition, helpe thy friend to fave.
So may thy paftures with their flowery feafts,
   As fuddenly as Lard, fat thy leane beafts;
So may thy woods oft poll'd, yet ever weare   15
   A greene, and when thee lift, a golden haire;
So may all thy fheepe bring forth Twins; and fo
   In chace and race may thy horfe all out goe;
So may thy love and courage ne'r be cold;
   Thy Sonne ne'r Ward; Thy lov'd wife ne'r feem old;
But maift thou wifh great things, and them attaine,   21
   As thou telft her, and none but her, my paine.

To Sir *H. W.* at his going Ambaffador to *Venice.*

AFter thofe reverend papers, whofe foule is
   Our good and great Kings lov'd hand and fear'd name,
By which to you he derives much of his,
   And (how he may) makes you almoft the fame,

A Taper of his Torch, a copie writ   5
   From his Originall, and a faire beame
Of the fame warme, and dazeling Sun, though it
   Muft in another Sphere his vertue ftreame:

11–12 *these lines from W: they have not previously been printed*   16
when thee lift, *Ed :* when thee lift *1633, A18, N, TC:* (when fhe lift)
1635–69, O'F: when thou wilt *W*   20 lov'd wife] fair wife *W*   22
her, . . . her, *Ed :* her . . . her *1633:* her, . . . her *1635–69*
    To Sir H. W. at his *&c. 1633–54:* To Sir Henry Wotton, at his *&c.*
1669, A18, N, O'F, TCC, TCD: printed in Walton's Life of Sir Henry
Wotton, 1670, *as a* 'letter, fent by him to Sir *Henry Wotton*, the morning
before he left *England*', *i. e. July 13* (O. S.), *1604*

                                    After

After thofe learned papers which your hand
   Hath ftor'd with notes of ufe and pleafure too,   10
From which rich treafury you may command
   Fit matter whether you will write or doe:

After thofe loving papers, where friends fend
   With glad griefe, to your Sea-ward fteps, farewel,
Which thicken on you now, as prayers afcend   15
   To heaven in troupes at'a good mans paffing bell:

Admit this honeft paper, and allow
   It fuch an audience as your felfe would aske;
What you muft fay at Venice this meanes now,
   And hath for nature, what you have for taske: 20

To fweare much love, not to be chang'd before
   Honour alone will to your fortune fit;
Nor fhall I then honour your fortune, more
   Then I have done your honour wanting it.

But'tis an eafier load (though both oppreffe)   25
   To want, then governe greatneffe, for wee are
In that, our owne and onely bufineffe,
   In this, wee muft for others vices care;

'Tis therefore well your fpirits now are plac'd
   In their laft Furnace, in activity;   30
Which fits them (Schooles and Courts and Warres o'rpaft)
   To touch and teft in any beft degree.

For mee, (if there be fuch a thing as I)
   Fortune (if there be fuch a thing as fhee)
Spies that I beare fo well her tyranny,   35
   That fhe thinks nothing elfe fo fit for mee;

---

10 pleafure *1635–69, A18, N, O'F, TC, Walton*: pleafures *1633*   13
where *1633, A18, N, TC*: which *1635–69, O'F, Walton*   16 in troupes]
on troops *Walton*   19 muft . . . meanes] would . . . fayes *Walton*
20 hath] has *Walton*   taske: *Ed:* taske. *1633–69*   21 not] nor
Walton   24 honour wanting it. *1633*: noble-wanting-wit. *1635–69,*
O'F: honour-wanting-wit. *Walton:* noble wanting it. *A18, N, TCC, TCD*
31 Warres *Ed:* warres *1633–69:* tents *Burley MS.*   32 teft] taft
1669 and Walton   35 Spies] Finds *Walton*

                                                             But

But though fhe part us, to heare my oft prayers
  For your increafe, God is as neere mee here;
And to fend you what I fhall begge, his ftaires
  In length and eafe are alike every where.   40

To Mrs *M. H.*

Mad paper ftay, and grudge not here to burne
  With all thofe fonnes whom my braine did create,
At left lye hid with mee, till thou returne
  To rags againe, which is thy native ftate.

What though thou have enough unworthinefle   5
  To come unto great place as others doe,
That's much; emboldens, pulls, thrufts I confeffe,
  But'tis not all; Thou fhould'ft be wicked too.

And, that thou canft not learne, or not of mee;
  Yet thou wilt goe? Goe, fince thou goeft to her   10
Who lacks but faults to be a Prince, for fhee,
  Truth, whom they dare not pardon, dares preferre.

But when thou com'ft to that perplexing eye
  Which equally claimes *love* and *reverence*,
Thou wilt not long difpute it, thou wilt die;   15
  And, having little now, have then no fenfe.

Yet when her warme redeeming hand, which is
  A miracle; and made fuch to worke more,
Doth touch thee (faples leafe) thou grow'ft by this
  Her creature; glorify'd more then before.   20

To Mrs M. H. *O'F:* To M. M. H. *1633–69,A18,N,TCC,TCD:* no title, *A25,B,C,P:* Elegie. *S96*   2 fonnes] Sunnes *B,S96*   my *1633:* thy *1635–69: Chambers attributes* thy *to 1633*   3 returne] returne.*1633*   7 That's much; emboldens, *A18,N,TC:* That's much, emboldens, *1633–54:* That's much emboldnefs, *1669:* That's much, it emboldens, *B,P*   8 all; Thou *A18,N,TC:* all, thou *1633–69*   10 goe? Goe, *Ed:* goe, Goe, *1633–69*   14 *reverence, Ed: reverence.* *1633: reverence: 1635–69*

Then

Then as a mother which delights to heare
 Her early child miſ-ſpeake halfe uttered words,
Or, becauſe majeſty doth never feare
 Ill or bold ſpeech, ſhe Audience affords.

And then, cold ſpeechleſſe wretch, thou dieſt againe, 25
 And wiſely; what diſcourſe is left for thee?
For, ſpeech of ill, and her, thou muſt abſtaine,
 And is there any good which is not ſhee?

Yet maiſt thou praiſe her ſervants, though not her,
 And wit, and vertue,'and honour her attend, 30
And ſince they'are but her cloathes, thou ſhalt not erre,
 If thou her ſhape and beauty'and grace commend.

Who knowes thy deſtiny? when thou haſt done,
 Perchance her Cabinet may harbour thee,
Whither all noble ambitious wits doe runne, 35
 A neſt almoſt as full of Good as ſhee.

When thou art there, if any, whom wee know,
 Were ſav'd before, and did that heaven partake,
When ſhe revolves his papers, marke what ſhow
 Of favour, ſhe alone, to them doth make. 40

Marke, if to˙get them, ſhe o'r skip the reſt,
 Marke, if ſhee read them twice, or kiſſe the name;
Marke, if ſhe doe the ſame that they proteſt,
 Marke, if ſhe marke whether her woman came.

Marke, if ſlight things be'objected, and o'r blowne, 45
 Marke, if her oathes againſt him be not ſtill
Reſerv'd, and that ſhee grieves ſhe's not her owne,
 And chides the doctrine that denies Freewill.

22 miſ-ſpeake] miſpeake *1633* 27 For, *1633*: From *1635-69,*
and MSS. her, *Ed*: her *1633-69* 31 erre, *1669*: erre *1633-54*
40 ſhe alone, *1633*: ſhe, alone, *1635-69* 41 get them, ſhe o'r skip]
get them, ſhe do skip *A18* (doth), *N, TC*: get them, ſhe skip oare *A25*,
C, O'F(skips): get to them, ſhee skipp *B, P* 44 whether *1633*:
whither *1635-69* 47 grieves *1633*: grieve *1635-69*
    I bid

I bid thee not doe this to be my fpie;
 Nor to make my felfe her familiar;   50
But fo much I doe love her choyce, that I
 Would faine love him that fhall be lov'd of her.

To the Counteffe of Bedford.

HOnour is fo fublime perfection,
 And fo refinde; that when God was alone
And creatureleffe at firft, himfelfe had none;

But as of the elements, thefe which wee tread,
Produce all things with which wee'are joy'd or fed,   5
And, thofe are barren both above our head:

So from low perfons doth all honour flow;
Kings, whom they would have honoured, to us fhow,
And but *direct* our honour, not *beftow.*

For when from herbs the pure part muft be wonne 10
From groffe, by Stilling, this is better done
By defpif'd dung, then by the fire or Sunne.

Care not then, Madame,'how low your prayfers lye;
In labourers balads oft more piety
God findes, then in *Te Deums* melodie.   15

And, ordinance rais'd on Towers, fo many mile
Send not their voice, nor laft fo long a while
As fires from th'earths low vaults in *Sicil* Ifle.

Should I fay I liv'd darker then were true,
Your radiation can all clouds fubdue;   20
But one,'tis beft light to contemplate you.

To the Counteffe of Bedford. *1633–69, B, O'F, S96:* To the Countefs
of B. *N, TCD* 10 part] parts *N, O'F, TCD* 12 or Sunne. *1633,
B, N, O'F, S96, TCD:* or Sun: *1669:* of Sunne: *1635–54, Chambers*
13 prayfers *N, O'F, TCD:* prayers *S96:* prayfes *1633–69* 16 Towers,]
Towers *1633* 20–1 fubdue; But one, *Ed:* fubdue; But One *Chambers:*
fubdue, But one, *1633–69:* fubdue But one; *Grolier and Grofart. See note*
                     You,

You, for whofe body God made better clay,
Or tooke Soules ftuffe fuch as fhall late decay,
Or fuch as needs fmall change at the laft day.

This, as an Amber drop enwraps a Bee,   25
Covering difcovers your quicke Soule; that we
May in your through-fhine front your hearts thoughts fee.

You teach (though wee learne not) a thing unknowne
To our late times, the ufe of fpecular ftone,
Through which all things within without were fhown.   30

Of fuch were Temples; fo and of fuch you are;
Beeing and *feeming* is your equall care,
And *vertues* whole *fumme* is but *know* and *dare*.

But as our Soules of growth and Soules of fenfe
Have birthright of our reafons Soule, yet hence   35
They fly not from that, nor feeke prefidence:

Natures firft leffon, fo, difcretion,
Muft not grudge zeale a place, nor yet keepe none,
Not banifh it felfe, nor religion.

Difcretion is a wifemans Soule, and fo   40
Religion is a Chriftians, and you know
How thefe are one; her *yea,* is not her *no.*

Nor may we hope to fodder ftill and knit
Thefe two, and dare to breake them; nor muft wit
Be colleague to religion, but be it.   45

26 Covering difcovers] Coverings difcover *1669*   27 your hearts
thoughts *B,N,O'F,S96,TCD:* our hearts thoughts *1633–69. See note*
31 fo and of fuch *N,TCD:* fo and fuch *1633–69,B,O'F,S96*   33
is but to know and dare. *N*
36–7   They fly not from that, nor feeke prefidence :
        Natures firft leffon, fo, difcretion, *&c. 1633–69* (prefidence. *1633;*
precedence : *1669*)
        They fly not from that, nor feek precedence,
        Natures firft leffon ; fo difcretion *&c.*   *Chambers and Grolier*
(difcretion, *Grolier*). *See note*   40–2] *These lines precede* 34–9 *in*
1635–69,B,N,S96,TCD: om. *O'F*   42 one ; *Ed:* one, *1633–69*
yea, . . . no] *ital. Ed.*

In

In thofe poor types of God (round circles) fo
Religions tipes the peecleffe centers flow,
And are in all the lines which all wayes goe.

If either ever wrought in you alone
Or principally, then religion   50
Wrought your ends, and your wayes difcretion.

Goe thither ftil, goe the fame way you went,
Who fo would change, do covet or repent;
Neither can reach you, great and innocent.

To the Counteffe of Bedford.
Begun in France but never perfected.

THough I be *dead*, and buried, yet I have
        (Living in you,) Court enough in my grave,
As oft as there I thinke my felfe to bee,
        So many refurrections waken mee.
That thankfullneffe your favours have begot   5
        In mee, embalmes mee, that I doe not rot.
This feafon as 'tis Eafter, as 'tis fpring,
        Muft both to growth and to confeffion bring
My thoughts difpos'd unto your influence; fo,
        Thefe verfes bud, fo thefe confeffions grow.   10
Firft I confeffe I have to others lent
        Your ftock, and over prodigally fpent
Your treafure, for fince I had never knowne
        Vertue or beautie, but as they are growne

48 all wayes *1719:* always *1633–69*
50–1   'twas Religion,
                    Yet you neglected not Difcretion. *S96*
53 do covet] doth covet *1669, O'F, S96*
        To the Counteffe &c. *1633–69 (following in 1635–69* That unripe fide
&c., *p.* 417, *and* If her difdaine &c., *p.* 430), *O'F*   5 begot] forgot *1633
some copies*   6 embalmes mee, *Ed:* embalmes mee; *1633–69*   rot. *Ed:*
rot; *1633–69*   9 influence; *Ed:* influence, *1633–69*   10 grow. *Ed:*
grow; *1633–69*   14 or *1633–39:* and *1650–69*

                                                                    In

In you, I fhould not thinke or fay they fhine,   15
　(So as I have) in any other Mine.
Next I confeffe this my confeffion,
　For, 'tis fome fault thus much to touch upon
Your praife to you, where half rights feeme too much,
　And make your minds fincere complexion blufh.   20
Next I confeffe my'impenitence, for I
　Can fcarce repent my firft fault, fince thereby
Remote low Spirits, which fhall ne'r read you,
　May in leffe leffons finde enough to doe,
By ftudying copies, not Originals,   25
　　　　　Defunt cætera.

A Letter to the Lady Carey, *and* M*rs* Effex
Riche, *From* Amyens.

MADAME,

HEre where by All All Saints invoked are,
　'Twere too much fchifme to be fingular,
And 'gainft a practife generall to warre.

Yet turning to Saincts, fhould my'humility
To other Sainct then you directed bee,   5
That were to make my fchifme, herefie.

Nor would I be a Convertite fo cold,
As not to tell it; If this be too bold,
Pardons are in this market cheaply fold.

Where, becaufe Faith is in too low degree,   10
I thought it fome Apoftlefhip in mee
To fpeake things which by faith alone I fee.

---

16 Mine. *Ed:* Mine; *1633-69*　　　　18 upon *Ed:* upon, *1633-69*
　A Letter to *&c. 1633-69, D, H49, Lec:* To the Lady Carey and her
Sifter M*rs* Effex Rich. From Amiens. *O'F:* To the Lady Co: of C. *N,*
TCD: To the Ladie Carey. *or* A Letter to the Ladie Carey. *B, Cy, S96:*
no title, P: To M*rs* Effex Rich and her fifter frô Amiens. *M*

　　　　　　　　　　　　　　　　　　　　That

That is, of you, who are a firmament
Of virtues, where no one is growne, or spent,
They'are your materials, not your ornament.   15

Others whom wee call vertuous, are not so
In their whole substance, but, their vertues grow
But in their humours, and at seasons show.

For when through tastlesse flat humilitie
In dow bak'd men some harmelessenes we see,   20
'Tis but his *flegme* that's *Vertuous*, and not Hee:

Soe is the Blood sometimes; who ever ran
To danger unimportun'd, he was than
No better then a *sanguine* Vertuous man.

So cloysterall men, who, in pretence of feare   25
All contributions to this life forbeare,
Have Vertue in *Melancholy*, and only there.

Spirituall *Cholerique* Crytiques, which in all
Religions find faults, and forgive no fall,
Have, through this zeale, Vertue but in their Gall.   30

We'are thus but parcel guilt; to Gold we'are growne
When Vertue is our Soules complexion;
Who knowes his Vertues name or place, hath none.

Vertue'is but aguish, when 'tis severall,
By occasion wak'd, and circumstantiall.   35
True vertue is *Soule*, Alwaies in all deeds *All*.

This Vertue thinking to give dignitie
To your soule, found there no infirmitie,
For, your soule was as good Vertue, as shee;

13 who are] who is *1633*   19 humilitie *1633-54, B, Cy, D, H49,
Lec, M, N, O'F, P, S96, TCD:* humidity *1669, Chambers*   26 con-
tributions] contribution *B, D, N, TCD*   30 this zeale, *1635-69, B, Cy,
D, H49, N, O'F, P, S96, TCD:* their zeale, *1633, Lec*   31 Gold] Golds
1633 some copies   33 aguish,] anguish, *1650-54*

Shee

Shee therefore wrought upon that part of you   40
Which is scarce lesse then soule, as she could do,
And so hath made your beauty, Vertue too.

Hence comes it, that your Beauty wounds not hearts,
As Others, with prophane and sensuall Darts,
But as an influence, vertuous thoughts imparts.   45

But if such friends by the honor of your sight
Grow capable of this so great a light,
As to partake your vertues, and their might,

What must I thinke that influence must doe,
Where it findes sympathie and matter too,   50
Vertue, and beauty of the same stuffe, as you?

Which is, your noble worthie sister, shee
Of whom, if what in this my Extasie
And revelation of you both I see,

I should write here, as in short Galleries   55
The Master at the end large glasses ties,
So to present the roome twice to our eyes,

So I should give this letter length, and say
That which I said of you; there is no way
From either, but by the other, not to stray.   60

May therefore this be enough to testifie
My true devotion, free from flattery;
He that beleeves himselfe, doth never lie.

57 our eyes,] your eyes, *Cy, D, H49, Lec, P*   60 by the] to the
1669   other, *1669:* other *1633–54*

To the Counteſſe of Salisbury. Auguſt. 1614.

FAire, great, and good, ſince ſeeing you, wee ſee
 What Heaven can doe, and what any Earth can be:
Since now your beauty ſhines, now when the Sunne
Growne ſtale, is to ſo low a value runne,
That his diſſhevel'd beames and ſcattered fires   5
Serve but for Ladies Periwigs and Tyres
In lovers Sonnets: you come to repaire
Gods booke of creatures, teaching what is faire.
Since now, when all is withered, ſhrunke, and dri'd,
All Vertues ebb'd out to a dead low tyde,   10
All the worlds frame being crumbled into ſand,
Where every man thinks by himſelfe to ſtand,
Integritie, friendſhip, and confidence,
(Ciments of greatnes) being vapor'd hence,
And narrow man being fill'd with little ſhares,   15
Court, Citie, Church, are all ſhops of ſmall-wares,
All having blowne to ſparkes their noble fire,
And drawne their ſound gold-ingot into wyre;
All trying by a love of littleneſſe
To make abridgments, and to draw to leſſe,   20
Even that nothing, which at firſt we were;
Since in theſe times, your greatneſſe doth appeare,
And that we learne by it, that man to get
Towards him that's infinite, muſt firſt be great.
Since in an age ſo ill, as none is fit   25
So much as to accuſe, much leſſe mend it,
(For who can judge, or witneſſe of thoſe times
Where all alike are guiltie of the crimes?)

  To the Counteſſe *&c. 1633–69, D, H49, Lec:* To the Counteſs of
Saliſbury. *O'F:* To the Counteſs of S. *N, TCD
1669, D, H49, Lec:* what *1635–54, N, O'F, TCD
1669*   17 noble fire,] nobler fire, *O'F*
that's *1650–69:* thats *1633–39*   2 and what *1633,*
   16 Court,] Courts,
   24 him] him, *1633*

            Where

Where he that would be good, is thought by all
A monſter, or at beſt fantaſticall;   30
Since now you durſt be good, and that I doe
Diſcerne, by daring to contemplate you,
That there may be degrees of faire, great, good,
Through your light, largeneſſe, vertue underſtood:
If in this ſacrifice of mine, be ſhowne   35
Any ſmall ſparke of theſe, call it your owne.
And if things like theſe, have been ſaid by mee
Of others; call not that Idolatrie.
For had God made man firſt, and man had ſeene
The third daies fruits, and flowers, and various greene, 40
He might have ſaid the beſt that he could ſay
Of thoſe faire creatures, which were made that day;
And when next day he had admir'd the birth
Of Sun, Moone, Stars, fairer then late-praiſ'd earth,
Hee might have ſaid the beſt that he could ſay,   45
And not be chid for praiſing yeſterday;
So though ſome things are not together true,
As, that another is worthieſt, and, that you:
Yet, to ſay ſo, doth not condemne a man,
If when he ſpoke them, they were both true than.   5⊃
How faire a proofe of this, in our ſoule growes?
Wee firſt have ſoules of growth, and ſenſe, and thoſe,
When our laſt ſoule, our ſoule immortall came,
Were ſwallowed into it, and have no name.
Nor doth he injure thoſe ſoules, which doth caſt   55
The power and praiſe of both them, on the laſt;
No more doe I wrong any; I adore
The ſame things now, which I ador'd before,
The ſubject chang'd, and meaſure; the ſame thing
In a low conſtable, and in the King   60

29–30 *Chambers includes in parenthesis*   30 fantaſticall; *Ed:* fan-
taſticall: *1633–69*   34 light, largeneſſe,] lights largeneſs, *1669*   38
Idolatrie.] Adulterie: *N,TCD*   40 greene,] greene *1633*   42 day;
Ed: day: *1633–69*   46 yeſterday; *Ed:* yeſterday: *1633–69*   54
name. *1633–39:* name *1654–69*   57 any; I adore *1633,D,Lec,N,*
TCD: any, if I adore *1635–69,O'F* (if *being inserted*)

I reverence;

I reverence; His power to work on mee:
So did I humbly reverence each degree
Of faire, great, good; but more, now I am come
From having found their *walkes,* to find their *home.*
And as I owe my firft foules thankes, that they   65
For my laft foule did fit and mould my clay,
So am I debtor unto them, whofe worth,
Enabled me to profit, and take forth
This new great leffon, thus to ftudy you;
Which none, not reading others, firft, could doe.   70
Nor lacke I light to read this booke, though I
In a darke Cave, yea in a Grave doe lie;
For as your fellow Angells, fo you doe
Illuftrate them who come to ftudy you.
The firft whom we in Hiftories doe finde   75
To have profeft all Arts, was one borne blinde:
He lackt thofe eyes beafts have as well as wee,
Not thofe, by which Angels are feene and fee;
So, though I'am borne without thofe eyes to live,
Which fortune, who hath none her felfe, doth give,   80
Which are, fit meanes to fee bright courts and you,
Yet may I fee you thus, as now I doe;
I fhall by that, all goodneffe have difcern'd,
And though I burne my librarie, be learn'd.

61 mee: *D,N,TCD:* mee; *1633–69*   63 good; *Ed:* good,
1633–69   77–8 *om. D,H49,Lec*

To the Lady Bedford.

YOu that are fhe and you, that's double fhee,
   In her dead face, halfe of your felfe fhall fee;
Shee was the other part, for fo they doe
   Which build them friendfhips, become one of two;
So two, that but themfelves no third can fit,   5
   Which were to be fo, when they were not yet;
Twinnes, though their birth *Cufco*, and *Mufco* take,
   As divers ftarres one Conftellation make;
Pair'd like two eyes, have equall motion, fo
   Both but one meanes to fee, one way to goe.   10
Had you dy'd firft, a carcaffe fhee had beene;
   And wee your rich Tombe in her face had feene;
She like the Soule is gone, and you here ftay,
   Not a live friend; but th'other halfe of clay.
And fince you act that part, As men fay, here   15
   Lies fuch a Prince, when but one part is there,
And do all honour and devotion due
   Unto the whole, fo wee all reverence you;
For, fuch a friendfhip who would not adore
   In you, who are all what both were before,   20
Not all, as if fome perifhed by this,
   But fo, as all in you contracted is.
As of this all, though many parts decay,
   The pure which elemented them fhall ftay;
And though diffus'd, and fpread in infinite,   25
   Shall recollect, and in one All unite:

To the &c. *1635–69, O'F:* Elegie to the Lady Bedford. *1633, Cy, H40,
L74, N, P, TCD:* Elegia Sexta. *S: In 1633, Cy, H40, N, TCD it follows, in
P precedes, the Funerall Elegy Death (p. 284), to which it is apparently
a covering letter: In L74 it follows the Elegy on the Lady Marckham:
O'F places it among the Letters, S among the Elegies*   1 fhe and you,]
fhe, and you *1633–69, Chambers. See note*   4 two;] the two; *1669*
6 yet; *Ed:* yet *1633–39:* yet. *1650–69*   8 make; *Ed:* make, *1633–69*
10 goe. *Ed:* goe; *1633–69*   13 ftay,] ftay *1633–35*   th'other]
thother *1633*   clay. *Ed:* clay; *1633–69*   16 there, *Ed:* there; *1633–69*
17 honour] honour: *1633*   due] due; *1633*   20 were] was *1633*
22 as all in you] as in you all *O'F:* that in you all *Cy, H40, L74, N, S*
is. *Ed:* is; *1633–69*

So

So madame, as her Soule to heaven is fled,
 Her fleſh reſts in the earth, as in the bed;
Her vertues do, as to their proper ſpheare,
 Returne to dwell with you, of whom they were: 30
As perfect motions are all circular,
 So they to you, their ſea, whence leſſe ſtreames are.
Shee was all ſpices, you all metalls; ſo
 In you two wee did both rich Indies know.
And as no fire, nor ruſt can ſpend or waſte 35
 One dramme of gold, but what was firſt ſhall laſt,
Though it bee forc'd in water, earth, ſalt, aire,
 Expans'd in infinite, none will impaire;
So, to your ſelfe you may additions take,
 But nothing can you leſſe, or changed make. 40
Seeke not in ſeeking new, to ſeeme to doubt,
 That you can match her, or not be without;
But let ſome faithfull booke in her roome be,
 Yet but of *Iudith* no ſuch booke as ſhee.

28 the bed;] a bed; *Cy, H40, L74, N, O'F, S:* her bed; *P* 30
were:] were; *1633* 32 are.] are; *1633* 34 know.] know; *1633*
41 doubt, *1633:* doubt; *1635–69* 42 can] *twice in 1633*

A N

AN ANATOMIE
OF THE WORLD.

Wherein,

By occaſion of the untimely death of
Miſtris ELIZABETH DRVRY,
the frailty and the decay of this
whole World is repreſented.

The firſt Anniverſary.

To the praiſe of the dead,
and the ANATOMIE.

WEll dy'd the World, that we might live to ſee
   This world of wit, in his Anatomie:
No evill wants his good; ſo wilder heires
Bedew their Fathers Tombes, with forced teares,
Whoſe ſtate requites their loſſe: whiles thus we gain,   5
Well may wee walke in blacks, but not complaine.
Yet how can I conſent the world is dead
While this Muſe lives? which in his ſpirits ſtead

An Anatomie &c. *1611–33:* Anatomie &c. *1635–69*   The firſt
Anniverſary. *1612–69: om. 1611. See note*   To the praiſe of the
dead &c. *1611–69* (Dead *1611*)   8 While] Whiles *1639–69*

                                              Seemes

Seemes to informe a World; and bids it bee,
In fpight of loffe or fraile mortalitie?   10
And thou the fubject of this welborne thought,
Thrice noble maid, couldft not have found nor fought
A fitter time to yeeld to thy fad Fate,
Then whiles this fpirit lives, that can relate
Thy worth fo well to our laft Nephews eyne,   15
That they fhall wonder both at his and thine:
Admired match! where ftrives in mutuall grace
The cunning pencill, and the comely face:
A taske which thy faire goodneffe made too much
For the bold pride of vulgar pens to touch;   20
Enough is us to praife them that praife thee,
And fay, that but enough thofe prayfes bee,
Which hadft thou liv'd, had hid their fearfull head
From th'angry checkings of thy modeft red:
Death barres reward and fhame: when envy's gone,   25
And gaine, 'tis fafe to give the dead their owne.
As then the wife Egyptians wont to lay
More on their Tombes, then houfes: thefe of clay,
But thofe of braffe, or marble were: fo wee
Give more unto thy Ghoft, then unto thee.   30
Yet what wee give to thee, thou gav'ft to us,
And may'ft but thanke thy felfe, for being thus:
Yet what thou gav'ft, and wert, O happy maid,
Thy grace profeft all due, where 'tis repayd.
So thefe high fongs that to thee fuited bin   35
Serve but to found thy Makers praife, in thine,
Which thy deare foule as fweetly fings to him
Amid the Quire of Saints, and Seraphim,
As any Angels tongue can fing of thee;
The fubjects differ, though the skill agree: 40
For as by infant-yeares men judge of age,

21 is] it is *1669*   25 fhame: *1611, 1612–25*: fhame, *1633–69*
26 gaine, *1633–69*: gaine; *1612–25*   34 where] were *1621–25*   35
bin *1633–39*: bine *1611*: bine, *1612–21*: bine, *1625*: bin, *1650–69*   36
praife, in thine, *1611, 1612–25*: praife and thine, *1633–69*   38 Quire
1611, 1612–25: quire *1633–69*   39 tongue *1611, 1612–39*: tongues
1650–69   41 infant-yeares *1611, 1621–25*: infant yeares *1633–69*
                                                                          Thy

Thy early love, thy vertues, did prefage
What an high part thou bear'ft in thofe beft fongs,
Whereto no burden, nor no end belongs.
Sing on thou virgin Soule, whofe lofsfull gaine   45
Thy lovefick parents have bewail'd in vaine;
Never may thy Name be in our fongs forgot,
Till wee fhall fing thy ditty and thy note.

An Anatomy of the World.

The firft Anniverfary.

WHen that rich Soule which to her heaven is gone,   *The entrie*
Whom all do celebrate, who know they have one,   *into the*
(For who is fure he hath a Soule, unleffe   *worke.*
It fee, and judge, and follow worthineffe,
And by Deedes praife it? hee who doth not this,   5
May lodge an In-mate foule, but 'tis not his.)
When that Queene ended here her progreffe time,
And, as t'her ftanding houfe to heaven did climbe,
Where loath to make the Saints attend her long,
She's now a part both of the Quire, and Song,   10
This World, in that great earthquake languifhed;
For in a common bath of teares it bled,
Which drew the ftrongeft vitall fpirits out:
But fuccour'd then with a perplexed doubt,
Whether the world did lofe, or gaine in this,   15
(Becaufe fince now no other way there is,

42 vertues, *1611, 1612-25*: vertues *1633-69*   prefage *1612-25*: prefage,
1633-69   43 What an hie . . . beft fongs, *1611-12* : What hie . . .
beft fongs *1621-25* : What high . . . beft of fongs, *1633-69*   47 our
1611, 1612-54: om. *1669*   forgot,] forgot. *1621-25*
An Anatomy *&c. 1611-69*   The firft Anniverfary. *1612-69* (First
1612-25): om. *1611*   2 Whom *1611, 1612-25, 1669*: Who *1633*: whõ
1635-54   5 Deedes *1611, 1612-25* : deeds, *1633-69*   6 In-mate
1611-12: Inmate *1621-25*: immate *1633* : inmate *1635-69*   10 Song,
1611: Song. *1612-33*: Song: *1635-69*   14 then *1611, 1612-39*:
them *1650-69*   *The entrie &c. 1612-21*: om. *1625-33*: *1611 and
1635-69 have no notes*

But

But goodneſſe, to ſee her, whom all would ſee,
All muſt endeavour to be good as ſhee,)
This great conſumption to a fever turn'd,
And ſo the world had fits; it joy'd, it mourn'd;   20
And, as men thinke, that Agues phyſick are,
And th'Ague being ſpent, give over care,
So thou ſicke World, miſtak'ſt thy ſelfe to bee
Well, when alas, thou'rt in a Lethargie.
Her death did wound and tame thee than, and than   25
Thou might'ſt have better ſpar'd the Sunne, or Man.
That wound was deep, but 'tis more miſery,
That thou haſt loſt thy ſenſe and memory.
'Twas heavy then to heare thy voyce of mone,
But this is worſe, that thou art ſpeechleſſe growne.   30
Thou haſt forgot thy name, thou hadſt; thou waſt
Nothing but ſhee, and her thou haſt o'rpaſt.
For as a child kept from the Font, untill
A prince, expected long, come to fulfill
The ceremonies, thou unnam'd had'ſt laid,   35
Had not her comming, thee her Palace made:
Her name defin'd thee, gave thee forme, and frame,
And thou forgett'ſt to celebrate thy name.
Some moneths ſhe hath beene dead (but being dead,
Meaſures of times are all determined)   40
But long ſhe'ath beene away, long, long, yet none
Offers to tell us who it is that's gone.
But as in ſtates doubtfull of future heires,
When ſickneſſe without remedie empaires
The preſent Prince, they're loth it ſhould be ſaid,   45
The Prince doth languiſh, or the Prince is dead:
So mankinde feeling now a generall thaw,
A ſtrong example gone, equall to law,
The Cyment which did faithfully compact,
And glue all vertues, now reſolv'd, and ſlack'd,   50

18 ſhee, *1611:* ſhee *1612, 1669:* ſhee. *1621–54*   22 care, *1611–21:*
care. *1625–33*   24 Lethargie.] Letargee. *1611, 1612–25*   26
Man. *1611, 1621–25:* man. *1633–69*   31 name, *1611, 1612–25:* name
1633–69   33 Font, *1611:* Fount, *1612–69*   36 Palace *1611–12,
1621–25:* palace *1633–69*   40 times *1611, 1612–33:* time *1635–69*
48 law, *1612, 1669:* law. *1611, 1621–25:* law; *1633–54*   50 glue]
give *1650–69*

Thought

Thought it fome blafphemy to fay fh'was dead,
Or that our weakneffe was difcovered
In that confeffion; therefore fpoke no more
Then tongues, the Soule being gone, the loffe deplore.
But though it be too late to fuccour thee,   55
Sicke World, yea, dead, yea putrified, fince fhee
Thy'intrinfique balme, and thy prefervative,
Can never be renew'd, thou never live,
I (fince no man can make thee live) will try,
What wee may gaine by thy Anatomy.   60
Her death hath taught us dearely, that thou art
Corrupt and mortall in thy pureft part.
Let no man fay, the world it felfe being dead,
'Tis labour loft to have difcovered
The worlds infirmities, fince there is none   65
Alive to ftudy this diffection;
For there's a kinde of World remaining ftill,   *What life*
Though fhee which did inanimate and fill   *the world*
The world, be gone, yet in this laft long night,   *hath ftil.*
Her Ghoft doth walke; that is, a glimmering light,   70
A faint weake love of vertue, and of good,
Reflects from her, on them which underftood
Her worth; and though fhe have fhut in all day,
The twilight of her memory doth ftay;
Which, from the carcaffe of the old world, free,   75
Creates a new world, and new creatures bee
Produc'd: the matter and the ftuffe of this,
Her vertue, and the forme our practice is:
And though to be thus elemented, arme
Thefe creatures, from home-borne intrinfique harme,   80
(For all affum'd unto this dignitie,
So many weedleffe Paradifes bee,
Which of themfelves produce no venemous finne,
Except fome forraine Serpent bring it in)

What life &c. 1612-21: om. 1625-33   70 walke; *1611, 1612-25:*
walke, *1633-69*   71 good, *1633:* good *1612-25, 1635-69*   75 old
world, free, *1611-12, 1633-69:* old world, free *1621-25*   79 though |
thought *1621-33*   80 home-borne] homborne *1611, 1621-25:*
homeborne *1633-69*
Yet,

Yet, becaufe outward ftormes the ftrongeft breake,   85
And ftrength it felfe by confidence growes weake,
This new world may be fafer, being told
The fickneffes The dangers and difeafes of the old:
of the World For with due temper men doe then forgoe,
Or covet things, when they their true worth know.   90
Impoffibili- There is no health; Phyfitians fay that wee,
ty of health At beft, enjoy but a neutralitie.
And can there bee worfe fickneffe, then to know
That we are never well, nor can be fo?
Wee are borne ruinous: poore mothers cry,   95
That children come not right, nor orderly;
Except they headlong come and fall upon
An ominous precipitation.
How witty's ruine! how importunate
Upon mankinde! it labour'd to fruftrate   100
Even Gods purpofe; and made woman, fent
For mans reliefe, caufe of his languifhment.
They were to good ends, and they are fo ftill,
But acceffory, and principall in ill;
For that firft marriage was our funerall: 105
One woman at one blow, then kill'd us all,
And fingly, one by one, they kill us now.
We doe delightfully our felves allow
To that confumption; and profufely blinde,
Wee kill our felves to propagate our kinde.   110
And yet we do not that; we are not men:
There is not now that mankinde, which was then,
When as, the Sunne and man did feeme to ftrive,
Shortneffe (Joynt tenants of the world) who fhould furvive;
of life. When, Stagge, and Raven, and the long-liv'd tree,   115
Compar'd with man, dy'd in minoritie;

85 Yet, *1612–25:* Yet *1633–69*   *The fickneffes &c. 1612: The
fickneffe &c. 1621: The ficknes &c. 1625–33*   89 then] them *1650–69*
99 ruine! *Ed:* ruine? *1611, 1612–25:* ruine, *1633–69*   100 mankinde!
Ed: mankinde? *1611, 1612–69*   113 When as, the Sunne and man
1633–39: no commas 1650–69: When as the Sunne and man, *1611,
1612–25*   114 furvive; *1650–69:* furvive. *1611, 1612–39*   116
minoritie; *1650–69:* minoritee. *1611, 1621–25:* minoritie, *1633–39*
                                                            When,

When, if a flow pac'd ftarre had ftolne away
From the obfervers marking, he might ftay
Two or three hundred yeares to fee't againe,
And then make up his obfervation plaine;   120
When, as the age was long, the fife was great;
Mans growth confefs'd, and recompenc'd the meat;
So fpacious and large, that every Soule
Did a faire Kingdome, and large Realme controule:
And when the very ftature, thus erect,   125
Did that foule a good way towards heaven direct.
Where is this mankinde now? who lives to age,
Fit to be made *Methufalem* his page?
Alas, we fcarce live long enough to try
Whether a true made clocke run right, or lie.   130
Old Grandfires talke of yefterday with forrow,
And for our children wee referve to morrow.
So fhort is life, that every peafant ftrives,
In a torne houfe, or field, to have three lives.
And as in lafting, fo in length is man   135
Contracted to an inch, who was a fpanne;   *Smalneffe*
For had a man at firft in forrefts ftray'd,   *of ftature.*
Or fhipwrack'd in the Sea, one would have laid
A wager, that an Elephant, or Whale,
That met him, would not haftily affaile   140
A thing fo equall to him: now alas,
The Fairies, and the Pigmies well may paffe
As credible; mankinde decayes fo foone,
We'are fcarce our Fathers fhadowes caft at noone:
Onely death addes t'our length: nor are wee growne   145
In ftature to be men, till we are none.
But this were light, did our leffe volume hold
All the old Text; or had wee chang'd to gold
Their filver; or difpos'd into leffe glaffe
Spirits of vertue, which then fcatter'd was.   150

131 Grandfires *1611, 1612–21* : Granfires *1625–69*   forrow,
1611–21 : forrow. *1625* : forrow: *1633–69*   133 peafant *1611, 1612–25* :
pefant *1633–69*   134 lives. *1611, 1633* : lives *1612* : lives, *1621–25*
135 man *1611* : man. *1612–25·* : man, *1633–69*   145 addes *1611–21* :
adds *1635–69* : ads *1625, 1633*   149 filver ; *1611–12* : filver
1621–25 : filver, *1633–69*   150 fcatter'd] fcattred *1612–25*

But

But 'tis not fo: w'are not retir'd, but dampt;
And as our bodies, fo our mindes are crampt:
'Tis fhrinking, not clofe weaving that hath thus,
In minde, and body both bedwarfed us.
Wee feeme ambitious, Gods whole worke t'undoe;   155
Of nothing hee made us, and we ftrive too,
To bring our felves to nothing backe; and wee
Doe what wee can, to do't fo foone as hee.
With new difeafes on our felves we warre,
And with new Phyficke, a worfe Engin farre.   160
Thus man, this worlds Vice-Emperour, in whom
All faculties, all graces are at home;
And if in other creatures they appeare,
They're but mans Minifters, and Legats there,
To worke on their rebellions, and reduce   165
Them to Civility, and to mans ufe:
This man, whom God did wooe, and loth t'attend
Till man came up, did downe to man defcend,
This man, fo great, that all that is, is his,
Oh what a trifle, and poore thing he is!   170
If man were any thing, he's nothing now:
Helpe, or at leaft fome time to waft, allow
T'his other wants, yet when he did depart
With her whom we lament, hee loft his heart.
She, of whom th'Ancients feem'd to prophefie,   175
When they call'd vertues by the name of *fhee*;
Shee in whom vertue was fo much refin'd,
That for Allay unto fo pure a minde
Shee tooke the weaker Sex; fhee that could drive
The poyfonous tincture, and the ftaine of *Eve*,   180
Out of her thoughts, and deeds; and purifie
All, by a true religious Alchymie;

152 bodies, *1611–25*: bodies *1633–39*   153 clofe weaving
1633–69: clofe-weaning *1611–12*: clofe weaning *1621–25*   161 Thus
man, *1611, 1612–33*: This man, *1635–69, Chambers*   166 ufe:]
ufe. *1611, 1621–33*   167 t'attend] t'atend *1633*   169 man, *1611*:
man *1612–69*   171 any thing, *1611–12*: any thing; *1621–33*   172
waft, *1633*: waft *1611*: wafte, *1635–69*   178 Allay *1611,1612–25*:
allay *1633–69*   179 Sex; *1611*: Sex, *1621–25*: Sex: *1633–69*
181 thoughts, *1611–12,1635–69*: thought, *1621–33*

Shee,

Shee, fhee is dead; fhee's dead: when thou knoweft this,
Thou knoweft how poore a trifling thing man is.
And learn'ft thus much by our Anatomie,   185
The heart being perifh'd, no part can be free.
And that except thou feed (not banquet) on
The fupernaturall food, Religion,
Thy better Growth growes withered, and fcant;
Be more then man, or thou'rt leffe then an Ant.   190
Then, as mankinde, fo is the worlds whole frame
Quite out of joynt, almoft created lame:
For, before God had made up all the reft,
Corruption entred, and deprav'd the beft:
It feis'd the Angels, and then firft of all   195
The world did in her cradle take a fall,
And turn'd her braines, and tooke a generall maime,
Wronging each joynt of th'univerfall frame.
The nobleft part, man, felt it firft; and than
Both beafts and plants, curft in the curfe of man.   200 *Decay of*
So did the world from the firft houre decay,   *nature in*
That evening was beginning of the day,   *other parts.*
And now the Springs and Sommers which we fee,
Like fonnes of women after fiftie bee.
And new Philofophy calls all in doubt,   205
The Element of fire is quite put out;
The Sun is loft, and th'earth, and no mans wit
Can well direct him where to looke for it.
And freely men confeffe that this world's fpent,
When in the Planets, and the Firmament   210
They feeke fo many new; they fee that this
Is crumbled out againe to his Atomies.
'Tis all in peeces, all cohaerence gone;
All juft fupply, and all Relation:

183 Shee, fhee *1611, 1612–25:* She, fhe *1633–69*   186 no]
no no *1621*   188 Religion, *1611,1650–69:* Religion. *1612–25:*
Religion: *1633–39*   189 Growth *1611:* grouth *1612–25:* growth
1633–69   withered] whithered *1621–25*   191 Then, *1611,*
1621–25: Then *1633–69*   195 Angels, *1612–69:* Angells: *1611*
200 man. *1611, 1612–25:* man, *1633–39:* man: *1650–69*   210
Firmament *1611–12:* firmament *1621–69*   212 Atomies.] Atomis.
1611, 1612–25   213 cohaerence *1611, 1612–25:* coherence *1633–69*

Prince, Subject, Father, Sonne, are things forgot,   215
For every man alone thinkes he hath got
To be a Phœnix, and that then can bee
None of that kinde, of which he is, but hee.
This is the worlds condition now, and now
She that should all parts to reunion bow,   220
She that had all Magnetique force alone,
To draw, and faften fundred parts in one;
She whom wife nature had invented then
When fhe obferv'd that every fort of men
Did in their voyage in this worlds Sea ftray,   225
And needed a new compaffe for their way;
She that was beft, and firft originall
Of all faire copies, and the generall
Steward to Fate; fhe whofe rich eyes, and breft
Guilt the Weft Indies, and perfum'd the Eaft;   230
Whofe having breath'd in this world, did beftow
Spice on thofe Iles, and bad them ftill fmell fo,
And that rich Indie which doth gold interre,
Is but as fingle money, coyn'd from her:
She to whom this world muft it felfe refer,   235
As Suburbs, or the Microcofme of her,
Shee, fhee is dead; fhee's dead: when thou knowft this,
Thou knowft how lame a cripple this world is.
And learn'ft thus much by our Anatomy,
That this worlds generall fickeneffe doth not lie   240
In any humour, or one certaine part;
But as thou faweft it rotten at the heart,
Thou feeft a Hectique feaver hath got hold
Of the whole fubftance, not to be contrould,
And that thou haft but one way, not t'admit   245
The worlds infection, to be none of it.
For the worlds fubtilft immateriall parts

217 then *1611, 1612–69*: there *Grosart, who with Chambers attributes to
1669*   223 invented] innented *1621*   228 copies, *1633–69*: copies;
1611–12: copies *1621–25*   229 Fate; *1612–69*: Fate: *1611*   breft
1611: breft: *1612–25*: breaft, *1633*   230 Weft Indies, *1611*: Weft-
Indies, *1621–69*   Eaft; *1611*: Eaft, *1621–69*   234 money, *1611–21*:
money *1625–69*   237 knowft *1611*: knoweft *1612–69*: and so in 238
237 this,] this *1633–35*   238 is. *1611, 1612–33*: is, *1635–69*   244
contrould,] contrould. *1611, 1612–25*

Feele this confuming wound, and ages darts.
For the worlds beauty is decai'd, or gone,
Beauty, that's colour, and proportion.
We thinke the heavens enjoy their Sphericall,
Their round proportion embracing all.
But yet their various and perplexed courfe,
Obferv'd in divers ages, doth enforce
Men to finde out fo many Eccentrique parts,
Such divers downe-right lines, fuch overthwarts,
As difproportion that pure forme: It teares
The Firmament in eight and forty fheires,
And in thefe Conftellations then arife
New ftarres, and old doe vanifh from our eyes:
As though heav'n fuffered earthquakes, peace or war,
When new Towers rife, and old demolifh't are.
They have impal'd within a Zodiake
The free-borne Sun, and keepe twelve Signes awake
To watch his fteps; the Goat and Crab controule,
And fright him backe, who elfe to either Pole
(Did not thefe Tropiques fetter him) might runne:
For his courfe is not round; nor can the Sunne
Perfit a Circle, or maintaine his way
One inch direct; but where he rofe to-day
He comes no more, but with a couzening line,
Steales by that point, and fo is Serpentine:
And feeming weary with his reeling thus,
He meanes to fleepe, being now falne nearer us.
So, of the Starres which boaft that they doe runne
In Circle ftill, none ends where he begun.
All their proportion's lame, it finkes, it fwels.
For of Meridians, and Parallels,
Man hath weav'd out a net, and this net throwne
Upon the Heavens, and now they are his owne.
Loth to goe up the hill, or labour thus
To goe to heaven, we make heaven come to us.
We fpur, we reine the ftarres, and in their race

250 *Disformity*
of parts.

255

260

265

270

275

280

251 Sphericall, *1650–69*: Sphericall *1611, 1612–39*   252 all. *1611,
1612–25*: all, *1633–69*   257 forme: *1633–69*: forme. *1611, 1612–25*
258 fheires, *1633–35*: fheeres, *1611, 1612–25*: fhieres, *1639–69*   267
Tropiques *1611, 1612–25*: tropiques *1633–69*   273 with] of *1635–69*
They're

They're diverfly content t'obey our pace.
But keepes the earth her round proportion ftill?   285
Doth not a Tenarif, or higher Hill
Rife fo high like a Rocke, that one might thinke
The floating Moone would fhipwracke there, and finke?
Seas are fo deepe, that Whales being ftrooke to day,
Perchance to morrow, fcarfe at middle way   290
Of their wifh'd journies end, the bottome, die.
And men, to found depths, fo much line untie,
As one might juftly thinke, that there would rife
At end thereof, one of th'Antipodies:
If under all, a Vault infernall bee,   295
(Which fure is fpacious, except that we
Invent another torment, that there muft
Millions into a ftraight hot roome be thruft)
Then folidneffe, and roundneffe have no place.
Are thefe but warts, and pock-holes in the face   300
Of th'earth? Thinke fo: but yet confeffe, in this
The worlds proportion disfigured is;

Diforder in the world.
That thofe two legges whereon it doth rely,
Reward and punifhment are bent awry.
And, Oh, it can no more be queftioned,   305
That beauties beft, proportion, is dead,
Since even griefe it felfe, which now alone
Is left us, is without proportion.
Shee by whofe lines proportion fhould bee
Examin'd, meafure of all Symmetree,   310
Whom had that Ancient feen, who thought foules made
Of Harmony, he would at next have faid
That Harmony was fhee, and thence infer,
That foules were but Refultances from her,
And did from her into our bodies goe,   315

284 pace.] peace. *1612–33*   286 Tenarif, *1611, 1612–25:* Tenarus
1633–69   Hill *1611, 1612–25:* hill *1633–69*   288 there, *1611,
1612–21:* there *1625–69*   289 ftrooke *1611, 1612–25:* ftrucke *1633–69*
290 to morrow, *1611, 1612–25:* to morrow *1633–69*   295 Vault
1611, 1612–25: vault *1633–69*   298 straight] strait *1611–25*   300
pock-holes] pockholes *1633–69*   301 th'earth?] th'earth; *1633*   306
beauties beft, proportion, *1611, 1612–39:* beauty's best proportion *Chambers:*
1650–69 drop the second comma   313 infer, *1611–12:* infer. *1621–25:*
infer *1633–69*

As

As to our eyes, the formes from objects flow:
Shee, who if thofe great Doctors truly faid
That the Arke to mans proportions was made,
Had been a type for that, as that might be
A type of her in this, that contrary   320
Both Elements, and Paffions liv'd at peace
In her, who caus'd all Civill war to ceafe.
Shee, after whom, what forme fo'er we fee,
Is difcord, and rude incongruitie;
Shee, fhee is dead, fhee's dead; when thou knowft this 325
Thou knowft how ugly a monfter this world is:
And learn'ft thus much by our Anatomie,
That here is nothing to enamour thee:
And that, not only faults in inward parts,
Corruptions in our braines, or in our hearts,   330
Poyfoning the fountaines, whence our actions fpring,
Endanger us: but that if every thing
Be not done fitly'and in proportion,
To fatisfie wife, and good lookers on,
(Since moft men be fuch as moft thinke they bee)   335
They're lothfome too, by this Deformitee.
For good, and well, muft in our actions meete;
Wicked is not much worfe than indifcreet.
But beauties other fecond Element,
Colour, and luftre now, is as neere fpent.   340
And had the world his juft proportion,
Were it a ring ftill, yet the ftone is gone.
As a compaffionate Turcoyfe which doth tell
By looking pale, the wearer is not well,
As gold falls ficke being ftung with Mercury,   345
All the worlds parts of fuch complexion bee.
When nature was moft bufie, the firft weeke,
Swadling the new borne earth, God feem'd to like
That fhe fhould fport her felfe fometimes, and play,

318 proportions *1611–12:* proportion *1621–69*   321 Elements,
1611–12: Elements *1621–69*   325 Shee, fhee *1611, 1612–25:* She, fhe
1633–69   fhee's] fhe's *1633–69*   knowft *1611:* knoweft *1612–25:*
know'ft *1633–69*   326 knowft *1611, 1612–25:* knoweft *1633–69*
336 Deformitee. *1611, 1612–25:* deformitie. *1633–69*
                                                            To

To mingle, and vary colours every day: 350
And then, as though ſhee could not make inow,
Himſelfe his various Rainbow did allow.
Sight is the nobleſt ſenſe of any one,
Yet ſight hath only colour to feed on,
And colour is decai'd: ſummers robe growes   355
Duskie, and like an oft dyed garment ſhowes.
Our bluſhing red, which us'd in cheekes to ſpred,
Is inward ſunke, and only our ſoules are red.
Perchance the world might have recovered,
If ſhe whom we lament had not beene dead: 360
But ſhee, in whom all white, and red, and blew
(Beauties ingredients) voluntary grew,
As in an unvext Paradiſe; from whom
Did all things verdure, and their luſtre come,
Whoſe compoſition was miraculous,   365
Being all colour, all Diaphanous,
(For Ayre, and Fire but thick groſſe bodies were,
And livelieſt ſtones but drowſie, and pale to her,)
Shee, ſhee, is dead; ſhee's dead: when thou know'ſt this,
Thou knowſt how wan a Ghoſt this our world is: 370
And learn'ſt thus much by our Anatomie,
That it ſhould more affright, then pleaſure thee.
And that, ſince all faire colour then did ſinke,
'Tis now but wicked vanitie, to thinke
Weakneſſe in To colour vicious deeds with good pretence,   375
the want of Or with bought colors to illude mens ſenſe.
correſpondence Nor in ought more this worlds decay appeares,
of heaven and Then that her influence the heav'n forbeares,
earth. Or that the Elements doe not feele this,
The father, or the mother barren is.   380
The cloudes conceive not raine, or doe not powre,
In the due birth time, downe the balmy ſhowre;

351 inow, *1611, 1612–25:* enough, *1633:* enow, *1635–69*   352
allow.] allow, *1621–33*   366 Diaphanous, *1611, 1612–25:* diaphanous,
1633–69   369 Shee, ſhee, *1611, 1612–25* (ſhee *1625*): She, ſhe
1633–69 (but Shee, *1633, in paſs-over word*)   370 knowſt *1611:*
knoweſt *1621–69*   374 vanitie, to thinke *1633–69:* vanity to think,
1611, 1612–25   379–80 feele this, . . . barren is. *1611, 1612–69:* feele
this. . . . barren is; *Chambers. See note*

Th'Ayre

Th'Ayre doth not motherly fit on the earth,
To hatch her feafons, and give all things birth;
Spring-times were common cradles, but are tombes; 385
And falfe-conceptions fill the generall wombes;
Th'Ayre fhowes fuch Meteors, as none can fee,
Not only what they meane, but what they bee;
Earth fuch new wormes, as would have troubled much
Th'Ægyptian *Mages* to have made more fuch. 390
What Artift now dares boaft that he can bring
Heaven hither, or conftellate any thing,
So as the influence of thofe ftarres may bee
Imprifon'd in an Hearbe, or Charme, or Tree,
And doe by touch, all which thofe ftars could doe? 395
The art is loft, and correfpondence too.
For heaven gives little, and the earth takes leffe,
And man leaft knowes their trade and purpofes.
If this commerce twixt heaven and earth were not
Embarr'd, and all this traffique quite forgot, 400
She, for whofe loffe we have lamented thus,
Would worke more fully, and pow'rfully on us:
Since herbes, and roots, by dying lofe not all,
But they, yea Afhes too, are medicinall,
Death could not quench her vertue fo, but that 405
It would be (if not follow'd) wondred at:
And all the world would be one dying Swan,
To fing her funerall praife, and vanifh than.
But as fome Serpents poyfon hurteth not,
Except it be from the live Serpent fhot, 410
So doth her vertue need her here, to fit
That unto us; fhee working more then it.
But fhee, in whom to fuch maturity
Vertue was growne, paft growth, that it muft die;
She, from whofe influence all Impreffions came, 415
But, by Receivers impotencies, lame,

383 Th'Ayre *1611, 1612–21:* Th'ayre *1625–69*   387 Th'Ayre
1611: Th'ayre *1612–69*   390 *Mages*] *No change of type, 1611–12*
394 Charme, *1611–21:* Charme *1625–54*   404 Afhes *1611, 1612–25:*
afhes *1633–69*   407 Swan, *1611, 1612–25:* fwan, *1633–69*   415
Impreffions *1611:* Impreffion *1612–25:* impreffion *1633–69*   416 But,
1611: But *1621–69*   Receivers *1611–12: rest no capital*

Who,

Who, though fhe could not tranfubftantiate
All ftates to gold, yet guilded every ftate,
So that fome Princes have fome temperance;
Some Counfellers fome purpofe to advance   420
The common profit; and fome people have
Some ftay, no more then Kings fhould give, to crave;
Some women have fome taciturnity,
Some nunneries fome graines of chaftitie.
She that did thus much, and much more could doe,   425
But that our age was Iron, and ruftie too,
Shee, fhee is dead; fhee's dead; when thou knowft this,
Thou knowft how drie a Cinder this world is.
And learn'ft thus much by our Anatomy,
That 'tis in vaine to dew, or mollifie   430
It with thy teares, or fweat, or blood: nothing
Is worth our travaile, griefe, or perifhing,
But thofe rich joyes, which did poffeffe her heart,
Of which fhe's now partaker, and a part.

Conclufion. But as in cutting up a man that's dead,   435
The body will not laft out, to have read
On every part, and therefore men direct
Their fpeech to parts, that are of moft effect;
So the worlds carcaffe would not laft, if I
Were punctuall in this Anatomy;   440
Nor fmels it well to hearers, if one tell
Them their difeafe, who faine would think they're well.
Here therefore be the end: And, bleffed maid,
Of whom is meant what ever hath been faid,
Or fhall be fpoken well by any tongue,   445
Whofe name refines courfe lines, and makes profe fong,
Accept this tribute, and his firft yeares rent,
Who till his darke fhort tapers end be fpent,
As oft as thy feaft fees this widowed earth,
Will yearely celebrate thy fecond birth,   450
That is, thy death; for though the foule of man
Be got when man is made, 'tis borne but than

421 have] have, *1633*   427 is dead;] is dead, *1633–69*   fhee's
dead; *1611–25*: fhe's dead; *1633–69*   431 nothing] no thing *1611–21*
442 they're] thy're *1633*   443 And, *1611, 1612–25*: and, *1633–69*

When

When man doth die; our body's as the wombe,
And, as a Mid-wife, death directs it home.
And you her creatures, whom fhe workes upon, 455
And have your laft, and beft concoction
From her example, and her vertue, if you
In reverence to her, do thinke it due,
That no one fhould her praifes thus rehearfe,
As matter fit for Chronicle, not verfe; 460
Vouchfafe to call to minde that God did make
A laft, and lafting'ft peece, a fong. He fpake
To *Mofes* to deliver unto all,
That fong, becaufe hee knew they would let fall
The Law, the Prophets, and the Hiftory, 465
But keepe the fong ftill in their memory:
Such an opinion (in due meafure) made
Me this great Office boldly to invade:
Nor could incomprehenfibleneffe deterre
Mee, from thus trying to emprifon her, 470
Which when I faw that a ftrict grave could doe,
I faw not why verfe might not do fo too.
Verfe hath a middle nature: heaven keepes Soules,
The Grave keepes bodies, Verfe the Fame enroules.

A Funerall ELEGIE.

'TIs loft, to truft a Tombe with fuch a gueft,
Or to confine her in a marble cheft.
Alas, what's Marble, Jeat, or Porphyrie,
Priz'd with the Chryfolite of either eye,
Or with thofe Pearles, and Rubies, which fhe was? 5
Joyne the two Indies in one Tombe, 'tis glaffe;
And fo is all to her materials,
Though every inch were ten Efcurials,

467 (in due meafure) *1611, 1612–25* (*but 1625 drops fecond bracket*): commas *1633–69* 468 Office *1611, 1612–25*: office *1633–69* 473 nature: *1611–25*: nature, *1633–69*
A Funerall ELEGIE. *1611, 1612–69: whole poem printed in italics 1612–25: in roman 1611* 1 loft, *1611, 1612–25*: loft *1633*: loffe *1635–69* 2 cheft. *1611–21*: cheft, *1625–69* 8 Efcurials,] efcurials. *1611–25*

Yet

Yet fhe's demolifh'd : can wee keepe her then
In works of hands, or of the wits of men?　　　　10
Can thefe memorials, ragges of paper, give
Life to that name, by which name they muft live?
Sickly, alas, fhort-liv'd, aborted bee
Thofe carcaffe verfes, whofe foule is not fhee.
And can fhee, who no longer would be fhee,　　　　15
Being fuch a Tabernacle, ftoop to be
In paper wrapt; or, when fhee would not lie
In fuch a houfe, dwell in an Elegie?
But 'tis no matter; wee may well allow
Verfe to live fo long as the world will now,　　　　20
For her death wounded it. The world containes
Princes for armes, and Counfellors for braines,
Lawyers for tongues, Divines for hearts, and more,
The Rich for ftomackes, and for backes, the Poore ;
The Officers for hands, Merchants for feet,　　　　25
By which, remote and diftant Countries meet.
But thofe fine fpirits which do tune, and fet
This Organ, are thofe peeces which beget
Wonder and love ; and thefe were fhee ; and fhee
Being fpent, the world muft needs decrepit bee ;　　　　30
For fince death will proceed to triumph ftill,
He can finde nothing, after her, to kill,
Except the world it felfe, fo great as fhee.
Thus brave and confident may Nature bee,
Death cannot give her fuch another blow,　　　　35
Becaufe fhee cannot fuch another fhow.
But muft wee fay fhe's dead ? may't not be faid
That as a fundred clocke is peecemeale laid,
Not to be loft, but by the makers hand
Repollifh'd, without errour then to ftand,　　　　40
Or as the Affrique Niger ftreame enwombs

　　13 aborted *1611, 1612–33:* abortive *1635–69*　　17 or, *1612–25:* or
1633–69　　18 a] an *1635–69*　　22–5 Princes, Counfellors *&c. all in
capitals except* Officers *1611, 1612–25: later editions erratic*　　24 backes,
1611: backes *1612–25:* backs *1633–69*　　　　Poore] *spelt* Pore *1611–12*
28 peeces] peeces, *1633–69*　　30 *1625 inserts marginal note,* Smalneffe
of ftature. *See p.* 235　　33 as *1611–21: om. 1625:* was *1633–69*

　　　　　　　　　　　　　　　　　　　　　　　　　It

It felfe into the earth, and after comes
(Having firft made a naturall bridge, to paffe
For many leagues) farre greater then it was,
May't not be faid, that her grave fhall reftore   45
Her, greater, purer, firmer, then before?
Heaven may fay this, and joy in't, but can wee
Who live, and lacke her, here this vantage fee?
What is't to us, alas, if there have beene
An Angell made a Throne, or Cherubin?   50
Wee lofe by't: and as aged men are glad
Being taftleffe growne, to joy in joyes they had,
So now the fick ftarv'd world muft feed upon
This joy, that we had her, who now is gone.
Rejoyce then Nature, and this World, that you,   55
Fearing the laft fires haftning to fubdue
Your force and vigour, ere it were neere gone,
Wifely beftow'd and laid it all on one.
One, whofe cleare body was fo pure and thinne,
Becaufe it need difguife no thought within.   60
'Twas but a through-light fcarfe, her minde t'inroule;
Or exhalation breath'd out from her Soule.
One, whom all men who durft no more, admir'd:
And whom, who ere had worth enough, defir'd;
As when a Temple's built, Saints emulate   65
To which of them, it fhall be confecrate.
But, as when heaven lookes on us with new eyes,
Thofe new ftarres every Artift exercife,
What place they fhould affigne to them they doubt,
Argue, and agree not, till thofe ftarres goe out: 70
So the world ftudied whofe this peece fhould be,
Till fhee can be no bodies elfe, nor fhee:
But like a Lampe of Balfamum, defir'd
Rather t'adorne, then laft, fhe foone expir'd,
Cloath'd in her virgin white integritie,   75

47 in't,] in't; *1612–21*: in'ts, *1625*   48 her, here *1611, 1612–25:*
her, here, *1633:* her here, *1635–69*   58 one. *1612–25:* one; *1633–69*
64 worth] worke *1633*   74 expir'd, *1633–69:* expir'd; *1611, 1612–25*
75 integritie, *1633–69:* integritie; *1611–25*

For

For marriage, though it doe not ſtaine, doth dye.
To ſcape th'infirmities which wait upon
Woman, ſhe went away, before ſh'was one;
And the worlds buſie noyſe to overcome,
Tooke ſo much death, as ſerv'd for *opium*;   80
For though ſhe could not, nor could chuſe to dye,
She'ath yeelded to too long an extaſie:
Hee which not knowing her ſaid Hiſtory,
Should come to reade the booke of deſtiny,
How faire, and chaſt, humble, and high ſhe'ad been,   85
Much promis'd, much perform'd, at not fifteene,
And meaſuring future things, by things before,
Should turne the leafe to reade, and reade no more,
Would thinke that either deſtiny miſtooke,
Or that ſome leaves were torne out of the booke.   90
But 'tis not ſo; Fate did but uſher her
To yeares of reaſons uſe, and then inferre
Her deſtiny to her ſelfe, which liberty
She tooke but for thus much, thus much to die.
Her modeſtie not ſuffering her to bee   95
Fellow-Commiſſioner with Deſtinie,
She did no more but die; if after her
Any ſhall live, which dare true good prefer,
Every ſuch perſon is her deligate,
T'accompliſh that which ſhould have beene her Fate.   100
They ſhall make up that Booke and ſhall have thanks
Of Fate, and her, for filling up their blankes.
For future vertuous deeds are Legacies,
Which from the gift of her example riſe;
And 'tis in heav'n part of ſpirituall mirth,   105
To ſee how well the good play her, on earth.

76 it doe *1611, 1612–25*: it doth *1633–69*   dye. *1611, 1612–69 (ſpelt die 1633–69): Chambers cloſes the ſentence at 74* expir'd *and prints 75–7 thus—*   Clothed in her virgin white integrity
   —For marriage, though it doth not ſtain, doth dye—
   To 'ſcape *&c.*
83 ſaid *1611, 1612–33*: ſad *1635–69*   94 tooke *1611, 1612–25*: tooke, *1633–69*   98 prefer, *1611, 1612–25*: prefer; *1633–69*

OF

OF THE
PROGRESSE
OF THE SOULE.

Wherein,

By occaſion of the Religious death of
Miſtris ELIZABETH DRVRY,
the incommodities of the Soule in
this life, and her exaltation in
the next, are contemplated.

The ſecond Anniverſary.

The Harbinger to the
PROGRESSE.

TWo Soules move here, and mine (a third) muſt move
Paces of admiration, and of love;
Thy Soule (deare virgin) whoſe this tribute is,
Mov'd from this mortall Spheare to lively bliſſe;
And yet moves ſtill, and ſtill aſpires to ſee   5
The worlds laſt day, thy glories full degree:
Like as thoſe ſtarres which thou o'r-lookeſt farre,

Of the Progreſſe &c. *1612–69:* The ſecond Anniverſary. *1612–69*
(*in 1612–21 it stands at head of page*)
The Harbinger &c.] *In 1612–25 this poem printed in italics*

Are

Are in their place, and yet ftill moved are:
No foule (whiles with the luggage of this clay
It clogged is) can follow thee halfe way;   10
Or fee thy flight, which doth our thoughts outgoe
So faft, that now the lightning moves but flow:
But now thou art as high in heaven flowne
As heaven's from us; what foule befides thine owne
Can tell thy joyes, or fay he can relate   15
Thy glorious Journals in that bleffed ftate?
I envie thee (Rich foule) I envy thee,
Although I cannot yet thy glory fee:
And thou (great fpirit) which hers follow'd haft
So faft, as none can follow thine fo faft;   20
So far, as none can follow thine fo farre,
(And if this flefh did not the paffage barre
Hadft caught her) let me wonder at thy flight
Which long agone hadft loft the vulgar fight,
And now mak'ft proud the better eyes, that they   25
Can fee thee lefs'ned in thine ayery way;
So while thou mak'ft her foule by progreffe knowne
Thou mak'ft a noble progreffe of thine owne,
From this worlds carkaffe having mounted high
To that pure life of immortalitie;   30
Since thine afpiring thoughts themfelves fo raife
That more may not befeeme a creatures praife,
Yet ftill thou vow'ft her more; and every yeare
Mak'ft a new progreffe, while thou wandreft here;
Still upward mount; and let thy Makers praife   35
Honor thy Laura, and adorne thy laies.
And fince thy Mufe her head in heaven fhrouds,
Oh let her never ftoope below the clouds:
And if thofe glorious fainted foules may know
Or what wee doe, or what wee fing below,   40
Thofe acts, thofe fongs fhall ftill content them beft
Which praife thofe awfull Powers that make them bleft.

    8 are:] are *1612–25*   1 2 that now] as now *1635–69, Chambers*   27
foule] foules *1612*   28 owne, *1635–69:* owne. *1612–33*   34 while]
whilft *1669*   35 upward] upwards *1612*

O F

OF
THE PROGRESSE
OF THE SOULE.

The second Anniverſarie.

NOthing could make me ſooner to confeſſe   *The entrance.*[1]
　　That this world had an everlaſtingneſſe,
Then to conſider, that a yeare is runne,
Since both this lower world's, and the Sunnes Sunne,
The Luſtre, and the vigor of this All,   5
Did ſet; 'twere blaſphemie to ſay, did fall.
But as a ſhip which hath ſtrooke ſaile, doth runne
By force of that force which before, it wonne:
Or as ſometimes in a beheaded man,
Though at thoſe two Red ſeas, which freely ranne,   10
One from the Trunke, another from the Head,
His ſoule be ſail'd, to her eternall bed,
His eyes will twinckle, and his tongue will roll,
As though he beckned, and cal'd backe his ſoule,
He graſpes his hands, and he pulls up his feet,   15
And ſeemes to reach, and to ſtep forth to meet
His ſoule; when all theſe motions which we ſaw,
Are but as Ice, which crackles at a thaw:
Or as a Lute, which in moiſt weather, rings
Her knell alone, by cracking of her ſtrings: 20
So ſtruggles this dead world, now ſhee is gone;
For there is motion in corruption.

[1] *The entrance. 1612–21: om. 1625–33: no notes, 1635–69*   5 All,
1612: all, *1625–69*   10 Though] Through *1612–25*   12 be ſail'd,]
he ſail'd, *1621–33*   13 twinckle] twincke *1625*   20 ſtrings: *Ed:*
ſtrings. *1612–69*

As

As some daies are at the Creation nam'd,
Before the Sunne, the which fram'd daies, was fram'd,
So after this Sunne's set, some shew appeares,   25
And orderly vicissitude of yeares.
Yet a new Deluge, and of *Lethe* flood,
Hath drown'd us all, All have forgot all good,
Forgetting her, the maine reserve of all.
Yet in this deluge, grosse and generall,   30
Thou seest me strive for life ; my life shall bee,
To be hereafter prais'd, for praysing thee ;
Immortall Maid, who though thou would'st refuse
The name of Mother, be unto my Muse
A Father, since her chast Ambition is,   35
Yearely to bring forth such a child as this.
These Hymnes may worke on future wits, and so
May great Grand children of thy prayses grow.
And so, though not revive, embalme and spice
The world, which else would putrifie with vice.   40
For thus, Man may extend thy progeny,
Untill man doe but vanish, and not die.
These Hymnes thy issue, may encrease so long,
As till Gods great *Venite* change the song.

<table>
<tr><td>*A iust dis-*
estimation[1] *of*
this world.</td><td>Thirst for that time, O my insatiate soule,   45
And serve thy thirst, with Gods safe-sealing Bowle.
Be thirstie still, and drinke still till thou goe
To th'only Health, to be Hydroptique so.</td></tr>
</table>

Forget this rotten world ; And unto thee
Let thine owne times as an old storie bee.   50
Be not concern'd : studie not why, nor when ;
Doe not so much as not beleeve a man.
For though to erre, be worst, to try truths forth,

23 are *Ed:* are, *1612–69*   24 was fram'd, *1612–25:* was fram'd :
1633–69   27 Deluge, *1612–25:* deluge, *1633–69*   29 all. *Ed:* all,
1612–33: all ; *1635–69*   33 Maid, *1612–25,1669:* maid, *1633–54*
35 is, *1612–25:* is *1633–69*   43 thy] they *1621–25*   issue,
1612–33: issue *1635–69. See note*   [1] *disestimation*] *estimation 1625*
46 safe-sealing] safe-fealing *1621–39*   47 goe] goe ; *1612–25*   48
Health, *1612–33:* Health ; *1635–69,* Chambers and Grolier   so. *1612–21:*
so, *1625–69,* Chambers and Grolier. See note   50 bee. *Ed:* bee *1612–35:*
bee, *1639–69*   51 why, *1612–21:* why *1625–69*   nor] or *1669*

Is far more bufineffe, then this world is worth.
The world is but a carkaffe; thou art fed   55
By it, but as a worme, that carkaffe bred;
And why fhould'ft thou, poore worme, confider more,
When this world will grow better then before,
Then thofe thy fellow wormes doe thinke upon
That carkaffes laft refurrection.   60
Forget this world, and fcarce thinke of it fo,
As of old clothes, caft off a yeare agoe.
To be thus ftupid is Alacritie;
Men thus Lethargique have beft Memory.
Look upward; that's towards her, whofe happy ftate   65
We now lament not, but congratulate.
Shee, to whom all this world was but a ftage,
Where all fat harkning how her youthfull age
Should be emploi'd, becaufe in all fhee did,
Some Figure of the Golden times was hid.   70
Who could not lacke, what e'r this world could give,
Becaufe fhee was the forme, that made it live;
Nor could complaine, that this world was unfit
To be ftaid in, then when fhee was in it;
Shee that firft tried indifferent defires   75
By vertue, and vertue by religious fires,
Shee to whofe perfon Paradife adher'd,
As Courts to Princes, fhee whofe eyes enfphear'd
Star-light enough, t'have made the South controule,
(Had fhee beene there) the Star-full Northerne Pole,   80
Shee, fhee is gone; fhe is gone; when thou knoweft this,
What fragmentary rubbidge this world is
Thou knoweft, and that it is not worth a thought;
He honors it too much that thinkes it nought.
Thinke then, my foule, that death is but a Groome,   85 *Contempla-*
Which brings a Taper to the outward roome,   *tion of our*
Whence thou fpieft firft a little glimmering light,   *ftate in our*
And after brings it nearer to thy fight: *death-bed.*
For fuch approaches doth heaven make in death.
Thinke thy felfe labouring now with broken breath,   90

57 more, *1612–25:* more *1633–69*   67 was but] twas but *1612–25*
81 Shee, fhee *1621–25:* Shee, fhe *1633–69*   82 is] is. *1612–25*

And

And thinke thofe broken and foft Notes to bee
Divifion, and thy happyeft Harmonie.
Thinke thee laid on thy death-bed, loofe and flacke;
And thinke that, but unbinding of a packe,
To take one precious thing, thy foule from thence.   95
Thinke thy felfe parch'd with fevers violence,
Anger thine ague more, by calling it
Thy Phyficke; chide the flackneffe of the fit.
Thinke that thou hear'ft thy knell, and think no more,
But that, as Bels cal'd thee to Church before,   ICO
So this, to the Triumphant Church, calls thee.
Thinke Satans Sergeants round about thee bee,
And thinke that but for Legacies they thruft;
Give one thy Pride, to'another give thy Luft:
Give them thofe finnes which they gave thee before,   105
And truft th'immaculate blood to wafh thy fcore.
Thinke thy friends weeping round, and thinke that they
Weepe but becaufe they goe not yet thy way.
Thinke that they clofe thine eyes, and thinke in this,
That they confeffe much in the world, amiffe,   110
Who dare not truft a dead mans eye with that,
Which they from God, and Angels cover not.
Thinke that they fhroud thee up, and think from thence
They reinveft thee in white innocence.
Thinke that thy body rots, and (if fo low,   115
Thy foule exalted fo, thy thoughts can goe,)
Think thee a Prince, who of themfelves create
Wormes which infenfibly devoure their State.
Thinke that they bury thee, and thinke that right
Laies thee to fleepe but a Saint Lucies night.   120
Thinke thefe things cheerefully: and if thou bee
Drowfie or flacke, remember then that fhee,
Shee whofe Complexion was fo even made,
That which of her Ingredients fhould invade

96 parch'd *1612-21, 1639-69:* pach'd *1625:* patch'd *1633-35*   99
knell,] knell *1633*   101 So this, *1612-33:* So, this *1635-69*   103
thruft;] truft; *1669*   113 fhroud] fhourd *1621-25*   116 exalted]
exhalted *1621*   goe,] goe. *1612-21*   123 Complexion *1612-25:*
complexion *1633-69*   124 Ingredients *1612-25:* ingredients *1633-69*
The

The other three, no Feare, no Art could gueffe :   125
So far were all remov'd from more or leffe.
But as in Mithridate, or juft perfumes,
Where all good things being met, no one prefumes
To governe, or to triumph on the reft,
Only becaufe all were, no part was beft.   130
And as, though all doe know, that quantities
Are made of lines, and lines from Points arife,
None can thefe lines or quantities unjoynt,
And fay this is a line, or this a point,
So though the Elements and Humors were   135
In her, one could not fay, this governes there.
Whofe even conftitution might have wonne
Any difeafe to venter on the Sunne,
Rather then her : and make a fpirit feare,
That hee to difuniting fubject were.   140
To whofe proportions if we would compare
Cubes, th'are unftable ; Circles, Angular ;
She who was fuch a chaine as Fate employes
To bring mankinde all Fortunes it enjoyes ;
So faft, fo even wrought, as one would thinke,   145
No Accident could threaten any linke ;
Shee, fhee embrac'd a fickneffe, gave it meat,
The pureft blood, and breath, that e'r it eate ;
And hath taught us, that though a good man hath
Title to heaven, and plead it by his Faith,   150
And though he may pretend a conqueft, fince
Heaven was content to fuffer violence,
Yea though hee plead a long poffeffion too,
(For they're in heaven on earth who heavens workes do)
Though hee had right and power and place, before,   155
Yet Death muft ufher, and unlocke the doore.
Thinke further on thy felfe, my Soule, and thinke   *Incommodities*
How thou at firft waft made but in a finke ;   *of the Soule in*
Thinke that it argued fome infirmitie,   *the Body.*[1]

134 a point, *1612–21:* a-point. *1625:* a point : *1633–69*   136 there.
1612–25: there, *1633–69*   137 wonne] worne *1612–25:* woon *1633*
140 to *1612–25:* too *1633–69*   146 Accident *1612–25:* accident
1633–69   156 Death *1612–25:* death *1633–69*   [1] *Incommodities*
&c. 1612–21: om. *1625–33*

That

That thofe two foules, which then thou foundft in me, 160
Thou fedft upon, and drewft into thee, both
My fecond foule of fenfe, and firft of growth.
Thinke but how poore thou waft, how obnoxious;
Whom a fmall lumpe of flefh could poyfon thus.
This curded milke, this poore unlittered whelpe   165
My body, could, beyond efcape or helpe,
Infect thee with Originall finne, and thou
Couldft neither then refufe, nor leave it now.
Thinke that no ftubborne fullen Anchorit,
Which fixt to a pillar, or a grave, doth fit   170
Bedded, and bath'd in all his ordures, dwels
So fowly as our Soules in their firft-built Cels.
Thinke in how poore a prifon thou didft lie
After, enabled but to fuck, and crie.
Thinke, when'twas growne to moft,'twas a poore Inne, 175
A Province pack'd up in two yards of skinne,
And that ufurp'd or threatned with the rage
Of ficknefles, or their true mother, Age.
But thinke that Death hath now enfranchis'd thee,
Her liberty   Thou haft thy'expanfion now, and libertie;   180
by death.   Thinke that a ruftie Peece, difcharg'd, is flowne
In peeces, and the bullet is his owne,
And freely flies: This to thy Soule allow,
Thinke thy fhell broke, thinke thy Soule hatch'd but now.
And think this flow-pac'd foule, which late did cleave 185
To'a body, and went but by the bodies leave,
Twenty, perchance, or thirty mile a day,
Difpatches in a minute all the way
Twixt heaven, and earth; fhe ftayes not in the ayre,
To looke what Meteors there themfelves prepare;   190
She carries no defire to know, nor fenfe,
Whether th'ayres middle region be intenfe;

161 thee, both *1612–25:* thee both *1633–69*   172 firft-built
1612–25: firft built *1633–69*   173 didft] doft *1669*   177 the
rage *1612–25:* a rage *1633–69*   179 Death *1612–25:* death
1633–69   181 Peece, difcharg'd, *1612:* Peece, difcharg'd *1625:* Peece
difcharg'd *1633:* Peece difcharg'd, *1635–69*   183 This *1612–25:* this
1633–69   185 foule, *1612–21:* foule *1625–69*   187 Twenty,
perchance,] Twentie, perchance *1625:* Twenty perchance *1633–69*

For

For th'Element of fire, fhe doth not know,
Whether fhe paft by fuch a place or no;
She baits not at the Moone, nor cares to trie   195
Whether in that new world, men live, and die.
Venus retards her not, to'enquire, how fhee
Can, (being one ftarre) *Hefper*, and *Vefper* bee;
Hee that charm'd *Argus* eyes, fweet *Mercury*,
Workes not on her, who now is growne all eye;   200
Who, if fhe meet the body of the Sunne,
Goes through, not ftaying till his courfe be runne;
Who findes in *Mars* his Campe no corps of Guard;
Nor is by *Iove*, nor by his father barr'd;
But ere fhe can confider how fhe went,   205
At once is at, and through the Firmament.
And as thefe ftarres were but fo many beads
Strung on one ftring, fpeed undiftinguifh'd leads
Her through thofe Spheares, as through the beads, a ftring,
Whofe quick fucceffion makes it ftill one thing: 210
As doth the pith, which, left our bodies flacke,
Strings faft the little bones of necke, and backe;
So by the Soule doth death ftring Heaven and Earth;
For when our Soule enjoyes this her third birth,
(Creation gave her one, a fecond, grace,)   215
Heaven is as neare, and prefent to her face,
As colours are, and objeƈts, in a roome
Where darkneffe was before, when Tapers come.
This muft, my Soule, thy long-fhort Progreffe bee;
To'advance thefe thoughts, remember then, that fhe,   220
She, whofe faire body no fuch prifon was,
But that a Soule might well be pleas'd to paffe
An age in her; fhe whofe rich beauty lent
Mintage to other beauties, for they went
But for fo much as they were like to her;   225
Shee, in whofe body (if we dare preferre

197 *Venus*] no ital. *1612–25, and so with* Hefper *&c.*   retards] recards
1612–25   201 Who, if *1612–25 :* Who if *1633–69*   204 barr'd ;]
bard ; *1612–39*   209 the] thofe *1669*   214 her] om. *1650–69*
219–20 *text 1612–25 (but* foul *1612–25, and then 1625 and* fhee *1612–25) :*
          This muft, my Soule, thy long-fhort Progreffe bee,
          To'advance thefe thoughts ; Remember then that fhe,
                    1633–69, Chambers and Grolier.   *See note*
                                                            This

This low world, to fo high a marke as fhee,)
The Wefterne treafure, Eafterne fpicerie,
Europe, and Afrique, and the unknowne reft
Were eafily found, or what in them was beft;   230
And when w'have made this large difcoverie
Of all, in her fome one part then will bee
Twenty fuch parts, whofe plenty and riches is
Enough to make twenty fuch worlds as this;
Shee, whom had they knowne who did firft betroth   235
The Tutelar Angels, and affign'd one, both
To Nations, Cities, and to Companies,
To Functions, Offices, and Dignities,
And to each feverall man, to him, and him,
They would have given her one for every limbe;   240
She, of whofe foule, if wee may fay, 'twas Gold,
Her body was th'Electrum, and did hold
Many degrees of that; wee underftood
Her by her fight; her pure, and eloquent blood
Spoke in her cheekes, and fo diftinctly wrought,   245
That one might almoft fay, her body thought;
Shee, fhee, thus richly and largely hous'd, is gone:
And chides us flow-pac'd fnailes who crawle upon
Our prifons prifon, earth, nor thinke us well,
Longer, then whil'ft wee beare our brittle fhell.   250

Her igno- But 'twere but little to have chang'd our roome,
rance in If, as we were in this our living Tombe
this life Opprefs'd with ignorance, wee ftill were fo.
and know- Poore foule, in this thy flefh what doft thou know?
ledge in the Thou know'ft thy felfe fo little, as thou know'ft not,   255
next.[1] How thou didft die, nor how thou waft begot.
Thou neither know'ft, how thou at firft cam'ft in,
Nor how thou took'ft the poyfon of mans finne.
Nor doft thou, (though thou know'ft, that thou art fo)
By what way thou art made immortall, know.   260
Thou art too narrow, wretch, to comprehend

231 difcoverie] Difcoveree. *1612–25*   232 Of all,] Of all *1612–25*
236 affign'd *Ed:* affigned *1612–69*   238 Dignities, *1612–25* : dignities,
1633–69   241 Gold, *1612–25*: gold, *1633–69*   243 underftood]
unftood *1621–25*   249 well,] well *1612–25*   251 little] litrle *1633*
[1] *Her ignorance &c.: 1612–25 : om. 1633*

Even

Even thy felfe: yea though thou wouldft but bend
To know thy body. Have not all foules thought
For many ages, that our body'is wrought
Of Ayre, and Fire, and other Elements?   265
And now they thinke of new ingredients,
And one Soule thinkes one, and another way
Another thinkes, and 'tis an even lay.
Knowft thou but how the ftone doth enter in
The bladders cave, and never breake the skinne?   270
Know'ft thou how blood, which to the heart doth flow,
Doth from one ventricle to th'other goe?
And for the putrid ftuffe, which thou doft fpit,
Know'ft thou how thy lungs have attracted it?
There are no paffages, fo that there is   275
(For ought thou know'ft) piercing of fubftances.
And of thofe many opinions which men raife
Of Nailes and Haires, doft thou know which to praife?
What hope have wee to know our felves, when wee
Know not the leaft things, which for our ufe be?   280
Wee fee in Authors, too ftiffe to recant,
A hundred controverfies of an Ant;
And yet one watches, ftarves, freefes, and fweats,
To know but Catechifmes and Alphabets
Of unconcerning things, matters of fact;   285
How others on our ftage their parts did Act;
What *Cæfar* did, yea, and what *Cicero* faid.
Why graffe is greene, or why our blood is red,
Are myfteries which none have reach'd unto.
In this low forme, poore foule, what wilt thou doe?   290
When wilt thou fhake off this Pedantery,
Of being taught by fenfe, and Fantafie?
Thou look'ft through fpectacles; fmall things feeme great
Below; But up unto the watch-towre get,
And fee all things defpoyl'd of fallacies: 295
Thou fhalt not peepe through lattices of eyes,

265 Ayre, and Fire, *1612-25*: aire, and fire, *1633-69*   266 in-
gredients, *1612*: ingredients. *1621-69*   268 'tis] ty's *1612-21*   270
breake *1612*: brake *1621-33*: break *1635-69*   287 faid. *1612-25*: faid,
1633-69   291 Pedantery] Pedantry *1650-69*   292 taught]
thought *1612-25*

Nor heare through Labyrinths of eares, nor learne
By circuit, or collections to difcerne.
In heaven thou ftraight know'ft all, concerning it,
And what concernes it not, fhalt ftraight forget.   300
There thou (but in no other fchoole) maift bee
Perchance, as learned, and as full, as fhee,
Shee who all libraries had throughly read
At home in her owne thoughts, and practifed
So much good as would make as many more: 305
Shee whofe example they muft all implore,
Who would or doe, or thinke well, and confeffe
That all the vertuous Actions they expreffe,
Are but a new, and worfe edition
Of her fome one thought, or one action: 310
She who in th'art of knowing Heaven, was growne
Here upon earth, to fuch perfection,
That fhe hath, ever fince to Heaven fhe came,
(In a far fairer print,) but read the fame:
Shee, fhee not fatisfied with all this waight,   315
(For fo much knowledge, as would over-fraight
Another, did but ballaft her) is gone
As well t'enjoy, as get perfection.
And cals us after her, in that fhee tooke,

Of our com-   (Taking her felfe) our beft, and worthieft booke.   320
pany in this   Returne not, my Soule, from this extafie,
life, and in   And meditation of what thou fhalt bee,
the next.   To earthly thoughts, till it to thee appeare,
With whom thy converfation muft be there.
With whom wilt thou converfe? what ftation   325
Canft thou choofe out, free from infection,
That will not give thee theirs, nor drinke in thine?
Shalt thou not finde a fpungie flacke Divine
Drinke and fucke in th'inftructions of Great men,
And for the word of God, vent them agen?   330
Are there not fome Courts (and then, no things bee

    300 fhalt] fhall *1612–25, 1669*   308 all] aie *1612–21:* are *1625*
314 print,] point, *1612–33*   323 earthly] early *1625*   324 there.]
there, *1633–39*   326 choose *1612–25:* chose *1633–69*   327 will not]
will nor *1612–25*   328 Divine *1612–25:* Divine, *1633–69*   329
Great *1612–25:* great *1633–69*

So

So like as Courts) which, in this let us fee,
That wits and tongues of Libellers are weake,
Becaufe they do more ill, then thefe can fpeake?
The poyfon's gone through all, poyfons affect   335
Chiefly the chiefeft parts, but fome effect
In nailes, and haires, yea excrements, will fhow;
So lyes the poyfon of finne in the moft low.
Up, up, my drowfie Soule, where thy new eare
Shall in the Angels fongs no difcord heare;   340
Where thou fhalt fee the bleffed Mother-maid
Joy in not being that, which men have faid.
Where fhe is exalted more for being good,
Then for her intereft of Mother-hood.
Up to thofe Patriarchs, which did longer fit   345
Expecting Chrift, then they'have enjoy'd him yet.
Up to thofe Prophets, which now gladly fee
Their Prophefies growne to be Hiftorie.
Up to th'Apoftles, who did bravely runne
All the Suns courfe, with more light then the Sunne. 350
Up to thofe Martyrs, who did calmly bleed
Oyle to th'Apoftles Lamps, dew to their feed.
Up to thofe Virgins, who thought, that almoft
They made joyntenants with the Holy Ghoft,
If they to any fhould his Temple give.   355
Up, up, for in that fquadron there doth live
She, who hath carried thither new degrees
(As to their number) to their dignities.
Shee, who being to her felfe a State, injoy'd
All royalties which any State employ'd;   360
For fhee made warres, and triumph'd; reafon ftill
Did not o'rthrow, but rectifie her will:
And fhe made peace, for no peace is like this,
That beauty, and chaftity together kiffe:
She did high juftice, for fhe crucified   365
Every firft motion of rebellious pride:

333 wits *1612–25:* wits, *1633–69*   336 fome] fome, *1633*
338 lyes] wife *1612–25*   353 thought] thoughts *1612–25*   366
rebellious] rebellions *1635–69*

And

And fhe gave pardons, and was liberall,
For, onely her felfe except, fhe pardon'd all:
Shee coy'nd, in this, that her impreffions gave
To all our actions all the worth they have: 370
She gave protections; the thoughts of her breft
Satans rude Officers could ne'r arreft.
As thefe prerogatives being met in one,
Made her a foveraigne State; religion
Made her a Church; and thefe two made her all.   375
She who was all this All, and could not fall
To worfe, by company, (for fhe was ftill
More Antidote, then all the world was ill,)
Shee, fhee doth leave it, and by Death, furvive
All this, in Heaven; whither who doth not ftrive   380
The more, becaufe fhees there, he doth not know
That accidentall joyes in Heaven doe grow.
But paufe, my foule; And ftudy, ere thou fall
On accidentall joyes, th'effentiall.
Still before Acceffories doe abide   385
A triall, muft the principall be tride.
And what effentiall joy can'ft thou expect
Here upon earth? what permanent effect
Of tranfitory caufes? Doft thou love
Beauty? (And beauty worthy'ft is to move)   390
Poore coufened coufenor, *that* fhe, and *that* thou,
Which did begin to love, are neither now;
You are both fluid, chang'd fince yefterday;
Next day repaires, (but ill) laft dayes decay.
Nor are, (although the river keepe the name)   395
Yefterdaies waters, and to daies the fame.
So flowes her face, and thine eyes, neither now
That Saint, nor Pilgrime, which your loving vow
Concern'd, remaines; but whil'ft you thinke you bee
Conftant, you'are hourely in inconftancie.   400

Of effentiall joy in this life and in the next.

369 impreffions *1612–25: rest* impreffion   378 ill,)] *last bracket dropped 1612–33*   380 whither] *spelt* whether *1612–33*   383 ftudy, *1635–69:* ftudy *1612–33*   391 *that . . . that] no italics 1612–25*   397 eies, *1612–21:* eyes *1625:* eyes; *1633–69, Chambers. See note*   398 Saint, *1612–25:* Saint *1633–69*   vow] row *1612–25*   399 remaines;] remaines, *1612–25*

Honour

Honour may have pretence unto our love,
Becaufe that God did live fo long above
Without this Honour, and then lov'd it fo,
That he at laft made Creatures to beftow
Honour on him; not that he needed it,   405
But that, to his hands, man might grow more fit.
But fince all Honours from inferiours flow,
(For they doe give it; Princes doe but fhew
Whom they would have fo honor'd) and that this
On fuch opinions, and capacities   410
Is built, as rife and fall, to more and leffe:
Alas, 'tis but a cafuall happineffe.
Hath ever any man to'himfelfe affign'd
This or that happineffe to'arreft his minde,
But that another man which takes a worfe,   415
Thinks him a foole for having tane that courfe?
They who did labour Babels tower to'erect,
Might have confidered, that for that effect,
All this whole folid Earth could not allow
Nor furnifh forth materialls enow;   420
And that this Center, to raife fuch a place,
Was farre too little, to have beene the Bafe;
No more affords this world, foundation
To erect true joy, were all the meanes in one.
But as the Heathen made them feverall gods,   425
Of all Gods Benefits, and all his Rods,
(For as the Wine, and Corne, and Onions are
Gods unto them, fo Agues bee, and Warre)
And as by changing that whole precious Gold
To fuch fmall Copper coynes, they loft the old,   430
And loft their only God, who ever muft
Be fought alone, and not in fuch a thruft :

402 that] *in italics 1633–69*   404 Creatures *1612–25:* creatures
1633–69   416 Thinks] Thinke *1612–25*   420 enow] enough *1633*
421 this *1612:* his *1621–69*   421–2 place, ... little, *1612:* place ... little,
1621–33   423 affords] affoords *1612–25*   world, foundation *1633–69:*
worlds, foundatione *1612–25*   426 Benefits ... Rods] *capitals from*
1612–25   428 Warre] *no capital 1612–39*   429 that] the *1625*
So

So much mankinde true happineſſe miſtakes;
No Joy enjoyes that man, that many makes.
Then, Soule, to thy firſt pitch worke up againe;   435
Know that all lines which circles doe containe,
For once that they the Center touch, doe touch
Twice the circumference; and be thou ſuch;
Double on heaven thy thoughts on earth emploid;
All will not ſerve; Only who have enjoy'd   440
The ſight of God, in fulneſſe, can thinke it;
For it is both the object, and the wit.
This is eſſentiall joy, where neither hee
Can ſuffer diminution, nor wee;
'Tis ſuch a full, and ſuch a filling good;   445
Had th'Angels once look'd on him, they had ſtood.
To fill the place of one of them, or more,
Shee whom wee celebrate, is gone before.
She, who had Here ſo much eſſentiall joy,
As no chance could diſtract, much leſſe deſtroy;   450
Who with Gods preſence was acquainted ſo,
(Hearing, and ſpeaking to him) as to know
His face in any naturall Stone, or Tree,
Better then when in Images they bee:
Who kept by diligent devotion,   455
Gods Image, in ſuch reparation,
Within her heart, that what decay was growne,
Was her firſt Parents fault, and not her owne:
Who being ſolicited to any act,
Still heard God pleading his ſafe precontract;   460
Who by a faithfull confidence, was here
Betroth'd to God, and now is married there;
Whoſe twilights were more cleare, then our mid-day;
Who dreamt devoutlier, then moſt uſe to pray;
Who being here fil'd with grace, yet ſtrove to bee,   465
Both where more grace, and more capacitie
At once is given: ſhe to Heaven is gone,
Who made this world in ſome proportion

A heaven,

A heaven, and here, became unto us all,
Joy, (as our joyes admit) effentiall.   470
But could this low world joyes effentiall touch,
Heavens accidentall joyes would paffe them much.
How poore and lame, muft then our cafuall bee?
If thy Prince will his fubjects to call thee
My Lord, and this doe fwell thee, thou art than,   475
By being greater, growne to bee leffe Man.
When no Phyfitian of redreffe can fpeake,
A joyfull cafuall violence may breake
A dangerous Apoftem in thy breaft;
And whil'ft thou joyeft in this, the dangerous reft,   480
The bag may rife up, and fo ftrangle thee.
What e'r was cafuall, may ever bee.
What fhould the nature change? Or make the fame
Certaine, which was but cafuall, when it came?
All cafuall joy doth loud and plainly fay,   485
Only by comming, that it can away.
Only in Heaven joyes ftrength is never fpent;
And accidentall things are permanent.
Joy of a foules arrivall ne'r decaies;
For that foule ever joyes and ever ftaies.   490
Joy that their laft great Confummation
Approaches in the refurrection;
When earthly bodies more celeftiall
Shall be, then Angels were, for they could fall;
This kinde of joy doth every day admit   495
Degrees of growth, but none of lofing it.
In this frefh joy, 'tis no fmall part, that fhee,
Shee, in whofe goodneffe, he that names degree,
Doth injure her; ('Tis loffe to be cal'd beft,
There where the ftuffe is not fuch as the reft)   500
Shee, who left fuch a bodie, as even fhee
Only in Heaven could learne, how it can bee
Made better; for fhee rather was two foules,

*Of acciden-
tall joys in
both places.*

475 *My Lord*] *no italics 1612-25*   477 redreffe] Reders *1612-25*
482 What e'r] What eye *1612-25*   500 where] waere *1612*
501 even] ever *1625*
VOL. I. T   Or

Or like to full on both fides written Rols,
Where eyes might reade upon the outward skin,   505
As ftrong Records for God, as mindes within;
Shee, who by making full perfection grow,
Peeces a Circle, and ftill keepes it fo,
Long'd for, and longing for it, to heaven is gone,
Where fhee receives, and gives addition.   510

Conclufion.   Here in a place, where mif-devotion frames
A thoufand Prayers to Saints, whofe very names
The ancient Church knew not, Heaven knows not yet:
And where, what lawes of Poetry admit,
Lawes of Religion have at leaft the fame,   515
Immortall Maide, I might invoke thy name.
Could any Saint provoke that appetite,
Thou here fhould'ft make me a French convertite.
But thou would'ft not; nor would'ft thou be content,
To take this, for my fecond yeares true Rent,   520
Did this Coine beare any other ftampe, then his,
That gave thee power to doe, me, to fay this.
Since his will is, that to pofteritie,
Thou fhould'ft for life, and death, a patterne bee,
And that the world fhould notice have of this,   525
The purpofe, and th'authoritie is his;
Thou art the Proclamation; and I am
The Trumpet, at whofe voyce the people came.

506 within; *Ed:* within, *1612–39:* within. *1650–69*   516
invoke] inroque *1612–25*   518 French *1635–69:* french *1612–33*
520 Rent] Rent. *1633*

EPICEDES

EPICEDES AND OBSEQVIES

Vpon

The deaths of fundry Perfonages.

Elegie upon the untimely death of the incomparable Prince Henry.

Looke to mee faith, and looke to my faith, God;
For both my centers feele this period.
Of waight one center, one of greatneffe is;
And Reafon is that center, Faith is this;
For into'our reafon flow, and there do end   5
All, that this naturall world doth comprehend:
Quotidian things, and equidiftant hence,
Shut in, for man, in one circumference.
But for th'enormous greatneffes, which are
So difproportion'd, and fo angulare,   10
As is Gods effence, place and providence, .
Where, how, when, what foules do, departed hence,
Thefe things (eccentrique elfe) on faith do ftrike;
Yet neither all, nor upon all, alike.
For reafon, put to'her beft extenfion,   15
Almoft meetes faith, and makes both centers one.
And nothing ever came fo neare to this,
As contemplation of that Prince, wee miffe.
For all that faith might credit mankinde could,
Reafon ftill feconded, that this prince would.   20

Epicedes &c. 1635–69: Elegie upon &c. 1613, in the Lachrymae
Lachrymarum &c. of Joshua Sylvester. See note: Elegie on Prince Henry.
1633–54, O'F: similarly, Cy, N, TCD: An Elegie on the untimely &c. 1669
8 man 1633–69: men 1613   17 neare] nere 1633   18 that 1633–69:
the 1613,   19 might credit 1633–69: could credit 1613

If

If then leaft moving of the center, make
More, then if whole hell belch'd, the world to fhake,
What muft this do, centers diftracted fo,
That wee fee not what to beleeve or know?
Was it not well beleev'd till now, that hee,   25
Whofe reputation was an extafie
On neighbour States, which knew not why to wake,
Till hee difcover'd what wayes he would take;
For whom, what Princes angled, when they tryed,
Met a *Torpedo*, and were ftupified;   30
And others ftudies, how he would be bent;
Was his great fathers greateft inftrument,
And activ'ft fpirit, to convey and tie
This foule of peace, through Chriftianity?
Was it not well beleev'd, that hee would make   35
This generall peace, th'Eternall overtake,
And that his times might have ftretch'd out fo farre,
As to touch thofe, of which they emblems are?
For to confirme this juft beleefe, that now
The laft dayes came, wee faw heav'n did allow,   40
That, but from his afpect and exercife,
In peacefull times, Rumors of war did rife.
But now this faith is herefie: we muft
Still ftay, and vexe our great-grand-mother, Duft.
Oh, is God prodigall? hath he fpent his ftore   45
Of plagues, on us; and onely now, when more
Would eafe us much, doth he grudge mifery;
And will not let's enjoy our curfe; to dy?
As, for the earth throwne loweft downe of all,
T'were an ambition to defire to fall,   50
So God, in our defire to dye, doth know
Our plot for eafe, in being wretched fo.

21 moving *1633–69:* movings *1613*   22 fhake, *1650–69:* fhake.
1633–39   26 extafie *Ed:* exftafie, *1633–69*   31 bent; *Ed:* bent,
1613,1633–69   34 through *1613–33:* to *1635–69*   Chriftianity?
1669: Chriftianity: *1633–54*   42 did *1633:* fhould *1613,1635–69*
44 great-grand-mother, *1613:* greatgrand mother, *1633:* greatgrand-mother,
1635–69   46 us;] us, *1633*   48 to dy? *Ed:* to dy. *1633:* to die!
1635–54: no stop, 1669

Therefore

Therefore we live; though such a life wee have,
As but so many mandrakes on his grave.
What had his growth, and generation done,   55
When, what we are, his putrefaction
Suftaines in us; Earth, which griefes animate?
Nor hath our world now, other Soule then that.
And could griefe get so high as heav'n, that Quire,
Forgetting this their new joy, would defire   60
(With griefe to fee him) hee had ftaid below,
To rectifie our errours, They foreknow.
Is th'other center, Reafon, fafter then?
Where fhould we looke for that, now we'are not men?
For if our Reafon be'our connexion   65
Of caufes, now to us there can be none.
For, as, if all the fubftances were fpent,
'Twere madneffe, to enquire of accident,
So is't to looke for reafon, hee being gone,
The onely fubject reafon wrought upon.   70
If Fate have fuch a chaine, whofe divers links
Induftrious man difcerneth, as hee thinks;
When miracle doth come, and fo fteale in
A new linke, man knowes not, where to begin:
At a much deader fault muft reafon bee,   75
Death having broke off fuch a linke as hee.
But now, for us, with bufie proofe to come,
That we'have no reafon, would prove wee had fome.
So would juft lamentations: Therefore wee
May fafelyer fay, that we are dead, then hee.   80
So, if our griefs wee do not well declare,
We'have double excufe; he'is not dead; and we are.
Yet I would not dy yet; for though I bee

57 animate?] animate; *1633*   66 Of *1633–69*: With *1613*   67
as, *1613*: as *1633–69*   69 So is't to] So is' to *1669*   71 Fate
1633–69: Faith *1613*   72 thinks; *Ed*: thinks, *1613*, *1633–69*   73
come, *1633–69*: joine; *1613*   fo fteale in *1633–69*: to fteal-in *1613*
77 proofe *1633–69*: proofes *1613*   78 fome. *1633*: fome, *1635–69*
80 hee. *1633*: hee, *1635–69*   82 and we are. *1633–54*: we are. *1613*,
1669   83 I would not *1633–54*: would not I *1669*

Too narrow, to thinke him, as hee is hee,
(Our Soules beſt baiting, and midd-period,   85
In her long journey, of conſidering God)
Yet, (no diſhonour) I can reach him thus,
As he embrac'd the fires of love, with us.
Oh may I, (ſince I live) but ſee, or heare,
That ſhe-Intelligence which mov'd this ſpheare,   90
I pardon Fate, my life: Who ere thou bee,
Which haſt the noble conſcience, thou art ſhee,
I conjure thee by all the charmes he ſpoke,
By th'oathes, which onely you two never broke,
By all the ſoules yee ſigh'd, that if you ſee   95
Theſe lines, you wiſh, I knew your hiſtory.
So much, as you, two mutuall heav'ns were here,
I were an Angell, ſinging what you were.

To the Counteſſe of Bedford.

MADAME,

I Have learn'd by thoſe lawes wherein I am a [1] little converſant,
*that hee which beſtowes any coſt upon the dead, obliges him
which is dead, but not the* [2] *heire; I do not therefore ſend this
paper to your Ladyſhip, that you ſhould thanke mee for it, or
thinke that I thanke you in it; your favours and benefits to mee
are ſo much above my merits, that they are even above my
gratitude, if that were to be judged by words which muſt expreſſe
it: But, Madame, ſince your noble brothers fortune being yours,
the evidences alſo concerning it are yours,* [3] *ſo his vertue* [4] *being
yours, the evidences concerning it,* [5] *belong alſo to you, of which by
your acceptance this may be one peece, in which quality I humbly
preſent it, and as a teſtimony how intirely your familie poſſeſſeth*

Your Ladiſhips moſt humble
and thankfull ſervant

JOHN DONNE.

    91 Who *Ed:* who *1633–69*   92 ſhee, *1633–69:* she. *Chambers*
97 So much, as you, *1633–69:* So, much as you *Chambers*
    To the Counteſſe *&c. 1633–69, and in most of the MSS. as next page*   [1] a
1633–54: om. 1669   [2] the] his *1669*   [3] yours, *1633:* yours: *1635–69*
[4] vertue *1633:* vertues *1635–69*   [5] it, *1633:* that *1635–69*

Obsequies to the Lord Harrington, brother to the Lady Lucy, Countesse of Bedford.

FAire foule, which waſt, not onely, as all foules bee,
  Then when thou waſt infuſed, harmony,
But did'ſt continue ſo; and now doſt beare
A part in Gods great organ, this whole Spheare:
If looking up to God; or downe to us,   5
Thou finde that any way is pervious,
Twixt heav'n and earth, and that mans actions doe
Come to your knowledge, and affections too,
See, and with joy, mee to that good degree
Of goodneſſe growne, that I can ſtudie thee,   10
And, by theſe meditations refin'd,
Can unapparell and enlarge my minde,
And ſo can make by this ſoft extaſie,
This place a map of heav'n, my ſelfe of thee.
Thou ſeeſt mee here at midnight, now all reſt;   15
Times dead-low water; when all mindes deveſt
To morrows buſineſſe, when the labourers have
Such reſt in bed, that their laſt Church-yard grave,
Subject to change, will ſcarce be'a type of this,
Now when the clyent, whoſe laſt hearing is   20
To morrow, ſleeps, when the condemned man,
(Who when hee opes his eyes, muſt ſhut them than
Againe by death,) although ſad watch hee keepe,
Doth practice dying by a little ſleepe,
Thou at this midnight ſeeſt mee, and as ſoone   25
As that Sunne riſes to mee, midnight's noone,

Obſequies to &c. *B,S96 and similarly A25,C,D,H49,JC,Lec,N,O'F, S,TCD:* Obſequies to the Lord Harringtons brother. To the Counteſſe of Bedford. *1633-54:* Obſequies on the Lord Harrington, &c. To the Counteſs of Bedford. *1669*   7 mans *1633,D,H49:* mens *1635-69 and most MSS.*   11 theſe *1633-69:* thoſe *B,D,H49,JC,O'F,S,TCD* 15 midnight, now *1633-69:* midnight; now *Chambers:* midnight now, *Grolier*   26 that Sunne] this Sunne *N,TCD*

All the world growes tranfparent, and I fee
Through all, both Church and State, in feeing thee;
And I difcerne by favour of this light,
My felfe, the hardeft object of the fight.   30
God is the glaffe; as thou when thou doft fee
Him who fees all, feeft all concerning thee,
So, yet unglorified, I comprehend
All, in thefe mirrors of thy wayes, and end.
Though God be our true glaffe, through which we fee 35
All, fince the beeing of all things is hee,
Yet are the trunkes which doe to us derive
Things, in proportion fit, by perfpective,
Deeds of good men; for by their living here,
Vertues, indeed remote, feeme to be neare.   40
But where can I affirme, or where arreft
My thoughts on his deeds? which fhall I call beft?
For fluid vertue cannot be look'd on,
Nor can endure a contemplation.
As bodies change, and as I do not weare   45
Thofe Spirits, humors, blood I did laft yeare,
And, as if on a ftreame I fixe mine eye,
That drop, which I looked on, is prefently
Pufht with more waters from my fight, and gone,
So in this fea of vertues, can no one   50
Bee'infifted on; vertues, as rivers, paffe,
Yet ftill remaines that vertuous man there was.
And as if man feed on mans flefh, and fo
Part of his body to another owe,

30 hardeft] hardyeft *1669*   34 end. *D:* end; *1633–69*   35 our
true glaffe, *1633–69* (glaff, *1633*): truly our glafs *A25,B,D,H49, JC,Lec,
N,O'F,S,S96,TCD*   fee] fee. *1633 some copies, 1635*   38 Things, in
proportion fit, by perfpective, *D:* Things, in proportion fit by perfpective,
1633: Things, in proportion, fit by perfpective, *1635–54, Chambers:* Things
in proportion, fit by perfpective, *1669. See note*   39 men; *D:* men,
1633: men: *1635–69*   living *1633:* beeing *1635–69, Chambers and
Grolier*   40 neare. *1635–69:* nere; *1633*   44 contemplation. *Ed:*
contemplation; *1633–69*   51 on; *Ed:* on, *1633–69*   52 was. *Ed:*
was; *1633–69*   53 feed *1635–69 and MSS.:* feeds *1633*

                                                             Yet

Yet at the laſt two perfect bodies riſe, 55
Becauſe God knowes where every Atome lyes;
So, if one knowledge were made of all thoſe,
Who knew his minutes well, hee might diſpoſe
His vertues into names, and ranks; but I
Should injure Nature, Vertue, and Deſtinie, 60
Should I divide and diſcontinue ſo,
Vertue, which did in one intireneſſe grow.
For as, hee that would ſay, ſpirits are fram'd
Of all the pureſt parts that can be nam'd,
Honours not ſpirits halfe ſo much, as hee 65
Which ſayes, they have no parts, but ſimple bee;
So is't of vertue; for a point and one
Are much entirer then a million.
And had Fate meant to have his vertues told,
It would have let him live to have beene old; 70
So, then that vertue in ſeaſon, and then this,
We might have ſeene, and ſaïd, that now he is
Witty, now wiſe, now temperate, now juſt:
In good ſhort lives, vertues are faine to thruſt,
And to be ſure betimes to get a place, 75
When they would exerciſe, lacke time, and ſpace.
So was it in this perſon, forc'd to bee
For lack of time, his owne epitome:
So to exhibit in few yeares as much,
As all the long breath'd Chronicles can touch. 80
As when an Angell down from heav'n doth flye,
Our quick thought cannot keepe him company,
Wee cannot thinke, now hee is at the Sunne,
Now through the Moon, now he through th'aire doth
    run,

63 would *1633*: ſhould *1635–69*   69 to have his *1633, A25, D, H49,
JC, Lec, N, S, S96, TCD*: to'have had his *1635–69, O'F, Chambers*   70
old; *Ed*: old, *1633–39*: old. *1650–69*   71 So, then that *Ed*: So then,
that *1633*: So, then, that *1635–69*   76 exerciſe] exercſe *1633 some
copies*: encreaſe *D, H49, Lec*: exerciſe: they *S*   lacke *1633–54*: laſt
1669   time] room *A25, B, JC, O'F, S, S96, TCD*   78 epitome: *D*:
epitome. *1633–69*   80 Chronicles] Chroniclers *1669*   can touch.]
can touch; *1633*   84 he] *om. 1669, O'F*

                                                            Yet

Yet when he's come, we know he did repair   85
To all twixt Heav'n and Earth, Sunne, Moon, and Aire;
And as this Angell in an inſtant knowes,
And yet wee know, this ſodaine knowledge growes
By quick amaſſing ſeverall formes of things,
Which he ſucceſſively to order brings;   90
When they, whoſe ſlow-pac'd lame thoughts cannot goe
So faſt as hee, thinke that he doth not ſo;
Juſt as a perfect reader doth not dwell,
On every ſyllable, nor ſtay to ſpell,
Yet without doubt, hee doth diſtinctly ſee   95
And lay together every A, and B;
So, in ſhort liv'd good men, is'not underſtood
Each ſeverall vertue, but the compound good;
For, they all vertues paths in that pace tread,
As Angells goe, and know, and as men read.   100
O why ſhould then theſe men, theſe lumps of Balme
Sent hither, this worlds tempeſts to becalme,
Before by deeds they are diffus'd and ſpred,
And ſo make us alive, themſelves be dead?
O Soule, O circle, why ſo quickly bee   105
Thy ends, thy birth and death, clos'd up in thee?
Since one foot of thy compaſſe ſtill was plac'd
In heav'n, the other might ſecurely'have pac'd
In the moſt large extent, through every path,
Which the whole world, or man the abridgment hath.   110
Thou knowſt, that though the tropique circles have
(Yea and thoſe ſmall ones which the Poles engrave,)
All the ſame roundneſſe, evenneſſe, and all
The endleſneſſe of the equinoctiall;
Yet, when we come to meaſure diſtances,   115
How here, how there, the Sunne affected is,

86 Aire; *1669:* Aire. *1633–35:* Air, *1639–54*   87 inſtant]
inſtant, *1633*   98 good; *Ed:* good. *1633–69*   102 this *A25,*
B,C,D,H49,JC,N,O'F,S,TCD: the *1633–69*   tempeſts *A25,D,H49,*
JC,N,S96,TCD: tempeſt *1633–69,O'F,S*   106 death, *Ed:* death
1633–69   110 man] man, *1633*   hath.] hath, *1633 some copies,1635–39*
                                                                        When

When he doth faintly worke, and when prevaile,
Onely great circles, than can be our ſcale:
So, though thy circle to thy ſelfe expreſſe
All, tending to thy endleſſe happineſſe,   120
And wee, by our good uſe of it may trye,
Both how to live well young, and how to die,
Yet, ſince we muſt be old, and age endures
His Torrid Zone at Court, and calentures
Of hot ambitions, irrelegions ice,   125
Zeales agues, and hydroptique avarice,
Infirmities which need the ſcale of truth,
As well as luſt, and ignorance of youth;
Why did'ſt thou not for theſe give medicines too,
And by thy doing tell us what to doe?   130
Though as ſmall pocket-clocks, whoſe every wheele
Doth each miſmotion and diſtemper feele,
Whoſe *hand* gets ſhaking palſies, and whoſe *ſtring*
(His ſinewes) ſlackens, and whoſe *Soule*, the ſpring,
Expires, or languiſhes, whoſe pulſe, the *flye*,   135
Either beates not, or beates unevenly,
Whoſe voice, the *Bell*, doth rattle, or grow dumbe,
Or idle,'as men, which to their laſt houres come,
If theſe clockes be not wound, or be wound ſtill,
Or be not ſet, or ſet at every will;   140
So, youth is eaſieſt to deſtruction,
If then wee follow all, or follow none.
Yet, as in great clocks, which in ſteeples chime,
Plac'd to informe whole towns, to'imploy their time,
An error doth more harme, being generall,   145
When, ſmall clocks faults, only'on the wearer fall;

117 When . . when *1633–69, D, H49, Lec:* Where . . where *rest of MSS.*
118 circles, than can *D:* circles, then, can *1633–69*   121 it] that *many
MSS.*   125 ambitions,] ambition, *1669*   126 agues, *Ed:* agues ;
1633–69   127–8 *in brackets 1635–69*   128 As well as luſt, *1669:*
As well, as luſt *1633–54*   130 tell us *1633, 1669, A25, D, H49, N, S,
TCD:* ſet us *1635–54, B, O'F, S96, and Chambers*   133 *hand gets A25,
B, C, D, H49, JC, N, S, TCD:* hands get *1633–54:* hands gets *1669. See
note*   135 *flye, 1633:* flee, *1635–69*   138 houres come, *1633–54:* hour
come, *1669:* hours are come, *Chambers*   142 none. *1635–69:* none ;
1633   146 fall ; *Ed:* fall. *1633–69*

So

So worke the faults of age, on which the eye
Of children, servants, or the State relie.
Why wouldst not thou then, which hadst such a soule,
A clock so true, as might the Sunne controule,   150
And daily hadst from him, who gave it thee,
Instructions, such as it could never be
Disordered, stay here, as a generall
And great Sun-dyall, to have set us All?
O why wouldst thou be any instrument   155
To this unnaturall course, or why consent
To this, not miracle, but Prodigie,
That when the ebbs, longer then flowings be,
Vertue, whose flood did with thy youth begin,
Should so much faster ebb out, then flow in?   160
Though her flood was blowne in, by thy first breath,
All is at once sunke in the whirle-poole death.
Which word I would not name, but that I see
Death, else a desert, growne a Court by thee.
Now I grow sure, that if a man would have   165
Good companie, his entry is a grave.
Mee thinkes all Cities, now, but Anthills bee,
Where, when the severall labourers I see,
For children, house, Provision, taking paine,
They'are all but Ants, carrying eggs, straw, and grain;   170
And Church-yards are our cities, unto which
The most repaire, that are in goodnesse rich.
There is the best concourse, and confluence,
There are the holy suburbs, and from thence
Begins Gods City, New Jerusalem,   175
Which doth extend her utmost gates to them.
At that gate then Triumphant soule, dost thou
Begin thy Triumph; But since lawes allow

154 great] grave *A25, C*   155 wouldst] wouldest *1639-54*   any
1633-35, and MSS.: an *1639-69, Chambers*   158 when *1633-69*:
where *C, D, H49, N, O'F, S, TCD*: whereas *B*   161 was *1633*: were
1635-69   165 grow sure, *1633, D, H49, Lec*: am sure, *1635-69*   170
and *1633-69*: or *A25, B, C, N, O'F, S, S96, TCD*   176 them. *D*: them;
1633,169-69: them, *1635*   178 Triumph; *1633*: Triumph. *1635-69*
                                                                  That

That at the Triumph day, the people may,
All that they will, 'gainſt the Triumpher ſay,   180
Let me here uſe that freedome, and expreſſe
My griefe, though not to make thy Triumph leſſe.
By law, to Triumphs none admitted bee,
Till they as Magiſtrates get victorie;
Though then to thy force, all youthes foes did yield, 185
Yet till fit time had brought thee to that field,
To which thy ranke in this ſtate deſtin'd thee,
That there thy counſailes might get victorie,
And ſo in that capacitie remove
All jealouſies 'twixt Prince and ſubjects love, 190
Thou could'ſt no title, to this triumph have,
Thou didſt intrude on death, uſurp'dſt a grave.
Then (though victoriouſly) thou hadſt fought as yet
But with thine owne affections, with the heate
Of youths deſires, and colds of ignorance, 195
But till thou ſhould'ſt ſucceſſefully advance
Thine armes 'gainſt forraine enemies, which are
Both Envy, and acclamations popular,
(For, both theſe engines equally defeate,
Though by a divers Mine, thoſe which are great,) 200
Till then thy War was but a civill War,
For which to Triumph, none admitted are.
No more are they, who though with good ſucceſſe,
In a defenſive war, their power expreſſe;
Before men triumph, the dominion   205
Muſt be *enlarg'd*, and not *preſerv'd* alone;
Why ſhould'ſt thou then, whoſe battailes were to win
Thy ſelfe, from thoſe ſtraits nature put thee in,
And to deliver up to God that ſtate,
Of which he gave thee the vicariate,   210

184 victorie; *Ed:* victorie, *1633-69* 186 brought] wrought *1639,*
Chambers 192 uſurp'dſt *B,D,H49,N,TCD:* uſurp'ſt *1633, Lec, S96:*
uſurpe *1635-69, A25, JC,O'F, Chambers* 193 Then *1635-69:* That
1633 198 acclamations *1669,A25,B,D,H49,JC,Lec,N,O'F,S,S96,TCD:*
acclamation *1633-54* 202 are. *D:* are ; *1633-69* 204 expreſſe ;
Ed: expreſſe. *1633-69*

             (Which

(Which is thy foule and body) as intire
As he, who takes endeavours, doth require,
But didſt not ſtay, t'enlarge his kingdome too,
By making others, what thou didſt, to doe;
Why ſhouldſt thou Triumph now, when Heav'n no more
Hath got, by getting thee, then't had before?   216
For, Heav'n and thou, even when thou livedſt here,
Of one another in poſſeſſion were.
But this from Triumph moſt diſables thee,
That, that place which is conquered, muſt bee   220
Left ſafe from preſent warre, and likely doubt
Of imminent commotions to breake out:
And hath he left us ſo? or can it bee
His territory was no more then Hee?
No, we were all his charge, the Diocis   225
Of ev'ry exemplar man, the whole world is,
And he was joyned in commiſſion
With Tutelar Angels, ſent to every one.
But though this freedome to upbraid, and chide
Him who Triumph'd, were lawfull, it was ty'd   230
With this, that it might never reference have
Unto the Senate, who this triumph gave;
Men might at Pompey jeaſt, but they might not
At that authoritie, by which he got
Leave to Triumph, before, by age, he might;   235
So, though, triumphant ſoule, I dare to write,
Mov'd with a reverentiall anger, thus,
That thou ſo earely wouldſt abandon us;
Yet I am farre from daring to diſpute
With that great ſoveraigntie, whoſe abſolute   240
Prerogative hath thus diſpenſ'd with thee,
'Gainſt natures lawes, which juſt impugners bee

212   endeavours,   *1633–54, A25, B, D, H49, JC, Lec, N, O'F, S, S96,*
TCD: Indentours, *1669, Chambers*   216 'thad] t'had *1633–39*   218
were. *D:* were; *1633–69*   222 out: *1635–69:* out. *1633*   224
His *1633–54:* This *1669*   then *1633–69:* but *D, H49, N, O'F, S, S96,*
TCD   231 reference] reverence *1650–54*   239 I am] am I *B,*
O'F, S, S96   241 with *1633–69, O'F:* for *A25, D, H49, Lec, N, TCD*
                                                                    Of

Of early triumphs; And I (though with paine)
Leſſen our loſſe, to magnifie thy gaine
Of triumph, when I ſay, It was more fit,   245
That all men ſhould lacke thee, then thou lack it.
Though then in our time, be not ſuffered
That teſtimonie of love, unto the dead,
To die with them, and in their graves be hid,
As Saxon wives, and French foldurii did;   250
And though in no degree I can expreſſe
Griefe in great Alexanders great exceſſe,
Who at his friends death, made whole townes deveſt
Their walls and bullwarks which became them beſt:
Doe not, faire foule, this ſacrifice refuſe,   255
That in thy grave I doe interre my Muſe,
Who, by my griefe, great as thy worth, being caſt
Behind hand, yet hath ſpoke, and ſpoke her laſt.

Elegie on the Lady Marckham.

MAn is the World, and death th'Ocean,
    To which God gives the lower parts of man.
This Sea invirons all, and though as yet
    God hath ſet markes, and bounds, twixt us and it,
Yet doth it rore, and gnaw, and ſtill pretend,   5
    And breaks our bankes, when ere it takes a friend.
Then our land waters (teares of paſſion) vent;
    Our waters, then, above our firmament,
(Teares which our Soule doth for her ſins let fall)
    Take all a brackiſh taſt, and Funerall,   10

247 time,] times, *1669,B,,JC,O'F,N,S,S96,TCD*   250 foldurii *D,
H49,Lec:* foldarii *1633–69*   251 expreſſe] expreſſe, *1633*   257
Who, *1633:* Which, *1639–69*
    Elegie *&c. 1633–54:* An Elegie *&c. 1669: similarly, A18,A25,B,
C,Cy,D,H40,H49,JC,L74,Lec,N,P,S96,TC*   6 And breaks
1633–54: To break *1669*   bankes *D,Cy,H40,H49,JC,Lec,O'F,P,
TCC:* bounds *A25,C:* banke, *1633–69,N* (s *added*),*TCD*   8 firmament,]
firmament. *1633*   10 Funerall, *Ed:* Funerall. *1633–69*

And

And even thefe teares, which fhould wafh fin, are fin.
  We, after Gods *Noe,* drowne our world againe.
Nothing but man of all invenom'd things
  Doth worke upon itfelfe, with inborne ftings.
Teares are falfe Spectacles, we cannot fee   15
  Through paffions mift, what wee are, or what fhee.
In her this fea of death hath made no breach,
  But as the tide doth wafh the flimie beach,
And leaves embroder'd workes upon the fand,
  So is her flefh refin'd by deaths cold hand.   20
As men of China,'after an ages ftay,
  Do take up Porcelane, where they buried Clay;
So at this grave, her limbecke, which refines
  The Diamonds, Rubies, Saphires, Pearles, and Mines,
Of which this flefh was, her foule fhall infpire   25
  Flefh of fuch ftuffe, as God, when his laft fire
Annuls this world, to recompence it, fhall,
  Make and name then, th'Elixar of this All.
They fay, the fea, when it gaines, lofeth too;
  If carnall Death (the yonger brother) doe   30
Ufurpe the body,'our foule, which fubject is
  To th'elder death, by finne, is freed by this;
They perifh both, when they attempt the juft;
  For, graves our trophies are, and both deaths duft.
So, unobnoxious now, fhe'hath buried both;   35
  For, none to death finnes, that to finne is loth,
Nor doe they die, which are not loth to die;
  So hath fhe this, and that virginity.

11 thefe *D,H49,Lec:* thofe *1633–69*   12 after Gods *Noe,* drowne *1633–54 (No, 1635–54):* after God, new drown *1669*   our world *1669,B,D,H49,L74,Lec,N,O'F,P,S96,TCD:* the world *1633–54,A18, A25,JC,TCC*   16 mift] miftes *Cy,L74,N,TCD*   19 embroder'd *1635–54:* embroderd *1633:* embroider'd *1669*   21 ftay, *Ed:* ftay *1633–69*   25 which *Ed:* which, *1633–69*   28 then, *1633:* then *1635–39:* them *1650–69*   34 and both deaths duft. *Ed:* and both Deaths' dust. *Grolier:* and both, deaths duft. *1633:* and both death's duft. *1635–69 and Chambers:* and both dead duft. *D,Cy,H40, H49,JC,Lec,S96. See note*   36 loth, *Ed:* loth. *1633–69*   37 die; *Ed:* die, *1633–69*

Grace

Grace was in her extremely diligent,
    That kept her from finne, yet made her repent.   40
Of what fmall fpots pure white complaines! Alas,
    How little poyfon cracks a chriftall glaffe!
She finn'd, but juft enough to let us fee
    That God's word muft be true, All, finners be.
Soe much did zeale her confcience rarefie,   45
    That, extreme truth lack'd little of a lye,
Making omiffions, acts; laying the touch
    Of finne, on things that fometimes may be fuch.
As *Mofes* Cherubines, whofe natures doe
    Surpaffe all fpeed, by him are winged too: 50
So would her foule, already'in heaven, feeme then,
    To clyme by teares, the common ftaires of men.
How fit fhe was for God, I am content
    To fpeake, that Death his vaine haft may repent.
How fit for us, how even and how fweet,   55
    How good in all her titles, and how meet,
To have reform'd this forward herefie,
    That women can no parts of friendfhip bee ;
How Morall, how Divine fhall not be told,
    Left they that heare her vertues, thinke her old: 60
And left we take Deaths part, and make him glad
    Of fuch a prey, and to his tryumph adde.

42 cracks *1633–69,A25,Cy,P* (crackt): breakes *A18,D,H40,H49,JC,*
L74,Lec,N,O'F,S96,TC   glaffe ! *Ed:* glaffe ? *1633–69*   44–5 *omitted*
in 1633 between foot of one page and top of next   45 rarefie,] rectify, *D,H40,*
H49,JC,Lec,S96   48 fometimes *1633 and MSS.:* fometime *1635–69,*
and Chambers   52 teares,] tears *Chambers*   the . . . men *in brackets A18,*
N,TC   54 Death *D:* death *1633–69*   58 women *1635–69,A18,*
A25,D,H49,JC,L74,Lec,N,P,TC: woman *1633, Cy*   parts] parte *Cy,*
JC. This line written in large letters in several MSS.   60 vertues,
1633–35, 1669: vertue, *1639–54*   thinke] thinks *1639*   old: *Ed:*
old. *1633–69*   62 tryumph *1633–69,A25,D,H40,Lec:* triumphes
A18,B,H49,JC,L74,N,O'F,P,S96,TC

Elegie on M*ris* Boulſtred.

DEath I recant, and ſay, unſaid by mee
  What ere hath ſlip'd, that might diminiſh thee.
Spirituall treaſon, atheiſme 'tis, to ſay,
 That any can thy Summons diſobey.
Th'earths face is but thy Table; there are ſet   5
 Plants, cattell, men, diſhes for Death to eate.
In a rude hunger now hee millions drawes
 Into his bloody, or plaguy, or ſterv'd jawes.
Now hee will ſeeme to ſpare, and doth more waſt,
 Eating the beſt firſt, well preſerv'd to laſt.   10
Now wantonly he ſpoiles, and eates us not,
 But breakes off friends, and lets us peecemeale rot.
Nor will this earth ſerve him; he ſinkes the deepe
 Where harmeleſſe fiſh monaſtique ſilence keepe,
Who (were Death dead) by Roes of living ſand,   15
 Might ſpunge that element, and make it land.
He rounds the aire, and breakes the hymnique notes
 In birds (Heavens choriſters,) organique throats,
Which (if they did not dye) might ſeeme to bee
 A tenth ranke in the heavenly hierarchie.   20
O ſtrong and long-liv'd death, how cam'ſt thou in?
 And how without Creation didſt begin?
Thou haſt, and ſhalt ſee dead, before thou dyeſt,
 All the foure Monarchies, and Antichriſt.
How could I thinke thee nothing, that ſee now   25
 In all this All, nothing elſe is, but thou.
Our births and lives, vices, and vertues, bee
 Waſtfull conſumptions, and degrees of thee.

Elegie on Mris Boulſtred. *1633–69, A18,A25,B, Cy, D,H40,H49,L74,
Lec, N,O'F,P,S,TCC,TCD: in Cy,O'F, P this and the* Elegie, Death, be
not proud (*p.* 416) *are given as one poem. See note* 5 there are ſet]
and the meate *A18. L74,N,TC*   6 diſhes *1633,1650–69:* diſhed
1635–39, A18,L74,N,O'F,S96,TC   10 firſt,] fruite *or* fruites *A18,
H49,L74,N,TC:* firſt fruit *P*   14 keepe, *1635–39:* keepe. *1633,
1650–69*   15 by Roes *1633:* the Roes *1635–54:* the Rows *1669:*
by rows *A18,N,O'F,P,S96,TC*   18 birds *Ed:* birds, *1633–69*
(Heavens choriſters)] *brackets from HN*   27 lives, *1635–69,A25.
Cy,O'F,P,S:* lifes, *HN:* life, *1633,A18. D,H49,L74,Lec,N,TC*

For, wee to live, our bellowes weare, and breath,
    Nor are wee mortall, dying, dead, but death.   30
And though thou beeſt, O mighty bird of prey,
    So much reclaim'd by God, that thou muſt lay
All that thou kill'ſt at his feet, yet doth hee
    Reſerve but few, and leaves the moſt to thee.
And of thoſe few, now thou haſt overthrowne   35
    One whom thy blow makes, not ours, nor thine own.
She was more ſtories high : hopeleſſe to come
    To her Soule, thou'haſt offer'd at her lower roome.
Her Soule and body was a King and Court:
    But thou haſt both of Captaine miſt and fort.   40
As houſes fall not, though the King remove,
    Bodies of Saints reſt for their ſoules above.
Death gets 'twixt ſoules and bodies ſuch a place
    As ſinne inſinuates 'twixt juſt men and grace,
Both worke a ſeparation, no divorce.   45
    Her Soule is gone to uſher up her corſe,
Which ſhall be'almoſt another ſoule, for there
    Bodies are purer, then beſt Soules are here.
Becauſe in her, her virtues did outgoe
    Her yeares, would'ſt thou, O emulous death, do ſo?   50
And kill her young to thy loſſe? muſt the coſt
    Of beauty,'and wit, apt to doe harme, be loſt?
What though thou found'ſt her proofe 'gainſt ſins of
        youth?
    Oh, every age a diverſe ſinne purſueth.
Thou ſhould'ſt have ſtay'd, and taken better hold,   55
    Shortly, ambitious; covetous, when old,
She might have prov'd : and ſuch devotion
    Might once have ſtray'd to ſuperſtition.

---

    34 to thee. *1633:* for thee. *1635–69*   35 thou haſt *1633–69:* haſt
thou *HN*   36 blow] blow, *1633*   41 King *1633, A18, A25, B, Cy,*
D, H49, HN, Lec, N, O'F, P, TC: Kings *1635–69*   45 worke *1633–69,*
HN, O'F, S: workes *A18, Cy, D, H49, L74, N, P, TC:* makes *Lec.* *See*
note   56 Shortly,] Shortly *1633*   ambitious ; *1635–69:* ambitious,
1633

If

If all her vertues muſt have growne, yet might
    Abundant virtue'have bred a proud delight.   60
Had ſhe perſever'd juſt, there would have bin
    Some that would ſinne, miſ-thinking ſhe did ſinne.
Such as would call her friendſhip, love, and faine
    To ſociableneſſe, a name profane ;
Or ſinne, by tempting, or, not daring that,   65
    By wiſhing, though they never told her what.
Thus might'ſt thou'have ſlain more ſoules, had'ſt thou not
    croſt
    Thy ſelfe, and to triumph, thine army loſt.
Yet though theſe wayes be loſt, thou haſt left one,
    Which is, immoderate griefe that ſhe is gone.   70
But we may ſcape that ſinne, yet weepe as much,
    Our teares are due, becauſe we are not ſuch.
Some teares, that knot of friends, her death muſt coſt,
    Becauſe the chaine is broke, though no linke loſt.

Elegie.

Death.

L Anguage thou art too narrow, and too weake
    To eaſe us now ; great ſorrow cannot ſpeake ;
If we could ſigh out accents, and weepe words,
    Griefe weares, and leſſens, that tears breath affords.

    62 miſ-thinking] miſtaking *Cy, HN, O'F (but altered to text)*   64
profane ; *1669:* profane, *1635–54:* profane. *1633*   74 though *1635–69,*
A18, A25, HN, L74, N, O'F, P, S, S96, TC: but *1633, D, H40, H49, Lec*
    Here follow in 1635–54 By our firſt ſtrange (*p.* 111), Madame, That I
(*p.* 291), *and* Death be not proud, (*p.* 422). *In 1669* My Fortune and
(*p.* 292) *precedes* Madame, That I
    Elegie. *1633:* ElegieXI. Death. *1635–54 (being placed among the*Elegies):
Elegie XI. *1669:* An Elegie upon the death of Mʳⁱˢ Boulſtred. *A18, B,*
Cy, H40, L74, N, O'F, P, S, TCC, TCD: no title, *HN*   2 ſorrow *1633,*
B, Cy, H40, HN, L74, N, P, TC: ſorrowes *1635–69, O'F, S*

                                           Sad

Sad hearts, the leſſe they ſeeme the more they are,⠀⠀⠀5
⠀⠀(So guiltieſt men ſtand muteſt at the barre)
Not that they know not, feele not their eſtate,
⠀⠀But extreme ſenſe hath made them deſperate.
Sorrow, to whom we owe all that we bee;
⠀,Tyrant, in the fift and greateſt Monarchy,⠀⠀⠀10
Was't, that ſhe did poſſeſſe all hearts before,
⠀⠀Thou haſt kil'd her, to make thy Empire more?
Knew'ſt thou ſome would, that knew her not, lament,
⠀⠀As in a deluge periſh th'innocent?
Was't not enough to have that palace wonne,⠀⠀⠀15
⠀⠀But thou muſt raze it too, that was undone?
Had'ſt thou ſtaid there, and look'd out at her eyes,
⠀⠀All had ador'd thee that now from thee flies,
For they let out more light, then they tooke in,
⠀⠀They told not when, but did the day beginne.⠀⠀⠀20
She was too Saphirine, and cleare for thee;
⠀⠀Clay, flint, and jeat now thy fit dwellings be;
Alas, ſhee was too pure, but not too weake;
⠀⠀Who e'r ſaw Chriſtall Ordinance but would break?
And if wee be thy conqueſt, by her fall⠀⠀⠀25
⠀⠀Th'haſt loſt thy end, for in her periſh all;
Or if we live, we live but to rebell,
⠀⠀They know her better now, that knew her well.
If we ſhould vapour out, and pine, and die;
⠀⠀Since, ſhee firſt went, that were not miſerie.⠀⠀⠀30
Shee chang'd our world with hers; now ſhe is gone,
⠀⠀Mirth and proſperity is oppreſſion;
For of all morall vertues ſhe was all,
⠀⠀The Ethicks ſpeake of vertues Cardinall.

⠀⠀8 deſperate. *Ed:* deſperate; *1633–69*⠀⠀⠀10 Tyrant, *1633,1669*
(*no comma*)*:* Tyran, *1635–54*⠀⠀⠀20 beginne. *Ed:* beginne ; *1633–69*
21 for *1635–69:* to *1633*⠀⠀⠀26 for in her *1633 and all the MSS.:* in
her we *1635–69, Chambers*⠀⠀⠀28 They . . that . . well ; *1633, Cy, H40,*
HN, L74, N, S, TC: That know her better now, who knew her well.
1635–69, B, O'F, P, S96⠀⠀⠀29 and pine, and] or pine, or *Cy, H40, HN,*
O'F, P, S, S96: or pine, and *L74, TCC*⠀⠀⠀30 miſerie. *Ed:* miſerie ;
1633–69⠀⠀⠀34 The Ethicks ſpeake *1633, A18, Cy, H40, L74, N, P, TC:*
That Ethickes ſpeake *1635–69, B, O'F, S:* The ethenickes ſpake *HN*
Cardinall. *Ed:* Cardinall ; *1633–69*

⠀⠀⠀⠀⠀⠀⠀⠀⠀⠀⠀⠀⠀⠀⠀⠀⠀⠀⠀⠀⠀⠀⠀Her

Her foule was Paradife; the Cherubin   35
  Set to keepe it was grace, that kept out finne.
Shee had no more then let in death, for wee
  All reape confumption from one fruitfull tree.
God tooke her hence, left fome of us fhould love
  Her, like that plant, him and his lawes above,   40
And when wee teares, hee mercy fhed in this,
  To raife our mindes to heaven where now fhe is;
Who if her vertues would have let her ftay
  Wee'had had a Saint, have now a holiday.
Her heart was that ftrange bufh, where, facred fire,   45
  Religion, did not confume, but'infpire
Such piety, fo chaft ufe of Gods day,
  That what we turne to *feaft*, fhe turn'd to *pray*,
And did prefigure here, in devout taft,
  The reft of her high Sabaoth, which fhall laft.   50
Angels did hand her up, who next God dwell,
  (For fhe was of that order whence moft fell)
Her body left with us, left fome had faid,
  Shee could not die, except they faw her dead;
For from leffe vertue, and leffe beautioufneffe,   55
  The Gentiles fram'd them Gods and Goddeffes.
The ravenous earth that now wooes her to be
  Earth too, will be a *Lemnia*; and the tree
That wraps that chriftall in a wooden Tombe,
  Shall be tooke up fpruce, fill'd with diamond;   60
And we her fad glad friends all beare a part
  Of griefe, for all would wafte a Stoicks heart.

36 that kept out] to keep out *HN, P*   finne. *Ed:* finne; *1633–69*
37 'She had no more; then let in death for we *1669*   38 tree. *Ed:*
tree; *1633–69*   41–2 And when we fee his mercy fhewne in this
'Twill *&c. S*   44 holiday. *Ed:* holiday; *1633–69*   *All the MSS.*
omit have, *but O'F inserts it later*   48 That what *1633–69:* That
when *HN*   turne] turn'd *Cy, HN, P, S96*   to *feaft, Ed:* to feaft,
1633–69   feaft] feafts *L74, N, O'F, TC*   to *pray, Ed:* to pray,
1633–69   50 laft.] laft; *1633*   53 Her body left *1633, A18, HN,
N, TC:* Her bodie's left *1635–69*   56 fram'd] fain'd *Cy, P:* form'd
H40, HN   57 wooes] woes *1633*   be] be, *1633*   58 *All the
MSS.* omit a *before* Lemnia, *but O'F inserts*   61 fad glad *1633–69:*
glad fad *B, Cy, L74, N, O'F, P, S, S96*   62 wafte *1633, A18, Cy, H40,
HN, L74, N, P, TC:* breake *1635–69, B, O'F*

Elegie

Elegie on the L. C.

SOrrow, who to this houfe fcarce knew the way:
Is, Oh, heire of it, our All is his prey.
This ftrange chance claimes ftrange wonder, and to us
Nothing can be fo ftrange, as to weepe thus.
'Tis well his lifes loud fpeaking workes deferve,   5
And give praife too, our cold tongues could not ferve:
'Tis well, hee kept teares from our eyes before,
That to fit this deepe ill, we might have ftore.
Oh, if a fweet briar, climbe up by'a tree,
If to a paradife that tranfplanted bee,   10
Or fell'd, and burnt for holy facrifice,
Yet, that muft wither, which by it did rife,
As we for him dead: though no familie
Ere rigg'd a foule for heavens difcoverie
With whom more Venturers more boldly dare   15
Venture their ftates, with him in joy to fhare.
Wee lofe what all friends lov'd, him; he gaines now
But life by death, which worft foes would allow,
If hee could have foes, in whofe practife grew
All vertues, whofe names fubtile Schoolmen knew.   20
What eafe, can hope that wee fhall fee'him, beget,
When wee muft die firft, and cannot dye yet?
His children are his pictures, Oh they bee
Pictures of him dead, fenfeleffe, cold as he.
Here needs no marble Tombe, fince hee is gone,   25
He, and about him, his, are turn'd to ftone.

Elegie &c. *1635–69, following* Death be not proud (*p.* 422): Elegie,
Funerall Elegie, *or no title,* B, Cy,HN,O'F,S96: Elegie VI. (*being placed
among the* Elegies) *1633:* Elegie. (*being eighth among* Elegies) D, H49,Lec:
Elegia tercia. S: Elegie XIII[a]. JC,W   1 who *1633–39:* that *1650–69*
2 prey. *1633:* prey, *1635–54:* Pay. *1669*   4 thus. *1669:* thus; *1633–54*
13 dead: *1633–69:* dead. HN, Grolier   16 Venture their ftates] Venter
eftates B   fhare. D, H49,Lec,W: fhare *1633:* fhare, *1635–69, Chambers
and Grolier. See note*   17 him;] him, *1633*   20 names] name *1635–69*
knew. Ed: knew; *1635–69*   24 he. *1650–69:* he, *1633–39*

An

An hymne to the Saints, and to Marqueſſe
Hamylton.

To Sir Robert Carr.

S I R,

I Preſume you rather try what you can doe in me, then what
I can doe in verſe; you know my uttermoſt when it was beſt,
and even then I did beſt when I had leaſt truth for my ſubjeets.
In this preſent caſe there is ſo much truth as it defeats all Poetry.
Call therefore this paper by what name you will, and, if it
bee not worthy of him, nor of you, nor of mee, ſmother it, and
bee that the ſacrifice.   If you had commanded mee to have
waited on his body to Scotland and preached there, I would have
embraced the obligation with more alacrity; But, I thanke you
that you would command me that which I was loath to doe, for,
even that hath given a tinĉture of merit to the obedience of

> Your poore friend and
> ſervant in Chriſt Jeſus
>
> I. D.

WHether that ſoule which now comes up to you
    Fill any former ranke or make a new;
Whether it take a name nam'd there before,
Or be a name it ſelfe, and *order* more

An hymne *&c. 1633–69, in all of which it is claſſed with the* Divine
Poems, *following* Reſurreĉtion. *In 1635–69 it is preceded by the letter*
To Sir Robert Carr.: *in 1633 the letter follows, and has no heading:
similarly in A18,O'F,TCC. See note*   2 verſe ; *1635–69:* verſe, *1633*
3 beſt] at the beſt *A18,TCC*   ſubjeĉts. *1635–69:* ſubjeĉts, *1633:*
ſubjeĉt, *A18,TCC*   6–7 of him . . . ſacrifice. *1635–69:* of you nor
of him, we will ſmother it, and be it your ſacrifice. *1633:* of him, nor of
you, nor of anye ; ſmother it, and bee that the ſacrifice. *A18,TCC*   9 the
1635–69: your *1633,A18,TCC*   more] much *1633*   10 loath]
loather *1633*   in Chriſt Jeſus] *om. A18,TCC*
    1 Whether] Whither *1633, and so in* 3   2 new ; *Ed:* new, *1633–69*
                                                            Then

Then was in heaven till now; (for may not hee   5
Bee fo, if every feverall Angell bee
A *kind* alone?) What ever order grow
Greater by him in heaven, wee doe not fo.
One of your orders growes by his acceffe;
But, by his loffe grow all our *orders* leffe;   10
The name of *Father*, *Mafter*, *Friend*, the name
Of *Subject* and of *Prince*, in one are lame;
Faire mirth is dampt, and converfation black,
The *houfehold* widdow'd, and the *garter* flack;
The *Chappell* wants an eare, *Councell* a tongue;   15
Story, a theame; and *Muficke* lacks a fong;
Bleft *order* that hath him! the loffe of him
Gangreend all *Orders* here; all loft a limbe.
Never made body fuch haft to confeffe
What a foule was; All former comelineffe   20
Fled, in a minute, when the foule was gone,
And, having loft that beauty, would have none;
So fell our *Monafteries*, in one inftant growne
Not to leffe houfes, but, to heapes of ftone;
So fent this body that faire forme it wore,   25
Unto the fpheare of formes, and doth (before
His foule fhall fill up his fepulchrall ftone,)
Anticipate a Refurrection;
For, as in his fame, now, his foule is here,
So, in the forme thereof his bodie's there.   30
And if, faire foule, not with firft *Innocents*
Thy ftation be, but with the *Pænitents*,
(And, who fhall dare to afke then when I am
Dy'd fcarlet in the blood of that pure Lambe,

6 fo,] fo? *1633*   7 alone?) *1635–54:* alone;) *1633:* alone) *1669*
8 fo. *Ed:* fo; *1633–69*   12 are *1633, A18, TCC:* is *1635–69, O'F*
16 fong; *1633:* fong. *1635–69*   17 him. *Ed:* him, *1633–69*   18
Gangreend *1635–69:* Gangred *1633*   limbe. *1633–35:* limbe: *1639–69*
22 none; *Ed:* none: *1650–69:* none, *1633–39*   23 one inftant *1633:*
an inftant *1635–69*   25 this *1633, A18, TCC:* his *1635–69*   29
For, as in his *1633–39:* For, as it his *1650–54:* For, as it is his *1669*
30 there. *Ed:* there; *1633–39:* there, *1650–69*
                                                  Whether

Whether that colour, which is fcarlet then,   35
Were black or white before in eyes of men?)
When thou rememb'reft what fins thou didft finde
Amongft thofe many friends now left behinde,
And feeft fuch finners as they are, with thee
Got thither by repentance, Let it bee   40
Thy wifh to wifh all there, to wifh them cleane;
Wifh *him* a *David*, *her* a *Magdalen*.

36 in eyes] in the eyes *A18,O'F,TCC*

EPITAPHS.

EPITAPHS.

EPITAPH

ON HIMSELFE.

To the Counteſſe of Bedford.

MADAME,

THat I might make your Cabinet my tombe,
  And for my fame which I love next my ſoule,
Next to my ſoule provide the happieſt roome,
  Admit to that place this laſt funerall Scrowle.
    Others by Wills give Legacies, but I   5
    Dying, of you doe beg a Legacie.

My fortune and my will this cuſtome breake,
When we are ſenſeleſſe grown to make ſtones ſpeak,
Though no ſtone tell thee what I was, yet thou
In my graves inſide ſee what thou art now :   10
Yet th'art not yet ſo good ; till us death lay
To ripe and mellow there, w'are ſtubborne clay,
Parents make us earth, and ſoules dignifie
Vs to be glaſſe, here to grow gold we lie ;
Whilſt in our ſoules ſinne bred and pampered is,   15
Our ſoules become worme-eaten Carkaſſes.

Epitaph. *B, D, H40, H49*   On himſelfe. *1635–69*   To the
Counteſſe of Bedford. *O'F, S96: no heading, and epiſtle only, A25, C
The introductory epiſtle, and the firſt ten lines of the epitaph, the whole with
heading* Elegie., *is printed 1635–54 among the* Funerall Elegies. *The full
epitaph without epiſtle and with heading* On himſelfe. *is included among
the* Divine Poems, *where it follows the* Lamentations of Jeremy. *In
his note Chambers (*II. 234) *reverses these facts. In 1669* On himſelfe.
is transferred to the Funerall Elegies *and is followed immediately by the*
Elegie, *i.e. the epiſtle and incomplete epitaph. They are here given for the
firſt time in a separate group*   5 Others by Wills *1635–69:* Others by
teſtaments *A25, C, O'F(altered to* wills), *S96:* Men by teſtament *B:*
Then by teſtament *H40:* O then by teſtament *D, H49*   10 now :
1650–69: now, *1635–39*   12 there, *1635, 1669:* thee, *1639–54*

Omnibus

Omnibus.

MY Fortune and my choice this cuſtome break,
  When we are ſpeechleſſe grown, to make ſtones ſpeak,
Though no ſtone tell thee what I was, yet thou
In my graves inſide ſeeſt what thou art now:
Yet thou'art not yet ſo good, till death us lay   5
To ripe and mellow here, we are ſtubborne Clay.
Parents make us earth, and ſoules dignifie
Vs to be glaſſe; here to grow gold we lie.
Whilſt in our ſoules ſinne bred and pamper'd is,
Our ſoules become wormeaten carkaſes;   10
So we our ſelves miraculouſly deſtroy.
Here bodies with leſſe miracle enjoy
Such priviledges, enabled here to ſcale
Heaven, when the Trumpets ayre ſhall them exhale.
Heare this, and mend thy ſelfe, and thou mendſt me,   15
By making me being dead, doe good to thee,
    And thinke me well compos'd, that I could now
    A laſt-ſicke houre to ſyllables allow.

Omnibus. D, H49: To all. *H40, RP31:* Another on the ſame. (*i.e.
Mʳˢ Boulſtred) P:* On himſelfe. *1635–69: no title, B, S96: in MSS. this
complete epitaph follows the epistle (p.* 291*); but in B they are separated
by various poems and in P the epistle is not given*   3 tell] tel *1635*
4 ſeeſt] ſee *D, H49: compare incomplete version.*   5 Yet *1635–69:*
Nay *S96*   thou'art *Ed:* thou art *1635–69*   8 lie. *Ed:*
lie; *1635–69*   14 them] then *1669*   16 to thee, *B, D, H40, H49,
O'F, S96:* for thee, *1635–69*

INFINITATI SACRUM,

16. *Augusti* 1601.

METEMPSYCHOSIS.

Poêma Satyricon.

EPISTLE.

Thers at the Porches and entries of their Buildings set their Armes; I, my picture; if any colours can deliver a minde so plaine, and flat, and through light as mine. Naturally at a new Author, I doubt, and sticke, and doe not say quickly, good. I censure much and taxe; And this liberty costs mee more then others, by how much my owne things are worse then others. Yet I would not be so rebellious against my selfe, as not to doe it, since I love it; nor so unjust to others, to do it *sine talione.* As long as I give them as good hold upon mee, they must pardon mee my bitings. I forbid no reprehender, but him that like the Trent Councell forbids not bookes, but Authors, damning what ever such a name hath or shall write. None writes so ill, that he gives not some thing exemplary, to follow, or flie. Now when I beginne this booke, I have no purpose to come into any mans debt[1]; how my stocke will hold out I know not; perchance waste, perchance increase in use; if I doe

---

Infinitati &c. *1633–69:* (*in 1633 it is the first poem; in 1635–69 it follows the* Funerall Elegies, *from which it is separated by some prose letters, and precedes* Divine Poems *as here*), *A18, G, N, TCC, TCD* Metempsychosis. *1650–69:* Metempsycosis. *1633–39* [1] debt; *Ed:* debt, *1633–69*

borrow

borrow any thing of Antiquitie, befides that I make account that I pay it to pofterity, with as much and as good: You fhall ftill finde mee to acknowledge it, and to thanke not him onely that hath digg'd out treafure for mee, but that hath lighted mee a candle to the place. All which I will bid you remember, (for I will have no fuch Readers as I can teach) is, that the Pithagorian doctrine doth not onely carry one foule from man to man, nor man to beaft, but indifferently to plants alfo: and therefore you muft not grudge to finde the fame foule in an Emperour, in a Poft-horfe, and in a Mucheron,[1] fince no unreadineffe in the foule, but an indifpofition in the organs workes this. And therefore though this foule could not move when it was a Melon, yet it may remember, and now tell mee,[2] at what lafcivious banquet it was ferv'd. And though it could not fpeake, when it was a fpider, yet it can remember, and now tell me, who ufed it for poyfon to attaine dignitie. How ever the bodies have dull'd her other faculties, her memory hath ever been her owne, which makes me fo ferioufly deliver you by her relation all her paffages from her firft making when fhee was that apple [3] which Eve eate,[4] to this time when fhee is hee,[5] whofe life you fhall finde in the end of this booke.

[1] Mucheron, *1633, N, TC*: Mufhrome, *G*: Maceron, *1635–69, O'F*
[2] and can now tell mee, *1635–69*   [3] apple] aple *1633*   [4] eate, *1633–69*: ate, *O'F*: eat, *mod. editors*   [5] fhee is hee, *1633, A18, G, N, TC*: fhee is fhee, *1635–69*

THE

THE
PROGRESSE
OF THE SOULE.

Firſt Song.

I.

I Sing the progreſſe of a deathleſſe ſoule,
  Whom Fate, which God made, but doth not controule,
Plac'd in moſt ſhapes; all times before the law
Yoak'd us, and when, and ſince, in this I ſing.
And the great world to his aged evening;   5
From infant morne, through manly noone I draw.
What the gold Chaldee, or ſilver Perſian ſaw,
Greeke braſſe, or Roman iron, is in this one;
A worke t'outweare *Seths* pillars, bricke and ſtone,
    And (holy writt excepted) made to yeeld to none.   10

II.

Thee, eye of heaven, this great Soule envies not,
By thy male force, is all wee have, begot.
In the firſt Eaſt, thou now beginſt to ſhine,
Suck'ſt early balme, and Iland ſpices there,
And wilt anon in thy looſe-rein'd careere   15
At Tagus, Po, Sene, Thames, and Danow dine,
And ſee at night thy Weſterne land of Myne,
Yet haſt thou not more nations ſeene then ſhee,
That before thee, one day beganne to bee,
    And thy fraile light being quench'd, ſhall long, long out
      live thee.   20

                                              III.

III.

Nor, holy *Ianus*, in whofe foveraigne boate
The Church, and all the Monarchies did floate;
That fwimming Colledge, and free Hofpitall
Of all mankinde, that cage and vivarie
Of fowles, and beafts, in whofe wombe, Deftinie   25
Us, and our lateft nephewes did inftall
(From thence are all deriv'd, that fill this All,)
Did'ft thou in that great ftewardfhip embarke
So diverfe fhapes into that floating parke,
　As have beene moved, and inform'd by this heavenly
　　fparke.   30 .

IV.

Great Deftiny the Commiffary of God,
That haft mark'd out a path and period
For every thing; who, where wee of-fpring tooke,
Our wayes and ends feeft at one inftant; Thou
Knot of all caufes, thou whofe changeleffe brow   35
Ne'r fmiles nor frownes, O vouch thou fafe to looke
And fhew my ftory, in thy eternall booke:
That (if my prayer be fit) I may'underftand
So much my felfe, as to know with what hand,
　How fcant, or liberall this my lifes race is fpand.   40

V.

To my fixe luftres almoft now outwore,
Except thy booke owe mee fo many more,
Except my legend be free from the letts
Of fteepe ambition, fleepie povertie,
Spirit-quenching fickneffe, dull captivitie,   45

21 Nor, holy *Ianus*, *Ed:* Nor holy *Ianus 1633–69*　　27 From thence]
For, thence *G*　　All,)]All) *1633–69*　　31 Commiffary] commiffary *1633
some copies*　　33 every thing; *Ed:* every thing, *1633–69*　　34 inftant;
1633: inftant. *1635–69*　　36 vouch thou fafe *A18, G, N, O'F, TC:* vouch
fafe thou *1633–69*　　37 booke: *Ed:* booke. *1633–69*　　45 Spirit-
quenching] Spright-quenching *G*

Diftracting

Diftracting bufineffe, and from beauties nets,
And all that calls from this, and to others whets,
O let me not launch out, but let mee fave
Th'expenfe of braine and fpirit; that my grave
    His right and due, a whole unwafted man may have. 50

VI.

But if my dayes be long, and good enough,
In vaine this fea fhall enlarge, or enrough
It felfe; for I will through the wave, and fome,
And fhall, in fad lone wayes a lively fpright,
Make my darke heavy Poëm light, and light.   55
For though through many ftreights, and lands I roame,
I launch at paradife, and I faile towards home;
The courfe I there began, fhall here be ftaid,
Sailes hoifed there, ftroke here, and anchors laid
    In Thames, which were at Tigrys, and Euphrates
    waide.   60

VII.

For the great foule which here amongft us now
Doth dwell, and moves that hand, and tongue, and brow,
Which, as the Moone the fea, moves us; to heare
Whofe ftory, with long patience you will long;
(For 'tis the crowne, and laft ftraine of my fong)   65
This foule to whom *Luther*, and *Mahomet* were
Prifons of flefh; this foule which oft did teare,
And mend the wracks of th'Empire, and late Rome,
And liv'd when every great change did come,
    Had firft in paradife, a low, but fatall roome.   70

---

54 fhall, *Ed:* fhall *1633:* hold *1635–69*   lone *1635–69:* love *1633*,
A18,G,N,TC   wayes *Ed:* wayes, *1633–69*   fpright, *Ed:* fpright
1633–69   59 hoifed] hoifted *G*   61 For the] For this *G,N,TCD:*
For that *O'F*   63 Which, *Ed:* Which *1633–69*   us; *Ed:* us,
1633–69   69 when] where *A18,G,N,O'F,TC*

VIII.

Yet no low roome, nor then the greateſt, leſſe,
If (as devout and ſharpe men fitly gueſſe)
That Croſſe, our joy, and griefe, where nailes did tye
That All, which alwayes was all, every where;
Which could not ſinne, and yet all ſinnes did beare; 75
Which could not die, yet could not chuſe but die;
Stood in the ſelfe ſame roome in Calvarie,
Where firſt grew the forbidden learned tree,
For on that tree hung in ſecurity
   This Soule, made by the Makers will from pulling
    free.   80

IX.

Prince of the orchard, faire as dawning morne,
Fenc'd with the law, and ripe as ſoone as borne
That apple grew, which this Soule did enlive,
Till the then climing ſerpent, that now creeps
For that offence, for which all mankinde weepes, 85
Tooke it, and t'her whom the firſt man did wive
(Whom and her race, only forbiddings drive)
He gave it, ſhe, t'her huſband, both did eate;
So periſhed the eaters, and the meate:
   And wee (for treaſon taints the blood) thence die and
    ſweat.   90

X.

Man all at once was there by woman ſlaine,
And one by one we'are here ſlaine o'er againe
By them. The mother poiſon'd the well-head,
The daughters here corrupt us, Rivolets;
No ſmalneſſe ſcapes, no greatneſſe breaks their nets; 95

71 no low] nor low *Chambers*   74 every where; *Ed:* every where
1633: every where, *1635–69*   83 enlive, *G:* enlive *1633–69:* om. *1633
some copies, and A18,N,TC*   93 poyſon'd *1669:* poiſoned *1633–54*
94 corrupt us, *1635–69:* corrupts us, *1633:* corrupt as *G*   Rivolets;
Ed: Rivolets, *1635–69:* om. *1633,A18,N,TC*   95 breaks] breake
1633 some copies   nets; *Ed:* nets, *1633–69*

                                 She

She thruſt us out, and by them we are led
Aſtray, from turning, to whence we are fled.
Were priſoners Judges, 'twould seeme rigorous,
Shee ſinn'd, we beare; part of our paine is, thus
 To love them, whoſe fault to this painfull love yoak'd
  us.   100

XI.

So faſt in us doth this corruption grow,
That now wee dare aſke why wee ſhould be ſo.
Would God (diſputes the curious Rebell) make
A law, and would not have it kept? Or can
His creatures will, croſſe his? Of every man   105
For one, will God (and be juſt) vengeance take?
Who ſinn'd? t'was not forbidden to the ſnake
Nor her, who was not then made; nor is't writ
That Adam cropt, or knew the apple; yet
 The worme and ſhe, and he, and wee endure for it. 110

XII.

But ſnatch mee heavenly Spirit from this vaine
Reckoning their vanities, leſſe is their gaine
Then hazard ſtill, to meditate on ill,
Though with good minde; their reaſons, like thoſe toyes
Of glaſſie bubbles, which the gameſome boyes   115
Stretch to ſo nice a thinnes through a quill
That they themſelves breake, doe themſelves ſpill:
Arguing is heretiques game, and Exerciſe
As wraſtlers, perfeᶜts them; Not liberties
 Of ſpeech, but ſilence; hands, not tongues, end
  hereſies.   120

96 thruſt] thruſts *1633* (thruſt *in some copies*)   97 fled.] fled, *1633*
99 beare; *1635–69, G:* here, *1633:* heare, *A18, N, TC* 108 is't] i'ſt *1633*
112 vanities, *1633, G:* vanitie, *1635–69* 114 minde; *Ed:* minde, *1633–69*
reaſons, *Ed:* reaſons *1633:* reaſon's *1635–69, Chambers and Grolier* 115
which] with *1633 some copies*   117 breake, doe *1633, A18, G, N, TC:*
breake, and doe *1635–69, Chambers*   ſpill: *Ed:* ſpill, *1633–69*   119
perfeᶜts] perfeᶜt *1633 some copies*

                  XIII.

XIII.

Juſt in that inſtant when the ſerpents gripe,
Broke the ſlight veines, and tender conduit-pipe,
Through which this ſoule from the trees root did draw
Life, and growth to this apple, fled away
This looſe ſoule, old, one and another day.   125
As lightning, which one ſcarce dares ſay, he ſaw,
'Tis ſo ſoone gone, (and better proofe the law
Of ſenſe, then faith requires) ſwiftly ſhe flew
To a darke and foggie Plot; Her, her fates threw
  There through th'earths pores, and in a Plant houſ'd
    her anew.   130

XIV.

The plant thus abled, to it ſelfe did force
A place, where no place was; by natures courſe
As aire from water, water fleets away
From thicker bodies, by this root thronged ſo
His ſpungie confines gave him place to grow: 135
Juſt as in our ſtreets, when the people ſtay
To ſee the Prince, and have ſo fill'd the way
That weeſels ſcarce could paſſe, when ſhe comes nere
They throng and cleave up, and a paſſage cleare,
  As if, for that time, their round bodies flatned were.   140

XV.

His right arme he thruſt out towards the Eaſt,
Weſt-ward his left; th'ends did themſelves digeſt
Into ten leſſer ſtrings, theſe fingers were:
And as a ſlumberer ſtretching on his bed,
This way he this, and that way ſcattered   145

125 day. *1635–69:* day, *1633 (corrected in some copies)*   126 dares]
dare *1669*   127 proofe] proofes *O'F*   130 earths pores, *1669,
A18, G, N:* earths-pores, *1633:* earth-pores, *1633 (some copies), 1635–54*
anew] a new *1633*   135 grow: *1650–69:* grow, *1633–39*   137 the
Prince, and have ſo fill'd *G:* the Princeſſe, and ſo fill'd *1633 (but some copies
read* the Prince, and ſo fill'd*):* the Prince, and ſo fill up *1635–69:* the Prince,
and ſo fill'd *A18, N, TC*   144 bed, *Ed:* bed; *1633–69*

His

His other legge, which feet with toes upbeare.
Grew on his middle parts, the firſt day, haire,
To ſhow, that in loves buſineſſe hee ſhould ſtill
A dealer bee, and be uſ'd well, or ill:
    His apples kindle, his leaves, force of conception kill. 150

XVI.

A mouth, but dumbe, he hath; blinde eyes, deafe eares,
And to his ſhoulders dangle ſubtile haires;
A young *Coloſſus* there hee ſtands upright,
And as that ground by him were conquered
A leafie garland weares he on his head   155
Enchas'd with little fruits, ſo red and bright
That for them you would call your Loves lips white;
So, of a lone unhaunted place poſſeſt,
Did this ſoules ſecond Inne, built by the gueſt,
    This living buried man, this quiet mandrake, reſt. 160

XVII.

No luſtfull woman came this plant to grieve,
But 'twas becauſe there was none yet but Eve:
And ſhe (with other purpoſe) kill'd it quite;
Her ſinne had now brought in infirmities,
And ſo her cradled child, the moiſt red eyes   165
Had never ſhut, nor ſlept ſince it ſaw light;
Poppie ſhe knew, ſhe knew the mandrakes might,
And tore up both, and ſo çoold her childs blood;
Unvirtuous weeds might long unvex'd have ſtood;
    But hee's ſhort liv'd, that with his death can doe moſt
       good.   170

146 upbeare. *Ed:* upbeare; *1633:* up beare; *1635–69*   147 middle
parts *1633, G, O'F:* middle part *1635–69:* mid-parts *A18, N, TC*   150
kindle, *G:* kinde, *1633, A18, N, O'F, TC:* kindle; *1635–69*   157 white;
1633: white, *1635–69*   159 gueſt, *Ed:* gueſt *1633–69. See note*
165 moiſt red *1633–35:* moiſt-red *1639–69*   166 ſlept] ſleept *1633–35*
light; *Ed:* light, *1633–69*   167 mandrakes might, *Ed:* mandrakes
might; *1633–54:* mandrakes-might; *1669*

XVIII.

XVIII.

To an unfetterd foules quick nimble haft
Are falling ftars, and hearts thoughts, but flow pac'd:
Thinner then burnt aire flies this foule, and fhe
Whom foure new comming, and foure parting Suns
Had found, and left the Mandrakes tenant, runnes 175
Thoughtleffe of change, when her firme deftiny
Confin'd, and enjayld her, that feem'd fo free,
Into a fmall blew fhell, the which a poore
Warme bird orefpread, and fat ftill evermore,
 Till her inclos'd child kickt, and pick'd it felfe a
 dore. 180

XIX.

Outcrept a fparrow, this foules moving Inne,
On whofe raw armes ftiffe feathers now begin,
As childrens teeth through gummes, to breake with paine,
His flefh is jelly yet, and his bones threds,
All a new downy mantle overfpreads, 185
A mouth he opes, which would as much containe
As his late houfe, and the firft houre fpeaks plaine,
And chirps alowd for meat. Meat fit for men
His father fteales for him, and fo feeds then
 One, that within a moneth, will beate him from his
 hen. 190

XX.

In this worlds youth wife nature did make haft,
Things ripened fooner, and did longer laft;
Already this hot cocke, in bufh and tree,
In field and tent, oreflutters his next hen;
He asks her not, who did fo taft, nor when, 195

180 inclos'd *1635–69,G:* encloth'd *A18,N,TC:* encloth'd *altered to*
unclothed *then to* enclofed *O'F:* uncloath'd *1633*   pick'd] peck'd *A18,*
G,TC   181 Outcrept *1633–35:* Out crept *1639–69*   185
a new downy *1635–69,A18,G,TC:* downy a new *1633*   overfpreades,
1633–39: overfpreads *1650–69*   193 cocke, *Ed:* cocke *1633–69*
tree,] tree *1633*   194 tent, *Ed:* tent *1633–69*   hen; *Ed:* hen,
1633–69

Nor

Nor if his fifter, or his neece fhee be;
Nor doth fhe pule for his inconftancie
If in her fight he change, nor doth refufe
The next that calls; both liberty doe ufe;
    Where ftore is of both kindes, both kindes may freely
      chufe.   200

XXI.

Men, till they tooke laws which made freedome leffe,
Their daughters, and their fifters did ingreffe;
Till now unlawfull, therefore ill, 'twas not.
So jolly, that it can move, this foule is,
The body fo free of his kindneffes,   205
That felfe-preferving it hath now forgot,
And flackneth fo the foules, and bodies knot,
Which temperance ftreightens; freely on his fhe friends
He blood, and fpirit, pith, and marrow fpends,
    Ill fteward of himfelf, himfelfe in three yeares ends. 210

XXII.

Elfe might he long have liv'd; man did not know
Of gummie blood, which doth in holly grow,
How to make bird-lime, nor how to deceive
With faind calls, hid nets, or enwrapping fnare,
The free inhabitants of the Plyant aire.   215

---

  196 be; *Ed:* be, *1633–69*   202 ingreffe; *Ed:* ingreffe, *1633–69*
203–5   Till now unlawfull, therefore ill; 'twas not
        So jolly, that it can move this foule; Is
        The body fo free of his kindneffes, *1633, and 1669* (Till now,)*:*
        Till now, unlawfull, therefore ill 'twas not
        So jolly, that it can move this foule.   Is
        The body, fo free of his kindneffes,   *1635–54*
        Till now, unlawful, therefore ill 'twas not.
        So jolly, that it can move this soul, is
        The body, so free of his kindnesses, *Chambers, and Grolier but*
203 not; *and no commas in 204. See note*   206 felfe-preferving]
no hyphen 1633–39   207 foules,] fouls *1669*   208 temperance]
têperance *1633–39*   212 grow,] grow *1633–39*   214 hid *G:* his
1633–69, A18, N, TC   fnare,] fnare *1633–69*

                                     Man

Man to beget, and woman to conceive
Askt not of rootes, nor of cock-fparrowes, leave:
Yet chufeth hee, though none of thefe he feares,
Pleafantly three, then ftreightned twenty yeares
    To live, and to encreafe his race, himfelfe outweares. 220

XXIII.

This cole with overblowing quench'd and dead,
The Soule from her too active organs fled
T'a brooke. A female fifhes fandie Roe
With the males jelly, newly lev'ned was,
For they had intertouch'd as they did paffe,   225
And one of thofe fmall bodies, fitted fo,
This foule inform'd, and abled it to rowe
It felfe with finnie oares, which fhe did fit:
Her fcales feem'd yet of parchment, and as yet
    Perchance a fifh, but by no name you could call it. 230

XXIV.

When goodly, like a fhip in her full trim,
A fwan, fo white that you may unto him
Compare all whiteneffe, but himfelfe to none,
Glided along, and as he glided watch'd,
And with his arched necke this poore fifh catch'd.   235
It mov'd with ftate, as if to looke upon
Low things it fcorn'd, and yet before that one
Could thinke he fought it, he had fwallowed cleare
This, and much fuch, and unblam'd devour'd there
    All, but who too fwift, too great, or well armed were. 240

    220 encreafe his race,] encreafe, *1633*   223 brooke. A *Ed:* brooke;
a *1633–69*   225 they had intertouch'd *1635–69, G, O'F:* they intertouched
1633: they intertouch'd *A18, N, TC*   227 abled] able *1669*   rowe] roe
1633   228 fit: *Ed:* fit, *1633–69*   240 armed were.] arm'd were *1633*
                                       XXV.

XXV.

Now fwome a prifon in a prifon put,
And now this Soule in double walls was fhut,
Till melted with the Swans digeftive fire,
She left her houfe the fifh, and vapour'd forth;
Fate not affording bodies of more worth   245
For her as yet, bids her againe retire
T'another fifh, to any new defire
Made a new prey; For, he that can to none
Refiftance make, nor complaint, fure is gone.
    Weakneffe invites, but filence feafts oppreffion.   250

XXVI.

Pace with her native ftreame, this fifh doth keepe,
And journeyes with her, towards the glaffie deepe,
But oft retarded, once with a hidden net
Though with greate windowes, for when Need firft taught
Thefe tricks to catch food, then they were not wrought 255
As now, with curious greedineffe to let
None fcape, but few, and fit for ufe, to get,
As, in this trap a ravenous pike was tane,
Who, though himfelfe diftreft, would faine have flain
    This wretch; So hardly are ill habits left again.   260

XXVII.

Here by her fmallneffe fhee two deaths orepaft,
Once innocence fcap'd, and left the oppreffor faft.
The net through-fwome, fhe keepes the liquid path,
And whether fhe leape up fometimes to breath
And fuck in aire, or finde it underneath,   265

---

249 fure is gone. *1633–39*: is fure gone. *1650–54*: is fure gone, *1669*
251 her *A18, G, N, O'F, TC*: the *1633–69*   254–7 for when . . . ufe,
to get,] *in brackets 1635–69*   254 Need *G*: need *1633–69*   255 then]
thê *1633*   257 ufe, *Ed*: ufe *1633–69*   262 faft. *Ed*: faft; *1633–69*
                                                Or

Or working parts like mills or limbecks hath
To make the water thinne, and airelike faith
Cares not; but fafe the Place fhe's come unto
Where frefh, with falt waves meet, and what to doe
    She knowes not, but betweene both makes a boord or
      two. 270

XXVIII.

So farre from hiding her guefts, water is,
That fhe fhowes them in bigger quantities
Then they are. Thus doubtfull of her way,
For game and not for hunger a fea Pie
Spied through this traiterous fpectacle, from high, 275
The feely fifh where it difputing lay,
And t'end her doubts and her, beares her away:
Exalted fhe'is, but to the exalters good,
As are by great ones, men which lowly ftood.
    It's rais'd, to be the Raifers inftrument and food. 280

XXIX.

Is any kinde fubject to rape like fifh?
Ill unto man, they neither doe, nor wifh:
Fifhers they kill not, nor with noife awake,
They doe not hunt, nor ftrive to make a prey
Of beafts, nor their yong fonnes to beare away; 285
Foules they purfue not, nor do undertake
To fpoile the nefts induftrious birds do make;
Yet them all thefe unkinde kinds feed upon,
To kill them is an occupation, 289
    And lawes make Fafts, and Lents for their deftruction.

---

266 mills *Ed:* mills, *1633–69*   267 water *1635–69, G:* wether *1633,*
A18, TC   airelike *1633–35:* ayre like *1639–69 and Chambers*   faith
1633–69: faith, *Chambers. See note*   268 not; *Ed:* not, *1633–69*
270 two.] two *1633*   271 is,] is *1633*   273 Thus doubtfull
1633, A18, G, N, TC: Thus her doubtfull *1635–69*   277 away: *Ed:*
away, *1633–69*   279 *in brackets 1635–69*   ftood. *1633–39:* ftood,
1650–69   280 It's rais'd *1633–69:* It rais'd *some copies of 1633, A18,*
G, N, TC   287 industrious] industruous *1633*   290 Fafts, and Lents
1635–69: fafts, and lents *1633*

XXX.

XXX.

A fudden ftiffe land-winde in that felfe houre
To fea-ward forc'd this bird, that did devour
The fifh; he cares not, for with eafe he flies,
Fat gluttonies beft orator: at laft
So long hee hath flowen, and hath flowen fo faft   295
That many leagues at fea, now tir'd hee lyes,
And with his prey, that till then languifht, dies:
The foules no longer foes, two wayes did erre,
The fifh I follow, and keepe no calender
    Of the other; he lives yet in fome great officer.   300

XXXI.

Into an embrion fifh, our Soule is throwne,
And in due time throwne out againe, and growne
To fuch vaftneffe as, if unmanacled
From Greece, Morea were, and that by fome
Earthquake unrooted, loofe Morea fwome,   305
Or feas from Africks body had fevered
And torne the hopefull Promontories head,
This fifh would feeme thefe, and, when all hopes faile,
A great fhip overfet, or without faile
    Hulling, might (when this was a whelp) be like this
      whale.   310

XXXII.

At every ftroake his brazen finnes do take,
More circles in the broken fea they make
Then cannons voices, when the aire they teare:
His ribs are pillars, and his high arch'd roofe
Of barke that blunts beft fteele, is thunder-proofe: 315

296 That many leagues at fea, *G :* That leagues o'er-paft at fea, *1633–69 :*
That leagues at fea, *A18, N, O'F (which inserts* o'r paft), *TC.*   *See note*
297 dies:] dies, *1633*   301 throwne,] throwne *1633*   303 vaft-
neffe as, if *Grolier:* vaftneffe, as if *1633–69, Chambers*   307 head,
1633: head; *1635–69 :* head. *Chambers. See note*   311 take,] take *1633*
315 thunder-proofe: *Ed :* thunder-proofe, *1633–69*

                                Swimme

Swimme in him fwallow'd Dolphins, without feare,
And feele no fides, as if his vaſt wombe were
Some Inland fea, and ever as hee went
Hee fpouted rivers up, as if he ment
    To joyne our feas, with feas above the firmament.   320

XXXIII.

He hunts not fiſh, but as an officer,
Stayes in his court, at his owne net, and there
All fuitors of all forts themfelves enthrall;
So on his backe lyes this whale wantoning,
And in his gulfe-like throat, fucks every thing   325
That paſſeth neare. Fiſh chafeth fiſh, and all,
Flyer and follower, in this whirlepoole fall;
O might not ftates of more equality
Confiſt? and is it of neceſſity
    That thoufand guiltleſſe fmals, to make one great, muſt
    die?   330

XXXIV.

Now drinkes he up feas, and he eates up flocks,
He juſtles Ilands, and he ſhakes firme rockes.
Now in a roomefull houfe this Soule doth float,
And like a Prince ſhe fends her faculties
To all her limbes, diſtant as Provinces.   335
The Sunne hath twenty times both crab and goate
Parched, fince firſt lanch'd forth this living boate;
'Tis greateſt now, and to deſtruction
Neareſt; There's no paufe at perfection;
    Greatneſſe a period hath, but hath no ſtation.   340

    316 fwallow'd] fwallowed *1633*   322 at] as *A18, G, TCC*   337
this *1633*: his *1635–69*   boate; *Ed:* boate, *1635–69* : boate. *1633*
339 perfection; *Ed:* perfection. *1633–35*: perfection, *1639–69*

                      XXXV.

XXXV.

Two little fiſhes whom hee never harm'd,
Nor fed on their kinde, two not throughly arm'd
With hope that they could kill him, nor could doe
Good to themſelves by his death (they did not eate
His fleſh, nor ſuck thoſe oyles, which thence outſtreat) 345
Conſpir'd againſt him, and it might undoe
The plot of all, that the plotters were two,
But that they fiſhes were, and could not ſpeake.
How ſhall a Tyran wife ſtrong projects breake,
    If wreches can on them the common anger wreake? 350

XXXVI.

The flaile-finn'd Threſher, and ſteel-beak'd Sword-fiſh
Onely attempt to doe, what all doe wiſh.
The Threſher backs him, and to beate begins;
The ſluggard Whale yeelds to oppreſſion,
And t'hide himſelfe from ſhame and danger, downe 355
Begins to ſinke; the Swordfiſh upward ſpins,
And gores him with his beake; his ſtaffe-like finnes,
So well the one, his ſword the other plyes,
That now a ſcoffe, and prey, this tyran dyes, 359
    And (his owne dole) feeds with himſelfe all companies.

XXXVII.

Who will revenge his death? or who will call
Thoſe to account, that thought, and wrought his fall?
The heires of ſlaine kings, wee ſee are often ſo
Tranſported with the joy of what they get,
That they, revenge and obſequies forget, 365

344–5 *brackets, 1719:* death: . . . outſtreat, *1633–69*   did not eate]
doe not eate G   349 Tyran] Tyrant *1669*   351 flaile-finn'd] flaile-
find *1633:* flaile-finnd *1635–39*   358 well] were *1633*   359 tyran]
tyrant *1669*   365 they, revenge *1635–69:* they revenge, *1633:* they,
revenge, *1633 some copies*

Nor

Nor will againſt ſuch men the people goe,
Becauſe h'is now dead, to whom they ſhould ſhow
Love in that act; Some kings by vice being growne
So needy of ſubjects love, that of their own
    They thinke they loſe, if love be to the dead Prince
    ſhown.   370

XXXVIII.

This Soule, now free from priſon, and paſſion,
Hath yet a little indignation
That ſo ſmall hammers ſhould ſo ſoone downe beat
So great a caſtle. And having for her houſe
Got the ſtreight cloyſter of a wreched mouſe   375
(As baſeſt men that have not what to eate,
Nor enjoy ought, doe farre more hate the great
Then they, who good repos'd eſtates poſſeſſe)
This Soule, late taught that great things might by leſſe
    Be ſlain, to gallant miſchiefe doth herſelfe addreſſe.   380

XXXIX.

Natures great maſter-peece, an Elephant,
The onely harmleſſe great thing; the giant
Of beaſts; who thought, no more had gone, to make one
    wiſe
But to be juſt, and thankfull, loth to offend,
(Yet nature hath given him no knees to bend)   385
Himſelfe he up-props, on himſelfe relies,
And foe to none, ſuſpects no enemies,
Still ſleeping ſtood; vex't not his fantaſie
Blacke dreames; like an unbent bow, careleſly
    His ſinewy Proboſcis did remiſly lie: 390

367 h'is *1633*: he's *1635–69*   368 act; *Ed:* act. *1633–69*   383
who thought, no more had gone, to make one wiſe *1633, G, A18, N, TC* (*the
last four MSS. all drop* more, *N and TCD leaving a space*): who thought
none had, to make him wiſe, *1635–69*   386 relies,] relies *1633*   389
dreames; *Ed:* dreames, *1633–69*   390 lie: *1635:* lie. *1633,1639–69*
                                      XL.

XL.

In which as in a gallery this moufe
Walk'd, and furveid the roomes of this vaft houfe,
And to the braine, the foules bedchamber, went,
And gnaw'd the life cords there; Like a whole towne
Cleane undermin'd, the flaine beaft tumbled downe;   395
With him the murtherer dies, whom envy fent
To kill, not fcape, (for, only hee that ment
To die, did ever kill a man of better roome,)
And thus he made his foe, his prey, and tombe:
    Who cares not to turn back, may any whither come. 400

XLI.

Next, hous'd this Soule a Wolves yet unborne whelp,
Till the beft midwife, Nature, gave it helpe,
To iffue. It could kill, as foone as goe.
Abel, as white, and milde as his fheepe were,
(Who, in that trade, of Church, and kingdomes, there   405
Was the firft type) was ftill infefted foe,
With this wolfe, that it bred his loffe and woe;
And yet his bitch, his fentinell attends
The flocke fo neere, fo well warnes and defends,
    That the wolfe, (hopeleffe elfe) to corrupt her, intends. 410

XLII.

Hee tooke a courfe, which fince, fucceffully,
Great men have often taken, to efpie
The counfels, or to breake the plots of foes.
To Abels tent he ftealeth in the darke,
On whofe skirts the bitch flept; ere fhe could barke,   415

---

395 downe; *Ed:* downe, *1633–69*   396 dies,] dies *1633*   397–8
brackets, Ed: fcape, . . . roome, *1633:* fcape; . . . roome, *1635–69*
ment] went *A18,N,TC*   403 goe. *Ed:* goe, *1633:* goe: *1635–69*
405 Who,] Who *1633*   trade, *1635–69:* trade *1633*   413 foes. *Ed:*
foes, *1633–69*

Attach'd

Attach'd her with ftreight gripes, yet hee call'd thofe,
Embracements of love; to loves worke he goes,
Where deeds move more then words; nor doth fhe fhow,
Nor ⟨make⟩ refift, nor needs hee ftreighten fo
  His prey, for, were fhee loofe, fhe would nor barke, nor
    goe.   420

XLIII.

Hee hath engag'd her; his, fhe wholy bides;
Who not her owne, none others fecrets hides.
If to the flocke he come, and Abell there,
She faines hoarfe barkings, but fhe biteth not,
Her faith is quite, but not her love forgot.   425
At laft a trap, of which fome every where
Abell had plac'd, ends all his loffe, and feare,
By the Wolves death; and now juft time it was
That a quicke foule fhould give life to that maffe
  Of blood in Abels bitch, and thither this did paffe. 430

XLIV.

Some have their wives, their fifters fome begot,
But in the lives of Emperours you fhall not
Reade of a luft the which may equall this;
This wolfe begot himfelfe, and finifhed
What he began alive, when hee was dead;   435
Sonne to himfelfe, and father too, hee is
A ridling luft, for which Schoolemen would miffe
A proper name. The whelpe of both thefe lay
In Abels tent, and with foft Moaba,
  His fifter, being yong, it us'd to fport and play. 440

419 Nor ⟨make⟩ refift, *Ed:* Nor much refift, *1633–69:* Nowe muft refift *N:* Nowe much refift *A18,G,TC:* Refiftance much *O'F* needs] need *O'F*   420 nor barke, *1633–39:* not barke *1650–69,A18,N,TC*   422 hides.] hides, *1633*   427 plac'd, ends] plac'd end *1633 some copies* 435 dead; *Ed:* dead, *1633–39:* dead. *1650–69*

XLV.

XLV.

Hee foone for her too harfh, and churlifh grew,
And Abell (the dam dead) would ufe this new
For the field. Being of two kindes thus made,
He, as his dam, from fheepe drove wolves away,
And as his Sire, he made them his owne prey.   445
Five yeares he liv'd, and cofened with his trade,
Then hopeleffe that his faults were hid, betraid
Himfelfe by flight, and by all followed,
From dogges, a wolfe; from wolves, a dogge he fled;
 And, like a fpie to both fides falfe, he perifhed.   450

XLVI.

It quickned next a toyfull Ape, and fo
Gamefome it was, that it might freely goe
From tent to tent, and with the children play.
His organs now fo like theirs hee doth finde,
That why he cannot laugh, and fpeake his minde,   455
He wonders. Much with all, moft he doth ftay
With Adams fift daughter *Siphatecia*,
Doth gaze on her, and, where fhe paffeth, paffe,
Gathers her fruits, and tumbles on the graffe,
 And wifeft of that kinde, the firft true lover was.   460

XLVII.

He was the firft that more defir'd to have
One then another; firft that ere did crave
Love by mute fignes, and had no power to fpeake;
Firft that could make love faces, or could doe
The valters fomberfalts, or us'd to wooe   465

 443 field. Being *Ed:* field, being *1633–69*   thus] *om. 1633*   453
play. *Ed:* play, *1633–69*
 VOL. I. Y   With

With hoiting gambolls, his owne bones to breake
To make his miſtreſſe merry; or to wreake
Her anger on himſelfe. Sinnes againſt kinde
They eaſily doe, that can let feed their minde
 With outward beauty; beauty they in boyes and beaſts
  do find.   470

XLVIII.

By this miſled, too low things men have prov'd,
And too high; beaſts and angels have beene lov'd.
This Ape, though elſe through-vaine, in this was wiſe,
He reach'd at things too high, but open way
There was, and he knew not ſhe would ſay nay;   475
His toyes prevaile not, likelier meanes he tries,
He gazeth on her face with teare-ſhot eyes,
And up lifts ſubtly with his ruſſet pawe
Her kidskinne apron without feare or awe
 Of nature; nature hath no gaole, though ſhee hath
  law.   480

XLIX.

Firſt ſhe was ſilly and knew not what he ment.
That vertue, by his touches, chaft and ſpent,
Succeeds an itchie warmth, that melts her quite;
She knew not firſt, nowe cares not what he doth,
And willing halfe and more, more then halfe ⟨loth⟩,   485
She neither puls nor puſhes, but outright
Now cries, and now repents; when *Tethlemite*
Her brother, entred, and a great ſtone threw
After the Ape, who, thus prevented, flew.   489
 This houſe thus batter'd downe, the Soule poſſeſt a new.

---

470 beauty; *Ed:* beauty, *1633–69*   472 lov'd. *Ed:* lov'd; *1633–69*
479 or] of *1669*   480 ſhee hath] ſhee have *A18, N, TC*   481
ment. *Ed:* ment, *1633–69*   483 quite; *Ed:* quite, *1633–69*   484
nowe *1633, G:* nor *1635–69, Chambers:* then *A18, TC*   485 ⟨loth⟩,
Ed: Tooth *1633, G: A18, N, TC leave a blank space: in TCC a later hand
has inserted* loath: wroth, *1635–69*   487 Tethlemite *A18, G, N, O'F,
TC:* Tethelemite *1633:* Thelemite *1635–69*   489 flew. *1635–69:*
flew, *1633*

L.

And whether by this change fhe lofe or win,
She comes out next, where the Ape would have gone in.
Adam and *Eve* had mingled bloods, and now
Like Chimiques equall fires, her temperate wombe
Had ftew'd and form'd it: and part did become   495
A fpungie liver, that did richly allow,
Like a free conduit, on a high hils brow,
Life-keeping moifture unto every part;
Part hardned it felfe to a thicker heart,
   Whofe bufie furnaces lifes fpirits do impart.   500

LI.

Another part became the well of fenfe,
The tender well-arm'd feeling braine, from whence,
Thofe finowie ftrings which do our bodies tie,
Are raveld out; and faft there by one end,
Did this Soule limbes, thefe limbes a foule attend;   505
And now they joyn'd: keeping fome quality
Of every paft fhape, fhe knew treachery,
Rapine, deceit, and luft, and ills enow
To be a woman. *Themech* fhe is now,
   Sifter and wife to *Caine, Caine* that firft did plow.   510

LII.

Who ere thou beeft that read'ft this fullen Writ,
Which juft fo much courts thee, as thou doft it,
Let me arreft thy thoughts; wonder with mee,
Why plowing, building, ruling and the reft,
Or moft of thofe arts, whence our lives are bleft,   515

492 in. *1650–69:* in, *1633–39*   498 Life-keeping] Life keeping *1633*   part; *Ed:* part, *1633–69*   502 well-arm'd *1669:* well arm'd *1633–54*   503 finowie] finewy *1639–54:* finew *1669*   504 out; *Ed:* out, *1633–69*   505 this Soule] a Soule *A18, N, TC*   attend; *Ed:* attend, *1633–69*   506–7 joyn'd: . . . paft fhape, *1633:* joyn'd, . . . paft fhape; *1635–69, Chambers, Grolier. See note*   513 thoughts; *1650–69:* thoughts, *1633–39*

By

By curſed *Cains* race invented be,
And bleſt *Seth* vext us with Aſtronomie.
Ther's nothing ſimply good, nor ill alone,
Of every quality compariſon,
   The onely meaſure is, and judge, opinion.   520

The end of the Progreſſe of the Soule.

517 Aſtronomie.] Aſtronomie, *1633*   519 compariſon, *1633,1669*
(*no comma*): Compariſon, *1635–54*   520 opinion. *1633:* Opinion. *1635–69*
The end &*c.* *1635–69: om. 1633*

DIVINE

DIVINE POEMS.

To *E.* of *D.* with fix holy Sonnets.

SEe Sir, how as the Suns hot Mafculine flame
  Begets ftrange creatures on Niles durty flime,
   In me, your fatherly yet lufty Ryme
(For, thefe fongs are their fruits) have wrought the fame;
But though the ingendring force from whence they came 5
  Bee ftrong enough, and nature doe admit
   Seaven to be borne at once, I fend as yet
But fix; they fay, the feaventh hath ftill fome maime.
  I choofe your judgement, which the fame degree
   Doth with her fifter, your invention, hold,   10
As fire thefe droffie Rymes to purifie,
  Or as Elixar, to change them to gold;
You are that Alchimift which alwaies had
Wit, whofe one fpark could make good things of bad.

To the *Lady Magdalen Herbert*: *of St. Mary Magdalen.*

HEr of your name, whofe fair inheritance
  Bethina was, and jointure Magdalo:
An active faith fo highly did advance,
  That fhe once knew, more than the Church did know,

Divine Poems. *A18, N, TC: In 1635–69 this is the title at head of each page, but the new section is headed* Holy Sonnets.   To E. of D. &c. *so headed 1633–69 but placed among* Letters &c., *and so in* O'F *and (but* L. of D.) *W: removed hither by Grosart.*   4 their fruits] the fruit *W* 6 doe *1633:* doth *1635–69*   8 fix;] fix, *1633*   maime. *W:* maime; *1633–69*   11 droffie] droffe *1650–54*
    To the Lady Magdalen Herbert: &c. *Ed:* To the Lady Magdalen Herbert, of &c. *Walton's* The Life of Mr George Herbert. (*1670, pp.* 25–6.), *See note*   4 know, *1675:* know *1670*
                                         The

The Refurrection; fo much good there is   5
   Deliver'd of her, that fome Fathers be
Loth to believe one Woman could do this;
   But, think thefe Magdalens were two or three.
Increafe their number, Lady, and their fame:
   To their Devotion, add your Innocence;   10
Take fo much of th'example, as of the name;
   The latter half; and in fome recompence
That they did harbour Chrift himfelf, a Gueft,
   Harbour thefe Hymns, to his dear name addreft.   J.D.

HOLY SONNETS.

La Corona.

1. **D**Eigne *at my hands this crown of prayer and praife,*
    Weav'd in my low devout melancholie,
Thou which of good, haft, yea art treafury,
All changing unchang'd Antient of dayes;
But doe not, with a vile crowne of fraile bayes,   5
Reward my mufes white fincerity,
But what thy thorny crowne gain'd, that give mee,
A crowne of Glory, which doth flower alwayes;
The ends crowne our workes, but thou crown'ft our ends,
For, at our end begins our endleffe reft;   10
The firft laft end, now zealoufly poffeft,
With a ftrong fober thirft, my foule attends.
'Tis time that heart and voice be lifted high,
Salvation to all that will is nigh.

HOLY SONNETS. *1633–69, being general title to the two groups:* Holy Sonnets written 20 years fince. *H49.*
   La Corona. *1633–69, A18, D, H49, N, S, TCC, TCD, W:* The Crowne. *B, O'F, S96*   2 low *1633, A18, D, H49, N, TC, W* (*spelt* lowe *in MSS.*): lone *1635–69, B, O'F, S:* loves *S96*   3 treafury, *1633–69:* a Treafurie, *B, O'F, S, S96*   4 dayes; *Ed:* dayes, *1633–69*   10 For] So *W* end *1633, A18, B, D, H49, N, O'F, TC, W:* ends *1635–69, S96*   reft; *Ed:* reft, *1633–69*   11 The] This *B, S, S96, W*   zealoufly] foberly *B, S96, W: O'F corrects*   13 heart and voice] voice and heart *B, O'F, S, S96, W*   14 nigh.] nigh, *1633*

ANNVNCIATION.

ANNVNCIATION.

2. *Salvation to all that will is nigh;*
That All, which alwayes is All every where,
Which cannot finne, and yet all finnes muft beare,
Which cannot die, yet cannot chufe but die,
Loe, faithfull Virgin, yeelds himfelfe to lye   5
In prifon, in thy wombe; and though he there
Can take no finne, nor thou give, yet he'will weare
Taken from thence, flefh, which deaths force may trie.
Ere by the fpheares time was created, thou
Waft in his minde, who is thy Sonne, and Brother;   10
Whom thou conceiv'ft, conceiv'd; yea thou art now
Thy Makers maker, and thy Fathers mother;
Thou'haft light in darke; and fhutft in little roome,
Immenfity cloyfterd in thy deare wombe..

NATIVITIE.

3. *Immenfitie cloyfterd in thy deare wombe,*
Now leaves his welbelov'd imprifonment,
There he hath made himfelfe to his intent
Weake enough, now into our world to come;
But Oh, for thee, for him, hath th'Inne no roome?   5
Yet lay him in this ftall, and from the Orient,
Starres, and wifemen will travell to prevent
Th'effect of *Herods* jealous generall doome.
Seeft thou, my Soule, with thy faiths eyes, how he
Which fils all place, yet none holds him, doth lye?   10
Was not his pity towards thee wondrous high,
That would have need to be pittied by thee?
Kiffe him, and with him into Egypt goe,
With his kinde mother, who partakes thy woe.

Annunciation. 1 *nigh; 1669:* nigh, *1633–54*   9 created,] begotten,
B, S, S96, W: O'F corrects   10 Brother; *Ed:* Brother, *1633–69*   11
conceiv'ft, *1633:* conceiv'ft *1635–69:* conceiv'dft, *O'F, S, W, and Grolier*
conceiv'd;] conceived; *1635–69*   12 mother; *Ed:* mother, *1633–69*
   Nativitie. 6 this] his *1669*   7 will] fhall *B, O'F, S, S96, W*
8 effect *1669, A18, B, N, O'F, S, S96, TC, W:* effects *1633–54, D, H49*
jealous] dire and *B, O'F, S, S96, W:* zealous *A18, N, TC*   doome.]
doome; *1633*   9 eyes, *1633, B, D, H49, O'F, S, S96, W:* eye, *1635–69,
A18, N, TC*

TEMPLE.

4. With his kinde mother who partakes thy woe,
Ioſeph turne backe; ſee where your child doth ſit,
Blowing, yea blowing out thoſe ſparks of wit,
Which himſelfe on the Doctors did beſtow;
The Word but lately could not ſpeake, and loe,   5
It ſodenly ſpeakes wonders, whence comes it,
That all which was, and all which ſhould be writ,
A ſhallow ſeeming child, ſhould deeply know?
His Godhead was not ſoule to his manhood,
Nor had time mellowed him to this ripeneſſe,   10
But as for one which hath a long taske, 'tis good,
With the Sunne to beginne his buſineſſe,
He in his ages morning thus began
By miracles exceeding power of man.

CRVCIFYING.

5. By miracles exceeding power of man,
Hee faith in ſome, envie in ſome begat,
For, what weake ſpirits admire, ambitious, hate;
In both affections many to him ran,
But Oh! the worſt are moſt, they will and can,   5
Alas, and do, unto the immaculate,
Whoſe creature Fate is, now preſcribe a Fate,
Meaſuring ſelfe-lifes infinity to'a ſpan,
Nay to an inch. Loe, where condemned hee
Beares his owne croſſe, with paine, yet by and by   10
When it beares him, he muſt beare more and die.
Now thou art lifted up, draw mee to thee,
And at thy death giving ſuch liberall dole,
Moyſt, with one drop of thy blood, my dry ſoule.

Temple.   5 loe, *Ed:* loe *1633–69*   6 wonders, *1633–39:* wonders:
1650–69   11 for] to *W*   a long taske, *1633–69, D, H49:* long
taskes *B, N, O'F, S, S96, TCD, W:* longe taske *A18, TCC*   'tis] 'Tis
1633: thinks *W*
     Crucifying.   3 weake] meeke *B, O'F, S, S96, W*   8 to'a ſpan, *B, N,*
O'F, S, S96, TC, W: to ſpan, *1633–69, A18, D, H49*   9 inch. Loe,
1635–69: inch, loe, *1633*   11 die. *1635–69:* die; *1633*

RESVRRECTION.

RESVRRECTION.

6. Moyſt with one drop of thy blood, my dry ſoule
Shall (though ſhe now be in extreme degree
Too ſtony hard, and yet too fleſhly,) bee
Freed by that drop, from being ſtarv'd, hard, or foule,
And life, by this death abled, ſhall controule   5
Death, whom thy death ſlue; nor ſhall to mee
Feare of firſt or laſt death, bring miſerie,
If in thy little booke my name thou enroule,
Fleſh in that long ſleep is not putrified,
But made that there, of which, and for which 'twas;   10
Nor can by other meanes be glorified.
May then ſinnes ſleep, and deaths ſoone from me paſſe,
That wak't from both, I againe riſen may
Salute the laſt, and everlaſting day.

ASCENTION.

7 Salute the laſt and everlaſting day,
Joy at the upriſing of this Sunne, and Sonne,
Yee whoſe juſt teares, or tribulation
Have purely waſht, or burnt your droſſie clay;
Behold the Higheſt, parting hence away,   5
Lightens the darke clouds, which hee treads upon,
Nor doth hee by aſcending, ſhow alone,
But firſt hee, and hee firſt enters the way.
O ſtrong Ramme, which haſt batter'd heaven for mee,
Mild Lambe, which with thy blood, haſt mark'd the path; 10
Bright Torch, which ſhin'ſt, that I the way may ſee,
Oh, with thy owne blood quench thy owne juſt wrath,
And if thy holy Spirit, my Muſe did raiſe,
Deigne at my hands this crowne of prayer and praiſe.

Reſurrection.   1 *ſoule 1635: ſoule, 1633,1639-69*   5 this] thy
B,O'F,S,S96,W   6 ſhall to] ſhall nowe to *A18,N,O'F,TC*   8
little *1633,A18,D,H49,TC:* life *1635-69,B,O'F,S,S96,W*   9 that
long] that laſt long *O'F,S,S96,W:* that *D,H49*   11 glorified]
purified *S,S96,W,* and *O'F (which corrects to* glorified)   12 deaths
A18,N,S96,TC,W: death *1633-69,D,H49*
    Aſcention.   3 juſt *1633,A18,D,H49,N,TC:* true *1635-69,B,S,*
S96,W,   8 way.] way, *1633*   10 Lambe, *D,W:* lambe *1633-69*
11 Torch, *D,W:* torch, *1633-69*   the way] thy wayes *B,S,S96,W:*
thee *A18,TCC*

Holy

Holy Sonnets.

I.

THou haft made me, And ſhall thy worke decay?
   Repaire me now, for now mine end doth haſte,
I runne to death, and death meets me as faſt,
And all my pleaſures are like yeſterday;
I dare not move my dimme eyes any way,   5
Deſpaire behind, and death before doth caſt
Such terrour, and my feeble fleſh doth waſte
By ſinne in it, which it t'wards hell doth weigh;
Onely thou art above, and when towards thee
By thy leave I can looke, I riſe againe;   10
But our old ſubtle foe ſo tempteth me,
That not one houre my ſelfe I can ſuſtaine;
Thy Grace may wing me to prevent his art,
And thou like Adamant draw mine iron heart.

II.

AS due by many titles I reſigne
   My ſelfe to thee, O God, firſt I was made
By thee, and for thee, and when I was decay'd
Thy blood bought that, the which before was thine;
I am thy ſonne, made with thy ſelfe to ſhine,   5
Thy ſervant, whoſe paines thou haſt ſtill repaid,
Thy ſheepe, thine Image, and, till I betray'd
My ſelfe, a temple of thy Spirit divine;
Why doth the devill then uſurpe on mee?
Why doth he ſteale, nay raviſh that's thy right?   10
Except thou riſe and for thine owne worke fight,
Oh I ſhall ſoone deſpaire, when I doe ſee
That thou lov'ſt mankind well, yet wilt'not chuſe me,
And Satan hates mee, yet is loth to loſe mee.

Holy Sonnets. *1633–69* (*following* La Corona *as second group under the same general title*), *W:* Devine Meditations. *B,O'F,S96:* no title, *A18,D, H49,N,TCC,TCD. See note*   I. *1635–69,B,O'F,S96,W:* omitted *1633,A18,D,H49,N,TCC,TCD*   4 yeſterday; *Ed:* yeſterday, *1635–69*   7 feeble *1635–69:* febled *B,O'F,S96,W*   12 my ſelfe I can *1635–69:* I can myſelf *B,S96,W*   ſuſtaine; *1669:* ſuſtaine, *1635–54*
    II. *1635–69,B,O'F,S96,W:*   I. *1633,A18,D,H49,N,TCC,TCD*   2 God, fiiſt *1633:* God. Firſt *1635–69*   4 thine; *1650–69:* thine,

                                   III.

III.

O Might thofe fighes and teares returne againe
   Into my breaſt and eyes, which I have ſpent,
That I might in this holy diſcontent
 Mourne with ſome fruit, as I have mourn'd in vaine;
In mine Idolatry what ſhowres of raine   5
Mine eyes did waſte? what griefs my heart did rent?
That ſufferance was my ſinne; now I repent;
'Cauſe I did ſuffer I muſt ſuffer paine.
Th'hydroptique drunkard, and night-ſcouting thiefe,
The itchy Lecher, and ſelfe tickling proud   10
Have the remembrance of paſt joyes, for reliefe
Of comming ills. To (poore) me is allow'd
No eaſe; for, long, yet vehement griefe hath beene
Th'effect and cauſe, the puniſhment and ſinne.

IV.

OH my blacke Soule! now thou art ſummoned
   By ſickneſſe, deaths herald, and champion;
Thou art like a pilgrim, which abroad hath done
Treaſon, and durſt not turne to whence hee is fled,
Or like a thiefe, which till deaths doome be read,   5
Wiſheth himſelfe delivered from priſon;
But damn'd and hal'd to execution,
Wiſheth that ſtill he might be impriſoned.
Yet grace, if thou repent, thou canſt not lacke;
But who ſhall give thee that grace to beginne?   10
Oh make thy ſelfe with holy mourning blacke,
And red with bluſhing, as thou art with ſinne;
Or waſh thee in Chriſts blood, which hath this might
That being red, it dyes red ſoules to white.

1633–39: thine. *W*   7 and, *Ed:* and *1633–69*   9 on *1633–69, D,
H49:* in *A18, B, N, S96, TC, W*   10 ſteale,] ſteale *1633–39*   that's]
what's *A18, TCC*   12 doe *1633 and moſt MSS.:* ſhall *1635–69, O'F, S96*
13 me,] me. *1633*
     III. *1635–69, B, O'F, S96, W:* omitted *1633, A18, D, &c.*   7 ſinne;
now I *Ed:* ſinne, now I *B, W:* ſinne I now *1635–69*   repent; *Ed:*
repent, *1633–69*
     IV. *1635–69:* II. *1633, A18, D, &c.:* V. *B, O'F, S96, W*   1 Soule!
1633: Soule *1635–69*   8 impriſoned. *W:* impriſoned; *1633–69*

                                        V.

V.

I Am a little world made cunningly
  Of Elements, and an Angelike fpright,
But black finne hath betraid to endleffe night
My worlds both parts, and (oh) both parts muft die.
You which beyond that heaven which was moft high   5
Have found new fphears, and of new lands can write,
Powre new feas in mine eyes, that fo I might
Drowne my world with my weeping earneftly,
Or wafh it, if it muft be drown'd no more:
But oh it muft be burnt! alas the fire   10
Of luft and envie have burnt it heretofore,
And made it fouler; Let their flames retire,
And burne me ô Lord, with a fiery zeale
Of thee and thy houfe, which doth in eating heale.

VI.

THis is my playes laft fcene, here heavens appoint
  My pilgrimages laft mile; and my race
Idly, yet quickly runne, hath this laft pace,
My fpans laft inch, my minutes lateft point,
And gluttonous death, will inftantly unjoynt   5
My body, and foule, and I fhall fleepe a fpace,
But my'ever-waking part fhall fee that face,
Whofe feare already fhakes my every joynt:
Then, as my foule, to'heaven her firft feate, takes flight,
And earth-borne body, in the earth fhall dwell,   10
So, fall my finnes, that all may have their right,
To where they'are bred, and would preffe me, to hell.
Impute me righteous, thus purg'd of evill,
For thus I leave the world, the flefh, the devill.

V. *1635–69: omitted 1633, A18, D, &c.*: VII. *B, O' F, S96, W*   6 lands
B, S96, W: land *1635–69, O' F*   7 I *1635–54:* he *1669*   9 it,
Ed: it: *W:* it *1635–69*   10 burnt! *Ed:* burnt, *1635–69*   11
have *B, S96, W:* hath *O'F:* om. *1635–69*   12 fouler; *W:* fouler,
1635–69   their] those *W*   13 Lord] God *W*
    VI. *1635–69, B, O'F, S96, W:* III. *1633, A18, D, &c.*   6 and foule,
1635–69: and my foule, *1633*   7 Or prefently, I know not, fee that
Face, *B, D, H49, O' F, S, S96, W*   10 earth-borne *1635–69:* earth borne
1633   14 flefh,] flefh *1633*   the devill.] and devill. *A18, B, D, H49,
N, O' F, S96, TC, W*

VII.

VII.

AT the round earths imagin'd corners, blow
 Your trumpets, Angells, and arise, arise
From death, you numberleſſe infinities
Of ſoules, and to your ſcattred bodies goe,
All whom the flood did, and fire ſhall o'erthrow,   5
All whom warre, dearth, age, agues, tyrannies,
Deſpaire, law, chance, hath ſlaine, and you whoſe eyes,
Shall behold God, and never taſt deaths woe.
But let them ſleepe, Lord, and mee mourne a ſpace,
For, if above all theſe, my ſinnes abound,   10
'Tis late to aske abundance of thy grace,
When wee are there; here on this lowly ground,
Teach mee how to repent; for that's as good
As if thou'hadſt ſeal'd my pardon, with thy blood.

VIII.

IF faithfull ſoules be alike glorifi'd
 As Angels, then my fathers ſoule doth ſee,
And adds this even to full felicitie,
That valiantly I hels wide mouth o'rſtride:
But if our mindes to theſe ſoules be deſcry'd   5
By circumſtances, and by ſignes that be
Apparent in us, not immediately,
How ſhall my mindes white truth by them be try'd?
They ſee idolatrous lovers weepe and mourne,
And vile blaſphemous Conjurers to call   10
On Ieſus name, and Phariſaicall
Diſſemblers feigne devotion. Then turne
O penſive ſoule, to God, for he knowes beſt
Thy true griefe, for he put it in my breaſt.

VII. *1635–69:* IV. *1633, A18, D, &c.:* VIII. *B, O'F, S96, W*   5
o'erthrow] overthrow *1669*   6 dearth, *W:* death, *1633–69, A18, B,*
D, H49, N, O'F, S96, TC   8 woe. *W:* woe, *1633–54:* owe; *1669*
12 lowly] holy *1669*   14 thy] my *1669*
VIII. *1635–69: omitted 1633, A18, D, &c.:* X. *B, O'F, S96, W*   7
in us, *W:* in us *1635–69. See note*   8 by] to *B, S96, W*   10 vile *W:*
vilde *B, O'F, S96:* ſtile *1635–69*   14 true *W: om. 1635–69, B, S96*
in *W:* into *1635–69, B, O'F, S96*   my] thy *B, S96*

IX.

IX.

IF poyfonous mineralls, and if that tree,
 Whofe fruit threw death on elfe immortall us,
If lecherous goats, if ferpents envious
Cannot be damn'd; Alas; why fhould I bee?
Why fhould intent or reafon, borne in mee,   5
Make finnes, elfe equall, in mee more heinous?
And mercy being eafie, and glorious
To God; in his fterne wrath, why threatens hee?
But who am I, that dare difpute with thee
O God? Oh! of thine onely worthy blood,   10
And my teares, make a heavenly Lethean flood,
And drowne in it my finnes blacke memorie;
That thou remember them, fome claime as debt,
I thinke it mercy, if thou wilt forget.

X.

DEath be not proud, though fome have called thee
 Mighty and dreadfull, for, thou art not foe,
For, thofe, whom thou think'ft, thou doft overthrow,
Die not, poore death, nor yet canft thou kill mee.
From reft and fleepe, which but thy pictures bee,   5
Much pleafure, then from thee, much more muft flow,
And fooneft our beft men with thee doe goe,
Reft of their bones, and foules deliverie.
Thou art flave to Fate, Chance, kings, and defperate men,
And doft with poyfon, warre, and ficknefle dwell,   10
And poppie, or charmes can make us fleepe as well,
And better then thy ftroake; why fwell'ft thou then?
One fhort fleepe paft, wee wake eternally,
And death fhall be no more; death, thou fhalt die.

IX. *1635–69,B,O'F,S96,W:* V. *1633,A18,D,&c.* 1 poyfonous]
poyfons *1639–54*   and if that] or if the *B,O'F,S96*   2 (elfe
immortal) *1635–69*   5 or] and *B,O'F,S96*   6 mee] mee, *1633*
8 God;] God, *1633*   9–10 thee O God? *W:* thee? O God, *1633–69*
12 memorie;] memorie, *1633*   14 forget.] forget, *1633*
  X. *1635–69:* VI. *1633,A18,D,&c.:* XI. *B,O'F,S96,W*   4 mee.]
mee; *1633*   5 pictures *1633 and MSS.:* picture *1635–69*   8 deliverie.]
deliverie *1633–69*   9 Chance, *W:* chance, *1633–69*   10 doft] doth
1633   dwell,] dwell. *1633*   12 better] eafier *B,O'F,S96,W*   13
wake] live *B,S96,W*   14 more; death, *Ed:* more, death *1633–69*
XI.

XI.

SPit in my face you Jewes, and pierce my fide,
 Buffet, and fcoffe, fcourge, and crucifie mee,
For I have finn'd, and finn'd, and onely hee,
Who could do no iniquitie, hath dyed:
But by my death can not be fatisfied   5
My finnes, which paffe the Jewes impiety:
They kill'd once an inglorious man, but I
Crucifie him daily, being now glorified.
Oh let mee then, his ftrange love ftill admire:
Kings pardon, but he bore our punifhment.   10
And *Iacob* came cloth'd in vile harfh attire
But to fupplant, and with gainfull intent:
God cloth'd himfelfe in vile mans flefh, that fo
Hee might be weake enough to fuffer woe.

XII.

WHy are wee by all creatures waited on?
 Why doe the prodigall elements fupply
Life and food to mee, being more pure then I,
Simple, and further from corruption?
Why brook'ft thou, ignorant horfe, fubjection?   5
Why doft thou bull, and bore fo feelily
Diffemble weakneffe, and by'one mans ftroke die,
Whofe whole kinde, you might fwallow and feed upon?
Weaker I am, woe is mee, and worfe then you,
You have not finn'd, nor need be timorous.   10
But wonder at a greater wonder, for to us
Created nature doth thefe things fubdue,
But their Creator, whom fin, nor nature tyed,
For us, his Creatures, and his foes, hath dyed.

XI. *1635–69:* VII. *1633, A18, D, &c.: omitted B, S96: added among*
Other Meditations. *O'F:* XIII. *W*   3 onely] humbly *W*   6
impiety] iniquitye *D, H49*   8 glorified.] glorified; *1633*   12 intent:]
intent *1633*

XII. *1635–69:* VIII. *1633, A18, D, &c.: omitted B, S96: among* Other
Meditations. *O'F:* XIV. *W*   1 are wee] ame I *W*   4 Simple,
1633, D, H49, W: Simpler *1635–69, A18, N, O'F, TC, Chambers*   9
Weaker I am,] Alas I am weaker, *W*   10 timorous. *W:* timorous,
1633–69   11 a greater wonder, *1633, D, H49, N, O'F* (greate), *TC, W:*
a greater, *1635–69*

XIII.

XIII.

WHat if this prefent were the worlds laft night?
　　Marke in my heart, O Soule, where thou doft dwell,
The picture of Chrift crucified, and tell
Whether that countenance can thee affright,
Teares in his eyes quench the amafing light,　　　　　5
Blood fills his frownes, which from his pierc'd head fell.
And can that tongue adjudge thee unto hell,
Which pray'd forgiveneffe for his foes fierce fpight?
No, no; but as in my idolatrie
I faid to all my profane miftreffes,　　　　　　　10
Beauty, of pitty, foulneffe onely is
A figne of rigour: fo I fay to thee,
To wicked fpirits are horrid fhapes affign'd,
This beauteous forme affures a pitious minde.

XIV.

BAtter my heart, three perfon'd God; for, you
　　As yet but knocke, breathe, fhine, and feeke to mend;
That I may rife, and ftand, o'erthrow mee,'and bend
Your force, to breake, blowe, burn and make me new.
I, like an ufurpt towne, to'another due,　　　　　5
Labour to'admit you, but Oh, to no end,
Reafon your viceroy in mee, mee fhould defend,
But is captiv'd, and proves weake or untrue.
Yet dearely'I love you,'and would be loved faine,
But am betroth'd unto your enemie:　　　　　　10
Divorce mee,'untie, or breake that knot againe,
Take mee to you, imprifon mee, for I
Except you'enthrall mee, never fhall be free,
Nor ever chaft, except you ravifh mee.

　　XIII. *1635–69:* IX. *1633, A18, D, &c.: om.* B, S96: *among* Other
Meditations. O'F: XV. W　　2 Marke] Looke W　　4 that A18, N,
O'F, TC, W: his *1633–69,* D, H49　　6 fell. *1639–69:* fell *1633–35*
8 fierce] ranck W　　14 affures A18, D, H49, N, O'F, TC, W: affumes
1633–69
　　XIV. *1635–69:* X. *1633, A18, D, &c.: om.* B, O'F, S96: XVI. W
7 mee fhould] wee fhould *1669*　　　8 untrue. W: untrue, *1633–69*
9 loved MSS.: lov'd *1633–69*　　10 enemie: W: enemie, *1633–69*
　　　　　　　　　　　　　　　　　　　　　XV.

XV.

Wllt thou love God, as he thee! then digeſt,
   My Soule, this wholſome meditation,
How God the Spirit, by Angels waited on
In heaven, doth make his Temple in thy breſt.
The Father having begot a Sonne moſt bleſt,   5
And ſtill begetting, (for he ne'r begonne)
Hath deign'd to chuſe thee by adoption,
Coheire to'his glory,'and Sabbaths endleſſe reſt.
And as a robb'd man, which by ſearch doth finde
His ſtolne ſtuffe ſold, muſt loſe or buy'it againe: 10
The Sonne of glory came downe, and was ſlaine,
Us whom he'had made, and Satan ſtolne, to unbinde.
'Twas much, that man was made like God before,
But, that God ſhould be made like man, much more.

XVI.

FAther, part of his double intereſt
   Unto thy kingdome, thy Sonne gives to mee,
His joynture in the knottie Trinitie
Hee keepes, and gives to me his deaths conqueſt.
This Lambe, whoſe death, with life the world hath bleſt, 5
Was from the worlds beginning ſlaine, and he
Hath made two Wills, which with the Legacie
Of his and thy kingdome, doe thy Sonnes inveſt.
Yet ſuch are thy laws, that men argue yet
Whether a man thoſe ſtatutes can fulfill;   10
None doth; but all-healing grace and ſpirit
Revive againe what law and letter kill.
Thy lawes abridgement, and thy laſt command
Is all but love; Oh let this laſt Will ſtand!

XV. *1635–69:* XI. *1633, A18 D, &c.:* XII. *B, O'F, S96, W*   4 breſt.
W: breſt, *1633–69*   8 reſt.] reſt; *1633*   11 Sonne *1633:* Sunne *1635–69*
12 ſtolne, *1633, A18, D, H49, N, TC:* ſtole, *1635–69, B, O'F, S96, W, Chambers*
   XVI. *1635–69:* XII. *1633, A18, D, &c.:* IV. *B, O'F, S96, W*   3 Trinitie]
Trinitie, *1633*   8 doe *1633:* om. *1635–69:* doth *A18, B, D, H49, N, O'F,*
S96, TC, W   inveſt. *W:* inveſt, *1633–39:* inveſt: *1650–69*   9 thy *O'F,*
S96, W: theſe *1633–69:* thoſe *A18, D, H49, N, TC*   11 doth;] doth, *1633*
but all-healing *A18, D, H49, N, TC, W:* but thy all-healing *1633–69.* *See note*
ſpirit] Spirit, *1633–69*   12 Revive againe] Revive and quicken *B, O'F,*
S96, W   kill. *1635–69:* kill, *1633*   14 this *1633–69:* that *A18, D,*
H49, N, TC, W: thy *B, O'F, S96*

XVII.

SInce fhe whom I lov'd hath payd her laft debt
  To Nature, and to hers, and my good is dead,
And her Soule early into heaven ravifhed,
Wholly on heavenly things my mind is fett.
Here the admyring her my mind did whett   5
To feeke thee God; fo ftreames do fhew their head;
But though I have found thee, and thou my thirft haft fed,
A holy thirfty dropfy melts mee yett.
But why fhould I begg more Love, when as thou
Doft wooe my foule for hers; offring all thine: 10
And doft not only feare leaft I allow
My Love to Saints and Angels things divine,
But in thy tender jealofy doft doubt
Leaft the World, Flefhe, yea Devill putt thee out.

XVIII.

SHow me deare Chrift, thy fpoufe, fo bright and clear.
  What! is it She, which on the other fhore
Goes richly painted? or which rob'd and tore
Laments and mournes in Germany and here?
Sleepes fhe a thoufand, then peepes up one yeare?   5
Is fhe felfe truth and errs? now new, now outwore?
Doth fhe, and did fhe, and fhall fhe evermore
On one, on feaven, or on no hill appeare?
Dwells fhe with us, or like adventuring knights
Firft travaile we to feeke and then make Love?   10
Betray kind hufband thy fpoufe to our fights,
And let myne amorous foule court thy mild Dove,
Who is moft trew, and pleafing to thee, then
When fhe'is embrac'd and open to moft men.

XVII. *W: first printed in Gosse's* Life and Letters of John Donne,
1899   2 dead,] dead *W*   6 their] y^r *W*   head;] head, *W*
10 wooe] *spelt* woe *W*   12 divine,] divine *W*
  XVIII. *W: first printed in Gosse's* Life *&c.*   2 What!] What *W*
3 tore] *so I read W:* lore *Gosse*

XIX.

XIX.

OH, to vex me, contraryes meet in one:
  Inconſtancy unnaturally hath begott
A conſtant habit; that when I would not
I change in vowes, and in devotione.
As humorous is my contritione   5
As my prophane Love, and as ſoone forgott:
As ridlingly diſtemper'd, cold and hott,
As praying, as mute; as infinite, as none.
I durſt not view heaven yeſterday; and to day
In prayers, and flattering ſpeaches I court God: 10
To morrow I quake with true feare of his rod.
So my devout fitts come and go away
Like a fantaſtique Ague: ſave that here
Thoſe are my beſt dayes, when I ſhake with feare.

The Croſſe.

SInce Chriſt embrac'd the Croſſe it ſelfe, dare I
  His image, th'image of his Croſſe deny?
Would I have profit by the ſacrifice,
And dare the choſen Altar to deſpiſe?
It bore all other ſinnes, but is it fit   5
That it ſhould beare the ſinne of ſcorning it?
Who from the picture would avert his eye,
How would he flye his paines, who there did dye?
From mee, no Pulpit, nor miſgrounded law,
Nor ſcandall taken, ſhall this Croſſe withdraw,   10
It ſhall not, for it cannot; for, the loſſe
Of this Croſſe, were to mee another Croſſe;
Better were worſe, for, no affliction,
No Croſſe is ſo extreme, as to have none.

XIX. *W: first printed in Gosse's Life &c.*   3 that] yᵗ *W, so always*
4 and] & *W, so always*
    The Croſſe. *1633–69 (following, 1635–69,* In that, ô Queene *&c.
p.* 427*): similarly,* A18, A25, B, D, H49, JC, Lec, N, O'F, P, S, TCC, TCD
8 paines] pangs *JC*   12 Croſſe; *1635–69:* Croſſe. *1633*   13 affliction,
Ed: affliction *1633–69*   14 none. *Ed:* none; *1633–54:* none: *1669*
                                                                    Who

Who can blot out the Croſſe, which th'inſtrument   15
Of God, dew'd on mee in the Sacrament?
Who can deny mee power, and liberty
To ſtretch mine armes, and mine owne Croſſe to be?
Swimme, and at every ſtroake, thou art thy Croſſe;
The Maſt and yard make one, where ſeas do toſſe;   20
Looke downe, thou ſpieſt out Croſſes in ſmall things;
Looke up, thou ſeeſt birds rais'd on croſſed wings;
All the Globes frame, and ſpheares, is nothing elſe
But the Meridians croſſing Parallels.
Materiall Croſſes then, good phyſicke bee,   25
But yet ſpirituall have chiefe dignity.
Theſe for extracted chimique medicine ſerve,
And cure much better, and as well preſerve;
Then are you your own phyſicke, or need none,
When Still'd, or purg'd by tribulation.   30
For when that Croſſe ungrudg'd, unto you ſtickes,
Then are you to your ſelfe, a Crucifixe.
As perchance, Carvers do not faces make,
But that away, which hid them there, do take;
Let Croſſes, ſoe, take what hid Chriſt in thee,   35
And be his image, or not his, but hee.
But, as oft Alchimiſts doe coyners prove,
So may a ſelfe-diſpiſing, get ſelfe-love,
And then as worſt ſurfets, of beſt meates bee,
Soe is pride, iſſued from humility,   40
For, 'tis no child, but monſter; therefore Croſſe
Your joy in croſſes, elſe, 'tis double loſſe.
And croſſe thy ſenſes, elſe, both they, and thou
Muſt periſh ſoone, and to deſtruction bowe.
For if the'eye ſeeke good objects, and will take   45

19 Croſſe; *Ed:* Croſſe, *1633:* Croſſe. *1635–69*   20 make] makes
B, D, H49, Lec, S   where] when *O'F*   toſſe; *1635–69:* toſſe. *1633*
21 out] our *1669*   23 is] are *A25, B*   26 But yet] And yet
A18, D, JC, N, TC   27 medicine] medicines *A25, B, JC*   33 make,
1635–69: make: *1633*   34 take; *Ed:* take. *1633:* take: *1635–69*
37 oft *Ed:* oft, *1633–69*   38 ſelfe-love, *D:* ſelfe-love. *1633–69*   42
loſſe. *Ed:* loſſe, *1633–69*   44 deſtruction] corruption *O'F*   45
ſeeke] ſee *1650–69*

No

No croſſe from bad, wee cannot ſcape a ſnake.
So with harſh, hard, ſowre, ſtinking, croſſe the reſt,
Make them indifferent all; call nothing beſt.
But moſt the eye needs croſſing, that can rome,
And move; To th'other th'objects muſt come home.   50
And croſſe thy heart: for that in man alone
Points downewards, and hath palpitation.
Croſſe thoſe dejections, when it downeward tends,
And when it to forbidden heights pretends.
And as the braine through bony walls doth vent   55
By futures, which a Croſſes forme preſent,
So when thy braine workes, ere thou utter it,
Croſſe and correct concupiſcence of witt.
Be covetous of Croſſes, let none fall.
Croſſe no man elſe, but croſſe thy ſelfe in all.   60
Then doth the Croſſe of Chriſt worke fruitfully
Within our hearts, when wee love harmleſly
That Croſſes pictures much, and with more care
That Croſſes children, which our Croſſes are.

Reſurrection, imperfect.

SLeep ſleep old Sun, thou canſt not have repaſt
  As yet, the wound thou took'ſt on friday laſt;
Sleepe then, and reſt; The world may beare thy ſtay,
A better Sun roſe before thee to day,
Who, not content to'enlighten all that dwell   5
On the earths face, as thou, enlightned hell,
And made the darke fires languiſh in that vale,

48 all; call nothing beſt. *Ed:* indifferent; call nothing beſt. *1633 and MSS:* indifferent; all, nothing beſt. *1635–69*   50 To th'other th'objects *1633:* To th'others objects *1635–69*   52 Points *A18, A25,N,P,S,TC:* Pants *1633–69,B,D,H49,JC,Lec,O'F*   53 dejections *1633:* detorſions *1635–69,O'F*   55 the] thy *A18,D,H49,JC,Lec,N,O'F, P,TC*   61 fruitfully *A18,A25,B,D,H49,JC,Lec,N,O'F,P,S,TC:* faithfully *1633–69*   63 That *A18,A25,B,D,H49,JC,Lec,N,O'F,P, S,TC:* The *1633–69*
  Reſurrection, imperfect. *1633-69 (following* By Euphrates *&c. p.* 424*), A18,N,O'F,TCC,TCD*

As,

As, at thy prefence here, our fires grow pale.
Whofe body having walk'd on earth, and now
Hafting to Heaven, would, that he might allow   10
Himfelfe unto all ftations, and fill all,
For thefe three daies become a minerall;
Hee was all gold when he lay downe, but rofe
All tincture, and doth not alone difpofe
Leaden and iron wills to good, but is   15
Of power to make even finfull flefh like his.
Had one of thofe, whofe credulous pietie
Thought, that a Soule one might difcerne and fee
Goe from a body,'at this fepulcher been,
And, iffuing from the fheet, this body feen,   20
He would have juftly thought this body a foule,
If not of any man, yet of the whole.

Defunt cætera.

The Annuntiation and Pafsion.

TAmely, fraile body,'abftaine to day; to day
　My foule eates twice, Chrift hither and away.
She fees him man, fo like God made in this,
That of them both a circle embleme is,
Whofe firft and laft concurre; this doubtfull day   5
Of feaft or faft, Chrift came, and went away.
Shee fees him nothing twice at once, who'is all;
Shee fees a Cedar plant it felfe, and fall,
Her Maker put to making, and the head
Of life, at once, not yet alive, yet dead.   10

15 good, *1633-69 and MSS.: Chambers queries* gold   22 If] If,
1633-69
　　The Annuntiation and Pafsion. *1633-69:* Upon the Annuntiation and
Pafsion falling upon one day. Anno Dñi 1608. *B,O'F,S,S96: similarly,
N,TCD:* The Annuntiation. *D,H49,Lec: no title, P*   1 Tamely,
fraile body, *Ed:* Tamely fraile body *1633:* Tamely fraile flefh, *1635-69,
O'F,S96 (1650-69 accidentally drop second* to day)   6 away.] away;
1633: away, *1635-39*   10 yet dead. *Ed:* yet dead; *1633,B,P,S:*
and dead; *1635-69,D,H49,Lec,N,O'F,TCD (full stop, MSS.)*

　　　　　　　　　　　　　　　　　　　　　　　　She

She fees at once the virgin mother ftay
Recluf'd at home, Publique at Golgotha;
Sad and rejoyc'd fhee's feen at once, and feen
At almoft fiftie, and at fcarce fifteene.
At once a Sonne is promif'd her, and gone,   15
Gabriell gives Chrift to her, He her to John;
Not fully a mother, Shee's in Orbitie,
At once receiver and the legacie.
All this, and all betweene, this day hath fhowne,
Th'Abridgement of Chrifts ftory, which makes one   20
(As in plaine Maps, the furtheft Weft is Eaft)
Of the'Angels *Ave,*'and *Confummatum eft.*
How well the Church, Gods Court of faculties
Deales, in fome times, and feldome joyning thefe!
As by the felfe-fix'd Pole wee never doe   25
Direct our courfe, but the next ftarre thereto,
Which fhowes where the'other is, and which we fay
(Becaufe it ftrayes not farre) doth never ftray;
So God by his Church, neereft to him, wee know,
And ftand firme, if wee by her motion goe;   30
His Spirit, as his fiery Pillar doth
Leade, and his Church, as cloud; to one end both.
This Church, by letting thefe daies joyne, hath fhown
Death and conception in mankinde is one;
Or'twas in him the fame humility,   35
That he would be a man, and leave to be:
Or as creation he hath made, as God,
With the laft judgement, but one period,
His imitating Spoufe would joyne in one
Manhoods extremes: He fhall come, he is gone: 40
Or as though one blood drop, which thence did fall,
Accepted, would have ferv'd, he yet fhed all;

12 at Golgotha; *Ed:* at Golgotha. *1633–69*   13 Sad and rejoyc'd]
Rejoyc'd and fad *B,O'F,P,S,S96*   18 legacie. *Ed:* legacie; *1633–69*
24 thefe! *Ed:* thefe? *D,TCD:* thefe; *1633:* thefe. *1635–69*   31
as *1633:* and *1635–69*   32 both. *1635–69:* both: *1633*   33 thefe
B,D,H49,Lec,N,O'F,P,S96,TCD: thofe *1633–69*   daies *1633,D,H49,*
Lec,N,TCD: feafts *1635–69,O'F,P,S,S96*   34 one; *Ed:* one. *1633:*
are one. *1635–69* (one *1669*)   37 hath] had *B,N,O'F,P,S,S96,TCD*

So

So though the leaſt of his paines, deeds, or words,
Would buſie a life, ſhe all this day affords;
This treaſure then, in groſſe, my Soule uplay,　　45
And in my life retaile it every day.

Goodfriday, 1613.　*Riding Weſtward.*

LEt mans Soule be a Spheare, and then, in this,
　　The intelligence that moves, devotion is,
And as the other Spheares, by being growne
Subject to forraigne motions, loſe their owne,
And being by others hurried every day,　　5
Scarce in a yeare their naturall forme obey:
Pleaſure or buſineſſe, ſo, our Soules admit
For their firſt mover, and are whirld by it.
Hence is't, that I am carryed towards the Weſt
This day, when my Soules forme bends toward the Eaſt. 10
There I ſhould ſee a Sunne, by riſing ſet,
And by that ſetting endleſſe day beget;
But that Chriſt on this Croſſe, did riſe and fall,
Sinne had eternally benighted all.
Yet dare I'almoſt be glad, I do not ſee　　15
That ſpectacle of too much weight for mee.
Who ſees Gods face, that is ſelfe life, muſt dye;
What a death were it then to ſee God dye?
It made his owne Lieutenant Nature ſhrinke,
It made his footſtoole crack, and the Sunne winke.　　20
Could I behold thoſe hands which ſpan the Poles,
And turne all ſpheares at once, peirc'd with thoſe holes?

　　Goodfriday, &c. *1633–69:* Good Friday (*with or without date and*
Riding &c.) *A18,B,Cy,N,S,S96,TCC,TCD:* Good Friday. 1613.
Riding towards Wales. *D,Lec,O'F:* Good Friday. 1613. Riding to
Sʳ Edward Harbert in Wales. *H49:* Mʳ J. Duſi goeing from Sir H. G. on
good friday ſent him back this meditation on the way. *A25*　　4 motions
A18,B,Cy,D,H49,Lec,N,O'F,S,S96,TC: motion, *1633–69*　　8 and]
bis 1650–54　　10 toward *1633:* do. or towards *MSS.:* to *1635–69,O'F*
12 beget; *1633:* beget. *1635–69,Chambers*　　13 this Croſſe, *1633,*
A18,D,H49,Lec,O'F,S,S96,TCC: his Croſſe, *1635–69,* B,Cy,N,TCD
16 too] two *1639–69*　　22 turne *A18,B,Cy,N,S,TC:* tune *1633–69,*
D,H49,Lec,O'F,S96　　once,] once *1633*

Could

Could I behold that endleffe height which is
Zenith to us, and our Antipodes,
Humbled below us? or that blood which is   25
The feat of all our Soules, if not of his,
Made durt of duft, or that flefh which was worne
By God, for his apparell, rag'd, and torne?
If on thefe things I durft not looke, durft I
Upon his miferable mother caft mine eye,   30
Who was Gods partner here, and furnifh'd thus
Halfe of that Sacrifice, which ranfom'd us?
Though thefe things, as I ride, be from mine eye,
They'are prefent yet unto my memory,
For that looks towards them; and thou look'ft towards mee,
O Saviour, as thou hang'ft upon the tree;   36
I turne my backe to thee, but to receive
Corrections, till thy mercies bid thee leave.
O thinke mee worth thine anger, punifh mee,
Burne off my rufts, and my deformity,   40
Reftore thine Image, fo much, by thy grace,
That thou may'ft know mee, and I'll turne my face.

30 Upon his miferable *1633, A18, B, Cy, D, H49, Lec, N, O'F, S, S96, TC:*
On his diftreffed *1635-69*   40 rufts, *1633, B, Cy, D, H49, Lec. N, O'F,*
S96, TCD: ruft, *1635-69, A18, S, TCC*

THE LITANIE.

I.

The FATHER.

FAther of Heaven, and him, by whom
It, and us for it, and all elſe, for us
Thou madeſt, and govern'ſt ever, come
And re-create mee, now growne ruinous:
  My heart is by dejection, clay,   5
  And by ſelfe-murder, red.
From this red earth, O Father, purge away
All vicious tinctures, that new faſhioned
I may riſe up from death, before I'am dead.

II.

The SONNE.

O Sonne of God, who ſeeing two things,   10
Sinne, and death crept in, which were never made,
  By bearing one, tryed'ſt with what ſtings
The other could thine heritage invade;
  O be thou nail'd unto my heart,
  And crucified againe,   15
Part not from it, though it from thee would part,
But let it be, by applying ſo thy paine,
Drown'd in thy blood, and in thy paſſion ſlaine.

III.

The HOLY GHOST.

O Holy Ghoſt, whoſe temple I
Am, but of mudde walls, and condenſed duſt,   20
  And being ſacrilegiouſly
Halfe waſted with youths fires, of pride and luſt,

The Litanie. *1633-69:* A Letanie. *A18, B, D, H49, JC, Lec, N, O'F, S, S96, TCC, TCD* 17 be, *D:* be *1633-69*

Muſt

Muft with new ftormes be weatherbeat;
Double in my heart thy flame,
Which let devout fad teares intend; and let   25
(Though this glaffe lanthorne, flefh, do fuffer maime)
Fire, Sacrifice, Prieft, Altar be the fame.

IV.

The TRINITY.

O Bleffed glorious Trinity,
Bones to Philofophy, but milke to faith,
Which, as wife ferpents, diverfly   30
Moft flipperineffe, yet moft entanglings hath,
As you diftinguifh'd undiftinct
By power, love, knowledge bee,
Give mee a fuch felfe different inftinct
Of thefe; let all mee elemented bee,   35
Of power, to love, to know, you unnumbred three.

V.

The Virgin MARY.

For that faire bleffed Mother-maid,
Whofe flefh redeem'd us; That fhe-Cherubin,
Which unlock'd Paradife, and made
One claime for innocence, and diffeiz'd finne,   40
Whofe wombe was a ftrange heav'n, for there
God cloath'd himfelfe, and grew,
Our zealous thankes wee poure. As her deeds were
Our helpes, fo are her prayers; nor can fhe fue
In vaine, who hath fuch titles unto you.   45

30 ferpents, *Ed:* ferpents *1633–69*   34 a fuch *1633:* fuch *1635–69,*
JC: fuch a *A18, D, H49, Lec, N, S, TC*   inftinct *1633:* inftinct, *1635–69*
35 thefe; *Ed:* thefe, *D, H49, Lec:* thefe *1633–69:* thee *A18, N, TC*
VI.

VI.

The Angels.

And fince this life our nonage is,
And wee in Wardfhip to thine Angels be,
   Native in heavens faire Palaces,
Where we fhall be but denizen'd by thee,
     As th'earth conceiving by the Sunne,   50
     Yeelds faire diverfitie,
Yet never knowes which courfe that light doth run,
So let mee ftudy, that mine actions bee
Worthy their fight, though blinde in how they fee.

VII.

The Patriarches.

And let thy Patriarches Defire   55
(Thofe great Grandfathers of thy Church, which faw
   More in the cloud, then wee in fire,
Whom Nature clear'd more, then us Grace and Law,
     And now in Heaven ftill pray, that wee
     May ufe our new helpes right,)   60
Be fatisfy'd, and fructifie in mee;
Let not my minde be blinder by more light
Nor Faith, by Reafon added, lofe her fight.

VIII.

The Prophets.

Thy Eagle-fighted Prophets too,
Which were thy Churches Organs, and did found   65
   That harmony, which made of two
One law, and did unite, but not confound ;

---

48 Native] Natives *B, JC, S*   in heavens faire Palaces, *D:* in heavens
faire Palaces *1633–39:* in heavens Palaces, *1650–69*   52 which *1633:*
what *1635–69*   56 Grandfathers] Grandfathers, *1633*   58 then] that
1635–39   58 Grace and Law, *D:* grace and law, *1633–69*   61
fatisfy'd, *1635–69, A18, D, H49, JC, N, S96, TC:* fanctified, *1633*   fructifie]
fructified *A18, JC*   63 Faith, *D:* Faith *1633–69*

Thofe

Those heavenly Poëts which did see
Thy will, and it expresse
In rythmique feet, in common pray for mee, 70
That I by them excuse not my excesse
In seeking secrets, or Poëtiquenesse.

IX.

The Apostles.

And thy illustrious Zodiacke
Of twelve Apostles, which ingirt this All,
(From whom whosoever do not take 75
Their light, to darke deep pits, throw downe, and fall,)
As through their prayers, thou'hast let mee know
That their bookes are divine;
May they pray still, and be heard, that I goe
Th'old broad way in applying; O decline 80
Mee, when my comment would make thy word mine.

X.

The Martyrs.

And since thou so desiroufly
Did'ft long to die, that long before thou could'ft,
And long since thou no more couldft dye,
Thou in thy scatter'd mystique body wouldft 85
In Abel dye, and ever since
In thine; let their blood come
To begge for us, a discreet patience
Of death, or of worse life: for Oh, to some
Not to be Martyrs, is a martyrdome. 90

75–6 *no brackets 1633*   75 whosoever] whoever *most MSS.*   76 throw
downe, and fall, *1633, A18, D, H49, Lec, N, TC:* thrown down do fall)
1635–69   78 bookes] works *B, O'F, S96*   87 thine;] thine, *1633*
XI.

XI.

The Confeſſors.

Therefore with thee triumpheth there
A Virgin Squadron of white Confeſſors,
   Whoſe bloods betroth'd, not marryed were,
Tender'd, not taken by thoſe Raviſhers:
     They know, and pray, that wee may know,   95
     In every Chriſtian
Hourly tempeſtuous perſecutions grow;
Tentations martyr us alive; A man
Is to himſelfe a Dioclefian.

XII.

The Virgins.

The cold white ſnowie Nunnery,   100
Which, as thy mother, their high Abbeſſe, ſent
   Their bodies backe againe to thee,
As thou hadſt lent them, cleane and innocent,
     Though they have not obtain'd of thee,
     That or thy Church, or I,   105
Should keep, as they, our firſt integrity;
Divorce thou ſinne in us, or bid it die,
And call chaſt widowhead Virginitie.

XIII.

The Doctors.

Thy ſacred Academie above
Of Doctors, whoſe paines have unclaſp'd, and taught   110
   Both bookes of life to us (for love
To know thy Scriptures tells us, we are wrote

---

93 were, *Ed:* were; *1633–69*   97 grow; *Ed:* grow, *1633–69*
100 The] Thy *B, D, H49, O'F, S, S96*   109 Thy] The *1635–69*
Academie *1633, D, H49, Lec:* Academ *1635–69:* Academe *N, O'F, S96,*
TC   112 thy] the *1650–69*   Scriptures] Scripture *1669*   wrote]
ſpelt wrought *1633 and MSS.*

In thy other booke) pray for us there
That what they have mifdone
Or mif-faid, wee to that may not adhere;   115
Their zeale may be our finne. Lord let us runne
Meane waies, and call them ftars, but not the Sunne.

XIV.

And whil'ft this univerfall Quire,
That Church in triumph, this in warfare here,
   Warm'd with one all-partaking fire   120
Of love, that none be loft, which coft thee deare,
      Prayes ceaflefly,'and thou hearken too,
      (Since to be gratious
Our taske is treble, to pray, beare, and doe)
Heare this prayer Lord: O Lord deliver us   125
From trufting in thofe prayers, though powr'd out thus.

XV.

From being anxious, or fecure,
Dead clods of fadneffe, or light fquibs of mirth,
   From thinking, that great courts immure
All, or no happineffe, or that this earth   130
      Is only for our prifon fram'd,
      Or that thou art covetous
To them whom thou loveft, or that they are maim'd
From reaching this worlds fweet, who feek thee thus,
With all their might, Good Lord deliver us.   135

115 adhere; *Ed:* adhere, *1633–69*   122 too, *D:* too *1633–69*
125 Lord: *Ed:* Lord, *1633–69*   128 clods *1633:* clouds *1635–69,*
B, O'F (which corrects), S96   133 whom] *om. D, H49, Lec*   them]
om. A18, N, TC   134 fweet, *1633, D, H49, JC, Lec, S96:* fweets, *1635–*
69, A18, N, O'F, S, TC

XVI.

XVI.

From needing danger, to bee good,
From owing thee yefterdaies teares to day,
  From trufting fo much to thy blood,
That in that hope, wee wound our foule away,
     From bribing thee with Almes, to excufe   140
     Some finne more burdenous,
From light affecting, in religion, newes,
From thinking us all foule, neglecting thus
Our mutuall duties, Lord deliver us.

XVII.

From tempting Satan to tempt us,   145
By our connivence, or flack companie,
  From meafuring ill by vitious,
Neglecting to choake fins fpawne, Vanitie,
     From indifcreet humilitie,
     Which might be fcandalous,   150
And caft reproach on Chriftianitie,
From being fpies, or to fpies pervious,
From thirft, or fcorne of fame, deliver us.

XVIII.

Deliver us for thy defcent
Into the Virgin, whofe wombe was a place   155
  Of middle kind; and thou being fent
To'ungratious us, ftaid'ft at her full of grace;
     And through thy poore birth, where firft thou
     Glorifiedft Povertie,
And yet foone after riches didft allow,   160
By accepting Kings gifts in the Epiphanie,
Deliver, and make us, to both waies free.

137 owing] owning *1669*   139 foule] fouls *1669, JC, O'F, S*   153
fame,] flame, *1633*   154 for *1633, D, H49, N, S, TC:* through *1635-69,*
JC, O'F, S96, Chambers   156 middle] midle *1633, D*   157 grace;]
grace, *1633*   159 Glorifiedft] Glorifieft *1633 some copies, D, H49*
162 Deliver, and] Deliver us, and *Chambers*

XIX.

XIX.

And through that bitter agonie,
Which is ſtill the agonie of pious wits,
   Diſputing what diſtorted thee,   165
And interrupted evenneſſe, with fits;
     And through thy free confeſſion
     Though thereby they were then
Made blind, ſo that thou might'ſt from them have gone,
Good Lord deliver us, and teach us when   170
Wee may not, and we may blinde unjuſt men.

XX.

Through thy ſubmitting all, to blowes
Thy face, thy clothes to ſpoile; thy fame to ſcorne,
   All waies, which rage, or Juſtice knowes,
And by which thou could'ſt ſhew, that thou waſt born; 175
     And through thy gallant humbleneſſe
     Which thou in death did'ſt ſhew,
Dying before thy ſoule they could expreſſe,
Deliver us from death, by dying ſo,
To this world, ere this world doe bid us goe.   180

XXI.

When ſenſes, which thy ſouldiers are,
Wee arme againſt thee, and they fight for ſinne,
   When want, ſent but to tame, doth warre
And worke deſpaire a breach to enter in,
     When plenty, Gods image, and ſeale   185
     Makes us Idolatrous,
And love it, not him, whom it ſhould reveale,
When wee are mov'd to ſeeme religious
Only to vent wit, Lord deliver us.

163 through] though *1633*   that] thy *B, JC, O'F, S96*   164 is ſtill]
ſtill is *1633 some copies, 1635–69*   166 fits;] fits, *1633*   173 clothes
1633, 418, D, H49, Lec, N, S, TC: robes *1635–69, B*(robe), *JC, O'F, S96*
175 born; *Ed:* born, *1633–69*

XXII.

In Churches, when the'infirmitie   190
Of him which ſpeakes, diminiſhes the Word,
   When Magiſtrates doe miſ-apply
To us, as we judge, lay or ghoſtly ſword,
      When plague, which is thine Angell, raignes,
      Or wars, thy Champions, ſwaie,   195
When Hereſie, thy ſecond deluge, gaines;
In th'houre of death, the'Eve of laſt judgement day,
Deliver us from the ſiniſter way.

XXIII.

Heare us, O heare us Lord; to thee
A ſinner is more muſique, when he prayes,   200
   Then ſpheares, or Angels praiſes bee,
In Panegyrique Allelujaes;
      Heare us, for till thou heare us, Lord
      We know not what to ſay;
Thine eare to'our ſighes, teares, thoughts gives voice and
    word.   205
O Thou who Satan heard'ſt in Jobs ſicke day,
Heare thy ſelfe now, for thou in us doſt pray.

XXIV.

That wee may change to evenneſſe
This intermitting aguiſh Pietie;
   That ſnatching cramps of wickedneſſe   210
And Apoplexies of faſt ſin, may die;
      That muſique of thy promiſes,
      Not threats in Thunder may
Awaken us to our juſt offices;
What in thy booke, thou doſt, or creatures ſay,   215
That we may heare, Lord heare us, when wee pray.

196 When] Where *many MSS.*   197 laſt judgement] the laſt *JC, S :*
Gods judgement *B*   202 Allelujaes; *1635–69:* Allelujaes, *1633*   204
ſay; *D:* ſay. *1633–69*   209 Pietie; *Ed:* Pietie, *1633–69*   214
offices;] offices, *1633*

XXV.

XXV.

That our eares fickneffe wee may cure,
And rectifie thofe Labyrinths aright,
  That wee, by harkning, not procure
Our praife, nor others difpraife fo invite,   220
     That wee get not a flipperineffe
     And fenflefly decline,
From hearing bold wits jeaft at Kings excefle,
To'admit the like of majeftie divine,
That we may locke our eares, Lord open thine.   225

XXVI.

That living law, the Magiftrate,
Which to give us, and make us phyficke, doth
  Our vices often aggravate,
That Preachers taxing finne, before her growth,
     That Satan, and invenom'd men   230
     Which well, if we ftarve, dine,
When they doe moft accufe us, may fee then
Us, to amendment, heare them; thee decline:
That we may open our eares, Lord lock thine.

XXVII.

That learning, thine Ambaffador,   235
From thine allegeance wee never tempt,
  That beauty, paradifes flower
For phyficke made, from poyfon be exempt,
     That wit, borne apt high good to doe,
     By dwelling lazily   240
On Natures nothing, be not nothing too,
That our affections kill us not, nor dye,
Heare us, weake ecchoes, O thou eare, and cry.

---

217 wee *1633:* me *1635–69*   219 wee, *Ed:* wee *1633–69* harkning,
not *1633–69:* heark'ning not *Chambers*   231 well, *1633 (but altered to*
will, *in some copies*), *A18, B, D, H49, N, S, TC:* will, *1635–69, Lec, Chambers,*
Grolier   233 decline: *Ed:* decline ; *1633–69*   239 apt . . . doe,]
apt, . . . doe *1633*   243 weake ecchoes, O thou eare, and cry. *1633–69,*
A18, D, H49, Lec, N, TC: weake wretches, O thou eare and eye. *B, S, S96:*
Chambers adopts Eye *from S, O'F reads* eye, *and TCC alters* crye *to* eye,
all retaining ecchoes. *See note*

XXVIII.

XXVIII.

Sonne of God heare us, and since thou
By taking our blood, oweſt it us againe,   245
  Gaine to thy ſelf, or us allow;
And let not both us and thy ſelfe be ſlaine;
     O Lambe of God, which took'ſt our ſinne
     Which could not ſtick to thee,
O let it not returne to us againe,   250
But Patient and Phyſition being free,
As ſinne is nothing, let it no where be.

Vpon the tranſlation of the Pſalmes by Sir Phi-
lip Sydney, *and the Counteſſe of Pembroke
his Siſter.*

ETernall God, (for whom who ever dare
  Seeke new expreſſions, doe the Circle ſquare,
And thruſt into ſtrait corners of poore wit
Thee, who art cornerleſſe and infinite)
I would but bleſſe thy Name, not name thee now;   5
(And thy gifts are as infinite as thou:)
Fixe we our prayſes therefore on this one,
That, as thy bleſſed Spirit fell upon
Theſe Pſalmes firſt Author in a cloven tongue;
(For 'twas a double power by which he ſung   10
The higheſt matter in the nobleſt forme;)
So thou haſt cleft that ſpirit, to performe
That worke againe, and ſhed it, here, upon
Two, by their bloods, and by thy Spirit one;
A Brother and a Siſter, made by thee   15
The Organ, where thou art the Harmony.

---

245 againe,] againe *1633*   246 or us *1633, A18, D, H49, Lec, JC, N,
S, TC:* and us *1635–69, O'F, S96, Chambers*   248 O Lambe] O lambe
1633
    Vpon the &c. *1635–69: no extant MSS.*

Two

Two that make one *Iohn Baptifts* holy voyce,
And who that Pfalme, *Now let the Iles rejoyce,*
Have both tranflated, and apply'd it too,
Both told us what, and taught us how to doe. 20
They fhew us Ilanders our joy, our King,
They tell us *why,* and teach us *how* to fing;
Make all this All, three Quires, heaven, earth, and fphears;
The firft, Heaven, hath a fong, but no man heares,
The Spheares have Mufick, but they have no tongue, 25
Their harmony is rather danc'd than fung;
But our third Quire, to which the firft gives eare,
(For, Angels learne by what the Church does here)
This Quire hath all. The Organift is hee
Who hath tun'd God and Man, the Organ we: 30
The fongs are thefe, which heavens high holy Mufe
Whifper'd to *David, David* to the Iewes:
And *Davids* Succeffors, in holy zeale,
In formes of joy and art doe re-reveale
To us fo fweetly and fincerely too, 35
That I muft not rejoyce as I would doe
When I behold that thefe Pfalmes are become
So well attyr'd abroad, fo ill at home,
So well in Chambers, in thy Church fo ill,
As I can fcarce call that reform'd untill 40
This be reform'd; Would a whole State prefent
A leffer gift than fome one man hath fent?
And fhall our Church, unto our Spoufe and King
More hoarfe, more harfh than any other, fing?
For *that* we pray, we praife thy name for *this,* 45
Which, by this *Mofes* and this *Miriam,* is
Already done; and as thofe Pfalmes we call
(Though fome have other Authors) *Davids* all:
So though fome have, fome may fome Pfalmes tranflate,
We thy Sydnean Pfalmes fhall celebrate, 50

17 voyce, *1635-39:* voyce; *1650-69*   22 fing;] fing. *1635-69*
23 three Quires, *1669:* 3 Quires, *1635-54*   28 here *1669:* heare
1635-54 (the fame word, not hear *as in Chambers' note)*   46 this Mofes
Grofart: thy *Mofes 1635-69*

And,

And, till we come th'Extemporall fong to fing,
(Learn'd the firft hower, that we fee the King,
Who hath tranflated thofe tranflators) may
Thefe their fweet learned labours, all the way
Be as our tuning; that, when hence we part,   55
We may fall in with them, and fing our part.

Ode : Of our Senfe of Sinne.

1. VEngeance will fit above our faults; but till
        She there doth fit,
We fee *her* not, nor *them*. Thus, blinde, yet ftill
We leade her way; and thus, whil'ft we doe ill,
        We fuffer it.   5

2. Vnhappy he, whom youth makes not beware
        Of doing ill.
Enough we labour under age, and care;
In number, th'errours of the laft place, are
        The greateft ftill.   10

3. Yet we, that fhould the ill we now begin
        As foone repent,
(Strange thing!) perceive not; our faults are not feen,
But paft us; neither felt, but onely in
        The punifhment.   15

4. But we know our felves leaft; Mere outward fhews
        Our mindes fo ftore,
That our foules, no more than our eyes difclofe
But forme and colour. Onely he who knowes
        Himfelfe, knowes more.   20

I. D.

55 tuning; *1719:* tuning, *1635–69*   part, *1719:* part *1635–69*
Ode. *1635–69,O'F:* Of our Senfe of Sinne. *H40,RP31 (in margin,*
Sʳ Edw. Herbert): *no title, B,Cy,P,S*   2 doth *1635–39:* do *1650–69*
11 now] new *B*   15 The *1635–69,Cy,P:* Our *B,H40,O'F*

To

To Mr Tilman *after he had taken orders.*

THou, whofe diviner foule hath caus'd thee now
　　To put thy hand unto the holy Plough,
Making Lay-fcornings of the Miniftry,
Not an impediment, but victory;
What bringft thou home with thee? how is thy mind　5
Affected fince the vintage? Doft thou finde
New thoughts and ftirrings in thee? and as Steele
Toucht with a Loadftone, doft new motions feele?
Or, as a Ship after much paine and care,
For Iron and Cloth brings home rich Indian ware,　10
Haft thou thus traffiqu'd, but with farre more gaine
Of noble goods, and with lefle time and paine?
Thou art the fame materials, as before,
Onely the ftampe is changed; but no more.
And as new crowned Kings alter the face,　15
But not the monies fubftance; fo hath grace
Chang'd onely Gods old Image by Creation,
To Chrifts new ftampe, at this thy Coronation;
Or, as we paint Angels with wings, becaufe
They beare Gods meffage, and proclaime his lawes,　20
Since thou muft doe the like, and fo muft move,
Art thou new feather'd with cœleftiall love?
Deare, tell me where thy purchafe lies, and fhew
What thy advantage is above, below.
But if thy gainings doe furmount expreffion,　25
Why doth the foolifh world fcorne that profeffion,
Whofe joyes paffe fpeech? Why do they think unfit
That Gentry fhould joyne families with it?
As if their day were onely to be fpent
In dreffing, Miftreffing and complement;　30
Alas poore joyes, but poorer men, whofe truft
Seemes richly placed in fublimed duft;
(For, fuch are cloathes and beauty, which though gay,
Are, at the beft, but of fublimed clay.)

To Mr Tilman *&c. 1635–69: no extant MSS.*　18 Chrifts] Chifts
1635　34 clay.) *Ed:* clay) *1635–69*

Let

Let then the world thy calling difrefpect,   35
But goe thou on, and pitty their neglect.
What function is fo noble, as to bee
Embaffadour to God and deftinie?
To open life, to give kingdomes to more
Than Kings give dignities; to keepe heavens doore?   40
Maries prerogative was to beare Chrift, fo
'Tis preachers to convey him, for they doe
As Angels out of clouds, from Pulpits fpeake;
And bleffe the poore beneath, the lame, the weake.
If then th'Aftronomers, whereas they fpie   45
A new-found Starre, their Opticks magnifie,
How brave are thofe, who with their Engine, can
Bring man to heaven, and heaven againe to man?
Thefe are thy titles and preheminences,
In whom muft meet Gods graces, mens offences,   50
And fo the heavens which beget all things here,
And the earth our mother, which thefe things doth beare,
Both thefe in thee, are in thy Calling knit,
And make thee now a bleft Hermaphrodite.

A Hymne to Chrift, at the Authors laft going into Germany.

IN what torne fhip foever I embarke,
   That fhip fhall be my embleme of thy Arke;
What fea foever fwallow mee, that flood
Shall be to mee an embleme of thy blood;
Though thou with clouds of anger do difguife   5
Thy face; yet through that maske I know thofe eyes,
   Which, though they turne away fometimes,
      They never will defpife.

52 beare, *1650–69:* beare *1635–39*
    A Hymne *&c. 1633–69:* A Hymne to Chrift. *A18, N, TCC, TCD:*
At his going with my Lord of Doncafter 1619. *B,* and similarly, *O'F, P,
S96: in MSS. last two lines of each stanza given as one*   2 my . . .
thy] an . . . the *P*   3 foever fwallow mee, that] foe'er fwallows me up,
that *O'F*

I facrifice

I facrifice this Iland unto thee,
And all whom I lov'd there, and who lov'd mee;   10
When I have put our feas twixt them and mee,
Put thou thy fea betwixt my finnes and thee.
As the trees fap doth feeke the root below
In winter, in my winter now I goe,
   Where none but thee, th'Eternall root   15
     Of true Love I may know.

Nor thou nor thy religion doft controule,
The amoroufneffe of an harmonious Soule,
But thou would'ft have that love thy felfe: As thou
Art jealous, Lord, fo I am jealous now,   20
Thou lov'ft not, till from loving more, thou free
My foule: Who ever gives, takes libertie:
   O, if thou car'ft not whom I love
     Alas, thou lov'ft not mee.

Seale then this bill of my Divorce to All,   25
On whom thofe fainter beames of love did fall;
Marry thofe loves, which in youth fcattered bee
On Fame, Wit, Hopes (falfe miftreffes) to thee.
Churches are beft for Prayer, that have leaft light:
To fee God only, I goe out of fight: 30
   And to fcape ftormy dayes, I chufe
     An Everlafting night.

10 I lov'd there, *1633, A18, N, TCC:* I love here, *1635–69:* I love there *P*   who lov'ft mee; *1633, A18, N, TC:* who love mee; *1635–69, B, O'F, P, S96*   11 our feas *1633, A18, N, TC:* this flood *1635–69:* thefe (*or* thofe) feas *B, O'F, P, S96*   12 fea *A18, B, N, O'F, S96, TC:* feas *1633, P:* blood *1635–69*   15 thee, th'Eternall root] thy eternall work *B, O'F (where it is altered to reading of text), P* (externall workes), *S96*   28 Fame, *1633, A18, N, TC:* Face, *1635–69, B, O'F, P, S96*

The Lamentations of Ieremy, *for the moſt part according to* Tremelius.

CHAP. I.

1 HOw ſits this citie, late moſt populous,
    Thus ſolitary, and like a widdow thus!
Ampleſt of Nations, Queene of Provinces
    She was, who now thus tributary is!

2 Still in the night ſhee weepes, and her teares fall   5
    Downe by her cheekes along, and none of all
Her lovers comfort her; Perfidiouſly
    Her friends have dealt, and now are enemie.

3 Unto great bondage, and afflictions
    Juda is captive led; Thoſe nations   10
With whom ſhee dwells, no place of reſt afford,
    In ſtreights ſhee meets her Perſecutors ſword.

4 Emptie are the gates of Sion, and her waies
    Mourne, becauſe none come to her ſolemne dayes.
Her Prieſts doe groane, her maides are comfortleſſe,   15
    And ſhee's unto her ſelfe a bitterneſſe.

5 Her foes are growne her head, and live at Peace,
    Becauſe when her tranſgreſſions did increaſe,
The Lord ſtrooke her with ſadneſſe: Th'enemie
    Doth drive her children to captivitie.   20

6 From Sions daughter is all beauty gone,
    Like Harts, which ſeeke for Paſture, and find none,
Her Princes are, and now before the foe
    Which ſtill purſues them, without ſtrength they go.

The Lamentations &c. *1633–69* (Tremellius *1639–69*), B,N,O'F,TCD:
Tr in the notes stands for Tremellius, *Vulg for* Vulgate.   *See note: full-stops
after verse-numbers 1635–69*   2–4 thus! . . . is!] thus? . . . is?
1633–69   22 Harts] hearts *1669*

7 Now

7 Now in her daies of Teares, Jeruſalem 25
  (Her men ſlaine by the foe, none ſuccouring them)
Remembers what of old, ſhee eſteemed moſt,
  Whileſt her foes laugh at her, for what ſhe hath loſt.

8 Jeruſalem hath ſinn'd, therefore is ſhee
  Remov'd, as women in uncleanneſſe bee; 30
Who honor'd, ſcorne her, for her foulneſſe they
  Have ſeene; her ſelfe doth groane, and turne away.

9 Her foulneſſe in her skirts was ſeene, yet ſhe
  Remembred not her end; Miraculouſly
Therefore ſhee fell, none comforting: Behold 35
  O Lord my affliction, for the Foe growes bold.

10 Upon all things where her delight hath beene,
  The foe hath ſtretch'd his hand, for ſhee hath ſeene
Heathen, whom thou command'ſt, ſhould not doe ſo,
  Into her holy Sanctuary goe. 40

11 And all her people groane, and ſeeke for bread;
  And they have given, only to be fed,
All precious things, wherein their pleaſure lay:
  How cheape I'am growne, O Lord, behold, and weigh.

12 All this concernes not you, who paſſe by mee, 45
  O ſee, and marke if any ſorrow bee
Like to my ſorrow, which Jehova hath
  Done to mee in the day of his fierce wrath?

13 That fire, which by himſelfe is governed
  He hath caſt from heaven on my bones, and ſpred 50
A net before my feet, and mee o'rthrowne,
  And made me languiſh all the day alone.

25 her *O'F:* their *1633-69,N,TCD:* the *B:* diebus afflictionis ſuae
et ploratuum ſuorum *Tr*   28 Whileſt *B,O'F:* Whiles *1633-69*
32 ſeene;] ſeene, *1633*   43 pleaſure] pleaſures *N*

14 His

14 His hand hath of my finnes framed a yoake
   Which wreath'd, and caft upon my neck, hath broke
My ftrength. The Lord unto thofe enemies   55
   Hath given mee, from whom I cannot rife.

15 He under foot hath troden in my fight
   My ftrong men; He did company invite
To breake my young men; he the winepreffe hath
   Trod upon *Juda's* daughter in his wrath.   60

16 For thefe things doe I weepe, mine eye, mine eye
   Cafts water out; For he which fhould be nigh
To comfort mee, is now departed farre;
   The foe prevailes, forlorne my children are.

17 There's none, though *Sion* do ftretch out her hand, 65
   To comfort her, it is the Lords command
That *Iacobs* foes girt him. *Ierufalem*
   Is as an uncleane woman amongft them.

18 But yet the Lord is juft, and righteous ftill,
   I have rebell'd againft his holy will;   70
O heare all people, and my forrow fee,
   My maides, my young men in captivitie.

19 I called for my *lovers* then, but they
   Deceiv'd mee, and my Priefts, and Elders lay
Dead in the citie; for they fought for meat   75
   Which fhould refrefh their foules, they could not get.

20 Becaufe I am in ftreights, *Iehova* fee
   My heart o'rturn'd, my bowells muddy bee,
Becaufe I have rebell'd fo much, as faft
   The fword without, as death within, doth waft. 80

53 hand] hands *1650–69:* manu ejus *Tr*   56 from whom *1635–69,* B,N,O'F,TCD: from whence *1633*   58 invite *1633,N,TCD:* accite *1635–69,B,O'F*   59 men; *Ed:* men, *1633–69*   63 farre;] farre *1633*   65 hand,] hand *1633–35*   76 they could not get. *1633:* and none could get. *1635–69*   *Norton conjectures that in* 75 *we should read the sought-for meat: but see note*   78 o'rturn'd,] return'd, *1633*

21 Of all which heare I mourne, none comforts mee,
  My foes have heard my griefe, and glad they be,
That thou haſt done it; But thy promis'd day
  Will come, when, as I ſuffer, ſo ſhall they.

22 Let all their wickedneſſe appeare to thee,   85
  Doe unto them, as thou haſt done to mee,
For all my ſinnes: The ſighs which I have had
  Are very many, and my heart is ſad.

Chap. II.

1 HOw over Sions daughter hath God hung
  His wraths thicke cloud! and from heaven hath
    flung   90
To earth the beauty of *Iſrael*, and hath
  Forgot his foot-ſtoole in the day of wrath!

2 The Lord unſparingly hath ſwallowed
  All Jacobs dwellings, and demoliſhed
To ground the ſtrengths of *Iuda*, and prophan'd   95
  The Princes of the Kingdome, and the land.

3 In heat of wrath, the horne of *Iſrael* hee
  Hath cleane cut off, and left the enemie
Be hindred, his right hand he doth retire,
  But is towards *Iacob*, All-devouring fire.   100

4 Like to an enemie he bent his bow,
  His right hand was in poſture of a foe,
To kill what *Sions* daughter did deſire,
  'Gainſt whom his wrath, he poured forth, like fire.

5 For like an enemie *Iehova* is,   105
  Devouring *Iſrael*, and his Palaces,
Deſtroying holds, giving additions
  To *Iuda's* daughters lamentations.

81 heare I mourne, *1633-35*, B, O'F, TCD: heare me mourn, N: here
I mourn, *1639-69, and mod. edd.*: Audientium me in gemitu eſſe nemo
conſolatur me. Tr   87 ſighs] fights *1669*   90 cloud! *Ed*: cloud?
1633-69   flung] flung. *1633*   92 wrath! *Ed*: wrath? *1633-69*   95
ſtrengths *1633*, N, TCD: ſtrength *1635-69*, B, O'F: munitiones Tr and Vulg
6 Like

6 Like to a garden hedge he hath caſt downe
   The place where was his congregation,   110
And *Sions* feaſts and ſabbaths are forgot;
   Her King, her Prieſt, his wrath regardeth not.

7 The Lord forſakes his Altar, and deteſts
   His Sanctuary, and in the foes hand reſts
His Palace, and the walls, in which their cries   115
   Are heard, as in the true ſolemnities.

8 The Lord hath caſt a line, ſo to confound
   And levell *Sions* walls unto the ground;
He drawes not back his hand, which doth oreturne
   The wall, and Rampart, which together mourne.   120

9 Their gates are ſunke into the ground, and hee
   Hath broke the barres; their King and Princes bee
Amongſt the heathen, without law, nor there
   Unto their Prophets doth the Lord appeare.

10 There *Sions Elders* on the ground are plac'd,   125
   And ſilence keepe; Duſt on their heads they caſt,
In ſackcloth have they girt themſelves, and low
   The Virgins towards ground, their heads do throw.

11 My bowells are growne muddy, and mine eyes
   Are faint with weeping: and my liver lies   130
Pour'd out upon the ground, for miſerie
   That ſucking children in the ſtreets doe die.

12 When they had cryed unto their Mothers, where
   Shall we have bread, and drinke? they fainted there,
And in the ſtreets like wounded perſons lay   135
   Till 'twixt their mothers breaſts they went away.

110 where] which *B,O'F*: locum conventus ſui *Tr*.   112 regardeth]
regarded *1669*   114 hand *B, N, O'F, TCD*: hands *1633–69*: tradit in manum
inimici muros, palatia illius *Tr*   118–9 ground; . . . hand,] ground,
. . . hand; *1633*   121 Their *1633*: The *1635–69*   122 barres; *B,
O'F*: barre; *1633–69, N, TCD*: vectes ejus *Tr*   124 their] the *1669*
134 there,] there *1633–39*   135 ſtreets *B, O'F*: ſtreet *1633–69, N,
TCD*: in plateis civitatis *Tr*

13 *Daughter Ierusalem,* Oh what may bee
   A witnesse, or comparison for thee?
Sion, to ease thee, what shall I name like thee?
   Thy breach is like the sea, what help can bee?   140

14 For thee vaine foolish things thy Prophets sought,
   Thee, thine iniquities they have not taught,
Which might disturne thy bondage: but for thee
   False burthens, and false causes they would see.

15 The passengers doe clap their hands, and hisse,   145
   And wag their head at thee, and say, Is this
That citie, which so many men did call
   Joy of the earth, and perfectest of all?

16 Thy foes doe gape upon thee, and they hisse,
   And gnash their teeth, and say, Devoure wee this,   150
For this is certainly the day which wee
   Expected, and which now we finde, and see.

17 The Lord hath done that which he purposed,
   Fulfill'd his word of old determined;
He hath throwne downe, and not spar'd, and thy foe   155
   Made glad above thee, and advanc'd him so.

18 But now, their hearts against the Lord do call,
   Therefore, O walls of *Sion,* let teares fall
Downe like a river, day and night; take thee
   No rest, but let thine eye incessant be.   160

19 Arise, cry in the night, poure, for thy sinnes,
   Thy heart, like water, when the watch begins;
Lift up thy hands to God, lest children dye,
   Which, faint for hunger, in the streets doe lye.

141 For thee *1635-54:* For, the *1633:* For the *1669*   143 disturne
1633-54 and MSS.: dis-urn *1669:* disturb *Chambers:* ad avertendum
captivitatem tuam *Tr*   145 hisse, *Ed:* hisse *1633-39*   157 against
1633: unto *1635-69, and MSS.:* clamat cor istorum contra Dominum *Tr:*
ad Dominum *Vulg*   161 poure, for *1633 and MSS.:* poure out
1635-69, Chambers

20 Behold O Lord, confider unto whom   165
  Thou haft done this; what, fhall the women come
To eate their children of a fpanne? fhall thy
  Prophet and Prieft be flaine in Sanctuary?

21 On ground in ftreets, the yong and old do lye,
  My virgins and yong men by fword do dye;   170
Them in the day of thy wrath thou haft flaine,
  Nothing did thee from killing them containe.

22 As to a folemne feaft, all whom I fear'd
  Thou call'ft about mee; when his wrath appear'd,
None did remaine or fcape, for thofe which I   175
  Brought up, did perifh by mine enemie.

Chap. III.

1 I Am the man which have affliction feene,
     Under the rod of Gods wrath having beene,
2 He hath led mee to darkneffe, not to light,
     3 And againft mee all day, his hand doth fight.   180

4 Hee hath broke my bones, worne out my flefh and skinne,
     5 Built up againft mee; and hath girt mee in
With hemlocke, and with labour; 6 and fet mee
     In darke, as they who dead for ever bee.

7 Hee hath hedg'd me left I fcape, and added more 185
     To my fteele fetters, heavier then before.
8 When I crie out, he out fhuts my prayer: 9 And hath
     Stop'd with hewn ftone my way, and turn'd my path.

10 And like a Lion hid in fecrecie,
     Or Beare which lyes in wait, he was to mee.   190
11 He ftops my way, teares me, made defolate,
     12 And hee makes mee the marke he fhooteth at.

  174 his *1633:* thy *1635–69*   Chap.] *ital. 1633*   182 girt]
hemde *B, O' F*   186 before. *1650–69:* before, *1633–39*   187 8 *Ed:*
8. *1635–69; om. 1633*   190 mee.] mee, *1633*

                        13 Hee

13 Hee made the children of his quiver paſſe
   Into my reines, 14 I with my people was
All the day long, a ſong and mockery.   195
   15 Hee hath fill'd mee with bitterneſſe, and he

Hath made me drunke with wormewood. 16 He hath burſt
   My teeth with ſtones, and covered mee with duſt;
17 And thus my Soule farre off from peace was ſet,
   And my proſperity I did forget.   200

18 My ſtrength, my hope (unto my ſelfe I ſaid)
   Which from the Lord ſhould come, is periſhed.
19 But when my mournings I do thinke upon,
   My wormwood, hemlocke, and affliction,

20 My Soule is humbled in remembring this;   205
   21 My heart conſiders, therefore, hope there is.
22 'Tis Gods great mercy we'are not utterly
   Conſum'd, for his compaſſions do not die;

23 For every morning they renewed bee,
   For great, O Lord, is thy fidelity.   210
24 The Lord is, ſaith my Soule, my portion,
   And therefore in him will I hope alone.

25 The Lord is good to them, who on him relie,
   And to the Soule that ſeeks him earneſtly.
26 It is both good to truſt, and to attend   215
   (The Lords ſalvation) unto the end:

27 'Tis good for one his yoake in youth to beare;
   28 He ſits alone, and doth all ſpeech forbeare,
Becauſe he hath borne it. 29 And his mouth he layes
   Deepe in the duſt, yet then in hope he ſtayes.   220

30 He gives his cheekes to whoſoever will
   Strike him, and ſo he is reproched ſtill.
31 For, not for ever doth the Lord forſake,
   32 But when he'hath ſtrucke with ſadnes, hee doth take

202 periſhed. *1633:* periſhed, *1635-69*   203 mournings *1633-69,*
N,O'F,TCD: mourning *B*   216 (The Lords ſalvation) *1633:* no
brackets, *1635-69*
                Compaſſion,

Compaffion, as his mercy'is infinite; 225
   33 Nor is it with his heart, that he doth fmite;
34 That underfoot the prifoners ftamped bee,
   35 That a mans right the Judge himfelfe doth fee

To be wrung from him, 36 That he fubverted is
   In his juft caufe; the Lord allowes not this. 230
37 Who then will fay, that ought doth come to paffe,
   But that which by the Lord commanded was?

38 Both good and evill from his mouth proceeds;
   39 Why then grieves any man for his mifdeeds?
40 Turne wee to God, by trying out our wayes; 235
   41 To him in heaven, our hands with hearts upraife.

42 Wee have rebell'd, and falne away from thee,
   Thou pardon'ft not; 43 Ufeft no clemencie;
Purfueft us, kill'ft us, covereft us with wrath,
   44 Cover'ft thy felfe with clouds, that our prayer hath

No power to paffe. 45 And thou haft made us fall 241
   As refufe, and off-fcouring to them all.
46 All our foes gape at us. 47 Feare and a fnare
   With ruine, and with wafte, upon us are.

48 With watry rivers doth mine eye oreflow 245
   For ruine of my peoples daughter fo;
49 Mine eye doth drop downe teares inceffantly,
   50 Untill the Lord looke downe from heaven to fee.

51 And for my citys daughters fake, mine eye
   Doth breake mine heart. 52 Caufles mine enemy, 250
Like a bird chac'd me. 53 In a dungeon
   They have fhut my life, and caft on me a ftone.

    226 fmite; *Ed:* fmite, *1633–69*   229 wrung] wrong *1633*   him,
Ed: him. *1633–69*   230 this.] this: *1633*   231 doth] will *B,O'F*
238 not; *1650–69:* not. *1633–35:* not *1639*   239 covereft us with
wrath] covereft with thy wrath *B,O'F*   243 47 *Ed:* 47, *1633:*
47. *1635–69*   245 watry] water *1633*   246 daughter *B,N,O'F,*
TCD: daughters *1633–69:* propter contritionem filiae populi mei *Tr*   249
citys *O'F:* city *1633–69:* propter omnes filias civitatis meae *Tr*   252 on
me *B,N,TCD:* me on *1633–69:* projiciunt lapides in me. *Tr:* pofuerunt
lapidem fuper me. *Vulg*

54 Waters flow'd o'r my head, then thought I, I am
    Deſtroy'd; 55 I called Lord, upon thy name
Out of the pit. 56 And thou my voice didſt heare;   255
    Oh from my ſigh, and crye, ſtop not thine eare.

57 Then when I call'd upon thee, thou drew'ſt nere
    Unto mee, and ſaid'ſt unto mee, do not feare.
58 Thou Lord my Soules cauſe handled haſt, and thou
    Reſcud'ſt my life. 59 O Lord do thou judge now,   260

Thou heardſt my wrong. 60 Their vengeance all they
    have wrought;
    61 How they reproach'd, thou haſt heard, and what they
    thought,
62 What their lips uttered, which againſt me roſe,
    And what was ever whiſper'd by my foes.

63 I am their ſong, whether they riſe or ſit,   265
    64 Give them rewards Lord, for their working fit,
65 Sorrow of heart, thy curſe. 66 And with thy might
    Follow, and from under heaven deſtroy them quite.

Chap. IV.

1 HOw is the gold become ſo dimme? How is
    Pureſt and fineſt gold thus chang'd to this?   270
The ſtones which were ſtones of the Sanctuary,
    Scattered in corners of each ſtreet do lye.   ,

2 The pretious ſonnes of Sion, which ſhould bee
    Valued at pureſt gold, how do wee ſee
Low rated now, as earthen Pitchers, ſtand,   275
    Which are the worke of a poore Potters hand.

3 Even the Sea-calfes draw their breſts, and give
    Sucke to their young; my peoples daughters live,
By reaſon of the foes great cruelneſſe,
    As do the Owles in the vaſt Wilderneſſe.   280

256 ſigh,] ſight, *1650–69*   260 Reſcud'ſt *B, O'F:* Reſcueſt *1633–69,*
N, TCD: vindicabas *Tr*   now, *1633–39:* now. *1650–69, Chambers*
Chap.] Cap. *1633*   270 .Pureſt] P *dropped 1650–54*   274 at
1633–39: as *1650–69, B, N, O'F, TCD:* qui taxandi erant auro purgatiſſimo
Tr   278 live,] live *1633*

4 And

4 And when the fucking child doth ftrive to draw,
   His tongue for thirft cleaves to his upper jaw.
And when for bread the little children crye,
   There is no man that doth them fatisfie.

5 They which before were delicately fed,   285
   Now in the ftreets forlorne have perifhed,
And they which ever were in fcarlet cloath'd,
   Sit and embrace the dunghills which they loath'd.

6 The daughters of my people have finned more,
   Then did the towne of *Sodome* finne before;   290
Which being at once deftroy'd, there did remaine
   No hands amongft them, to vexe them againe.

7 But heretofore purer her Nazarite
   Was then the fnow, and milke was not fo white;
As carbuncles did their pure bodies fhine,   295
   And all their polifh'dneffe was Saphirine.

8 They are darker now then blacknes, none can know
   Them by the face, as through the ftreets they goe,
For now their skin doth cleave unto the bone,
   And withered, is like to dry wood growne.   300

9 Better by fword then famine 'tis to dye;
   And better through pierc'd, then through penury.
10 Women by nature pitifull, have eate
   Their children dreft with their owne hands for meat.

11 *Iehova* here fully accomplifh'd hath   305
   His indignation, and powr'd forth his wrath,
Kindled a fire in *Sion*, which hath power
   To eate, and her foundations to devour.

    283 little children] little *om. Chambers*   296 Saphirine. *1635–69:*
Seraphine. *1633:* Sapphirina polities eorum *Tr*   298 ftreets *B,O'F:*
ftreet *1633–69,N,TCD:* in vicis *Tr:* in plateis *Vulg*   299 the
B,O'F: their *1633–69*   302 through penury.] by penury, *1633,N,*
TCD: confoffi gladio quam confoffi fame. *Tr. See note*   304 hands
B,O'F: hand *1633–69*

12 Nor would the Kings of the earth, nor all which live
  In the inhabitable world beleeve, 310
That any adverſary, any foe
  Into *Ieruſalem* ſhould enter ſo.

13 For the Prieſts ſins, and Prophets, which have ſhed
  Blood in the ſtreets, and the juſt murthered:
14 Which when thoſe men, whom they made blinde, did
    ſtray 315
  Thorough the ſtreets, defiled by the way

With blood, the which impoſſible it was
  Their garments ſhould ſcape touching, as they paſſe,
15 Would cry aloud, depart defiled men,
  Depart, depart, and touch us not; and then 320

They fled, and ſtrayd, and with the *Gentiles* were,
  Yet told their friends, they ſhould not long dwell there;
16 For this they are ſcattered by Jehovahs face
  Who never will regard them more; No grace

Unto their old men ſhall the foe afford, 325
  Nor, that they are Prieſts, redeeme them from the ſword.
17 And wee as yet, for all theſe miſeries
  Deſiring our vaine helpe, conſume our eyes:

And ſuch a nation as cannot ſave,
  We in deſire and ſpeculation have. 330
18 They hunt our ſteps, that in the ſtreets wee feare
  To goe: our end is now approached neere,

Our dayes accompliſh'd are, this the laſt day.
  19 Eagles of heaven are not ſo ſwift as they
Which follow us, o'r mountaine tops they flye 335
  At us, and for us in the deſart lye.

312 ſo.] ſo; *1633*   316 Thorough] Through *1669*   318 gar-
ments *1633:* garment *1635–69:* quem non poſſunt quin tangant veſtimentis
ſuis *Tr*   320 not; *O'F,N,TCD:* not, *1633–69*   322 dwell there;
Ed: dwell; there. *1633:* dwell there. *1635–39:* dwell there *1650–54:*
dwell there: *1669*   325 their . . . the *1633–39:* the . . . their *1650–69*
333–4 day. 19 Eagles *Ed: The old editions place a comma after* day, *and*
19 *at the beginning of* 335, *wrongly.*   335 mountaine tops *1633–39:*
mountaines tops *1650–69, B*

20 The

20 The annointed Lord, breath of our noftrils, hee
  Of whom we faid, under his fhadow, wee
Shall with more eafe under the Heathen dwell,
  Into the pit which thefe men digged, fell.   340

21 Rejoyce O *Edoms daughter*, joyfull bee
  Thou which inhabitft *Huz*, for unto thee
This cup fhall paffe, and thou with drunkenneffe
  Shalt fill thy felfe, and fhew thy nakedneffe.

22 And then thy finnes O *Sion*, fhall be fpent,   345
  The Lord will not leave thee in banifhment.
Thy finnes O *Edoms daughter*, hee will fee,
  And for them, pay thee with captivitie.

Chap. V.

1 REmember, O Lord, what is fallen on us;
  See, and marke how we are reproached thus,   350
2 For unto ftrangers our poffeffion
  Is turn'd, our houfes unto Aliens gone,

3 Our mothers are become as widowes, wee
  As Orphans all, and without father be;
4 Waters which are our owne, wee drunke, and pay,   355
  And upon our owne wood a price they lay.

5 Our perfecutors on our necks do fit,
  They make us travaile, and not intermit,
6 We ftretch our hands unto th'*Egyptians*
  To get us bread; and to the *Affyrians*.   360

340 fell.] fell *1633*   342 which *1633*; that *1635–69*   Huz *B*:
Hus *N,TCD*: her, *1633*: U*z*, *1635–69*: in terra Hutzi *Tr*   345
And then] And *om. Chambers*   Chap.] Cap. *1633*   349 us;]
us, *1633–35*   354 father *B,O'F*: fathers *1633–69*: Pupilli fumus ac
nullo patre *Tr*: absque patre *Vulg*   355 drunke, *1633, N,TCD*: drinke
1635–69, B, O'F   356 lay. *1650–69*: lay, *1633–39*

7 Our

7 Our Fathers did thefe finnes, and are no more,
  But wee do beare the finnes they did before.
8 They are but fervants, which do rule us thus,
  Yet from their hands none would deliver us.

9 With danger of our life our bread wee gat;   365
  For in the wildernefle, the fword did wait.
10 The tempefts of this famine wee liv'd in,
  Black as an Oven colour'd had our skinne:

11 In *Iudaes* cities they the maids abus'd
  By force, and fo women in *Sion* us'd.   370
12 The Princes with their hands they hung; no grace
  Nor honour gave they to the Elders face.

13 Unto the mill our yong men carried are,
  And children fell under the wood they bare.
14 Elders, the gates; youth did their fongs forbeare, 375
15 Gone was our joy; our dancings, mournings were.

16 Now is the crowne falne from our head; and woe
  Be unto us, becaufe we'have finned fo.
17 For this our hearts do languifh, and for this
  Over our eyes a cloudy dimnefle is.   380

18 Becaufe mount *Sion* defolate doth lye,
  And foxes there do goe at libertie:
19 But thou O Lord art ever, and thy throne
  From generation, to generation.

20 Why fhould'ft thou forget us eternally?   385
  Or leave us thus long in this mifery?
21 Reftore us Lord to thee, that fo we may
  Returne, and as of old, renew our day.

22 For oughteft thou, O Lord, defpife us thus,
  And to be utterly enrag'd at us?   390

---

368 Oven *1635–69*: Ocean *1633*: Pelles noftrae ut furnus atratae funt
Tr   374 fell . . . bare. *1633–69*: fall . . . beare. *B,O'F*   376 15
Gone *&c.*] Old edd. *transfer* 15 *to next line, wrongly. In consequence, the
remaining verses are all a number short, but the complete number of* 22 *is
made up by breaking the last verse,* 'For oughteft thou *&c.*,' *into two. I have
corrected throughout.*   389 thus,] thus *1633*

Hymne

Hymne to God my God, in my ſickneſſe.

SInce I am comming to that Holy roome,
  Where, with thy Quire of Saints for evermore,
I ſhall be made thy Muſique; As I come
   I tune the Inſtrument here at the dore,
   And what I muſt doe then, thinke here before.   5

Whilſt my Phyſitians by their lore are growne
  Coſmographers, and I their Mapp, who lie
Flat on this bed, that by them may be ſhowne
   That this is my South-weſt diſcoverie
   Per fretum febris, by theſe ſtreights to die,   10

I joy, that in theſe ſtraits, I ſee my Weſt;
  For, though theire currants yeeld returne to none,
What ſhall my Weſt hurt me? As Weſt and Eaſt
   In all flatt Maps (and I am one) are one,
   So death doth touch the Reſurrection.   15

Is the Pacifique Sea my home? Or are
  The Eaſterne riches? Is *Ieruſalem?*
Anyan, and *Magellan,* and *Gibraltare,*
   All ſtreights, and none but ſtreights, are wayes to them,
   Whether where *Iaphet* dwelt, or *Cham,* or *Sem.*   20

We thinke that *Paradiſe* and *Calvarie,*
  Chriſts Croſſe, and *Adams* tree, ſtood in one place;
Looke Lord, and finde both *Adams* met in me;
   As the firſt *Adams* ſweat ſurrounds my face,
   May the laſt *Adams* blood my ſoule embrace.   25

    Hymn to God *&c. 1635–69, S96, and in part Walton* (Life of
Dr John Donne. 1670), *who adds* March 23, 1630   2 thy *1635
and Walton* (1670): the *1639–69*   4 the Inſtrument *1635–69:* my
inſtrument *Walton*   6 Whilſt . . . lore *Addl. MS. 34324:* Whilſt . . .
love *1635–69:* Since . . . loves *Walton*   10 to die, *1635:* to die. *1639–
54:* to dy· *1669*   12 theire *S96:* thoſe *1635–69*   18 *Gibraltare,
1635–54:* Gabraltare, *1669:* Gibraltar? *1719, Chambers:* Gibraltar are
Grosart. See note   19 but ſtreights, *Ed:* but ſtreights *1635–69*
24 firſt] ſiſt *1669*   So,

Corporis hæc Animæ sit Syndon, Syndon Jesu
Amen.

Martin (R) scup And are to be sould by R R and Ben: ffisher

JOHN DONNE
From the frontispiece to *Death's Duel*, 1632

So, in his purple wrapp'd receive mee Lord,
  By thefe his thornes give me his other Crowne ;
And as to others foules I preach'd thy word,
  Be this my Text, my Sermon to mine owne,
    Therfore that he may raife the Lord throws down. 30

A Hymne to God the Father :

I.

WIlt thou forgive that finne where I begunne,
  Which was my fin, though it were done before?
Wilt thou forgive that finne; through which I runne,
  And do run ftill: though ftill I do deplore?
    When thou haft done, thou haft not done, 5
      For, I have more.

II.

Wilt thou forgive that finne which I have wonne
  Others to finne? and, made my finne their doore?
Wilt thou forgive that finne which I did fhunne
  A yeare, or two: but wallowed in, a fcore? 10
    When thou haft done, thou haft not done,
      For I have more.

III.

I have a finne of feare, that when I have fpunne
  My laft thred, I fhall perifh on the fhore;
But fweare by thy felfe, that at my death thy fonne 15
  Shall fhine as he fhines now, and heretofore;
    And, having done that, Thou hafte done,
      I feare no more.

   28 others fouls] other fouls *Walton and S96*   30 That, he may raife; therefore, *Walton*
   A Hymne *&c. 1633–69:* To Chrift. *A18, N, TCC, TCD :* Chrifto Salvatori. *O'F, S96: for the text of the MSS. see next page*   2 Which] which *1633*   8 my fin] my fins *1639–69*   10 two: *1633:* two, *1635–69*
                                                To

To Chriſt.

Wᴵlt thou forgive that ſinn, where I begunn,
  Wᶜʰ is my ſinn, though it were done before?
Wilt thou forgive thoſe ſinns through wᶜʰ I runn
  And doe them ſtill, though ſtill I doe deplore?
    When thou haſt done, thou haſt not done,   5
        for I have more.

Wilt thou forgive that ſinn, by wᶜʰ I'have wonne
  Others to ſinn, & made my ſinn their dore?
Wilt thou forgive that ſinn wᶜʰ I did ſhunne
  A yeare or twoe, but wallowed in a ſcore?   10
    When thou haſt done, thou haſt not done,
        for I have more.

I have a ſinn of feare yᵗ when I have ſpunn
  My laſt thred, I ſhall periſh on the ſhore;
Sweare by thy ſelf that at my Death, thy Sunn   15
  Shall ſhine as it ſhines nowe, & heretofore;
    And having done that, thou haſt done,
        I have noe more.

  To Chriſt. *A18,N,TCC,TCD:* Chriſto Salvatori. *O'F,S96: text from*
TCD   1 begunn, *Ed:* begunn *TCD*   2 were *A18,N,TC:* was *O'F,S*
before? *Ed:* before *TCD*   4 them *A18,N,TC:* runne *O'F,S96*
5 done, *Ed:* done *TCD: and so* 11 *and* 17   14 ſhore; *Ed:* ſhore
TCD   15 thy Sunne *O'F,S:* this Sunn *A18,N,TC*   16 heretofore;
Ed: heretofore *TCD*

TO THE MEMORIE OF
MY EVER DESIRED FRIEND
D'. DONNE.

TO have liv'd eminent, in a degree
　　Beyond our lofty'ft flights, that is, like Thee,
Or t'have had too much merit, is not fafe;
For, fuch exceffes finde no Epitaph.
At common graves we have Poetique eyes　　　　5
Can melt themfelves in eafie Elegies,
Each quill can drop his tributary verfe,
And pin it, like the Hatchments, to the Hearfe:
But at Thine, Poeme, or Infcription
(Rich foule of wit, and language) we have none.　　10
Indeed a filence does that tombe befit,
Where is no Herald left to blazon it.
Widow'd invention juftly doth forbeare
To come abroad, knowing Thou art not here,
Late her great Patron; Whofe Prerogative　　　　15
Maintain'd, and cloth'd her fo, as none alive
Muft now prefume, to keepe her at thy rate,
Though he the Indies for her dowre eftate.
Or elfe that awfull fire, which once did burne
In thy cleare Braine, now falne into thy Urne　　20
Lives there, to fright rude Empiricks from thence,
Which might prophane thee by their Ignorance.
Who ever writes of Thee, and in a ftile
Unworthy fuch a Theme, does but revile
Thy precious Duft, and wake a learned Spirit　　25
Which may revenge his Rapes upon thy Merit.
For, all a low pitch't phanfie can devife,
Will prove, at beft, but Hallow'd Injuries.
　　Thou, like the dying Swanne, didft lately fing
Thy Mournfull Dirge, in audience of the King;　　30
When pale lookes, and faint accents of thy breath,
Prefented fo, to life, that peece of death,
That it was fear'd, and prophefi'd by all,
Thou thither cam'ft to preach thy Funerall.

　　To the &c. *Also in* Deaths Duell. *1632, Walton's* Lives *1670, King's*
Poems. *1657, 1664, 1700*　　　14 here] there *1632*　　　31 faint]
weak *1632*

　　　　　　　　　　　　　　　　O! had'ft

O! had'ſt Thou in an Elegiacke Knell   35
Rung out unto the world thine owne farewell,
And in thy High Victorious Numbers beate
The ſolemne meaſure of thy griev'd Retreat;
Thou might'ſt the Poets ſervice now have miſt
As well, as then thou did'ſt prevent the Prieſt;   40
And never to the world beholding bee
So much, as for an Epitaph for thee.
   I doe not like the office. Nor is 't fit
Thou, who did'ſt lend our Age ſuch ſummes of wit,
Should'ſt now re-borrow from her bankrupt Mine,   45
That Ore to Bury Thee, which once was Thine,
Rather ſtill leave us in thy debt; And know
(Exalted Soule) more glory 't is to owe
Unto thy Hearſe, what we can never pay,
Then, with embaſed Coine thoſe Rites defray.   50
   Commit we then Thee to Thy ſelfe: Nor blame
Our drooping loves, which thus to thy owne Fame
Leave Thee Executour. Since, but thine owne,
No pen could doe Thee Juſtice, nor Bayes Crowne
Thy vaſt deſert; Save that, wee nothing can   55
Depute, to be thy Aſhes Guardian.
   So Jewellers no Art, or Metall truſt
   To forme the Diamond, but the Diamonds duſt.

H. K.

To the deceaſed Author,

Upon the *Promiſcuous* printing of his Poems, the
Looſer ſort, with the *Religious.*

WHen thy *Looſe* raptures, *Donne,* ſhall meet with Thoſe
       That doe confine
     Tuning, unto the Duller line,
    And ſing not, but in *Sanctified Proſe*;
      How will they, with ſharper eyes,   5
    The *Fore-skinne* of thy phanſie circumciſe?
And feare, thy *wantonneſſe* ſhould now, begin
Example, that hath ceaſed to be *Sin*?

57 or] nor *1632*

And

And that *Feare* fannes their *Heat* ; whilſt knowing eyes
   Will not admire   10
    At this *Strange Fire,*
  That here is *mingled with thy Sacrifice* :
   But dare reade even thy *Wanton Story,*
  As thy *Confeſſion*, not thy *Glory.*
And will ſo envie *Both* to future times,   15
That they would buy thy *Goodneſſe*, with thy *Crimes.*

        Tho: Browne.

On the death of Dr DONNE.

I Cannot blame thoſe men, that knew thee well,
 Yet dare not helpe the world, to ring thy knell
In tunefull *Elegies* ; there's not language knowne
Fit for thy mention, but 'twas firſt thy owne ;
The *Epitaphs* thou writſt, have ſo bereft   5
Our tongue of wit, there is not phanſie left
Enough to weepe thee ; what henceforth we ſee
Of Art or Nature, muſt reſult from thee.
There may perchance ſome buſie gathering friend
Steale from thy owne workes, and that, varied, lend, 10
Which thou beſtow'ſt on others, to thy Hearſe,
And ſo thou ſhalt live ſtill in thine owne verſe ;
Hee that ſhall venture farther, may commit
A pitied errour, ſhew his zeale, not wit.
Fate hath done mankinde wrong ; vertue may aime 15
Reward of conſcience, never can, of fame,
Since her great trumpet's broke, could onely give
Faith to the world, command it to beleeve ;
 Hee then muſt write, that would define thy parts :
Here lyes the beſt Divinitie, All the Arts.   20

       Edw. Hyde.

On the *&c. Also in* Deaths Duell. *1632*   4 thy] thine *1632*
6 tongue] pens *1632*

            On

On Doctor Donne,
By D' C. B. of O.

HEe that would write an Epitaph for thee,
    And do it well, muft firft beginne to be
Such as thou wert; for, none can truly know
Thy worth, thy life, but he that hath liv'd fo;
He muft have wit to fpare and to hurle downe: 5
Enough, to keepe the gallants of the towne.
He muft have learning plenty; both the Lawes,
Civill, and Common, to judge any caufe;
Divinity great ftore, above the reft;
Not of the laft Edition, but the beft.   10
Hee muft have language, travaile, all the Arts;
Judgement to ufe; or elfe he wants thy parts.
He muft have friends the higheft, able to do;
Such as *Mecænas*, and *Auguftus* too.
He muft have fuch a fickneffe, fuch a death;   15
Or elfe his vaine defcriptions come beneath;
    Who then fhall write an Epitaph for thee,
    He muft be dead firft, let'it alone for mee.

An Elegie upon the incomparable
D' DONNE.

ALl is not well when fuch a one as I
    Dare peepe abroad, and write an *Elegie*;
When fmaller *Starres* appeare, and give their light,
Phœbus is gone to bed: Were it not night,
And the world witleffe now that DONNE is dead,   5
You fooner fhould have broke, then feene my head.
Dead did I fay? Forgive this *Injury*
I doe him, and his worthes *Infinity*,
To fay he is but dead; I dare averre
It better may be term'd a *Maffacre*,   10
Then *Sleepe* or *Death*; See how the *Mufes* mourne
Upon their oaten *Reeds*, and from his *Vrne*
Threaten the World with this *Calamity*,
    They fhall have *Ballads*, but no *Poetry*.

On &c. *Also in Corbet's* Poems *1647*

Language lyes fpeechleffe; and *Divinity*, 15
Loft fuch a *Trump* as even to *Extafie*
Could charme the Soule, and had an *Influence*
To teach beft *judgements*, and pleafe dulleft *Senfe*.
The *Court*, the *Church*, the *Vniverfitie*,
Loft *Chaplaine*, *Deane*, and *Doctor*, All thefe, Three. 20
   It was his *Merit*, that his *Funerall*
   Could caufe a loffe fo *great* and *generall*.

If there be any Spirit can anfwer give
Of fuch as hence depart, to fuch as live :
Speake, Doth his body there vermiculate, 25
Crumble to duft, and feele the lawes of Fate?
Me thinkes, *Corruption*, *Wormes*, what elfe is foule
Should fpare the *Temple* of fo faire a *Soule*.
I could beleeve they doe; but that I know
What inconvenience might hereafter grow : 30
   Succeeding ages would *Idolatrize*,
   And as his *Numbers*, fo his *Reliques* prize.

If that Philofopher, which did avow
The world to be but Motes, was living now :
He would affirme that th'*Atomes* of his mould 35
Were they in feverall bodies blended, would
Produce new worlds of *Travellers*, *Divines*,
Of *Linguifts*, *Poets*: fith thefe feverall *lines*
In him concentred were, and flowing thence
Might fill againe the worlds *Circumference*. 40
I could beleeve this too ; and yet my faith
Not want a *Prefident* : The *Phœnix* hath
(And fuch was He) a power to animate
Her afhes, and herfelfe perpetuate.
But, bufie Soule, thou doft not well to pry 45
Into thefe Secrets; *Griefe*, and *Iealoufie*,
The more they know, the further ftill advance,
And finde no way fo fafe as *Ignorance*.
Let this fuffice thee, that his *Soule* which flew
A pitch of all admir'd, known but of few, 50
(Save thofe of purer mould) is now tranflated
From Earth to Heavên, and there *Conftellated*.
   For, if each *Prieft* of God fhine as a *Starre*,
   His *Glory* is as his *Gifts*, 'bove others farre.

HEN, VALENTINE.

Au

An Elegie upon Dr Donne.

IS *Donne*, great *Donne* deceas'd? then England fay
　Thou'haft loft a man where language chofe to ftay
And fhew it's gracefull power. I would not praife
That and his vaft wit (which in thefe vaine dayes
Make many proud) but as they ferv'd to unlock   5
That Cabinet, his minde : where fuch a ftock
Of knowledge was repos'd, as all lament
(Or fhould) this generall caufe of difcontent.
　And I rejoyce I am not fo fevere,
But (as I write a line) to weepe a teare   10
For his deceafe ; Such fad extremities
May make fuch men as I write *Elegies.*
　And wonder not ; for, when a generall loffe
Falls on a nation, and they flight the croffe,
God hath rais'd *Prophets* to awaken them   15
From ftupifaction ; witneffe my milde pen,
Not us'd to upbraid the world, though now it muft
Freely and boldly, for, the caufe is juft.
　Dull age, Oh I would fpare thee, but th'art worfe,
Thou art not onely dull, but haft a curfe   20
Of black ingratitude ; if not, couldft thou
Part with *miraculous Donne,* and make no vow
For thee and thine, fucceffively to pay
A fad remembrance to his dying day?
　Did his youth fcatter *Poetrie,* wherein   25
Was all Philofophie? Was every finne,
Character'd in his *Satyres?* made fo foule
That fome have fear'd their fhapes, and kept their foule
Freer by reading verfe? Did he give *dayes*
Paft marble monuments, to thofe, whofe praife   30
He would perpetuate? Did hee (I feare
The dull will doubt :) thefe at his twentieth yeare?
　But, more matur'd : Did his full foule conceive,
And in harmonious-holy-numbers weave
A *Crowne of facred fonets,* fit to adorne   *La Corona.*   35
A dying Martyrs brow : or, to be worne
On that bleft head of *Mary Magdalen* :
After fhe wip'd Chrifts feet, but not till then?

An Elegie *&c.*   *See note*
1–3　　Our Donne is dead; England fhould mourne, may fay
　　　　We had a man where language chofe to stay
　　　　And fhew her gracefull power *1635–69*
35 *Crowne*] Crowme *1633*

Did

Did hee (fit for fuch penitents as fhee
And hee to ufe) leave us a *Litany*? 40
Which all devout men love, and fure, it fhall,
As times grow better, grow more claſſicall.
Did he write *Hymnes*, for piety and wit
Equall to thofe great grave *Prudentius* writ?
Spake he all *Languages*? knew he all *Lawes*? 45
The grounds and ufe of *Phyſicke*; but becaufe
'Twas mercenary wav'd it? Went to fee
That bleſſed place of *Chriſts nativity*?
Did he returne and preach him? preach him fo
As none but hee did, or could do? They know 50
(Such as were bleft to heare him know) 'tis truth.
Did he confirme thy age? convert thy youth?
Did he thefe wonders? And is this deare loſſe
Mourn'd by fo few? (few for fo great a croſſe.)
     But fure the filent are ambitious all 55
To be *Cloſe Mourners* at his Funerall;
If not; In common pitty they forbare
By repetitions to renew our care;
Or, knowing, griefe conceiv'd, conceal'd, confumes
Man irreparably, (as poyfon'd fumes 60
Do wafte the braine) make filence a fafe way
To'inlarge the Soule from thefe walls, mud and clay,
(Materialls of this body) to remaine
With *Donne* in heaven, where no promifcuous paine
Leſſens the joy wee have, for, with *him*, all 65
Are fatisfyed with *joyes eſſentiall.*
     My thoughts, Dwell on this *Ioy*, and do not call
Griefe backe, by thinking of his Funerall;
Forget he lov'd mee; Wafte not my fad yeares;
(Which hafte to *Davids* feventy, fill'd with feares 70
And forrow for his death;) Forget his parts,
Which finde a living grave in good mens hearts;
And, (for, my firft is daily paid for finne)
Forget to pay my fecond figh for him:
Forget his powerfull preaching; and forget 75
I am his *Convert.* Oh my frailtie! let
My flefh be no more heard, it will obtrude
This lethargie: fo fhould my gratitude,
My vowes of gratitude fhould fo be broke;
Which can no more be, then *Donnes* vertues fpoke 80
By any but himfelfe; for which caufe, I
     Write no *Encomium*, but an *Elegie.*

                                        IZ. WA.

An Elegie upon the death of the
Deane of Pauls, D[r]. Iohn Donne :
By M[r]. *Tho: Carie.*

CAn we not force from widdowed Poetry,
  Now thou art dead (Great DONNE) one Elegie
To crowne thy Hearfe ? Why yet dare we not truft
Though with unkneaded dowe-bak't profe thy duft,
Such as the uncifor'd Churchman from the flower   5
Of fading Rhetorique, fhort liv'd as his houre,
Dry as the fand that meafures it, fhould lay
Upon thy Afhes, on the funerall day ?
Have we no voice, no tune ? Did'ft thou difpenfe
Through all our language, both the words and fenfe ? 10
'Tis a fad truth ; The Pulpit may her plaine,
And fober Chriftian precepts ftill retaine,
Doctrines it may, and wholefome Ufes frame,
Grave Homilies, and Lectures, But the flame
Of thy brave Soule, that fhot fuch heat and light, 15
As burnt our earth, and made our darkneffe bright,
Committed holy Rapes upon our Will,
Did through the eye the melting heart diftill ;
And the deepe knowledge of darke truths fo teach,
As fenfe might judge, what phanfie could not reach ; 20
Muft be defir'd for ever. So the fire,
That fills with fpirit and heat the Delphique quire,
Which kindled firft by thy Promethean breath,
Glow'd here a while, lies quench't now in thy death ;
The Mufes garden with Pedantique weedes 25
O'rfpred, was purg'd by thee ; The lazie feeds
Of fervile imitation throwne away ;
And frefh invention planted, Thou didft pay
The debts of our penurious bankrupt age ;
Licentious thefts, that make poëtique rage 30
A Mimique fury, when our foules muft bee
Poffeft, or with Anacreons Extafie,
Or Pindars, not their owne ; The fubtle cheat
Of flie Exchanges, and the jugling feat
Of two-edg'd words, or whatfoever wrong 35
By ours was done the Greeke, or Latine tongue,
Thou haft redeem'd, and open'd Us a Mine
Of rich and pregnant phanfie, drawne a line

An Elegie &c. *Alfo in Carew's* Poems *1640. See note*

Of

Of mafculine expreffion, which had good
Old Orpheus feene, Or all the ancient Brood   40
Our fuperftitious fooles admire, and hold
Their lead more precious, then thy burnifh't Gold,
Thou hadft beene their Exchequer, and no more
They each in others duft, had rak'd for Ore.
Thou fhalt yield no precedence, but of time,   45
And the blinde fate of language, whofe tun'd chime
More charmes the outward fenfe ; Yet thou maift claime
From fo great difadvantage greater fame,
Since to the awe of thy imperious wit
Our ftubborne language bends, made only fit   50
With her tough-thick-rib'd hoopes to gird about
Thy Giant phanfie, which had prov'd too ftout
For their foft melting Phrafes. As in time
They had the ftart, fo did they cull the prime
Buds of invention many a hundred yeare,   55
And left the rifled fields, befides the feare
To touch their Harveft, yet from thofe bare lands
Of what is purely thine, thy only hands
(And that thy fmalleft worke) have gleaned more
Then all thofe times, and tongues could reape before ;   60
But thou art gone, and thy ftrict lawes will be
Too hard for Libertines in Poetrie.
They will repeale the goodly exil'd traine
Of gods and goddeffes, which in thy juft raigne
Were banifh'd nobler Poems, now, with thefe   65
The filenc'd tales o'th'Metamorphofes
Shall ftuffe their lines, and fwell the windy Page,
Till Verfe refin'd by thee, in this laft Age,
Turne ballad rime, Or thofe old Idolls bee
Ador'd againe, with new apoftafie ;   70
Oh, pardon mee, that breake with untun'd verfe
The reverend filence that attends thy herfe,
Whofe awfull folemne murmures were to thee
More then thefe faint lines, A loud Elegie,
That did proclaime in a dumbe eloquence   75
The death of all the Arts, whofe influence
Growne feeble, in thefe panting numbers lies
Gafping fhort winded Accents, and fo dies :
So doth the fwiftly turning wheele not ftand
In th'inftant we withdraw the moving hand,   80
But fome fmall time maintaine a faint weake courfe
By vertue of the firft impulfive force :

                                                  And

And fo whil'ft I caft on thy funerall pile
Thy crowne of Bayes, Oh, let it crack a while,
And fpit difdaine, till the devouring flafhes   85
Suck all the moyfture up, then turne to afhes.
I will not draw the envy to engroffe
All thy perfections, or weepe all our loffe ;
Thofe are too numerous for an Elegie,
And this too great, to be exprefs'd by mee.   90
Though every pen fhould fhare a diftinct part,
Yet art thou Theme enough to tyre all Art ;
Let others carve the reft, it fhall fuffice
I on thy Tombe this Epitaph incife.

> *Here lies a King, that rul'd as hee thought fit*   95
> *The univerfall Monarchy of wit ;*
> *Here lie two Flamens, and both thofe, the beft,*
> *Apollo's firft, at laft, the true Gods Prieft.*

An Elegie on D^r. DONNE: *By Sir Lucius Carie.*

POets attend, the Elegie I fing
    Both of a doubly-named Prieft, and King :
In ftead of Coates, and Pennons, bring your Verfe,
For you muft bee chiefe mourners at his Hearfe,
A Tombe your Mufe muft to his Fame fupply,   5
No other Monuments can never die ;
And as he was a two-fold Prieft ; in youth,
Apollo's ; afterwards, the voice of Truth,
Gods Conduit-pipe for grace, who chofe him for
His extraordinary Embaffador,   10
So let his Liegiers with the Poets joyne,
Both having fhares, both muft in griefe combine :
Whil'ft Johnfon forceth with his Elegie
Teares from a griefe-unknowing Scythians eye,
(Like Mofes at whofe ftroke the waters gufht   15
From forth the Rock, and like a Torrent rufht.)
Let Lawd his funerall Sermon preach, and fhew
Thofe vertues, dull eyes were not apt to know,
Nor leave that Piercing Theme, till it appeares
To be goodfriday, by the Churches Teares ;   20
                                                   Yet

Yet make not griefe too long oppreſſe our Powers,
Leaſt that his funerall Sermon ſhould prove ours.
Nor yet forget that heavenly Eloquence,
With which he did the bread of life diſpenſe,
Preacher and Orator diſcharg'd both parts   25
With pleaſure for our ſenſe, health for our hearts,
And the firſt ſuch (Though a long ſtudied Art
Tell us our ſoule is all in every part,)
None was ſo marble, but whil'ſt him he heares,
His Soule ſo long dwelt only in his eares.   30
And from thence (with the fierceneſſe of a flood
Bearing downe vice) victual'd with that bleſt food
Their hearts; His ſeed in none could faile to grow,
Fertile he found them all, or made them ſo:
No Druggiſt of the Soule beſtow'd on all   35
So Catholiquely a curing Cordiall.
Nor only in the Pulpit dwelt his ſtore,
His words work'd much, but his example more,
That preach't on worky dayes, His Poetrie
It ſelfe was oftentimes divinity,   40
Thoſe Anthemes (almoſt ſecond Pſalmes) he writ
To make us know the Croſſe, and value it,
(Although we owe that reverence to that name
Wee ſhould not need warmth from an under flame.)
Creates a fire in us, ſo neare extreme   45
That we would die, for, and upon this theme.
Next, his ſo pious Litany, which none can
But count Divine, except a Puritan,
And that but for the name, nor this, nor thoſe
Want any thing of Sermons, but the proſe.   50
Experience makes us ſee, that many a one
Owes to his Countrey his Religion;
And in another, would as ſtrongly grow,
Had but his Nurſe and Mother taught him ſo,
Not hee the ballaſt on his Judgement hung;   55
Nor did his preconceit doe either wrong;
He labour'd to exclude what ever ſinne
By time or careleſſeneſſe had entred in;
Winnow'd the chaffe from wheat, but yet was loath
A too hot zeale ſhould force him, burne them both;   60
Nor would allow of that ſo ignorant gall,
Which to ſave blotting often would blot all;
Nor did thoſe barbarous opinions owne,
To thinke the Organs ſinne; and faction, none;

                                    Nor

Nor was there expectation to gaine grace   65
From forth his Sermons only, but his face;
So Primitive a looke, fuch gravitie
With humbleneffe, and both with Pietie;
So milde was Mofes countenance, when he prai'd
For them whofe Satanifme his power gainfaid;   70
And fuch his gravitie, when all Gods band
Receiv'd his word (through him) at fecond hand,
Which joyn'd, did flames of more devotion move
Then ever Argive Hellens could of love.
Now to conclude, I muft my reafon bring,   75
Wherefore I call'd him in his title King,
That Kingdome the Philofophers beleev'd
To excell Alexanders, nor were griev'd
By feare of loffe (that being fuch a Prey
No ftronger then ones felfe can force away)   80
The Kingdome of ones felfe, this he enjoy'd,
And his authoritie fo well employ'd,
That never any could before become
So Great a Monarch, in fo fmall a roome;
He conquer'd rebell paffions, rul'd them fo,   85
As under-fpheares by the firft Mover goe,
Banifh't fo farre their working, that we can
But know he had fome, for we knew him man.
Then let his laft excufe his firft extremes,
His age faw vifions, though his youth dream'd dreams.   90

On D^r. D o n n e s *death:*

By M^r. Mayne *of Chrift-Church in Oxford.*

WHo fhall prefume to mourn thee, *Donne*, unleffe
    He could his teares in thy expreffions dreffe,
And teach his griefe that reverence of thy Hearfe,
To weepe lines, learned, as thy Anniverfe,
A Poëme of that worth, whofe every teare   5
Deferves the title of a feverall yeare.
Indeed fo farre above its Reader, good,
That wee are thought wits, when 'tis underftood,
There that bleft maid to die, who now fhould grieve?
After thy forrow, 'twere her loffe to live;   10

72 Receiv'd] Receiv' 1633

And

And her faire vertues in anothers line,
Would faintly dawn, which are made Saints in thine.
Hadft thou beene fhallower, and not writ fo high,
Or left fome new way for our pennes, or eye,
To fhed a funerall teare, perchance thy Tombe   15
Had not beene fpeechleffe, or our Mufes dumbe;
But now wee dare not write, but muft conceale
Thy Epitaph, left we be thought to fteale,
For, who hath read thee, and difcernes thy worth,
That will not fay, thy careleffe houres brought forth   20
Fancies beyond our ftudies, and thy play
Was happier, then our ferious time of day?
So learned was thy chance; thy hafte had wit,
And matter from thy pen flow'd rafhly fit,
What was thy recreation turnes our braine,   25
Our rack and paleneffe, is thy weakeft ftraine.
And when we moft come neere thee, 'tis our bliffe
To imitate thee, where thou doft amiffè.
Here light your mufe, you that do onely thinke,
And write, and are juft Poëts, as you drinke,   30
In whofe weake fancies wit doth ebbe and flow,
Juft as your recknings rife, that wee may know
In your whole carriage of your worke, that here
This flafh you wrote in Wine, and this in Beere,
This is to tap your Mufe, which running long   35
Writes flat, and takes our eare not halfe fo ftrong;
Poore Suburbe wits, who, if you want your cup,
Or if a Lord recover, are blowne up.
Could you but reach this height, you fhould not need
To make, each meale, a project ere you feed,   40
Nor walke in reliques, clothes fo old and bare,
As if left off to you from *Ennius* were,
Nor fhould your love, in verfe, call Miftreffe, thofe,
Who are mine hofteffe, or your whores in profe;
From this Mufe learne to Court, whofe power could move   45
A Cloyftred coldneffe, or a Veftall love,
And would convey fuch errands to their eare,
That Ladies knew no oddes to grant and heare;
But I do wrong thee, *Donne*, and this low praife
Is written onely for thy yonger dayes.   50
I am not growne up, for thy riper parts,
Then fhould I praife thee, through the Tongues, and Arts,
And have that deepe Divinity, to know,
What myfteries did from thy preaching flow,

                                                                        Who

Who with thy words could charme thy audience,   55
That at thy fermons, eare was all our fenfe ;
Yet have I feene thee in the pulpit ftand,
Where wee might take notes, from thy looke, and hand ;
And from thy fpeaking action beare away
More Sermon, then fome teachers ufe to fay.   60
Such was thy carriage, and thy gefture fuch,
As could divide the heart, and confcience touch.
Thy motion did confute, and wee might fee
An errour vanquifh'd by delivery.
Not like our Sonnes of Zeale, who to reforme   65
Their hearers, fiercely at the Pulpit ftorme,
And beate the cufhion into worfe eftate,
Then if they did conclude it reprobate,
Who can out pray the glaffe, then lay about
Till all Predeftination be runne out.   70
And from the point fuch tedious ufes draw,
Their repetitions would make Gofpell, Law.
No, In fuch temper would thy Sermons flow,
So well did Doctrine, and thy language fhow,
And had that holy feare, as, hearing thee,   75
The Court would mend, and a good Chriftian bee.
And Ladies though unhanfome, out of grace,
Would heare thee, in their unbought lookes, and face.
More I could write, but let this crowne thine Urne,
Wee cannot hope the like, till thou returne.   80

Upon Mr J. Donne, *and his* Poems.

WHo dares fay thou art dead, when he doth fee
    (Unburied yet) this living part of thee?
This part that to thy beeing gives frefh flame,
    And though th'art *Donne*, yet will preferve thy name.
Thy flefh (whofe channels left their crimfen hew,   5
    And whey-like ranne at laft in a pale blew)
May fhew thee mortall, a dead palfie may
    Seife on't, and quickly turne it into clay ;
Which like the Indian earth, fhall rife refin'd :
    But this great Spirit thou haft left behinde,   10
This Soule of Verfe (in it's firft pure eftate)
    Shall live, for all the World to imitate,

                                                                 But

But not come neer, for in thy Fancies flight
　Thou doſt not ſtoope unto the vulgar ſight,
But, hovering highly in the aire of Wit,　　　　　　　15
　Hold'ſt ſuch a pitch, that few can follow it;
Admire they may. Each objeƈt that the Spring
　(Or a more piercing influence) doth bring
T'adorne Earths face, thou ſweetly did'ſt contrive
　To beauties elements, and thence derive　　　　　20
Unſpotted Lillies white; which thou did'ſt ſet
　Hand in hand, with the veine-like Violet,
Making them ſoft, and warme, and by thy power,
　Could'ſt give both life, and ſenſe, unto a flower.
The Cheries thou haſt made to ſpeake, will bee　　25
　Sweeter unto the taſte, then from the tree.
And (ſpight of winter ſtormes) amidſt the ſnow
　Thou oft haſt made the bluſhing Roſe to grow.
The Sea-nimphs, that the watry cavernes keepe,
　Have ſent their Pearles and Rubies from the deepe　30
To deck thy love, and plac'd by thee, they drew
　More luſtre to them, then where firſt they grew.
All minerals (that Earths full wombe doth hold
　Promiſcuouſly) thou couldſt convert to gold,
And with thy flaming raptures ſo refine,　　　　　35
　That it was much more pure then in the Mine.
The lights that guild the night, if thou did'ſt ſay,
　They looke like eyes, thoſe did out-ſhine the day;
For there would be more vertue in ſuch ſpells,
　Then in Meridians, or croſſe Parallels:　　　　　40
What ever was of worth in this great Frame,
　That Art could comprehend, or Wit could name,
It was thy theme for Beauty; thou didſt ſee,
　Woman, was this faire Worlds Epitomie.
Thy nimble *Satyres* too, and every ſtraine　　　　45
　(With nervy ſtrength) that iſſued from thy brain,
Will loſe the glory of their owne cleare bayes,
　If they admit of any others praiſe.
But thy diviner Poëms (whoſe cleare fire
　Purges all droſſe away) ſhall by a Quire　　　　　50
Of Cherubims, with heavenly Notes be ſet
　(Where fleſh and blood could ne'r attaine to yet)
There pureſt Spirits ſing ſuch ſacred Layes,
　In Panegyrique Alleluiaes.
　　　　　　　　　　　　Arth. Wilſon.

In memory of Doctor Donne:
By Mr R. B.

Donne dead? 'Tis here reported true, though I
   Ne'r yet fo much defir'd to heare a lye,
'Tis too too true, for fo wee finde it ftill,
Good newes are often falfe, but feldome, ill:
But muft poore fame tell us his fatall day,   5
And fhall we know his death, the common way,
Mee thinkes fome Comet bright fhould have foretold
The death of fuch a man, for though of old
'Tis held, that Comets Princes death foretell,
Why fhould not his, have needed one as well?   10
Who was the Prince of wits, 'mongft whom he reign'd,
High as a Prince, and as great State maintain'd?
Yet wants he not his figne, for wee have feene
A dearth, the like to which hath never beene,
Treading on harvefts heeles, which doth prefage   15
The death of wit and learning, which this age
Shall finde, now he is gone; for though there bee
Much graine in fhew, none brought it forth as he,
Or men are mifers; or if true want raifes
The dearth, then more that dearth *Donnes* plenty praifes. 20
Of learning, languages, of eloquence,
And Poëfie, (paft rauifhing of fenfe,)
He had a magazine, wherein fuch ftore
Was laid up, as might hundreds ferve of poore.
  But he is gone, O how will his defire   25
Torture all thofe that warm'd them by his fire?
Mee thinkes I fee him in the pulpit ftanding,
Not eares, or eyes, but all mens hearts commanding,
Where wee that heard him, to our felves did faine
Golden Chryfoftome was alive againe;   30
And never were we weari'd, till we faw
His houre (and but an houre) to end did draw.
How did he fhame the doctrine-men, and ufe,
With helps to boot, for men to beare th'abufe
Of their tir'd patience, and endure th'expence   35
Of time, O fpent in hearkning to non-fenfe,
With markes alfo, enough whereby to know,
The fpeaker is a zealous dunce, or fo.
'Tis true, they quitted him, to their poore power,
They humm'd againft him; And with face moft fowre 40
Call'd

Call'd him a ftrong lin'd man, a Macaroon,
And no way fit to fpeake to clouted fhoone,
As fine words [truly] as you would defire,
But [verily,] but a bad edifier.
Thus did thefe beetles flight in him that good, 45
They could not fee, and much leffe underftood.
But we may fay, when we compare the ftuffe
Both brought; He was a candle, they the fnuffe.
Well, Wifedome's of her children juftifi'd,
Let therefore thefe poore fellowes ftand afide ; 50
Nor, though of learning he deferv'd fo highly,
Would I his booke fhould fave him ; Rather flily
I fhould advife his Clergie not to pray,
Though of the learn'dft fort ; Me thinkes that they
Of the fame trade, are Judges not fo fit, 55
There's no fuch emulation as of wit.
Of fuch, the Envy might as much perchance
Wrong him, and more, then th'others ignorance.
It was his Fate (I know't) to be envy'd
As much by Clerkes, as lay men magnifi'd ; 60
And why? but 'caufe he came late in the day,
And yet his Penny earn'd, and had as they.
No more of this, leaft fome fhould fay, that I
Am ftrai'd to Satyre, meaning Elegie.
No, no, had DONNE need to be judg'd or try'd, 65
A Jury I would fummon on his fide,
That had no fides, nor factions, paft the touch
Of all exceptions, freed from Paffion, fuch
As nor to feare nor flatter, e'r were bred,
Thefe would I bring, though called from the dead : 70
Southampton, Hambleton, Pembrooke, Dorfets Earles,
Huntingdon, Bedfords Counteffes (the Pearles
Once of each fexe.) If thefe fuffice not, I
Ten *decem tales* have of Standers by :
All which, for DONNE, would fuch a verdict give, 75
As can belong to none, that now doth live.
    But what doe I? A diminution 'tis
To fpeake of him in verfe, fo fhort of his,
Whereof he was the mafter ; All indeed
Compar'd with him, pip'd on an Oaten reed. 80
O that you had but one 'mongft all your brothers
Could write for him, as he hath done for others :
(Poets I fpeake to) When I fee't, I'll fay,
My eye-fight betters, as my yeares decay,

                                              Meane

Meane time a quarrell I fhall ever have   85
Againft thefe doughty keepers from the grave,
Who ufe, it feemes their old Authoritie,
When (Verfes men immortall make) they cry:
Which had it been a Recipe true tri'd,
Probatum effet, DONNE had never dy'd.   90
    For mee, if e'r I had leaft fparke at all
Of that which they Poetique fire doe call,
Here I confeffe it fetched from his hearth,
Which is gone out, now he is gone to earth.
This only a poore flafh, a lightning is   95
Before my Mufes death, as after his.
Farewell (faire foule) and deigne receive from mee
This Type of that devotion I owe thee,
From whom (while living) as by voice and penne
I learned more, then from a thoufand men: 100
So by thy death, am of one doubt releas'd,
And now beleeve that miracles are ceas'd.

Epitaph.

H*Eere lies Deane Donne*; Enough; Thofe words alone
    Shew him as fully, as if all the ftone
His Church of Pauls contains, were through infcrib'd
Or all the walkers there, to fpeake him, brib'd.
None can miftake him, for one fuch as Hee   5
DONNE, Deane, or Man, more none fhall ever fee.
Not man? No, though unto a Sunne each eye
Were turn'd, the whole earth fo to overfpie.
A bold brave word; Yet fuch brave Spirits as knew
His Spirit, will fay, it is leffe bold then true.   10

Epitaph upon Dr. DONNE,

By *Endy: Porter.*

THis decent Urne a fad infcription weares,
   Of *Donnes* departure from us, to the fpheares ;
And the dumbe ftone with filence feemes to tell
The changes of this life, wherein is well
Expreft, A caufe to make all joy to ceafe,   5
And never let our forrowes more take eafe ;
For now it is impoffible to finde
One fraught with vertues, to inrich a minde ;
But why fhould death, with a promifcuous hand
At one rude ftroke impoverifh a land ?   10
Thou ftrict Attorney, unto ftricter Fate,
Didft thou confifcate his life out of hate
To his rare Parts ? Or didft thou throw thy dart,
With envious hand, at fome Plebeyan heart ;
And he with pious vertue ftept betweene   15
To fave that ftroke, and fo was kill'd unfeene
By thee ? O 'twas his goodneffe fo to doe,
Which humane kindneffe never reacht unto.
Thus the hard lawes of death were fatisfi'd,
And he left us like Orphan friends, and di'de.   20
Now from the Pulpit to the peoples eares,
Whofe fpeech fhall fend repentant fighes, and teares ?
Or tell mee, if a purer Virgin die,
Who fhall hereafter write her Elegie ?
Poets be filent, let your numbers fleepe,   25
For he is gone that did all phanfie keepe ;
Time hath no Soule, but his exalted verfe ;
Which with amazements, we may now reherfe.

In

In obitum venerabilis viri *Iohannis Donne,* ſacræ

Theologiæ Doctoris, Eccleſiæ Cathedralis Divi *Pauli,* nu-
per Decani ; Illi honoris, tibi (multum mihi colende
Vir) obſervantiæ ergo Hæc ego.

*C*Onquerar? *ignavoᴙ ſequar tua funera planctu?*
  Sed lachrimæ clauſiſtis iter : nec muta querelas
Lingua poteſt proferre pias: ignoſcite manes
Defuncti, & tacito ſinite indulgere dolori.
  Sed ſcelus eſt tacuiſſe : cadant in mæſta lituræ   5
Verba. Tuis (docta umbra) tuis hæc accipe juſſis
Cæpta, nec officii contemnens pignora noſtri
Averſare tuâ non dignum laude Poëtam.
  O ſi Pythagoræ non vanum dogma fuiſſet:
Inᴙ meum â veſtro migraret pectore pectus   10
Muſa, repentinos tua noſceret urna furores.
Sed fruſtra, heu fruſtra hæc votis puerilibus opto:
Tecum abiit, ſummoᴙ ſedens jam monte Thalia
Ridet anhelantes, Parnaſſi & culmina vates
Deſperare jubet. Verum hâc nolente coactos   15
Scribimus audaces numeros, & flebile carmen
Scribimus (ô ſoli qui te dilexit) habendum.
  Siccine perpetuus liventia lumina ſomnus
Clauſit? & immerito merguntur funere virtus?
Et pietas? & quæ poterant feciſſe beatum,   20
Cætera, ſed nec te poterant ſervare beatum.
  Quo mihi doctrinam? quorſum impalleſcere chartis
Nocturnis juvat? & totidem olfeciſſe lucernas?
Decolor & longos ſtudiis deperdere Soles
Vt prius aggredior, longamque arceſſere famam.   25
Omnia ſed fruſtra: mihi dum cunctiſque minatur
Exitium crudele & inexorabile fatum.
  Nam poſt te ſperare nihil decet: hoc mihi reſtat
Vt moriar, tenues fugiatque obſcurus in auras
Spiritus: ô doctis ſaltem ſi cognitus umbris.   30
Illic te (venerande) iterum, (venerande) videbo.
Et dulces audire ſonôs, & verba diſerti
Oris, & æternas dabitur mihi carpere voces.
Quêis ferus infernæ tacuiſſet Ianitor aulæ
Auditis: Niluſᴙ minus ſtrepuiſſet: Arion   35

In obitum &c. *1635–69, taking the place of the lines by* Tho: Browne.
10 pectore] pectore, *1635*   21 beatum.] beatum *1635*   23 olfeciſſe]
olfeciſſe *1635*   25 prius aggredior, *1635–69:* prius, aggredior, *1719*
arceſſere *Ed:* acceſſere *1635–69*   26–7 mihi dum . . . Exitium *1719:*
mihi, dum . . . Exitium, *1635–39:* mihi dum, . . . Exitium, *1650–69*

Cederet,

Cederet, & fylvas qui poft fe traxerat Orpheus.
Eloquio fic ille viros, fic ille movere
Voce feros potuit: quis enim tam barbarus? aut tam
Facundis nimis infeftus non motus ut illo
Hortante, & blando victus fermone fileret?   40
  Sic oculos, fic ille manus, fic ora ferebat,
Singula fic decuere fenem, fic omnia. Vidi,
Audivi & ftupui quoties orator in Æde
Paulina ftetit, & mira gravitate levantes
Corda, oculos�q̃ viros tenuit: dum Neftoris ille   45
Fudit verba (omni quanto mage dulcia melle?)
Nunc habet attonitos, pandit myfteria plebi
Non conceffa prius nondum intellecta: revolvunt
Mirantes, tacitique arrectis auribus aftant.
  Mutatis mox ille modo, forma�q̃ loquendi   50
Triftia pertractat: fatum�q̃ & flebile mortis
Tempus, & in cineres redeunt quod corpora primos.
Tunc gemitum cunctos dare, tunc lugere videres,
Forfitan à lachrymis aliquis non temperat, atque
Ex oculis largum ftillat rorem; ætheris illo   55
Sic pater audito voluit fuccumbere turbam,
Affectuf�q̃ ciere fuos, & ponere notæ
Vocis ad arbitrium, divinæ oracula mentis
Dum narrat, roftrifque potens dominatur in altis.
  Quo feror? audaci & forfan pietate nocenti   60
In nimia ignofcas vati, qui vatibus olim
Egregium decus, et tanto excellentior unus
Omnibus; inferior quanto eft, et peffimus, impar
Laudibus hifce, tibi qui nunc facit ifta Poëta.
Et quo nos canimus? cur hæc tibi facra? Poëtæ   65
Definite: en fati certus, fibi voce canorâ
Inferias præmifit olor, cum Carolus Albâ
(Vltima volventem et Cycnæâ voce loquentem)
Nuper eum, turba & magnatum audiret in Aulâ.
  Tunc Rex, tunc Proceres, Clerus, tunc aftitit illi   70
Aula frequens. Solâ nunc in tellure recumbit,
Vermibus efca, pio malint nifi parcere: quidni
Incipiant & amare famem? Metuere Leones
Sic olim, facrofque artus violare Prophetæ
Bellua non aufa eft quàmquam jejuna, fitim�q̃   75
Optaret nimis humano fatiare cruore.
  At non hæc de te fperabimus; omnia carpit
Prædator vermis: nec talis contigit illi
Præda diu; forfan metrico pede ferpet ab inde:

38 Voce feros] Voceferos *1635, 1669*   79 inde:] inde *1635-39*
                                                                    Vefcere,

Vefcere, & exhaufto fatia te fanguine. Iam nos   80
Adfumus ; et poft te cupiet quis vivere ? Poft te
Quis volet, aut poterit ? nam poft te vivere mors eft.
  Et tamen ingratas ignavi ducimus auras:
Suftinet & tibi lingua vale, vale dicere : parce
Non feftinanti æternum requiefcere turbæ.   85
Ipfa fatis properat quæ nefcit Parca morari,
Nunc urgere colum, trahere atǵ occare videmus.
Quin rurfus (Venerande) Vale, vale : ordine nos te
Quo Deus, & quo dura volet natura fequemur.
  Depofitum interea lapides fervate fideles.   90
Fælices illâ quêis Ædis parte locari
Quâ jacet ifte datur. Forfan lapis inde loquetur,
Parturietǵ viro plenus teftantia luêtus
Verba: & carminibus quæ Donni *fuggeret illi*
Spiritus, infolitos teftari voce calores   95
Incipiet: (non fic Pyrrhâ jaêtante calebat.)
  Mole fub hâc tegitur quicquid mortale reliêtum eft
De tanto mortale viro. Qui præfuit Ædi huic,
Formofi pecoris paftor, formofior ipfe.
Ite igitur, dignifǵ illum celebrate loquelis,   100
Et quæ demuntur vitæ date tempora famæ.

Indignus tantorum meritorum Præco, virtutum
tuarum cultor religiofiffimus,

DANIEL DARNELLY.

Elegie *on* D. D.

NOw, by one yeare, time and our frailtie have
  Leffened our firft confufion, fince the Grave
Clos'd thy deare Afhes, and the teares which flow
In thefe, have no fprings, but of folid woe :
Or they are drops, which cold amazement froze   5
At thy deceafe, and will not thaw in Profe :
All ftreames of Verfe which fhall lament that day,
Doe truly to the Ocean tribute pay ;
But they have loft their faltneffe, which the eye
In recompence of wit, ftrives to supply :   10

86 Parca] parca *1635–69* morari,] morari *1635*   88 rurfus *1719:* rufus
1635: nufus *1639–69*   96 Incipiet : . . calebat. *1719: no stops, 1635–69*
  Elegie on D. D. *1635–69: it follows Walton's elegy.*

Paffions

Paffions exceffe for thee wee need not feare,
Since firft by thee our paffions hallowed were ;
Thou mad'ft our forrowes, which before had bin
Onely for the Succeffe, forrowes for finne,
We owe thee all thofe teares, now thou art dead,   15
Which we fhed not, which for our felves we fhed.
Nor didft thou onely confecrate our teares,
Give a religious tincture to our feares ;
But even our joyes had learn'd an innocence,
Thou didft from gladneffe feparate offence :   20
All mindes at once fuckt grace from thee, as where
(The curfe revok'd) the Nations had one eare.
Pious diffector : thy one houre did treate
The thoufand mazes of the hearts deceipt ;
Thou didft purfue our lov'd and fubtill finne,   25
Through all the foldings wee had wrapt it in,
And in thine owne large minde finding the way
By which our felves we from our felves convey,
Didft in us, narrow models, know the fame
Angles, though darker, in our meaner frame.   30
How fhort of praife is this? My Mufe, alas,
Climbes weakly to that truth which none can paffe,
Hee that writes beft, may onely hope to leave
A Character of all he could conceive
But none of thee, and with mee muft confeffe,   35
That fanfie findes fome checke, from an exceffe
Of merit moft, of nothing, it hath fpun,
And truth, as reafons task and theame, doth fhunne.
She makes a fairer flight in emptineffe,
Than when a bodied truth doth her oppreffe.   40
Reafon againe denies her fcales, becaufe
Hers are but fcales, fhee judges by the lawes
Of weake comparifon, thy vertue fleights
Her feeble Beame, and her unequall Weights.
What prodigie of wit and pietie   45
Hath fhe elfe knowne, by which to meafure thee?
Great foule : we can no more the worthineffe
Of what you were, then what you are, expreffe.

Sidney Godolphin.

On Dr John Donne, *late Deane of S.* Paules, *London.*

LOng ſince this taske of teares from you was due,
Long ſince, ô Poëts, he did die to you,
Or left you dead, when wit and he tooke flight
On divine wings, and ſoard out of your ſight.
Preachers, 'tis you muſt weep ; The wit he taught   5
You doe enjoy ; the Rebels which he brought
From ancient diſcord, Giants faculties,
And now no more religions enemies ;
Honeſt to knowing, unto vertuous ſweet,
Witty to good, and learned to diſcreet,   10
He reconcil'd, and bid the Vſurper goe ;
Dulneſſe to vice, religion ought to flow ;
He kept his loves, but not his objeĉts ; wit
Hee did not baniſh, but tranſplanted it,
Taught it his place and uſe, and brought it home   15
To Pietie, which it doth beſt become ;
He ſhew'd us how for ſinnes we ought to ſigh,
And how to ſing Chriſts Epithalamy :
The Altars had his fires, and there hee ſpoke
Incenſe of loves, and fanſies holy ſmoake :   20
Religion thus enrich'd, the people train'd,
And God from dull vice had the faſhion gain'd.
The firſt effeĉts ſprung in the giddy minde
Of flaſhy youth, and thirſt of woman-kinde,
By colours lead, and drawne to a purſuit,   25
Now once againe by beautie of the fruit,
As if their longings too muſt ſet us free,
And tempt us now to the commanded tree.
Tell me, had ever pleaſure ſuch a dreſſe,
Have you knowne crimes ſo ſhap'd? or lovelineſſe   30
Such as his lips did cloth religion in?
Had not reproofe a beauty paſſing ſinne?
Corrupted nature ſorrow'd when ſhe ſtood
So neare the danger of becomming good,
And wiſh'd our ſo inconſtant eares exempt   35
From piety that had ſuch power to tempt :
Did not his ſacred flattery beguile
Man to amendment? The law, taught to ſmile,

On Dr John Donne *&c. 1635–69, where it follows Godolphin's* Elegie
                                                    Penſion'd

Penfion'd our vanitie, and man grew well
Through the fame frailtie by which he fell.   40
O the fick ftate of man, health does not pleafe
Our tafts, but in the fhape of the difeafe.
Thriftleffe is charitie, coward patience,
Iuftice is cruell, mercy want of fenfe.
What meanes our Nature to barre vertue place,   45
If fhee doe come in her owne cloathes and face?
Is good a pill, we dare not chaw to know?
Senfe the foules fervant, doth it keep us fo
As we might ftarve for good, unleffe it firft
Doe leave a pawne of relifh in the guft?   50
Or have we to falvation no tie
At all, but that of our infirmitie?
Who treats with us muft our affections move
To th' good we flie by thofe fweets which we love,
Muft feeke our palats, and with their delight   55
To gaine our deeds, muft bribe our appetite.
Thefe traines he knew, and laying nets to fave,
Temptingly fugred all the health hee gave.
But, where is now that chime? that harmony
Hath left the world, now the loud organ may   60
Appeare, the better voyce is fled to have
A thoufand times the fweetneffe which it gave.
I cannot fay how many thoufand fpirits
The fingle happineffe this foule inherits,
Damnes in the other world, foules whom no croffe   65
O'th fenfe afflicts, but onely of the loffe,
Whom ignorance would halfe fave, all whofe paine
Is not in what they feele, but others gaine,
Selfe executing wretched fpirits, who
Carrying their guilt, tranfport their envy too: 70
But thofe high joyes which his wits youngeft flame
Would hurt to chufe, fhall not we hurt to name?
Verfe ftatues are all robbers, all we make
Of monument, thus doth not give but take
As Sailes which Seamen to a forewinde fit,   75
By a refiftance, goe along with it,
So pens grow while they leffen fame fo left;
A weake affiftance is a kinde of theft.
Who hath not love to ground his teares upon,
Muft weep here if he have ambition.
                              I. Chudleigh.

FINIS.

APPENDIX A.
LATIN POEMS AND TRANSLATIONS

DE LIBRO CVM MVTV-
aretur Impreſſo; Domi à pueris fru-
ſtatim lacerato; et poſt reddito
Manuſcripto.
Doctiſſimo Amiciſſimoque v.
D. D. Andrews.

P Arturiunt madido quae nixu praela, recepta,
    Sed quae ſcripta manu, ſunt veneranda magis.
Qui liber in pluteos, blattis cinerique reliĉtos,
    Si modo ſit praeli ſanguine tinĉtus, abit;
Accedat calamo ſcriptus, reverenter habetur,   5
    Involat et veterum ſcrinia ſumma Patrum.
Dicat Apollo modum; Pueros infundere libro
    Nempe vetuſtatem canitiemque novo.
Nil mirum, medico pueros de ſemine natos,
    Haec nova fata libro poſſe dediſſe novo.   10
Si veterem faciunt pueri, qui nuperus, Annon
    Ipſe Pater Iuvenem me dabit arte ſenem?
Hei miſeris ſenibus! nos vertit dura ſeneĉtus
    Omnes in pueros, neminem at in Iuvenem.
Hoc tibi ſervaſti praeſtandum, Antique Dierum,   15
    Quo viſo, et vivit, et juveneſcit Adam.
Interea, infirmae fallamus taedia vitae,
    Libris, et Coelorum aemulâ amicitiâ.
Hos inter, qui a te mihi redditus iſte libellus,
    Non mihi tam charus, tam meus, ante fuit.   20

⟨Epigramma⟩

Tranſiit in Sequanam Moenus; Viĉtoris in aedes;
    Et Francofurtum, te revehente, meat.

DE LIBRO &c. *1635–69 among certain prose letters in Latin and
English*   *Title*:—mutuaretur Impreſſo;] mutuaretur, Impreſſo, *1635–69*
fruſtatim] fruſtratim *1635–69*   lacerato;] lacer.ito, *1635–69*   2 manu,
ſunt] manu ſunt, *1635–69*   4 abit;] abit, *1635–69*
  ⟨Epigramma⟩ *Ed: in old edd. these lines are 3 and 4 of above poem. See
note*   1 aedes;] aedes, *1635–69*

Amiciſſimo

Amiciffimo, & meritiffimo B E N. J O N S O N. In Vulponem.

Q*Vod arte aufus es hic tuâ, Poeta,*
Q *Si auderent hominum Deique juris*
Confulti, veteres fequi aemularierque,
O omnes faperemus ad falutem.
His fed funt veteres araneofi ;   5
Tam nemo veterum eft fequutor, ut tu
Illos quod fequeris novator audis.
Fac tamen quod agis ; tuique primâ
Libri canitie induantur horâ :
Nam chartis pueritia eft neganda,   10
Nafcanturque fenes, oportet, illi
Libri, queis dare vis perennitatem.
Prifcis, ingenium facit, laborque
Te parem ; hos fuperes, ut et futuros,
Ex noftrâ vitiofitate fumas,   15
Quâ prifcos fuperamus, et futuros.

To Mr *George Herbert*, with one of my Seal(s), of the Anchor and Chrift.

Q*Vi prius affuetus Serpentum fafce Tabellas*
Q *Signare, (haec noftrae fymbola parva Domus)*
Adfcitus domui Domini, patrioque relicto
  Stemmate, nancifcor ftemmata jure nova.
Hinc mihi Crux primo quae fronti impreffa lavacro,   5
  Finibus extenfis, anchora facta patet.

Amiciffimo &c. *in sheets added 1650 : prefixed originally to Quarto*
edition of Jonson's Volpone. 1607, *later to Folio edition of* The Workes of
Beniamin Jonfon. 1616., *when* In Vulponem *was added : in both signed* I. D.
11 Nafcanturque *1607 :* Nafcunturque *1616, 1650–69*
    To Mr George Herbert &c. *1650–69, in sheets added 1650 : two and*
a half lines in Walton's Life of Donne (1658) : *for Herbert's reply see note*
Title :—fent him with one *Walton* (1670) Seal, *1650–69 :* Seales *Walton*
1 fafce] falce *Walton*   5 fronti] fronte *1650–69*

Anchorae

Anchorae in effigiem Crux tandem definit ipfam,
  Anchora fit tandem Crux tolerata diu.
Hoc tamen ut fiat, Chrifto vegetatur ab ipfo
  Crux, et ab Affixo, eft Anchora faĉta, Iefu.   10
Nec Natalitiis penitus ferpentibus orbor,
  Non ita dat Deus, ut auferat ante data.
Quâ fapiens, Dos eft ; Quâ terram lambit et ambit,
  Peftis ; At in noftra fit Medicina Cruce,
Serpens ; fixa Cruci fi fit Natura ; Crucique   15
  A fixo, nobis, Gratia tota fluat.
Omnia cum Crux fint, Crux Anchora faĉta, figillum
  Non tam dicendum hoc quam Catechifmus erit.
Mitto nec exigua, exiguâ fub imagine, dona,
  Pignora amicitiae, et munera ; Vota, preces.   20
Plura tibi accumulet, fanĉtus cognominis, Ille
  Regia qui flavo Dona figillat Equo.

A Sheafe of Snakes ufed heretofore to be
   My Seal, The Creft of our poore Family.
Adopted in Gods Family, and fo
Our old Coat loft, unto new armes I go.
The Croffe (my feal at Baptifm) fpred below,   5
Does, by that form, into an Anchor grow.
Croffes grow Anchors; Bear, as thou fhouldft do
Thy Croffe, and that Croffe grows an Anchor too.
But he that makes our Croffes Anchors thus,
Is Chrift, who there is crucifi'd for us.   10
Yet may I, with this, my firft Serpents hold,
God gives new bleffings, and yet leaves the old ;
The Serpent, may, as wife, my pattern be ;
My poifon, as he feeds on duft, that's me.

17 *facta,*] *fixa, 1650–69*   19 Mitto] *Mitto, 1650–69*
A fheafe &c.] *1650–69 and in Walton's Life of Donne (1658), in all
of which and in all subsequent editions except Grolier the first two lines are
printed as a title, Walton bracketing them :*—
        A fheafe of Snakes ufed heretofore to be
          my Seal, The Creft of our poore Family.
4 Our . . . unto] My . . . into *Walton*   5 at] in *Walton*   11 with
this I may *Walton*

And as he rounds the Earth to murder fure,   15
My death he is, but on the Croffe, my cure.
Crucifie nature then, and then implore
All Grace from him, crucified there before;
When all is Croffe, and that Croffe Anchor grown,
This Seal's a Catechifm, not a Seal alone.   20
Under that little Seal great gifts I fend,
⟨Wifhes,⟩ and prayers, pawns, and fruits of a friend.
And may that Saint which rides in our great Seal,
To you, who bear his name, great bounties deal.

Tranflated out of *Gazæus*, *Vota Amico*
facta. fol. 160.

God grant thee thine own wifh, and grant thee mine,
Thou, who doft, beft friend, in beft things outfhine;
May thy foul, ever chearfull, nere know cares,
Nor thy life, ever lively, know gray haires.
Nor thy hand, ever open, know bafe holds,   5
Nor thy purfe, ever plump, know pleits, or folds.
Nor thy tongue, ever true, know a falfe thing,
Nor thy word, ever mild, know quarrelling.
Nor thy works, ever equall, know difguife,
Nor thy fame, ever pure, know contumelies.   10
Nor thy prayers, know low objects, ftill Divine;
God grant thee thine own wifh, and grant thee mine.

15 to murder fure,] to murder, fure *Walton*   16 He is my death ;
Walton   22 Wifhes, *Ed:* Works, *1650–69:* Both works *Walton:* Lat.
vota   23–4   Oh may that Saint that rides on our great Seal,
               To you that bear his name large bounty deal. *Walton.*
  Translated *&c.*] *1650–69, in sheets added 1650 : for original see note*

APPENDIX B.

POEMS WHICH HAVE BEEN ATTRIBUTED TO JOHN DONNE IN THE OLD EDITIONS AND THE PRINCIPAL MS. COLLECTIONS, ARRANGED ACCORDING TO THEIR PROBABLE AUTHORS.

I.

POEMS

PROBABLY BY SIR JOHN ROE, KNT.

To Sr Nicholas Smyth.

SLeep, next Society and true friendſhip,
Mans beſt contentment, doth ſecurely ſlip
His paſſions and the worlds troubles. Rock me
O ſleep, wean'd from my dear friends company,
In a cradle free from dreams or thoughts, there   5
Where poor men ly, for Kings aſleep do fear.
Here ſleeps Houſe by famous Arioſto,
By ſilver-tongu'd Ovid, and many moe,
Perhaps by golden-mouth'd Spencer too pardie,
(Which builded was ſome dozen Stories high)   10
I had repair'd, but that it was ſo rotten,
As ſleep awak'd by Ratts from thence was gotten:
And I will build no new, for by my Will,
Thy fathers houſe ſhall be the faireſt ſtill

To Sr Nicholas Smyth. *Ed:* Satyra Sexta. To S^r *&c. S,:* Satires to S^r
Nic: Smith. 1602 *B:* A Satire,: to Sr Nicholas Smith. 1602, *L74:* A
Satyricall Letter to Sr Nich: Smith. Quere, if Donnes or S^r Th: Rowes.
O'F: no title *N,TCD(JR in margin):* Satyre VI. *1669 (on which the
present text is based)*   1 Sleep, next] Sleep next, *1669*   2 ſlip
1669,S: skipp *B,L74,N,O'F,TCD. In 1669 full stops after* ſlip *and*
rock me *and no stop after* troubles   3 Rock] rock *1669*   4 my
MSS.: thy *1669*   6 aſleep] all ſleap *B*   9 golden-mouth'd] gold-
mouth'd *B,S*   14 ſtill] ſtill. *1669*

In

In Excefter. Yet, methinks, for all their Wit,   15
Thofe wits that fay nothing, beft defcribe it.
Without it there is no Senfe, only in this
Sleep is unlike a long Parenthefis.
Not to fave charges, but would I had flept
The time I fpent in London, when I kept   20
Fighting and untruft gallants Company,
In which Natta, the new Knight, feized on me,
And offered me the experience he had bought
With great Expence. I found him throughly taught
In curing Burnes. His thing hath had more fcars   25
Then Things himfelfe; like Epps it often wars,
And ftill is hurt. For his Body and State
The Phyfick and Counfel which came too late,
'Gainft Whores and Dice, hee nowe on mee beftowes
Moft fuperficially: hee fpeaks of thofe   30
(I found by him) leaft foundly who moft knows:
He fwears well, fpeakes ill, but beft of Clothes,
What fits Summer, what Winter, what the Spring.
He had Living, but now thefe waies come in
His whole Revenues. Where each Whore now dwells, 35
And hath dwelt, fince his fathers death, he tells.
Yea he tells moft cunningly each hid caufe
Why Whores forfake their Bawds. To thefe fome Laws
He knows of the Duello, and touch his Skill
The leaft Iot in that or thofe he quarrell will,   40
Though fober; but fo never fought. I know

---

   25 hath had *L74,N,O'F,S,TCD*: had had *1669*: had *B*   26
Things *B,L74,N,O'F,S,TCD*: T   *1669*   28–31 *text from B,L74,*
N,O'F,S,TCD, which bracket which . . . late: *see note:*
           The Phyfick and Councel (which came too late
           'Gainft Whores and Dice) he now on me beftows:
           Moft fuperficially he fpeaks of thofe.
           I found, by him, leaft found him who moft knows. *1669*
33 what Winter] what What Winter *1669*   35 each *B,L74,N,O'F,S,*
TCD: his *1669*   37 cunningly *1669,L74,N,TCD*: perfectly *B,*
O'F,S   39 Duello, *B,N,O'F,S,TCD*: Duel, *1669*   touch *B,L74,*
O'F,S: on *1669*: only *N,TCD*   40 thofe *B,L74,O'F*: thefe *1669*
41 but fo never fought. *B,L74,O'F,S* (foe as), *TCD* (nere): but nere
                                   What

What made his Valour, undubb'd, Windmill go,
Within a Pint at moſt: yet for all this
(Which is moſt ſtrange) Natta thinks no man is
More honeſt than himſelf. Thus men may want   45
Conſcience, whilſt being brought up ignorant,
They uſe themſelves to vice. And beſides thoſe
Illiberal Arts forenam'd, no Vicar knows,
Nor other Captain leſs then he; His Schools
Are Ordinaries, where civil men ſeem fools,   50
Or are for being there; His beſt bookes, Plaies,
Where, meeting godly Scenes, perhaps he praies.
His firſt ſet prayer was for his father, ill
And ſick, that he might dye: That had, until
The Lands were gone, he troubled God no more: 55
And then ask'd him but his Right, That the whore
Whom he had kept, might now keep him: She ſpent,
They left each other on even terms; ſhe went
To Bridewel, he unto the Wars, where want
Hath made him valiant, and a Lieutenant   60
He is become: Where, as they paſs apace,
He ſteps aſide, and for his Captains place
He praies again: Tells God, he will confeſs
His ſins, ſwear, drink, dice and whore thenceforth leſs,
On this Condition, that his Captain dye   65
And he ſucceed; But his Prayer did not; They
Both caſhir'd came home, and he is braver now
Than'his captain: all men wonder, few know how.
Can he rob? No. Cheat? No. Or doth he ſpend
His own? No. Fidus, he is thy dear friend,   70
That keeps him up. I would thou wert thine own,
Or thou'hadſt as good a friend as thou art one.

fought. *1669*   42 Valour, undubb'd, Windmill go, *Ed:* Valour undubd
Windmill go. *1669:* valours undubb'd Wine-mill go. *L74, N, TCD:* his
undouted valour windmill goe. *B:* his undaunted valour windmill goe.
O'F, S   45 want] vaunt *S*   47 beſides] except *B, O'F, S*   49
he; *Ed:* he, *1669*   53 father, ill] fathers ill, *1669*   65 his] if his
1669   66 ſucceed; *Ed:* ſucceed, *1669*   They *Ed:* they *1669*
68 Than'his *Ed:* Than his *1669:* Then's *N, TCD*   how. *Ed:* how,
1669   69 Or *Ed:* or *1669*   72 thou'hadſt *L74, N, TCD:* thou
hadſt *1669*

No

No prefent Want nor future hope made me,
Defire (as once I did) thy friend to be:
But he had cruelly poffeft thee then, 75
And as our Neighbours the Low-Country men,
Being (whilft they were Loyal, with Tyranny
Oppreft) broke loofe, have fince refus'd to be
Subjeċt to good Kings, I found even fo,
Wer't thou well rid of him, thou't have no moe. 80
Could'ft thou but chufe as well as love, to none
Thou fhould'ft be fecond: Turtle and Damon
Should give thee place in fongs, and Lovers fick
Should make thee only Loves Hieroglyphick:
Thy Imprefs fhould be the loving Elm and Vine, 85
Where now an ancient Oak, with Ivy twine
Deftroy'd, thy Symbol is. O dire Mifchance!
And, O vile verfe! And yet your Abraham France
Writes thus, and jefts not. Good Fidus for this
Muft pardon me, Satyres bite when they kifs. 90
But as for Natta, we have fince faln out:
Here on his knees he pray'd, elfe we had fought.
And becaufe God would not he fhould be winner,
Nor yet would have the Death of fuch a finner,
At his feeking, our Quarrel is deferr'd, 95
I'll leave him at his Prayers, and (as I heard)
His laft; Fidus, and you, and I do know,
I was his friend, and durft have been his foe,
And would be either yet; But he dares be
Neither; Sleep blots him out and takes in thee. 100
"The mind, you know is like a Table-book,
"Which, th'old unwipt, new writing never took.

81 love, *Ed:* love *1669*   82 Damon] damon *1669*   83 thee]
the *1669*   86–7 Oak, with Ivy twine Deftroy'd, thy Symbol is.
L74,N,TCD: Oak with Ivy twine, Deftroy'd thy Symbole is. *1669:* Oak
with ivy twine. Destroy'd thy symbol is! *Chambers*   87 Mifchance!]
Mifchance? *1669*   88 your *B,L74,N,S,TCD:* our *1669*   92
knees] knees, *1669*   97 Fidus, and you, and I *N,TCD:* and Fidus,
you and I *1669:* Fidus, and you, and he *B,L74,O'F,S*   100 Neither;
L74,N,O'F,S,TCD: Neither yet. *1669*   Sleep] fleep *1669*   102
Which, th'old unwipt, *B,O'F,S,TCD:* "The old unwipt *1669*

Hear

Hear how the Huifhers Checques, Cupbord and Fire
I paff'd; by which Degrees young men afpire
In Court; And how that idle and fhe-ftate,   105
Whenas my judgment cleer'd, my foul did hate;
How I found there (if that my trifling Pen
Durft take fo hard a Task) Kings were but men,
And by their Place more noted, if they erre;
How they and their Lords unworthy men prefer;   110
And, as unthrifts had rather give away
Great Summs to flatterers, than fmall debts pay,
So they their weaknefs hide, and greatnefs fhow,
By giving them that which to worth they owe:
What Treafon is, and what did Effex kill,   115
Not true Treafon, but Treafon handled ill;
And which of them ftood for their Countries good,
Or what might be the Caufe of fo much Blood.
He faid fhe ftunck, and men might not have faid
That fhe was old before that fhe was dead.   120
His Cafe was hard, to do or fuffer; loth
To do, he made it harder, and did both.
Too much preparing loft them all their Lives,
Like fome in Plagues kill'd with prefervatives.
Friends, like land-fouldiers in a ftorm at Sea,   125
Not knowing what to do, for him did pray.
They told it all the world; where was their wit?
Cuffs putting on a fword, might have told it.
And Princes muft fear Favorites more then Foes,
For ftill beyond Revenge Ambition goes.   130
How fince Her death, with Sumpter-horfe that Scot
Hath rid, who, at his coming up, had not
A Sumpter-dog. But till that I can write
Things worth thy Tenth reading (dear Nick) goodnight.

104–6 *1669 has colon after* paff'd, *brackets by* which . . . Court *and*
Whenas . . . cleer'd, *and places comma after* hate   107 there (if that *1669:*
then that (if *B, O'F, S*   111 And, as unthrifts *Ed:* And, as unthrifts,
1669, Chambers   112 pay, *Ed:* pay; *1669:* pay. *Chambers*   113
weaknefs *B, L74, O'F, S:* greatnefs *1669, N, TCD*   116 ill; *Ed:* ill:
1669   118 Blood. *Ed:* Blood; *1669*   121 hard, *Ed:* hard *1669*
122 both. *Ed:* both *1669*   127 world; *Ed:* world, *1669*   132
Hath rid,] Doth ryde, *B*   133 till that *1669:* till *N, TCD:* untill
B, OF, S

Satyre.

Satyre.

MEn write that love and reafon difagree,
But I ne'r faw't expreft as 'tis in thee.
Well, I may lead thee, God muft make thee fee,
But, thine eyes blinde too, there's no hope for thee.
Thou fay'ft fhee's wife and witty, faire and free,   5
All thefe are reafons why fhe fhould fcorne thee.
Thou doft proteft thy love, and wouldft it fhew
By matching her as fhe would match her foe:
And wouldft perfwade her to a worfe offence,
Then that whereof thou didft accufe her wench.   10
Reafon there's none for thee, but thou may'ft vexe
Her with example. Say, for feare her fexe
Shunne her, fhe needs muft change; I doe not fee
How reafon e'r can bring that *muft* to thee.
Thou art a match a Iuftice to rejoyce,   15
Fit to be his, and not his daughters choyce.
Urg'd with his threats fhee'd fcarcely ftay with thee,
And wouldft th'have this to chufe thee, being free?
Goe then and punifh fome foone-gotten ftuffe,
For her dead husband this hath mourn'd enough,   20
In hating thee. Thou maift one like this meet;
For fpight take her, prove kinde, make thy breath fweet,
Let her fee fhe hath caufe, and to bring to thee
Honeft children, let her difhoneft bee.
If fhee be a widow, I'll warrant her   25
Shee'll thee before her firft hufband preferre,
And will wifh thou hadft had her maidenhead;
Shee'll love thee fo, for then thou hadft bin dead.

Satyre. *B,O'F:* A Satire: upon one who was his Rivall in a widdowes
Love. *A10:* Satyre VI. *1635–54:* Satyre. VII. *1669 (where* Satyre VI. *is*
Sleep, next Society *&c.*)   4 thine eyes *1635–69:* thy eye's *A10*
11 thee,] the, *1669*   13 fhe needs muft change; I *1635–69:* fhe muft
change, yet I *A10*   16 and *1635–69:* but *B*   17 Urg'd *A10,B,O'F:*
Dry'd *1635–69*   19 fome] *1635 duplicates*   22 fweet, *1639–69:*
fweet. *1635*   27 maidenhead; *Ed:* maidenhead, *1635–69*   28 (Shee'll
love thee fo) for, *1635–69*

But

But thou fuch ftrong love, and weake reafons haft,
Thou muft thrive there, or ever live difgrac'd. 30
Yet paufe a while; and thou maift live to fee
A time to come, wherein fhe may beg thee;
If thou'lt not paufe nor change, fhe'll beg thee now.
Doe what fhe can, love for nothing fhee'll allow.
Befides, her⟨s⟩ were too much gaine and merchandife, 35
And when thou art rewarded, defert dies.
Now thou haft odds of him fhe loves, he may doubt
Her conftancy, but none can put thee out.
Againe, be thy love true, fhee'll prove divine,
And in the end the good on't will be thine: 40
For thou muft never think on other love,
And fo wilt advance her as high above
Vertue as caufe above effect can bee:
'Tis vertue to be chaft, which fhee'll make thee.

AN ELEGIE.

Reflecting on his paffion for his miftriffe.

COme, Fates; I feare you not. All whom I owe
Are paid, but you. Then reft me ere I goe.
But, Chance from you all foveraignty hath got,
Love woundeth none but thofe whom death dares not;

29 ftrong] firm *A10*   32 thee; *Grosart:* thee. *1635–69*   33 now.
Grosart: now, *1635–69*   34 love for nothing fhee'll *1635–69:* fhe'le love
for nought *A10*   35 Befides, hers *Ed:* Befides, here *1635–69:* But
hers *A10:* Befides her *O'F*   38–9 out. Againe, *1635–69:* out Againe ;
A10   40 And in *1635–69:* And yet in *A10*   thine: *Ed:* thine.
1635–69   41 For thou muft never think on *H-K* (*Grosart*): And thou
muft never think on, *A10:* For though thou muft ne'r thinke of *1635–69*
42 And fo wilt advance her *1635–69:* For that will her advance *A10*
43 bee: *Ed:* bee, *1635–69*
    An Elegie. Reflecting on *&c. A10:* An Elegie. *H39, H40, L74,
RP31:* Eleg. XIII. *1635–69: no title, Cy:* Elegie. *P*

Elfe,

Elſe, if you were, and juſt, in equitie   5
I ſhould have vanquiſh'd her, as you did me.
Elſe Lovers ſhould not brave death's pains, and live,
But 'tis a rule, *Death comes not to relieve.*
Or, pale and wan deaths terrours, are they lay'd
So deepe in Lovers, they make death afraid?   10
Or (the leaſt comfort) have I company?
Orecame ſhe Fates, Love, Death, as well as mee?
    Yes, Fates doe ſilke unto her diſtaffe pay,
For their ranſome, which taxe on us they laye.
Love gives her youth, which is the reaſon why   15
Youths, for her ſake, ſome wither and ſome die.
Poore Death can nothing give; yet, for her ſake,
Still in her turne, he doth a Lover take:
And if Death ſhould prove falſe, ſhe feares him not;
Our Muſes, to redeeme her ſhe hath got.   20
That fatall night wee laſt kiſs'd, I thus pray'd,
Or rather, thus deſpair'd; I ſhould have ſaid:
Kiſſes, and yet deſpaire? The forbid tree
Did promiſe (and deceive) no more then ſhee.
Like Lambs that ſee their teats, and muſt eat Hay,   25
A food, whoſe taſt hath made me pine away.
Dives, when thou ſaw'ſt bliſſe, and crav'dſt to touch
A drop of water, thy great paines were ſuch.
Here griefe wants a freſh wit, for mine being ſpent,
And my ſighes weary, groanes are all my rent;   30

    5 Elſe, if you were, and juſt, in equitie *H39:* Elſe, if you were, and juſt in equitie, *1635–54, Grosart:* True, if you were, and juſt in equitie, *1669, Chambers* (True)   12 Orecame ſhe Fates, Love, Death, *MSS.:* Or can the Fates love death, *1635–69*   13 diſtaffe *1635–69, H39, L74:* diſtaves *A10, H40, RP31*   14 For their . . . on us they laye. *Cy, H39, H40, L74, P:* For ranſome, which taxe they on us doe lay. *1635–69:* For Ranſome, but a taxe on us they lay: *A10*   17–19 Death] death *1635–69*   18 take: *H40, L74:* take. *1635–69*   21 That fatall night we laſt kiſs'd *1635–69:* That laſt fatall night wee kiſs'd *A10, H39, H40, L74, P, RP31*   22 *in brackets 1635–69*   ſaid: *Ed:* ſaid, *1635–69*   23 deſpaire? *Ed:* deſpaire. *1635–69*   24 ſhee.] yee. *A10, H40*   28 A drop of water, thy greate *1635–69:* A ſmall little drop, thy *Cy, H39* (then thy), *H40, L74, P:* The pooreſt little drop, thy *A10*

Vnable

Vnable longer to indure the paine,
They breake like thunder, and doe bring down rain.
Thus, till dry teares foulder mine eyes, I weepe;
And then, I dreame, how you fecurely fleepe,
And in your dreames doe laugh at me. I hate, 35
And pray Love, All may: He pitties my ftate,
But fayes, I therein no revenge fhould finde;
The Sunne would fhine, though all the world were blind.
Yet, to trie my hate, Love fhew'd me your teare;
And I had dy'd, had not your fmile beene there. 40
Your frowne undoes me; your fmile is my wealth;
And as you pleafe to looke, I have my health.
Me thought, Love pittying me, when he faw this,
Gave me your hands, the backs and palmes to kiffe.
That cur'd me not, but to beare paine gave ftrength, 45
And what it loft in force, it tooke in length.
I call'd on Love againe, who fear'd you fo,
That his compaffion ftill prov'd greater woe;
For, then I dream'd I was in bed with you,
But durft not feele, for feare't fhould not prove true. 50
This merits not your anger, had it beene,
The Queene of Chaftitie was naked feene;
And in bed, not to feele, the paine I tooke,
Was more then for *Aĉtæon* not to looke.
And that breft which lay ope, I did not know, 55
But for the clearneffe, from a lump of fnowe,
Nor that fweet teat which on the top it bore
From the rofe-bud, which for my fake you wore.
Thefe griefs to iffue forth, by verfe, I prove,
Or turne their courfe, by travaile, or new love: 60

33 dry] dry'd *H39, H40, L74, RP31* 36 Love, *Ed:* Love *1635–69:*
Love: *A10* 37 fhould *most MSS.:* fhall *1635–69, Cy, P* 44 the
1635–69: their *A10, Cy, H40, L74, P, RP31* 46 it . . . it *all
MSS.:* is . . . is *1635–69* 50 prove *most MSS.:* be *1635–69, Cy, P*
51 your *all MSS.:* our *1635–69* beene, *Ed:* beene: *1635–69* 52
Chaftitie *Ed:* chaftitie *1635–69* feene; *Ed:* feene, *1635–69* 53
feele, *Ed:* feele *1635–69* 56 fnowe,] fnowe. *1635–69, Cy, L74, P,
which end here: text of rest from A10, H39, H40, RP31* 60 or new
love:] and new love, *A10*

    All

All would not doe. The beft at laft I tryde:
Vnable longer to hould out I dyed.
And then I found I loft life, death by flying:
Who hundreds live are but foe long a dying.
Charon did let me paffe: I'le him requite.   65
To marke the groves or fhades wrongs my delight.
I'le fpeake but of thofe ghofts I found alone,
Thofe thoufand ghofts, whereof myfelf made one,
All images of thee. I ask'd them, why?
The Judge told me, all they for thee did dye,   70
And therefore had for their Elifian bliffe,
In one another their owne Loves to kiffe.
O here I mifs'd not bliffe, but being dead;
For loe, I dream'd, I dream'd; and waking faid,
Heaven, if who are in thee there muft dwell,   75
How is't, I now was there, and now I fell.

An Elegie to M^{ris} Boulftred: 1602.

SHall I goe force an Elegie? abufe
My witt? and breake the Hymen of my mufe
For one poore houres love? Deferves it fuch
Which ferves not me, to doe on her as much?
Or if it could, I would that fortune fhunn: 5
Who would be rich, to be foe foone undone?
The beggars beft is, wealth he doth not know;
And but to fhew it him, encreafes woe.
But we two may enjoye an hour? when never

63 life] lif's *Grosart: spelt* lief *H40*   64 Who] Where *Grosart*
66 marke] walke *Grosart*   or] and *A10*   67 but] out *Grosart, from*
H39   68 Thofe thoufand] Thoufand *A10*   72 In one] *omit. Grosart*
74 (For loe I dreampt) *H39 and Grosart*   75 Heaven] O Heaven *A1ς*
    An Elegie *&c. A10, L74* (J. R. *in margin*), *RP31:* Elegie *N, TCD*
(J. R.)*:* Elegie to his M. promiffing to love him an hour. *HN* (*signed* J. R.)*:*
An Elegy 1602. To Mrs Boulftrede. *Le Prince d'Amour. &c. 1660*
7 *text from HN:* The beggers beft is, that wealth he doth ⟨not⟩ know,
A10: The beggar's beft, his *&c. L74, RP31, N, TCD, Sim:* The beggar's
best that *Grosart*   9 two *Sim:* om. *HN, L74, N, RP31, TCD:* But we
an hour may now enjoy when never *A10*   hour?] hour; *L74*

                                                                            It

It returnes, who would have a loffe for ever? 10
Nor can fo fhort a love, if true, but bring
A halfe howres feare, with the thought of lofing:
Before it, all howres were hope; and all are
(That fhall come after it,) yeares of difpaire.
This joye brings this doubt, whether it were more 15
To have enjoy'd it, or have died before?
T'is a loft paradife, a fall from grace,
Which I thinke, Adam felt more then his race.
Nor need thofe angells any other Hell;
It is enough for them, from Heaven they fell. 20
Befides, Conqueft in love is all in all;
That when I lifte, fhee under me may fall:
And for this turne, both for delight and view,
I'le have a Succuba, as good as you.
But when thefe toyes are paft, and hott blood ends, 25
The beft enjoying is, we ftill are frends.
Love can but be frendfhipps outfide; their two
Beauties differ, as myndes and bodies do.
Thus, I this great Good ftill would be to take,
Vnlefs one houre, another happy make: 30
Or, that I might forgett it inftantlie;
Or in that bleft eftate, that I might die. ·
But why doe I thus travaile in the skill
Of defpis'd poetrie, and perchance fpill
My fortune? or undoe myfelf in fport 35
By having but that dangerous name in Court?
I'le leave, and fince I doe your poet prove,
Keep you my lines as fecret as my Love.

10 It returnes] Again't returnes *A10*   16 or have] or elfe *A10*
21 Befides, *A10:* Befide, *L74*   23 delight] defpite *A10*   27 but
be] be but *Sim*   their *Ed:* there *A10, L74*   30 one] on *L74*   32
Poem clofes, A10   34 defpis'd poetrie,] deeper mysteries, *Sim*

An Elegie.

TRue Love findes witt, but he whofe witt doth move
   Him to love, confeffes he doth not love:
And from his witt, paffions and true defire
Are forc'd as hard, as from the flint is fire.
My love's all fire whofe flames my foule do nurfe,   5
Whofe fmokes are fighes; whofe every fparke's a verfe.
Doth meafure women win? Then I know why
Moft of our Ladies with the Scotts doe lie.
A Scott is meafur'd in each fyllable, terfe
And fmooth as a verfe: and like that fmooth verfe   10
Is fhallow, and wants matter, but in his handes,
And they are rugged; Her ftate better ftandes
Whom dauncing meafures tempted, not the Scott:
In brief fhe's out of meafure, loft, foe gott.
Greene-ficknefs wenches, (not needes muft but) may   15
Looke pale, breathe fhort; at Court none fo long ftay.
Good witt ne're defpair'd there, or *Ay me* faid:
For never Wench at Court was ravifhed.
And fhee but cheates on Heaven, whom you fo winne
Thinking to fhare the fport, but not the finne.   20

Song.

DEare Love, continue nice and chafte,
   For, if you yeeld you doe me wrong,
Let duller wits to loves end hafte,
I have enough to wooe thee long.

An Elegie. *A10: similarly,* B, H40, L74, O'F, RP31: Elegia Un-
decima. *S: no title,* Cy, P (J. D *in margin*): *first printed by Grosart* 1
findes] kindles *RP31* 5 do *A10, L74:* doth *Grosart and Chambers*
7 women win? *A10:* win women? *L74* 11 but in his handes, *A10,*
B, L74, O'F, P: but's in's bands *S:* cut in bands *Grosart and Chambers:*
writt in his hands *H-K (teste Grosart)* 14 fhe's *A10, L74, P, H-K*
(Grosart): theyre *S, Chambers* foe] if *A10* 17 ne're *A10:* neare *L74*
   Song. *1635-69: no title,* A10, B, HN (*signed* J. R.), L74 (Finis. ℞),
O'F, P, S96   Love,] Love *1635-69*

All

All paine and joy is in their way;   5
The things we feare bring leſſe annoy
Then feare; and hope brings greater joy;
But in themſelves they cannot ſtay.

Small favours will my prayers increaſe;
Granting my ſuit you give me all,   10
And then my prayers muſt needs ſurceaſe,
For, I have made your Godhead fall.

Beaſts cannot witt nor beauty ſee,
They mans affections onely move;
Beaſts other ſports of love doe prove,   15
With better feeling farre than we.

Then Love prolong my ſuite, for thus
By loſing ſport, I ſport doe win;
And that may vertue prove in us,
Which ever yet hath beene a ſinne.   20

My comming neare may ſpie ſome ill,
And now the world is given to ſcoffe;
To keepe my Love, (then) keepe me off,
And ſo I ſhall admire thee ſtill.

Say I have made a perfect choyce,   25
Satietie our Love may kill;
Then give me but thy face and voyce,
Mine eye and eare thou canſt not fill.

To make me rich (oh) be not poore,
Give me not all, yet ſomething lend,   30
So I ſhall ſtill my ſuite commend,
And you at will doe leſſe or more.
   But, if to all you condeſcend,
   My love, our ſport, your Godhead end.

13 witt] will, *1635–54*   14 They, *1635–69*: Thoſe *L74*   18
I ſport] I ſports *1635–54*   19 that may *A10,HN,L74*: that doth
1635–69: let that *B*   26 Satietie] Sacietie *1635–39,L74*   Love *A10,*
B,HN,L74,S96: ſelves *1635–69*   28 Mine *MSS.*: My *1635–39*
32 you at will] at your will *S96*

To

To Ben. Iohnſon, 6 *Ian.* 1603.

THe State and mens affaires are the beſt playes
　　Next yours; 'Tis nor more nor leſſe than due praiſe.
Write, but touch not the much deſcending race
Of Lords houſes, ſo ſettled in worths place,
As but themſelves none thinke them uſurpers.　　　　5
It is no fault in thee to ſuffer theirs.
If the Queene Maſque, or King a hunting goe,
Though all the Court follow, Let them. We know
Like them in goodneſſe that Court ne'r will be,
For that were vertue, and not flatterie.　　　　10
Forget we were thruſt out; It is but thus,
God threatens Kings, Kings Lords, as Lords doe us.
Iudge of ſtrangers, Truſt and believe your friend,
And ſo me; And when I true friendſhip end,
With guilty conſcience let me be worſe ſtonge,　　　15
Then with *Pophams* ſentence theeves, or *Cookes* tongue
Traitors are. Friends are our ſelves. This I thee tell
As to my friend, and to my ſelfe as Counſell;
Let for a while the times unthrifty rout
Contemne learning, and all your ſtudies flout.　　　20
Let them ſcorne Hell, they will a Sergeant feare,
More then wee *that*; ere long God may forbeare,
But Creditors will not. Let them increaſe
In riot and exceſſe as their meanes ceaſe;
Let them ſcorne him that made them, and ſtill ſhun　　25
His Grace, but love the whore who hath undone
Them and their ſoules. But; that they that allow

To Ben. Iohnſon, 6 Ian. 1603. *1635–69,O'F:* To Ben Johnſon 6 Jan:
1603 T. R. *B:* An Epiſtle to Ben Johnſon. S*r* J: R: *H40:* An Epiſtle
to Beniamin Johnſon. *RP31:* An Epiſtle: To M*r* Ben. Johnſon. Ja: 6:
1603 *L74:* To M*r* Ben Johnſon. S　　2 yours; *Ed:* yours, *1635–69*
nor more] noe more *L74*　　5 none thinke] none can thinke *1669*　　11
out; *Ed:* out. *1635–69*　　15 ſtonge, *L74: ſpelt* ſtũg, *1635*　　18
as Counſell;] is Counſell: *1635–54*　　22 More then wee *that*; *Ed:*
More then wee that *H40, L74:* More then wee them; that, *1635–69* (them
in ital. 1635–54)　　24 ceaſe; *Ed:* ceaſe, *1635–69*

But

But one God, fhould have religions enow
For the Queens Mafque, and their husbands, far more
Then all the Gentiles knew, or *Atlas* bore!   30
Well, let all paffe, and truft him who nor cracks
The bruifed Reed, nor quencheth fmoaking flaxe.

To Ben. Iohnfon, 9. Novembris, 1603.

IF great men wrong me, I will fpare my felfe;
If meane, I will fpare them. I know that pelf
Which is ill got the Owner doth upbraid.
It may corrupt a Iudge, make me afraid
And a Iury; But 'twill revenge in this,   5
That, though himfelfe be judge, hee guilty is.
What care I though of weakneffe men taxe me,
I had rather fufferer than doer be.
That I did truft, it was my Natures praife,
For breach of word I knew but as a phrafe.   10
That judgement is, that furely can comprife
The world in precepts, moft happy and moft wife.
What though? Though leffe, yet fome of both have we,
Who have learn'd it by ufe and mifery.
Poore I, whom every pety croffe doth trouble,   15
Who apprehend each hurt thats done me, double,
Am of this (though it fhould finke me) careleffe,
It would but force me to a ftricter goodneffe.
They have great odds of me, who gaine doe winne,
(If fuch gaine be not loffe) from every finne.   20
The ftanding of great mens lives would afford

---

28 enow *H40, L74:* enough *1635–69*   29 far *L74:* for *1635–69,*
H40   30 bore! *Ed:* bore? *H40:* bore. *1635–69, L74*
To Ben Johnfon, 9 Novembris, 1603 : *1635–69, B (subscribed* doubtfull
author), *O'F, S:* Another Epiftle to Mr Ben: Johnfon. No: 9. 1603. *L74:*
Another to Ben Johnfon. *H40*   2 them.] them, *1635–69*   that
B, H40, L74, S: the *1635–69*   3 upbraide. *Ed:* upbraide; *1635–69*
5 Iury; *Ed:* Iury. *1635–69*   18 goodneffe.] goodneffe *1635–39*
19 odds *B, H40, L74, S:* gaine *1635–69, O'F*

A pretty

A pretty fumme, if God would fell his Word.
He cannot; they can theirs, and breake them too.
How unlike they are that they are likened to?
Yet I conclude, they are amidft my evils,   25
If good, like Gods, the naught are fo like devils.

To Sr Tho. Roe 1603.

Deare Thom :

TEll her if fhe to hired fervants fhew
   Diflike, before they take their leave they goe;
When nobler fpirits ftart at no difgrace,
For who hath but one minde, hath but one face:
If then why I tooke not my leave fhe aske,   5
Aske her againe why fhe did not unmaske?
Was fhe or proud or cruell, or knew fhee
'Twould make my loffe more felt, and pittyed me?
Or did fhe feare one kiffe might ftay for moe?
Or elfe was fhe unwilling I fhould goe?   10
I thinke the beft, and love fo faithfully
I cannot chufe but thinke that fhe loves mee.
If this prove not my faith, then let her trie
How in her fervice I would fructifie.
Ladies have boldly lov'd; bid her renew   15
That decay'd worth, and prove the times paft true.
Then he whofe wit and verfe goes now fo lame,
With fongs to her will the wild Irifh tame.
Howe'r, I'll weare the black and white ribband,
White for her fortunes, blacke for mine fhall ftand.   20

To Sir Tho. Rowe, 1603. *1635–69,O'F:* An Elegie. To Sr Tho. Roe. *B (subscribed* J. R.), *L74:* An Elegie, complayning a want of complement in his miftriffe, at his leave-taking. *A10:* Elegia Vicefima Septima. To Sr Thomas Roe. 1603. *S*   *Thom: B,L74,O'F,S: Tom: 1635–69* 5 tooke *A10,B,L74,O'F,S:* take *1635–69*   14 I would *1635–69:* it will *A10,L74,S*   17 goes now,fo *Ed:* goe now fo *B:* growes now fo *1635–69,O'F:* now goes thus *A10,L74,S*

I doe

I doe efteeme her favours, not their ftuffe;
If what I have was given, I have enough:
And all's well; for had fhe lov'd, I had had
All my friends hate; for now, departing fad
I feele not that; Yet as the Rack the Gout   25
Cures, fo hath *this* worfe griefe *that* quite put out:
My firft difeafe nought but that worfe cureth,
Which (which I dare forefee) nought cures but death.
Tell her all this before I am forgot,
That not too late fhee grieve fhee lov'd me not.   30
   Burden'd with this, I was to depart leffe
   Willing, then thofe which die, and not confeffe.

II.

To the Counteffe of Huntington.

THat unripe fide of earth, that heavy clime
  That gives us man up now, like *Adams* time
Before he ate; mans fhape, that would yet bee
(Knew they not it, and fear'd beafts companie)
So naked at this day, as though man there   5
From Paradife fo great a diftance were,
As yet the newes could not arrived bee
Of *Adams* tafting the forbidden tree;
Depriv'd of that free ftate which they were in,
And wanting the reward, yet beare the finne.   10

21 favours, not their *B, L74, S*: favour, not the *1635–69*   22
enough: *Ed:* enough, *1635–69*   23 had had] had not had *1635–69,*
O'F   24 hate;] hate *1635*: hate, *1639–69*   now, *Ed:* now
1635–69: not *A10, B, L74, S*   26 out:] out. *1635*   28 Which (which
I dare forefee) nought *A10, B, L74, S*: Which (I dare forefay) nothing
1635–69   32 Willing, *Ed:* Willing *1635–69*: Willing; *A10*
   To the Counteffe of Huntington. *1635–69:* Sʳ Wal: Afhton to yᵉ Counteffe
of Huntingtowne *P, TCD (II)*   2 man] men *P*   3 ate; *1635–39:*
eat; *1650–69*

                                           But,

But, as from extreme hights who downward looks,
Sees men at childrens fhapes, Rivers at brookes,
And lofeth younger formes; fo, to your eye,
Thefe (Madame) that without your diftance lie,
Muft either mift, or nothing feeme to be,   15
Who are at home but wits mere *Atomi.*
But, I who can behold them move, and ftay,
Have found my felfe to you, juft their midway;
And now muft pitty them; for, as they doe
Seeme fick to me, juft fo muft I to you.   20
Yet neither will I vexe your eyes to fee
A fighing Ode, nor croffe-arm'd Elegie.
I come not to call pitty from your heart,
Like fome white-liver'd dotard that would part
Elfe from his flipperie foule with a faint groane,   25
And faithfully, (without you fmil'd) were gone.
I cannot feele the tempeft of a frowne,
I may be rais'd by love, but not throwne down.
Though I can pittie thofe figh twice a day,
I hate that thing whifpers it felfe away.   30
Yet fince all love is fever, who to trees
Doth talke, doth yet in loves cold ague freeze.
'Tis love, but, with fuch fatall weakneffe made,
That it deftroyes it felfe with its owne fhade.
Who firft look'd fad, griev'd, pin'd, and fhew'd his paine, 35
Was he that firft taught women, to difdaine.
      As all things were one nothing, dull and weake,
Vntill this raw difordered heape did breake,
And feverall defires led parts away,
Water declin'd with earth, the ayre did ftay,   40
Fire rofe, and each from other but unty'd,
Themfelves unprifon'd were and purify'd:

· 11 downward] inward *TCD*   14 without] *om. TCD*   17 who]
that *P,TCD*   20 you.] you, *1635–69*   26 faithfully, *1635–69:* finally
P,TCD   you fmil'd *1635–54:* your fmile *1669, P,TCD*   28 down.
1635–54: down, *1669*   30 whifpers] whifpered *P:* vapours *TCD*   31
fever] *feverifh 1669*   32 doth yet] yet doth *1669*   ague] feaver *P*
35 paine,] paine. *1635–39*   36 women] woman *TCD*   37 were
one] were but one *1669*

                                                                     So

So was love, firſt in vaſt confuſion hid,
An unripe willingneſſe which nothing did,
A thirſt, an Appetite which had no eaſe,   45
That found a want, but knew not what would pleaſe.
What pretty innocence in thoſe dayes mov'd?
Man ignorantly walk'd by her he lov'd;
Both ſigh'd and enterchang'd a ſpeaking eye,
Both trembled and were ſick, both knew not why.   50
That naturall fearefulneſſe that ſtruck man dumbe,
Might well (thoſe times conſider'd) man become.
As all diſcoverers whoſe firſt aſſay
Findes but the place, after, the neareſt way:
So paſſion is to womans love, about,   55
Nay, farther off, than when we firſt ſet out.
It is not love that ſueth, or doth contend;
Love either conquers, or but meets a friend.
Man's better part conſiſts of purer fire,
And findes it ſelfe allow'd, ere it deſire.   60
Love is wiſe here, keepes home, gives reaſon ſway,
And journeys not till it finde ſummer-way.
A weather-beaten Lover but once knowne,
Is ſport for every girle to practiſe on.
Who ſtrives through womans ſcornes, women to know, 65
Is loſt, and ſeekes his ſhadow to outgoe;
It muſt bee ſickneſſe, after one diſdaine,
Though he be call'd aloud, to looke againe.
Let others ſigh, and grieve; one cunning ſleight
Shall freeze my Love to Chriſtall in a night.   70
I can love firſt, and (if I winne) love ſtill;
And cannot be remov'd, unleſſe ſhe will.
It is her fault if I unſure remaine,
Shee onely can untie, and binde againe.

47 thoſe dayes] that day *1669*   50 both knew *1635–54:* but knew
P,TCD: yet, knew *1669*   52 conſider'd *Ed:* conſidered *1635–69*
57 ſueth, or] ſues and *P*   65 womans] womens *P*   women] woman
TCD   know, *1650–69:* know. *1635–39*   67 It muſt be] It is
meer *1669*   ſickneſſe,] ſickneſſe *1635–69*   69 ſigh *P,TCD:* ſinne,
1635–69   74 and *P:* I *1635–69, TCD*

The

The honefties of love with eafe I doe,   75
But am no porter for a tedious woo.
    But (madame) I now thinke on you ; and here
Where we are at our hights, you but appeare,
We are but clouds you rife from, our noone-ray
But a foule fhadow, not your breake of day.   80
You are at firft hand all that's faire and right,
And others good reflects but backe your light.
You are a perfectneffe, fo curious hit,
That youngeft flatteries doe fcandall it.
For, what is more doth what you are reftraine,   85
And though beyond, is downe the hill againe.
We'have no next way to you, we croffe to it :
You are the ftraight line, thing prais'd, attribute ;
Each good in you's a light ; fo many a fhade
You make, and in them are your motions made.   90
Thefe are your pictures to the life. From farre
We fee you move, and here your *Zani's* are :
So that no fountaine good there is, doth grow
In you, but our dimme actions faintly fhew.
    Then finde I, if mans nobleft part be love,   95
Your pureft lufter muft that fhadow move.
The foule with body, is a heaven combin'd
With earth, and for mans eafe, but nearer joyn'd.
Where thoughts the ftarres of foule we underftand,
We gueffe not their large natures, but command.   100
And love in you, that bountie is of light,
That gives to all, and yet hath infinite.
Whofe heat doth force us thither to intend,
But foule we finde too earthly to afcend,

    76 woo. *TCD :* wooe. *P :* woe. *1635–69, Chambers and Grolier*
77 I now] now I *TCD*   78 hights] height *TCD*   79 clouds you rise
from, our noone-ray *Grolier :* clouds, you rife from our noone-ray, *1635–69,*
TCD, and Chambers   81 right] bright *P*   83 a perfectneffe] all
perfections *P*   84 youngeft] quainteft *TCD*   flatteries] flatterers
P, TCD   86 though] what's *P*   87 We'have *Ed :* We have *1635–69*
88 ftraight line,] ftreight-lace *P*   attribute ; *Ed :* attribute. *1635 :*
attribute, *1639–69*   91 Thefe] Thofe *TCD*   98 With earth] *om.*
TCD   but] *om. 1650–69*   99 thoughts] through *P*

                                                         'Till

'Till flow acceffe hath made it wholy pure,   105
Able immortall clearneffe to endure.
Who dare afpire this journey with a ftaine,
Hath waight will force him headlong backe againe.
No more can impure man retaine and move
In that pure region of a worthy love: 110
Then earthly fubftance can unforc'd afpire,
And leave his nature to converfe with fire:
Such may have eye, and hand; may figh, may fpeak;
But like fwoln bubles, when they are high'ft they break.

  Though far removed Northerne fleets fcarce finde 115
The Sunnes comfort; others thinke him too kinde.
There is an equall diftance from her eye,
Men perifh too farre off, and burne too nigh.
But as ayre takes the Sunne-beames equall bright
From the firft Rayes, to his laft oppofite: 120
So able men, bleft with a vertuous Love,
Remote or neare, or howfoe'r they move;
Their vertue breakes all clouds that might annoy,
There is no Emptineffe, but all is Ioy.
He much profanes whom violent heats do move 125
To ftile his wandring rage of paffion, *Love*:
Love that imparts in every thing delight,
Is fain'd, which only tempts mans appetite.
Why love among the vertues is not knowne
Is, that love is them all contract in one.   130

105 wholy] holy *TCD* 106 endure.] endure *1635* 108 waight]
weights *P,TCD* 109 impure] vapore *P* 114 when they're higheft
break. *P,TCD* break.] break *1635–39:* brak *1650–54:* brake. *1669*
115 *In edd. new par. begins wrongly at* 113, *and so Chambers and Grolier*
fleets] Isles *1669* 116 comfort; *1635–54:* sweet comfort, *1669*
others] yet some *1669* 119 But as the aire takes all funbeams equall
bright *P* 120 the firft Rayes, *1635–54:* the Raies firft, *1669, TCD:*
the rife firft *P* 121 able men *P:* able man, *1635–54:* happy man, *1669:*
happy['s] man *Grosart and Chambers* 123 Their *1669,P,TCD:*
There *1635–54, Chambers and Grolier* 125 violent *P,TCD:* valiant
1635–69 126 *Love: Ed:* Love. *1635–54:* Love, *1669* 127
imparts] imports *1669,TCD* 128 Is fain'd, which ... appetite. *P:*
Is thought the manfion of fweet appetite. *TCD:* Is fancied *1635–39 (rest*
of line left blank): Is fancied in the Soul, not in the fight. *1650–54:* Is
fancied by the Soul, not appetite. *1669* 130 Is, that] Is, 'caufe *TCD*
contract in *1650–69,P:* contracted *1635–39,TCD*

                    III.

III.

Elegie.

DEath be not proud, thy hand gave not this blow,
Sinne was her captive, whence thy power doth flow;
The executioner of wrath thou art,
But to deftroy the juft is not thy part.
Thy comming, terrour, anguifh, griefe denounce;   5
Her happy ftate, courage, eafe, joy pronounce.
From out the Chriftall palace of her breaft,
The clearer foule was call'd to endleffe reft,
(Not by the thundering voyce, wherewith God threats,
But, as with crowned Saints in heaven he treats,)   10
And, waited on by Angels, home was brought,
To joy that it through many dangers fought;
The key of mercy gently did unlocke
The doores 'twixt heaven and it, when life did knock.
  Nor boaft, the faireft frame was made thy prey,   15
Becaufe to mortall eyes it did decay;
A better witneffe than thou art, affures,
That though diffolv'd, it yet a fpace endures;
No dramme thereof fhall want or loffe fuftaine,
When her beft foule inhabits it again.   20
Goe then to people curft before they were,
Their fpoyles in Triumph of thy conqueft weare.
Glory not thou thy felfe in thefe hot teares
Which our face, not for hers, but our harme weares,

Elegie. *Ed:* Elegye on the Lady Markham. By L. C. of B. *RP31:*
do. By C. L. of B. *H40:* Elegie on Miftris Boulftred. *1635–69: given as*
continuation of Death I recant *&c. O' F, P: no title,* B (*at foot of page* F. B.).
See Text and Canon *&c.* 2 flow; *Ed:* flow, *1635–69:* growe, B,
Cy, H40, O'F, P 5–6 comming, *1650–69:* comming *1635–39*
ftate, *1650–69:* ftate *1635–39* denounce; . . . pronounce. *B, Cy, H40,*
P: denounces; . . . pronounces. *1635–69* 12 To joy that *1635–69:*
To joy what *H40:* To joye, that *B* fought; *Ed:* fought, *1635–69*
22 fpoyles . . of . . weare. *B, Cy, H40* (beare), *P:* foules . . to . . beare,
1635–69. See note 24 hers, *H40, P:* her, *1635–69* weares,
Ed: weares. *1635–54:* weares: *1669*

The

The mourning livery given by Grace, not thee,   25
Which wils our foules in thefe ftreams wafht fhould be,
And on our hearts, her memories beft tombe,
In this her Epitaph doth write thy doome.
Blinde were thofe eyes, faw not how bright did fhine
Through flefhes mifty vaile the beames divine.   30
Deafe were the eares, not charm'd with that fweet found
Which did i'th fpirit-inftructed voice abound.
Of flint the confcience, did not yeeld and melt,
At what in her laft Act it faw, heard, felt.

   Weep not, nor grudge then, to have loft her fight,   35
Taught thus, our after ftay's but a fhort night:
But by all foules not by corruption choaked
Let in high rais'd notes that power be invoked.
Calme the rough feas, by which fhe fayles to reft,
From forrowes here, to a kingdome ever bleft;   40
And teach this hymne of her with joy, and fing,
   The grave no conqueft gets, Death hath no fting.

---

   30 the *B, Cy, H40, P :* thofe *1635–69*   31 not *1635–69:* that *B,*
Cy, P   32 Which did *1635–69:* Did *H40:* Did not *B, Cy, P*   fpirit-
inftructed *MSS.:* fpirits inftructed *1635–69*   34 faw, heard, felt. *B,*
Cy, H40, P : faw and felt. *1635–69*   38 rais'd *1635–69:* raisèd
Chambers   39 fhe fayles *1635–69:* fhee's fayl'd *B, H40:* fhee's fled
Cy, P   reft, *1650–69:* reft *1635–39*   40 here, *1650–69:* here
1635–39 ' bleft; *Ed:* bleft *1635:* bleft, *1639–54:* bleft. *1669*   41 And
preach this Hymn which hers (fhe *Cy, P*) with joy did fing, *B, Cy,*
H40, P   fing, *1650–69:* fing *1635–69*

IV.

Pfalme 137.

Probably by Francis Davison.

I.

BY Euphrates flowry fide
        We did bide,
From deare Juda farre abfented,
Tearing the aire with our cryes,
        And our eyes,   5
With their ftreames his ftreame augmented.

II.

When, poore Syons dolefull ftate,
        Defolate;
Sacked, burned, and inthrall'd,
And the Temple fpoil'd, which wee   10
        Ne'r fhould fee,
To our mirthleffe mindes wee call'd:

III.

Our mute harpes, untun'd, unftrung,
        Up wee hung
On greene willowes neere befide us,   15
Where, we fitting all forlorne;
        Thus, in fcorne,
Our proud fpoylers 'gan deride us.

IV.

IV.

Come, fad Captives, leave your moanes,
    And your groanes 20
Under Syons ruines bury;
Tune your harps, and fing us layes
    In the praife
Of your God, and let's be merry.

V.

Can, ah, can we leave our moanes? 25
    And our groanes
Under Syons ruines bury?
Can we in this Land fing Layes
    In the praife
Of our God, and here be merry? 30

VI.

No; deare Syon, if I yet
    Do forget
Thine affliction miferable,
Let my nimble joynts become
    Stiffe and numme, 35
To touch warbling harpe unable.

VII.

Let my tongue lofe finging skill,
    Let it ftill
To my parched roofe be glewed,
If in either harpe or voice 40
    I rejoyce,
Till thy joyes fhall be renewed.

22-3   To your Harpes fing us fome layes
         To the praife   *Crane*
24 merry.] merry, *1633-39*   25-6 moanes ... groanes] *interchanged*
Crane
31-2   if I faile
            To bewayle *Crane*
42 renewed.] renewed *1633*

                                        VIII.

VIII.

Lord, curfe Edom's traiterous kinde,
　　　　Beare in minde
In our ruines how they revell'd.　　　　　　　45
Sack, kill, burne, they cry'd out ftill,
　　　　Sack, burne, kill,
Downe with all, let all be levell'd.

IX.

And, thou Babel, when the tide
　　　　Of thy pride　　　　　　　　　　　50
Now a flowing, growes to turning;
Victor now, fhall then be thrall,
　　　　And fhall fall
To as low an ebbe of mourning.

X.

Happy he who fhall thee wafte,　　　　　　55
　　　　As thou haft
Us, without all mercy, wafted,
And fhall make thee tafte and fee
　　　　What poore wee
By thy meanes have feene and tafted.　　　　60

XI.

Happy, who, thy tender barnes
　　　　From the armes
Of their wailing mothers tearing,
'Gainft the walls fhall dafh their bones,
　　　　Ruthleffe ftones　　　　　　　65
With their braines and blood befmearing.

---

43 curfe] plague *Crane*　　　45 ruines] Ruine *Crane*　　　revell'd. *Ed:*
revell'd, *1633–39*　　　52–3 fhall...fhall] fhalt...fhalt *Crane*
59–60　　　　　　What by thee
　　　　Wee (poore wee) have &c. *Crane*

V.

V.

On the bleſſed Virgin Mary.

Probably by Henry Constable.

I N that, ô Queene of Queenes, thy birth was free
From that which others doth of grace bereave,
  When in their mothers wombe they life receive,
God, as his ſole-borne daughter loved thee.

To match thee like thy births nobilitie,   5
  He thee his Spirit for thy ſpouſe did leave,
  By whom thou didſt his onely ſonne conceive,
And ſo waſt link'd to all the Trinitie.

Ceaſe then, ô Queenes, that earthly Crownes doe weare,
  To glory in the Pompe of earthly things;   10
If men ſuch high reſpects unto you beare,
  Which daughters, wives, and mothers are to Kings,
What honour can unto that Queene be done
Who had your God for Father, Spouſe and Sonne?

VI.

On the Sacrament.

H E was the Word that ſpake it,
Hee tooke the bread and brake it;
And what that Word did make it,
I doe beleeve and take it.

On the *&c. 1635–69, A10, B, O'F, S, S96: also among* Spiritual Sonnets
by H. C. *in Harl. MS. 7553*   6 thy ſpouſe *A10, B:* his ſpouſe
1635–69   12 to *B:* of *1635–69*   Kings,] kings, *1635*
  On the *&c. 1635–69*

VII.

VII.

Abfence.

That time and abfence proves
Rather helps than hurts to loves.

Probably by John Hoskins.

A Bfence heare my proteftation
  Againft thy ftrengthe
  Diftance and lengthe,
Doe what thou canft for alteration:
  For harts of trueft mettall   5
  Abfence doth joyne, and time doth fettle.

Who loves a Miftris of right quality,
  His mind hath founde
  Affections grounde
Beyond time, place, and all mortality: 10
  To harts that cannot vary
  Abfence is prefent, time doth tary:

My Sences want their outward motion
  Which now within
  Reafon doth win,   15
Redoubled by her fecret notion:
  Like rich men that take pleafure
  In hidinge more then handling treafure.

Abfence. *The Grove (1721): do. or no title,* B, Cy, HN (*signed* J. H.),
L74, O'F, P, S, S96 (*the text here printed*): *also in* Davifon's Poetical Rhapfody
(PR) *1602 and* (*a maimed and altered version*) *in* Wit Reftored (WR) *1658*
1 heare B, S96, *Grove:* heare thou Cy, HN, L74, PR, S, WR   3
Diftance] Difdayne HN   4 you can PR: yee dare HN   5 For
hearts where love's refined WR 6 Are abfent joyned, by tyme com-
bined. WR 7 right S96: fuch *Grove,* HN, L74, PR 8 He foon hath
found PR 10 all] *om.* WR 11 To] That WR 12 prefent]
prefence B tary] carry WR 13 motion] motions PR 16 by
. . notion:] in . . notions: PR: in . . notion HN   18 hidinge]
finding *Grove*

                    By

By abfence this good means I gaine
That I can catch her   20
Where none can watch her
In fome clofe corner of my braine:
There I embrace and there kifs her,
And fo enjoye her, and fo miffe her.

VIII.

Song.

Probably by the Earl of Pembroke.

SOules joy, now I am gone,
And you alone,
(Which cannot be,
Since I muft leave my felfe with thee,
And carry thee with me)   5
Yet when unto our eyes
Abfence denyes
Each others fight,
And makes to us a conftant night,
When others change to light;   10
O give no way to griefe,
But let beliefe
Of mutuall love,
This wonder to the vulgar prove
Our Bodyes, not wee move.   15

19 means] mean *WR*   23 There I embrace and there kifs her, *S96:* There I embrace her, and *&c. L74:* There I embrace and there I kifs her, *B,O'F,WR:* There I embrace and kifs her, *Grove, HN, PR*   24 and fo miffe her *B, Cy, HN, L74, O'F, S96, WR:* while none miffe her. *Grove:* I both enjoy and mifs her. *PR*

Song. *1635–69, O'F: also in the* Poems *&c. (1660) of the Earle of Pembroke, and Sr Benjamin Ruddier, and the Lansdowne MS. 777, where it is signed* E. of Pembroke.   1 now] when *1660, L77*

Let

Let not thy wit beweepe
　　　Wounds but fenfe-deepe,
　　For when we miffe
By diftance our lipp-joying bliffe,
　　　Even then our foules fhall kiffe,　　　20
　　Fooles have no meanes to meet,
　　　But by their feet.
　　Why fhould our clay,
Over our fpirits fo much fway,
　　To tie us to that way?　　　25
　　　O give no way to griefe, &c.

A Dialogue.

EARLE OF PEMBROKE.

IF her difdaine leaft change in you can move,
　　　　　you doe not love,
For whilft your hopes give fuell to the fire,
　　　　　you fell defire.
　　Love is not love, but given free,　　　5
　　And fo is mine, fo fhould yours bee.

17 Wounds *L.77:* Words *1635–69,O'F* fenfe-deepe,] *no hyphen,*
1635–69 18 when] while *L77* 19 lipp-joyning *L77* (*not* lives
joining *as Chambers reports*): hopes joyning *1635–69,O'F*
　　A Dialogue. *Ed:* A Dialogue betweene Sʳ Henry Wotton and Mʳ Donne.
1635–69 among Letters to Severall Perfonages: *no heading but divided
between* Earle of Pembroke *and* Ben: Ruddier *H39, H40, P: and so between*
P *and* R *in the* Poems *&c.* (1660) *of* Pembroke *and* Ruddier. *See note:
only 18 lines and no dialogue, Cy: in TCD (II) the first part is given to* Earl
of Pembroke *and* Sʳ Henry Wotton, *the second to* Sʳ Ben. Ruddier *and*
Dʳ John Donne 3 whilft your hopes give *H39* (the), *H40, P:* when
the hope gives *1635–54:* when that hope gives *1669*
　　　　　　　　　　　　　　　　　　　　　Her

Her heart that melts at others moane,
              to mine is ftone.
Her eyes that weepe a ftrangers hurt to fee,
              joy to wound mee :   10
    Yet I fo much affeƈt each part,
    As (caus'd by them) I love my fmart.

Say her difdaynings juftly muft be grac't
              with name of chafte.
And that fhee frownes leaft longing fhould exceed,   15
              and raging breed;
    Soe can her rigor ne'er offend
    Unleffe felfe-love feeke private end.

BEN: RUDDIER·

'Tis love breeds love in mee, and cold difdaine
              kils that againe,   20
As water caufeth fire to fret and fume,
              till all confume.
    Who can of love more free gift make,
    Then to loves felf, for loves own fake.

7 melts at *H39,H40,P,TCD:* melts to hear of *1635-69*   9 a
ftrangers] anothers *P*   hurt *H39,H40,P,TCD:* eyes *1635-69 and
mod. edd.*   11 much *Cy,H39,H40,P,TCD:* well *1635-69*   13
Say *1635-69:* I think *H39:* Think *H40:* But thinke *P*   her dif-
daynings *1635-69:* her unkindnefs *H40:* that her difdaine *P*   muft
be] may well be *P*
17–18 *text H40,P,P and R:*
        So her difdaines can ne'er offend;
        Vnleffe felfe-love take private end. *1635-69*
21 caufeth] maketh *H40,P*
23–4   Who can of love more free gift make
        Then to loves felf, for loves owne fake   *H39,H40,P (but
H39 has* to love *in 23)*
        Who can of love more gift make,
        Then to love felfe for loves fake. *1635-39*
        Who can of love more rich gift make,
        Then to love felfe-love for loves fake? *1650-54*
        Who can of love more rich gift make,
        Then to Loves felf for loves own fake. *1669*

I'll

I'll never dig in Quarry of an heart   25
　　　　　　　　to have no part,
Nor roaſt in fiery eyes, which alwayes are
　　　　　　　　Canicular.
　　　Who this way would a Lover prove,
　　　May ſhew his patience, not his love.   30

A frowne may be ſometimes for phyſick good,
　　　　　　　　But not for food;
And for that raging humour there is ſure
　　　　　　　　A gentler Cure.
　　　Why barre you love of private end,   35
　　　Which never ſhould to publique tend?

IX.

Break of Daye.

Stanza prefixed to Donne's Poem (p. 23) in Stowe MS. 961 and
in Edition of 1669.

Probably by John Dowlands.

Stay, O ſweet, and do not riſe,
The light that ſhines comes from thine eyes;
The day breaks not, it is my heart,
Becauſe that you and I muſt part.
　　　Stay, or elſe my joys will die,   5
　　　And periſh in their infancie.

25 Quarry] quarryes *P*   27 roaſt *1669, H40*: reſt *1635-54*: waſte
H39, P   30 May] doth *H39, H40, P*
　Stanza &c.] *given as a separate poem in A25 (where it is written in at the
side), C, O'F, P: printed in John Dowland's* A Pilgrim's Solace (1612) 1
Stay, O ſweet] Lie still my dear *A25, C*   3 The day breakes not]
There breakes not day *S96*   4 Because that] To think that *S96*   5
Stay] Oh stay *S96*

APPENDIX

APPENDIX C.

A
SELECTION OF POEMS WHICH FREQUENTLY ACCOMPANY POEMS BY JOHN DONNE IN MANUSCRIPT COLLECTIONS OR HAVE BEEN ASCRIBED TO DONNE BY MODERN EDITORS.

I.

POEMS FROM ADDITIONAL MS. 25707.

A Letter written by S^r H: G: and J: D: alternis vicibus.

SInce ev'ry Tree beginns to bloſſome now
Perfuminge and enamelinge each bow,
Hartes ſhould as well as they, ſome fruits allow.

For ſince one old poore ſunn ſerves all the reſt,
You ſev'rall ſunns that warme, and light each breſt   5
Doe by that influence all your thoughts digeſt.

And that .you two may ſoe your vertues move,
On better matter then beames from above,
Thus our twin'd ſouls ſend forth theſe buds of love.

As in devotions men Joyne both there hands,   10
Wee make ours doe one Act to ſeale the bands,
By which we enthrall ourſelves to your commands,

And each for others faith and zeale ſtand bound:
As ſafe as ſpirits are from any wound,
Soe free from impure thoughts they ſhal be found.   15

A Letter written &c. *A25*: *published by Chambers, who completes the names*
2 bow, *Ed:* bow *A25*   9 twin'd *A25*: twined *Chambers*   10 hands,
Ed: hands *A25*   12–13 commands, . . . bound: *Ed:* command. . . .
bound, *A25*

Admit

Admit our magique then by which wee doe
Make you appeere to us, and us to you,
Supplying all the Mufes in you twoe.

Wee doe confider noe flower that is fweet,
But wee your breath in that exhaling meet,   20
And as true types of you, them humbly greet.

Heere in our Nightingales we heere you finge
Who foe doe make the whole yeare through a fpringe,
And fave us from the feare of Autumns ftinge.

In Anchors calme face wee your fmoothnes fee,   25
Your mindes unmingled, and as cleare as fhee
That keepes untoucht her firft virginitie.

Did all St. Edith nunns defcend againe
To honor Polefworth with their cloyftred traine,
Compar'd with you each would confeffe fome ftayne.   30

Or fhould wee more bleed out our thoughts in inke,
Noe paper (though it woulde be glad to drinke
Thofe drops) could comprehend what wee doe thinke.

For t'were in us ambition to write
Soe, that becaufe wee two, you two unite,   35
Our letter fhould as you, bee infinite.

O Frutefull Garden.

O Frutefull garden, and yet never tilde,
Box full of Treafure yet by noe man filde.
O thou which hafte, made him that firft made thee;
O neare of kinne to all the Trinetie;
O Pallace where the kinge of all, and more;   5
Went in, and out, yet never opened doore;

25 Anchors *Chambers*: Anchos *A25*   29 traine, *Ed*: traine *A25*
31 inke, *Ed*: inke *A25*
    O Frutefull Garden. *A25*: [TO THE BLESSED VIRGIN
MARY.] *Chambers*   6 out, *Ed*: out *A25*

Whofe

Whofe flefh is purer, than an others fperrit
Reache him our Prayers, and reach us down his merrit;
O bread of lyfe which fweld'fte up without Leaven;
O bridge which joynft togeather earth and heaven;   10
Whofe eyes fee me through thefe walles, and throughe glaffe,
And through this flefhe as thorowe Cipres paffe.
Behould a little harte made greate by thee
Swellinge, yet fhrinkinge at thy majeftie.
O dwell in it, for where foe ere thou go'fte   15
There is the Temple of the Holy Ghofte.

To my Lord of Pembroke.

FYe, Fye you fonnes of Pallas what madd rage
  Makes you contend that Love's, or God, or page?
Hee that admires, his weaknes doth confefs;
For as Love greater growes; foe hee growes lefs.
Hee that difdaines, what honor wynns thereby,   5
That he feeles not, or triumphes on a fly?
If love with queafie paine thy ftomack move,
Soe will a flutt whome none dare touch; or love.
If it with facred ftraines doe thee infpire
Of Poetrie; foe wee maye want admire.   10
If it thee valiant make, his ryvall hate
Can out doe that and make men defperate.
Yealdinge to us, all woemen conquer us,
By gentlenes we are betrayed thus.
We will not ftrive with Love that's a fhee beafte;   15
But playinge wee are bounde, and yeald in Jeft;
As in a Cobwebb toyle, a flye hath beene
Undone; fo have I fome fainte lover feene.
Love cannot take away our ftrength, but tame,
And wee lefs feele the thinge then feare the name;   20

8 merrit; *Ed:* merrit, *A25*   9 Leaven, *Ed:* Leaven *A25*
  To my Lord of Pembroke. *A25, Chambers*   3 confefs; *Ed:* confefs
A25   5 difdaines, *Ed:* difdaines *A25*   6 fly? *Ed:* fly; *A25*
19 tame, *Ed:* tame *A25*

                                Love

Love is a temperate bath; hee that feeles more
Heate or could there, was hott, or could before.
But as Suñ beames which would but norifhe, burne,
Drawne into hollow Chriftall, foe we turne
To fire her bewties Luftre willingly,   25
By gatheringe it in our falfe treacherous eye.
Love is nor you, nor you; but I a balme,
Sword to the ftiff, unto the wounded balme.
Prayes noe thinge adds, if it be infinite,
If it be nothing, who can leffen it?   30

Of a Lady in the Black Mafque.

WHy chofe fhee black; was it that in whitenes
   Shee did Leda equal? whofe brightnes
Muft fuffer lofs to put a bewtie on
Which hath no grace but from proportion.
It is but Coullor, which to loofe is gayne,   5
For fhee in black doth th'Æthiopian ftaine,
Beinge the forme that beautifies the creature
Her rarenefs not in Coullor is; but feature.
Black on her receaves foe ftrong a grace
It feemes the fitteft beautie for the face.   10
Coullor is not, but in æftimation,
Faire, or foule, as it is ftild by fafhion.
Kinges wearinge fackcloath it doth royall make;
Soe black⟨ne⟩s from her face doth beautie take.
It not in Coullor but in her, inheres,   15
For what fhe is, is faire, not what fhe weares;
The Moore fhalle envye her, as much, or more,
As did the Ladies of our Court before.
The Sunn fhall mourne that hee had weftwarde beene,
To feeke his Love; whilft fhee i'th North was feene.   20

27 I a balme, *A25* : Aye a calm, *Chambers conjectures*
  Of a Lady *&c. A25, Chambers*   10 face. *Ed :* face *A25*
13 make; *Ed:* make *A25*   14 black⟨ne⟩s *Chambers :* blacks *A25*
16 weares; *Ed :* weares, *A25*

Her

Her blacknes lends like luftre to her eyes,
As in the night pale Phoebe glorifyes.
Hell, fynne, and vice their attributes fhall loofe
Of black, for it wan, and pale whitenes choofe,
As like themfelves, Common, and moft in ufe: 25
Sad of that Coulor is the late abufe.

II.

POEMS FROM THE BURLEY MS.

⟨ *Life.* ⟩

THis lyfe it is not life, it is a fight
  That wee haue of yᵉ earth, yᵉ earth of vs;
It is a feild, where fence & reafon fight,
The foules & bodies quarrells to difcus;
  It is a iorney where wee do not goe,   5
  but fly wᵗʰ fpeedy wings t'our bliffe or woe.
It is a chaine yᵗ hath but two fmale links
Where⟨with⟩ oʳ graue is to oʳ bodie ioyned;
It is a poyfned feaft wherein who thinks
To taft ioyes cup, yᵉ cup of death doth find.   10
  It is a play, prefented in heauens eye,
  Wherein oʳ parts are to do naught but dye.

⟨ *My Love.* ⟩

MY love doth fly wᵗʰ wings of feare
  And doth a flame of fire refemble,
wᶜʰ mounting high & burning cleere
yet ever more doth wane & tremble.

⟨Life.⟩ *Ed : no title, Bur*   2 vs; *Ed : vs Bur*   3 feild, *Ed :* feild *Bur*   4 difcus; *Ed :* difcus *Bur*   6 woe. *Ed :* woe *Bur* 8 Where⟨with⟩ *Ed :* where *Bur*   ioyned; *Ed :* ioyned *Bur*
  ⟨My Love.⟩ *Ed: no title and no punctuation, Bur*   4 wane *Ed :* weane *Bur*

My

My loue doth fee & ftill admire,   5
Admiring breedeth humblenes;
blind loue is bold, but my defire
the more it loues p^{re}fumes ye leffe.
My loue feekes no reward or glory
but wth it felf it felf contenteth,   10
is never fullaine, never fory,
never repyneth or repenteth.
O'who the funne beames can behold
but hath fome paffion, feeles fome heat,
for though the funn himfelf be cold   15
his beames reflecting fire begett.
O y^t myne eyes, ô that myne hart
Were both enlarged to contayne
the beames & ioyes fhee doth impart,
whilft fhee this bowre doth not difdayne;   20
this bowre vnfit for fuch a guefte,
but fince fhe makes it now her Inn,
Would god twere like her facred breaft
moft fayre wthout, moft rich wthin.

⟨ *O Eyes !* ⟩

O Eyes, what do you fee?
o eares what do you heare?
that makes y^o wifh to bee
All eyes or elfe all eare?
I fee a face as fayre   5
As mans eye ever faw,
I here as fweet an ayre
as y^t wch rocks did draw,

12 never *Ed:* ne're *Bur*
⟨O Eyes!⟩ *Ed: no title and no punctuation, Bur*

I wifh,

I wifh, when in fuch wife
I fee or heare ye fame,   10
I had all Argus eyes
or elfe ye eare⟨s⟩ of fame.

⟨*Silence Beſt Praiſe.*⟩

COmend her? no. I dare not terme her fayre,
nor fugred fweet, nor tall, nor louely browne;
fuffice it y^t fhe is w^{th}out compare;
but how, I dare not tell left fhe fhould frowne.
but thofe parts ⟨leaft⟩ wch others make theyre pryde,   5
and feed there fancies wth devifed lyes;
giue me but leaue to pull my faint afyde,
and tell her in her eare that fhe is wife.
to write of beauties rare ther is noe art,
for why tis common to there fex & kind,   10
but making choice of natures better part
my Mufe doth moft defire to prayfe her mind.
    But as her vertue⟨s⟩ clayme a crowne of bayes,
    So manners makes me fylent in her prayfe.

---

12 eare⟨s⟩ *Ed :* eare *Bur :*

Cui, quot sunt corpore plumae,
   Tot vigiles oculi subter, mirabile dictu,
   Tot linguae, totidem ora sonant, *tot subrigit auris.*
                                    Virgil : *Aen.* iv. 181–3.

⟨Silence Beſt Praiſe.⟩ *Ed: no title, Bur*   1 fayre, *Ed:* fayre *Bur*
2 fweet, . . . tall, . . . browne; *Ed: no stops, Bur*   3 compare; *Ed:*
compare *Bur*   4 frowne. *Ed:* frowne *Bur*   5 ⟨leaft⟩ *Ed:*
left *Bur*   pryde, *Ed:* pryde *Bur*   6 lyes; *Ed:* lyes *Bur*   7
afyde, *Ed:* afyde *Bur*   8 wife. *Ed:* wife *Bur*   9–10 art, . . . kind,
Ed: no commas, Bur   10 common] cõmõ *Bur*   12 mind. *Ed:* mind
Bur   13 vertue⟨s⟩ *Ed:* vertue *Bur*   bayes, *Ed:* bayes *Bur*
                                                        ⟨*Beauty*

⟨*Beauty in Little Room.*⟩

THofe droffy heads & irrepurged braynes
    wᶜʰ facred fyre of loue hath not refined
may groffly think my loue fmale worth contaynes
becaufe fhee is of body fmale combined.
Not diving to yᵉ depth of natures reach,   5
Wᶜʰ on fmale things doth greateft guifts beftow:
fmall gems & pearls do witt more truly teach
Wᶜʰ little are yet great in vertue grow,
of flowers moft part yᵉ leaft wee fweeteft fee,
of creatures having life & fence yᶜ annt   10
is fmalft, yet great her guifts & vertues bee,
frugall & provident for feare of want.
    Wherfore who fees not natures full intent ?
    fhe made her fmale to make her excellent.

⟨*Loves Zodiake.*⟩

I That yᵉ higher half of loues
    Round Zodiake haue rune,
And in the figne of crabbed chaunce
My Tropick haue begun,
Am taught to teach yᵉ man is bleft   5
Whofe loues lott lights fo badd,
as his folftitium fooneft makes
And fo growes Retrograde.

⟨*Fortune, Love, and Time.*⟩

WHen fortune, loue, and Tyme bad me be happie,
    Happy I was by fortune, loue, and tyme.
Thefe powres at higheft then began to vary,
and caft him downe whome they had caus'd to clyme ;
    They prun'd theire wings, and tooke theire flight in rage ;
    fortune to fooles, loue to gold, and tyme to age.   6

⟨Beauty in Little Room.⟩ *Ed: no title,* Bur   5 depth *Ed:* depht *Bur*
reach, *Ed:* reach *Bur*   6 beftow: *Ed:* beflow *Bur*   8 grow, *Ed:*
grow *Bur*   11 bee, *Ed:* bee *Bur*   13 intent ? *Ed:* intent *Bur*
    ⟨Loves Zodiake⟩ *Ed: no title,* Bur
    ⟨Fortune, Love, and Time.⟩ *Ed: no title and no punctuation,* Bur

Fooles

Fooles, gold, and age, (o foolifh golden age!)
Witt, fayth, and loue muft begg, muft brybe, muft dy;
Thefe are the actors and the world's the ftage,
Defert and hope are as but ftanders by :   10
   True lovers fit and tune this reftleffe fong;
   Fortune, loue, and tyme haue done me wrong.

⟨ *Life a Play.* ⟩

WHat is oʳ life? a play of pafsion.
   oʳ mirth? the mufick of diuifion.
Oʳ mothers wombs the tyring houfes bee
Where we are dreft for liues fhort comedy.
The earth the ftage, heauen yᵉ fpectator is,   5
Who ftill doth note who ere do act amiffe.
Oʳ graues that hyde vs, frõ the all-feeing fuñ,
Are but drawne curtaynes whẽ the play is done.

A Kiffe.

O What a bliffe
  is this?
   heaven is effected
   and loues eternity contracted
     In one fhort kiffe.   5
For not tymes meafure
    makes pleafure
      more full.
   tedious and dull
   all ioyes are thought   10
  yᵗ are not in an inftant wrought.

   ⟨Life a Play.⟩ *Ed: no title, and no punctuation except the two marks of interrogation,* Bur
   A Kiffe. *Bur*   8 full. *Ed:* full *Bur*

                              Cupi⟨d⟩s

Cupi⟨d⟩s bleſt and higheſt ſpheare
    is heare.
  heere on his throne
  in his bright imperial crowne   15
    hee ſitts.
    Thoſe witts
That thinke to proue
that mortals know
in any place below   20
  a bliſſe ſo great
    ſo ſweet
Are heretiques in loue.
Theſe pleaſures high
    now dye,   25
  but ſtill beginning
new & greater glory wiñing
    gett freſh ſupply.
No ſhort breath'd panting
    nor faynting   30
    is heere,
fuller and freer
more pleaſinge is
this pleaſure ſtill, & none but this.
Heer'es no bluſh nor labor great,   35
    no ſweat;
  Heres no payne
nor repentance when againe
    Loue cooles.
    O fooles   40
That fondly glory
  in baſe condition
  of ſenſual fruition,
you do miſtake
    & make   45
    yʳ heaven purgatory.

12 Cupi⟨d⟩s *Ed:* Cupis *Bur*   27 new *Ed:* now *Bur*   28
ſupply. *Ed:* ſupply *Bur*   31 heere, *Ed:* heere *Bur*   35 great,
Ed: great *Bur*   39 cooles. *Ed:* cooles *Bur*   43 fruition, *Ed:*
fruition *Bur*

                                              Epi:

Epi: B: Jo:

TEll me who can when a player dies
  In wᶜʰ of his ſhapes againe hee ſhall riſe?
What need hee ſtand at the iudgment throne
Who hath a heaven and a hell of his owne.
  Then feare not Burbage heavens angry rodd,   5
  When thy fellows are angells & old Hemmĩgs is God.

Epi: Hen: Princ: Hugᵒ Holland.

LOe now hee ſhineth yonder
  A fixed ſtarr in heaven,
Whoſe motion is vnder
None of the planetts ſeaven;
  And if the ſoñ ſhould tender
  The moone his loue and marry,   5
  They never could engender
  So fayre a ſtarr as Harry.

III

POEMS FROM VARIOUS MSS.

⟨*The Annuntiation.*
Additional Lines.⟩

NAture amaz'd ſawe man without mans ayde
  Borne of a mother nurſed by her a mayd,
The child the Parent was, the worke the word,
No word till then did ſuch a worke affoord.

Epi: B: Jo: (i.e. Epitaph: Ben Ionſon) *Bur: no punctuation*
Epi: Hen: Princ: Hugᵒ Holland. *Bur: no punctuation*
⟨The Annuntiation. Additional Lines.⟩ *Ed: these lines run straight
on as part of* The Annuntiation and Passion *in* O'F   2 a mayd]
Norton supplies a mayd, *Ed:* mayd O'F   3 was, . . . word, *Ed: no
commas,* O'F

Twas

Twas leſſe from nothing the world's all to growe 5
Then all-Creato^{rs} height to ſtoope ſo lowe.
A virgin mother to a child bredd wonder,
T'was more a child ſhould bee the God of thunder.
Th'omnipotent was ſtrangely potent heere
To make the powerfull God peareleſſe appeare. 10
Hee in our body cladd, for our ſoules love
Came downe to us, yet ſtay'd vnchanged above.
Yet God through man ſhind ſtill in this cleere brooke,
Through meane ſhewes into maieſty wee looke.
Sinnes price ſeemd payd with braſſe, fewe ſawe the gold,
Yet true ſtones ſet in lead theyr luſtre hold. 16
His birth though poore, Prophets foretold his ſtory,
Hee breathd with beaſts, but Angels ſung his glory.
Hee, ſo farr of, ſo weake, yet Herod quakes,
The citty dreads, babes, murderd, feare miſtakes. 20
His Circumciſion bore ſinne, payne, and ſhame,
Young bloud new budd, hence bloomd a ſauiours name.
His paynes and paſſion bredd compaſſion, wonder;
Earth trembling, heavens darke, rocks rent aſunder.
His birth, life, death, his words, his workes, his face 25
Shewd a rich Jewell ſhining through the caſe,
Caſt thus, ſince man at gods high preſence trembles.
Heere man mans troth loves whome his ſheepe reſembles.
The bright Sunne beame a ſickly eye may dim̃e,
A little babe in ſhallow heart may ſwim̃. 30
Hee heavens wealth to a poore ſtable brings,
Th'oxeſtall the Court unto the king of kings.
No Shadowes now nor lightning flames give terro^r.
This light tells with our tongue, and beares o^r erro^r.
Pure infant teares, moiſt pearle adornd his cheeke, 35
Aſſignd, ere borne, our erring ſoules to ſeeke.
Hee firſt wept teares, then bloud, a deare redemption;
This bought what Adam ſould, that ſeemd preemption.

6 lowe. *Ed:* lowe *O'F*   7 wonder, *Ed:* wonder *O'F*   8 thunder.
Ed: thunder *O'F*   13 brooke, *Ed:* brooke *O'F*   21 ſhame, *Ed:*
ſhame *O'F*   23 wonder; *Ed:* wonder *O'F*   24 trembling, *Ed:*
trembling *O'F*   26 caſe, *Ed:* caſe *O'F*   27 trembles. *Ed:* trembles
O'F   28 reſembles. *Ed:* reſebles *O'F*   29 dim̃e, *Ed:* dim̃e *O'F*
31 brings, *Ed:* brings *O'F*   35 cheeke, *Ed:* cheeke *O'F*   37 redemp-
tion; *Ed:* redemption *O'F*   38 preemption. *Ed:* preemption *O'F*

Cleare

Cleare droppe, deare feede, the corne had bloudy eares,
Rich harveft reapd in bloud and fowne in teares. 40
Who this Corne in theyr hart nor threfh, nor lay,
Breake for finnes debt, unthrifty never pay.
Ufe wealth, it waftes, a ftayd hand heapes the ftore,
But this the more wee ufe wee have the more;
Ufe, not like ufury whofe growth is lending, 45
Rich thoughts this treafure keepe and thrive by fpending;
Th'expenfe runnes circular, turning returning,
Such love no hart confumes, yet ever burning.

Elegy.   To Chaft Love.

CHaft Love, let mee embrace thee in mine armes
Without the thought of luft. From thence no harmes
Enfue, no difcontent attende thofe deeds
So innocently good wch thy love breeds.
Th'approche of day brings to thy fence no feares, 5
Nor is the black nights worke wafhd in thy teares;
Thou takft no care to keepe thy lover true,
Nor yet by flighte, nor fond inventions new
To hold him in, who with like flame of love
Muft move his fpirit too, as thine doth move; 10
wch ever mounts aloft with golden wings
And not declines to lowe defpifed things.
Thy foule is bodyd within thy quiet breft
In fafety, free from trouble and unreft.
Thou fearft no ill becaufe thou doft no ill, 15
Like miftrefs of thy felfe, thy thought, and will,

39 eares, *Ed:* eares *O'F*   41 lay, *Ed:* lay *O'F*   43 ftore, *Ed:*
ftore *O'F*   44 more; *Ed:* more *O'F*   45 Ufe, . . . lending, *Ed:*
no commas, O'F   46 fpending; *Ed:* fpending *O'F*   47 returning,
Ed: returning *O'F*   48 confumes, *Ed:* confumes *O'F*
   Elegy.   To Chaft Love. *O'F*   5 feares, *Ed:* feares *O'F*   6
teares; *Ed:* teares *O'F*   7 true, *Ed:* true *O'F*   9 in, *Ed:* in *O'F*
10 move; *Ed:* move *O'F*   15 ill, *Ed:* ill *O'F*   16 will, *Ed:*
will *O'F*

Obey

Obey thy mind, a mind for ever fuch
As all may prayfe, but none admire too much.
　Then come, Chaſt Love, choyfe part of womankind
　Infufe chaſt thoughts into my loving mind.　20

Upon his fcornefull Miſtreſſe.　Elegy.

CRuell fince that thou doſt not feare the curfe
　Wᶜʰ thy difdayne, and my defpayre procure,
My prayer for thee fhall torment thee worfe
　Then all the payne thou coudſt thereby endure.
May, then, that beauty wᶜʰ I did conceave　5
　In thee above the height of heavens courfe,
When firſt my Liberty thou didſt bereave,
　Bee doubled on thee and with doubled force.
Chayne thoufand vaſſalls in like thrall with mee,
　Wᶜʰ in thy glory mayſt thou ſtill defpife,　10
As the poore Trophyes of that victory
　Which thou haſt onely purchaſd by thine eyes;
And when thy Triumphs fo extended are
　That there is nought left to bee conquered,
Mayſt thou with the great Monarchs mournfull care　15
　Weepe that thine Honoʳˢ are fo limited;
So thy difdayne may melt it felfe to love
　By an unlookd for and a wondrous change,
Wᶜʰ to thy felfe above the reſt muſt prove
　In all th'effects of love paynefully ſtrange,　20
　　While wee thy fcorned fubjects live to fee
　　Thee love the whole world, none of it love thee.

Upon his fcornefull Miſtreſſe. *O'F: no title,* B, *which adds note,* This hath relation to 'When by thy fcorne'. *See* The Apparition, *p.* 191　2 defpayre B: difdayne *O'F* procure, *Ed:* procure *O'F* 6 courfe, *Ed:* courfe *O'F* 7 bereave, *Ed:* bereave *O'F* 8 force. *Ed:* force *O'F* 9 Chayne B: Stay *O'F* mee, *Ed:* mee *O'F* 10 defpife, *Ed:* defpife *O'F* 12 eyes; *Ed:* eyes *O'F* 14 conquered, *Ed:* conquered *O'F* 16 limited; *Ed:* limited *O'F* 18 change, *Ed:* change *O'F* 20 ſtrange, *Ed:* ſtrange *O'F*

⟨*Abfence.*⟩

⟨*Abſence.*⟩

WOnder of Beautie, Goddeſſe of my ſenſe,
　You that have taught my ſoule to love aright,
You in whoſe limbes are natures chief expenſe
Fitt inſtrument to ſerve your matchleſs ſpright,
If ever you have felt the miſerie　　　　　　　5
Of being baniſh'd from your beſt deſier,
By Abſence, Time, or Fortunes tyranny,
Sterving for cold, and yet denied for fier:
Deare miſtreſſe pittie then the like effects
The which in mee your abſence makes to flowe,　　10
And haſte their ebb by your divine aſpect
In which the pleaſure of my life doth growe:
Stay not ſo long for though it ſeem a wonder
You keepe my bodie and my ſoule aſunder.
　　　　　　　FINIS.

⟨*Tongue-tied Love.*⟩

FAire eies do not think ſcorne to read of Love
　That to your eies durſt never it preſume,
Since abſence thoſe ſweet wonders do⟨th⟩ remove
That nouriſh thoughts, yet ſence and wordes conſume;
This makes my pen more hardy then my tongue,　　5
Free from my feare yet feeling my deſire,
To utter that I have conceal'd ſo long
By doing what you did yourſelf require.
Believe not him whom Love hath left ſo wiſe
As to have power his owne tale for to tell,　　10
For childrens greefes do yield the loudeſt cries,
And cold deſires may be expreſſed well:
In well told Love moſt often falſehood lies,
But pittie him that only ſighes and dies.
　　　　　　　FINIS.

⟨Abſence.⟩ ⟨Tongue-tied Love.⟩　*Ed: whole ſonnets without titles in*
L74 : the laſt ſix lines of the ſecond appear among Donne's poems in B, O'F, S96
⟨Tongue-tied Love.⟩　12 cold deſires] coldeſt Ayres *O'F*
　　　　　　　　　　　　　　　　　⟨*Love,*

⟨ *Love, if a God thou art.* ⟩

Love if a god thou art
   then evermore thou muſt
  Bee mercifull and juſt;
If thou bee juſt, ô wherefore doth thy dart
Wound mine alone and not my miſtreſſe hart?   5

If mercifull, then why
  Am I to payne reſervd
  Who have thee truely ſerv'd,
When ſhee that by thy powre ſets not a fly
Laughs thee to ſcorne and lives at liberty?   10

Then if a God thou woulds accounted bee,
Heale mee like her, or elſe wound her like mee.

⟨ *Great Lord of Love.* ⟩

Greate Lord of love, how buſy ſtill thou art
  To give new wounds and fetters to my hart!
Is't not enough that thou didſt twice before
      It ſo mangle
      And intangle   5
      By ſly arts
      of falſe harts.
  Forbeare mee, Ile make love no more.

Fy buſy Lord, will it not thee ſuffice
To uſe the Rhetorique of her tongue and eyes   10
When I am waking, but that abſent ſo
      They invade mee
      To perſwade mee,
      When that ſleepe
      Oft ſhould keepe   15
  And lock out every ſence of woe.

⟨ Love if a God thou art. ⟩ ⟨ Great Lord of Love. ⟩ ⟨ Loves Exchange. ⟩
all without titles in O'F: punctuation mainly the Editor's

If

If thou perſwade mee thus to ſpeake, I dye
And ſhee the murdreſſe, for ſhe will deny;
And if for ſilence I bee preſt, Her good
        Yet I cheriſh   20
        Though I periſh,
        For that ſhee
        Shall bee free
From that foule guilt of ſpilling bloud.

⟨ *Loves Exchange.* ⟩

1. **T**O ſue for all thy Love, and thy whole hart
                were madneſſe.
    I doe not ſue, nor can admitt,
    (Fayreſt) from yoᵘ to have all yet;
  Who giveth all, hath nothing to impart   5
           But ſadneſſe.

2. Hee who receaveth all can have no more,
          Then ſeeing
    My love by length of every howre
    Gathers new ſtrength, new growth, new power:
  You muſt have dayly new rewards in ſtore   11
          Still beeing.

3. You cannot every day give mee yoʳ hart
          For merit;
    Yet if you will, when yours doth goe   15
    You ſhall have ſtill one to beſtow,
  For you ſhall mine, when yours doth part,
          Inherit.

4. Yet if you pleaſe weele find a better way
        Then change them,   20
    For ſo alone (deareſt) wee ſhall
    Bee one and one another all;
  Let us ſo joyne our harts, that nothing may
        Eſtrange them.

                              Song.

Song.

NOw y'have killd mee with yor ſcorne
Who ſhall live to call yo^u fayre?
What new foole muſt now bee borne
    To prepare
Dayly ſacrifice of ſervice new,   5
Teares too good for woemen true?
  Who ſhall ſorrow when yo^u crye
  And to pleaſe yo^u dayly dye?
    Men ſucceeding ſhall beware
    And woemen cruell, no more fayre.   10

2.

Now y'have killd mee, never looke
  Any left to call yo^u trewe;
Who more madd muſt now bee tooke
    To renewe
My oblations dayly, loſt?   15
Vowes too good for woemen chaſt!
  Who ſhall call yo^u ſweete, and ſweare
  T"is yor face renews the yeare?
    Men by my Death ſhall beleeve,
    And woemen cruell yet ſhall greeve.   20

Love, bred of glances.

LOve bred of Glances twixt amorous eyes
Like Childrens fancies, ſone borne, ſone dyes.
  Guilte, Bitternes, and ſmilinge woe
  Doth ofte deceaue poore lovers ſoe,
As the fonde Sence th'unwary ſoule deceives   5
With deadly poiſon wrapt in Lily leaves.

Song. *O'F*: *punctuation mainly Editor's*
Love *&c.* ⟨True Love.⟩ *Chambers, who prints from RP117: no title,*
O'F, P, S96 (*from which present text is taken*)   2 borne *B, P, O'F, S96*:
bred *Chambers*   4 Doth *S96*: does *B, O'F*: doe *P*   5 As] And
Chambers

But

But harts fo chain'd as Goodnes ftands
With truthe unftain'd to couple hands,
    Love beinge to all beauty blinde
    Save the cleere beauties of the minde,   10
There heaven is pleafd, continuall bleffings fheddinge,
Angells are guefts and dance at this bleft weddinge.

To a Watch reftored to its Myftres.

GOe and Count her better howers.
For they are happier than oures.
The day that gives her any blifs,
Make it as long againe as 'tis.
The hower fhee fmyles in, lett it bee   5
By thy acte multiplyde to three.
But if fhee frowne on thee or mee,
Know night is made by her, not thee;
Be fwifte in fuch an hower & soone,
See thou make night, ere it be noone.   10
Obey her tymes, whoe is the free
Faire Sunne that governes thee & mee.

⟨Ad Solem.⟩

WHerfore peepft thou, envious daye?
We can kiffe without thee.
Lovers hate the golden raye,
    Which thou bearft about thee.

7 as Goodnes] 'tis goodnes *Chambers*   8 hands, *Ed:* hands *S96*
10 minde, *B:* minde *S96*   11 There heav'n is *O'F, P, S96:* Where
Reason is *Chambers*   fheddinge, *Ed:* fheddinge *S96*   12 this] his
Chambers
    To a Watch *&c. B, where note below title says* none of J. D. *and poem
is signed* W. L.
    ⟨Ad Solem.⟩ *Ed: no title, Add. MSS. 22603, 33998, Egerton MS. 2013,
Harleian MS. 791, S, TCD (II): printed J. Wilton: Cheerful Ayres* (1659),
Grosart and Chambers: text from Eg. MS. 2013: punctuation partly Editor's
2 kiffe] live *E20*
                        Goe

Goe and give them light that forowe 5
    Or the faylor flyinge:
Our imbraces need noe morowe
    Nor our bliffes eying.

We fhall curfe thy curyous eye
    For thy foone betrayinge, 10
And condemn thee for a fpye
    Yf thou catch us playinge.
Gett thee gone and lend thy flafhes
    Where there's need of lendinge,
Our affections are not afhes 15
    Nor our pleafures endinge.

Weare we cold or withered heare
    We would ftay thee by us,
Or but one anothers feare
    Then thou fhouldft not flye us. 20
Wee are yongue, thou fpoilft our pleafure;
    Goe to fea and flumber,
Darknes only gives us leafure
    Our ftolne joyes to number.

⟨ *If She Deride.* ⟩

GReate and goode if fhe deryde mee
    Let me walke Ile not defpayre,
Ere to morrowe Ile provide mee
    One as greate, leffe prowd, more faire.
They that feeke Love to conftraine 5
Have theire labour for their paine.

    9 curyous *A22, A33, H79, S, TCD*: envious *E20*   19 one anothers
feare *TCD*: one another fear *E20*: one anothers fphere *A22, A33, S*
23 gives] lends *A22, A33*
    ⟨If She Deryde.⟩ *Chambers*: no title, *S*: also, *Chambers reports, in C.C.C.
Oxon. MS. 327, f. 26: printed by Grosart and Chambers*

They

They that ſtrongly can importune
   And will never yeild nor tyre,
Gaine the paye in ſpight of Fortune
   But ſuch gaine Ile not deſyre.   10
Where the prize is ſhame or ſynn,
Wynners looſe and looſers wynn.

Looke upon the faythfull lover,
   Griefe ſtands paynted in his face,
Groanes, and Teares and ſighs diſcover   15
   That they are his onely grace:
Hee must weepe as children doe
That will in the faſhion wooe.

I whoe flie theſe idle fancies
   Which my deareſt reſt betraye,   20
Warnd by others harmfull chances,
   Vſe my freedome as I may.
When all the worlde ſays what it cann
'Tis but—Fie, vnconſtant mann!

⟨*Fortune Never Fails.*⟩

WHat if I come to my miſtris bedd
   The candles all ecclipſt from ſhyninge,
Shall I then attempt for her mayden-head
   Or ſhowe my ſelfe a coward by declyninge?
       Oh noe   5
     Fie doe not ſoe,
For thus much I knowe by devyninge,
     Blynd is Love
     The dark it doth approve,

---

11 Where the prize is *Chambers*: Where they prize this ('t' *struck out*) *S*: Where they prize is *Grosart*   14 Teares and ſighs] *Chambers reverses*

⟨Fortune Never Fails.⟩ *Grosart: no title, RP31,S: also, Chambers reports, in C.C.C. Oxon. MS. 327, f. 21: printed Grosart and Chambers, and, last two verses only, Simeon*

To

To pray on pleasures pantinge;   10
  What needeth light
  For Cupid in the night,
If jealous eyes be wantinge.

Fortune never failes, if fhe badd take place,
 To fhroude all the faire proceedings: 15
Love and fhe though blynd, yet each other embrace,
 To favor all their fervants meetings:
  Venture I fay
  To fport and to play,
If in place all be fitting;   20
  Though fhe fay fie
  Yet doth fhe not denie:
For fie is but a word of tryall:
  Jealofie doth fleepe,
  Then doe not weepe   25
At force of a faynt denyall.

Glorious is my love, with tryumphs in her face,
 Then to to bould were I to venter:
Who loves deferves to live in a princes grace,
 Why ftand you then affraid to enter?   30
  Lights are all out
  Then make noe doubt
A lover bouldly maye take chufinge.
  Bewtie is a baite
  For a princely mate.   35
Fy, why ftand you then a mufinge?
  You'll repent too late
  If fhe doe you hate,
For loves delight refufinge.

10 pantinge;] hauntinge: *RP31* 14 fhe badd *S:* fhe bidd *Grosart:* she bids *Chambers:* the bould *RP31* 19 and to play *RP31, S:* and play *Grosart and Chambers* 26 faynt] fair *Chambers* 28 were] was *RP31* 29 princes] Princess *Chambers* 33 lover] woer *Chambers* chufinge] a choosing *Chambers*

To His Miſtreſſ.

1. BEleeve yoᵘ Glaſſe, and if it tell you (Deare)
      Yoᵘ Eyes inſhrine
      A brighter ſhine
    Then faire Apollo, looke if theere appeare
      The milkie ſkye   5
      The Crimſon dye
    Mixt in your cheeks, and then bid Phoebus ſett,
    More Glory then hee owes appears.   But yet

2. Be not deceived with fond Alteration

            10

          .   .   .   .   .

      .   .   .   .

      As Cynthias Globe,
      A ſnow white robe
    Is ſooneſt ſpotled, a Carnation dye   15
    Fades, and diſcolours open'd but to Eie.

3. Make uſe of youth, and bewty whileſt they flouriſh :
      Tyme never ſleepes,
      Though it but creeps
    It ſtill gets forward. Do not vainly nouriſh   20
      Them to ſelfe-use,
      It is Abuse;
    The richeſt Grownds lying waſt turne Boggs and rott,
    And ſoe beinge uſeles, were as good were not.

4. Walke in a meddowe by a Rivers ſide,   25
      Upon whoſe Bancks
      Grow milk-white Ranks
    Of full blown Lyllies in their height of Pryde,

To His Miſtreſs. *Le Prince D'Amour (1660): no title,* S *(whence text):
printed by Simeon, Grosart, Chambers: punctuation partly Editor's*   1 if
it tell] it will tell *Chambers*   9 deceived] deceiv'd *S*   16 open'd]
opened *S*   24 were not] as not *LePD'A*

                                                    Which

Which downward bend
And nothing tend   30
Save their owne Bewties in the Glaſſie ſtreame:
Looke to yor ſelfe : Compare yo^rſelfe to them.

5.   In ſhow, in bewtie, marke what followes then :
        Sommer muſt end,
        The ſunn muſt bend   35
His Longe Abſented beames to others : then
        Their ſpring being croſt
        By wynters froſt
And ſneap'd by bytter ſtorms againſt wch nought boots,
They bend their prowd topps lower then their roots.

6.   Then none regard them; but wth heedles feet   41
        In durt each treads
        Their declyned heads.
So when youthe waſted, Age, and yo^u ſhall meet,
        Then I alone   45
        Shall ſadly moane
That Interviewe; others it will not move,
So light regard we, what we little Love.
          FINIS.

A Paradoxe of a Painted Face.

NOt kiſſe? By Jove I muſt, and make impreſſion!
   As longe as Cupid dares to holde his Seſſion
Vpon my fleſh and blood: our kiſſes ſhall
Outminute Time and without number fall.

31 the Glaſſie *S :* a Glaſſie *LePD'A :* their Glaſſie *Chambers*   32
to them. *S :* with them. *Chambers*   36 then] when *Chambers*   39
ſneap'd *Ed :* ſnep'd *S :* ſwept *LePD'A :* snipped *Chambers*
   A Paradoxe of a Painted Face. *H39,S,S96,TCD (II)* Pembroke and
Ruddier (*1660*), Le Prince D'Amour (*1660*), Simeon (*1856–7*), Grosart
(*from S*), Chambers (*from Simeon, and Pembroke and Ruddier*): text from
S96: punctuation partly Editor's

                                   Doe

Doe I not know thefe Balls of blufhinge Red   5
That on thy Cheekes thus amorouflie are fpred?
Thy fnowy necke, thofe veynes upon thy Browe
Which with their azure crincklinge fweetly bowe
Are artificiall? Borrowed? and no more thine owne
Then Chaines which on St. George's Day are fhowne,   10
Are proper to the wearers? Yet for this
I idole thee, and beg a lufcious kiffe.
The fucus, and Cerufe, which on thy face
Thy Cunninge hand layes on to add new Grace,
Detaine me with fuch pleafing fraude, that I   15
Finde in thy art, what can in nature Lie.
Much like a painter that upon fome Wall
On which the radiant Sun-beames ufe to fall
Paints with fuch art a Gilded butterflye
That filly maides with flowe-moved fingers trye   20
To Catch it, and then blufh at theire miftake,
Yet of this painted flye moft reckonynge make:
Such is our ftate; fince what we looke upon
Is nought but Coullor and Proportion.
Take me a face, as full of fraud and Lies   25
As Gypfies in your cunninge Lotteries,
That is more falfe, and more Sophifticate
Than are Saints reliques, or a man of ftate.
Yet fuch being Glazed by the fleight of arte,
Gaines admiration, winninge many a Harte.   30
Put cafe there be a difference in the molde,
Yet may thy Venus be more Chafte, and holde
A dearer treafure: oftentimes we fee
Rich Candian wines in woodden Boules to bee.
The odoriferous Civet doth not lie   35
Within the mufkat's nofe, or eare, or eye,
But in a bafer place; for prudent nature

8 azure crincklinge *S96:* azure winckles *P and R:* azure twinklinge *S:*
azur'd wrinklings *TCD:* azure wrinkles *Chambers*   15 Detaine]
Deceive *H39. P and R, Le P D' A. TCD. Chambers*   pleafing] cunning *TCD*
18 radiant *S96:* cadent *H39. TCD, Le P D' A, Grosart,* and *Chambers:*
fplendent *P and R*   21 then] yet *S96*   32 Chafte] choife *P and R.
Le P D' A, TCD*

In drawinge us of various formes and ſtature
Gives from the curious ſhop of hir rich treaſure
To faire parts comelineſs, to baſer, pleaſure.   40
The faireſt flowers, which in the Springe doe growe
Are not ſo much for uſe, as for the ſhowe,
As Lillies, Hyacinths, and the georgious birthe
Of all pide flowers that diaper the earthe,
Pleaſe more with their diſcoloured purple traine   45
Then wholeſome pothearbs which for uſe remaine.
Shall I a Gaudy Speckled Serpent kiſs
For that the colours which he weares are his?
A perfumed Cordevant who will not wear
Becauſe the ſente is borrowed elſewhere?   50
The roabes and veſtiments, which grace us all
Are not our owne, but adventitiall.
Time rifles Natures beauty, but ſlye Arte
Repaires by cunninge this decayinge parte.
Fills here a wrinckle, and there purles a veyne,   55
And with a nimble hand runs o're againe
The breaches dented in by th'arme of time,
And makes Deformity to be no crime.
As when great men be grip't by ſicknes hand,
Induſtrious Phyſicke pregnantly doth ſtand   60
To patch up foule diſeaſes, and doth ſtrive
To keepe theire totteringe Carcaſſes alive.
Beautie is a candlelight which every puffe
Blowes out, and leaves nought but a ſtinking ſnuffe
To fill our noſtrills with; this boldelie thinke,   65
The cleereſt Candle makes the greateſt ſtincke,
As your pure fode and cleereſt nutryment
Gets the moſt hott, and noſe ſtronge excrement.
Why hange we then on thinges ſo apt to varie,
So fleetinge, brittle, and ſo temporarie?   70

39 ſhop] ſhape *S96*   rich] largeſt *S96*: large *P and R, Grosart, and Chambers*   45 diſcoloured] diſcovered *H39: but* diſcoloured *is here* variegated   53 rifles] rifled *S96*   55 purles] fills *S*: purls *is* embroiders as with gold or silver thread   67 cleereſt] choiceſt *P and R*: cleaneſt *S*: fineſt *Chambers*   68 moſt hott] moſt ſtronge *S96*

That

That agues, Coughes, the toothache, or Catarr
(Slight hanfells of difeafes) fpoile and marr.
But when olde age theire beauties hath in Chace,
And plowes up furrowes in theire once-fmoothe face,
Then they become forfaken, and doe fhowe   75
Like ftately abbeyes ruin'd longe agoe.
Nature but gives the modell, and firft draught
Of faire perfection, which by art is taught
To fpeake itfelfe, a compleat form and birthe,
Soe ftands a Copie to thefe fhapes on earthe.   80
Jove grante me then a reparable face
Which, whiles that Colours are, can want no grace.
Pigmalions painted ftatue I coulde love,
Soe it were warme and fofte, and coulde but move.

Sonnett.

Madam that flea that Crept between your brefts
I envied, that there he fhould make his reft:
The little Creatures fortune was foe good
That Angells feed not on fo pretious foode.
How it did fucke how eager tickle you   5
(Madam fhall fleas before me tickle you?)

Oh I can not holde; pardon if I kild it.
Sweet Blood, to you I afke this, that which fild it
Ran from my Ladies Breft. Come happie flea
That dide for fuckinge of that milkie Sea.   10

72 hanfells *H39:* houfes *S, S96, Chambers:* touches *P and R:* caufes
Le P D'A   73 beauties] brav'ries *H39*   79 To fpeake itfelfe *TCD,*
P and R: Speake to itfelfe *S, S96:* Speake for itfelfe *H39:* To make it-
felfe *Simeon, Grofart, and Chambers*

    Sonnett. *O'F, S96: no title, S:* On A Flea on His Miftrefs's Bofom
Simeon, Grofart, Chambers (from Simeon): text from S96   7 I can not
holde] I not hold can *Chambers*   kild *Ed:* killed *Chambers:* kill *S96*

Oh now againe I well could wifhe thee there,
About hir Hart, about hir anywhere;
I would vowe (Deareſt flea) thou ſhouldſt not dye,
If thou couldſt ſucke from hir hir crueltye.

On Black Hayre and Eyes.

IF ſhaddowes be the pictures excellence;
  And make it ſeeme more lively to the ſence;
If ſtarres in the bright day are hid from ſight
And ſhine moſt glorious in the maſque of night;
Why ſhould you thinke (rare creature) that you lack   5
Perfection cauſe your haire and eyes are blacke,
Or that your heavenly beauty which exceedes
The new ſprung lillies in their mayden weeds,
The damaſke coullour of your cheekes and lipps
Should ſuffer by their darkneſſe an eclipps?   10
Rich diamonds ſhine brighteſt, being ſett
And compaſſed within a foyle of Jett.
Nor was it fitt that Nature ſhould have mayde
So bright a ſunne to ſhine without a ſhade.
It ſeemes that Nature when ſhe firſt did fancie   15
Your rare compoſure ſtudied Necromancie,
That when to you this guift ſhe did impart
She uſed altogether the black art.
By which infuſed power from Magique tooke
You doe command all ſpiritts with a looke: 20

13 vowe] now *Chambers*   Deareſt *S96:* deare *S,O'F, Chambers*
thou] that thou *Chambers*
     On Black Hayre and Eyes *Add. MS. 11811, on which text is
based: in several MSS. including A25, TCD (II), L77: printed in
Parnaſſus Biceps* (1656), *Pembroke and Ruddier's* Poems (1660), *Simeon
(1856–7), Grosart, and Chambers*   2 it *A21,H60,TCD:* them *A11:*
things *L77*   4 ſhine *H39,TCD:* ſeem *A11,Grosart, and Chambers*
8 mayden weeds,] maidenheads, *H39,TCD, Grosart, and Chambers*   9
The damaſque coullor of] That cherry colour of *H39,TCD:* Or that the
cherries of *Some MSS.*   12 compaſſed] compoſ'd *A11*   foyle] field
Chambers   19 tooke] book *Grosart and Chambers*   20 all ſpiritts]
like spirits *Grosart and Chambers*

                      Shee

Shee drew thofe Magique circles in your eyes,
And mayde your hayre the chaines wherewith fhee ties
Rebelling hearts: thofe blew veines which appeare,
Winding Meander about either fpheare,
Mifterious figures are, and when you lift   25
Your voice commandeth like the Exorcift,
And every word which from your Pallett falleth
In a deep charme your hearer's heart inthralleth.
Oh! If in Magique you have fkill fo farre,
Vouchfafe me to be your familiar.   30
Nor hath kind Nature her black art reveal'd
To outward partes alone, fome lie conceal'd,
And as by heads of fprings men often knowe
The nature of the ftreames that run belowe,
So your black haire and eyes do give direction   35
To make me thinke the reft of like complexion:
That reft where all reft lies that blefleth Man,
That Indian mine, that ftraight of Magellan,
That worlde dividing gulfe where he that venters,
With fwelling fayles and ravifht fenfes enters   40
To a new world of blifle. Pardon, I pray,
If my rude mufe prefumeth to difplay
Secretts unknowne, or hath her bounds orepaft
In prayfing fweetnefle which I ne're did taft;
Sterved men doe know there's meate, and blind men may
Though hid from light prefume there is a day.   46
The rover in the marke his arrowe fticks
Sometimes as well as he that fhootes att prickes,
And if I might direct my fhaft aright,
The black mark would I hitt and not the white.   50

25 figures] fables *A11* 26 commandeth] commands *A11* 29
you have fkill *L77, TCD, &c.*: your power *A11*: you have power *Grosart
and Chambers* 33 For (And) as by the fpringhead a man may (men
often) know *L77, TCD, and other MSS.* 34 ftreame . . runs *L77, &c.*
44 did] fhall *TCD and other MSS.* 47 fticks] strikes *Grosart and
Chambers* 49 direct *L77, TCD, &c.*: ayme *A11, Grosart, and Chambers*

Fragment

Fragment of an Elegy.

ANd though thy glaffe a burning one become
And turne us both to afhes on her urne,
Yet to our glory till the later day
Our duft fhall daunce like attomes in her ray.
And when the world fhall in confufion burne, 5
And Kinges and peafantes fcramble at an urne,
Like tapers new blowne out wee happy then
Will at her beames catch fire and live againe.
But this is fence, and fome one may-be glad
That I fo good a caufe of forrow had, 10
Will wifh all thofe whome I affect may dye
So I might pleafe him with an elegie.
O let there never line of witt be read
To pleafe the living that doth fpeake thee dead;
Some tender-harted mother good and mild, 15
Who on the deare grave of her tender child
So many fad teares hath beene knowne to rayne
As out of duft would mould him up againe,
And with hir plaintes enforce the wormes to place
Themfelves like veynes fo neatly on his face, 20
And every lymne, as if that they wer ftriving
To flatter hir with hope of his reviving:
Shee fhould read this, and hir true teares alone
Should coppy forth thefe fad lines on the ftone
Which hides thee dead, and every gentle hart 25
That paffeth by fhould of his teares impart
So great a portion, that if after times
Ruine more churches for the Clergyes crimes,
When any fhall remove thy marble hence,
Which is leffe ftone then hee that takes it thence, 30
Thou fhalt appeare within thy tearefull cell
Much like a faire nymph bathing in a well.

Fragment of an Elegy. *From P, where it appears as portion of an 'heroical epistle' from Lady Penelope Rich to Sir Philip Sidney: punctuation Ed.*

But

But when they find thee dead ſo lovely fair,
Pitty and ſorrow then ſhall ſtraight repaire
And weepe beſide thy grave with cipreſſe cround,   35
To ſee the ſecound world of beauty dround,
And add ſufficient teares as they condole
'Twould make thy body ſwimme up to thy ſoule.
Such eyes ſhould read the lines are writ of thee;
But ſuch a loſſe ſhould have no elegie   40
To palliate the wound wee tooke in hir,
Who rightly greeves admittes no comforter.
He that had tane to heart thy parting hence
Should have beene chain'd to Bedlam two houres thence,
And not a frind of his ere ſhed a teare   45
To ſee him for thy ſake diſtracted there,
But hugge himſelfe for loving ſuch as hee
That could runne mad with greefe for looſing thee.
I, hapleſſe ſoule, that never knew a frend
But to bewayle his too untimely end,   50
Whoſe hopes (cropt in the bud) have never come
But to ſitt weeping on a ſenceleſſe tombe,
That hides not duſt enough to count the teares
Which I have fruitleſſe ſpent in ſo few yeares,
I that have truſted thoſe that would have given   55
For our deare Saviour and the Sonne of heaven
Ten times the valew Judas had of yore,
Onely to ſell him for three peeces more;
I that have lov'd and truſted thus in vaine
Yet weepe for thee, and till the clowdes ſhall daigne   60
To throw on Egipt more then Nile ere ſweld,
Theſe teares of mine ſhalbee unparellell'd.
He that hath lov'd, enjoy'd, and then beene croſt,
Hath teares at will to mourne for what he loſt;
He that hath truſted and his hope appeares   65
Wrong'd but by death may ſoone diſſolve in teares;
But hee unhappy man whoſe love and truſt
Nere met fruition nor a promiſe juſt,
For him (unleſſe like thee hee deadly ſlepe)
'Tis eaſier to runn mad then 'tis to weepe;   70

And

And yet I can. Fall then yee mournefull ſhowers,
And as old time leades on the winged howers,
Bee you their minutes, and let men forgett
To count their ages from the plague of ſweat,
From eighty eight, the Poulder-plot, or when   75
Men were affrayd to talke of it againe;
And in their numerations be it ſayd
Thus old was I when ſuch a teare was ſhed,
And when that other fell a comett roſe
And all the world tooke notice of my woes.   80
Yet finding them paſt cure, as doctores fly
Their patientes paſt all hope of remedy,
No charitable ſoule will once impart
One word of comfort to ſo ſicke a heart;
But as a hurt deare beaten from the heard,   85
Men of my ſhadow allmoſt now affeard
Fly from my woes, that whilome wont to greet mee,
And well nigh thinke it ominous to meete mee.
Sad lines go yee abroad; go ſaddeſt muſe,
And as ſome nations formerly did uſe   90
To lay their ſicke men in the ſtreet, that thoſe,
Who of the ſame diſeaſe had ſcapt the throwes,
Might miniſter releefe as they went by
To ſuch as felt the ſelfſame malady,
So hapleſſe lynes fly through the faireſt land,   95
And if ye light into ſome bleſſed hand,
That hath a heart as merry as the ſhine
Of golden dayes, yet wrong'd as much as mine,
Pitty may lead that happy man to mee,
And his experience worke a remedy   100
To thoſe ſad fittes which (ſpight of nature's lawes)
Torture a poore hart that out-lives the cauſe.
But this muſt never bee, nor is it fitt
An ague or ſome ſickenes leſſe then itt
Should glory in the death of ſuch as hee,   105
That had a heart of fleſh and valued thee.
Brave Roman, I admire thee that would'ſt dy
At no leſſe rate then for an empery.

                             Some

Some maſſy diamond from the center drawne,
For which all Europ wer an equall pawne,   110
Should (beaten into duſt) bee drunke by him
That wanted courage good enough to ſwimme
Through ſeas of woes for thee, and much deſpiſe
To meet with death at any lower prize,
Whilſt greefe alone workes that effect in mee,   115
And yet no greefe but for the loſſe of the .
Fortune now doe thy worſt, for I have gott
By this her death ſo ſtrong an antidote,
That all thy future croſſes ſhall not have
More then an angry ſmile, nor ſhall the grave   120
Glory in my laſt day: theſe lines ſhall give
To us a ſecond life, and we will live
To pull the diſtaffe from the hand of fate;
And ſpinn our own thrides for ſo long a date,
That death ſhall never ſeize uppon our fame   125
Till this ſhall periſh in the whole world's frame.

⟨ *Farewel, ye guilded follies.* ⟩

FArewel ye guilded follies, pleaſing troubles,
  Farewel ye honour'd rags, ye glorious bubbles;
Fame's but a hollow echo, gold pure clay,
Honour the darling but of one ſhort day.
Beauty (th'eyes idol) but a damasked ſkin,   5
State but a golden priſon, to keepe in
And torture free-born minds; imbroidered trains
Meerly but Pageants, proudly ſwelling vains,

⟨Farewell, Ye Guilded Follies.⟩ *Ed: variously titled, Add. MS. 18220,
C.C.C. Oxon. MS. 324, Egerton MS. 2603, Harleian MS. 6057: printed
in Walton's Compleat Angler (1653), Wits Interpreter (1655) Hannah's
Courtly Poets: Grosart prints from MS. Dd. 643 in Cambridge University
Library, and Chambers follows—a very inferior version: text from Walton*
2 ye glorious] ye chriſtal *A18, E26, H60:* the chriſtall *WI*   6 keepe
A18, E26, H60: live *Walton*   8 proudly] proud *Walton*

And

And blood ally'd to greatnefs, is a loane
Inherited, not purchafed, not our own. 10
   Fame, honor, beauty, ftate, train, blood and birth,
   Are but the fading bloffomes of the earth.

I would be great, but that the Sun doth ftill
Level his rayes againft the rifing hill :
I would be high, but fee the proudeft Oak 15
Moft fubject to the rending Thunder-ftroke ;
I would be rich, but fee men too unkind
Dig in the bowels of the richeft mine ;
I would be wife, but that I often fee
The Fox fufpected whilft the Afs goes free ; 20
I would be fair, but fee the fair and proud
Like the bright fun, oft fetting in a cloud ;
I would be poor, but know the humble grafs
Still trampled on by each unworthy Affe :
Rich, hated ; wife, fufpected ; fcorn'd, if poor ; 25
Great, fear'd ; fair, tempted ; high, ftil envied more :
   I have wifh'd all, but now I wifh for neither,
   Great, high, rich, wife, nor fair, poor I'l be rather.

Would the world now adopt me for her heir,
Would beauties Queen entitle me the Fair, 30
Fame fpeak me fortune's Minion, could I vie
Angels with India, with a fpeaking eye

9 a loane *Ed:* a lone *Walton:* but loane *MSS.* 18 mine *E26,*
CCC: mind *Walton, A182, H60, WI:* minds *Grosart and Chambers*
19–20 I would be wife but that the fox I fee
   Sufpected guilty when the Afs goes free
         A182, E26, H60, Grosart, and Chambers
21–2 I would be fair, but fee that Champion proud
   The bright fun often fetting in a cloud
    WI and MSS., but with The worlds bright eye *or* fair eye
31–2   could I vie
Angels with India, *Walton, A182, E26, H60*
      could I joy
The bliffe of angells, *CCC*
      could I vie (vey *Grosart*)
The blisse of angells, *Grosart and Chambers*

                   Command

Command bare heads, bow'd knees, ſtrike Juſtice dumb
As wel as blind and lame, or give a tongue
To ſtones, by Epitaphs, be called great Maſter   35
In the looſe rhimes of every Poetaſter;
Could I be more then any man that lives,
Great, fair, rich, wiſe in all Superlatives;
Yet I more freely would theſe gifts reſign
Then ever fortune would have made them mine,   40
   And hold one minute of this holy leaſure,
   Beyond the riches of this empty pleaſure.

Welcom pure thoughts, welcom ye ſilent groves,
Theſe gueſts, theſe Courts, my ſoul moſt dearly loves,
Now the wing'd people of the Skie ſhall ſing   45
My cheerful Anthems to the gladſome Spring;
A Pray'r book now ſhall be my looking-glaſſe,
Wherein I will adore ſweet vertues face.
Here dwell no hateful looks, no Pallace cares,
No broken vows dwell here, nor pale-faced fears,   50
Then here I'l ſit and ſigh my hot loves folly,
And learn t'affect an holy melancholy.
   And if contentment be a ſtranger, then
   I'l nere look for it, but in heaven again.

43 ye ſilent groves, *Walton:* the ſilent Groves, *WI:* ye carelefs groves,
H60: the carelefs grove, *CCC:* ye careless groans, *Grosart and Chambers*
44 Theſe are the courts my ſoul entire loves, *A182 :* Theſe are my gueſts,
this is the court I love, *CCC :* These are my guests, this is that courtage
tones, *Grosart and Chambers :* the court age loves, *Ash38*   46 My
Anthem; be my Selah gentle Spring. *A182:* Mine anthems; be my cellar,
gentle spring. *Grosart and Chambers*   48 wherein] In which *Walton*
49–50 Here dwells no hartleſſe Love, no palſey fears,
   No ſhort joys purchaſed with eternal tears. *A182, H60*
51 hot loves *Walton:* hot youths *H60:* paſt years *A182*   53 be]
prove *A182*

INDEX OF FIRST LINES.

*The poems marked * are contained in Appendixes B and C of doubtful or unauthentic poems. Those marked † are poems to or on Donne.*